MAR DEL CARIBE
Barranquilla
Cartagena
CARACAS
LLANOS
VENEZUELA
GUYANA
SURINAM
GUAYANA FRANCESA
Medellín
Río Orinoco
BOGOTÁ
Cali
COLOMBIA
Ecuador
QUITO
ECUADOR
Guayaquil
Manaus
Río Amazonas
Belén
Iquitos
BRASIL
PERÚ
LIMA
ANDES
Cuzco
Lago Titicaca
BOLIVIA
La Paz
BRASILIA
OCÉANO PACÍFICO
Arica
SUCRE
Iquique
PARAGUAY
ANDES
OCÉANO ATLÁNTICO
São Paulo
Río de Janeiro
Antofagasta
ASUNCIÓN
Santos
Tucumán
CHILE
Río Paraná
Córdoba
Mendoza
Rosario
Valparaíso
URUGUAY
SANTIAGO
BUENOS AIRES
MONTEVIDEO
Río de la Plata
Concepción
ARGENTINA
ANDES
Bahía Blanca
PATAGONIA
América del Sur
Islas Malvinas
Estrecho de Magallanes
Punta Arenas
Tierra del Fuego
Cabo de Hornos
0
600
1200
Kilómetros

M000288387

PASAPORTE

First-Year
SPANISH

First-Year SPANISH

Richard Woehr
California State University, Hayward

Fausto Vergara

Bárbara Mujica
Georgetown University

John Wiley & Sons

New York Chichester Brisbane Toronto

COVER DESIGN Vladimir Yevtikhiev
TEXT DESIGN Patricia Smythe
PHOTO EDITOR Marian Griffith
MAPS Rino Dussi
DRAWINGS Sergio Aragonés

Copyright © 1980 by John Wiley & Sons, Inc.

All rights reserved. Published simultaneously in Canada.

Reproduction or translation of any part of this work beyond that permitted by Sections 107 or 108 of the 1976 United States Copyright Act without the permission of the copyright owner is unlawful. Requests for permission or further information should be addressed to the Permissions Department, John Wiley & Sons, Inc.

Library of Congress Cataloging in Publication Data:

Woehr, Richard, 1942–
Pasaporte : first-year Spanish.

Includes index.
1. Spanish language–Grammar–1950–
I. Vergara, Fausto, joint author. II. Mujica, Barbara Kaminar de, joint author. III. Title.
PC4112.W59 468.2'421 79-26709
ISBN 0-471-02758-8

Printed in the United States of America

10 9 8 7 6 5 4 3 2

Preface

Pasaporte is a new program for first-year college Spanish. It presents the fundamentals of the Spanish language in the context of culturally authentic, contemporary settings. The conscious application of grammar in settings of interpersonal communication is emphasized. A workbook, laboratory recordings (available for copying or purchase), instructor's manual, and tapescript accompany the textbook.

Scope and organization of the text

The textbook has twenty basic chapters plus a series of supplementary interchapters. In chapter 1, in place of a formal presentation of grammatical structures, there are five short related dialogs, each followed by notes on pronouncing and writing Spanish as well as short sections of *Aplicación* that serve as an introduction to classroom exercise procedures. Chapters 2 through 20 have the following divisions:

Despegue and *Diálogo*
Estructura I
Pausa oral
Estructura II
Repaso oral

Beginning with chapter 3, the odd-numbered chapters have a *Lectura* following the *Estructura II.*

The *Despegue* section is a short oral and visual introduction to the themes and vocabulary of the dialog. Selected aspects of Spanish pronunciation are singled out for special attention. The *Diálogo* itself is followed by a translation, a section of *Variaciones* containing additional basic words and expressions, cultural *Glosas,* short exercises, and a *Vocabulario* containing all the active vocabulary for the chapter.

The *Estructura* sections introduce the major points of Spanish grammar. Examples from the dialog are highlighted at the outset; often a short *Repaso* recalls a structure taught in an earlier chapter, for purposes of contrast or comparison or to establish continuity. Further examples, with translations in a second column, illustrate each point discussed. Exercises follow each segment of explanation; these range from closely controlled drills with predictable responses to more open-ended activities.

The *Pausa oral* is a conversational interlude that affords students a further opportunity to use the vocabulary and structures presented in the context of a single theme. The *Pausa* also serves to divide the presentation of grammar into manageable units.

The *Lecturas,* which appear in alternate chapters, are short reading selections that relate to the themes of the chapters in which they are found.

Several optional interchapter sections appear as follows:

Comunicación, after chapters 4, 8, 12, and 16. These four sections contain vocabulary and communicative activities relating to the topics *La casa, La comida, Las diversiones,* and *El teléfono y el banco.*

Grammatical *Repasos,* after chapters 5, 10, 15, and 20. The most important grammatical materials are synthesized for the student and drilled once again for reinforcement.

Two *Lecturas sobre civilización hispánica,* after chapters 10 and 20. These are longer readings about Hispanic history and culture.

Special features

Thematic unity. Each chapter is organized around a particular theme: travel, job hunting, food, sports, politics, etc. As the chapter progresses and the students learn more language structure, they discuss aspects of the theme in diverse sections of *Aplicación.*

Natural-sounding language. The language of the dialogs, grammar examples, exercises, and *Lecturas* is authentic. Each dialog is linguistically accurate, thanks in part to the careful scrutiny of a large number of native-speaking reviewers and consultants from several countries. The language is based on a variety of situations and is meant to suggest something of the spirit and life of the Hispanic peoples.

Vocabulary spheres. Following the dialog, a *Variaciones* section introduces words associated with those in the dialog. If a color is mentioned in a dialog, for example, the *Variaciones* section may include the rest of the colors. This allows the students to react to the situations in the dialogs and to use the structures of the chapter to express their own thoughts.

Concise grammar explanations. Each explanation begins with an example from the dialog and continues with illustrative examples highlighted with a yellow tint, to keep the reader's focus on them rather than on their English equivalents. Important paradigms are presented in boxes to facilitate memorization and review. Difficult linguistic terminology is avoided; basic grammar terms are explained in context.

Graded exercises. The exercises in *Pasaporte* are especially varied in format and progress from the purely manipulative to those encouraging free expression. Most exercises are short so that classroom activities will change often. Where possible, the exercise lines are held in a thematic context: even in manipulative exercises, the lines frequently form a story.

Flexibility. Since each chapter is thematically integrated, an instructor may choose to begin with the dialog, with grammar, with conversation, or with reading. When time is short, the *Pausa oral* and *Lectura* may be omitted without disturbing the lexical progression from chapter to chapter. The interchapter sections are also optional.

Hispanic culture. Pasaporte has been written to help American students recognize and appreciate the differences and similarities between Hispanic and Anglo-American culture. Dialogs, readings, and cultural *Glosas* touch on nearly all the Spanish-speaking countries; drawings, photographs, and maps also help to depict the Hispanic world, including that part of the Hispanic world brought to the United States by the large Spanish-speaking population living within its borders.

A word of thanks

The organization and content of *Pasaporte* evolved as the book was first drafted, reviewed, rewritten, classroom tested, reviewed again, and finally edited. The authors would like to acknowledge the lively criticism and suggestions of the following persons:

> Milton M. Azevedo of the University of California, Berkeley, Paul W. Borgeson, Jr., of the University of North Carolina at Chapel Hill, Fé Brittain of Pima Community College, Agnes L. Dimitriou of the University of San Francisco, Sara L. de la Vega of Los Angeles Valley College, Katherine C. Richards of Texas A&M University, Dorothy Rissel of Indiana University, Robert Russell of Dartmouth College, Maureen Weissenrieder of Ohio University, and Leslie N. Wilson of Florida State University.

Marilyn Pérez-Abreu, Baruch College, CUNY, supervised the book's program of vocabulary control, prepared the Spanish-English vocabulary, and suggested many substantial improvements in the text.

R.W.
F.V.
B.M.

Contents

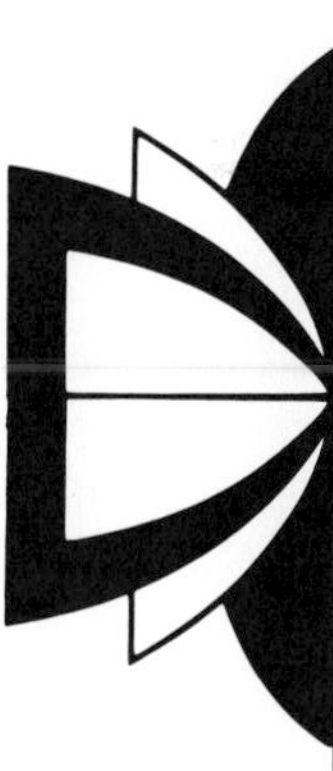

Capítulo 1

Despegue

DIÁLOGO En la universidad

Pronouncing Spanish

Writing Spanish

Repaso oral

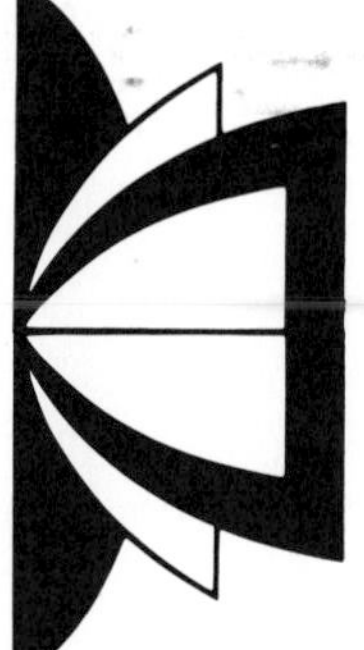

Despegue

Look at the following drawings. Can you tell the meaning of the Spanish words associated with each of them?

la universidad

Lola

Susana

el profesor

la clase

Aplicación

I. Practice saying each of the following words, imitating the pronunciation of your instructor.

1. la universidad
2. Lola
3. Susana
4. el profesor
5. la clase

II. Now tell what is shown in each of the following drawings. Pronounce each item very clearly.

1. 

2. 

3. 

4. 

5.

Theme of the dialog

The following dialog has five parts. Susana and Lola meet and discuss a young man. Lola decides to take English. After class she tells Susana about the class.

Students at the University of the Americas in Puebla, Mexico, at the beginning of a new school year.

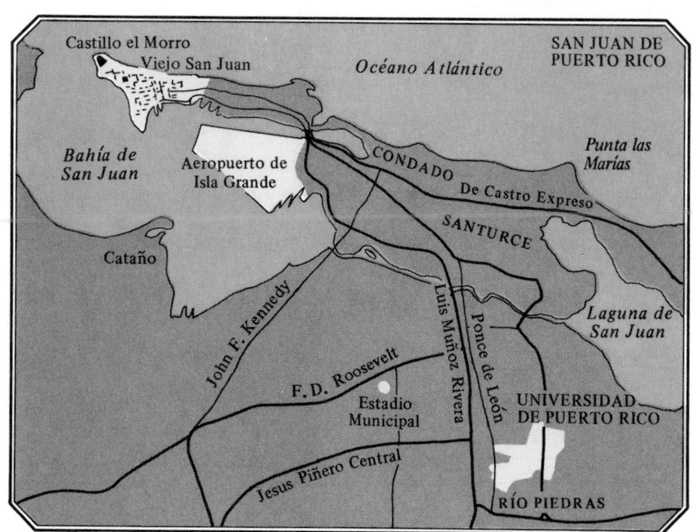

DIÁLOGO

En la universidad

1. Lola y Susana

Lola and Susana meet before class.

SUSANA ¡Lola, Lola!
LOLA ¡Susana! Hola, chica. ¿Cómo estás?
SUSANA Yo, muy bien. ¿Y tú?
LOLA Yo, como siempre.

VARIACIONES

¡Roberto! Hola, chico. ¿Cómo estás?	Roberto! Hi (boy). How are you?
Yo, muy mal.	Me, awful (very bad).

Pronouncing Spanish

Different sounds are used to pronounce Spanish and English. Listen carefully to your instructor, and imitate what you hear as exactly as you can. Notice the following points.

1. Spanish /a/ is pronounced with the mouth open quite wide.
   Susana estás universidad
2. Spanish /o/ is pronounced with the lips fairly rounded.
   Lola yo profesor
3. Spanish /u/ is pronounced with the lips forming a small, round opening.
   Susana tú universidad

Students on their way to class at the University of Madrid.

Here is a translation of the dialog.

DIALOG **At the university**

1. Lola and Susana

S: Lola, Lola!
L: Susana! Hi (girl). How are you?
S: Me, I'm very well. And you?
L: Like always.

Writing Spanish

To write a question or an exclamation in Spanish, put an inverted punctuation mark at the beginning of the sentence and the familiar punctuation mark at the end.

¡Lola, Lola! **¿Cómo estás?**
¡Susana! **¿Y tú?**

Aplicación

I. Repeat the following words after your instructor, paying special attention to:

1. the /a/ sound: **Lola, hola, Susana, estás**
2. the /o/ sound: **Lola, hola, como, yo**
3. the /u/ sound: **Susana, tú, universidad**

II. Now repeat the entire dialog several times after the instructor. Pronounce each line very clearly.

III. Complete the answers to the following questions.

1. ¿Cómo estás? Yo, muy _____.
2. ¿Y tú? Yo, como _____.

2. Un nuevo profesor

Lola and Susana discuss a young man standing nearby.

LOLA ¿Quién es ese chico?
SUSANA ¿Cuál? ¿Ése?
LOLA Sí. ¿Es un nuevo estudiante?
SUSANA No, chica. Es un nuevo profesor.
LOLA ¡No! ¡Imposible!
SUSANA Sí, chica. Enseña inglés.

VARIACIONES

¿Qué enseña?	What does he teach?
Enseña español.	He teaches Spanish.

2. A new professor

L: Who is that guy?
S: Which? That one?
L: Yes. Is he a new student?
S: No (girl). He is a new professor.
L: No! Impossible!
S: Yes (girl). He teaches English.

Pronouncing Spanish

1. Spanish /e/ is pronounced with the lips more closed than for /a/. The tongue is toward the front of the mouth.
   ese **estudiante** **enseña**
2. Spanish /i/ is pronounced with the lips in a slit position. The tongue nearly touches the front of the roof of the mouth.
   chica **sí** **inglés**

Writing Spanish

1. The combination **qu** is used only before **e** and **i** (**que, qui**). **Qu** is pronounced as a single /k/ sound.
   ¿qué? **¿quién?**

2. In the Spanish alphabet, **ch** and **c** are different letters.
   chica **¿cuál?**
   chico **¿cómo?**

Aplicación

I. Repeat the following words after your instructor, paying special attention to:

1. the /e/ sound: **ese, profesor, enseña**
2. the /i/ sound: **sí, chica, inglés**

II. Repeat the dialog several times after your instructor.

III. Complete the answers to the following questions.

1. 
   ¿Es Lola? — No, es ____.
2. 
   ¿Es Susana? — No, es ____.
3. ¿Quién es ese chico? — ¿Cuál? ¿____?
4. ¿Es un nuevo estudiante? — No, es un nuevo ____.
5. ¿Qué enseña? — Enseña ____.

3. La clase de inglés

Lola decides to take an English class with the new professor.

LOLA Buenos días, señor.
PROFESOR Buenos días, señorita.
LOLA ¿Es ésta la clase de inglés?
PROFESOR Sí, señorita. Adelante, por favor.
LOLA Gracias, señor.
PROFESOR ¿Cómo se llama usted?
LOLA Lola Núñez Gimeno.

VARIACIONES

Buenos días, señora.	Hello (ma'am).
¿Es ésta la clase de español?	Is this the Spanish class?
De nada.	You're welcome.
Adiós.	Good-bye.

Pronouncing Spanish

1. The sound /ñ/ is pronounced in a manner similar to the *ny* of English *canyon.*
   señor **señorita** **Núñez**
2. Spanish /t/ is pronounced by placing the tip of the tongue against the back of the upper front teeth. Spanish /t/ is never followed by the puff of air (the *h* sound) heard in English.
   estás **tú** **estudiante** **señorita** **adelante**
3. The letter **z** is pronounced exactly like /s/ in most of the Hispanic world. (In northern and in central Spain **z** is pronounced /th/.)
   Núñez

3. English Class

L: Hello (sir).
P: Hello (miss).
L: Is this the English class?
P: Yes (miss). Come in, please.
L: Thank you, sir.
P: What is your name?
L: Lola Núñez Gimeno.

Writing Spanish

1. Double *s* is never used in Spanish.
   clase **profesor** **imposible**
2. Notice that **n** and **ñ** are two separate letters, each with a different pronunciation.

Susana	enseña
nuevo	señor
bueno	señora
inglés	señorita

Aplicación

I. Repeat the following words after your instructor, paying special attention to:

1. the /ñ/ sound: **señor, señorita, Núñez, enseña**
2. the /t/ sound: **tú, estudiante, señorita, adelante**
3. the /s/ sound: **clase, profesor, Susana, Núñez**

II. Review the dialog several times imitating the pronunciation of your instructor.

III. Complete the answers to the following statements and questions.

1. Buenos días, señor. — Buenos días, _____.
2. ¿Es ésta la clase de inglés? — Sí, ésta es la clase _____.
3. Adelante. — Gracias, _____.
4. ¿Cómo se llama usted? — _____________.

4. ¿Y la clase de inglés?

After the English class Lola and Susana meet again.

SUSANA Bueno, ¿y la clase de inglés?
LOLA Es excelente. El nuevo profesor es muy bueno.
SUSANA Y joven y guapo.
LOLA Sí, chica, y también muy inteligente.

VARIACIONES

La profesora.	The (woman) professor.

Pronouncing Spanish

1. The letters **b** and **v** are pronounced exactly alike. In most positions Spanish **b** is much softer than English *b*. The lips do not close tightly, and the airstream continues to pass between them.
   muy bien nuevo por favor joven muy bueno
2. The sound of the Spanish letter **j,** and also of Spanish **g** when it comes before **e** or **i** (**ge, gi**), is similar to the sound of English *h* in *hip*.
   joven Gimeno inteligente
3. In most positions, **g** (in **ga, go, gu**) is similar to the soft *g* of rapidly pronounced *Chicago*.
   . . . y guapo

4. What about the English class?

S: Well, what about the English class?
L: It's excellent. The new professor is very good.
S: And young and handsome.
L: He sure is (yes, girl), and also very intelligent.

Writing Spanish

1. Look at the following words which have no written accent.
   Lola siempre chico joven buenos
   If a word ends in a vowel, in **-n** or in **-s** and is stressed on the next-to-last syllable, no written accent is used.
2. Now look at the following words which do have a written accent mark.
   estás inglés también
   If a word ends in a vowel, in **-n,** or in **-s** but is not stressed on the next-to-last syllable, a written accent mark must be placed over the stressed vowel.

The University of Madrid. Too many activities, or something for everybody?

3. Several words are used with a written accent only if they appear in a question or exclamation.

   ¿cómo? **¿quién?** **¿cuál?** **¿qué?**

4. A few words of one syllable are used with a written accent.

   tú *you* **sí** *yes*

Aplicación

I. Repeat the following words after your instructor, paying special attention to:

1. the /b/ sound: **muy bien, nuevo, por favor, joven, muy bueno**
2. the /h/ sound: **joven, Gimeno, inteligente**

II. Repeat the dialog several times after your instructor.

III. Complete the answers to the following questions.

1. Bueno, ¿y la clase de inglés? Es _____.
2. ¿Cómo es el profesor? El profesor es _____.
3. ¿Es joven el profesor? Sí, el profesor es _____.
4. ¿Es guapo también? Sí, es muy _____.
5. ¿Es inteligente? Sí, también es _____.

5. ¿Cuándo hay clase?

Lola and Susana continue to discuss the English class.

SUSANA ¿Es americano el profesor?
LOLA Sí, pero habla español muy bien.
SUSANA ¿Cuándo hay clase?
LOLA Los lunes, martes, miércoles y viernes.

VARIACIONES

Los jueves, sábados y domingos. On Thursdays, Saturdays, and Sundays.

Pronouncing Spanish

1. The letter *h* is never pronounced in any word.
   hola habla hay
2. In most positions **d** is pronounced like the weak *th* sound in English *this.*
   estudiante buenos días adelante

5. When is there class?

S: Is the professor American?
L: Yes, but he speaks Spanish very well.
S: When is there class?
L: On Mondays, Tuesdays, Wednesdays, and Fridays.

Writing Spanish

1. Look at the following words which have no written accent mark.
   profesor señor español universidad
   If a word ends in a consonant (other than **-n** or **-s**) and is pronounced with the stress on the last syllable, no written accent is used.
2. Now look at the following word which does have a written accent.
   Núñez
   If a word ends in a consonant (other than **-n** or **-s**) but is not stressed on the last syllable, a written accent mark is placed over the vowel of the accented syllable.
3. In Spanish the names of languages, nationalities, and the days of the week are written with a small letter and not a capital.
   inglés, español, americano, lunes, sábado

Aplicación

I. Repeat the following words after your instructor.

1. silent **h: hola, habla, hay**
2. the weak /d/ sound: **estudiante, buenos días, adelante**

II. Repeat the dialog several times after your instructor.

III. Complete the answer to each question.

1. ¿Es americano el profesor?	Sí, pero habla español ____.
2. ¿Hay clase los lunes y los martes?	Sí, hay clase ____.
3. ¿Hay clase los miércoles y los viernes?	Sí, hay clase ____.

IV. Say the days of the week. Then answer the following questions.

1. ¿Cuándo hay clase de español?
2. ¿Cuándo hay clase de inglés?

VOCABULARIO

nouns

la **aplicación**	application
el **capítulo**	chapter
la **clase**	class
la **chica**	girl
el **chico**	boy
el **despegue**	takeoff (airplane)
el **día**	day
el **diálogo**	dialog
el **español**	Spanish language
el, la **estudiante**	student
el **inglés**	English language
el **profesor,** la **profesora**	professor
la **universidad**	university
la **variación**	variation
el **vocabulario**	vocabulary

days of the week

lunes	Monday
martes	Tuesday
miércoles	Wednesday
jueves	Thursday
viernes	Friday
sábado	Saturday
domingo	Sunday

verbs

enseña	(he) teaches
es	(he) is
estás	you are
habla	(he) speaks
hay	there is, there are

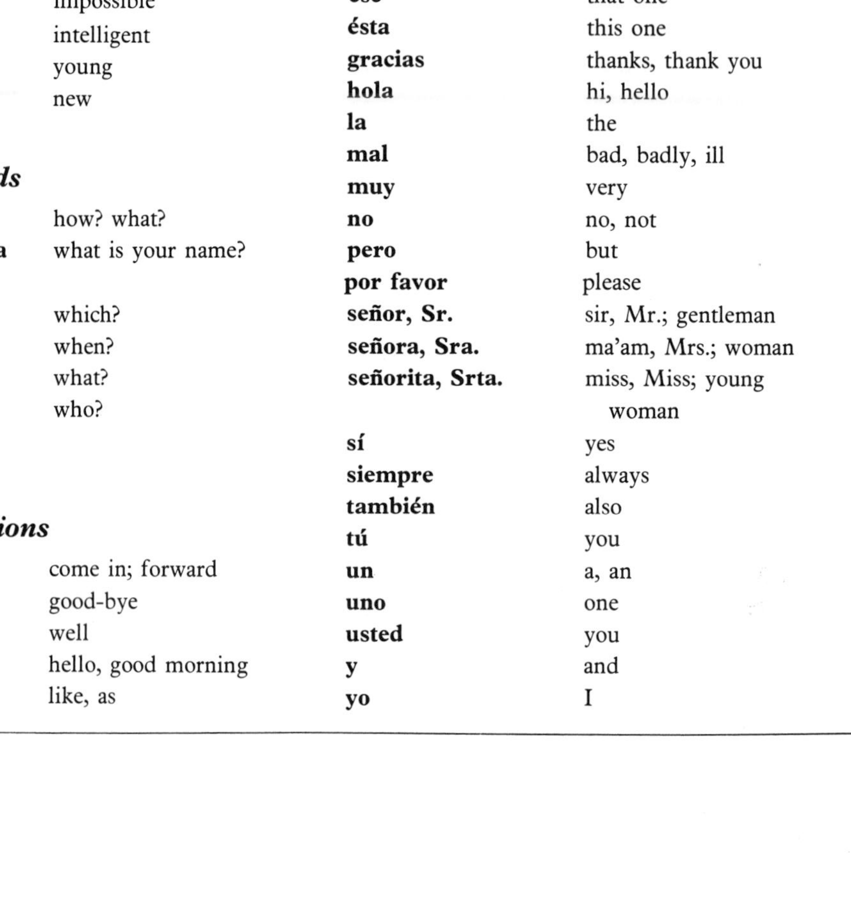

adjectives

americano	American
bueno	good
ese	that
excelente	excellent
guapo	handsome
imposible	impossible
inteligente	intelligent
joven	young
nuevo	new

question words

¿cómo?	how? what?
¿cómo se llama usted?	what is your name?
¿cuál?	which?
¿cuándo?	when?
¿qué?	what?
¿quién?	who?

other expressions

adelante	come in; forward
adiós	good-bye
bien	well
buenos días	hello, good morning
como	like, as
de	of
la clase de inglés	English class
de nada	you're welcome
el	the
en	in, at
ése	that one
ésta	this one
gracias	thanks, thank you
hola	hi, hello
la	the
mal	bad, badly, ill
muy	very
no	no, not
pero	but
por favor	please
señor, Sr.	sir, Mr.; gentleman
señora, Sra.	ma'am, Mrs.; woman
señorita, Srta.	miss, Miss; young woman
sí	yes
siempre	always
también	also
tú	you
un	a, an
uno	one
usted	you
y	and
yo	I

INGRESO A LA UNIVERSIDAD
15 AÑOS DE EXPERIENCIA EN INGRESOS UNIVERSITARIOS
Instituto
GRANADEROS
PLAZA FLORES: RIVERA INDARTE 174
ECO

Repaso oral[1]

A. Read the following words, being careful to stress the next-to-last syllable.

Lola, hola, clase, guapo, bueno, adelante, inteligente, martes, joven, señora

B. Read the following words, being careful to stress the last syllable.

señor, profesor, español, universidad

C. Read the following words, being careful to stress the syllable that has a written accent mark.

estás, inglés, también, Núñez, miércoles

D. Para describir.[2]

¿Qué hay en la universidad?

[1] *Oral review.* [2] *To be described.*

Capítulo 2

Despegue

DIALOGO **Dos mundos**

Nouns and gender • Singular and plural • Definite articles • The contractions **al** and **del**

PAUSA ORAL **Un viaje a México**

Subject pronouns (I) • Present tense of **-ar** verbs • Subject pronouns (II)

Repaso oral

Despegue

el aeropuerto

la aduana

el hotel

la casa

el club campestre

la recepción

Pronunciación[1]

Here are some further points to remember as you pronounce Spanish.

aeropuerto **club campestre**	Each vowel sound is pronounced very clearly (**a/e/ro /puer/to**).
México **mexicano**	The **x** in these words is pronounced like Spanish **j.**
hablan **hotel** **ahora**	Remember that the letter **h** is not pronounced in any Spanish word.

[1] *Pronunciation.*

Aplicación

I. Practice saying each of the following words, imitating the pronunciation of your instructor.

1. **hablan** **hotel** **ahora**
2. **México** **mexicano**
3. **aeropuerto** **aduana** **casa**
4. **recepción** **club campestre**

II. Tell what is shown in each of the following drawings; pronounce each item clearly.

1.

2.

3.

4.

5.

6.

Tema del diálogo[1]

Do both Latins and North Americans approach business deals in the same way? Here's what happened when two businessmen (one from Mexico, one from the U.S.A.) met in Mexico City.

[1] *Theme of the dialog.*

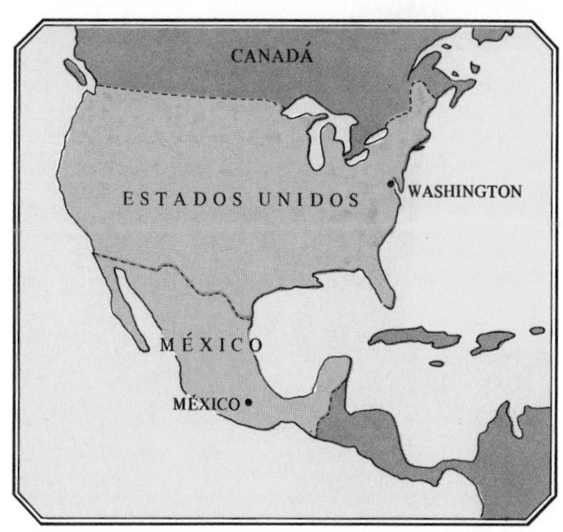

DIÁLOGO

Dos mundos

Un lunes por la tarde en el Aeropuerto Internacional del D.F.[1], *dos hombres de negocios hablan: José Antonio Díaz, mexicano de 30 (treinta) años, y Fred Williams, de 24 (veinticuatro) años, de los Estados Unidos*[2].

DÍAZ ¿Fred Williams? ¡Mucho gusto! Yo soy José Antonio Díaz, de la Nacional Financiera[3]. (Da la mano.)

WILLIAMS Buenas tardes, señor Díaz. ¡Qué bueno llegar! Los viajes siempre cansan un poco. Afortunadamente, para el extranjero no hay problemas con la aduana en México.

DÍAZ Cierto. Pero para el mexicano. . .es una lata.[4]

* * *

WILLIAMS Bien, ahora al Hotel María Isabel. Y dentro de un rato hablamos de negocios, ¿no?

DÍAZ Tal vez. Primero, cenamos en casa esta noche. Y mañana por la tarde hay una recepción para usted en el club campestre.

WILLIAMS ¿Y el contrato? ¿Cómo anda?

DÍAZ Bien. El miércoles en mi oficina hablamos de la situación.

Two Worlds

On a Monday afternoon in the International Airport of D.F. two businessmen are talking: José Antonio Díaz, a 30-year-old Mexican, and Fred Williams, 24 years old, from the United States.

D: Fred Williams? Glad to meet you. I'm José Antonio Díaz, from the National Finance Corporation. (He puts out his hand.)

W: Hello (good afternoon), Mr. Díaz. How good to arrive! Trips always tire (you out) a little. Luckily, for the foreigner there are no problems with customs in Mexico.

D: Right. But for the Mexican . . .it's a pain.

* * *

W: O.K. Now to the Hotel María Isabel. And in a little while we'll talk business, correct?

D: Maybe. First, we'll have dinner at home this evening. And tomorrow afternoon there's a reception for you at the country club.

W: And the contract? How's it going?

D: Fine. Wednesday in my office we'll discuss the situation.

Reception at a country club in Mexico City.

VARIACIONES

Dos hombres hablan.	Two men are talking.
mujeres	women
Sí, hombre.	Oh yes. (Yes, man.)
Los viajes cansan un poco.	Trips tire (you out) a little.
mucho	a lot
Buenos días.	Good morning.
Buenas tardes.	Good afternoon.
Buenas noches.	Good evening.
¿Qué necesitamos para viajar?	What do we need (in order) to travel?
el pasaporte	the passport
la maleta	the suitcase
¿Adónde vamos?	Where are we going?
al restaurante	to the restaurant
al café	to the cafe

Glosas[1]

1. **D.F.** stands for **Distrito Federal** *Federal District.* Mexico City is known as **México, D.F.;** its political status is similar to that of Washington, D.C. Besides the **Distrito Federal,** the Republic of Mexico has 31 states. The Republic's full name is **Estados Unidos Mexicanos** *United Mexican States.*
2. The proper term for the U.S.A. in Spanish is **Estados Unidos de América.** The term **América** includes all of the Americas—North, Central, and South America and the

[1] *Notes.*

Mexico City is a spectacular sight from the air on a clear day.

Aplicación

I. Change from singular to plural.

MODELO problema → **problemas**

1. mundo 2. mujer 3. aduana 4. recepción 5. hombre 6. mano 7. aeropuerto 8. casa 9. universidad 10. clase 11. pasaporte 12. problema

II. Change from plural to singular.

MODELO profesores → **profesor**

1. contratos 2. pasaportes 3. casas 4. oficinas 5. viajes 6. restaurantes 7. universidades 8. situaciones 9. cafés 10. negocios 11. mujeres 12. problemas

C. Definite articles; the contractions **al** and **del**

la tarde
el aeropuerto **del** D.F.
al café

1. The definite article in English is *the* (*the* person, *the* place).

2. The Spanish definite article appears in front of nouns and has four forms: **el, la, los, las.**

MASCULINE SINGULAR	FEMININE SINGULAR
el contrato	la casa
el problema	la mano
el viaje	la tarde
el estudiante	la estudiante

MASCULINE PLURAL	FEMININE PLURAL
los contratos	las casas
los problemas	las manos
los viajes	las tardes
los estudiantes	las estudiantes

3. In Spanish, when **el** follows the preposition **de** *of,* a contraction occurs.

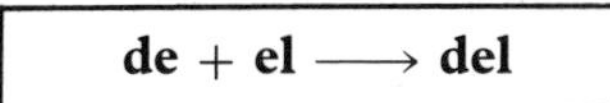

de + el ⟶ del

del mundo	of the world
del hotel	of the hotel
del hombre	of the man

4. When **el** follows the preposition **a** *to,* a second contraction occurs.

a + el ⟶ al

al aeropuerto	to the airport
al estudiante	to the student

5. No contraction ever occurs with the other three forms of the article: **a la estudiante, a los estudiantes, a las estudiantes, de la oficina, de los hoteles, de las casas.**

Aplicación

I. Supply the correct definite article.

MODELO problema → **el problema**

1. mundo 2. universidad 3. aduana 4. recepción 5. hombres 6. manos 7. aeropuertos 8. casas 9. club campestre 10. mujeres 11. pasaportes 12. problemas

II. Respond using the pattern shown in the model.

MODELO ¿Diálogo? ¿Qué diálogo? → **¡El diálogo, hombre, el diálogo!**

1. ¿Viaje? ¿Qué viaje?
2. ¿Pasaporte? ¿Qué pasaporte?
3. ¿Recepción? ¿Qué recepción?
4. ¿Casa? ¿Qué casa?
5. ¿Clase? ¿Qué clase?
6. ¿Negocios? ¿Qué negocios?
7. ¿Hoteles? ¿Qué hoteles?
8. ¿Contrato? ¿Qué contrato?
9. ¿Maletas? ¿Qué maletas?
10. ¿Problemas? ¿Qué problemas?

III. Supply the correct form of the definite article.

1. Un martes por _____ tarde dos hombres hablan en _____ aeropuerto.
2. José Antonio Díaz es de _____ Nacional Financiera.
3. Para _____ mexicano, _____ aduana es una lata.
4. Afortunadamente no hay problemas con _____ maletas de Fred.
5. En _____ hotel, Fred y José Antonio hablan de _____ recepción.
6. ¡Qué bueno llegar! _____ viajes cansan mucho.
7. Esta noche cenamos en _____ casa de José Antonio y mañana en _____ club campestre.
8. Hablan de negocios _____ viernes, en _____ oficina de la Nacional Financiera.

IV. Restate the sentences, each time replacing the noun with a new noun suggested by the cue.

MODELO ¿Cuándo hablan de la recepción? (hotel, universidad) →
¿Cuándo hablan del hotel?
¿Cuándo hablan de la universidad?

1. ¡Qué bueno llegar al hotel! (recepción, aeropuerto, Estados Unidos, oficina, club campestre, café, restaurante, clase de español)
2. Es de la Nacional Financiera. (Estados Unidos, hotel, club campestre, aduana, recepción, aeropuerto)
3. Hablan de la clase. (negocio, contrato, pasaporte, aduana, problemas, club)

V. Say **no** and give the correct information, as suggested by the cue.

MODELO ¿Hablamos del negocio? (recepción) → **No, hablamos de la recepción.**

1. ¿Vamos a la universidad? (aeropuerto)
2. ¿Vamos a México? (Estados Unidos)
3. ¿Vamos al café? (casa de José Antonio)
4. ¿Hablamos del contrato? (recepción)
5. ¿Vamos al Aeropuerto Internacional? (oficina)

VI. If the noun is singular, change it to plural. If the noun is plural, change it to singular.

MODELO Para el mexicano, es bueno. → **Para los mexicanos, es bueno.**

1. Hablan con el estudiante.
2. Cenamos con los hombres.
3. Necesitamos hablar de los contratos.
4. Vamos a la recepción.
5. No hay problemas.
6. Hablan de los hoteles.
7. Vamos el lunes.
8. Hablamos de la mujer.

Don Roberto Hernández Ramírez, chairman of the Mexican Stock Exchange.

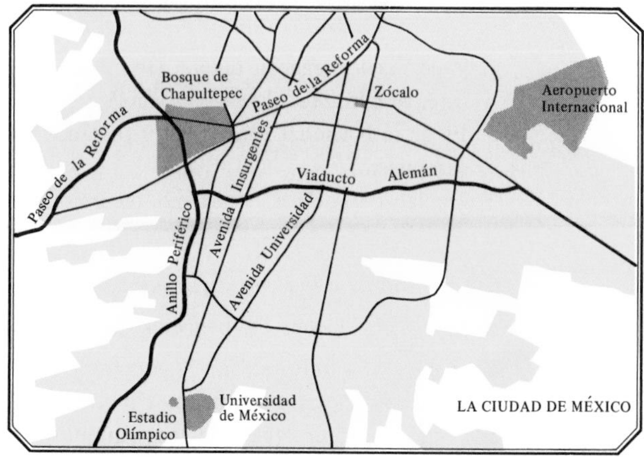

Pausa oral

Un viaje a México

Mexico is the first Spanish-speaking country which most North Americans visit. Imagine that you are there right now and find yourself speaking Spanish for the first time.

I. Para combinar[1]

Make complete statements by combining the phrase at left with an item from the right-hand column.

MODELO ¿Cómo anda. . . ? → **¿Cómo anda el contrato?**

1. ¿Cómo es. . . ?	para el viaje
2. Los viajes. . .	el aeropuerto
3. Esta noche. . .	el contrato
4. José Antonio. . .	siempre cansan
5. ¡Qué bueno. . . !	llegar
6. Necesitamos una maleta. . .	cenamos en casa
	da la mano

II. Para completar

Each of the following questions is one that someone might ask you while you are in Mexico. Complete the answer to each with any logical ending.

MODELO Cenamos en el Hotel María Isabel esta noche, ¿no? No, cenamos _____.
→ **No, cenamos en casa.**

1. Usted es José Antonio Díaz, ¿no?	No, yo soy _____.
2. Los viajes siempre cansan, ¿no?	Sí, los viajes siempre _____.
3. Usted es de México, ¿no?	Yo soy de _____.
4. Cenamos en casa, ¿no?	No, cenamos en _____.

[1] *To be combined.*

5. Necesitamos un pasaporte, ¿no?	Sí, necesitamos _____.
6. Hablamos de negocios ahora, ¿no?	No, ahora hablamos de _____.
7. Hay clases de español, ¿no?	Sí, hay _____.
8. Usted es estudiante, ¿no?	Yo soy _____.
9. Hay restaurantes en el hotel, ¿no?	Sí, hay _____.
10. José Antonio es extranjero, ¿no?	No, Fred Williams es _____.
11. Hay problemas con la aduana, ¿no?	Siempre hay _____.
12. ¿Hay estudiantes en la universidad?	Sí, hay _____.

III. Para conversar[1]

Make two or three statements about each of the following drawings. You may want to use some of the words which appear below the drawing.

MODELO

campestre
internacional

Possible statements **Es un club campestre.**
Es un club internacional.
Hay una recepción en el club campestre esta noche.

1. 

Los Ángeles
México

2. 

esta noche
mañana

3. 

una lata
un problema

4. 

el domingo
ahora

5. 

hay
necesitamos

[1] *To be discussed.*

ESTRUCTURA II

A. Subject pronouns (I)

Yo soy José Antonio Díaz.

1. The subject pronouns in English are *I, you, he, she, it, we, they.* Pronouns stand in place of nouns.

2. The Spanish subject pronouns are shown in the following chart.

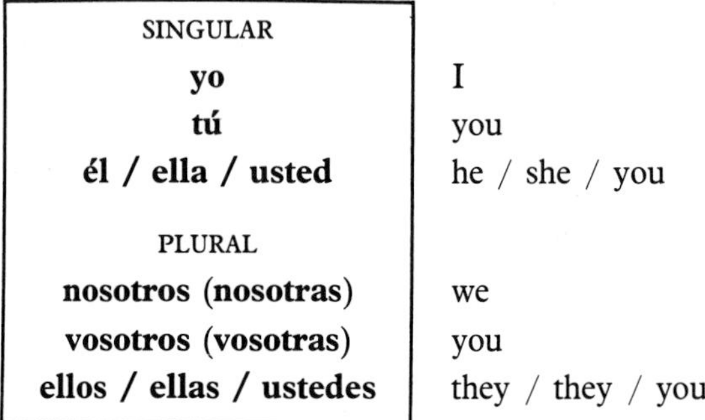

SINGULAR	
yo	I
tú	you
él / ella / usted	he / she / you
PLURAL	
nosotros (nosotras)	we
vosotros (vosotras)	you
ellos / ellas / ustedes	they / they / you

1. **Yo** *I* is first-person singular.

2. **Tú** *you* is second-person singular. Using the intimate **tú** when talking to someone shows that a bond is felt to exist between the speaker and the person addressed. Typically, **tú** is used when talking to family members and to friends of one's own age.

3. **Él** *he,* **ella** *she,* and **usted** *you* are third-person singular. The formal pronoun **usted** is often written **Ud.** Using **usted** shows the degree of courtesy or respect called for in more formal situations—for example, in a business discussion or when speaking to an older person. In most language classes, students address each other as **tú** but use **usted** when talking to the instructor.

TWO STUDENTS

Yo soy Lola Núñez Gimeno. ¿Y tú? — I'm Lola Núñez Gimeno. And you?

TWO BUSINESSMEN

Yo soy José Antonio Díaz. ¿Y usted? — I'm José Antonio Díaz. And you?

4. **Nosotros, nosotras** *we* is first-person plural. It refers to the speaker (**yo**) plus one or more other persons. **Nosotros** is the form used unless all persons referred to are female.
   a) Speaker (**yo**) is a man.

   tú y yo; Ana y yo; Ana, José y yo = **nosotros**

b) Speaker (**yo**) is a woman, but at least one other person referred to by the pronoun is a man.

tú [*man*] y yo; Ana, José y yo = **nosotros**

c) Speaker (**yo**) and everyone else referred to is female.

tú [*woman*] y yo; Ana y yo = **nosotras**

5. **Ellos, ellas** *they*, and **ustedes** *you* are third-person plural.

a) **Ellos** refers to two or more persons, at least one of which is male.

José y Alberto; Ana y Alberto = **ellos**

b) **Ellas** refers to two or more persons, all female.

Alicia y Ana = **ellas**

c) **Ustedes,** often abbreviated in writing to **Uds.,** is the plural form of **usted.** It is used in all parts of the Spanish-speaking world when talking to two or more persons in a formal situation.

José Antonio Díaz y usted = **ustedes**

d) In Spanish America **ustedes** also serves as the plural form of **tú.** (In Spain **vosotros, vosotras** is used instead.)

José Antonio Díaz y tú = **ustedes**

Aplicación

I. Supply the corresponding subject pronoun.

MODELO los hombres de negocios → **ellos**

1. Alicia y yo 2. Roberto y tú 3. Beatriz, Jorge y yo 4. el hombre 5. Teresa 6. Claudia, Sara y Pablo 7. José Antonio Díaz 8. Teresa Sánchez 9. María, Teresa y Lola 10. Jesús, Francisco y ella 11. los estudiantes 12. el hombre y la mujer

II. The speaker isn't sure who is supposed to meet with Fred Williams tomorrow. Say that his guess is wrong, as shown in the model.

MODELO ¿yo? → **Usted, no.**

1. ¿usted? 2. ¿Pedro y José Antonio? 3. ¿Ricardo y yo? 4. ¿el hombre de negocios y Roberto? 5. ¿Lola Núñez Gimeno? 6. ¿usted y ella? 7. ¿la estudiante? 8. ¿usted, ella y yo? 9. ¿Susana y Lola? 10. ¿yo?

III. Tell whether you would use **tú, usted,** or **ustedes** in the following situations described in English.

MODELO You are talking with a travel agent. → **usted**

1. You are talking with your best friend.
2. You are talking on the phone with the Department of Motor Vehicles.
3. You are talking with two of your father's associates.
4. You are talking with two of your cousins.
5. You are talking with Mrs. Ortiz, your mother's boss.

IV. Tell whether you would use **tú, usted,** or **ustedes** in the following situations described in Spanish.

MODELO Usted habla con un estudiante. → **tú**

1. Usted habla con dos hombres de negocios.
2. Usted habla con una chica en la clase de español.
3. Usted habla con una señora de la Nacional Financiera.
4. Usted habla con el profesor de español.
5. Usted habla con dos estudiantes en el club campestre.
6. Usted habla con dos chicos en la universidad.

B. Present tense of -ar verbs

Los viajes siempre **cansan** un poco.

1. A sentence has two basic parts, the subject and the verb phrase. The verb tells what its subject does or is. In the sentence above, **los viajes** is the subject. What do **los viajes** do? The word **cansan** tells the answer—it is the verb.

2. The form of the verb found in a dictionary or vocabulary list is called the infinitive. Spanish infinitives end in **-ar, -er,** or **-ir.**

hablar	to talk
comer	to eat
vivir	to live

3. The stem of the verb indicates what the verbal idea is. The endings change in order to indicate when the verbal idea takes place (tense) and who the subject is (person and number). Each regular **-ar** verb adds exactly the same endings to its stem. Here are the present tense forms of **cenar** *to have dinner.*

	cenar		
	stem	*endings*	
yo	**cen**	**o**	Ceno en el aeropuerto.
tú	**cen**	**as**	¿Cenas con José Antonio?
él, ella, usted	**cen**	**a**	Ella cena en el hotel.
nosotros	**cen**	**amos**	Cenamos en el restaurante.
vosotros	**cen**	**áis**	Cenáis en casa, ¿no?
ellos, ellas, ustedes	**cen**	**an**	Cenan ahora.

4. A few verbs which follow this pattern are **hablar, llegar,** and **cansar.**

¿Cuándo hablamos de negocios?	When do we talk business?
Llego al Hotel María Isabel.	I'm arriving at the Hotel María Isabel.
Los viajes siempre cansan.	Trips always tire (you out).

The subject pronouns are often omitted in Spanish. Note that in the first two sentences, the subject of the verb is made clear by the verb ending.

5. The present tense in Spanish is generally equivalent to three structures in English.

Hablan.	They speak They do speak. They are speaking.	¿Hablan?	They speak? Do they speak? Are they speaking?

6. When used in a question, the verbs corresponding to **yo** and to **nosotros** can mean *Should (Shall) I (we)?* + verb. The context of the sentence will clarify the meaning.

¿Llego al aeropuerto mañana?	Should I arrive at the airport tomorrow?
¿Hablamos español?	Shall we speak Spanish?
¿Cenamos en casa esta noche?	Should we eat at home tonight?

Aplicación

I. Tell who the subject of each sentence is. In some cases there may be more than one possible subject.

MODELOS Viajas poco. → **tú**
Dan la mano. → **ellos / ellas / ustedes**

1. Hablamos de negocios.
2. Llego esta noche.
3. Cenas en el club campestre.
4. Necesitan el pasaporte.
5. Viajamos mañana.

II. Following the model, respond using the **yo** verb form.

MODELO ¿Hablas ahora? → **Sí, ahora hablo.**

1. ¿Cenas ahora?
2. ¿Llegas al hotel ahora?
3. ¿Necesitas la maleta ahora?
4. ¿Viajas a México ahora?
5. ¿Hablas ahora?

III. Now respond using the **nosotros** verb form.

MODELO ¿Llegan ustedes esta noche? → **Sí, llegamos esta noche.**

1. ¿Cenan ustedes en el café?
2. ¿Necesitan ustedes las maletas?
3. ¿Llegan ustedes el sábado?
4. ¿Viajan ustedes mucho?
5. ¿Hablan ustedes español?

IV. Restate each sentence, changing the subject and verb as suggested by the cues.

MODELO Hablo de negocios. (ustedes, ella) → **Ustedes hablan de negocios. Ella habla de negocios.**

1. Cenamos en casa. (él, ustedes, yo, nosotros, José Antonio, tú)
2. Llegan a México. (Marta, los estudiantes, él y yo, tú, usted, yo)
3. Viajamos mucho. (Luisa y yo, él, tú, usted y ella, yo, usted)
4. Dan la mano. (nosotros, tú, los hombres, Eva, Eva y tú)
5. Hablo de la situación. (José Antonio, ustedes, tú y yo, el profesor)

V. Respond negatively according to the model.

MODELO ¿Llega Luisa ahora? → **No, ella llega dentro de un rato.**

1. ¿Llega Pedro al hotel ahora?
2. ¿Cenan los estudiantes ahora?
3. ¿Habla usted ahora?
4. ¿Ceno yo ahora?
5. ¿Llegamos nosotros ahora?

VI. If the subject and verb are singular, change them to the plural. If they are plural, change them to the singular.

MODELOS Llegamos ahora. → **Llego ahora.**
El estudiante cena en el restaurante. → **Los estudiantes cenan en el restaurante.**

1. Los hombres hablan.
2. La recepción cansa.
3. ¿Cómo anda el contrato?
4. ¿Qué necesita usted?
5. Viajas mucho.
6. Ustedes llegan por la tarde.

VII. Give an affirmative response to each question.

MODELO ¿Hablan los estudiantes? → **Sí, los estudiantes hablan.**

1. ¿Hablan los profesores también?
2. ¿Habla usted mucho?
3. ¿Habla bien?
4. ¿Cansan las clases?
5. ¿Cansan las recepciones?
6. ¿Necesita usted el pasaporte?
7. ¿Viaja usted mucho?
8. ¿Cenan ustedes en casa o en el restaurante?
9. ¿Hablo mucho yo?
10. ¿Cómo andan las clases?

C. Subject pronouns (II)

Primero, cenamos en casa.

1. As mentioned on page 30, the subject pronoun in Spanish is often omitted—using it would seem redundant to the Spanish-speaker. Spanish verb endings clearly indicate whether the subject is **yo, tú, nosotros,** or **vosotros** in the present tense.

¿Cuándo hablamos de negocios?	When do we talk about business?
Soy americano.	I am American.

2. The subject pronouns are used, however, for emphasis or contrast. **Usted** is also used to be especially polite.

¿Fred Williams? Yo soy José Antonio Díaz.	Fred Williams? I am José Antonio Díaz.
Usted es de México, ¿no?	You're from Mexico, correct?

3. The range of possible subjects is greater when the verb is third person. To clarify who the subject is, the pronouns **él, ella, usted** (in the singular) and **ellos, ellas, ustedes** (plural) are often used.

Él (ella, usted) habla de negocios.	He talks (she talks, you talk) about business.
Ellas (ellos, ustedes) cenan en casa.	They (you) are eating at home.

4. Spanish has no equivalent for the subject pronoun *it* or *they* when referring to things. In these cases a verb (third person singular or plural) is used with no pronoun.

¿La aduana? ¡Es una lata!	Customs? It's a pain!
¿Los viajes? Siempre cansan un poco.	Trips? They always tire (you out) a little.

Aplicación

I. Respond in the negative according to the models.

MODELOS ¿Soy estudiante yo? → **¿Usted? No.**
¿Es usted estudiante? → **¿Yo? No.**

1. ¿Habla usted?
2. ¿Llegan Pedro y José Antonio?
3. ¿Necesitamos el pasaporte Ricardo y yo?
4. ¿Cenan los hombres de negocios?
5. ¿Viaja mucho Lola Núñez Gimeno?
6. ¿Soy yo José Antonio Díaz?
7. ¿Habla del viaje el estudiante?
8. ¿Hablan mucho usted y ella?
9. ¿Llegan esta noche Susana y Lola?
10. ¿Hablamos primero usted y yo?

II. Respond in the affirmative. Since no confusion about the subject of your sentence is possible, omit the subject pronoun or noun.

MODELOS ¿Viaja usted a México? → **Sí, viajo a México.**
¿Hablan los profesores? → **Sí, hablan.**

1. ¿Habla usted del contrato?
2. ¿Habla usted de la situación?
3. ¿Necesita usted cenar ahora?
4. ¿Cenan ustedes en casa?
5. ¿Siempre dan la mano los mexicanos?
6. ¿Hablo mucho yo?
7. ¿Llego por la tarde?
8. ¿Andan bien los negocios?
9. ¿Cena usted con los estudiantes?
10. ¿Viajan mucho los hombres de negocios?
11. ¿Necesita usted viajar mucho?
12. ¿Cansa mucho la clase de español?

III. Para expresar en español[1]

MODELO She speaks. → **Habla.**
She speaks. → **Ella habla.**

1. We travel. *We* travel.
2. They arrive. *They* arrive.
3. You have dinner. *You* have dinner.
4. I need the suitcase. *I* need the suitcase.
5. He is very good. *He* is very good.

[1] *To be expressed in Spanish.*

Repaso oral

I. Para conversar

In this review you will have short conversations with another person.

MODELO You run into a friend one afternoon. Person B responds. →
(Person A) **Buenas tardes, José.**
(Person B) **Buenas tardes, Susana.**

1. You introduce yourself. Person B says "hello."
2. You say that for foreigners there are no problems with customs. Person B agrees.
3. You want to talk about business. Person B thinks it's boring.
4. You want to know how the contract is going. Person B says there aren't any problems.
5. You say that tonight the two of you will have dinner in the hotel. Person B says "O.K."
6. You say that the two of you need passports. Person B says that it's good to travel.

II. Para describir

How many statements can you make about the people and places you see in the following drawing? Use words which you already know to describe all that you can, telling: 1) who they are, 2) what they are doing, and 3) what they are discussing.

Capítulo 3

Despegue

DIÁLOGO **El amor es internacional**

Present tense of **-er** and **-ir** verbs • Saying no and asking questions • Use and non-use of the definite article

PAUSA ORAL **En Madrid**

The expressions **hay** and **hay que** • The irregular verb **ir** • The indefinite article

Preparing to read in Spanish

LECTURA **Amigos y novios**

Repaso oral

Despegue

el amor

España

un banco

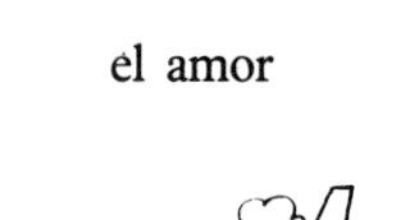

un avión

un matrimonio

una familia

Pronunciación

tú **pero** **matrimonio**	All vowels are pronounced very clearly.
tarde **Navidad** **Estados Unidos**	Most of the time Spanish **d** has a soft *th* sound (as in *this*).
tú **tarde** **todo**	Spanish **t** is pronounced with the tip of the tongue against the back of the upper teeth.

Aplicación

I. Practice saying each of the following words, first very slowly and then at a normal speed, imitating the pronunciation of your instructor.

1. tú / pero / matrimonio
2. tarde / Navidad / Estados Unidos
3. hotel / tarde / todo
4. amor / banco / España
5. avión / amor / familia

II. Tell what is shown in each of the following drawings.

1. 

3. 

5. 

2. 

4. 

6. 

Tema del diálogo

Love and marriage. Is there anything left to think over?

Seriously considering getting married during the Christmas holidays.

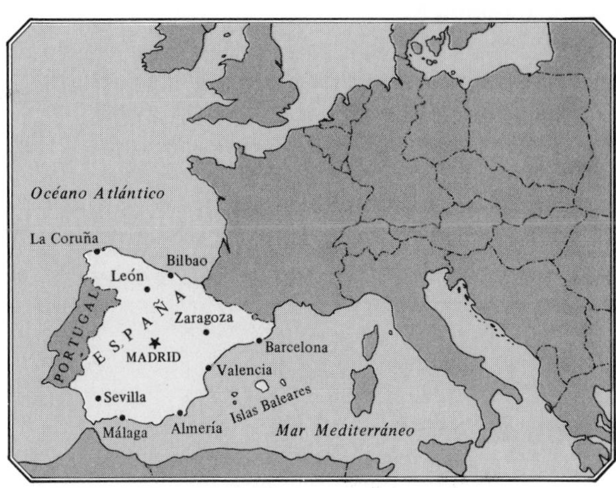

DIÁLOGO

El amor es internacional

Jane Robinson, joven americana que estudia en España; Miguel Sánchez Cordero[1], *joven economista español que trabaja en el Banco de Bilbao.*

JANE Miguel, ya es muy tarde.

MIGUEL No, unos minutos más, por favor. Mañana partes y en el avión vas a dormir como un lirón.

JANE De acuerdo. Pero sólo quince minutos más. Hay que salir a comer todavía.[2]

* * *

MIGUEL Comprendes que en Navidades[3] voy a los Estados Unidos a visitar a tu familia, ¿no?

JANE Sí, sí, seguro. Así vamos a pasar la Navidad y el Año Nuevo juntos. . .tú y yo.

MIGUEL Con tus padres. . .para discutir cierto caso concreto.

JANE ¿Qué caso concreto?

MIGUEL Los detalles del matrimonio. ¿Qué otra cosa?

JANE Esto. . .sí, claro. Pero no hay que apresurar las cosas. Necesitamos analizar todo muy bien otra vez.

MIGUEL ¿Por qué? No veo problema. Pero tú, mi vida, ¿vas a cambiar de opinión ahora?

Love is international

Jane Robinson, a young American who is studying in Spain; Miguel Sánchez Cordero, a young Spanish economist who works at the Bank of Bilbao.

J: Miguel, it's already late.

M: No (it's not), a few minutes more please. Tomorrow you're leaving and on the plane you'll sleep like a log [dormouse].

J: O.K. But only fifteen minutes more. We've still got to go out to eat.

* * *

M: You know that at Christmas time I'm going to the United States to visit your family, right?

J: Yes, of course. That way we'll have (spend) Christmas and New Year's together. . .you and I.

M: With your parents. . .to discuss a certain special matter.

J: What special matter?

M: The details of the wedding. What else?

J: Uh. . . Sure, of course. But we shouldn't rush things. We need to analyze everything very well again.

M: Why? I don't see any problem. But you, sweetheart, are you going to change your mind now?

VARIACIONES

Usted parte mañana.	You leave tomorrow.
hoy	today
¿Es muy tarde?	Is it very late?
No, es temprano.	No, it's early.
¿Hay muchas personas en tu familia?	Are there many people in your family?
Hay siete.	Yes, there are seven.
mi madre (mi mamá)	my mother (my mom)
mi padre (mi papá)	my father (my dad)
cinco hijos	five children (sons and daughters)
el hijo	son
la hija	daughter
dos hermanos	two brothers
dos hermanas	two sisters
los hermanos	brothers and sisters
¿Cuántos hay en tu familia?	How many are there in your family?
Uno, dos, tres, cuatro, cinco, seis, siete, ocho, nueve, diez.	One, two, three, four, five, six, seven, eight, nine, ten.

Glosas

1. In the Hispanic world each person uses one or two first names, then the father's last name, often followed by the mother's maiden name. For example:

first name	*(optional)*	*father's name*	*mother's name*
Miguel	Ángel	Sánchez	Cordero

A person with this name would be addressed as **Sr. Sánchez** or **Sr. Sánchez Cordero,** but never "Sr. Cordero." If Jane marries Miguel, she will be known as either **Jane Robinson de Sánchez** or, more briefly, **Señora (Sra.) Sánchez** or, more formally, **Sra. de Sánchez.**

2. In many Spanish-speaking countries, lunch is served at two or three o'clock in the afternoon. Dinner (or supper) is served after nine or even ten at night.

3. **La Navidad** means Christmas Day. **Las Navidades** refers to the Christmas season.

SOBRE EL DIÁLOGO

I. ¿Sí o no? If the information contained in the statement is true, say **sí** and repeat the statement. If the information is false, say **no** and make a statement which is true.

MODELO Jane Robinson es de México. → **No, Jane Robinson es de los Estados Unidos.**

1. Jane Robinson estudia en los Estados Unidos.
2. Miguel es un economista que trabaja en California.
3. Jane parte en avión esta noche.
4. Ella va a dormir muy bien en el avión.
5. Miguel va a pasar las Navidades en los Estados Unidos.
6. Miguel va a discutir los detalles del viaje con los padres de Jane.
7. Jane y Miguel necesitan analizar todo otra vez.

II. Para contestar[1] Answer each of the following questions concerning the dialog.

MODELO ¿Trabaja Jane o estudia? → **Jane estudia.**

1. ¿Estudia Jane en España o en Colombia?
2. ¿Es Miguel hombre de negocios o economista?
3. ¿Hay que comer en casa o en el restaurante?
4. ¿Pasa Miguel las Navidades en España o en los Estados Unidos?
5. ¿Necesitan Jane y Miguel discutir el matrimonio o las clases?
6. ¿Necesitan apresurar las cosas o analizar todo muy bien?

III. Para completar Choose an appropriate word from the list and complete each sentence.

banco, avión, España, familia, hermana, trabaja, tarde, hijos, temprano

MODELO Vamos al aeropuerto. Parte el _____. → **Vamos al aeropuerto. Parte el avión.**

1. Mario es mi hermano y Lilia es mi _____.
2. ¡Las once de la noche! Ya es _____.
3. Hablan español en _____.
4. Hay siete personas en mi _____.
5. No es tarde; es _____.
6. Miguel no estudia. Él _____.
7. Miguel es economista. Trabaja en un _____.
8. El señor Sánchez siempre pasa la Navidad con los _____.

IV. React to each statement choosing a logical response from the list.

Buenas tardes.	**Sí, sí, seguro.**
De acuerdo.	**¿Por qué?**
Sí, por favor.	**Siempre cambia de opinión.**

MODELO ¿Cenamos ahora? → **Sí, por favor.**

1. Hola, Miguel.
2. Vamos a visitar a tu familia en Madrid, ¿no?
3. Necesitamos ver el pasaporte otra vez.

[1] *To be answered.*

4. Primero Jane no ve problema; ahora necesita analizar todo.
5. No voy a cenar en casa esta noche.

V. Count from one to ten.

VI. Say the following numbers.

5 2 4 6 9 1 3 7 10 8

VOCABULARIO

nouns

el **amor**	love
el **Año Nuevo**	New Year
el **avión**	airplane
el **banco**	bank
el **caso**	matter, case
la **cosa**	thing
el **detalle**	detail
el (la) **economista**	economist
la **familia**	family
el (la) **joven**	young man (woman)
el **lirón**	dormouse
dormir como un lirón	to sleep like a log
el **matrimonio**	wedding, marriage
el **minuto**	minute
la **Navidad**	Christmas
las **Navidades**	Christmas season
la **opinión**	opinion
la **persona**	person
la **vez**	time
la **vida**	life
mi vida	sweetheart

verbs

analizar (**c**)[1]	to analyze; to think over
apresurar	to hurry; to rush
cambiar	to change
cambiar de opinión	to change one's mind
comer	to eat
comprender	to understand
discutir	to discuss; to argue
dormir (**ue**)[1]	to sleep
estudiar	to study
hay que (+ infinitive)	it is necessary (to do something)
hay que salir	it is necessary to (one has to) go out
ir	to go
ir a (+ infinitive)	to be going to (do something)

[1]Certain Spanish verbs change a stem vowel or consonant in specific circumstances. Vocabulary lists note the change with parenthetical letters. The changes involved are explained in the Appendix.

necesitar (+ infinitive)	to need (to do something)
pasar	to spend (time)
partir	to leave, to depart
salir	to go out, to leave (a place)
yo salgo	I go out.
son	they are
trabajar	to work
ver	to see
veo	I see
visitar	to visit

adjectives

cierto	(a) certain
cierto caso	a certain matter
concreto	particular, concrete, special
español	Spanish
juntos, juntas	together
mucho(s)	much (many)
otro	other, another
otra vez	again, another time
tu, tus	your
unos, unas	some, a few

family relations

la **familia**	family
la **hermana**	sister
el **hermano**	brother
los **hermanos**	brothers (or) brothers and sisters
la **hija**	daughter
el **hijo**	son
los **hijos**	sons, children
la **madre**	mother
la **mamá**	mom
el **padre**	father
el **papá**	dad
los **padres**	mother and father, parents

other expressions

así	so, this (that) way
claro	of course, sure
¿cuánto (-a, -os, -as)?	how much, how many?
de acuerdo	O.K.; agreed
esto...	uh...
hoy	today
más	more
por	for
¿por qué?	why?
que	who, that
seguro	of course, (for) sure
sólo	only
tarde	late
temprano	early
todavía	still, yet
todo	everything
¿verdad?	true?, right?, isn't it?
ya	already
ya es tarde	it's already late

numbers

uno	one
dos	two
tres	three
cuatro	four
cinco	five
seis	six
siete	seven
ocho	eight
nueve	nine
diez	ten
quince	fifteen

additional vocabulary

considerar	to consider
seriamente	seriously

ESTRUCTURA I

A. Present tense of -er and -ir verbs

Hay que **salir** a **comer** todavía, **¿comprendes?**

1. Here are the present tense forms of **comprender.** All regular **-er** verbs add the same endings to their stem.

	comprender		
yo	**comprend**	**o**	Comprendo el diálogo.
tú	**comprend**	**es**	No comprendes los negocios.
él, ella, usted	**comprend**	**e**	Ella comprende el problema.
nosotros	**comprend**	**emos**	Comprendemos las cosas.
vosotros	**comprend**	**éis**	¿Comprendéis el caso?
ellos, ellas, ustedes	**comprend**	**en**	Ustedes comprenden la lectura, ¿no?

Another verb that follows this pattern is **comer.**

Como en el aeropuerto.	I eat at the airport.
Jane y Miguel comen juntos.	Jane and Miguel eat together.

2. **Discutir** is a regular **-ir** verb. Other regular **-ir** verbs add the same endings to their stem in the present tense.

discutir		
discut	**o**	Discuto el problema.
discut	**es**	¿Discutes negocios?
discut	**e**	Él discute el viaje.
discut	**imos**	Discutimos todo.
discut	**ís**	Discutís un caso concreto.
discut	**en**	Ellas discuten la situación.

Another **-ir** verb which follows this pattern is **partir.**

Mañana partes en el avión.	Tomorrow you're leaving on the plane.
Partimos para México.	We're leaving for Mexico.

3. Notice that **-er** and **-ir** verbs use the same present-tense endings except for the **nosotros** and **vosotros** forms.

comer		**partir**
como	**-o**	parto
comes	**-es**	partes
come	**-e**	parte
comemos	**-emos / -imos**	partimos
coméis	**-éis / -ís**	partís
comen	**-en**	parten

4. **Ver** is regular except for the first person singular: **veo.**

Veo el contrato.	I see the contract.
Vemos el problema.	We see the problem.

Aplicación

I. Repeat each sentence, changing the subject according to the cue.

MODELO Sale ahora. (nosotros, tú) → **Salimos ahora. Sales ahora.**

1. Parten temprano. (yo, el avión, ellos, el hijo, tú, ustedes, Miguel y yo)
2. Comprende el problema. (el estudiante, yo, nosotros, tú, mamá y papá, usted, tu hermano)
3. Comes mucho. (mi hijo, los señores, yo, Pedro y tú, ella y yo, tú)
4. Discutimos el contrato. (tú, los hombres, ustedes, yo, la señorita, Teresa y yo, María y usted)
5. Veo el avión. (ellos, tú, yo, tú y yo, usted)

II. Answer each question according to the model.

MODELO ¿Necesitan partir ustedes? → **Sí, partimos ahora.**

1. ¿Necesitan comer ustedes?
2. ¿Necesitan salir ustedes?
3. ¿Necesitan ver el contrato ustedes?
4. ¿Necesitan discutir los detalles ustedes?
5. ¿Necesitan partir ustedes?

III. Respond using **necesitar** + infinitive. Note that some of the infinitives end in **-ar,** some in **-er,** and some in **-ir.**

MODELO ¿Parte Juan? → **Sí, necesita partir.**

1. ¿Viaja Juan?
2. ¿Ve el contrato Juan?
3. ¿Sale Juan?
4. ¿Discute los detalles Juan?
5. ¿Estudia Juan?
6. ¿Come Juan?

IV. Para contestar

MODELO ¿Parte usted para México? → **Sí, parto para México.**

1. ¿Comprende usted el diálogo?
2. ¿Discuten Miguel y Jane el matrimonio?
3. ¿Parte Juan mañana?
4. ¿Parten ustedes para Madrid?
5. ¿Discuten ustedes los hoteles?
6. ¿Salen ustedes mucho?
7. ¿Discute usted los problemas?
8. ¿Como yo en casa?
9. Y usted, ¿come en casa?
10. ¿Comprende usted el español?

A wedding in the state of Jalisco, Mexico. Afterwards, a fiesta for two days.

V. Make sentences by combining the words in each list.

MODELO ellos / discutir / detalles → **Ellos discuten los detalles.**

1. yo / siempre / comer / en casa
2. mi hermano / trabajar / Banco de Bilbao
3. él y yo / comprender / problemas
4. los detalles / cansar / mucho
5. tú / partir / para España / mañana

VI. Complete the following dialog by supplying the correct form of the verbs indicated in the key.

A: ¿___1___ esta noche?
B: Sí, con Mario. Vamos al club campestre.
A: Qué bueno.
B: Esto...no. No es muy bueno. Él siempre ___2___ del matrimonio, de pasar la vida juntos, ¿___3___?
A: Sí, sí, yo ___4___. Él ___5___ las cosas. Y tú ___6___ analizar la situación y hablar con tus padres.
B: Claro. Y hay otro problema... Mario no ___7___. Es estudiante. Es muy joven.
A: ¿Sí? ¿Qué ___8___?
B: Negocios. Dentro de poco ___9___ para Madrid.
A: Mmmm, ya ___10___.
B: Pero él ya ___11___ de pasar las Navidades con mi familia y de discutir los detalles del matrimonio.
A: ¿Y tú?
B: Yo...yo ___12___ salir con otros.
A: ¿Por qué no ___13___ el problema con él? Él necesita ___14___ de opinión.
B: Oh, él y yo no ___15___ de otra cosa.

1. salir (tú)
2. hablar
3. ver (tú)
4. comprender
5. apresurar
6. necesitar
7. trabajar
8. estudiar (él)
9. partir (él)
10. ver
11. hablar
12. necesitar
13. discutir (tú)
14. cambiar
15. hablar

B. Saying no and asking questions

No veo problema.
Hablamos de negocios, ¿no?

1. To make a negative statement, the word **no** is placed directly before the verb.

No hay problemas con la aduana.	There aren't any problems with customs.
No es muy tarde.	It's not very late.
No necesitas analizar todo.	You don't need to analyze everything.

2. One type of simple question seeks a yes-or-no answer. Almost any statement may be converted into a simple question by changing the intonation to rising pitch at the end.

Hay problemas con la aduana.	There are problems with customs.
→ ¿Hay problemas con la aduana?	Are there problems with customs?
Hablamos de negocios.	We're talking business.
→ ¿Hablamos de negocios?	Are we talking business?
Vas a cambiar.	You're going to change.
→ ¿Vas a cambiar?	Are you going to change?

3. Another type of simple question is formed by inverting the word order from subject + verb to verb + subject.

Usted es Miguel Sánchez.	You are Miguel Sánchez.
→ ¿Es usted Miguel Sánchez?	Are you Miguel Sánchez?
Ellas son mexicanas.	They are Mexican.
→ ¿Son ellas mexicanas?	Are they Mexican?

4. An agreement question asks for confirmation or rejection of what is stated. Simply add the word **¿no?** or **¿verdad?** to the end of a sentence.

Hay una recepción mañana por la tarde, ¿no?	There's a reception tomorrow afternoon, isn't there?
Usted es José Díaz, ¿verdad?	You are José Díaz, aren't you?
El amor es internacional, ¿no?	Love is international, right?

Aplicación

I. Change each sentence to the negative.

MODELO Pasamos las Navidades juntos. → **No pasamos las Navidades juntos.**

1. Hablo con tu familia.
2. Cenamos juntos esta noche.
3. Discutimos el matrimonio.
4. Tu padre ve problemas.
5. Cambias de opinión.
6. Parto para Madrid otra vez.

II. Answer each question in the negative.

MODELO ¿Es una lata estudiar? → **No, no es una lata estudiar.**

1. ¿Salen ustedes ahora?
2. ¿Trabaja usted en el Banco de Bilbao?
3. ¿Es internacional el amor?
4. ¿Apresuran las cosas los hombres?
5. ¿Comprende usted el matrimonio?
6. ¿Estudia usted en España?

III. Change the following statements to questions. Two questions are possible in each case.

MODELO Miguel trabaja en el banco. → **¿Miguel trabaja en el banco?** *or* **¿Trabaja Miguel en el banco?**

1. Jane estudia en España.
2. Miguel y Jane van a los Estados Unidos.
3. El avión parte mañana.
4. Ellos necesitan discutir cierto caso.
5. Jane y Miguel hablan del matrimonio.

IV. Change each of the following statements to an agreement question. Two questions are possible for each one.

MODELO Federico y José Antonio cenan en el club. → **Federico y José Antonio cenan en el club, ¿verdad?** *or* **Federico y José Antonio cenan en el club, ¿no?**

1. Federico habla de negocios.
2. Él apresura las cosas mucho.
3. José Antonio necesita analizar el contrato.
4. Necesita hablar con otros.
5. Pero Federico discute y discute.
6. José Antonio siempre cambia de opinión.
7. Él ve muchos problemas.
8. Pero Federico no comprende la situación.

V. Respond to each of the following statements with any suitable question.

MODELO Voy a dormir como un lirón. →
Possible responses **Los viajes cansan mucho, ¿verdad?**
¿No es muy temprano para dormir?

1. Para el extranjero no hay problemas con la aduana.
2. No necesito discutir los detalles del matrimonio.
3. Paso el Año Nuevo con mi familia.
4. Siempre hay que analizar todo muy bien.
5. ¡Qué lata! Hay que estudiar ahora.

C. Use and non-use of the definite article

La estudiante americana estudia en **El** Salvador.

The definite article is used in the following cases.

1. When making a general, blanket statement about a thing or an idea.

El amor es internacional.	Love is international.
Los viajes siempre cansan.	Trips are always tiring.
La aduana no es problema.	Customs is no problem.

2. When talking about a person and using a title such as **señor, señora, señorita,** or **profesor.**

El señor Díaz es de México.	Mr. Díaz is from Mexico.
Hay una recepción para la profesora Fernández.	There's a reception for Professor Fernández.

But When speaking directly to a person, the article is not used.

Buenos días, profesor Sánchez.	Good morning, Professor Sánchez.
¿Cuándo hablamos de negocios, señor Díaz?	When do we talk business, Mr. Díaz?

3. With reference to parts of the body.

Mario da la mano.	Mario extends his hand.

4. With days of the week, when used to tell when an event or activity takes place.

Vamos a Madrid el lunes.	We're going to Madrid on Monday.
Hay una recepción el miércoles.	There is a reception on Wednesday.

5. With reference to certain geographical names. In the following names, the article is always used.

El Salvador, La Habana, El Escorial, el Atlántico, el Pacífico, el Caribe, el Amazonas	El Salvador, Havana, El Escorial [outside of Madrid], the Atlantic, the Pacific, the Caribbean, the Amazon

With the following names, the article may be used or omitted. The tendency to omit the article with these names is growing.

(el) África, (la) América Latina, (la) Argentina, (el) Brasil, (el) Canadá, (la) China, (el) Ecuador, (los) Estados Unidos, (el) Paraguay, (el) Perú, (el) Uruguay	Africa, Latin America, Argentina, Brazil, Canada, China, Ecuador, the United States, Paraguay, Peru, Uruguay

The article is not used with these and most other names of countries.

México, Portugal, España, Costa Rica, Colombia	Mexico, Portugal, Spain, Costa Rica, Colombia

6. The definite article is *not* used in the following cases.

   a. With the day of the week when it is identified by a word such as **hoy** or **mañana.**

Hoy es viernes.	Today is Friday.
Mañana es sábado.	Tomorrow is Saturday.

b. When referring to an indefinite quantity of things.

No hay problemas.	There aren't any problems.
¿Cuándo hablamos de negocios?	When do we talk business?
Necesito amor.	I need love.

c. Often after the verbs **hablar** and **estudiar,** before the name of a language.

Hablo inglés.	I speak English.
Estudiamos inglés y español.	We study English and Spanish.

Aplicación

I. Supply a definite article—but only when required. In some cases you will have to use the contraction **al** or **del.**

MODELO ¿Es usted _____ Sr. Díaz? Mucho gusto, _____ Sr. Díaz. → **¿Es usted el Sr. Díaz? Mucho gusto, Sr. Díaz.**

__1__ Sr. Arce va a una recepción. Ve que __2__ doctora Solé habla con un joven economista español __3__ Banco de Bilbao. En un rato ve que ella no habla más con el joven.

A: Buenas tardes, __4__ Doctora. (Da __5__ mano.)
S: Ah, __6__ Sr. Arce. ¡Qué recepción! Hay muchas personas.
A: A veces __7__ recepciones cansan un poco, ¿verdad?
S: Sí, sí, seguro.
A: Usted es de __8__ Argentina, ¿no?
S: No, de __9__ Chile. ¿Y usted?
A: Yo soy de __10__ Caribe. De __11__ Cuba.
S: ¿Ah? ¿De __12__ Habana?
A: No, de __13__ Santiago de Cuba.
S: Ah, ya veo.
A: Ya es un poco tarde, __14__ Doctora. ¿Por qué no vamos a mi club a cenar?
S: Mmmm... esto...
A: ¿ __15__ martes tal vez?
S: Mmmm, hoy es __16__ viernes. __17__ miércoles tal vez.
A: Muy bien, __18__ Doctora.

LOS MEJORES
PAVOS RELLENOS
PARA NAVIDAD Y
AÑO NUEVO.
CASA DE BANQUETES
DON GABOR
Reservaciones: Tel. 2482643
Calle 74 No. 15-39

Pausa oral

En Madrid

Imagine that you are just about to land in Madrid, Spain. Practice the Spanish you already know with a friend.

I. Para conversar

Formulate two or three simple questions concerning the following aspects of your life in Madrid. You may want to use the words or expressions listed with each drawing. Another member of the class should be able to answer your questions.

MODELO

trabajar
hay

Possible questions **¿Trabajas en un banco?**
¿Hay muchos bancos en Madrid?
¿Trabajas en el Banco de Bilbao?

1. 

apresurar
comprender

3. 

estudiar
hay

5. 

Navidad
Año Nuevo

2. 

viaje
pasaporte

4. 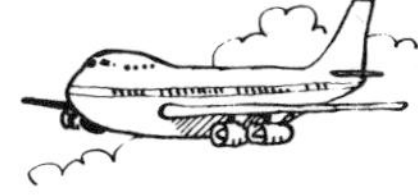

tarde
temprano

II. Para contestar

During your stay in Madrid someone might ask you the following questions. How would you answer them?

MODELO ¿Trabaja usted o estudia? → **Estudio en la universidad.** *or* **No trabajo pero estudio mucho.**

1. ¿Habla usted español?
2. ¿Estudia usted en la universidad o trabaja en un banco?
3. ¿Estudia usted en Madrid o en Barcelona?
4. ¿Pasa las Navidades en casa con la familia?
5. ¿Es tarde ahora o es temprano?
6. ¿Hay que salir a comer o hay que estudiar?
7. ¿Viaja usted mucho en avión?
8. ¿Es una lata estudiar? ¿Es una lata viajar?

ESTRUCTURA II

A. The expressions **hay** and **hay que**

Hay una recepción mañana.
Hay que salir a comer.

1. The combination **hay** + (singular or plural) noun means both *there is* and *there are.*

Hay un avión que parte mañana.	There's a plane that leaves tomorrow.
No hay problemas con la aduana en México.	There aren't any problems with customs in Mexico.

2. **Hay** is always singular and should not be confused with **es** *it is* nor **son** *they are.*

Sólo hay quince minutos más.	There are only fifteen minutes more.

3. The combination **hay que** + infinitive indicates that something should or must be done.

Hay que dormir.	It is necessary to sleep. (One should sleep.)
¿Hay que ir a la recepción?	Is it necessary to go to the reception?

Aplicación

I. Respond to each question using **hay.**

MODELO ¿Una familia? ¿en la oficina? → **Sí, hay una familia en la oficina.**

1. ¿Un matrimonio? ¿en el hotel?
2. ¿Una recepción? ¿en el club?
3. ¿Un aeropuerto? ¿en Barcelona?
4. ¿Una oficina? ¿en la casa?
5. ¿Unos estudiantes? ¿en el café?
6. ¿Cinco personas? ¿en la familia?

II. Respond to each statement using **Pero hay que** + infinitive.

MODELO No necesito dormir. → **Pero hay que dormir.**

1. No necesito comer.
2. No necesito estudiar.
3. No necesito trabajar.
4. No necesito partir.
5. No necesito hablar.
6. No necesito cenar.

III. Para expresar en español

1. There's a problem, right?
2. There are a lot of foreigners. Luckily, there's no problem with customs.
3. One has to eat, one has to sleep, and one has to study Spanish.
4. There's a reception tomorrow. Is it necessary to go?
5. There are cafés and restaurants in Bilbao.
6. It's necessary to eat at home tonight.
7. There are five children: two sons and three daughters.
8. Are you José Antonio?

B. The irregular verb **ir**

> **Vas** a dormir como un lirón.
> **Vamos** a pasar la Navidad juntos.

1. All the forms of a regular verb can be predicted from the form of the infinitive. An irregular verb has at least one form that does not follow the standard pattern. In English, *to be* is irregular: *I am, you are, she is...*
2. The verb **ir** is irregular. Its forms must be memorized.

ir	
voy	Voy a México.
vas	Vas a llegar tarde.
va	Ella va a la recepción.
vamos	Vamos a cenar en casa.
vais	¿Vais a partir en avión?
van	Ustedes van al banco.

3. **Ir a** + infinitive is often used in conversation to express the future.

Vas a llegar tarde.	You're going to arrive late.
Ella va a partir mañana.	She's going to leave tomorrow.
Ustedes no van a apresurar las cosas, ¿verdad?	You (people) are not going to rush things, right?

Aplicación

I. Repeat each sentence, changing the subject as indicated.

MODELO Van al hotel. (yo, usted) → **Voy al hotel. Va al hotel.**

1. Va a la recepción. (yo, Miguel y yo, mi hermana, ustedes, tú)
2. ¿No va él? (tú, nosotros, los padres, yo, tu hermana, usted)

II. Answer each question using verb + **claro**.

MODELO ¿Van a la recepción? → **Van, claro.**

1. ¿Vas al hotel?
2. ¿Voy a casa?
3. ¿Vamos al banco él y yo?
4. ¿Van ustedes al aeropuerto?
5. ¿Va tu hermana a España?

III. Change the verb to **ir a** + infinitive.

MODELO Parto para el banco. → **Voy a partir para el banco.**

1. Partimos para Madrid.
2. Estudiamos español.
3. Ceno en casa esta noche.
4. Comprende el diálogo.
5. ¿No sales con él?
6. Cambian de opinión.
7. Trabajas muy poco.
8. No hablamos con ellos.

San Sebastián, Spain. Young women enjoying themselves at a café.

IV. Answer in the negative, using **ir a** + infinitive and the word **mañana.**

MODELO ¿Hablamos de negocios hoy? → **No, vamos a hablar de negocios mañana.**

1. ¿Van al café hoy?
2. ¿Parte usted hoy?
3. ¿Estudio hoy?
4. ¿Cenamos en el club hoy?
5. ¿Vamos a la recepción hoy?
6. ¿Comemos con ellos hoy?
7. ¿Trabajo hoy?
8. ¿Partimos mamá y yo hoy?

V. Review. Complete each sentence with any logical ending.

MODELO Hay que _____ → **Hay que hablar de negocios.**

1. Hay _____
2. Voy a _____
3. No vas a _____
4. Marta y Mateo van a _____
5. Hay que _____
6. No hay _____
7. ¿Vas a _____?
8. Vamos a _____

C. The indefinite article

Es **una** lata.

1. The English indefinite articles are *a* and *an.*

2. The indefinite article has the following forms in Spanish.

masculine singular	**un**	un aeropuerto
feminine singular	**una**	una familia
masculine pural	**unos**	unos minutos
feminine plural	**unas**	unas maletas

3. The indefinite article is used to refer to a noun which has not been previously identified.

Un viaje siempre es bueno.	A trip is always good.
Hay una recepción mañana.	There's a reception tomorrow.
Miguel trabaja en un banco.	Miguel works in a bank.

4. The combination **unos (unas)** + plural noun is used to express an indefinite number or quantity; it means *a few* or *some.*

Unos minutos más, por favor.	A few minutes more, please.
Voy a analizar unas cosas.	I'm going to analyze some things.
Hay que discutir unos problemas.	We have to discuss some problems.

Aplicación

I. Identify each of the drawings using **es** + indefinite article.

MODELO 

→ **Es un hotel.**

1. 

2. 

3. 

4. 

5. 

6. 

II. Repeat each sentence making the indicated substitutions.

MODELO Hay un hotel. (casa, club) → **Hay una casa. Hay un club.**

1. Necesito un pasaporte. (cosas, maleta, profesor de inglés, contratos)
2. Hablan de unos problemas. (señor, cosas, club, casos concretos, casa)
3. Sale con un español. (mexicanos, chico, estudiante, señores, americana)
4. Discuten unos detalles. (problema internacional, recepción, situación, negocios, nuevo diálogo)

III. Make sentences by combining all the elements in the list. Use an indefinite article in each sentence.

MODELO mañana / yo / ir / a / recepción → **Mañana yo voy a una recepción.**

1. yo / necesitar / maletas
2. hombres de negocios / hablar de / contratos
3. ¿tú / ver / hotel?
4. hay / estudiantes / en Bilbao
5. el amor / es / problema

Preparing to read in Spanish

One of the pleasures of studying Spanish is that you learn to read Spanish menus and advertisements, newspapers, magazines, and books. With a little advance preparation, you can acquire this ability more rapidly. Certain points should be kept in mind as you begin to read.

1. First of all, reading does not mean translating, word for word, a passage from Spanish into English. You should start, right from the beginning, to read directly in Spanish. Rather than attempting to interpret each word separately, your task will be to understand whole groups of words: phrases, sentences, and entire paragraphs.

   What is a natural sounding (rather than literal) translation of this sentence into English?

   No hay problemas con la aduana.

2. Dictionaries and vocabulary lists are useful aids; overuse of either, however, slows you down. Before you consult any list to find the English equivalent of a particular word, read ahead to the end of the sentence (or even the entire paragraph) in which the word appears. Many times you will be able to grasp the meaning of the word because you can understand what appears before and after it. If you do decide to consult a vocabulary or dictionary for the meaning of a particular word, underline the Spanish word in the text and write the English equivalent in the margin. Never write the English equivalent directly above the Spanish word.

   What is the meaning of the underlined word, which is associated with sports?

   el <u>partido</u> de tenis, un <u>partido</u> de fútbol

3. Cognate words in two languages are words that are historically related to each other—for example, they may both have descended from the same ancestor word in Latin. Such cognates are often similar or even identical in form and meaning. Spanish and English share an enormous number of cognates; recognize them, and reading Spanish will become easier.

   What is the English equivalent of the following cognates?

   aeropuerto, compañía, afortunadamente, tenis

4. As you read, one of the differences you will note between Spanish and English is word order. Although both languages normally follow the basic pattern of subject + verb + remainder, Spanish word order is a little freer than English. Adjectives are a good example. In Spanish, adjectives often follow the noun: **aeropuerto internacional, club campestre.** Sometimes, however, adjectives appear before the noun: **mucho gusto, buenas tardes.** You should expect Spanish sentences to be arranged somewhat differently from English sentences.

   Go back to the dialog at the beginning of the chapter and pick out two examples of the combination noun + adjective. Then find two cases of adjective + noun.

Aplicación

1. Look at the following passage in Spanish. What is the general theme? Identify all the verbs by marking them with a *V*; identify the nouns by marking them *N*.
2. Now, consulting only those English equivalents which are provided, read the passage through several times until the meaning is clear.

Cartagena, Colombia. Hispanic people love to walk downtown.

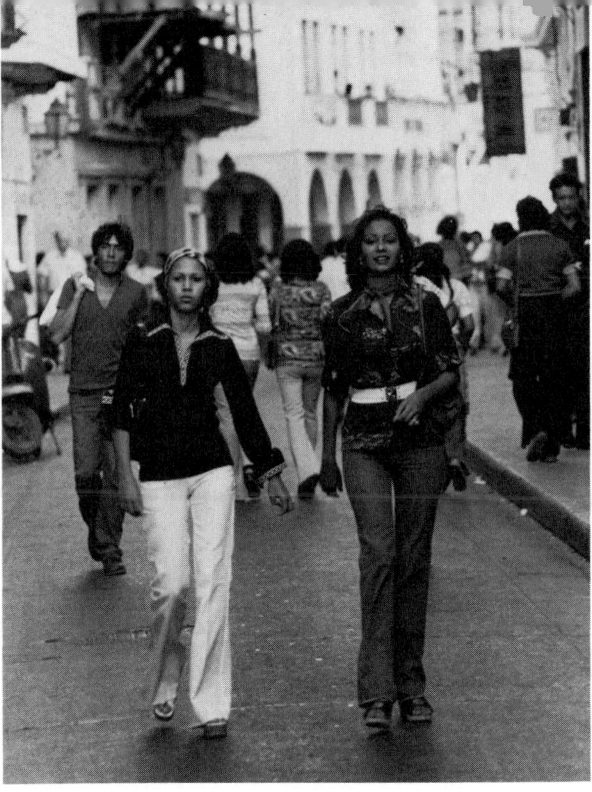

LECTURA[1]

Amigos y novios

Es necesario comprender la diferencia entre la categoría de **amigos** y la categoría de **novios.**[1] Normalmente en los países hispánicos, después de las clases o el trabajo, la gente joven forma grupos de tres, cuatro, cinco, o más amigos de uno y otro sexo. Juntos organizan un paseo a un parque o una reunión en un café. Si desean ver una película, pues entonces, naturalmente, seleccionan un programa interesante y pasan un rato agradable en un cine. Las discotecas[2] son lugares ideales para bailar y para conversar un poco.

Cuando una chica y un chico deciden no andar en grupos, la acción de formar una pareja para salir solos significa que existe la intención de formalizar sus relaciones. Es decir, ya no son simplemente **amigos.** Ahora pueden considerar que entran en la categoría de **novios.** Hay ahora más intensidad y profundidad en sus relaciones personales y, lógicamente, también más responsabilidades, pues todo el mundo comprende que su situación es seria.[3]

between
friends / countries
people
después de after **uno y otro** both
outing / meeting
they wish / film / **pues...** in that case
pleasant / movie theater / places
dance
go around
couple / alone
their / That is / no longer
they can
for / **todo...** everybody

[1] *Reading selection.*

Glosas

1. The specific term **novio (novia)** will be explained. In general, dating customs in Hispanic countries differ somewhat from those in the U.S.A. Middle-class girls may have many **amigos,** and couples typically go out in groups. The dating customs of U.S. Hispanics vary depending on socioeconomic factors and the general degree of adaptation to America's Anglo culture.
2. **Discotecas** *discotheques* have in recent years become quite popular in the Hispanic world. Hispanic countries have no "blue laws;" no one needs to be any particular legal age to enter a bar, night club, or discotheque.
3. When a man has been accepted by the young woman's family as her **novio,** he is included in social functions at their home or in the home of relatives. In earlier times a girl was always accompanied by a **dueña** or chaperone, commonly a cousin, aunt, or even a maid. This custom has not completely disappeared from rural areas. Young men, however, worry less about their reputations, making the double standard somewhat more visible in Hispanic countries than in the U.S.A.

SOBRE LA LECTURA

I. Basing your selection on the information contained in the **lectura,** choose the correct answer.

1. En los países hispánicos, los jóvenes salen a) en parejas b) en grupos c) solos
2. En los grupos hay a) hombres b) chicos y chicas c) sólo chicas
3. Cuando salen los jóvenes, normalmente van a) a un parque o a un café b) a un lugar ideal para estudiar c) al club campestre a cenar
4. Si desean ver una película, van a) a una discoteca b) al cine c) a una reunión
5. Cuando un chico y una chica deciden andar solos, esto significa que ellos son a) amigos b) novios c) hermanos
6. Cuando los jóvenes salen en grupos, la gente considera que ellos son a) amigos b) novios c) estudiantes
7. Si son novios, esto significa que a) ya no van al parque y a las discotecas b) sus relaciones son intensas y serias c) no hablan con la otra gente
8. Es decir, los novios probablemente a) ya hablan del matrimonio b) ya no salen juntos c) no hablan del amor

II. Para contestar

1. ¿Hay una diferencia entre **amigo** y **novio?**
2. ¿Qué tipo de grupos forman los jóvenes después de las clases o el trabajo?
3. Y los jóvenes americanos, ¿salen en grupos o en parejas?
4. ¿A qué lugares van los jóvenes hispánicos?
5. ¿A qué lugares van los jóvenes americanos?
6. ¿Qué es una discoteca?
7. ¿Son populares las discotecas en los Estados Unidos?
8. ¿Va usted a las discotecas?
9. ¿Baila usted bien?

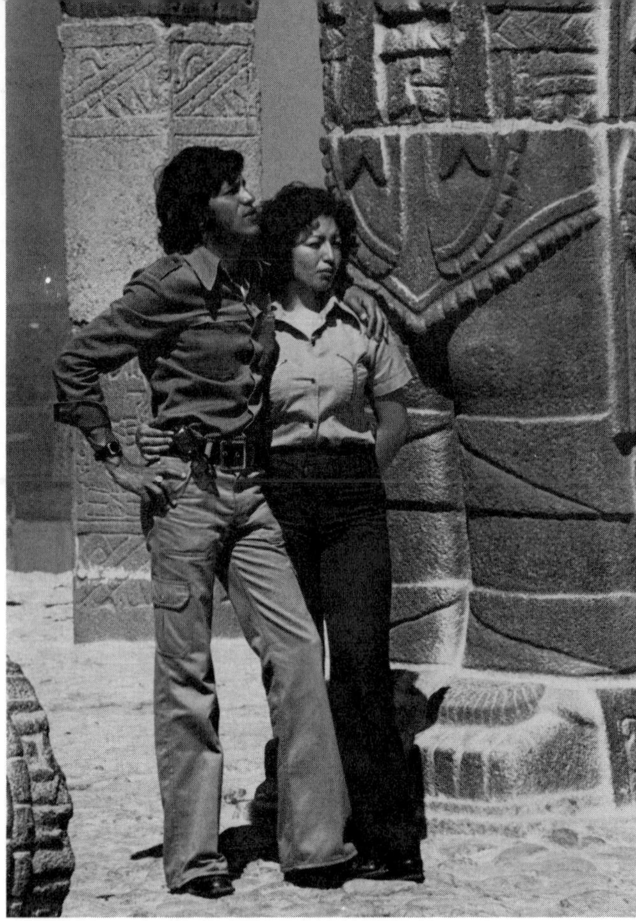
The civilization of the ancient Toltecs comes alive for a young Mexican couple visiting Tula.

10. ¿Va usted al cine con su amigo (amiga)?
11. ¿Ve usted películas de amor?
12. En un país hispánico, cuando una chica y un chico deciden no andar en grupos, ¿qué significa?
13. Si un chico y una chica americanos salen solos, ¿significa que ellos son **novios?**

Glory's
DISCOTHEQUE IBIZA
Carretera San Antonio Km. 1,7
Tel. 971-30 29 20 - Ibiza

Repaso oral

I. Para conversar

In this review you will have short conversations with another member of the class.

MODELO You say not to rush things because there are lots of problems. Person B says you're always changing your mind. →
—No hay que apresurar las cosas. Hay muchos problemas.
—¡Siempre cambias de opinión!

1. You need to go out to eat because it's late. Person B needs to study a few minutes more.
2. You need to have dinner at home. Person B agrees.
3. You ask your friend how many people there are in his/her family. Person B tells you.
4. You tell your friend you'll be spending Christmas and New Year's Day with him or her in Madrid. Person B says, "Yes, yes, of course."
5. You say, "We need to discuss everything again." Person B asks why and says that you're always changing your mind.

II. Para describir

Make eight to ten complete statements about Jane and Miguel; use the following sketch for some ideas. You might mention what each one does, where they're going, Jane's family, their concerns, etc.

Capítulo 4

Despegue

DIÁLOGO **De sobremesa**

Stem-changing verbs • Non-use of the indefinite article • The verb **ser**

PAUSA ORAL **El dinero y la vida**

The information question • Descriptive adjectives

Repaso oral

Despegue

Look at the following drawings and the Spanish words associated with each of them.

una taza

el café

las nubes

la doctora

un burro

la plata

Pronunciación

sugiere **jóvenes** **viejos**	When **g** precedes **e** or **i**, it represents the same sound as **j**.
economizar **optimista**	In long words, each syllable must be pronounced clearly: (**e** / **co** / **no** / **mi** / **zar**).

Aplicación

I. Practice saying each of the following words first very slowly and then at a normal speed, imitating the pronunciation of your instructor.

a. **la taza** **el café** **las nubes**
b. **sugiere** **jóvenes** **viejos**
c. **un médico** **un burro** **la plata**
d. **economizar** **optimista**

II. Answer each question following the model.

MODELO ¿Es una casa? → **No, no es una casa; es una taza.**

1.  ¿Es un hombre de negocios?

2.  ¿Es una maleta?

3.  ¿Es la aduana?

4.  ¿Es estudiante?

5.  ¿Es una mano?

Tema del diálogo

What must a middle-class family in Argentina do to make ends meet?

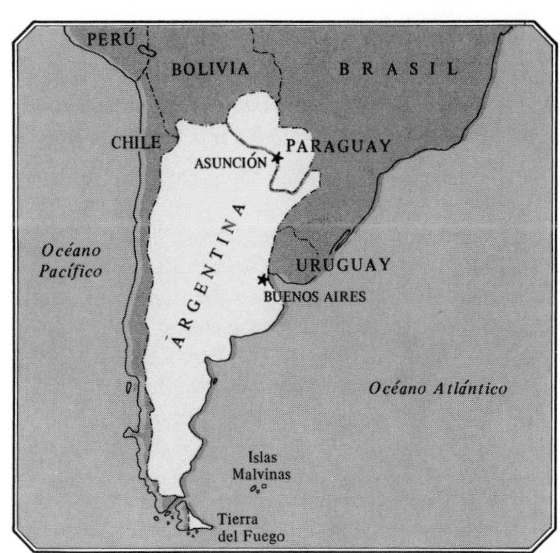

DIÁLOGO

De sobremesa

Una noche los Alessandri[1] hablan de sobremesa[2]. Jorge Alessandri es empleado bancario y además trabaja por la noche en una casa comercial argentina[3]. Sandra es ama de casa. Juan Carlos es estudiante de medicina.

MADRE ¿Qué quieren? ¿Más café? ¿Un poco más de postre?

JUAN CARLOS Otro café mamá, por favor.

PADRE Yo, no pido nada. El médico quiere disminuir el número de tazas de café que tomo...y ¡ni hablar del postre!

MADRE Más vale escuchar al Dr. Varela. Además, como los precios de todo están por las nubes, yo sugiero tratar de economizar un poco[4].

JUAN CARLOS Cierto. Hay que comprar menos porque todo cuesta más cada día. Papá no puede seguir con dos trabajos.

PADRE ¡Qué cosa! ¿Por qué no? Los Alessandri somos gente fuerte.

MADRE Che, Jorge[5], no podemos trabajar como burros todos los días. También hay que disfrutar de la vida un poco.

PADRE Es verdad. Pero pienso que con el nuevo gobierno militar el país puede mejorar.

JUAN CARLOS ¡Ojalá! De otra manera, si la economía no mejora, parto para el Paraguay. Allá buscan médicos jóvenes. Puedo hacer muy buena plata así.

MADRE Pues yo soy optimista. Y creo que la situación económica va a mejorar mucho.

PADRE No vas a necesitar abandonar a los viejos.

After dinner

One evening the Alessandri family is talking after dinner. Jorge Alessandri is a bank employee and also works evenings in an Argentine company. Sandra is a housewife. Juan Carlos is a medical student.

M: What would you like? More coffee? A little more dessert?

JC: Another (cup of) coffee, Mother, please.

P: Me, I don't need (ask for) anything. The doctor wants to cut down the number of cups of coffee I drink...not to mention dessert!

M: It's better to listen to Dr. Varela. Besides, as the prices of everything are sky high (in the clouds), I suggest trying to economize a little.

JC: Right. It's necessary to buy less because everything costs more each day. Dad can't continue with two jobs.

P: Hey! Why not? The Alessandris are strong people.

M: Listen, Jorge, we can't work like mules every day. One also has to enjoy life a little.

P: That's true. But I think that with the new military government the country can (could) improve.

JC: I hope so! Otherwise, if the economy doesn't improve, I'm leaving for Paraguay. They're looking for young doctors there. I can make good money that way.

M: Well, I'm optimistic. And I think the economic situation is going to improve a lot.

P: You're not going to have to abandon your parents (the old folks).

VARIACIONES

¿Quiere usted ser médico?	Do you want to be a doctor?
No, abogado.	No, a lawyer.
¿Quiere usted trabajar?	Do you want to work?
No, prefiero jugar tenis con mis amigos.	No, I prefer to play tennis with my friends.
¿Hace usted buena plata?	Do you make good money?
Sí, gano mucho dinero.	Yes, I earn lots of money.
¿Cómo es Juan Carlos?	What's Juan Carlos like?
Es alto.	He's tall.
bajo	short
simpático	nice
malo	bad
¿De qué color es tu casa?	What color is your house?
Es blanca.	It's white.
negra	black
roja	red
verde	green
azul	blue
amarilla	yellow

General Jorge Videla, left, President of Argentina, surrounded by pillars of the political establishment.

Glosas

1. The name **Alessandri,** spelled with a double **s,** is of Italian origin. Between 1857 and 1926, some 2,718,000 Italians immigrated to Argentina, 47.4% of all immigrants to the country during the period.
2. **La sobremesa** is a custom that Hispanics in all countries cultivate. After a meal (**la comida** or **la cena**) people remain at the table sipping coffee, tea, or **licores** and conversing for as long as one or even two hours.
3. In many Hispanic countries, the head of a middle-class household has to hold down two jobs in order to make ends meet. Although younger wives are beginning to work full-time in large cities, the man is still expected to be the main breadwinner. Young Latin American students find practically no opportunities to work part-time; consequently, most of those enrolled in universities are full-time students.
4. Americans are beginning to understand what it is like to spend exorbitant amounts of money on basic items such as coffee, flour, meat, and eggs. In several Hispanic countries, and Argentina is a good example, inflation at an annual rate of 100% or even 200% is not unheard of.
5. In Argentina **che** + name of person is used profusely. **Che** functions as an interjection—such as *hey* in *Hey, Joe!* Argentinians use **che** so much in casual situations that other Hispanics refer to them as **"los Ches."**

SOBRE EL DIÁLOGO

I. ¿Sí o no? If the information contained in the statement is true, say **sí** and repeat the statement. If the information is false, say **no** and make a statement which is true.

MODELO La familia Alessandri es de Chile. → **No, es de la Argentina.**

1. Los Alessandri cenan ahora.
2. Hablan de la situación de los estudiantes en la Argentina.
3. Jorge Alessandri trabaja en un banco y en el aeropuerto.
4. Sandra es profesora.
5. Juan Carlos estudia inglés.
6. Juan Carlos pide más postre.
7. El Sr. Alessandri también quiere más postre.
8. El Sr. Alessandri toma mucho café.
9. La familia quiere economizar.
10. El Sr. Alessandri va a seguir con dos trabajos.
11. La Sra. de Alessandri piensa que Jorge necesita disfrutar de la vida.
12. El Sr. Alessandri piensa que hay muchos problemas con el nuevo gobierno.
13. Juan Carlos va a abandonar la medicina si la economía no mejora.
14. La mamá es optimista y cree que el país va a mejorar mucho.
15. El papá piensa que Juan Carlos necesita ir a Paraguay.

II. Choosing from the list below, complete each of the following sentences.

bancario / **amarilla** / **café** / **simpático** / **trabajo** / **gana** / **dinero** / **abogado** / **alto** / **malo** / **un poco**

1. Miguel no es bajo, es ______.
2. Trabaja como burro pero no ______ mucho.
3. Hay que economizar ______.
4. La casa es blanca y ______.
6. Jorge trabaja en un banco. Es un empleado ______.
7. Una ama de casa hace mucho ______.
8. Antonio no es médico, es ______.
9. Ese chico no es bueno, es ______.
10. El nuevo profesor es guapo y joven y muy ______.

III. Para contestar

1. ¿Toma usted mucho café? ¿Es bueno tomar mucho café por la noche?
2. ¿Come usted postre todos los días? ¿Es bueno comer mucho postre?
3. ¿Estudia usted medicina?
4. ¿Gana usted mucho dinero ahora?
5. ¿Es usted una persona optimista?

VOCABULARIO

nouns

el **abogado**	lawyer
el **ama de casa** (feminine gender)	housewife
el **amigo,** la **amiga**	friend
el **burro**	donkey
el **café**	coffee
la **casa comercial**	business firm, company
el **color**	color
el **dinero**	money
el **doctor,** la **doctora**	doctor
la **economía**	economy; economics
el **empleado,** la **empleada**	employee
la **gente**	people
el **gobierno**	government
la **medicina**	medicine
el **médico,** la **médica**	doctor
la **nube**	cloud
por las nubes	sky-high (literally, in the clouds)
el **número**	number
el **país**	country
la **plata**	money (literally, silver)
el **postre**	dessert
el **precio**	price
la **sobremesa**	after-dinner conversation
la **taza**	cup
el **tenis**	tennis
el **trabajo**	work, job
la **verdad**	truth
los **viejos** (=los **padres**)	parents (literally, old people)

verbs

abandonar	to abandon
buscar (qu)	to look (for)
comprar	to buy
costar (ue)	to cost
creer	to think; to believe
disfrutar de (+ noun)	to enjoy
disminuir (y)	to diminish; to cut down
economizar (c)	to save
escuchar	to listen (to)
ganar	to earn
hacer	to make
yo hago	I make
jugar (ue)	to play
mejorar	to improve
pedir (i)	to ask (for)
pensar (ie)	to think
poder (ue, u)	to be able; can; may
preferir (ie, i)	to prefer
querer (ie)	to want; to love
seguir (i)	to follow; to continue
ser	to be
sugerir (ie, i)	to suggest
tomar	to drink, to take
tratar de (+ infinitive)	to try to (+ verb)

adjectives

alto	tall
amarillo	yellow
argentino	Argentine
azul	blue
bajo	short
bancario	bank, banking
blanco	white
comercial	commercial, business
económico	economic
fuerte	strong

malo	bad	**más vale**	one had better..., it would be better...
militar	military	**menos**	less; minus
negro	black	**nada**	nothing, anything
optimista	optimistic	**ni hablar (de)**	don't even mention
rojo	red	**¡ojalá!**	I hope so.
simpático	nice	**un poco más (de)**	a little more
verde	green	**por la noche**	at night
viejo	old	**porque**	because
		pues	well
		¡qué cosa!	hey
		si	if
		todos los días	every day

other expressions

además	besides
allá	there
así	thus, this way, that way
cada	each
che	Listen!, hey
cierto	right
como	since, as
de otra manera	otherwise
de sobremesa	after dinner
es verdad	it's true; that's true

additional vocabulary

aquí	here
donde	where
¿dónde?	where?
¿de dónde?	(from) where?
¿quién?, ¿quiénes?	who?, whom?

ESTRUCTURA I

A. Stem-changing Verbs

Repaso. Verbs generally have one stem only. This stem remains constant regardless of the verb ending: **ceno, cenas, cena, cenamos, cenan.**

> **Puedes** ganar muy buena plata.
> **Pienso** que la situación va a mejorar.

1. A limited number of verbs are known as stem-changing verbs. These verbs have an alternate stem that is used in certain of their present-tense forms. For example:

INFINITIVE	STEM ONE (+ ENDING)	STEM TWO (+ ENDING)
querer to want, to love	**queremos**	**quiero, quieres...**
poder to be able	**podemos**	**puedo, puedes...**
pedir to ask (for)	**pedimos**	**pido, pides...**

2. The stem-changes are of three types: **e** becomes **ie** (**quiero**), **o** becomes **ue** (**puedo**), and **e** becomes **i** (**pido**). The following chart is a summary of these stem changes. Note that **ie, ue,** and **i** occur *only* when the stem itelf is *stressed.*

Stem-changing verbs

MODEL	TYPICAL VERBS	
e → ie querer		
quiero quieres quiere queremos queréis quieren	pensar preferir querer sugerir	¿Qué piensas tú? Prefiero disfrutar de la vida. Juan quiere otro café. Sandra sugiere economizar. ***But*** No queremos más postre, gracias.
o → ue poder		
puedo puedes puede podemos podéis pueden	costar dormir poder	Todo cuesta más cada día. Duermo muy bien aquí. Papá no puede seguir con dos trabajos. ***But*** Podemos economizar.
e → i pedir		
pido pides pide pedimos pedís piden	pedir seguir	La empleada pide más dinero. ¿Sigues con dos trabajos? ***But*** Pedimos muchas cosas, ¿no?

3. The verb **jugar** is special since **u** changes to **ue**. Its forms are: **juego, juegas, juega, jugamos, jugáis, juegan.**

4. In the vocabulary lists in this book, a parenthesis following the infinitive signals that the verb changes its stem: **pensar** (**ie**), **costar** (**ue**), **seguir** (**i**).

Avenida de Mayo, one of many important avenues in Buenos Aires, cosmopolitan capital of Argentina.

Aplicación

I. Repeat each sentence, changing the subject according to the cue.

MODELO ¿Qué piensas? (Miguel, ustedes) → **¿Qué piensa? ¿Qué piensan?**

1. Quiero salir. (los hombres, el ama de casa, tú, nosotras, yo)
2. No sugiere nada. (yo, el médico, ustedes, mis hermanos y yo, tú)
3. Puedo trabajar. (los profesores, la chica y yo, tú, yo, el empleado)
4. No duermo bien. (mi papá, mis hermanos, yo, ustedes, nosotros)
5. ¿Qué pide? (las empleadas, tú y él, yo, tu papá, tú)
6. Sigue con dos trabajos. (Jorge, los estudiantes, yo, tú y yo, ustedes)

II. Change the verb to the form that corresponds to **nosotros.**

MODELO Duermo muy bien. → **Dormimos muy bien.**

1. Pienso así.
2. No sugiero nada.
3. Prefiero economizar.
4. Juego con ellos.
5. Pido más plata.
6. ¿Puedo hablar con usted?
7. ¿Sigo con el trabajo?
8. Quiero partir ahora.

III. Change the verb to the form that corresponds to **yo.**

MODELO Podemos partir ahora. → **Puedo partir ahora.**

1. Seguimos aquí.
2. Queremos ganar más.
3. No jugamos.
4. Podemos escuchar.
5. No dormimos aquí.
6. ¿Por qué no pedimos otra cosa?
7. Pensamos así.
8. Sugerimos escuchar más.

IV. Answer each question using **querer** + infinitive.

MODELO ¿Vas a salir mañana? → **Quiero salir ahora.**

1. ¿Van ellos a dormir aquí mañana?
2. ¿Vamos a sugerir otra cosa mañana?
3. ¿Van ustedes a poder trabajar mañana?
4. ¿Va a jugar el mexicano mañana?
5. ¿Van ustedes a pedir más plata mañana?
6. ¿Vas a seguir con el trabajo mañana?

V. Say **no** and correct the suggestion, using the information in the cue.

MODELO ¿Trabaja Miguel? (dormir) → **No, no trabaja. Duerme.**

1. ¿Estudian los estudiantes? (jugar)
2. ¿Duerme usted? (pensar)
3. ¿Parten ustedes? (seguir con el trabajo)
4. ¿Necesita usted más dinero? (pedir otra cosa)
5. ¿Toman ustedes más café? (querer más postre)
6. ¿Cena papá? (dormir)

VI. Para contestar en español

1. ¿Duerme usted ahora o piensa?
2. ¿Hablan ustedes en inglés o en español?
3. ¿Qué quieren hacer los estudiantes ahora, escuchar o jugar?
4. ¿Pido mucho trabajo yo?
5. ¿Qué sugiero, estudiar más o dormir más?
6. ¿Piensan ustedes en inglés o en español? ¿Y yo?
7. ¿Seguimos con la clase o vamos al aeropuerto?
8. ¿Cuesta mucho una casa?

B. Non-use of the indefinite article

Repaso. Singular **un** or **una** is used in most situations in which English requires *a* or *an*. Plural **unos** or **unas** corresponds to English *some*.

> ¿Otro café, papá?
> Juan Carlos es estudiante.

1. The indefinite article is not used with the verb **ser** to state someone's occupation or nationality. (Note that words describing occupation and nationality are seldom capitalized in Spanish.)

Sandra es doctora.	Sandra is a doctor.
Miguel es español y Jane es americana.	Miguel is Spanish and Jane is American.

But If the occupation or nationality is further described with an adjective, the indefinite article is used.

Juan Carlos es un estudiante bueno.	Juan Carlos is a good student.
Son unos argentinos muy jóvenes.	They are very young Argentinians.

2. The article does not appear before the words **cierto** *a certain,* **otro** *another,* nor after **¡qué!** *what a!*.

Vamos a discutir cierto caso concreto.	We're going to discuss a certain specific issue.
Mañana hay otra recepción.	There's another reception tomorrow.
¡Qué problema!	What a problem!

3. The article is absent from negative sentences which express the idea *any* (+ noun).

No quiero postre.	I don't want any dessert.
No hay problemas con la aduana.	There aren't any problems with customs.

Aplicación

I. Fill in the indefinite article whenever appropriate.

Parte A

Chela y Luisa son ___1___ hermanas. Ahora visitan los Estados Unidos.

CH: ¡Qué ___2___ precios!

L: Quiero comprar ___3___ cosas pero todo está por las nubes.

CH: Es cierto.

L: ¡Qué ___4___ lata! Necesito comprar ___5___ cosas.

CH: ¡Qué ___6___ situación! ¿Qué vamos a hacer?

L: Esto...hay que pedir más dinero.

CH: Hay que economizar.

L: No podemos seguir así. Necesito ___7___ otra maleta.

CH: Es verdad, pero por ahora, hermana, no veo ___8___ solución.

Parte B

Carlos es ___1___ joven abogado que trabaja con ___2___ casa comercial americana. María Elena es ___3___ estudiante. Carlos y María Elena son ___4___ amigos, pero Carlos quiere ser mucho más que amigo de ella. Ah, el amor. ¡Qué ___5___ problema! María Elena es ___6___ estudiante muy buena y estudia y estudia todo el día.

___7___ día Carlos y María Elena hablan.

C: ¿Vamos a tomar ___8___ café?

ME: Muy bien.

C: Quiero discutir ___9___ cierta situación.

ME: ¿Ah? ¿Qué situación?

C: Esto...es que...tú y yo somos jóvenes, fuertes...

ME: Cierto...

C: Creo que tú y yo...

ME: ¿Sí...?

C: Es que...

ME: Tú puedes ser ___10___ abogado, pero no hablas muy claro.

C: Esto... María Elena, pienso en *(I'm thinking about)* el matrimonio, en nosotros dos.
ME: ¡El matrimonio!
C: Sí...
ME: No veo __11__ problema. Claro que hay __12__ detalles que hay que discutir con mis padres.
C: Puedo ir a tu casa en Navidades. Ay, ¡qué __13__ día!

II. Construct sentences by combining the words in each list; make any necessary verb agreements.

MODELO Soy / estudiante / muy malo → **Soy un estudiante muy malo.**

1. Nosotros / necesitar / otra taza / café
2. Juan / es / médico
3. Teresa / es / empleada / muy buena
4. ¡Qué / postre! Yo / querer / poco más
5. No / hay / empleados / aquí
6. Yo / sugerir / hablar de / ciertos detalles
7. Ella / no / querer / ser / ama de casa
8. Él / es / abogado / muy bueno

C. The verb **ser**

Yo **soy** optimista.

1. Here are the present tense forms of **ser.**

soy	Soy José Antonio Díaz.
eres	¿Eres mexicano?
es	María Isabel es estudiante.
somos	Somos españoles.
sois	Sois gente fuerte.
son	Lola y Carlos son movios.

2. **Ser** is one of two principal verbs which correspond to English *to be.* The special situations in which **ser** is used will be presented in the following chapter.

Aplicación

I. Supply the correct form of **ser.**

Yo __1__ de los Estados Unidos, pero mi mamá __2__ de México. Ella __3__ profesora de español en la universidad. Ella y yo __4__ buenos amigos, pero a veces ella no comprende mi situación. Mis hermanos Juan y Carlos __5__ estudiantes, y mi hermana __6__ profesora. Yo __7__ la persona que más trabaja en la casa. Yo __8__ estudiante y por la noche __9__ empleado en un hotel. Quiero __10__ abogado y necesito estudiar y trabajar mucho. Mamá cree que trabajo como burro, pero ¿por qué no? Los García __11__ fuertes. Y tú, ¿también __12__ fuerte?

II. Answer each question using a form of **ser,** according to the model.

MODELO ¿Nosotros? ¿Gente fuerte? → **Sí, ustedes son gente fuerte.**

1. ¿Esta casa? ¿De Sandra?
2. ¿Usted? ¿De Chile?
3. ¿Yo? ¿El profesor de español?
4. ¿Hoy? ¿Domingo?
5. ¿Nosotros? ¿Americanos?
6. ¿Jesús y Antonio? ¿Hermanos?
7. ¿Yo? ¿Un problema para mamá?
8. ¿Roberto? ¿Estudiante de medicina?

III. Answer each question using a form of **ser.**

MODELO ¿Es usted médico? → **No, no soy médico. Soy estudiante.**

1. ¿Soy yo profesor (profesora) de español?
2. ¿Es usted una persona optimista?
3. ¿Quiere usted ser médico?
4. ¿Son ustedes estudiantes?
5. ¿Es simpático ese chico?
6. ¿Es guapo el nuevo profesor de inglés?

Argentina and Brazil share Iguazu Falls.

Pausa oral

El dinero y la vida

For better or for worse, economics play as active a role in the Hispanic world as in the U.S.A. You are already able to make certain comments on the economy.

I. Para reaccionar

Choosing from the following list of expressions, react to each statement. You may be able to respond to some statements in more than one way.

Cierto. / **¡Qué cosa!** / **¿Por qué no?** / **Es verdad.** / **¡Ojalá!** / **Ni hablar.** / **Nada, gracias.** / **Trabaja como burro.**

MODELO ¿Trabaja mucho el Sr. Alessandri? → **Sí, trabaja como burro.**

1. Creo que la economía va a mejorar mucho.
2. No quiero trabajar en un banco.
3. Miguel gana muy buena plata.
4. Hay muchos abogados en los Estados Unidos.
5. Hay que economizar.
6. Miguel trabaja día y noche.

II. Para preguntar

Make up two or three questions for each of the following drawings; you may want to use the words which appear with each drawing. Another member of the class should be able to answer your questions.

MODELO

viajar
querer

Possible questions **¿Cuesta mucho dinero viajar?**
¿Quieres ganar mucha plata?

1. 

trabajar
buscar

2. 

precios
aviones

3. 

empleado
dinero

4. 

necesitar
escuchar

5. 

trabajo
abogado

III. Para contestar

Student A asks a question. Student B answers with a complete sentence.

MODELO A: **¿Trabajas mucho?**
B *(possible answers):* **¿Yo? ¡Trabajo como burro!** *or* **No trabajo mucho. Disfruto de la vida.**

1. ¿Hablas de la economía con los amigos? ¿Prefieres hablar del amor?
2. ¿Trabajas por la noche? ¿Ganas mucho dinero?
3. ¿Es tu mamá ama de casa?
4. ¿Estudias español? ¿Qué estudias?
5. ¿Quieres ser profesor (profesora)? ¿Qué quieres ser?
6. ¿Cuestan mucho las cosas en los Estados Unidos?
7. ¿Crees que todo cuesta más en la Argentina o en los Estados Unidos?
8. ¿Economizas mucho?
9. ¿Prefieres trabajar o dormir?
10. ¿Disfrutas de la vida o trabajas como burro?
11. ¿En qué trabajos puedes hacer muy buena plata?
12. ¿Crees que la economía de los Estados Unidos va a mejorar?

* PEONES

$ 550.000
Total de ingresos
Mensuales por todo concepto
Para tareas de depósito y
limpieza
MONASTERIO 265
CAPITAL

ESTRUCTURA II

A. The information question

¿Qué quieren?

1. An information question requests specific information concerning the subject of the sentence. Some of the question words used have only one form (**qué, cuándo...**). Another word has two forms (**cuál, cuáles**), and one word has four forms (**cuánto, cuánta, cuántos, cuántas**). Each of the question words has a written accent mark.

Question words

<table>
<tr><td colspan="4">INVARIABLE
¿qué? what?
¿por qué? why?
¿cuándo? when?
¿cómo? how? (what?)
¿dónde? where?[1]</td></tr>
<tr><td colspan="2">SINGULAR
¿quién?
¿cuál?</td><td colspan="2">PLURAL
¿quiénes? who? (whom?)
¿cuáles? which? (what?)</td></tr>
<tr><td>MASCULINE SINGULAR
¿cuánto?</td><td>FEMININE SINGULAR
¿cuánta?</td><td>MASCULINE PLURAL
¿cuántos?</td><td>FEMININE PLURAL
¿cuántas? how much?
how many?</td></tr>
</table>

¿Qué es un lirón?	What's a dormouse?
¿Por qué no?	Why not?
¿Cuándo hablamos de negocios?	When do we talk business?
¿Cómo es la Universidad de Buenos Aires?	What is the University of Buenos Aires like?
¿Dónde estudias?	Where do you study?
¿Cuál es el precio?	What's the price?
¿Cuáles son los detalles?	What are the details?
¿Cuál de las chicas es Lola?	Which of the girls is Lola?
¿Cuántos estudiantes hay en la clase?	How many students are there in the class?

[1]The question word **¿adónde?** is used to ask about direction toward: **¿Adónde vas?**

2. The normal word order used in information questions follows this pattern: interrogative word + verb (+subject) (+remainder).

¿Quién eres?	Who are you?
¿Qué discuten los hombres de negocios?	What are the businessmen discussing?
¿Dónde cenan Mario y Susana esta noche?	Where are Mario and Susana eating tonight?

3. The words **¿qué?** and **¿cuál(es)?** may both mean *what?* and *which?* The difference is that **¿qué?** asks for a definition or general explanation while **¿cuál(es)?** asks for definite selection from a group.

DEFINITION

¿Qué es el amor?	What is love?
¿Qué es la aduana?	What is customs?

SELECTION

¿Cuál es un hotel bueno en México, D.F.?	What's (the name of) a good hotel in Mexico City?
Hay dos bancos. ¿Cuál es el Banco de Bilbao?	There are two banks. Which is the Bank of Bilbao?
¿Cuáles quieres?	Which (ones) do you want?

4. **¡Qué!, ¡Cómo!,** and **¡Cuánto!** may be used as exclamations. The written accent mark is retained.

¡Qué bueno llegar!	How good (it is) to arrive!
¡Cómo cansan las clases!	How classes tire (you out)!
¡Cuánto vas a cambiar!	How (much) you're going to change!

Aplicación

I. Ask two questions suggested by each of the following statements.

MODELO El Sr. Alessandri no toma café. → **¿Qué no toma el Sr. Alessandri? ¿Quién no toma café?**

1. Los Alessandri cenan en casa.
2. Jorge no come mucho porque el médico no quiere.
3. Jorge Alessandri trabaja como burro.
4. Gana poca plata.
5. "Plata" es "dinero".
6. Hay cuatro personas en la familia.
7. Hay dos hijos: Juan Carlos y María Elena.
8. La hermana de Juan Carlos llega dentro de un rato.

9. Ella trabaja en la aduana.
10. María Elena es muy optimista, pero Juan Carlos, no.
11. Los Alessandri siempre hablan de la economía.
12. Los Alessandri son más optimistas que los García.

II. Make up as many information questions as you can about the dialog.

MODELOS **¿Cuándo hablan los Alessandri? ¿Qué personas hay en la familia?**

III. Ask your teacher as many information questions about himself or herself as you can think of. Use the **usted** verb form.

MODELOS **¿De qué país es usted? ¿Cuántas clases enseña usted?**

IV. Ask a classmate as many information questions about himself or herself as you can think of. He or she should answer each question. Use the **tú** verb form.

MODELOS **¿Qué estudias? → Estudio medicina.**
¿Quién es tu profesor de inglés? → Mi profesor de inglés es el Dr. Walters.

V. Change each of the following statements to an exclamation with **¡cómo!**

MODELO Enrique estudia mucho. → **¡Cómo estudia Enrique!**

1. Jorge trabaja mucho.
2. Nosotros jugamos mucho.
3. Tú duermes mucho.
4. Los hombres hablan mucho.
5. Ustedes discuten mucho.

VI. Respond to the following statements with any suitable exclamation.

MODELO Juan trabaja día y noche. →
Possible responses **¡Cuánto trabaja Juan!**
¡Qué hombre!
¡Qué fuerte es Juan!
¡Cómo trabaja Juan!

1. Miguel gana mucha plata.
2. Hay diez hijos en la familia Fernández.
3. Los viajes cansan mucho.
4. Es un gobierno muy fuerte.
5. Soy una persona muy optimista.

A Paraguayan farmer from the Chaco region takes time to sip **mate**, the ever-present green tea.

B. Descriptive adjectives

una empleada **argentina** / el gobierno **militar**

1. Descriptive adjectives answer the question *What kind of?*

2. *Masculine and feminine forms.* Most adjectives have a masculine form ending in **-o** and a feminine form ending in **-a.** These adjectives agree in gender and in number with the nouns they modify.

un caso concreto	a particular case
una cosa concreta	a particular thing
el chico mexicano	the Mexican boy
la chica mexicana	the Mexican girl

3. *Invariable forms.* Adjectives which end in a consonant, in **-e,** or in **-ista** have only one form for both masculine and feminine in the singular.

el Aeropuerto Internacional	International Airport
una casa internacional	an international house
un pasaporte verde	a green passport
una casa verde	a green house
un hombre optimista	an optimistic man
una persona optimista	an optimistic person

Exception: Adjectives indicating geographical origin have a feminine form ending in **-a: española, inglesa. . .**

un economista español	a Spanish economist
una casa española	a Spanish house
un estudiante inglés	an English student (from England)
una profesora inglesa	an English professor (one from England)

4. *Plural forms.* All adjectives which end in a vowel form their plural by adding **-s.** Adjectives which end in a consonant form the plural by adding **-es.**

el banco mexicano	the Mexican bank
los bancos mexicanos	the Mexican banks
el aeropuerto internacional	the international airport
los aeropuertos internacionales	the international airports
un pasaporte inglés	an English passport
unos pasaportes ingleses	some English passports

5. If a feminine noun is combined with a masculine noun, a masculine plural adjective is used to modify the combination.

Juana y Miguel son simpáticos.	Juana and Miguel are nice.

6. *Adjective position.* Adjectives which describe the characteristic or class of a person or object are normally placed after the noun.

el aeropuerto internacional	the international airport
un hotel americano	an American hotel
una estudiante inglesa	an English student

7. The adjectives **bueno** and **malo** commonly appear before the noun they modify. In this position special short forms are used.

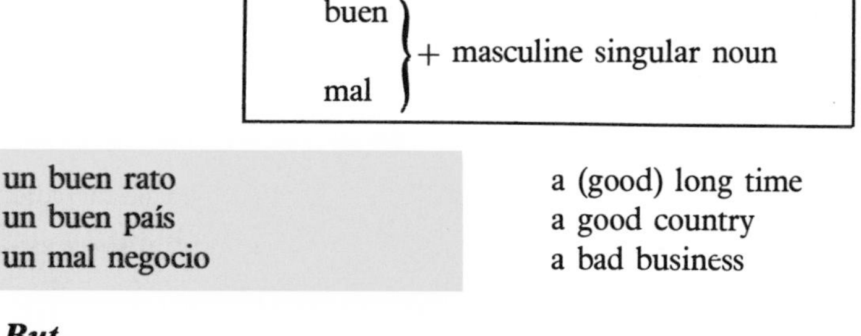

buen } + masculine singular noun
mal }

un buen rato	a (good) long time
un buen país	a good country
un mal negocio	a bad business

But

una buena vida	a good life
unas clases muy malas	some very bad classes

Aplicación

I. Repeat each sentence following the model. Make the adjectives (and articles) agree in each case.

MODELO Necesito una maleta nueva. (pasaporte, tazas) → **Necesito un pasaporte nuevo. Necesito unas tazas nuevas.**

1. Somos gente fuerte. (hijos, estudiantes, personas)
2. Ceno con el señor mexicano. (profesores, chicas, empleado, abogados, doctora)
3. Hay un banco internacional. (restaurante, problemas, situación, hotel, casa)
4. Compran una casa blanca. (maleta, tazas, cosas)
5. Sale con un chico simpático. (doctor, señorita, chicos, chica, estudiantes)
6. Hay una taza azul. (tazas, pasaporte, casa, maletas)

II. Respond to the questions in the pattern shown by the model.

MODELO ¿Es español el médico? → **Sí, es español.**
¿Y la empleada? → **Es española también.**
¿Y los abogados? → **Son españoles también.**

1. ¿Es optimista el padre? ¿Y la mamá? ¿Y los hijos?
2. ¿Es español el médico? ¿Y los abogados? ¿Y la doctora?
3. ¿Es bueno el café? ¿Y el postre? ¿Y los precios?

4. ¿Es inglesa la economista? ¿Y los médicos? ¿Y el abogado?
5. ¿Es joven el profesor? ¿Y la profesora? ¿Y ustedes?
6. ¿Es amarilla la casa? ¿Y las otras casas? ¿Y el hotel?
7. ¿Es guapo el profesor? ¿Y los estudiantes? ¿Y el abogado?
8. ¿Es alta la mamá? ¿Y el papá? ¿Y las hijas? ¿Y los hijos?

III. Repeat each sentence making the indicated substitutions. Several changes are required in each new sentence.

MODELO El es empleado bancario. (Ella, ellos) → **Ella es empleada bancaria. Ellos son empleados bancarios.**

1. Alessandri es muy fuerte. (Sandra, nosotros, los profesores)
2. Sandra es una estudiante extranjera. (Pablo, los hijos de Jorge, nosotros)
3. Soy muy joven. (ustedes, las extranjeras, el economista)
4. Pedro es un economista español. (la señora, el señor Fernández, ellos)
5. Otra familia americana llega. (estudiantes, profesoras, empleado)

IV. Supply an adjective in its correct form. The following list contains the adjectives you will need.

militar / **económico** / **bancario** / **nuevo** / **mucho** / **optimista** / **español** / **extranjero** / **todo** / **joven** / **fuerte**

Mónica y Luis son __1__. Mónica es empleada __2__ y Luis es empleado en una casa comercial __3__. __4__ los días parten para el trabajo muy temprano y llegan a casa muy tarde. También hacen __5__ trabajo en casa.

Una noche hablan de sobremesa.

L: Nosotros trabajamos como burros.

M: Pues con la situación __6__ del país, hay que trabajar mucho. Pero tú y yo somos __7__, ¿no es cierto, mi amor?

L: Claro, pero ¿cuándo vamos a disfrutar de la vida? Necesito unas cosas __8__. También quiero una familia, un hijo. . .

M: Sí, sí seguro, mi vida. Pero no va a ser por __9__ años más. Con el gobierno __10__ todo va a mejorar. Vas a ver.

L: Ojalá. ¡Qué __11__ eres!

V. Using an adjective in each sentence, tell as much as you can about yourself.

MODELOS **Soy un estudiante americano. Soy una persona muy optimista.**

VI. Now tell as much as you can about a friend or a member of your family.

MODELO **Mi hermano es alto y guapo. Es muy simpático.**

VII. Tell the colors of as many objects in the classroom as you can.

Repaso oral

I. Para conversar

Act out the following situations with another student.

MODELO You want to know if your friend would like more dessert. Person B says, "No thanks, I don't want any more." →
— ¿Quieres más postre?
— No gracias, no quiero más.

1. You offer your friend another cup of coffee. Person B says the doctor wants to cut down the number of cups he/she takes.
2. You suggest that one ought to economize. Person B agrees and says that everything costs more each day.
3. You say to your friend that he/she can't go on carrying two jobs. Person B disagrees and says that he's/she's strong.
4. You ask your friend if he/she wants to be a doctor. Person B says no, that he/she wants to be an English professor.
5. You ask your friend if he's/she's a good student. He/she says no, that he's/she's a bad student.

II. Make original sentences by combining the words in each pair.

MODELO gobierno / mejorar → **Con el gobierno militar todo va a mejorar.** *or* **Creo que con el nuevo gobierno la situación va a mejorar.**

1. mamá / ama de casa
2. hablar / inglés
3. estudiar / medicina
4. hermano / abogado
5. trabajar / burro
6. tomar / café
7. hablar / sobremesa
8. más vale / llegar temprano

EL MAS ALTO INTERES
GARANTIZA
RENTABILIDAD POSITIVA
PARA SU INVERSION
Entidad adherida al régimen de garantía
de los depósitos - Ley Nº: 21.526

76%
A 30 DIAS
tasa efectiva anual: 109,01%

banco Santurce
UN BANCO CAPAZ
RECONQUISTA 353
Tel. 32-2608/2567/1806/1774/1646
Buenos Aires - Rep. Argentina

Comunicación 1

La casa

la casa	el apartamento estar en casa limpiar la casa la renta	house	apartment to be (at) home to clean house rent
la cocina	el refrigerador la cocina cocinar preparar la comida	kitchen	refrigerator stove to cook to prepare a meal
el comedor	la mesa las sillas comer cenar servir la comida	dining room	table chairs to eat to have dinner (in the evening) to serve the food
el cuarto	la ventana la puerta el cuarto de baño el excusado tomar un baño tomar una ducha	room	window door bathroom toilet to have a bath to take a shower

el dormitorio	dormir (como un lirón) la cama el radio tender la cama escuchar el radio	bedroom	to sleep (like a log) bed radio to make the bed to listen to the radio
la sala	los muebles el sofá el televisor ver televisión	living room	furniture sofa television set to watch television
el patio	el árbol la hierba las flores cortar la hierba tomar el sol	patio, yard	tree grass (lawn) flowers to cut the grass to sunbathe

I. Los cuartos

Using vocabulary from each of the seven groups above, make a statement about each section of the house.

MODELO **Mañana por la tarde hay que limpiar la cocina.**

II. Seis estudiantes están en casa

Lupe, Alicia, Teresa, Pablo, Ricardo, and Alfredo are the six children of Enrique Pérez, a widower. State what each is doing in a different room of the house.

MODELO **En la cocina Alfredo prepara la comida.**

III. Tú estás en casa

Now place yourself in this house and create an imaginary day. State two activities which you carry out in the morning (**por la mañana**), afternoon (**por la tarde**), and evening (**por la noche**).

MODELO **Por la mañana tomo una ducha en el cuarto de baño.**

IV. Unos amigos están en casa

Form groups of from two to four people each. Pretend that you are sharing a house and are discussing your activities. One person may be going to Mexico; a second person may be getting married; a third may be looking for a job; and a fourth may be staying home. How do these friends interact? Ask each other questions about what everyone is going to do.

Capítulo 5

Despegue

Begin by looking at the following drawings and the sentence associated with each of them.

Josefa espera a Marco Antonio.

Josefa y Marco Antonio charlan.

Marco llama.

Marco deja los estudios.

Pronunciación

esperé **pasó** **llamamos** **contaron**	In the preterit tense, regular verbs are stressed on the verb ending (and not on the stem).
un poco **un puesto**	In the combination **n** + **p, n** is pronounced **m.**
esperé‿ayer **va‿a‿estar** **ahora‿está‿en Caracas**	When two vowels occur next to each other, one glides into the other, even if they are in different words.

Aplicación

I. Practice saying each of the following words and phrases first very slowly and then at a normal speed.

1. **esperé** / **pasó** / **llamamos** / **contaron**
2. **un poco** / **un puesto**
3. **esperé ayer** / **va a estar** / **ahora está en Caracas**

II. Preguntas

1. 

¿Qué hace Josefa, trabaja o espera? ¿Epera usted a un amigo ahora?

2. 

¿Llama Marco a su amigo o sale con él? ¿A quién llama usted?

3. 

¿Qué hacen Josefa y Marco, estudian o charlan? Y ustedes, ¿charlan ahora?

4. 

¿Marco sigue con los estudios o deja los estudios? ¿Usted también deja los estudios?

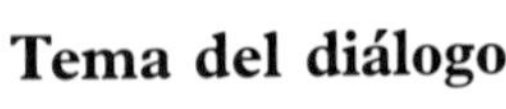

Tema del diálogo

A Colombian student with the possibility of living and working in Caracas explains the situation to a friend.

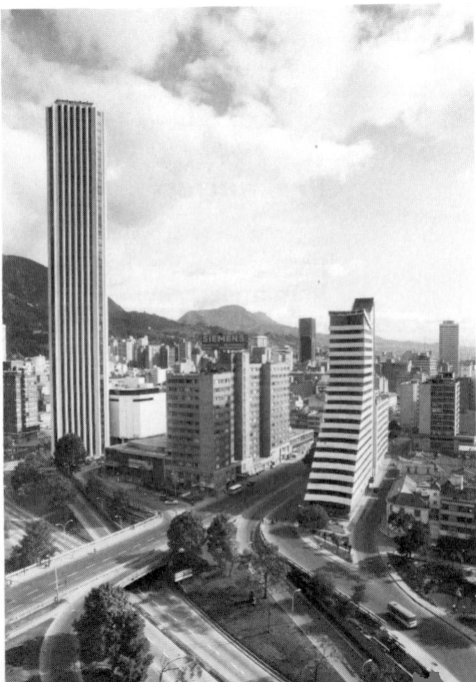

Modern structures in Bogotá, Colombia.

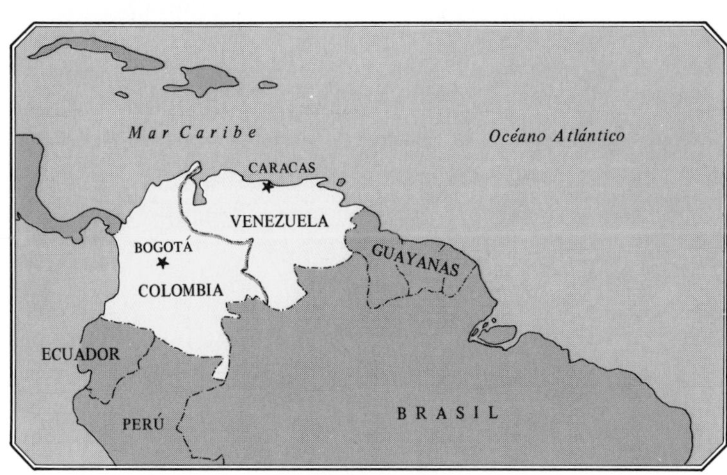

DIÁLOGO

Un puesto estupendo

Dos amigos colombianos charlan. Ella es Josefa Ortiz, estudiante de química; él se llama Marco Antonio Gaviria, y estudia leyes[1].

JOSEFA Esperé ayer toda la tarde pero nunca llegaste. ¿Qué pasó?

MARCO Nada, nada. Un poco antes de salir en el carro de mi hermano, llamó mi primo, Bernardo.

JOSEFA ¿Bernardo? No sé quién es.

MARCO Sí, hombre[2]. Bernardo Páez. Ahora está en Caracas donde trabaja con una compañía venezolana.

JOSEFA Bueno, y ¿qué hay con eso?

MARCO Pues bien. Estoy muy emocionado porque me contó que hay un puesto estupendo en la compañía para alguien como yo. Con un gran futuro.

JOSEFA ¡Ya doy! Y dejaste tus estudios de leyes.

MARCO Sí, efectivamente. Ahora sólo tengo que convencer a mi padre. Mamá no es problema. . .pero claro está, va a estar preocupada.[3]

JOSEFA ¡Y yo también!

MARCO ¡No, hombre! ¡Qué va! Yo pongo en orden todos mis asuntos aquí y allá todo va a salir chévere.

JOSEFA ¿Vamos a tomar un café y conversamos más?

MARCO Vamos. Quiero tomar una cerveza bien fría. Ah. . .y yo invito. Voy a comenzar a gastar mis treinta mil bolívares.

There's a great job in the company for someone like me.

A great job

Two Colombian friends are talking. She is Josefa Ortiz, a chemistry student; his name is Marco Antonio Gaviria, and he is studying law.

J: I waited all afternoon yesterday but you never arrived. What happened?

M.A.: Nothing, nothing. A little before leaving in my brother's car, my cousin Bernardo called.

J: Bernardo? I don't know who he is.

M.A.: Of course (you do). Bernardo Páez. He's in Caracas now where he works for a Venezuelan company.

J: O.K., and what's the story?

M.A.: Well. . .I'm very excited because he told me that there's a great job in the company for someone like me. With a great future.

J: I get it! And you quit your law studies.

M.A.: Yes, as a matter of fact. Now I have only to convince my father. Mom is no problem. . . but, of course, she's going to be worried.

J: And me too!

M.A.: Come on! Quit it! I'm putting all my affairs in order here and everything is going to turn out great there.

J: Shall we go for coffee and talk some more?

M.A.: Let's go. I want to have a nice cold beer. Ah. . .and I'm treating. I'm going to start spending my 30,000 bolivars.

VARIACIONES

¿Cuáles son los cuartos de una casa?	What are the rooms of a house?
la cocina	kitchen
el comedor	dining room
el dormitorio	bedroom
la sala	living room
el cuarto de baño (el baño)	bathroom
¿Vive usted en una casa?	Do you live in a house?
No, vivo en un apartamento.	No, I live in an apartment.

¿Cómo es su casa?	What's your house like?
Es bonita.	It's pretty.
fea	ugly
grande	big
pequeña	little
Hay un garage.	There's a garage.
Pero no hay patio.	But there's no patio.
¿A quién traes al café?	Whom do you bring to the café?
Traigo a mi amiga.	I bring my friend.
¿Cuántos hay en la clase?	How many are in the class?
Once, doce, trece, catorce, quince.	Eleven, twelve, thirteen, fourteen, fifteen.

Glosas

1. Nowadays in Hispanic countries more and more young women are going to college; the once all-male universities are changing. Of the women in college, a high percentage study for a profession, since the universities are basically professional schools; medicine, dentistry, architecture, and chemistry in particular have attracted a large number of women in the last two decades. Obstacles other than admissions policies can still block a Hispanic woman's effort to obtain a college education, however. If her own city is too small to have a university, for example, and her family has no relatives or close friends in the capital with whom she can stay, her parents may oppose her wish to attend the national university, out of fear of the assumed dangers of urban living.
2. **Hombre, Sí hombre, No hombre** are very common expressions of emphasis. They do not refer to any particular sex or number of people.
3. Middle-class Hispanic parents would like to see every member of the family remain within "walking distance" of the family home. Normally only lack of economic opportunities will prevent families from staying in the same city or even in the same residential area.
4. **Yo invito** *I'll treat.* Dutch treat is unusual in Latin America and in Spain. Friends usually take turns treating each other to drinks and snacks, though when a man and woman have a drink together, the man nearly always pays.

SOBRE EL DIÁLOGO

I. Complete each sentence by choosing an appropriate word from the following list.

química / **llama** / **esperamos** / **venezolana** / **preocupados** / **pequeño** / **asunto** / **invitar** / **patio** / **cuartos** / **dejo** / **puesto** / **bonita**

MODELO Josefa tiene un buen _____ en la compañía. → **Josefa tiene un buen puesto en la compañía.**

1. Susana es de Venezuela. Es _____.
2. No estudio _____ ahora.
3. Mañana voy a _____ a los Gaviria a cenar en casa.

4. Los chicos juegan en el ______.
5. Dos dormitorios, la cocina, el comedor, el baño y la sala. La casa tiene seis ______.
6. María siempre me ______ por teléfono.
7. Si llegas tarde vamos a estar ______.
8. Siempre ______ mis cosas en el dormitorio.
9. Mamá y yo siempre ______ a papá para comer.
10. Necesito hablar de un ______ con mamá.
11. No tenemos un patio grande, tenemos un patio ______.
12. La casa no es fea, es ______.

II. Name the room described.

MODELO el cuarto en que dormimos → **el dormitorio**

1. el cuarto en que comemos
2. el cuarto en que hacemos el postre y el café
3. el cuarto en que hablamos con la gente
4. el cuarto en que hacemos las cosas personales
5. el cuarto en que dormimos
6. donde dejamos el carro

III. Para contestar

MODELO ¿Llega usted tarde a clase? → **No, no llego tarde a clase.**

1. ¿Es usted colombiano (colombiana)?
2. ¿Cómo se llama el profesor (la profesora)? ¿Es de Colombia?
3. ¿Estudia leyes usted? ¿Estudia leyes una persona que quiere ser médico?
4. ¿Estudia usted química? ¿Inglés? ¿Qué estudia?
5. ¿Esperan ustedes al profesor si llega tarde?
6. Si usted quiere salir por la noche, ¿tiene que convencer a sus padres?
7. ¿Está preocupado (preocupada) usted? ¿Por qué? ¿Hay mucho trabajo?
8. ¿Siempre deja usted su cuarto en orden?
9. ¿Cuántos cuartos hay en su casa? ¿Cuáles son?
10. ¿Hay un comedor en su casa? ¿un patio? ¿un garage?
11. ¿Cómo es su casa?
12. ¿Vive usted en una casa o en un apartamento?

Con paso firme
y seguro,
llegamos a Belén
...para asegurarle su futuro.
CAJA DE AHORRO Y CREDITO
SOCIEDAD COOPERATIVA LTDA.
Nueva Sucursal Belén Carrera 76 No. 30-44.
Ed. Mariscal Tel: 561016

VOCABULARIO

nouns

el **apartamento**	apartment
el **asunto**	matter
el **bolívar**	monetary unit of Venezuela
el **carro**	car
la **cerveza**	beer
la **compañía**	company
el **cuarto**	room
el **estudio**	study
los **estudios**	studies
el **futuro**	future
la **ley**	law
el **orden**	order
el **primo**, la **prima**	cousin
el **puesto**	position, job
la **química**	chemistry

divisions of a house

la **cocina**	kitchen
el **comedor**	dining room
el **cuarto de baño** (el **baño**)	bathroom
el **dormitorio**	bedroom
el **garage**	garage
el **patio**	patio, yard
la **sala**	living room

numbers

See summary, pages 97–98.

adjectives

bonito	pretty
colombiano	Colombian
emocionado	excited
estupendo	wonderful
feo	ugly
frío	cold
gran, grande	big, great
gran futuro	great future
pequeño	small, little
preocupado	worried
venezolano	Venezuelan

verbs

comenzar a (ie, c)	to begin to, start
contar (ue)	to tell, relate
convencer (z)	to convince
charlar	to converse, chat
dejar	to leave, quit
esperar	to wait, hope
estar	to be
estoy	I am
gastar	to spend
invitar	to invite, treat
llamar	to call
pasar	to happen
poner	to put
pongo	I put
saber	to know (information)
sé	I know
tener (ie)	to have
tengo	I have
tener que	to have to
traer	to bring
traigo	I bring
vivir	to live

other expressions

alguien	someone
antes de	before
ayer	yesterday
bien	very
claro está	of course
chévere	(regional) great, fantastic

efectivamente	exactly, as a matter of fact
nada	nothing
¡No, hombre!	Not at all!
nunca	never, ever
pues bien	well
¡Qué va!	Go on! Of course not!
se llama	his name is
toda la tarde	the whole afternoon
¿Y qué hay con eso?	So what? What's the story?
Ya doy.	I see; I get it.
Vamos a (+infinitive)	Let's (+verb)
Vamos a comer.	Let's eat.

additional vocabulary

caer	to fall
yo caigo	I fall
la libertad de expresión	freedom of expression
más	plus; more, most
la chica más bonita	the prettiest girl
menos	minus
la **novia**	fiancée, steady girlfriend
el **novio**	suitor, fiancé, steady boyfriend
la **observación**	observation
personal	personal
el presidente	president

ESTRUCTURA I

A. Preterit tense of regular -ar verbs

Repaso. Remember that, in the present tense, regular **-ar** verb forms follow a standard pattern of stem + endings. Regular **-er** and **-ir** verbs also follow a standard pattern.

> **Esperé** ayer pero no **llegaste.** ¿Qué **pasó?**

1. The preterit tense conveys what happened. It focuses on a state or event as a single point in the past.

2. Regular **-ar** verbs in the preterit follow a standard pattern of forms: verb stem + **-é, -aste, -ó, -amos, -asteis, -aron.**

cenar		
stem	endings	
cen	**é**	Cené en casa.
cen	**aste**	¿Dónde cenaste anoche?
cen	**ó**	Josefa cenó con Miguel.
cen	**amos**	Ayer cenamos tarde.
cen	**asteis**	¿Cenasteis en Caracas?
cen	**aron**	Mis padres ya cenaron.

Note the difference in stress between present tense **(yo) ceno** *I eat,* and preterit **(él) cenó** *he ate.*

Llamó mi primo Bernardo.	My cousin Bernard called.
Dejaste tus estudios.	You quit your studies.
Yo invité.	I invited (I treated).
Esperamos ayer toda la tarde.	We waited all afternoon yesterday.
Ustedes nunca llegaron.	You never arrived.

3. The first person plural (**nosotros**) verb form is the same in the present and preterit tenses. The context of the conversation indicates either a present or a past situation.

Ayer cenamos juntos.	Yesterday we had dinner together.
¿Cenamos aquí esta noche?	Shall we have dinner here tonight?
Siempre charlamos mucho.	We always talk a lot.

4. The stem-changes **e** → **ie** and **o** → **ue** occur in the present tense only; they do not occur in the preterit.

pensar	
present	preterit
pienso	pensé
piensas	pensaste
piensa	pensó
pensamos	pensamos
pensáis	pensasteis
piensas	pensaron

5. **Bernardo llamó** can mean *Bernard called* or *Bernard did call.*

Dos hombres de negocios hablaron.	Two businessmen talked.
Mamá tomó una taza de café.	Mom had a cup of coffee.
Esperé y esperé pero no llegaste.	I waited and waited but you didn't arrive.
¿Ya llamó mi primo Bernardo?	Did my cousin Bernardo call already?

Aplicación

I. Repeat each sentence, substituting the subjects in parentheses for the one in the original sentence.

MODELO Ayer hablé con él. (tú, nosotros) →
Ayer hablaste con él.
Ayer hablamos con él.

1. Esperé y esperé. (Josefa, tú, las dos hermanas, mamá y yo, yo)
2. ¿Llamaste temprano. (el hombre, ustedes, nosotros, tú, yo)

3. Contaron muchas cosas. (yo, tú, el abogado, tú y él, ella y yo)
4. Yo invité. (el extranjero, ustedes, tú, nosotros, las estudiantes)

II. Express each sentence in the preterit.

MODELO Espero a Marta. → **Esperé a Marta.**

1. Marta llega tarde.
2. Hablamos del futuro.
3. Ella gasta su plata.
4. Tomamos café y conversamos.
5. Yo invito.
6. ¿Tú hablas con ella también?

III. Answer each question using **¡Qué va!** and **ya** + the preterit tense.

MODELO ¿Van ustedes a cenar ahora? → **¡Qué va! Ya cenamos.**

1. ¿Tú vas a llamar ahora?
2. ¿Josefa va a estudiar ahora?
3. ¿Voy a hablar del puesto ahora?
4. ¿Ustedes van a tomar un café ahora?
5. ¿Ellos van a dejar las cosas en casa ahora?
6. ¿El profesor va a llegar ahora?

IV. Complete each sentence by supplying the correct form of the verb indicated in the key. Add any other words you wish to include.

MODELO Tomaron un café y __C__. → **Tomaron un café y hablaron toda la tarde.**

1. Hablé con Juan y él me __A__.
2. María Elena llamó a María y __B__.
3. Cenamos juntos y __C__.
4. Me invitó a casa y nosotros __D__.
5. Llegamos a California y __E__ las Navidades allá.
6. Esperé toda la tarde pero él no __F__.

A. invitar
B. charlar
C. hablar
D. cenar
E. pasar
F. llamar

V. Tell what you did yesterday, using the items listed as a guide. Add other items if you wish.

MODELO llegar / aquí → **Llegué aquí temprano.**

1. charlar / amigos
2. estudiar / por la mañana
3. tomar / Coca-Cola / amigos
4. hablar / profesor
5. llegar / casa
6. llamar / María
7. cenar / familia
8. estudiar / un rato más

VI. Answer the following questions with any logical response.

1. ¿Cenó usted ayer en casa o en un restaurante?
2. ¿De qué hablamos ayer?
3. ¿Trabajé yo por la tarde?
4. ¿Pasaron ustedes las Navidades aquí o en casa?
5. ¿Llegaron ustedes tarde esta mañana?
6. ¿Tomó usted un café con un amigo ayer? ¿Quién invitó, usted o él?

B. Counting from 11 to the thousands

Quince mil y quince mil son treinta mil.

1. To begin, learn the numbers that are multiples of ten.

(20)	veinte	(60)	sesenta	(*note:* seis / sesenta)
(30)	treinta	(70)	setenta	(*note:* siete / setenta)
(40)	cuarenta	(80)	ochenta	
(50)	cincuenta	(90)	noventa	(*note:* nueve / noventa)

Note that **veinte** and **treinta** are both spelled with **ei** (and not **ie**).

2. Here are the numbers 11–15.

(11)	once	(13)	trece	(15)	quince
(12)	doce	(14)	catorce		

3. The numbers between 16 and 29 are usually written as one word. To count from 16 to 29, follow this combination:

multiple + **-i-** + smaller number

(16)	dieciséis	(23)	veintitrés
(17)	diecisiete	(24)	veinticuatro
(18)	dieciocho	(25)	veinticinco
(19)	diecinueve	(26)	veintiséis
(20)	veinte	(27)	veintisiete
(21)	veintiuno	(28)	veintiocho
(22)	veintidós	(29)	veintinueve

3. Starting with 31, three words are used.

multiple + **y** + smaller number

(30)	treinta	(42)	cuarenta y dos
(31)	treinta y uno	(93)	noventa y tres

4. Now learn the multiples of 100.

(100)	ciento[1]	(500)	quinientos	(*note:* cinco / quinientos)
(200)	doscientos	(600)	seiscientos	
(300)	trescientos	(700)	setecientos	(*note:* siete / setecientos)
(400)	cuatrocientos	(800)	ochocientos	
		(900)	novecientos	(*note:* nueve / novecientos)

[1]**Cien,** a variant of **ciento,** occurs when counting and before nouns: **cien estudiantes.**

5. To count beyond 100, use **ciento(s)** + smaller number; **y** is not used between them.

(101)	ciento uno	(220)	doscientos veinte
(102)	ciento dos	(331)	trescientos treinta y uno
(103)	ciento tres	(999)	novecientos noventa y nueve

6. 1,000 and its multiples are as follows.

(1.000)	mil	(3.000)	tres mil
(2.000)	dos mil	(4.000)	cuatro mil

Spanish uses a period, not a comma, in large number combinations. Note also that **un** is not used before **mil.**

7. To count beyond **mil,** the smaller number follows **mil** directly; **y** is not used.

(1.001)	mil uno
(2.016)	dos mil dieciséis
(3.031)	tres mil treinta y uno
(9.999)	nueve mil novecientos noventa y nueve

Spanish renders dates like 1984 as **mil novecientos ochenta y cuatro;** do not translate "nineteen hundred. . ." directly from English; use **mil** instead.

1898	mil ochocientos noventa y ocho
1984	mil novecientos ochenta y cuatro

Aplicación

I. Count by tens from 10 to 1000.

MODELO **diez, veinte, treinta. . .**

II. State the following numbers.

MODELO 64 → **sesenta y cuatro**

1. 38	6. 49	11. 114	16. 913	21. 2.479
2. 90	7. 77	12. 597	17. 881	22. 5.532
3. 17	8. 51	13. 233	18. 406	23. 7.075
4. 23	9. 82	14. 783	19. 614	24. 8.791
5. 19	10. 6	15. 362	20. 1.693	25. 9.783

III. State the number that precedes, the number indicated, and the number that follows.

MODELO 104 → **ciento tres, ciento cuatro, ciento cinco**

1. 178 2. 1.983 3. 3.742 4. 10.659 5. 99.876

IV. Answer the following questions.

1. ¿Cuántos son veinticinco más *(plus)* veinticinco?
2. ¿Cuántos son treinta más treinta?
3. ¿Cuántos son sesenta y dos más diez?
4. ¿Cuántos son doscientos menos *(minus)* veinticinco?
5. ¿Cuántos son cincuenta menos veinte?
6. ¿Cuántos son setenta menos diez?
7. ¿En qué año estamos ahora?
8. ¿En qué año llegó Cristóbal Colón[1] a América?

C. The verb **estar**

Bernardo está en Caracas.

1. Here are the present tense forms of **estar** *to be.*

estoy	Estoy aquí.
estás	¿Estás en el hotel?
está	Miguel está con su familia.
estamos	Estamos con mamá.
estáis	¿Ya estáis en casa?
están	Los precios están por las nubes.

2. **Estar** is used for location: it indicates where someone or something is to be found.

Juan Carlos está en el Paraguay.	Juan Carlos is in Paraguay.
Las maletas están en el dormitorio.	The suitcases are in the bedroom.

3. **Estar** is also used with **bien, mal,** and **cómo** to state how people are feeling and to inquire about their health.

Hola, chica. ¿Cómo estás?	Hi there. How are you?
Yo estoy bien, gracias.	I am well, thank you.

Aplicación

I. Repeat each sentence, changing the verb to agree with the new subject.

MODELO Estamos aquí. (yo, ella) → **Estoy aquí. Está aquí.**

1. Está en Caracas. (mis primos, yo, tú, Josefa, nosotros)
2. ¿Dónde estás? (el abogado, el estudiante y ella, yo, tú y yo, tú)

[1] Christopher Columbus.

II. Answer each question according to the model.

MODELO ¿Cómo están ustedes? → **¿Nosotros? Estamos bien, gracias.**

1. ¿Cómo está mamá?
2. ¿Cómo está usted?
3. ¿Cómo están los amigos?
4. ¿Cómo están todos ustedes?
5. Y la señorita mexicana, ¿cómo está?

D. Uses of **ser** / **Ser** and **estar** + adjective

Mamá no es problema.

1. **Ser** is used in the following situations:

   a) Linking: to link two nouns, a noun + pronoun, or two numbers.

Jorge es colombiano.	Jorge is a Colombian.
Yo soy estudiante de español.	I'm a Spanish student.
Somos profesores.	We are teachers.
Dos y dos son cuatro.	Two and two are four.

Two views of Caracas, the dynamic capital of Venezuela. Since 1955 the country has enjoyed progressive, democratically elected governments and large revenues from the sale of oil.

b) Origin or material: **ser de** + name of place indicates where someone is from; **ser de** + material tells what something is made of.

Soy de Bogotá.	I'm from Bogotá.
Juan Carlos es de Chile.	Juan Carlos is from Chile.
Somos de los Estados Unidos.	We're from the United States.
La taza es de plata.	The cup is (made of) silver.

c) Possession. In order to indicate who something belongs to, English uses *'s* or *s'*: *Sandy's books, the gamblers' money.* Spanish, instead, uses **ser de** + name of person.

La casa es de mis padres.	The house is my parents'.
Las maletas son de Sandra.	The suitcases are Sandra's.
Juan Carlos es el novio de María.	Juan Carlos is María's boyfriend.

d) Time: **ser** is used to indicate time of day.

Es temprano.	It is early.
Ya es muy tarde.	It's already late.
Son las once de la mañana.	It's eleven in the morning.

2. Both **ser** and **estar** may be used with adjectives, but with the following differences.

a) **Ser** + adjective is used to mention a quality that is viewed as normal for the person or object being described. **Ser** + adjective categorizes the subject as being one of a group (strong people, young persons, etc.).

Bernardo es fuerte.	Bernardo is strong.
Mis hijos son jóvenes.	My children are young.
La clase de inglés es muy buena.	The English class is very good
La casa no es muy grande, pero la cocina es estupenda.	The house is not very big, but the kitchen is great.

b) **Estar,** on the other hand, is used with adjectives (and with some adverbs) to indicate a state or a condition of the subject. **Estar** + adjective expresses the speaker's personal reaction or feelings concerning the person or object being described.

¡Qué preocupado estoy!	How worried I am!
La cerveza no está fría.	The beer isn't cold.
Mis padres están bien.	My parents are well.
Estamos muy emocionados.	We're very excited.

c) Used with an adjective, **estar** sometimes corresponds to English words such as *to look, to seem, to feel, to taste.*

¡Qué joven estás, Josefa!	How young you look, Josefa.
La comida está buena.	The food tastes good.

Aplicación

I. Supply the correct form of **ser** or **estar.**

Me llamo Sara González Peña y __1__ de Colombia. Yo __2__ estudiante de medicina en mi pais, pero ahora __3__ en los Estados Unidos donde estudio inglés. __4__ muy emocionada porque __5__ en un país extranjero. Mis padres __6__ un poco preocupados porque yo __7__ la hija más joven, pero ellos comprenden que el viaje __8__ estupendo para mi futuro. Mi hermano José __9__ en España ahora. Él __10__ economista y __11__ con una compañía en Madrid. Claro que José no __12__ problema para mis padres porque él __13__ hombre.

II. Answer each question choosing **ser** or **estar** according to the context.

MODELOS ¿Usted? ¿estudiante de leyes? → **Sí, soy estudiante de leyes.**
¿Ellos? ¿aquí? → **Sí, ellos están aquí.**

1. ¿Usted? ¿de los Estados Unidos?
2. ¿Ellos? ¿en México?
3. ¿El profesor? ¿muy preocupado?
4. ¿Yo? ¿un poco emocionado?
5. ¿Los precios? ¿por las nubes?
6. ¿Ustedes? ¿americanos?
7. ¿La señora? ¿en la cocina?
8. ¿El puesto? ¿estupendo?
9. ¿Yo? ¿español?
10. ¿Nosotros? ¿aquí?
11. ¿Ahora? ¿muy tarde?
12. ¿Los estudiantes? ¿en el comedor?
13. ¿Las maletas? ¿de los extranjeros?
14. ¿Marco Aurelio? ¿estudiante de inglés?
15. ¿María? ¿una chica muy bonita?

III. Para expresar en español

MODELOS She is young. → **Ella es joven.**
She looks young. → **Ella está joven.**

1. The job is great.
   You look great.
2. Coffee is good.
   The coffee tastes good.
3. They are old.
   They look old.
4. The house is new.
   The house seems new.
5. I'm optimistic.
   I feel optimistic.
6. We are strong.
   We feel strong.
7. She is pretty.
   She looks pretty.
8. The car is ugly.
   The car looks ugly.

IV. Using **ser** and **estar,** make as many statements about yourself as you can.

MODELO **Soy una persona muy optimista. Ahora estoy un poco preocupado (preocupada).**

V. Make as many statements about a friend as you can.

MODELO **Mi amiga (amigo) es de California. Ahora está en Nueva York.**

Pausa oral

Una familia venezolana

If you went to Caracas and stayed a month, you might end up living with a Venezuelan family. How much could you tell your friends about the family members when you got home?[1]

I. In the left-hand column below, statements are made about the Sánchez family of Bogotá, Colombia. Make up names for your Venezuelan family and describe its members. Use complete sentences.

MODELO Es la familia Sánchez. → **Es la familia Hernández.**

1. Es la familia Sánchez. ____________
2. El padre es José. Es el señor Sánchez. ____________
3. La madre es María. Es la señora María Cordero de Sánchez. ____________
4. El hijo es Miguel. Es el señor Sánchez. ____________
5. La hija es Lilia. Es la señorita Sánchez. ____________
6. El novio de Lilia es Mario. ____________
7. La novia de Miguel es Teresa. ____________
8. Lilia y Miguel son estudiantes. ____________

II. Using the names you have just created, explain the relationships of the family members. Once again, statements about the Sánchez family are provided as a guide. Use complete sentences.

MODELO El señor Sánchez es el padre de Miguel y de Lilia. → **El señor Hernández es el padre de Juan y de Marta.**

1. El señor Sánchez es el padre de Miguel y de Lilia. ____________
2. La señora Sánchez es la madre de Miguel y de Lilia. ____________
3. Miguel es el hijo de José y de María. Es el hijo de los señores Sánchez. ____________
4. Lilia es la hija de José y de María. Es la hija de los señores Sánchez. ____________
5. Miguel y Lilia son hermanos. ____________
6. Lilia es la novia de Mario. ____________
7. Lilia y Mario son novios. ____________
8. Miguel y Teresa son novios también. ____________

[1]Review **glosa** 1, page 38.

III. Now identify the members of your own family, your friends, and your **novio** or **novia** if you have one.

MODELO **Somos la familia Lewis. Hay tres hijos: Ann, Robert, y yo, Susana. Fred es mi novio; trabaja con una casa comercial.**

IV. Para contestar

1. ¿Cuántas personas hay en la familia venezolana? ¿Quiénes son?
2. ¿Cuántos cuartos hay en la casa de usted? ¿Cuáles son?
3. Después de la cena, ¿charlan ustedes de sobremesa? ¿De qué hablan ustedes?
4. ¿Gasta usted mucho dinero? ¿En qué gasta dinero?

ESTRUCTURA II

A. Possession

Repaso. The phrase **ser de** is used to express to whom something belongs: **El dinero es de Josefa.**

Llamó mi primo Bernardo.

1. Spanish never uses the form apostrophe + **s ('s)** in order to express possession. Instead, one way to express ownership is as follows:

object possessed + **de** + name of owner
la casa de Josefa

To ask the question *Whose . . . ?* , use the form **¿De quién(es) . . . ?**

¿De quién es el café? — Whose coffee is it?
¿De quiénes son los pasaportes? — Whose passports are they?

2. Another way to express ownership is to use a possessive adjective. Study the set of possessive adjectives in the following chart.

	SINGULAR MASCULINE	SINGULAR FEMININE	PLURAL MASCULINE	PLURAL FEMININE	
my	**mi**		**mis**		Mi dormitorio es muy grande.
your	**tu**		**tus**		¿Dónde está tu casa?
his, her, your	**su**		**sus**		Sus padres están preocupados.
our	**nuestro**	**nuestra**	**nuestros**	**nuestras**	Nuestro país va a mejorar.
your	**vuestro**[1]	**vuestra**	**vuestros**	**vuestras**	¿Vuestros primos viven aquí?
their, your	**su**		**sus**		Su mamá no es problema.

[1]In most of the Spanish-speaking world, the forms **su, sus** (or **de ustedes**) are used instead of **vuestro (-a, -os, -as)** since the **vosotros** forms are not used.

3. Note that all possessive adjectives have both a singular and a plural form. But none except **nuestro** (and **vuestro**) change ending to show gender agreement.

¿Dónde estás, en tu cuarto?	Where are you, in your room?
Dejaste tus estudios de leyes.	You quit your law studies.
Nuestra familia es muy grande.	Our family is very large.
Aquí están nuestros pasaportes.	Here are our passports.

4. In Spanish, the possessive adjective agrees in number and gender with the object possessed, not with the owner.

No quiero abandonar mis estudios.	I don't want to abandon my studies.
Nuestro gobierno es militar.	Our government is a military one.

5. In order to be more specific, the forms **su** and **sus** are often replaced by **de** + third-person pronoun:

sus negocios → los negocios de {él, ella, usted / ellos, ellas, ustedes}

Los padres de ella viven en Venezuela.	Her parents live in Venezuela.
La casa de ellos es estupenda.	Their home is wonderful.
¿Es de usted el dinero?	Is the money yours?

Aplicación

I. Para expresar en español

MODELO the gentleman's house → **la casa del señor**

1. María's sister 2. Mr. Arce's passport 3. Juan's job 4. the woman's cup 5. the president's problems 6. the daughter's room

II. Combine each pair of sentences into one by using **de.**

MODELO Los Alessandri tienen una casa. La casa es nueva. →
La casa de los Alessandri es nueva.

1. Chela tiene un hermano. Él es muy guapo.
2. Luis tiene un puesto. Es estupendo.
3. Las estudiantes tienen un amigo. Es extranjero.
4. Luisa tiene unas maletas. Son viejas.
5. El gobierno tiene unos problemas. Son económicos.

III. Restate each sentence making the indicated substitution and any necessary changes.

MODELO Habla con su amigo. (profesores) → **Habla con sus profesores.**

1. Luis llamó a su hermano. (novia)
2. Espero a mi mamá. (padres)
3. No comprendes mis problemas. (situación)
4. Discuten nuestro caso. (problemas)
5. ¿Hablaste con tus padres? (primo)
6. Hablamos con nuestros amigos. (profesora)

IV. Supply the possessive adjective which corresponds to the subject of the sentence.

MODELO María está en ______ cuarto. → **María esta en su cuarto.**

1. Nosotros salimos con ______ padres.
2. Josefa habla con ______ amigos.
3. María y Teresa invitan a ______ profesor a cenar.
4. Estudio en ______ dormitorio.
5. No comprendes a ______ padres.
6. Roberto cenó con ______ hermana ayer.
7. Ustedes no hacen ______ trabajo.
8. Ella y yo hablamos de ______ futuro.
9. ¿Habló usted con ______ abogado?
10. Los médicos van a ______ oficina.

V. Express in Spanish using **de.**

MODELO his cousins and her sister → **los primos de él y la hermana de ella**

1. your house and their garage
2. his patio and your dining room
3. their bathroom and your bedroom
4. her job and his studies
5. your problems and their situation

VI. Para contestar

1. ¿Dónde está su casa?
2. ¿Tiene nuestro país un gobierno militar?
3. ¿Están preocupados sus padres?
4. ¿Quién es el profesor de ustedes?
5. ¿Con quién hablan los estudiantes de sus problemas?
6. ¿Dónde están mis cosas?

B. Irregular (yo) verb forms (present tense)

Repaso. The irregular verbs studied up to now show irregularities in all of their present tense forms (for example, **ser: soy, eres, es, somos, sois, son**).

No **sé** quién es.

1. Several verbs are irregular only in the first person (**yo**) form. Here are the most common:

saber *to know*	**sé**		**caer** *to fall*	**caigo**
ver *to see*	**veo**		**traer** *to bring*	**traigo**
			hacer *to do*	**hago**
dar *to give*	**doy**		**poner** *to put*	**pongo**
estar *to be*	**estoy**		**salir** *to leave*	**salgo**

Sé que los viajes cansan un poco.	I know that trips are a little tiring.
No veo problema.	I see no problem.
Estoy en una mala situación.	I'm in a bad situation.
Traigo unas cosas.	I'm bringing some things.
Salgo a comer.	I am going out to eat.
¿Qué hago esta noche?	What shall I do tonight?

2. The other present-tense forms of these verbs are all regular. Here are three examples.

saber	dar	hacer	
sé	**doy**	**hago**	No sé quién es.
sabes	das	haces	¿Sabes cómo se llama?
sabe	da	hace	Ella no da la mano.
sabemos	damos	hacemos	No le damos nada.
sabéis	dais	hacéis	¿Qué hacéis?
saben	dan	hacen	Ellas hacen mucho trabajo.

Aplicación

I. Change from singular to plural or from plural to singular.

MODELOS No sé nada. → **No sabemos nada.**
¿Cuándo salimos? → **¿Cuándo salgo?**

1. ¿Qué ponemos aquí?
2. ¿Dónde estamos?
3. ¿A qué hora salimos?
4. No sé nada.
5. No veo problema.
6. Damos una recepción.
7. Hago muy buena plata.
8. Traigo a Sara.
9. Sabemos cómo se llama.
10. ¿Qué hacemos ahora?

II. Respond in the first person (**yo**).

MODELO El señor ve problemas, ¿y usted? → **Yo veo problemas también.**

1. Mamá está preocupada, ¿y usted?
2. Nosotros salimos temprano, ¿y usted?
3. El profesor sabe inglés, ¿y usted?
4. Nosotros damos plata, ¿y usted?
5. El trae su pasaporte, ¿y usted?
6. Los estudiantes hacen el trabajo, ¿y usted?

Farming in San Andrés, Ecuador, at an altitude of 11,200 feet, calls for modern technology and ancient clothing. Chimborazo, the volcano in the background, reaches a height of 20,561 feet.

III. Para contestar

1. ¿Traigo café a clase? ¿Trae usted café?
2. ¿Hace usted mucho trabajo? Y yo, ¿también hago mucho trabajo?
3. ¿Está usted preocupado porque hay mucho trabajo?
4. ¿Dan muchos problemas los estudiantes? ¿Usted da muchos problemas?
5. ¿Sé hablar español yo? ¿Y usted? ¿Y su padre?
6. ¿Siempre pone usted sus cosas en orden antes de salir?

C. Personal **a**

> Tengo que convencer **a** mi padre.

1. Personal **a** is used between a verb and a direct object noun or pronoun that refers to a definite, particular person.

> verb + **a** + person (or group of people)

Juan no quiere abandonar a sus padres.	Juan doesn't want to leave his parents.
Visitamos a tu familia, ¿no?	We're visiting your family, right?

2. This **a** is not translated into English. The **a** contracts with the article **el** (but not with the pronoun **él**).

Más vale escuchar al Dr. Varela.	It would be better to listen to Dr. Varela.

3. Personal **a** is seldom used when talking about non-specific people, or with the verb **tener** *to have.*

Veo mucha gente en el aeropuerto.	I see lots of people in the airport.
Los señores Alessandri tienen un hijo.	Mr. and Mrs. Alessandri have a son.

Aplicación

I. Make the indicated substitutions, using personal **a** when required.

MODELO Espero a la señorita. (las Navidades, médico) → **Espero las Navidades. Espero al médico.**

1. Veo los problemas. (hombres, gente, casas, dinero, profesor)
2. Paquita no comprende la situación. (americanos, caso, asunto, negocios, muchacho español)
3. No necesitamos al doctor. (profesora, pasaporte, maletas, dinero)

II. Supply personal **a** wherever necessary.

Tengo __1__ un amigo que se llama Perico Pérez. Perico tiene __2__ un problema. Quiere *(He loves)* __3__ una señorita que es muy buena pero que no es muy optimista. Cuando Perico invita __4__ su amiga Paquita a salir, ella siempre piensa en los problemas. "¿Cómo podemos salir? Primero tengo que convencer __5__ mi padre. Y tengo que hacer __6__ mucho trabajo. Y tengo que visitar __7__ mi amiga Lupita, porque no está bien. Y tú, Perico, no ganas __8__ mucha plata. ¿Cómo me invitas a salir, hombre? ¿No ves que hay __9__ problemas?" Pero Perico no es como su amiga. Él es optimista. Esta noche va a llamar __10__ Paquita otra vez. . .para ver si ella cambia de opinión. ¡Qué problema!

"I shall save the Fatherland from anarchy and demagoguery. Free elections will again be held when the country is ready." Bolivia—an often repeated scene.

 LECTURA

Economía y política

"En un país en que no se puede contar con una situación económica estable, rara vez se va a encontrar un sistema político democrático."[1] Así explicó el presidente de una república latinoamericana, Venezuela, cuyo sistema político sí es democrático, la falta de gobiernos civiles democráticos en muchos países hispánicos.

La historia de los últimos años confirma esta verdad. Si la economía de un país depende en gran parte de la exportación de uno o dos productos como la carne y la lana, en el caso del Uruguay, o el café solamente, en el caso de El Salvador, una transformación adversa en los mercados internacionales puede ocasionar grandes desórdenes en la situación política de ese país. Cuando un país sufre un desequilibrio grave, es común observar diferentes facciones extremistas tratar de subvertir el orden con acciones violentas y terroristas. En ese momento entran las fuerzas armadas para restablecer la paz y el orden. Muchos de los ciudadanos del país reciben a los militares con cierta resignación, pues piensan que un gobierno militar no tolera la anarquía que el gobierno civil democrático no es capaz de eliminar.[2]

no. . . one cannot count on
rara. . . one will seldom
whose / **sí es** is indeed
lack, absence
depende de depends upon
la carne. . . meat and wool
create / that
sufre. . . suffers a serious imbalance
extremist groups / **tratar. . .** try to disrupt
armed forces / **la. . .** law and order
citizens
capable of

Glosas

1. The constitutions of most Hispanic countries are loosely patterned after that of the U.S.A. On paper they are quite elaborate in protecting human rights, natural resources, cultural heritage, and sovereignty. Most countries, however, have not enjoyed free democratic governments during most of their histories. Some of the reasons have been foreign intervention, economic upheaval, national uprisings designed to establish a new order, and even counterrevolutions aimed at bringing back former systems. In the 1970's only Venezuela, Colombia, Costa Rica, and Mexico enjoyed relatively democratic governments. In Spain, after the death of Generalissimo Francisco Franco, who ruled for nearly forty years (1939–1975), a constitutional monarchy was established. In 1979 Ecuador returned to an elective form of government.
2. Most people of the Hispanic world would like to enjoy fully democratic governments. Nonetheless, whenever things get out of hand, a military regime may appear to be the lesser of two evils to a large percentage of the population.

SOBRE LA LECTURA

I. Make a statement about each of the following topics.

MODELO la observación del presidente de Venezuela →
Si no hay una situación económica estable, no se va a encontrar un sistema político democrático.

1. la clase de gobierno que hay en Venezuela
2. la economía de un país que depende de uno o de dos productos
3. los productos de exportación del Uruguay y El Salvador
4. las fuerzas armadas
5. la resignación de los ciudadanos
6. un gobierno militar y un gobierno civil

II. Para contestar

1. ¿Hay un gobierno democrático o un gobierno militar en los Estados Unidos?
2. ¿Qué tipo de gobierno prefiere usted?
3. ¿Cuáles son unos países latinoamericanos donde hay un gobierno militar?
4. ¿En qué países latinoamericanos hay un gobierno democrático?
5. ¿Exportan los Estados Unidos muchos productos? ¿Cuáles son dos o tres de ellos?
6. ¿Qué productos exportan en Latinoamérica?
7. ¿Hay grandes desórdenes políticos en los Estados Unidos ahora?
8. ¿Son fuertes las fuerzas armadas norteamericanas?
9. En su opinión, ¿hay que eliminar las facciones extremistas o hay que tolerar estas facciones?
10. ¿Es más importante la paz y el orden o la libertad de expresión?

Repaso oral

I. Complete each of the sentences below with any logical ending that will reflect the content of the dialog and the **Variaciones.**

MODELO Las dos personas que charlan son. . . →
Las dos personas que charlan son de Colombia.

1. Josefa estudia. . .
2. Marco Antonio es estudiante. . .
3. Josefa esperó a Marco Antonio. . .
4. Marco Antonio no llegó porque. . .
5. Bernardo trabaja. . .
6. Marco Antonio está. . .
7. Marco tiene que. . .
8. Su mamá no. . .
9. También Josefa. . .
10. Marco Antonio va a poner. . .
11. Josefa y Marco Antonio van. . .
12. Cinco cuartos de la casa son. . .

II. Para describir

Repaso 1

I. NOUN GROUPS: Possession and numbers

A noun is often accompanied by additional words which, together with it, form a group. Two such noun groups are formed by combining a possessive adjective + noun, or a number + noun.

A. Possession

The possessive adjectives are as follows: **mi(s)**, **tu(s)**, **su(s)**, **nuestro (-a, -os, -as)**, **vuestro (-a, -os, -as)** and **su(s)**. Each agrees with the object possessed, not with the owner. **Su** and **sus** are often replaced by **de** + third person pronoun (**de él, de ella, de usted, de ellos. . .**).

Aplicación

Combine each pair of sentences into one sentence by using a possessive adjective or **de** + third person pronoun.

MODELOS Tienes tres hermanos. Son muy optimistas. → **Tus tres hermanos son muy optimistas.**
Los Arce tienen una casa. Es muy grande. → **La casa de ellos es muy grande.**

1. José Antonio tiene unas maletas. Son nuevas.
2. Ustedes tienen un primo. Llegó ayer por la tarde.
3. Tengo un pasaporte. Está en el hotel.
4. Tenemos unas tazas. Son de Guadalajara.
5. Miguel tiene cuatro profesores. Cambian mucho de opinión.
6. Los Arce tienen una casa. Tiene una cocina estupenda.
7. Tenemos un doctor. Quiere disminuir el número de tazas de café.
8. Tenemos unos asuntos. Van a salir muy bien.
9. Ellos tienen un gobierno. Va a mejorar.
10. Tienes una compañía. Gana mucho dinero, ¿no?
11. Tengo un abogado. No tiene oficina.
12. Tienes una familia. Sale ahora a comer.

B. Counting in Spanish

1. In order to count from 11 to 15, learn the words that correspond to each number: **once, doce, trece, catorce, quince.** From 16 to 19 and from 21 to 29, use a multiple of 10 + **i** + a smaller number, all written as one word: **dieciséis, diecisiete, (veinte), veintiuno, veinticinco, veintinueve.**

2. To count from 31 to 99, use a multiple of ten + **y** + a smaller number, written as three words: **treinta y uno, cuarenta y dos, cincuenta y seis. . .**

3. To count by hundreds from 100 to 900, use **cien** or a smaller number + **cientos: cien, doscientos, cuatrocientos, seiscientos.** There are three special forms: (500) **quinientos,** (700) **setecientos,** and (900) **novecientos.** To count beyond an even hundred, use **ciento(s)** + smaller number; **y** is not used between them: **ciento tres, quinientos cincuenta y cinco.**

4. For 1,000 to 900,000 use a smaller number + **mil.** Note that in Spanish a period, not a comma, is used when writing large numbers (2.000; 4.896. . .): **mil, seis mil, setecientos mil.**

5. When used with nouns, only the numbers **un** (**una, unos, unas**) and **cientos** (**cientas**) agree in gender and number with the noun which follows: **un viaje, una botella, unos problemas, unas casas; quinientos mexicanos, novecientas personas; cuarenta y un libros, cincuenta y una chicas. Cien** does not agree: **cien hombres, cien mujeres.**

Aplicación

State the following in Spanish.

1. 21 colombianos
2. 38 extranjeros
3. 500 españoles
4. 900 personas
5. 12.000 jóvenes
6. 1 amor
7. 32 casas
8. 99 muchachas
9. 2.000 aviones
10. 129 médicos
11. 1.984 años
12. 71 noches

II. Verbs: Present Tense

Verbs in Spanish are either completely regular or they contain a stem-change or some irregularity which appears in certain forms. Review the following examples.

A. Regular verbs

-ar verbs	**-er** verbs	**-ir** verbs
(disfrutar)	(comprender)	(partir)
disfruto	comprendo	parto
disfrutas	comprendes	partes
disfruta	comprende	parte
disfrutamos	comprendemos	partimos
disfrutáis	comprendéis	partís
disfrutan	comprenden	parten

B. Stem-changing verbs

Changes in the stem-vowel appear in all persons except **nosotros** (and **vosotros**).

e → ie	**o → ue**	**e → i**
(preferir)	(dormir)	(seguir)
prefiero	duermo	sigo
prefieres	duermes	sigues
prefiere	duerme	sigue
preferimos	dormimos	seguimos
preferís	dormís	seguís
prefieren	duermen	siguen

C. Irregular verbs

Several verbs are irregular only in the **yo** form. Still others are irregular in all their forms.

irregular **yo** forms	
saber	**sé**
ver	**veo**
dar	**doy**
estar	**estoy**
caer	**caigo**
traer	**traigo**
hacer	**hago**
poner	**pongo**
salir	**salgo**

all irregular forms
ir
voy
vas
va
vamos
vais
van

Aplicación

Student A asks a question. Student B responds in the negative, then gives the information suggested by the cue.

MODELO A: **¿Trabaja Miguel?** (dormir)
B: **No, Miguel no trabaja. Duerme.**

1. ¿Estudia el señor Díaz? (trabajar en México)
2. ¿Quieres más café? (estar muy bien así)
3. ¿Sales ahora? (ir a dormir)
4. ¿Marco y Josefa toman café? (pedir dos cervezas bien frías)
5. ¿Estudiamos ahora? (comer)
6. ¿Parto para el Uruguay? (salir para la Argentina)
7. ¿Esperamos aquí todo el día? (poder llamar más tarde)
8. ¿Jorge quiere escuchar al abogado? (sugerir otra cosa)
9. ¿Quieres disfrutar de la vida? (preferir trabajar como burro)

10. ¿Duerme Juan Carlos? (seguir con dos trabajos)
11. ¿Traes cerveza? (salir a comprar café)
12. ¿Ves el pasaporte? (ver al extranjero)
13. ¿Van ustedes a economizar? (ir a disfrutar de la vida)
14. ¿Ves problema? (saber que todo está bien)

III. To be: **Ser** and **Estar**

Ser and **estar** both correspond to one verb, *to be,* in English. Each of the Spanish verbs is used in different situations.

A. Ser

The forms of **ser** are: **soy, eres, es, somos, sois, son. Ser** is used:

1. To indicate identification: ¿Quién **es** usted? **Soy** argentino. **Somos** gente fuerte.
2. To state origin or possession: Jorge **es** de Buenos Aires. Los libros **son** de Sandra.
3. In expressions of time: **Es** muy tarde.
4. With adjectives to classify the subject in a category: Mis padres **son** estupendos. **Somos** jóvenes y fuertes.

B. Estar

The forms of **estar** are: **estoy, estás, está, estamos, estáis, están. Estar** is used:

1. To indicate location: **Estamos** en Caracas. ¿Dónde **estás** ahora?
2. With adjectives (and some adverbs) to indicate states and conditions: **Estamos** muy bien. Elena **está** preocupada.

Aplicación

Student A asks a question. Student B answers, choosing **ser** or **estar** according to the context.

MODELO ¿El pasaporte? ¿del Sr. Gaviria? → **Sí, el pasaporte es del Sr. Gaviria.**
¿Tú? ¿bien? → **No, no estoy bien.**

1. ¿Tú? ¿de Bogotá?
2. ¿La profesora? ¿española?
3. ¿Ustedes? ¿en el comedor?
4. ¿La casa? ¿de tus padres?
5. ¿Los profesores? ¿muy buenos?
6. ¿El café? ¿frío?
7. ¿Yo? ¿en Texas?
8. ¿Jane y Miguel? ¿americanos?
9. ¿Sandra? ¿empleada bancaria?
10. ¿El médico? ¿preocupado?
11. ¿Papá? ¿con dos trabajos?
12. ¿Las tazas? ¿de mamá?
13. ¿Nosotros? ¿optimistas?

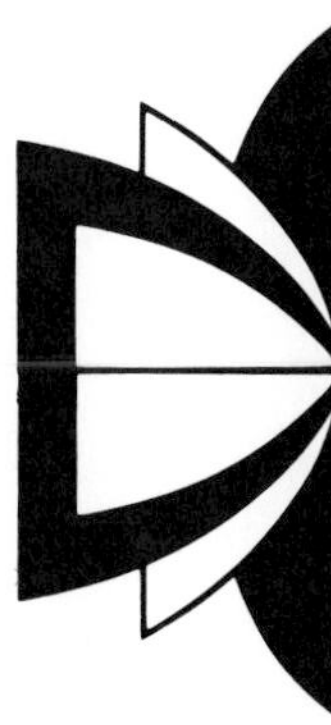

Capítulo 6

Despegue

DIÁLOGO **Fin de semana en el monte**

Present tense: **conocer, tener, venir** • The verb **decir** • Indirect and direct object pronouns (I)

PAUSA ORAL **En el monte tropical**

Indirect and direct object pronouns (II) and (III) • Preterit of **-er** and **-ir** verbs

Repaso oral

Despegue

tres muchachos

Los tres muchachos caminan.

las botas

el tigre

un mapa

El muchacho saca un mapa.

Pronunciación

¡Vamos! **Voy**	The two Spanish letters **v** and **b** are pronounced exactly alike. Following a pause (e.g., as the first letter in a word starting a sentence), Spanish **v** and **b** sound like the English *b* of *boy*.
rápido **restos**	To pronounce trilled Spanish **r**, the tongue tip flaps against the hard upper gum ridge.
pirámide **jóvenes** **víbora**	Certain words are accented on the third-from-the-last syllable. Each syllable is pronounced clearly.

Aplicación

I. Pronounce the following groups of words first very slowly, then at a normal speed.

1. vamos / voy
2. rápido / restos
3. muchachos / mochila / mapa
4. pirámide / jóvenes / víbora

II. Para contestar

1\.  ¿Son muchachos o muchachas?
¿Cuántos muchachos hay en esta clase?

2\. 

¿Qué hacen los muchachos?
¿Camina usted mucho?

3\. 

¿Qué hay aquí?
¿Hay un mapa de México en la clase?

4\. 

¿Qué hace el muchacho con el mapa?
¿Qué hace usted cuando quiere ver dónde está un país?

5\. 

¿Qué son, unas tazas?
¿Tiene usted botas?

6\. 

¿Qué es?
¿Son bonitos o feos los tigres?

Tema del diálogo

Have you ever dreamed of entering a tropical jungle and exploring the unknown? It is possible in Guatemala.

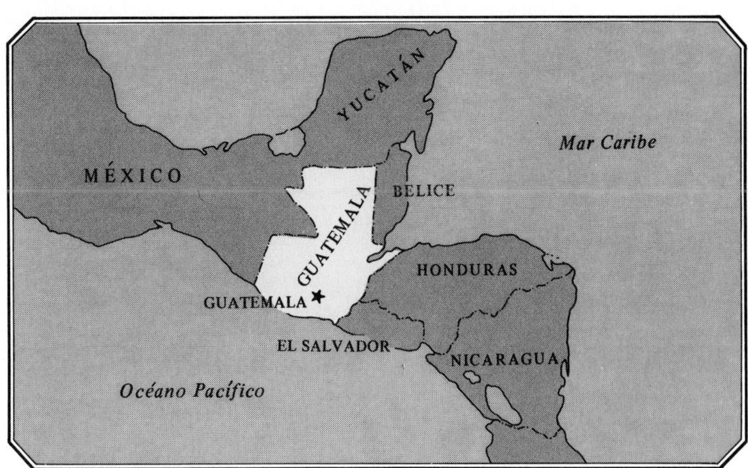

DIÁLOGO

Fin de semana en el monte

Alberto Domínguez, Guillermo Rayón y Felipe Sánchez, tres jóvenes, pasan el fin de semana en el monte en Guatemala[1].

ALBERTO ¡Vamos! ¡Vamos!
GUILLERMO ¡Voy! No puedo caminar más rápido.
FELIPE Tenemos tres horas de luz solamente.
GUILLERMO Esta colina y estas botas me van a matar.
FELIPE Un momento. Necesito tu machete, Guillermo.
GUILLERMO ¿Qué? ¿Una víbora?
FELIPE No, no, y la pala también. ¿Quién la tiene?
ALBERTO Yo la tengo aquí. Pero, ¿qué pasó? ¿Qué viste?
FELIPE Calma, ahora se lo enseño a ustedes. Uff, ¡qué difícil!

* * *

FELIPE Por fin quité la maleza. . .
GUILLERMO ¡Dios mío! ¡Parte de una escalera!
ALBERTO Sí, parece ser parte de una pirámide maya.
FELIPE Y la maleza la cubrió toda. . .
(Felipe mete la mano en su mochila y saca un mapa del gobierno.)
FELIPE Ajá, esta pirámide no está catalogada.[2]
GUILLERMO Nunca pensé, jamás soñé. . .
FELIPE Vamos a la cima. A ver qué más encontramos.
(Los tres muchachos suben rápidamente. Felipe es el primero.)
FELIPE Así lo pensé: restos de un templo. . .
ALBERTO ¡Qué maravilla! ¿Qué dices, Memo?[3]
GUILLERMO Yo digo que una pirámide bien vale ocho tigres.

A farmyard in remote San Jorge, Guatemala. With its 800 inhabitants, San Jorge is a hamlet like thousands of others in Latin America.

Weekend in the jungle

Alberto Domínguez, Guillermo Rayón, and Felipe Sánchez, three young men, are spending the weekend in the jungle in Guatemala.

A: Come on! Come on!
G: I'm coming! I can't walk any faster.
F: We only have three hours of light.
G: This hill and these boots are going to kill me.
F: Wait a minute. I need your machete, Guillermo.
G: What? A snake?
F: No, no, and the shovel, too. Who has it?
A: I have it here. But what happened? What did you see?
F: Take it easy; I'll show it to you. Uff, this is hard!

* * *

F: Finally I've pulled away the vegetation. . .
G: My gosh! Part of a stairway!
A: Yes, it seems to be part of a Mayan pyramid.
F: And the vegetation covered it all (up). . .
(Felipe puts his hand in his backpack and takes out a government map.)
F: Hey! This pyramid is not catalogued.
G: Never in my wildest dreams. . . (I never thought, I never dreamed. . .)
F: Let's go up to the top. Let's see what else we'll find.
(The three boys climb up quickly. Felipe is the first one.)
F: Just as I thought: the remains of a temple. . .
A: How fantastic! What do you say, Memo?
G: I say that one pyramid is worth eight cougars.

VARIACIONES

¿Cuándo vienes a Guatemala?	When are you coming to Guatemala?
en (el) verano	in the summer
en (el) otoño	in the fall
en (el) invierno	in the winter
en (la) primavera	in the spring
la semana que viene	next week
durante las vacaciones	during the vacation
¿Qué quiere decir **pirámide?**	What does **pirámide** mean?
¿Cuándo encontraron la pirámide?	When did they find the pyramid?
hoy	today
anoche	last night
ayer	yesterday
la semana pasada	last week
¿Es difícil encontrar pirámides?	Is it difficult to find pyramids?
No, es fácil.	No, it's easy.

Glosas

1. Hunting can be very exciting in the southern part of Mexico and in Guatemala. Ocelots, pumas, jaguars, and cougars abound together with deer, tapir, and a variety of tropical snakes and large exotic game birds.
2. The governments of Mexico and Guatemala spend a great deal of time and money trying to identify and catalog major archeological sites and their contents, such as figurines, jewels, and artifacts. It is a never-ending task for which there are not enough resources, since new discoveries are constantly being made either in the jungles or in the very cities which are being modernized. Several major finds were made during the construction of Mexico City's **metro** (subway).
3. **Memo** is the nickname for **Guillermo.** There are many such **apodos** or nicknames in Spanish:

José → **Pepe**	Concepción → **Concha**
Francisco → **Pancho, Paco**	Guadalupe → **Lupe**
Roberto, Alberto → **Beto**	Graciela → **Chela**

SOBRE EL DIÁLOGO

I. ¿Sí o no? If the information contained in the sentence is true, say **sí** and repeat the sentence. If the information is false, say **no** and make a sentence which is true.

MODELO Los muchachos son de México. → **No, son de Guatemala.**

1. Los tres jóvenes pasan una semana en el monte.
2. Es temprano por la mañana.
3. Guillermo tiene problemas con las botas.

4. Felipe necesita el machete porque va a matar una víbora.
5. La escalera que ven los muchachos es parte de una pirámide maya.
6. La pirámide ya está catalogada.
7. Los muchachos ven la escalera y van a casa.
8. Los muchachos ven restos de un templo.

II. Fill in the appropriate word from the following list:
fin de semana, botas, enseña, maleza, encuentro, soñé, fácil, vacaciones, luz.

MODELO No veo nada; no hay ____. → **No veo nada; no hay luz.**

1. El inglés no es difícil; es ____.
2. Hay mucha ____ en el monte.
3. ¿Dónde están mis cosas? No ____ nada.
4. Nuestras ____ son en el verano.
5. El sábado y el domingo son el ____.
6. Carlos me ____ el mapa.
7. No duermo bien. Anoche ____ mucho.
8. No puedo caminar. Estas ____ me matan.

III. Match each expression with the situation described.

¡Vamos! / ¡Dios mío! / ¡Qué maravilla! / Un momento.

1. Usted ve una cosa estupenda.
2. Usted quiere apresurar las cosas.
3. Usted quiere esperar un rato más.
4. Usted no sabe qué pensar.

Tikal VI, 210 feet high, one of six pyramids in Tikal, Northern Guatemala, the largest known city of the ancient Mayas.

IV. Para contestar

1. ¿Cuándo hay vacaciones, en el invierno?
2. ¿Pasa usted las vacaciones aquí o en un país extranjero?
3. ¿Estudian ustedes en el verano? ¿Cuándo estudian?
4. ¿Dónde pasó usted el fin de semana?
5. Cuando usted está en el monte, ¿es bueno tener un machete y una pala?
6. ¿Soñó usted anoche? ¿Sueña usted mucho?
7. ¿Qué va a hacer usted el fin de semana que viene?
8. ¿Es fácil o difícil el español?

VOCABULARIO

nouns

la **bota**	boot
la **cima**	top (of a hill)
la **colina**	hill
la **escalera**	staircase, stairway
la **hora**	the hour
la **luz**	light, sunlight
el **machete**	machete
la **maleza**	vegetation, growth, weed
el **mapa**	map
la **maravilla**	wonder, marvel
la **mochila**	backpack
el **momento**	moment
el **monte**	wilderness, jungle, forest
la **muchacha**	girl
el **muchacho**	boy
la **pala**	shovel
la **parte**	part
la **pirámide**	pyramid
los **restos**	ruins; remains
el **templo**	temple
el **tigre**	tiger[1]
las **vacaciones**	vacation
la **víbora**	snake

[1]In Latin America, **tigre** refers to jaguars and bobcats as well as tigers.

verbs

caminar	to walk
cubrir	to cover
decir (digo, i)	to say
encontrar (ue)	to find
enseñar	to show, to teach
matar	to kill
meter	to put into, to stick, to insert
parecer (zc)	to seem
quitar	to remove, to take from
sacar (qu)	to pull out; to remove
soñar (ue)	to dream
subir (a)	to climb; to go up
valer (valgo)	to be worth
venir (vengo, ie)	to come

expressions of time

anoche	last night
durante	during
el fin de semana	weekend
el invierno	winter
el otoño	fall
pasado	past, last
el año pasado	last year

la primavera	spring
la semana	week
la semana pasada	last week
la semana que viene	next week
el verano	summer

adjectives

catalogado	catalogued
difícil	difficult
este (esta; estos, estas)	this; these
fácil	easy
maya	Mayan; of the Mayan Indians
rápido	fast
más rápido	faster

other expressions

¡ajá!	Hey!
así lo pensé	just as I thought
a ver	let's see
bien vale	is well worth
calma	take it easy
¡Dios mío!	Oh my gosh!, my God
un momento	just a minute
nunca pensé, jamás soñé	never in my wildest dreams
por fin	finally, at last
¡Qué maravilla!	How fantastic!
querer decir	to mean
¿Qué quiere decir?	What does it mean?
rápidamente	rapidly, quickly
rápido	rapidly, quickly
solamente	only
uff	wow (used to express great difficulty)
Vamos.	Come on; let's go.
Voy.	I'm coming.

additional vocabulary

condùcir (zc)	to drive
conocer (zc)	to know
decir que sí (**no**)	to say yes (no)
el **dólar**	dollar
la **oración**	sentence
traducir (zc)	to translate

ESTRUCTURA I

A. Present tense: **conocer, tener, venir**

Repaso. Besides regular **-ar, -er,** and **-ir** verbs, we have studied stem-changing verbs (**quiero, cuesta, pide**) and irregular **yo**-forms (**sé, traigo, hago. . .**).

> Yo lo **tengo** aquí.

1. One additional present-tense stem change is from **c** in the infinitive to **zc** in the first-person (**yo**) form; the other forms are all regular. A common verb of this group is **conocer** *to know, to be acquainted with.*

conocer	
conozco	Conozco a Alberto Domínguez.
conoces	¿Conoces a Alberto?
conoce	Manolo no conoce a Roberto.
conocemos	Conocemos a muchas personas.
conocéis	Ya conocéis muy bien Madrid.
conocen	Ellos conocen Guadalajara.

2. Also included in this group are all verbs whose infinitive ends in **-ucir,** for example **conducir** *to drive* (**conduzco, conduces, conduce**) and **traducir** *to translate* (**traduzco, traducimos, traducen**).

Yo conduzco ahora; tú conduces más tarde.	I'll drive now; you drive later.
Traduzco las oraciones en casa.	I'm translating the sentences at home.

3. **Tener** and **venir** also have irregular **yo** forms. Additionally, these two verbs are stem-changing in the **tú, él,** and **ellos** forms.

tener	venir	
tengo	**vengo**	No vengo mucho a Guatemala.
tienes	vienes	¿Cuántos hermanos tienes?
tiene	viene	La casa tiene dos baños.
tenemos	venimos	Venimos aquí en verano.
tenéis	venís	Venís la semana que viene.
tienen	vienen	Ellos no tienen tiempo.

Note that the **yo, nosotros,** and **vosotros** forms do not show the stem-change **e** → **ie.**

Tengo vacaciones en el otoño.	I have vacation in the fall.
Vengo con mis amigos.	I'm coming with my friends.
Tenemos muy poco dinero.	We have very little money.
Venimos en avión.	We're coming by plane.

Aplicación

I. If the verb is singular, change it to plural, and vice versa.

MODELO Conocemos a Pancho. → **Conozco a Pancho.**

1. Traduzco del inglés.
2. Él conduce bien.
3. ¿Conoces a José Miguel?
4. ¿Conducimos nosotros?
5. Conozco a toda la familia.
6. Traducen muy rápido.
7. Parece inteligente.
8. Conocemos a esta señora.

II. Replace the verb in the original sentence with the verb in parentheses.

MODELO ¿Hablas bien? (traducir) → **¿Traduces bien?**

1. Invito a los muchachos. (conocer)
2. No salimos ahora. (conducir)
3. No comprenden. (traducir)
4. Vemos al profesor. (conocer)
5. Estudio mucho. (traducir)
6. ¿Cuándo salgo? (conducir)
7. Usted no camina mucho. (conducir)
8. Es difícil. (parecer)
9. Ellos no invitan a mucha gente. (conocer)
10. Son simpáticos. (parecer)

III. Repeat each sentence changing the subject as indicated.

MODELO Tengo vacaciones en verano. (tú, ellos) →
Tienes vacaciones en verano.
Tienen vacaciones en verano.

1. No tiene problemas. (la profesora, yo, los estudiantes, tú, mi prima y yo)
2. Vienen temprano. (tú, ustedes, el muchacho, yo, tú y yo)

IV. Answer each question using a form of **tener que estudiar.**

MODELO ¿Sales ahora? → **No, tengo que estudiar.**

1. ¿Sale Juan ahora?
2. ¿Salimos Juan y yo ahora?
3. ¿Salgo yo ahora?
4. ¿Salen ustedes ahora?
5. ¿Sale usted ahora?
6. ¿Salen los muchachos ahora?

V. Answer each question using the appropriate form of **ir** followed by a clause with **si** *if.*

MODELO ¿Vienes con nosotros? → **Voy si tengo plata.**

1. ¿Viene ella con nosotros?
2. ¿Vienen ustedes con nosotros?
3. ¿Vienen los muchachos con nosotros?
4. ¿Viene usted con nosotros?
5. ¿Viene el primo de Pepe con nosotros?

B. The verb **decir**

Yo **digo** que es una pirámide.

1. The verb **decir** has the following present-tense forms.

decir	
digo	Digo que es un templo.
dices	¿Qué dices, Memo?
dice	Mamá dice que todo cuesta mucho.
decimos	¿Qué decimos ahora?
decís	¿Decís que sois estudiantes?
dicen	Dicen que es difícil.

2. Several common expressions are formed with **decir.**

decir que sí	to say yes
decir que no	to say no
Mamá dice que sí. Digo que no.	Mom says yes. I say no.
querer decir	to mean
¿Qué quiere decir **mochila?** ¿Qué quieres decir?	What does **mochila** mean? What do you mean?

3. Whereas **decir** means *to say, to tell,* **hablar** means *to speak* or *to talk.* Some common expressions formed with **hablar** are the following.

hablar español (inglés)	to speak Spanish (English)
En casa hablamos inglés. Pero en la universidad hablamos inglés y español.	At home we speak English. But at the university we speak English and Spanish.
hablar de (negocios, viajes. . .)	to talk about (business, travel. . .)
Vamos a hablar de Guatemala y de Honduras.	We're going to talk about Guatemala and Honduras.

4. **Contar** means to tell in the sense of to recount (e.g., a story).

¿Le cuenta sus problemas?	Are you telling her your problems?

Aplicación

I. Answer each question in the pattern suggested by the model.

MODELO Papá dice muchas cosas. ¿y usted? ¿y Paco? → **Yo digo muchas cosas también. Paco dice muchas cosas también.**

1. Ellos dicen la verdad. ¿y el médico? ¿y usted? ¿y yo? ¿y usted y su amigo? ¿y los tres jóvenes?
2. Él dice que sí. ¿y yo? ¿y usted? ¿y los muchachos? ¿y la profesora? ¿y ustedes?

II. Answer using a form of **decir que** and an original phrase.

MODELO Él, ¿qué piensa? → **Él dice que es una maravilla.**

1. Ustedes, ¿qué piensan?
2. Los muchachos, ¿qué piensan?
3. Usted, ¿qué piensa?
4. Los extranjeros, ¿qué piensan.
5. Yo, ¿qué pienso?
6. Tú y yo, ¿qué pensamos?

III. Para contestar

1. ¿Conoce usted a muchas extranjeras?
2. ¿Traducimos del inglés en clase?
3. ¿Traduce usted bien?
4. ¿Sabe usted conducir? ¿Conduce mucho?
5. ¿Tiene usted que estudiar más?
6. ¿Tienen ustedes mucho trabajo?
7. ¿Tengo mucho trabajo yo?
8. ¿Siempre dice usted la verdad?
9. ¿Vienen ustedes aquí los sábados y los domingos? ¿Qué días vienen?
10. ¿Qué dice usted, es fácil o difícil el español?

C. Indirect and Direct Object Pronouns (I)

Repaso. Of the many pronouns in Spanish, we have studied only the subject pronouns: **yo, tú, él, ella, usted. . .** Two other types of pronouns are the indirect object pronoun and the direct object pronoun. Like all pronouns, the object pronouns take the place of nouns.

Necesito el machete. **¿Lo** tienes tú?

1. Pronouns take the place of nouns: Give *it* to *him.*

2. The third-person singular forms of the indirect and direct object pronouns are as follows.

indirect	**le**	*to him, to her, to you*
direct	**lo**	*him, it, you* (masculine)
	la	*her, it, you* (feminine)

Note that **le** means to (sometimes *for* or *from*) *him, her,* and also *you* (formal). **Lo** means *him, it,* and also *you* (masculine formal). **La** means *her, it,* and *you* (feminine formal).

Le escribo.	I'm writing to you (to him, to her).
Lo veo.	I see you (him, it).
No la comprendo.	I don't understand you (her, it).

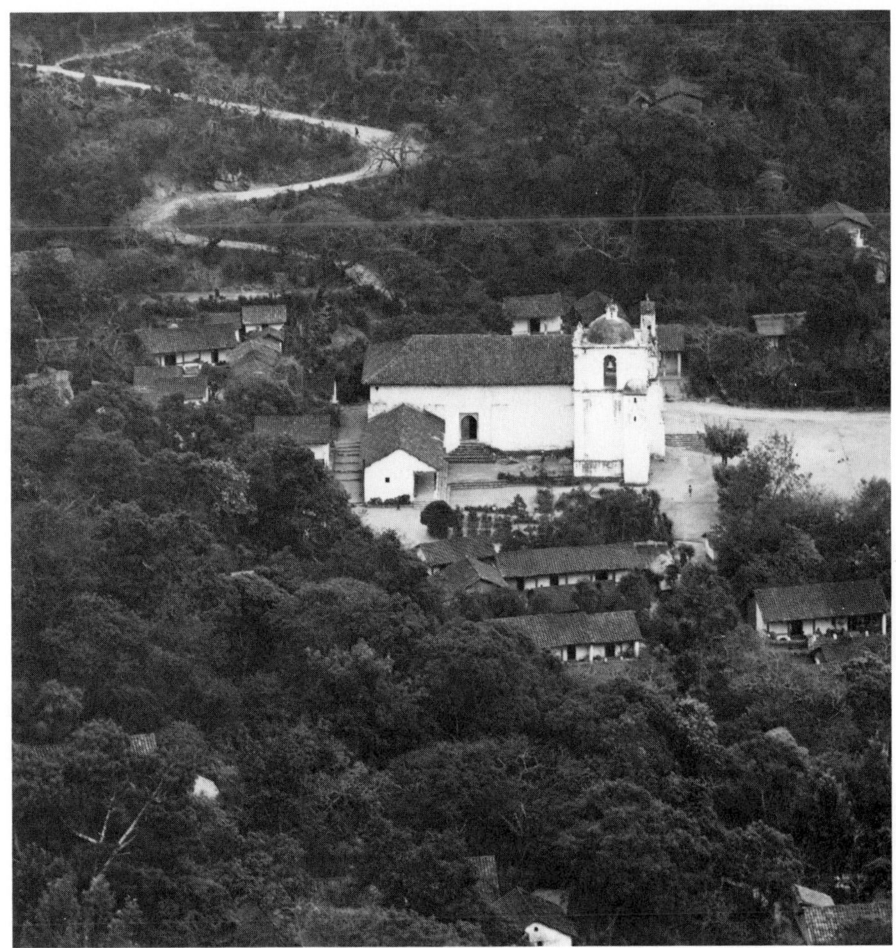

San Jorge, Guatemala. If unopposed by human effort, the jungle would again cover everything.

3. To find the direct object in a sentence, ask who or what is the receiver of the action of the verb: I see *him.* Do you have *it?*

(Necesitamos el pasaporte) → **Lo** necesitamos.	We need it.
(Necesitamos la maleta.) → **La** necesitamos.	We need it.

4. To find the indirect object in a sentence, ask the question *to whom?, for whom?,* or *from whom?:* I gave *her* the machete. I bought *him* a ticket.

Le digo la verdad.	I'm telling you the truth.
Le hablé ayer.	I spoke to him yesterday.
¿No **le** enseñamos el mapa?	Didn't we show the map to her?

5. Certain verbs may be used with an indirect object while others are used with a direct object. Many are used with both, with different meanings. The following summary shows some verbs as typically used with each object pronoun.

INDIRECT OBJECT

Le doy.	I give to you (him, her).
Le pido.	I ask you (him, her).
Le traigo.	I bring to you (him, her).
Le enseño.	I show you (him, her).
Le digo.	I tell you (him, her).
Le hablo.	I speak to you (him, her).
Le sugiero.	I suggest to you (him, her).
Le cuento.	I tell you (him, her).

DIRECT OBJECT

masculine	*feminine*
Lo comprendo.	La comprendo.
I understand you (him, it).	I understand you (her, it).
Lo necesito.	La necesito.
I need you (him, it).	I need you (her, it).
Lo veo.	La veo.
I see you (him, it).	I see you (her, it).
Lo quiero.	La quiero.
I love you (him, it).	I love you (her, it).
Lo tomo.	La tomo.
I take you (him, it).	I take you (her, it).
Lo llamo.	La llamo.
I call you (him, it).	I call you (her, it).
Lo espero.	La espero.
I wait for you (him, it).	I wait for you (her, it).

6. To use a direct object pronoun in Spanish with the meaning *it*, you need to know the gender of the noun for which the pronoun stands.

DIRECT OBJECT

masculine	*feminine*	
Lo doy.	La doy.	I give it.
Lo tengo.	La tengo.	I have it.
Lo pongo.	La pongo.	I put it.

Lo traigo.	La traigo.	I bring it.
Lo encuentro.	La encuentro.	I find it.
Lo digo.	La digo.	I say (tell) it.
Lo conozco.	La conozco.	I know it.

7. In a declarative sentence, all pronouns are placed directly before the conjugated verb.

Le hablé ayer.	I spoke to him (her, you) yesterday.
La maleza la cubrió toda.	The vegetation covered it all.

8. If a sentence is negative, **no** appears before the pronoun(s).

No lo veo.	I do not see it.
No le hablamos la semana pasada.	We didn't speak to her last week.

Aplicación

I. Replace the direct object noun with the corresponding pronoun.

MODELO Felipe pide la pala. → **Felipe la pide.**

1. Guillermo tiene el machete.
2. Los muchachos encuentran la escalera.
3. La maleza cubrió la pirámide.
4. Felipe quita la maleza.
5. Guillermo necesita las botas.
6. Los jóvenes pasan los días en el monte.
7. Conozco a los muchachos.
8. Visité a los jóvenes la semana pasada.

II. A. Elaborate the following statements by adding **le** or **lo** as required by the verb.

MODELO Siempre invito → **Siempre lo invito.**

1. Llamo mañana.
2. Digo la verdad.
3. No pido nada.
4. ¿Qué sugieres?
5. Enseño el mapa.
6. Esperé anoche.
7. Hablé en español.
8. No comprendo.

B. Repeat part A, this time using **le** or **la.**

MODELO Siempre invito. → **Siempre la invito.**

III. Complete with either **lo** or **le,** as required by each verb.

Juan es un muchacho muy bueno. __1__ conozco bien. Siempre __2__ invito a mi casa y __3__ hablo de mis cosas. Cuando tengo un problema, __4__ llamo y __5__ cuento todo. Antes de la clase __6__ enseño mi trabajo y él dice si está bien o no. Juan es un buen amigo y __7__ quiero mucho. Muchas veces cuando voy a su casa __8__ encuentro con sus libros, pero cuando __9__ digo que necesito hablar con él, deja sus cosas. No le puedes pedir más a un amigo, ¿verdad?

Pausa oral

En el monte tropical

Imagine that you are spending a weekend with two friends exploring the tropical jungles of Guatemala. Discuss what happens by carrying out the following activities.

I. Para completar

Form complete sentences by combining the elements in the list and making all necessary changes.

MODELO mis / tres / amigo / ser / Guatemala → **Mis tres amigos son de Guatemala.**

1. nosotros / pasar / fin de semana / monte
2. Guillermo / no poder / caminar / rápido
3. Felipe / necesitar / machete / y / pala
4. yo / por fin / quitar / maleza
5. nosotros / ver / parte / escalera
6. nosotros / subir / cima

II. Para contestar

1. ¿Pasa usted las vacaciones en el monte? ¿Pasa las vacaciones aquí o en un país extranjero?
2. ¿Hay hoteles en el monte? ¿Hay médicos? ¿víboras? ¿pirámides?
3. ¿Cuando alguien está en el monte, ¿es bueno tener un machete y una pala?
4. ¿Dónde pasó usted el fin de semana?
5. ¿Cuándo son las vacaciones, en el otoño?
6. ¿Estudian ustedes en el verano? ¿Cuándo estudian?

III. Para charlar

Formulate two questions concerning the following aspects of your weekend spent in the jungle. Another member of the class should be able to answer your questions.

MODELO

viaje
Estados Unidos

Possible questions **¿Necesitas un mapa para el viaje al monte?**
¿Es un mapa de los Estados Unidos?

1. 

ir
visitar

2. 

costar
matar

3. 

Estados Unidos
monte

ESTRUCTURA II

A. Indirect and Direct Object Pronouns (II)

¿Me das la pala?

1. The following chart contains the indirect and direct object pronouns for all persons.

me	to me / me
te	(familiar singular) to you / you
le **lo, la**	to him, to her, to you (formal) him, her, you (formal), it
nos	to us / us
os	(familiar plural, Spain) to you / you
les **los, las**	to them, to you them, you

2. Four of the pronouns have the same form whether indirect or direct: **me, te, nos, os.**

INDIRECT

Te digo la verdad.	I'm telling you the truth.
Concha nos habló anoche.	Concha spoke to us last night.

DIRECT

Te llamó Bernardo ayer.	Bernardo called you yesterday.
¿Dónde nos esperaste?	Where did you wait for us?

3. The third-person pronouns (singular and plural) have different forms for indirect and direct objects.

INDIRECT

Le hablo todos los días.	I speak to him (her, you) every day.
No les pedimos nada.	We're not asking anything from them (you).

DIRECT

La llamé el miércoles pasado.	I called you (her) last Wednesday.
Los conocemos muy bien.	We know them (you) very well.

4. The third-person direct object pronouns also differ between masculine (**lo, los**) and feminine (**la, las**).

No lo veo.	I don't see you (him, it).
¿Los conoces bien?	Do you know them well?
La quiero mucho.	I love her very much.
Las encontramos allá.	We found them there.

Aplicación

I. Direct each sentence to the persons indicated.

MODELO Lo llamo mañana.

(a su amiga) → **Te llamo mañana.**
(a la profesora) → **La llamo mañana.**
(a unos estudiantes) → **Los llamo mañana.**

1. ¿Dónde la encuentro?
   (al profesor de química) (a unas amigas de su mamá)
   (a sus amigos) (a su primo)
   (a su hermana) (a los hijos del Sr. López)
2. Yo te invito.
   (a la doctora Vargas) (a una estudiante)
   (a unos profesores) (a unos muchachos)
3. No las vimos.
   (a un extranjero) (a una buena amiga)
   (a unas muchachas) (al médico)
   (a la hermana de su amiga)

II. Direct each sentence to the person indicated.

MODELO Te hablé en la universidad.
(a la profesora) → **Le hablé en la universidad.**
(a su hermana) → **Te hablé en la universidad.**

1. ¿Qué le sugieren?
   (a unos buenos amigos)
   (a sus hermanos)
   (al abogado de sus padres)
   (a un extranjero)
   (a su prima)
2. No te puedo dar la plata.
   (a su amigo)
   (a dos muchachos)
   (a un joven)
   (al médico)
   (a sus padres)
3. ¿Qué les dicen?
   (a su hermana)
   (a una persona que usted no conoce bien)
   (a su hermano)
   (a una señora de Guatemala)
   (a sus profesores)

III. Complete each sentence using the object pronoun that corresponds to the first subject.

MODELOS Tú nos invitas y nosotros. . . → **Tú nos invitas y nosotros te invitamos.**
Yo lo conozco y él. . . → **Yo lo conozco y él me conoce.**

1. Nosotros la llamamos y ella. . .
2. Tú me ves y yo. . .
3. Yo los visito y ellos. . .
4. Ella te invita y tú. . .
5. Juan me conoce y yo. . .
6. Ellos nos necesitan y nosotros. . .
7. Tú me quieres y yo. . .
8. Ellas nos llaman y nosotros. . .

IV. Para expresar en español

1. He says it. / He tells him.
2. They speak it. / They speak to her.
3. I ask for it. / I ask him.
4. We show it. / We show her.
5. She tells it. (**contar**) / She tells you.

V. Answer each question, always including an indirect or direct object pronoun in each response.

MODELOS ¿Me habló usted esta mañana? → **Sí, le hablé esta mañana.**
¿Llamas a María? → **Sí, la llamo.**

1. ¿Conoce usted a los otros estudiantes de la clase?
2. ¿Me conoce usted?
3. ¿Va usted a llamar a su amiga esta noche?
4. ¿A quién llama usted? ¿Le cuenta sus problemas?
5. ¿Conocen ustedes a todos sus profesores?
6. ¿Siempre hacen ustedes el trabajo?
7. ¿Tiene usted el trabajo para hoy?
8. Si usted no viene, ¿quién le cuenta qué pasó?
9. ¿Dónde pasa usted las vacaciones?
10. ¿Me pide usted dinero?
11. ¿Trabajan los estudiantes o les dan dinero sus padres?

B. Indirect and direct object pronouns (III)

Ahora **se lo** enseño.

1. A sentence may contain both an indirect and direct object pronoun. The indirect pronoun always appears before the direct.

Bernardo me contó el asunto.	Bernardo told me about the matter.
Bernardo me lo contó.	Bernardo told me about it.
Te voy a enseñar la pirámide.	I'm going to show you the pyramid.
Te la voy a enseñar.	I'm going to show it to you.

2. When two third-person object pronouns appear together, the first one (**le** or **les**) changes to **se.**

se lo(s) / **se la(s)**

Bernardo le contó el asunto.	Bernardo told him (her, you) about the matter.
Bernardo se lo contó.	Bernardo told him about it (it to him, her, you).
Le voy a enseñar las botas.	I'm going to show you (him, her) the boots.
Se las voy a enseñar.	I'm going to show them to you (to him, to her).

Aplicación

I. Replace the direct object noun with a pronoun.

MODELO Los muchachos me enseñan el mapa. → **Me lo enseñan.**

1. Te pido la plata ahora.
2. Nos contaron sus problemas.
3. ¿Me dices la verdad?
4. Nos dan los pasaportes.
5. Te quité el dinero.

II. Replace the direct object noun with a pronoun, and change **le** or **les** to **se.**

MODELO Le enseñamos la escalera. → **Se la enseñamos.**

1. Les damos el dinero.
2. Felipe le pide las cosas.
3. Le quito el dinero.
4. Les pasamos el postre.
5. Alberto le enseña las maletas.

C. Preterit of **-er** and **-ir** verbs

Repaso. The preterit tense focuses upon states and events at a specific point in the past. A typical **-ar** verb in the preterit is **caminar: caminé, caminaste, caminó, caminamos, caminasteis, caminaron.**

¿Qué viste?

1. To form the preterit tense for regular **-er** and **-ir** verbs, add the following endings to the stem of the verb:

   (stem +) **-í, -iste, -ió, -imos, -isteis, -ieron**

meter		subir		
met	**í**	**sub**	**í**	Subí la escalera.
met	**iste**	**sub**	**iste**	Lo metiste en la mochila.
met	**ió**	**sub**	**ió**	Subió al apartamento.
met	**imos**	**sub**	**imos**	Metimos el mapa allá.
met	**isteis**	**sub**	**isteis**	Subisteis muy rápido.
met	**ieron**	**sub**	**ieron**	Metieron la mochila en el carro.

¿Qué comiste?	What did you eat?
La maleza cubrió toda la pirámide.	The growth covered the whole pyramid.
Los tres jóvenes subieron rápidamente.	The three young people climbed quickly.

2. The **nosotros** form of **-ir** verbs, as of **-ar** verbs, is the same in the present and preterit. The context of the conversation usually indicates whether a present or past situation is meant.

Discutimos las vacaciones todos los días.	We discuss (our) vacation every day.
Subimos al templo anoche.	We climbed up to the temple last night.

Aplicación

I. Answer each question in the pattern suggested by the model.

MODELO Yo comprendí. ¿y ellos? ¿y usted? → **Ellos comprendieron también. Yo comprendí también.**

1. Papá ya comió. ¿y usted? ¿y la muchacha? ¿y ustedes? ¿y ellos? ¿y yo? ¿y usted y yo?
2. Ellos vieron el mapa. ¿y yo? ¿y tú? ¿y nosotros? ¿y el profesor? ¿y el presidente?
3. El salió temprano. ¿y ustedes? ¿y María Teresa? ¿y yo? ¿y nosotros? ¿y los jóvenes?
4. Los profesores discutieron el problema. ¿y ustedes? ¿y papá y yo? ¿y usted? ¿y los abogados? ¿y yo?

II. Restate each sentence using a verb in the preterit.

MODELO Nosotros comemos temprano. → **Nosotros comimos temprano.**

1. Felipe y Guillermo parten para el monte.
2. Yo salgo temprano.
3. Metemos el mapa en la mochila.
4. En el monte vemos una escalera.
5. La maleza la cubre toda.
6. Felipe y Guillermo suben a la cima.
7. Me parece una maravilla.
8. ¿Tú ves la pirámide?

Repaso oral

I. Tell what you and your friends did the other day, using the following items as a guide.

MODELO mis amigos y yo / salir / temprano → **Mis amigos y yo salimos temprano.**

1. primero / visitar / Concha
2. hablar / rato / con ella
3. después / partir / para / banco
4. Carlos / meter / dinero / banco
5. yo / sacar / diez / dólares
6. todos nosotros / discutir / dónde comer
7. yo / pensar / en el Restaurante Bilbaín
8. Felipe / contar / que / Casa de Madrid / es / bueno
9. nosotros / llegar / allá / dentro de un rato
10. subir / por la escalera
11. pero / no / parecer / bueno
12. y no / comer / allí

II. Para contestar

1. ¿Salió usted anoche o estudió?
2. ¿Comprendieron ustedes el diálogo? ¿Les pareció fácil o difícil?
3. ¿Soñó usted anoche o no sueña usted cuando duerme?
4. ¿Hacen ustedes mucho trabajo para mí? ¿Vi su trabajo hoy?
5. ¿Van ustedes a comer más tarde o ya comieron?
6. ¿Donde comió usted ayer, aquí o en casa?

III. Para describir

What does the following picture suggest to you? Make as many statements as you can think of which could relate to a weekend expedition into the jungle.

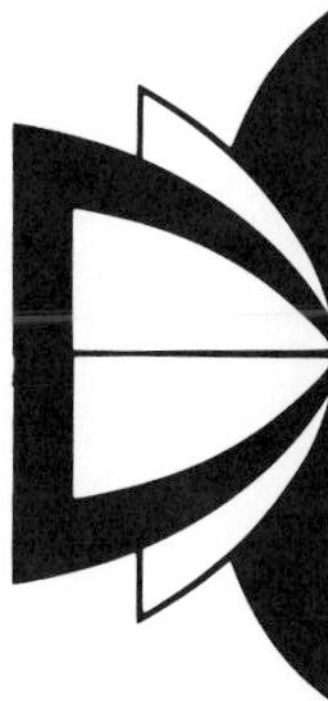

Capítulo 7

Despegue

la comida

¡Qué comida más sabrosa!

la botella de vino

El señor prueba el vino.

el viejo

El viejo no oye bien.

Pronunciación

el cebiche **la botella de vino**	When pronouncing **b** or **v** in most positions, the lips never close tightly.
un brindis **un momento** **en Perú**	In the groups **n** + **b**, **n** + **v**, **n** + **m**, **n** + **p**, **n** is pronounced **m.**
José **usa** **hizo**	Spanish **s** and **z** do not sound like English *z*. They are pronounced *s*.[1]

[1]In most parts of Spain, **z** is pronounced *th*.

Aplicación

I. Para pronunciar

1. el cebiche / la botella de vino
2. ¡Qué comida más sabrosa!
3. un brindis / un momento / en Perú
4. El señor prueba el vino.
5. José / usa / hizo
6. El viejo no oye bien.

II. Para contestar

1. ¿Qué hay aquí?
¿Es bueno tomar mucho vino?

2. ¿Qué hace el señor?
¿Probamos vino en la clase de español?

3. 
¿Qué hay aquí?
¿A usted le gusta la comida mexicana?

4. 
¿Qué dice el señor?
¿Cree usted que está sabrosa la comida?

5. 
¿Es joven o viejo este señor?
¿Es usted joven o viejo?

6. 
¿Qué problema tiene el señor?
¿Oye bien su padre? ¿Oye cuando usted dice que necesita dinero?

Tema del diálogo

An ambitious young Peruvian can still enjoy the traditions of family and country.

DIÁLOGO

¡Qué comida más sabrosa!

José María Roldán, teniente del ejército peruano, llega a su pueblo para visitar a sus padres, Juan José y Hortensia Roldán, de 70 y 62 años respectivamente. Son las dos de la tarde.

JOSÉ MARÍA ¡Te felicito, madre! ¡Qué comida más sabrosa! El cebiche está rico.[1]

MADRE ¿Qué te parecen los anticuchos?[2] ¿Te gustan?

JOSÉ MARÍA Sí, todo me gusta. Todo está estupendo.

PADRE Tu tío vino ayer y te trajo una botella de vino. Hay que probarlo.

JOSÉ MARÍA Por supuesto. Vamos a hacer un brindis.

PADRE ¿Qué dijo este muchacho? No oigo nada con estos setenta años que tengo.

* * *

MADRE José María, de ahora en adelante vas a tener que hablar más fuerte. El viejo ya casi no oye nada.

JOSÉ MARÍA Sí, mamá. Pero, ¿qué le hizo a su aparato? ¿Por qué no lo usa?

MADRE Ya lo conoces. Es muy terco. Nunca lo usa. Y a veces lo esconde. A él le molestan todas esas cosas modernas.

JOSÉ MARÍA Bueno, ¿qué remedio? Ahora vamos a brindar por la salud de los Roldán y el progreso de la patria.

PADRE Salud, hijo. Te deseo un gran futuro.[3]

JOSÉ MARÍA Gracias. Y en diez años, ¡la presidencia!

What a Delicious Meal!

José María Roldán, a lieutenant in the Peruvian army, arrives in his hometown to visit his parents, Juan José and Hortensia Roldán, 70 and 62 years old, respectively. It is two o'clock in the afternoon.

JM: Congratulations, mother! What a delicious meal. The cebiche is tasty.

M: What do you think of the anticuchos? Do you like them?

JM: Yes, I like everything. Everything is great.

P: Your uncle came by yesterday and brought you a bottle of wine. We've got to taste it.

JM: Of course. Let's make a toast.

P: What did this boy say? I don't hear anything with these seventy years (that I have).

M: José María, from now on you're going to have to talk louder. The old fellow can hardly hear anything anymore.

JM: O.K., mom. But what did he do with his hearing aid? Why doesn't he use it?

M: You (already) know him. He's very stubborn. He never uses it. And sometimes he hides it. All those modern things bother him.

JM: Well, what's to be done? Now let's drink to the health of the Roldán family and to the progress of the homeland.

P: To your health, son. I wish you a great future.

JM: Thanks. And in ten years, the presidency!

* * *

VARIACIONES

¿Qué te parece el cebiche?	What do you think of the cebiche?
la carne	meat
la ensalada	salad
la fruta	fruit
el pan	bread
el pescado	fish
¿Qué te parecen las legumbres?	What do you think of the vegetables?
las papas	potatoes
A veces pruebo el vino.	Sometimes I try the wine.
el agua	water
la leche	milk
Le molesta todo.	Everything bothers him.
duele	hurts
importa	is important to
interesa	interests
Le queda algo.	He has something left.
aquel vino	that wine

Glosas

1. **Cebiche** (marinated raw fish) is a dish characteristic of Peru. The Hispanic world possesses a great array of dishes. Each country has national dishes of its own, and even within the borders of the larger countries, dishes vary from region to region. On the other hand, quite a few dishes are found everywhere in the Hispanic world—**arroz con pollo** (chicken with rice) and **empanadas** (turnovers) are examples. And the fame of the best local dishes does

not remain local; people in places as far from Lima as Acapulco and Mexico City will treat themselves to **cebiche** on Sundays and other holidays.

2. **Anticuchos** is the Peruvian version of shish kebab, a Middle Eastern delicacy. Geographers and historians sometimes try to determine whether particular dishes originated in America or abroad. **Tortillas** (corn cakes) were first prepared in ancient Mexico. **Lechón** (suckling pig roasted on a spit over hot coals) is a dish brought by the Spaniards from the Iberian Peninsula. **Mole poblano,** a Mexican Colonial dish containing twenty-odd ingredients, represents a superb combination of pre-Columbian and Spanish elements. Some pre-Columbian ingredients are tomatoes, turkey, chilies, raw chocolate; some Spanish ingredients are almonds, sesame seeds, lard, and raisins.
3. In Latin America it is not uncommon to see ambitious young men from low and middle socio-economic groups join the armed forces as a way to improve their status.

SOBRE EL DIÁLOGO

I. For each word, choose an appropriate definition from the list.

MODELO esconder → **c. poner una cosa donde otras personas no la encuentran**

1. **sabroso**	a. el país de una persona
2. **agua**	b. claro
3. **carne**	c. poner una cosa donde otras personas no la encuentran
4. **la patria**	d. algo que tomamos
5. **por supuesto**	e. algo que comemos
6. **terco**	f. rico
	g. que hace las cosas como quiere

II. For each statement, choose an appropriate response from the list.

Te felicito.	**Bueno, ¿qué remedio?**
Por supuesto.	**Salud.**
¡Qué comida más sabrosa!	

1. Voy a ser presidente del Club de Español el año que viene.
2. Hay cebiche y carne con papas y ensalada.
3. Brindo por la salud de la familia.
4. Ya no sé qué hacer. Papá no quiere usar su aparato.
5. Vamos al club campestre. ¿Quieres ir con nosotros?

III. Para contestar

1. ¿Es estudiante José María? ¿Qué es? 2. ¿Por qué va José María a su pueblo? 3. ¿Qué comen los Roldán? ¿Qué toman? 4. ¿Por qué no oye casi nada el papá? 5. ¿Por qué no usa su aparato el papá? 6. ¿Qué brindis hace el padre? 7. ¿Qué quiere ser José María en el futuro? 8. ¿Qué come usted? ¿Qué toma?

IV. Complete each sentence in any logical way.

MODELO Te felicito porque ——. → **Te felicito porque la carne está muy sabrosa.**

1. Me gusta comer ——.
2. También me parece rico (rica) ——.
3. Me gusta tomar ——.
4. Hago un brindis cuando ——.
5. Mi patria ——.
6. Yo a veces escondo ——.
7. A mí me molesta (molestan) ——.
8. Brindo por ——.
9. Quiero probar ——.
10. Hay que ——.

Machu Picchu, fortress city of the Incas built on a mountain peak some fifty miles northwest of Cuzco, Peru.

VOCABULARIO

nouns

el **agua** (feminine in gender)	water
los **anticuchos**	Peruvian *shish kebab*
el **aparato**	device, gadget; hearing aid
la **botella**	bottle
el **brindis**	toast
la **carne**	meat
el **cebiche**	marinated raw fish
la **comida**	meal; food; lunch, dinner
la **ensalada**	salad
el **ejército**	army
la **fruta**	fruit
la **leche**	milk
la **legumbre**	vegetable
el **pan**	bread
la **papa**	potato
la **patria**	fatherland, homeland
el **pescado**	fish
la **presidencia**	presidency
el **progreso**	progress
el **pueblo**	town, village
la **salud**	health
¡Salud!	To your health!
el **teniente**	lieutenant
el **tío,** la **tía**	uncle, aunt
los **tíos**	aunt and uncle
el **vino**	wine

verbs

brindar	to toast
desear	to desire; to wish
doler (ue)	to hurt, to ache
esconder	to hide
felicitar	to congratulate
gustar	to be pleasing
importar	to be important
interesar	to interest
molestar	to bother, to annoy
oír (oigo, y)	to hear
probar (ue)	to try, to taste
quedar	to be left, to remain
usar	to use

adjectives

aquel, aquella	that
aquellos, aquellas	those
fuerte	loud; strong
moderno	modern
peruano	Peruvian
rico	tasty, delicious; rich (wealthy)
sabroso	tasty, delicious
terco	stubborn

time expressions

See list, page 159.

other expressions

algo	something
a veces	sometimes, at times
de ahora en adelante	from now on
casi	almost
de 70 años	70 years old
fuerte	loudly
por supuesto	of course
¿qué remedio?	what's to be done?, there's nothing you can do about it
¡qué!	what! how!
¡Qué comida más sabrosa!	What a delicious meal!

¿qué te parece. . . ?	what do you think of. . . ?, how do you like. . . ?		
respectivamente	respectively		
tener 70 años	to be 70 years old		

additional vocabulary

la **conversación**	conversation
el **laboratorio de lenguas**	language laboratory
la **lengua**	language

ESTRUCTURA I

A. Preterit tense (II): irregular verb forms

Repaso. In the preterit tense, regular verbs have the following forms:

-ar VERBS

hablar **hablé, hablaste, habló, hablamos, hablasteis, hablaron**

-er AND **-ir** VERBS

esconder **escondí, escondiste, escondió, escondimos, escondisteis, escondieron**

> Tu tío **vino** ayer y te **trajo** una botella de vino.

1. Many verbs which have irregular stems have these endings in the preterit tense: **-e, -iste, -o, -imos, -isteis, -ieron** (or **-eron**); none of these endings has a written accent mark.

2. Verbs with **u** stems

   Model verb, **andar** **anduve, anduviste, anduvo, anduvimos, anduvisteis, anduvieron**

Here are some verbs of this same type.

Verb	**yo** form	Examples with other forms
andar	**anduve**	Anduvimos con el tío Lorenzo.
estar	**estuve**	¿Estuviste en el Paraguay?
poder	**pude**	Sandra no pudo ir.
poner	**puse**	Lo pusimos en el banco.
saber	**supe**	¿Supo usted adónde voy?
tener	**tuve**	No tuvieron tiempo.

Saber in the preterit usually means *find out.*

¿Qué supiste? — What did you find out?

3. Verbs with **i** stems

Model verb, **hacer** **hice, hiciste, hizo, hicimos, hicisteis, hicieron**

Verb	**yo** form	Examples with other forms
hacer querer venir	**hice** **quise** **vine**	¿Qué hiciste anoche? Bernardo quiso salir de casa. Vinimos a Lima en 1979.

Querer in the preterit usually means *try* in the affirmative and *refuse* in the negative.

Quisieron entrar.	They tried to enter.
No quisieron venir.	They refused to come.

4. Verbs with **j** stems

Model verb, **conducir** **conduje, condujiste, condujo, condujimos, condujisteis, condujeron**

Note that the ending for the **ellos** form is **-eron,** not **-ieron.**

Verb	**yo** form	Examples with other forms
conducir decir traducir traer	**conduje** **dije** **traduje** **traje**	Condujiste mucho. ¿Qué dijo Manolo? Tradujeron algo al español. El señor González trajo el dinero.

Aplicación

I. Repeat each sentence, changing the subject to the new one given.

MODELO Tuve que salir. (nosotros, mamá) → **Tuvimos que salir. Tuvo que salir.**

1. ¿Dónde puso las tazas? (ustedes, el muchacho, yo, tú, nosotros)
2. No pude hacer nada. (ellos, tú y yo, yo, tú, el médico)
3. ¿Qué supiste? (el abogado, ustedes, nosotros, yo, tú)

II. Change the verbs from the present to the preterit.

MODELO No puedo ir. → **No pude ir.**

1. ¿Por dónde andan?
2. Tengo un problema.
3. ¿Sabe algo?
4. ¿Puedes dormir?
5. Estamos aquí.
6. No sé nada.
7. ¿Con quién anda?
8. Tenemos que estudiar.
9. ¿Dónde pones tus cosas?
10. ¿Con quiénes está?

Statue of *El Libertador,* Simón Bolívar, in Lima, Peru. Bolívar helped Colombia, Venezuela, Ecuador, Peru, and Bolivia achieve independence from Spain.

III. Answer each question following the model.

MODELO Ella hizo una ensalada, ¿y las muchachas? ¿y usted? → **Las muchachas hicieron una ensalada también. Yo hice una ensalada también.**

1. Ellos quisieron salir, ¿y ustedes? ¿y José María? ¿y usted? ¿y yo?
2. Viniste temprano, ¿y los tíos? ¿y el muchacho? ¿y usted?
3. Hice un postre, ¿y María? ¿y ustedes? ¿y las chicas?

IV. Say each sentence, replacing the verb as indicated.

MODELO Llegaron tarde. (venir) → **Vinieron tarde.**

1. Desearon hacer algo. (querer)
2. Me enseñó el trabajo. (hacer)
3. No llegó. (venir)
4. No pedimos nada. (querer)
5. No escuché nada. (hacer)
6. Salimos temprano. (venir)

V. Answer each question using the preterit tense, according to the model.

MODELO ¿Vas a conducir esta tarde? → **No, hombre. Conduje ayer.**

1. ¿Vas a traer la comida esta tarde?
2. ¿Van ustedes a decir algo esta tarde?
3. ¿Ella va a traducir el diálogo esta tarde?
4. ¿Yo voy a conducir esta tarde?
5. ¿Ellas van a traer las cosas esta tarde?

VI. Para contestar

1. ¿Pudo usted hacer todo su trabajo anoche? 2. ¿Estuvo usted en México el año pasado? 3. ¿Dónde puse mis cosas? 4. ¿Tradujeron ustedes el diálogo al inglés? 5. ¿Trajo usted muchas cosas hoy? 6. ¿Qué hicimos ayer, el diálogo? 7. ¿Condujo usted esta mañana? 8. ¿Vinieron ustedes a clase ayer?

B. Object pronouns (IV): preposition + pronoun

A él le molestan esas cosas.

1. In order to express the words *me, you, him, her, we, they* after a preposition, the following pronouns are used.

mí	**nosotros**
ti	**vosotros**
él / ella / usted	**ellos / ellas / ustedes**

Note the written accent mark over **mí** but not over **ti**.

A mí me gustan las cosas modernas.	I like modern things.
No hay postre para nosotros.	There's no dessert for us.
Sólo hablamos de ellos, no de ustedes.	We only talked about them, not about you.

2. Two special forms are used with **con**.

conmigo / contigo

Los dos argentinos hablaron conmigo.	The two Argentinians spoke with me.
Hoy no puedo ir contigo.	I can't go with you today.

3. Any object pronoun may be clarified or emphasized by adding the phrase **a** + prepositional pronoun.

INDIRECT OBJECT

José María me habló a mí.	José María spoke to me.
¿Les doy mucho trabajo a ustedes?	Do I give you (people) lots of work?
Se lo dijimos a ella anoche.	We told it to her last night.
No le hablo a él pero a veces le hablo a ella.	I don't speak to him but sometimes I speak to her.

DIRECT OBJECT

Ellos me esperaron a mí.	They waited for me.
No te comprendo a ti.	I don't understand you.
¿Felipe la llamó a usted hoy?	Did Felipe call you today?
Las vimos a ellas esta tarde.	We saw them this afternoon.
No lo veo a él pero a veces la veo a ella.	I don't see him but sometimes I see her.

4. In conversational Spanish, if a sentence contains an indirect object noun, it also contains **a** + the corresponding indirect object pronoun. This is called the redundant construction.

Le di el libro a Sandra.	I gave Sandra the book.
Les escribe a sus amigos.	He writes to his friends.

5. The use of a redundant pronoun is always necessary when **a** + object (indirect or direct) appears at the beginning of a sentence.

a + object + pronoun

¿A ti te gusta el café?	Do you like coffee?
A Josefa la vi esta tarde.	I saw Josefa this afternoon.
A nosotros nos llegó el dinero ayer.	The money reached (arrived to) us yesterday.
¿A quién le pide usted dinero?	Whom do you ask for money?
¿A quién le cuenta sus problemas?	Whom do you tell your problems to?

Aplicación

I. Replace the noun with a prepositional pronoun.

MODELO José María habla con su mamá. → **José María habla con ella.**

1. Hablo con mis amigos.
2. Carlos habla de la nueva profesora.
3. Esta fruta es para mi primo.
4. ¿Le gusta a María?
5. Cenamos con las estudiantes extranjeras.

II. Complete each sentence with the appropriate prepositional pronoun.

MODELO Ellos quieren la ensalada. Es para _____. →
Ellos quieren la ensalada. Es para ellos.

1. Yo quiero la plata. Es para _____.
2. Ella tiene los anticuchos. Son de _____.
3. Nosotros tenemos la comida. Es de _____.
4. Tú quieres el pan. Es para _____.
5. El tiene las cosas. Son de _____.
6. Usted tiene el dinero. Es de _____.
7. Ellas quieren la cerveza. Es para _____.
8. Ustedes quieren el postre. Es para _____.

III. Respond to each statement using a preposition and a prepositional pronoun, in the pattern shown by the model.

MODELO Este dinero es para usted. → **¿Para mí? ¡Qué bien!**

1. Esta comida es para ustedes.
2. Toman una cerveza con Susana López.
3. Quieren hablar contigo.
4. Esta plata es para mí.
5. Charlan con el nuevo estudiante.
6. Hablan de nosotros.
7. El carro azul es de Pedro.
8. Esta noche cenan conmigo.
9. El cebiche es para ti.
10. Salgo con María y Javier.

IV. Para expresar en español

MODELO I know him. → **Lo conozco.**
I know <u>him</u>. → **Lo conozco a él.** *or* **A él lo conozco.**

1. They invite us. / They invite <u>us</u>.
2. I need you (formal singular). / I need <u>you</u>.
3. We visited them. / We visited <u>them</u>.
4. We found her. / We found <u>her</u>.
5. I don't see you (plural). / I don't see <u>you</u> (plural).

V. Combine the following elements into sentences containing the redundant construction.

MODELO yo / escribir / mis amigos → **Yo les escribo a mis amigos.**

1. mi tío / traer / botella de vino / mamá
2. Sandra / dar / comida / sus hijos
3. José / decir / verdad / sus padres
4. el señor / enseñar / aparato / su médico
5. yo / dar / dinero / mi abogado

VI. Answer each question with a sentence containing a redundant pronoun.

MODELOS ¿A quién le dice usted la verdad? → **Le digo la verdad a mi amiga.**

1. ¿A quién le pide usted dinero?
2. ¿A quién le cuenta usted sus problemas?
3. ¿A quién le da usted cerveza?
4. ¿A quién le enseña usted su trabajo?
5. ¿A quién le habla usted todos los días?
6. ¿A quiénes les hace usted un brindis?
7. ¿A quiénes les compra usted los carros?
8. ¿A quiénes les da usted una botella de vino?

C. The use of **gustar** and similar verbs

¿Te **gusta** la comida? ¿Te **parece** buena?

1. The verb **gustar** means *to please* or *be appealing.* Thus, English *I like wine* must be converted into Spanish **Me gusta el vino** *Wine pleases me.* To formulate the question *How do you like. . . ?*, do not use the word **¿cómo?**, but rather **¿Le (te) gusta. . . ?**

2. A common word order with **gustar** is:

Indirect object pronoun	+ verb	+ subject
Me	gusta	el vino.
Me	gustan	los vinos.

If what you like is one thing, singular **gusta** is used. If more than one thing pleases you, plural **gustan** is used because what you like is the subject of the sentence.

Me gusta la leche.	I like milk.
Me gustan mis clases.	I like my classes.

3. The indirect object (**me, te, le, nos, os, les**) indicates the person who is pleased.

¿Te gusta la ensalada?	Do you like the salad?
Nos gusta mucho la carne.	We like the meat a lot.
Les gusta mucho la carne.	They like the meat a lot.
No le gustan a papá las cosas modernas.	Dad doesn't like modern things.

4. If the indirect object is named, the name is always introduced by **a.**

A José Antonio le gusta el trabajo.	José Antonio likes the work.
A mis padres les gustan los viajes.	My parents like trips.
A mí no me gustan los problemas.	I don't like problems.

5. The subject of **gustar** may be a noun, a pronoun, or an infinitive.

Me gustan las lenguas.	I like languages.
A papá no le gusta probar las cosas modernas.	Dad doesn't like to try modern things.
A nosotros nos gusta comer bien.	We like to eat well.

6. Here are some other common verbs which follow the same pattern as **gustar.**

Verb	object + verb	
doler	**Me duele(n)**	Me duelen las manos.
importar	**Te importa(n)**	¿Te importa comer aquí?
interesar	**Le interesa(n)**	Le interesa mucho la patria.
molestar	**Nos molesta(n)**	Nos molestan estos problemas.
parecer	**Les parece(n)**	¿Les parecen buenas las papas?
quedar	**Les queda(n)**	¿A ustedes les queda algo?

7. **Gustar** and the other verbs above may, of course, be used in different tenses.

¿Les gustó el club?	Did they like the club?
¿Qué te pareció la recepción?	What did you think of the reception?
Me interesaron mucho los detalles del matrimonio.	The details of the marriage interested me a lot.

Aplicación

I. Repeat each sentence using the new subjects given.

MODELO Me quedan tres horas. (un día, dos años) → **Me queda un día. Me quedan dos años.**

1. Me gusta la leche. (el vino, las papas, la carne, las legumbres)
2. Me interesó la recepción. (las clases, el matrimonio, la conversación, las muchachas)
3. No me molestan esas cosas. (el caso, sus problemas, la situación, los aparatos)

II. Change each sentence, substituting the indirect objects given.

MODELO A ti te gusta la fruta. (a los muchachos, a Juan) → **A los muchachos les gusta la fruta. A Juan le gusta la fruta.**

1. A mí no me duele la mano. (a la empleada, a mis hermanos, a ti, a ustedes, a nosotros)
2. A Sandra le interesa la química. (a mí, a las muchachas, a ustedes, a nosotros)
3. A Hortensia no le importa. (a ellas, al médico, a mí, a Pedro y a Felipe)

III. Complete the following sentences any way you wish. Note whether the verb is singular or plural.

MODELO Me quedan _____. → **Me quedan cinco botellas de vino.**

1. Me pareció fácil _____.
2. A mí no me gusta _____.
3. ¿A ustedes les interesa _____?
4. Ya no me quedan _____.
5. A ti no te importa _____.
6. ¿A usted le duele _____?
7. A las muchachas les molestó _____.
8. A mi padre no le gustaron _____.

IV. Para contestar

1. A usted le interesan los estudios, ¿verdad? ¿Qué le gusta estudiar? 2. ¿A los estudiantes les importa el futuro? 3. ¿A ustedes les interesan los negocios? ¿Qué les interesa? 4. A los muchachos, ¿qué les interesa más, el español o las muchachas? 5. Y a usted, señorita, ¿le interesa más la química o los muchachos? 6. ¿Cuántas horas de clase le quedan a usted hoy? 7. ¿A mí me gusta el español? ¿Cuál me parece más fácil a mí, el español o el inglés? ¿Y a ustedes? 8. ¿A los jóvenes les molestan las cosas modernas? ¿Qué les molesta? 9. ¿Qué comió usted anoche? ¿Le pareció rica la comida? 10. A ustedes no les gusta tomar vino, ¿verdad? ¿Y a mí?

Spanish peasants. Their ancestors created the largest empire in recorded history.

Pausa oral

¡Vamos a comer!

No one can last very long in a foreign country before it is time to eat. Luckily, you can already say quite a bit about food and drinks.

I. Para completar

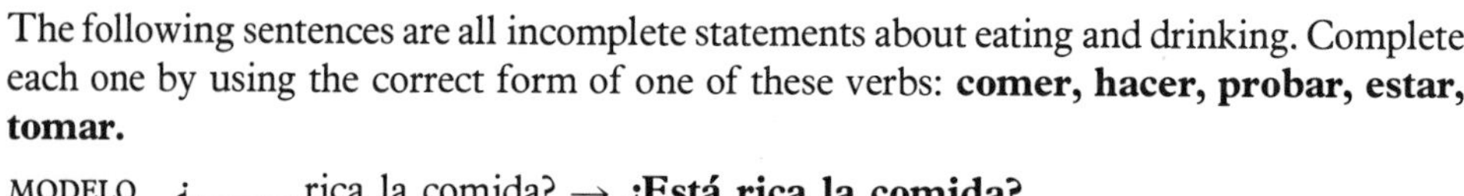

The following sentences are all incomplete statements about eating and drinking. Complete each one by using the correct form of one of these verbs: **comer, hacer, probar, estar, tomar.**

MODELO ¿_____ rica la comida? → **¿Está rica la comida?**

1. ¿Vamos a _____ una taza de café?
2. Quiero _____ una cerveza bien fría.
3. ¿Quieres _____ el vino?
4. ¿_____ nosotros un brindis?
5. ¿Qué quiere usted _____: café o leche?
6. ¿_____ sabrosas las papas?
7. ¡Qué rica _____ la comida!
8. Ahora voy a _____ las legumbres.
9. Hay que salir a _____ todavía.
10. ¡Me gusta _____ el vino español.

II. Para dialogar[1]

Together with another person, complete the following mini-conversations. Person A asks a question or makes a statement by completing each sentence at the left. Person B responds by suggesting a different food or drink.

PERSON A	PERSON B
1. Voy a tomar. . .	Bueno, yo voy a tomar. . .
2. ¿Está rica. . . ?	Sí, pero está(n) más rica(s). . .
3. Quiero tomar. . .	Yo quiero tomar. . .
4. ¿Quieres probar. . . ?	Voy a probar. . .
5. Me parece muy bueno. . .	A mí me parece(n) bueno(s). . .
6. ¡Qué sabroso está. . . !	También está(n) muy sabroso(s). . .
7. Mi tío me trajo. . .	Mi mamá me trajo. . .
8. Brindo por . . .	Y yo brindo por. . .

[1] *In order to converse.*

III. Para preguntar

Ask a classmate two or three questions which are suggested by each of the following drawings.

IV. Para contestar

1. ¿Dónde come usted por la mañana? ¿por la tarde? ¿por la noche? 2. Cuando come con sus amigos, ¿hablan mucho de sobremesa? ¿De qué hablan ustedes? 3. ¿Toma usted café o leche por la mañana? ¿Qué toma por la noche? 4. ¿Están por las nubes los precios de la comida? ¿Qué cuesta más, la carne o las legumbres? 5. ¿Disfruta usted más de la vida cuando come mucho o cuando come poco? ¿Disfruta más cuando toma mucho vino o poco vino?

ESTRUCTURA II

A. Demonstrative adjectives and pronouns

Con **estos** 70 años que tengo, yo no oigo nada.

1. A demonstrative adjective is one which points to a particular noun by answering the question *Which one?* In English the demonstrative adjectives are *this, that, these, those.* The following chart contains all of the demonstratives.

	MASCULINE	FEMININE	English
SINGULAR	**este** / **ese** / **aquel** } **abogado**	**esta** / **esa** / **aquella** } **casa**	this that that (far away)
PLURAL	**estos** / **esos** / **aquellos** } **casos**	**estas** / **esas** / **aquellas** } **botellas**	these those those (far away)

2. Note that the plural forms of **este** and **ese** are **estos** and **esos.**

Este templo y estos restos son de los mayas.	This temple and these remains are of the Mayans (the Mayan Indians).
Esos profesores son muy buenos.	Those professors are very good.

3. The difference in use between **ese (esa. . .)** and **aquel (aquella . . .)** is subtle: **aquel** refers to something farther removed in space (or in time) than **ese.**

Aquel puesto con la compañía venezolana es estupendo.	That job with the Venezuelan company is great.
Esas legumbres parecen estar muy buenas.	Those vegetables seem to be very good.

4. Each of the demonstratives may replace a specific noun by being used alone (and written with an accent mark). In this case the adjective becomes a demonstrative pronoun (English *this one, that one, those*).

¿Cuál es mi café, éste o ése?	Which is my coffee, this one or that one?
Éstos son los médicos argentinos y ésos son los médicos colombianos.	These are the Argentinian doctors and those are the Colombian doctors.

5. Three special demonstrative pronouns are the following:

   esto *this*
   eso *that*
   aquello *that (far away)*

   These words refer to an idea or an unidentified object but show no agreement for number or gender. They never take a written accent mark.

¿Qué es esto?	What is this?
Eso no me importa.	That doesn't matter to me.
Ya hablé de aquello con mi novia.	I already spoke about that with my **novia.**

Aplicación

I. Change from singular to plural, and vice versa.

MODELO Este muchacho es mexicano. → **Estos muchachos son mexicanos.**

1. Esta casa es nueva.
2. Ese profesor es muy bueno.
3. ¡Qué viejos son esos hoteles!
4. ¿Es fácil este diálogo?
5. ¿Ves aquel avión?
6. No conozco a esas señoras.
7. Aquellos apartamentos son modernos.
8. ¿Quiénes son aquellas muchachas?

II. Repeat each sentence, replacing the noun with the new ones given.

MODELO Necesito esta maleta. (botellas, aparato) → **Necesito estas botellas. Necesito este aparato.**

1. Quiero probar este cebiche. (leche, vino, ensalada, legumbres)
2. Ella trajo esos anticuchos. (fruta, papas, pan, vinos)
3. ¿Conoces aquel hotel? (casa comercial, aeropuerto, países, restaurante)

III. Say each sentence, deleting the noun. Then tell what the meaning is in English.

MODELO Este puesto es estupendo → **Éste es estupendo.** *This one is great.*

1. Este médico es muy bueno.
2. Esa clase es fácil.
3. Esos muchachos no hablan inglés.
4. Esta profesora es simpática.
5. Ya estudié aquellos problemas.
6. Esa casa es blanca y roja.
7. ¿Conoce usted a estas personas?
8. ¿Ves aquel hotel?
9. Estos estudiantes son argentinos.
10. Ella no sabe nada de aquella situación.

IV. Para expresar en español

MODELO This is a problem. → **Esto es un problema.**

1. What's this?
2. He's coming tomorrow? That's great.
3. I don't understand all this.
4. Do they discuss that?
5. We have to (one has to) try that.

V. Supply the correct demonstrative adjective or pronoun in each case.

Mi padre es un hombre estupendo. Otros señores que tienen 70 años ya no trabajan, pero __1__ trabaja todos los días. __2__ no le gusta a mamá.—__3__ puesto te va a matar, Jorge—le dice—. Hay que disfrutar de __4__ vida.

—Disfruto, Sandra—le dice papá—. __5__ semana gané seis contratos. __6__ no es trabajar. __7__ es disfrutar.

Y la verdad es que papá disfruta de la vida. __8__ tarde, como todas las tardes, pasó dos o tres horas con sus amigos. __9__ señores, como él, trabajan mucho. A veces hablan de la situación económica. El país está ahora en manos del ejército y __10__ puede ser un problema. Pero papá no está preocupado.

Así es mi papá. Siempre muy optimista.

B. Time-telling

Son las dos de la tarde.

1. The following are some expressions used to ask and tell time.

¿Qué hora es?	What time is it?[1]
(el) mediodía	noon
(la) medianoche	midnight
la una	one o'clock
de la mañana	in the morning
cuarto	quarter (15 minutes)
media	half-past
menos	before (minus)
en punto	on the dot, exactly
como a	at about
a eso de	at about
¿A qué hora?	At what time?
¿Tiene usted la hora?	Do you have the time?

[1]In some parts of Spanish America, the question *What time is it?* is asked, **¿Qué horas son?** Spanish has no word equivalent to English *o'clock.*

2. Es + **mediodía, medianoche,** or **la una**
   Singular **es** is used with **(el) mediodía, (la) medianoche,** and with **la una.**

Es (el) mediodía.	It's noon.
Es (la) medianoche. ¡Qué tarde!	It's midnight. How late!
Es la una de la tarde.	It's one in the afternoon.

3. Note that if the hour is given, **de la** (and not **por la**) is used to express *in the.*

Es la una de la mañana.	It's one in the morning.
Es la una de la tarde.	It's one in the afternoon.

4. **Son** + **las** + hour
   Plural **son** is used with all other hours.

¿Qué hora es?

Son las dos.

Son las tres.

Son las cuatro.

Son las cinco.

Notice that **Son las** + hour corresponds to English *It is* (+ hour).

5. Hour + **y** + minutes (or **cuarto** or **media**)
   To tell time between the hour and half hour, the word **y** is used.

¿Qué hora es?

Son las cinco y diez.

Son las cinco y cuarto.

Son las siete y veinte.

Son las ocho y media.

6. Hour + **menos** + minutes or **cuarto**
   To tell time between the half hour and before the hour, use **menos.**

¿Qué hora es?

Son las 8 menos 25.

Son las 9 menos 20.

Son las 11 menos cuarto.

Son las 12 menos 5.

7. Additional time expressions

   a) **¿A qué hora. . . ?** *At what time. . . ?*

   ¿A qué hora llamó Bernardo?

   b) **en punto** *exactly*

   Llegamos a las 3 en punto.

   c) **como a** / **a eso de** } *at about*

   Como a las cinco voy a salir.

   d) On train, bus, and plane timetables a 24-hour clock is used.

a las 13 horas	*at 1* PM
a las 14 horas	*at 2* PM
a las 15 horas	*at 3* PM
a las 23 horas 30	*at 11:30* PM

   El avión parte a las 16 horas y llega a Lima a las 22 horas 30.

Aplicación

I. Look at each clock and tell what time it is.

MODELO  → **Son las tres en punto.**

1.  **2.**  **3.**  **4.**  **5.** 

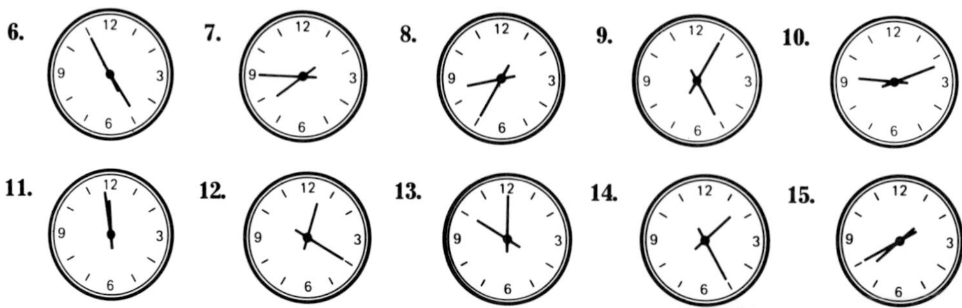

II. Answer the following questions.

1. ¿Qué hora es ahora? 2. ¿A qué hora llegó usted? 3. ¿Están ustedes aquí a las ocho de la mañana? ¿A las ocho de la noche? 4. ¿A qué hora cena usted? 5. ¿Viene usted a la universidad a eso de las once? 6. El avión parte a las 13 horas y llega a las 18 horas. ¿A qué hora parte el avión? ¿A qué hora llega? 7. La recepción es a las 20 horas. ¿A qué hora es la recepción? 8. ¿Va usted a estar en casa a eso de las cuatro de la tarde? ¿Lo puedo llamar como a las cuatro y media? 9. ¿Llegan los profesores a las nueve en punto? ¿A qué hora llegan? 10. ¿Tiene usted la hora? ¿Qué hora es?

C. The irregular verb **oír**

Ya no **oigo** nada.

1. The present tense forms of **oír** are as follows.

oigo	Oigo muy bien.
oyes	¿Me oyes tú?
oye	Juan José no oye bien.
oímos	No oímos eso.
oís	¿Oís todo?
oyen	No oyen al profesor.

2. The preterit tense forms of **oír** are **oí, oíste, oyó, oímos, oísteis, oyeron.**

No oí nada anoche.	I didn't hear anything last night.
¿Qué oyó usted?	What did you hear?
Juan José y Hortensia oyeron muchas cosas.	Juan José and Hortensia heard lots of things.

3. Note the difference between **escuchar** and **oír:**

escuchar = *to listen (to)*
oír = *to hear*

Escuchamos y escuchamos, pero no pudimos oír.

Aplicación

I. Respond using the appropriate form of **escuchar** and **no oír nada.**

MODELO ¿Escuchan ellos la conversación? → **Escuchan, pero no oyen nada.**

1. ¿Escucha usted la conversación?
2. ¿Escucha la muchacha la conversación?
3. ¿Escuchan ustedes la conversación?
4. ¿Escucho yo el diálogo?
5. ¿Escuchan los jóvenes el diálogo?
6. ¿Escucha usted el diálogo?

II. Para contestar

1. ¿Oye bien su papá o necesita un aparato? 2. ¿Siempre escucha cuando el profesor (la profesora) habla? 3. ¿Qué dice usted cuando no oye bien? 4. ¿Qué hace la gente que no oye bien? 5. ¿Siempre escucha el diálogo cuando viene a clase? 6. ¿Dónde oyen ustedes el diálogo primero, aquí o en el laboratorio de lenguas? 7. ¿Qué otras cosas hacen ustedes cuando vienen a clase? 8. ¿Qué oyó usted en clase el otro día?

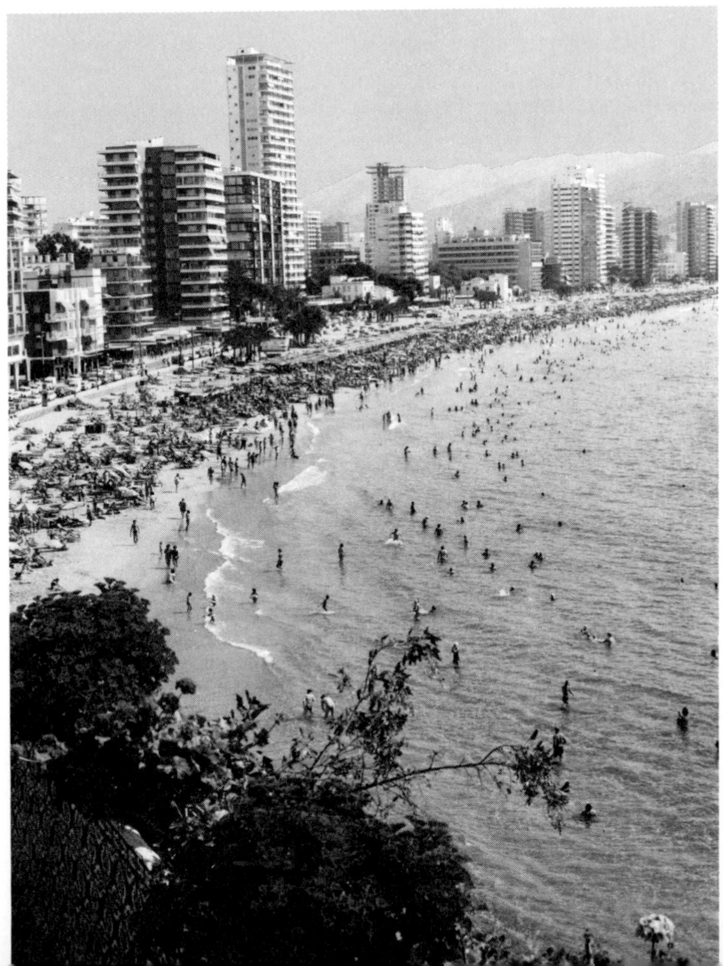

Foreign and national tourists flock to Benidorm (Alicante) and other beautiful areas of Spain's Mediterranean coast.

Urubamba Valley in Peru.

LECTURA

La variedad hispánica

El mundo hispánico es tan grande que, necesariamente, presenta una infinidad de climas y regiones y una gran variedad de tipos étnicos. Es legítimo decir que podemos encontrar prácticamente todos los tipos de terrenos o regiones geográficos en los países que forman el mundo hispano. Existen montañas, lagos, desiertos, selvas, llanuras y playas de todos estilos y tamaños. El clima, naturalmente, es bastante diverso; podemos hablar del infierno de las selvas del Amazonas[1] *(tierra caliente[2])* o del intenso frío de los Andes[3] *(tierra fría).* También existen los climas ideales en donde la persona piensa que sólo hay una estación—la primavera. Estos lugares son normalmente conocidos como *tierra templada.* Los guatemaltecos afirman que Guatemala es la tierra de la eterna primavera. Y los españoles dicen que la Costa del Sol[4] en España es el paraíso terrenal.

variety
so / **-mente** = -ly
climates
terrain
There exist mountains, lakes, deserts, jungles, plains, and beaches of all kinds and sizes.
quite
season
known
earthly paradise

El aspecto físico del hispánico' no es, realmente, mucho menos variado' que su geografía. También es cierto que casi todos los tipos raciales y étnicos existen en el mundo hispano. España misma' es una colección de distintos grupos étnicos y de diversas razas. Ahora bien', los españoles viajan al Nuevo Mundo y se mezclan' con las razas' indias y poco después, especialmente en las zonas tropicales, también se mezclan con los negros traídos' de África. Cuando termina' la dominación española en las Américas, otros grupos raciales y étnicos vienen a Hispanoamérica como inmigrantes. Los grupos más numerosos son los chinos, los libaneses y los italianos[5].

Debido a' estos acontecimientos', en cuestión de' climas y fisionomías', el mundo hispánico es un supermercado muy bien abastecido' con productos para todos los gustos'.

Hispanic person
varied
itself
Now then
se mezclan mix / races
brought / ends
Due to / events / **en. . .** when it comes to
facial features
stocked / tastes

Glosas

1. The Amazon River originates in Peru and travels 6300 kilometers (3915 miles) through Northern Brazil to the Atlantic Ocean. The term **Amazonas** also refers to the territories and provinces of Bolivia, Peru, Ecuador, Colombia, Venezuela, and Brazil located in the 2,500,000-square-mile basin drained by the Amazon and its tributaries.
2. The terms **tierra caliente** *hot lands,* **tierra fría** *cold lands,* and **tierra templada** *temperate lands* usually refer to Latin America's tropical, cold mountainous, and moderately warm areas, respectively.
3. The Andes mountain system in South America runs from the Caribbean Sea to Tierra del Fuego. Its total length is estimated to be 8500 kilometers (5300 miles). Eighteen separate peaks, located in five different countries and all higher than any peak in North America, have altitudes over 6250 meters (20,500 feet); Argentina's Aconcagua, at 22,831 feet, is the grand champion. The Andes chain is traditionally divided into seven sections: The Venezuelan Andes, the Colombian Andes, the Ecuatorian Andes, the Peruvian Andes, the Bolivian Andes, and the Argentine-Chilean Andes.
4. **Costa del Sol** *Coast of the Sun,* the southern coast of Spain from Estepona to Motril. About a hundred miles of fabulous beaches, the area is a mecca for foreign and national tourists. Main cities, Marbella, Torremolinos, and Málaga.
5. Chinese immigrants to Spanish America settled mainly on the West Coast of Mexico, in Central America, and in Peru. The Lebanese concentrated in the large cities of Mexico, Colombia, Ecuador, Venezuela, and Argentina. The Italians settled principally in Argentina.

SOBRE LA LECTURA

I. Para completar

Complete each sentence using the items in parentheses.

MODELO El mundo hispánico es tan grande que ____. (climas / tipos étnicos) → **El mundo hispánico es tan grande que presenta una infinidad de climas y de tipos étnicos.**

1. En el mundo hispánico existen ____. (montañas / lagos / desiertos / selvas / llanuras)
2. El clima es diverso; podemos hablar de ____. (intenso calor / intenso frío / primavera)
3. España es una colección ____. (grupos étnicos / diversas razas)
4. Los españoles viajan al Nuevo Mundo y ____. (se mezclan / razas indias / negros)
5. También llegan inmigrantes de otras partes del mundo como ____. (chinos / libaneses / italianos)

II. Para explicar[1]

1. ¿En los Estados Unidos hay climas y regiones muy diversos? ¿Puede usted hablar de esto? 2. ¿Hay más variedad geográfica en Latinoamérica o en los Estados Unidos? ¿Por qué dice usted esto? 3. ¿Hay diferentes tipos étnicos en los Estados Unidos? 4. Cuando los ingleses llegaron al Nuevo Mundo, ¿se mezclaron con los indios? ¿Qué pasó? 5. ¿Dónde hay más variedad étnica, en Latinoamérica o en los Estados Unidos? ¿Por qué dice usted esto?

[1] *To be explained.*

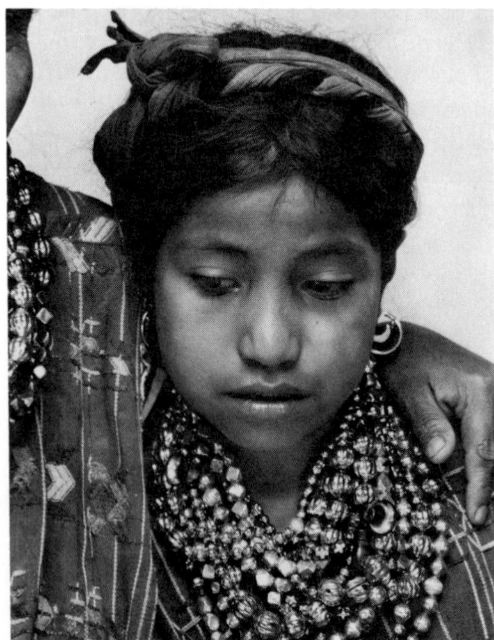

An Indian girl from Guatemala dressed for the village fiestas.

Repaso oral

I. Para conversar

You invite a friend over for dinner. During dinner you have the following discussions.

MODELO You ask if your friend likes the wine. Person B says he or she likes everything →
—¿Te gusta el vino?
—Sí, claro. Todo me gusta.

1. You congratulate your friend saying that the food is delicious. Person B says "thank you" and asks if you like the meat.
2. You say that your uncle came by yesterday and brought a bottle of wine. Person B says that it's got to be tasted.
3. You say you cannot hear anything. Person B says that from now on he's / she's going to have to talk louder.
4. You say, "Let's drink to health and to progress." Person B wishes you a bright future.
5. You say that Hortensia is very stubborn. Person B agrees and says that all modern things bother her.

II. Para describir

¿Quiénes comen? ¿Dónde comen? ¿Es la cena? ¿Qué comen? ¿Qué hora es? ¿Qué hacen después de *(after)* la comida? ¿Charlan de sobremesa?

Capítulo 8

Despegue

¿Entramos?

Usted primero, doctora.

Es usted muy amable.

Estoy para servirle.

Pronunciación

la doctora **es verdad** **millones de dólares**	Remember that, in most positions, Spanish **d** has a soft *th* sound.
una cerveza **conozco** **empiezan** **razón**	In most countries Spanish **z** is pronounced *s*.
negocios **llegar** **larga** **náufrago**	Within a word the **g** in **ga, gue, gui, go, gu** normally has a soft *g* sound.

Aplicación

I. Pronounce each of the following words and word groups first very slowly and then at a normal speed.

1. la doctora / es verdad / millones de dólares
2. Usted primero, doctora.
3. una cerveza / conozco / empiezan /razón
4. Es usted muy amable.
5. negocios / llegar / larga / náufrago
6. Estoy para servirle.

II. Para identificar

1. ¿Qué dice la señora?
¿Entran ellos o salen?

2. 

¿Qué dice el señor?
¿Quién entra primero?

3. 

¿Qué dice la señora?
¿Qué dice usted cuando alguien lo invita a un restaurante?

4. 

¿Qué dice el señor?
¿Cuándo dice usted "estoy para servirle"?

Tema del diálogo

A Chilean and a Bolivian diplomat in Madrid find themselves with a moment to relax after making an important trade agreement.

DIÁLOGO

Dos sudamericanos en Madrid

La doctora Olga Velasco, economista chilena, y Federico Ovando, primer secretario de la embajada boliviana en Madrid, conversan después de una larga sesión de negocios.

VELASCO ¿Qué le pareció la sesión, don Federico?

OVANDO ¡Estupenda! Sé que fue muy provechosa para todos los participantes.

VELASCO Es verdad. Yo no esperaba un pacto así de bueno.

OVANDO Ya era tiempo. Doscientos millones de dólares en camiones y autobuses para nuestros países. . .

VELASCO A cambio del cobre chileno y el estaño boliviano a precios fijos, ¿eh?[1]

* * *

(Salen a la calle y empiezan a caminar.[2])

VELASCO Pensándolo bien, es aún muy temprano para ir a la fiesta de los Andrade.

OVANDO Tiene usted razón. Y como no tenemos prisa, ¿por qué no tomamos una copa y unas tapas primero?

VELASCO Sí. Es preferible llegar un poco tarde y no antes de tiempo.[3]

OVANDO Una cerveza me va a caer muy bien. ¡Tengo una sed de náufrago!

VELASCO ¡Y yo tengo un hambre de huérfano![4] A ver. . .yo conocía un sitio por aquí que no estaba mal. Ah. . . ¡qué bien! Aquí está todavía. . . el mismo lugar. ¿Entramos?

OVANDO Usted primero, doctora. (Abre la puerta.)

VELASCO Gracias, don Federico. Es usted muy amable.

OVANDO Estoy para servirle.

A sidewalk café on Madrid's famous Gran Vía.

Two South Americans in Madrid

Doctor Olga Velasco, a Chilean economist, and Federico Ovando, First Secretary of the Bolivian Embassy in Madrid, are conversing after a long business session.

V: What did you think of the session, Don Federico?

O: Great! I know it was very beneficial for all the participants.

V: That's true. I was not expecting such a good pact.

O: It was about time. Two hundred million dollars in trucks and buses for our countries.

V: In exchange for Chilean copper and Bolivian tin at fixed prices, hmmm?

* * *

(They go out to the street and start to walk.)

V: Thinking it over, it's still very early to go to the Andrades' party.

O: You're right. And since we're in no hurry, why don't we have a drink and some snacks first?

V: Yes. It's preferible to arrive a little late and not ahead of time.

O: A beer will hit the spot (is going to please me very well). I'm parched (as thirsty as a shipwrecked person).

V: And I'm famished (hungry as an orphan). Let's see. . .I used to know a place around here that wasn't bad. Ah. . .good! Here it still is. . .the same place. Shall we go in?

O: You first, Doctor. (Opens the door.)

V: Thank you, Don Federico. You are very kind.

O: It's my pleasure.

VARIACIONES

¿Qué hace el Sr. Ovando?	What does Mr. Ovando do?
Es arquitecto.	He's an architect.
Es contador.	He's an accountant.
Es diplomático.	He's a diplomat.
Es ingeniero.	He's an engineer.

Y usted, ¿qué hace?	And what do you do?
Estudio para economista.	I'm studying to become an economist.
Trabajo de mesero (mesera).	I work as a waiter (waitress).
Voy a reuniones.	I go to meetings.
Leo un libro.	I'm reading a book.
Escribo algo.	I'm writing something.
¿Vas a leer el libro antes o después?	Are you going to read the book beforehand or afterwards?

Glosas

1. Many Latin American countries are said to have "one-product economies" because their exports of a single raw material or agricultural product—for example, wheat or copper—produce a high percentage of the foreign currency they need to purchase oil, computers, and other goods. Changes in the price of the key product, caused by international conditions beyond the control of the country, can mean hectic economic expansion or sudden depression. To protect themselves against such fluctuations, Latin American governments attempt to negotiate trade agreements involving fixed prices, and they also encourage the manufacture of additional items for export, such as clothing, electrical appliances, and automobiles.
2. Madrid's busiest thoroughfares, such as **la Gran Vía** and **la Castellana,** are ideal places for taking a walk or for finding a sidewalk cafe. **Madrileños** (people from Madrid) and tourists sit at a table and watch life go by as they sip drinks and eat **tapas** (snacks) or have coffee.
3. Well-bred Hispanics consider it poor taste to show up early or right on time for any social function.
4. Spanish is full of colorful metaphors used to describe hunger, anger, fear, happiness, etc. To have the thirst of a shipwrecked person (**náufrago**) or the hunger of an orphan (**huérfano**) are examples. English has set phrases of its own: *fresh as a cucumber, clean as a whistle,* etc.

Afternoon traffic on the Avenida del Prado, Madrid.

SOBRE EL DIÁLOGO

I. In each list there is a word that does not logically belong with the others. Tell which it is.

MODELO ingeniero / abogado / médico / padre → **padre**

1. economista / secretario / hijo / arquitecto
2. hija / hermana / profesora / prima
3. tapas / anticuchos / náufrago / leche
4. mujer / muchacha / joven / copa
5. carne / plata / estaño / cobre
6. cerveza / vino / legumbres / agua
7. contador / mesero / secretaria / señorita
8. ingeniero / arquitecto / oficina / empleado

II. Choosing from the list below, respond to each of the following statements. There may be more than one possible response.

Ya era tiempo. / **Tiene usted razón.** / **Tengo mucha sed.** / **Usted primero, señora.** / **Gracias, es usted muy amable.** / **Estoy para servirle.** / **Sí, señorita.**

MODELO Es un pacto muy bueno. → **Tiene usted razón.**

1. Por fin nos dieron el dinero.
2. ¿Quiere usted agua, señora?
3. Voy con usted a la oficina.
4. Este café parece muy bonito. ¿Entramos?
5. Mesero, ¿me puede usted traer un poco de vino?

III. Ask questions about the dialog that will elicit the following answers.

MODELO Ella es una economista chilena y él es primer secretario de la embajada boliviana. → **¿Quiénes son Olga Velasco y Federico Ovando?**

1. En Madrid.
2. Después de una larga sesión de negocios.
3. Le pareció muy provechosa para todos los participantes.
4. Doscientos millones de dólares en camiones y autobuses.
5. Porque aún es muy temprano para ir a la fiesta.
6. Una copa y unas tapas.
7. Es mejor llegar un poco tarde.
8. Quiere tomar una cerveza.
9. Sí, tiene un hambre de huérfano.
10. Usted primero, doctora.

IV. Use both words to form complete sentences.

MODELO médico / oficina → **El médico no está en su oficina.**

1. secretaria / compañía
2. estudiar para / arquitecto
3. trabajar en / pequeño restaurante
4. comer / tapas
5. sitio / no estar mal
6. ingeniero / muy amable
7. mesero / restaurante
8. leer / escribir
9. abrir / puerta
10. postre / después

VOCABULARIO

nouns

el **arquitecto**	architect
el **autobús**	bus
la **calle**	street
el **cambio**	change, exchange
el **camión**	truck
el **cobre**	copper
el **contador**	accountant
la **copa**	drink; stem glass, wine glass
el, la **diplomático**	diplomat
la **embajada**	embassy
el **estaño**	tin
la **fiesta**	party
el **huérfano,** la **huérfana**	orphan
el **ingeniero**	engineer
el **libro**	book
el **lugar**	place
el **mesero**	waiter
la **mesera**	waitress
el **millón**	millon
dos millones de dólares	two million dollars
el **náufrago,** la **náufraga**	shipwrecked person
el **pacto**	pact
el, la **participante**	participant
la **puerta**	door
la **reunión**	meeting
el **secretario,** la **secretaria**	secretary
la **sesión**	session
el **sitio**	place
el **sudamericano,** la **sudamericana**	South American
las **tapas**	snacks, hors d'oeuvres (regional, Spain)
el **tiempo**	time

verbs

abrir	to open
conversar	to converse
empezar (ie) (a)	to start
entrar (en) (a)	to enter
escribir	to write
esperar	to expect
leer (y)	to read
servir (i)	to serve

adjectives

amable	kind
boliviano	Bolivian
chileno	Chilean
largo	long
mismo	same
preferible	preferable
primer, primero	first
provechoso	beneficial

other expressions

a cambio de	in exchange for
a precios fijos	at fixed prices
antes	before, beforehand
antes de tiempo	ahead of time
así de bueno	so good, such a good, that good
aún	still
caer bien	to please, to be just right, to hit the spot
después	afterwards
después de	after
don, doña	title of respect
¿eh?	hm?
estoy para servirle	it's my pleasure
estudiar para	to study to be
pensándolo bien	thinking it over

por	around, through, by	el **favor**	favor
por aquí	around here	**la profesión**	profession
tener hambre	to be hungry	el **rifle**	rifle
tener un hambre *f* **de huérfano**	to be dying of hunger	el **secreto**	secret
tener prisa	to be in a hurry	**tener. . .años**	to be. . .years old
tener razón	to be right	**tener calor**	to be warm, hot
tener sed	to be thirsty	**tener frío**	to be cold
tener una sed de náufrago	to be dying of thirst	**tener ganas de** + infinitive	to feel like (doing something)
trabajar de	to work as	**tener miedo**	to be afraid
ya era tiempo	it was about time	**tener que** + infinitive	to have to (do something)
ya no	not any more	**tener sueño**	to be sleepy
		tener suerte	to be lucky

additional vocabulary

contestar	to answer

Statues of Cervantes, Don Quijote, and Sancho in the Plaza de España, in the heart of the Spanish capital, Madrid.

A. Formation of the imperfect tense: regular verbs

Repaso. The preterit tense pinpoints states and events in the past: **Salieron** a la calle y **empezaron** a caminar.

> Yo **conocía** un sitio que no **estaba** mal.

1. Unlike the preterit, the imperfect tense conveys states and events in the past which were habitual or continuous. To form the imperfect of **-ar** verbs, add these endings to the stem of the verb: **-aba, -abas, -aba, -ábamos, -abais, -aban.**

estar	
estaba	Yo estaba en casa.
estabas	¿Estabas con Josefa?
estaba	Ella estaba en un restaurante.
estábamos	Estábamos juntos, tú y yo.
estabais	Estabais aquí.
estaban	Ustedes estaban en la fiesta.

Note the written accent and pronunciation of the **nosotros** form.

2. For both **-er** and **-ir** verbs, the imperfect endings are **-ía, -ías, -ía, -íamos, -íais, -ían.**

traer	vivir	
traía	vivía	Yo traía a mi hijo.
traías	vivías	¿Por qué no traías dinero?
traía	vivía	Usted traía quince dólares.
traíamos	vivíamos	Vivíamos en este sitio.
traíais	vivíais	¿Vivíais aquí?
traían	vivían	Ellos vivían en mi casa.

Note the pronunciation of the **nosotros** (and **vosotros**) forms.

3. The imperfect of **hay** is **había.**

Aplicación

I. Repeat each sentence, changing the subject according to the cue.

MODELO ¿Con quién hablabas? (ellos, Olga) → **¿Con quién hablaban? ¿Con quién hablaba?**

1. Cenaba en el club. (tú, yo, los diplomáticos, el abogado, ustedes)
2. Caminábamos por el pueblo. (los chicos, el hombre, yo, mis amigos y yo, tú)
3. Tomaban una cerveza. (los dos arquitectos, el economista, nosotros, usted, yo)
4. No hacía nada. (yo, tú, el empleado, ellos y yo, los estudiantes)
5. Salían a la calle. (yo, tú, la secretaria, los estudiantes, mi amiga y yo)

II. Change the verbs in the following sentences to the imperfect.

MODELO Siempre llego temprano a la oficina. → **Siempre llegaba temprano a la oficina.**

1. La secretaria me trae los contratos.
2. Yo los leo.
3. Llamo a mi abogado.
4. Él y yo conversamos.
5. Vienen los ingenieros.
6. Hablamos de nuestros negocios.
7. Salimos a tomar una copa.
8. Hay mucha gente en el café.
9. Charlamos por un largo rato.
10. Y así pasan los días.

III. Answer the questions using **antes** (+ imperfect) and **ya no.**

MODELO ¿Lee usted mucho? → **Antes leía mucho, pero ya no.**

1. ¿Trabaja Juan mucho?
2. ¿Conversan ellos mucho?
3. ¿Estudian ustedes mucho?
4. ¿Salgo yo mucho?
5. ¿Caminan los muchachos mucho?
6. ¿Hablo yo inglés mucho?

IV. Using the imperfect tense, tell what you used to do during the summer when you were a child. Add some additional information to complete each sentence.

MODELO siempre / pasar / verano → **Yo siempre pasaba el verano en la casa de mis primos.**

1. mis amigos y yo / jugar / patio
2. yo / salir / todos los días
3. nosotros / no / estudiar
4. a veces / nosotros / leer / libros
5. cuando / tener tiempo / yo
6. también / me / gustar
7. yo / siempre / hacer / muchas cosas
8. nosotros / disfrutar / mucho

B. Uses of **para**

Millones de dólares **para** el país. . .

The preposition **para** is used to express three basic concepts: destination, deadline, and disproportion.

1. *Destination.* **Para** indicates to whom or to what something or someone is directed.

Hay un puesto estupendo para alguien como yo.	There's a great job for someone like me.
Esta botella de vino es para ti.	This bottle of wine is for you.
Salimos para Madrid esta noche.	We're leaving for Madrid tonight.
Vamos para la tienda.	We're heading for the store.

2. There are two set phrases which indicate destination or purpose:

para + infinitive = purpose of an action
estudiar para + profession = goal

Trabajan para ganar dinero.	They work in order to earn money.
Estudio para profesor.	I'm studying to become a professor.

3. *Deadline.* **Para** also indicates a point in time which is a deadline. Sometimes **para** is translated *due* in this context.

Este trabajo es para mañana.	This work is for (due) tomorrow.
Para la semana que viene quiero poner en orden mis asuntos.	By next week I want to put my affairs in order.

4. *Disproportion.* **Para** is used to express how a person, place, or thing differs from what we might expect it to be.

Para una casa pequeña, la cocina es muy grande.	For a small house, the kitchen is very large.
Esta taza de café está fuerte para café americano.	This cup of coffee is strong for American coffee.

Aplicación

I. Para expresar en español

MODELO: This wine is for Luis. → **Este vino es para Luis.**

1. For a foreigner, she speaks well.
2. This work is for next week.
3. I need a book to read.
4. You need a lot of money in order to have a party.
5. We're leaving for the hotel.
6. This book is for Friday.
7. She called in order to talk to Marta.
8. For an old house, the price is sky high.

II. Complete each sentence by adding a phrase that starts with **para.**

MODELO Es muy fuerte. . . → **Es muy fuerte para un viejo.**

1. Necesitas mucha plata. . .
2. Hay un puesto estupendo. . .
3. Vamos. . .
4. Ellas vinieron. . .
5. Fue una sesión muy provechosa. . .
6. Voy a dejar la fiesta. . .
7. Es muy temprano. . .
8. El está muy alto. . .
9. Estudio. . .
10. Este dólar es. . .

C. Ir, ser, and dar in the preterit

Repaso. In the preterit tense, we have seen regular **-ar** verbs (**caminé, caminaste. . .**), regular **-er** and **-ir** verbs (**conocí, saliste. . .**); also irregular verbs with **u** (**estuve, estuviste. . .**), with **i** (**hice, hiciste. . .**), and with **j** (**dije, dijiste. . .**).

1. **Ir** *to go* and **ser** *to be* have identical forms in the preterit.

ir ser	
fui	Le di una cerveza.
fuiste	No le diste nada.
fue	Ella me dio unos anticuchos.
fuimos	Dimos una fiesta.
fuisteis	Disteis cien dólares.
fueron	¿Qué le dieron?

The meaning of the entire sentence establishes whether the verb used is **ir** or **ser.**

Fui Primer Secretario.	I was First Secretary.
Federico fue el primero.	Federico was the first one.
Fuimos en autobús.	We went by bus.
Todos fueron a mi casa.	Everyone went to my house.

2. **Dar** has the following preterit forms.

dar	
di	Fui a Caracas el mes pasado.
diste	Fuiste a ver a tu familia.
dio	Mi primo Bernardo fue profesor.
dimos	Fuimos a Sevilla.
disteis	Fuisteis al café.
dieron	Todas las sesiones fueron buenas.

At a cattle auction in Argentina.

Flower market, Mexico City.

Vegetable vendor, Lima, Peru.

Cherry picker, Chile.

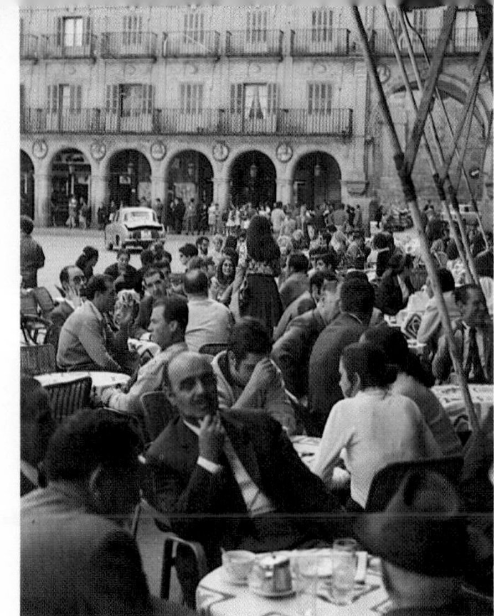

Salamanca, Spain. A Roman bridge over the River Tormes. Right: Salamanca's central plaza.

Madrid. The Prado Museum, on one of the capital's principal avenues.

San Juan, Puerto Rico. Part of the Condado section.

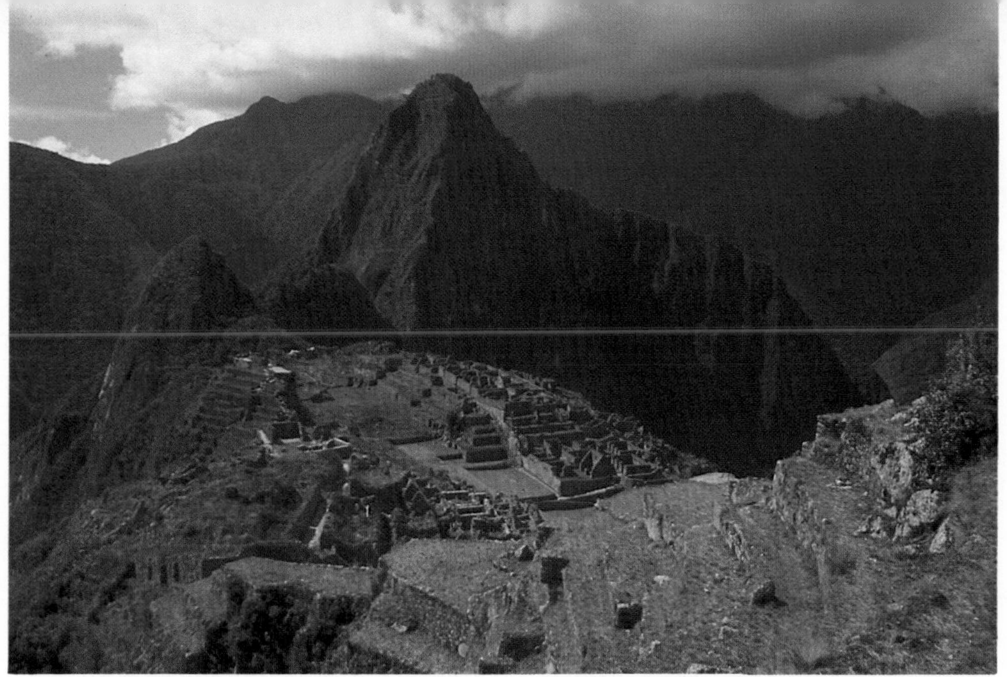

Machu Picchu, fortress city built by the Incas on a peak in the Peruvian Andes.

Above: An Uro Indian on a reed island, Lake Titicaca, in the Andes between Bolivia and Peru. Right: Mount Huascarán, in the Peruvian Andes.

Left: Quito, Ecuador. The Convent of San Francisco, showing ornamentation characteristic of one phase of Colonial architecture. Above: San Augustín, Colombia. A pre-Columbian statue discovered in the forest. Below: Tula, Mexico, ancient capital of the Toltec civilization. Carved pillars at the top of a pyramid.

Aplicación

I. Answer each question using the preterit and **también.**

MODELO María fue a la oficina, ¿y Pedro? ¿y los abogados? → **Pedro fue a la oficina también. Los abogados fueron a la oficina también.**

1. Elena fue a la recepción, ¿y yo? ¿y ustedes? ¿y el arquitecto? ¿y los estudiantes? ¿y el secretario?
2. Ellos fueron participantes, ¿y ustedes? ¿y la profesora? ¿y usted?
3. Yo di una fiesta, ¿y ellos? ¿y ustedes? ¿y la secretaria?

II. Para contestar

1. ¿Adónde fue usted ayer?
2. ¿Fue usted el mejor estudiante de su *high school?*
3. ¿Dieron ustedes una fiesta anoche?
4. ¿Quién dio una fiesta la semana pasada?
5. ¿Fueron todos ustedes al mismo *high school?*
6. ¿Adónde fueron la doctora Velasco y el señor Ovando, a una clase de inglés?
7. ¿Les di mucho trabajo a ustedes para hoy?
8. ¿Fuimos a un café español todos juntos? ¿Quieren ustedes ir?

Pausa oral

El trabajo y los estudios

Most university students are concerned with academic matters and eventually with job prospects. You are already prepared to make some remarks about these topics.

I. Two people each make statements about themselves by completing the following exchanges.

PERSON A	PERSON B
1. Estudio para. . .	Yo estudio para. . .
2. Trabajo en. . .	Yo trabajo en. . .
3. El año pasado trabajé en. . .	El año pasado no trabajé; yo. . .
4. Una cosa que no quiero ser es. . .	Y yo no quiero ser. . .
5. Una secretaria trabaja en. . .	Y un empleado bancario trabaja en. . .
6. Este año voy a dejar. . .	Yo no quiero dejar los estudios porque. . .
7. Un puesto que me gusta mucho es. . .	A mí me gusta. . .
8. Tengo un amigo que trabaja de. . .	Tengo una amiga que trabaja de. . .

II. Para contestar

1. ¿Qué estudia usted? ¿Le gusta estudiar? ¿Puede usted disfrutar de la vida cuando estudia? ¿Qué le gusta más, estudiar o ir a fiestas?
2. ¿Qué quiere usted ser? ¿Qué profesión no le interesa?
3. ¿En qué profesión puede usted ganar buen dinero? ¿En qué profesión gana la gente poco dinero?
4. ¿Prefiere usted trabajar en un banco, en una casa comercial o en un restaurante? ¿Por qué?
5. ¿Qué clases tiene usted ahora en la universidad? ¿Qué le parece cada clase: estupenda, provechosa, buena o mala?

III. Para describir

Discuss with a friend or the class what it would be like to work in the places shown in the drawings which follow. You might want to use some of the words provided with each drawing.

aduana
avión

recepción
médico

dinero
economista

ESTRUCTURA II

A. The preterit and imperfect tenses contrasted

> Velasco y Ovando **conversaron** esta mañana.
> Antes Velasco y Ovando **conversaban** mucho.

When you want to express an idea in the past, you must choose between two different tenses: the preterit and the imperfect. Each conveys a different picture of the past.

1. The preterit is like a snapshot of a past situation and often answers the question, *What specifically happened?* It confines a past action or series of actions, or a state, to a specific unit of time which is viewed as completed.

¿Qué pasó? ¿Qué viste?	What happened? What did you see?
Esperé ayer toda la tarde pero no llegaste.	I waited yesterday all afternoon but you didn't arrive.
Tu tío vino ayer y te trajo esta botella de vino.	Your uncle came (by) yesterday and brought you this bottle of wine.
Fui a Guatemala cinco veces pero no vi una pirámide maya.	I went to Guatemala five times but I didn't see a Mayan pyramid.

2. The imperfect, on the other hand, is like a motion picture of the past and often anwers the question, *What was generally true?* or *What was happening?* It focuses on the middle of an action or condition and presents it as on-going, in progress.

Había cien personas en la fiesta.	There were one hundred people at the party.
Antes yo vivía en Caracas donde trabajaba con una compañía venezolana.	I used to live in Caracas where I worked for a Venezuelan company.
Todo costaba más cada día y papá seguía con dos trabajos.	Everything cost more each day and Dad continued with two jobs.

3. The imperfect also conveys states or conditions that were continuous in the past. These include mental states, emotional states, calendar time in the past, and the time of day.

¿Qué querías ver?	What did you want to see?
Yo no estaba preocupado porque no veía problema.	I wasn't worried because I didn't see any problem.
Era un lunes por la mañana.	It was a Monday morning.
Eran las cinco de la tarde.	It was five in the afternoon.

4. The preterit and the imperfect sometimes occur in the same sentence.

specific point preterit	+	continuum imperfect

Olga dijo que salía ayer.	Olga said she was leaving yesterday.
Cuando llegaste a casa anoche yo dormía.	When you arrived home last night I was sleeping.

Aplicación

I. Using the words in the list, make sentences that contain the imperfect and the preterit joined by **cuando.**

MODELO yo / leer / ustedes / llamar → **Yo leía cuando ustedes llamaron.**

1. él / comer / yo / llegar
2. ellas / conversar / nosotros / entrar
3. el abogado / trabajar en su oficina / usted / venir
4. los chicos / jugar / su mamá / salir
5. ella y yo / hablar / nuestros amigos / llamar

II. Para expresar en español

MODELO He left at ten. / He used to leave at ten. → **Salió a las diez.** / **Salía a las diez.**

1. They had dinner at eight (last night). / They used to have dinner at eight.
2. He came last Tuesday. / He always came on Tuesday.
3. I spoke to him (that time). / I was speaking to him.
4. We spent last summer there. / We always spent the summer there.
5. Did you wait all afternoon? / Were you waiting at home?

III. Complete the sentences any way you wish, using the preterit or the imperfect according to the meaning of the entire sentence.

MODELOS Yo _____ y tú _____. → **Yo leía y tú escribías.** Tú _____ cuando yo _____. → **Tú dormías cuando yo llegué.**

1. El contador _____ y el abogado _____.
2. El ingeniero _____ cuando nosotros _____.
3. El profesor _____ cuando los estudiantes _____.
4. Ellas _____ y nosotros _____.
5. Yo _____ y ustedes _____.

IV. Supply the correct past form of the verb in the list.

MODELO __0__ el verano pasado con mi primo en el monte. → **pasamos**

0. pasar, nosotros
1. salir, nosotros
2. tener, nosotros
3. caminar, nosotros
4. oír, nosotros
5. pensar, yo
6. tomar, yo
7. decir
8. buscar
9. ser
10. saber
11. encontrar, nosotros
12. matar, nosotros

Todos los días __1__ con él. En la mochila siempre __2__ comida, agua y un mapa. Un día, cuando __3__ por el monte, __4__ algo. —Es un tigre— __5__, y __6__ mi rifle. —Es una víbora— __7__ mi primo, y __8__ su machete. ¿Qué __9__? Yo no sé, y nunca __10__, porque no __11__ nada. La verdad es que no __12__ nada en todo el verano.

V. Write the following passage using a past tense, either the preterit or imperfect as appropriate.

a) Todos los días don Pedro hace las mismas cosas. Llega a su oficina temprano y empieza a trabajar. Lee contratos, va a reuniones, habla con los otros hombres de negocios. Nunca conversa con las secretarias porque no tiene tiempo. Nunca llama a un amigo. A las dos come en casa y después va a la oficina y trabaja toda la tarde. Y ¿quién sabe[1] cuántas tazas de café toma? A don Pedro no le parece mala su vida porque piensa que el trabajo es bueno.

b) Pero un día don Pedro cambia de opinión. Hace las maletas, no le dice adiós a nadie, y parte. Viaja por diez semanas. Va a Perú, a Chile y a Argentina. Ve Machu Picchu[2], los Andes y muchas otras cosas. Conoce a gente nueva y conversa con muchas personas. Por fin llega a su país otra vez. Va a su oficina y empieza a trabajar. Los mismos contratos están en el mismo lugar. Los mismos hombres de negocios esperan una sesión con él. Las mismas secretarias hacen el mismo trabajo en el mismo sitio que antes. Nadie sabe nunca el secreto de don Pedro.

VI. Para contestar

1. ¿Estaban aquí los otros estudiantes cuando usted llegó a clase? 2. ¿Qué hacían ustedes cuando entré yo? 3. ¿Qué hizo usted esta mañana? 4. ¿Fue usted a una fiesta la semana pasada? ¿Había mucha gente? 5. ¿Cómo pasaba usted los veranos antes? ¿y ahora? 6. ¿Puede usted contar algo que pasó el verano pasado? 7. ¿Llamó usted a un amigo anoche? ¿Estaba en casa esa persona? 8. ¿De qué hablaron usted y su amigo?

B. The verbs **saber** and **conocer** contrasted

Conozco un sitio por aquí.
Sé que el sitio no está mal.

Saber (sé, sabes, sabe. . .) and **conocer (conozco, conoces, conoce. . .)** both correspond to English *to know.* Each of the Spanish verbs is used in different situations.

1. **Saber** refers to intellectual knowledge; it means *to know information.*

¿Sabe usted dónde viven los Andrade?	Do you know where the Andrades live?
Sabemos que Federico es un mesero muy bueno.	We know that Federico is a very good waiter.

2. **Saber,** but not **conocer,** may be followed by an infinitive. In this use, it indicates a skill and has the meaning *to know how.*

Sé hacer café, nada más.	I know how to make coffee, nothing else.
¿Sabes llegar a casa de los Andrade?	Do you know how to get to the Andrade's house?

[1]Do not change to the past.
[2]A fortress city in the mountains of Peru, built by the Incas.

3. **Conocer** refers to personal familiarity with a person, a place, or a thing (music, wines, books, etc.). The meaning is often *to be familiar with.*

No conozco a Olga Velasco.	I don't know Olga Velasco.
Conocemos Madrid muy bien, pero sólo conocemos Barcelona un poco.	We know Madrid very well but we only know Barcelona a little.
¿Conoces este libro?	Are you familiar with this book?

4. When **saber** and **conocer** are used in the imperfect, they mean *to know.*

¡Hombre! ¡No sabíamos que estabas aquí en Madrid!	Hey! We didn't know that you were here in Madrid!
Cuando yo era joven conocía a mucha gente hispánica.	When I was young I knew lots of Hispanic people.

When used in the preterit, **saber** and **conocer** have different meanings. In the preterit, **saber** means *found out;* **conocer** means *met.*

Supe que estabas en España este verano.	I found out (learned) that you were in Spain this summer.
Conocí a Federico Ovando en la fiesta.	I met Federico Ovando at the party.

Aplicación

I. Supply the present tense form of either **saber** or **conocer** as required.

Yo __1__ a una muchacha que __2__ hablar inglés y español. ¿__3__ tú de quién hablo? Creo que tú la __4__ también. Es una chica simpática, pero tiene un problema. Cuando no __5__ decir una cosa en español, la dice en inglés. Cuando no __6__ decir algo en inglés, lo dice en español. Si tú no __7__ inglés y también español, no __8__ de qué habla ella.

II. Para expresar en español

MODELO I know the Spanish girl. / I know how to speak Spanish. →
Conozco a la chica española. / Sé hablar español.

1. Do you know Los Angeles? / Do you know how to get to (arrive at) Los Angeles?
2. Does she know that book? / Does she know how to read that book?
3. She knows Spanish. / She knows Madrid.
4. We know where his house is. / We know his house.
5. I know them. / I don't know where they live.

III. Ask a question with **conocer** or **saber** that will elicit the following answers.
MODELO ¿Yo? ¿Hablar inglés? Sí, claro. → **¿Sabe usted hablar inglés?**

1. ¿A María Teresa? Sí, muy bien.
2. ¿Dónde está ella ahora? No.
3. ¿Llegar a su casa? Cómo no.
4. ¿En qué calle está? Sí, sí.
5. ¿A toda su familia? No.

G. Expressions with tener

Tiene usted razón.

Spanish uses **tener** in many common expressions in which English uses *to be.*

1. Several expressions are used without an indirect object.

tener. . .años, to be. . .years old	Tengo diecinueve años.
tener calor, to be warm (hot)	Tengo calor en verano.
tener frío, to be cold	Tengo frío en invierno.
tener hambre, to be hungry	¡Qué hambre tengo!
tener prisa, to be in a hurry	Siempre tienes prisa.
tener razón, to be right	Josefa siempre tiene razón.
tener sed, to be thirsty	¿No tienen ustedes sed?
tener sueño, to be sleepy	Teníamos mucho sueño.
tener suerte, to be lucky	¡Qué suerte tiene mi hermano!

2. When these expressions are modified, an adjective is used.

Tengo mucha hambre.	I'm very hungry.

3. Other expressions may be used alone, with an indirect object, or with **de.**

tener miedo (or **tenerle miedo a**), to be afraid (of someone)	¿Por qué les tienes miedo a tus padres?
tener ganas (de + infinitive) to feel like (doing something)	Tenemos ganas de comer una ensalada bien grande.
tener que (+ infinitive), to have to (do something)	Tengo que estudiar esta noche.

Madrid's stock exchange. Trading, light to moderate.

Aplicación

I. Para expresar en español

MODELO He's thirsty. → **Tiene sed.**
He's very thirsty. → **Tiene mucha sed.**

1. You're right. / You're very right.
2. She's sleepy. / She's very sleepy.
3. I'm hungry. / I'm very hungry.
4. They're lucky. / They're very lucky.
5. We're thirsty. / We're very thirsty.
6. You're twenty years old. / She's thirty-five years old.
7. He's afraid. / He's afraid of the professor.
8. I don't feel like doing it. / I don't feel like reading.
9. You (plural) have to arrive early. / You have to leave a little late.
10. We're cold. / They're warm.

II. Respond to each statement with a sentence that includes an expression with **tener.**

MODELO Hicieron un pacto muy provechoso. → **Tuvieron mucha suerte.** *or* **Tiene usted razón.**

1. No tengo ganas de comer ahora.
2. Ella es muy vieja.
3. Parece que él quiere dormir.
4. Hay tigres y víboras en este monte.
5. Quiero llegar a las diez en punto a la fiesta.
6. Yo necesito salir ahora, ¿y usted?
7. El cobre chileno es muy necesario.
8. Quiero tomar algo.
9. ¡Encontró mil dólares!
10. ¡Quiero dormir!

BAR
LA PLAZA

★ DEGUSTACION DE CAFE
★ TAPAS DE COCINA
★ COCINA CASERA
★ CERVEZA
★ VINO
Y ALEGRIA

GENERAL ZABALA, 37 - MADRID

Repaso oral

I. Para conversar

1. You ask your friend what he/she thought of the session. Person B says that it was profitable but that it was very long.
2. You say that it is still very early to go to the Andrade's party. Person B thinks it is preferible to arrive a little late and not early.
3. You say that you're very thirsty. Person B says that some cold water will hit the spot.
4. You say that you're very hungry. Person B asks if you know a good restaurant.
5. You say that you used to know of a restaurant which wasn't bad. Person B asks, "Shall we go in?"
6. You ask Person B what type of work he/she does. Person B says that he/she works as a waiter (waitress).

II. Para contestar

1. Cuando usted va a la casa de un amigo, ¿le gusta llegar tarde o prefiere llegar temprano? ¿Por qué?
2. ¿Le gusta a usted la cerveza? ¿Qué le gusta tomar? ¿Dónde?
3. ¿Tiene usted mucha hambre ahora? ¿Tiene mucha sed? ¿Qué va a comer o tomar?
4. ¿En qué restaurante le gusta a usted comer? ¿Hay buena comida? ¿Son muy buenos los meseros? ¿Siempre come usted en el mismo lugar?
5. ¿Prefiere usted trabajar en una oficina o en otro sitio? ¿De qué trabaja usted?
6. ¿Estudia usted para contador? ¿Para qué estudia?
7. ¿Es interesante trabajar en una embajada? ¿Qué hace el primer secretario de una embajada?
8. Cuando usted entra en un lugar con una señora, ¿le abre usted la puerta?
9. ¿Cómo llega usted a la universidad? ¿en carro? ¿en autobús?

GRAN CHAPSUY CHIFA

KUO WA

ALMUERZO Y COMIDA — SERVICIO COMPLETO

LOCAL DE LUJO Y APROPIADO PARA BANQUETES

Pasaje Santa Rosa 115 (Sótano del Club de la Unión)

Plaza de Armas — Teléfono 2-79489

Comunicación 2

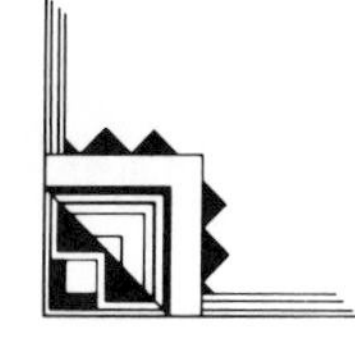

La comida

tener hambre	entrar en un restaurante comer un plato	to be hungry	to enter a restaurant to have a dish
tener sed	beber el vaso	to be thirsty	to drink glass
pedir	pedir la carta (el menú) el mesero (la mesera)	to order	to ask for the menu waiter (waitress)
desayunar	el desayuno	to have breakfast	breakfast
comer	la comida a la mesa	to eat	the meal; lunch at the table
comer mucho	engordar estar gordo (gorda)	to eat a lot	to gain weight to be heavy
comer poco	estar a dieta estar delgado (delgada)	to eat little	to be on a diet to be thin
cenar	la cena	to have dinner (supper)	dinner; supper

traer la cuenta	pagar dejar una propina	to bring the bill	to pay to leave a tip
salir del restaurante	la salida	to leave the restaurant	the exit

I. ¿Sí o no?

MODELO (Student A) Cuando tienes hambre, comes poco. →
(Student B) **¡No hombre! Cuando tengo hambre, como mucho.**

1. Cuando tienes hambre, comes mucho.
2. Cuando tienes sed, bebes poco.
3. Cuando el mesero trae la carta, sales del restaurante.
4. Comes en un comedor.
5. Cenas por la manaña.
6. Siempre dejas una propina en un restaurante.
7. Primero sales de un restaurante, después pides la carta.
8. Si comes mucho, vas a engordar.
9. Si estás delgado (delgada), debes comer mucho.
10. Si la comida es mala, no pagas la cuenta.
11. Engordar y estar a dieta son la misma cosa.

II. ¿Qué pide usted en un restaurante?

la bebida	los refrescos	drink	soft drinks
el café	café solo café con leche el azúcar	coffee	black coffee coffee with milk sugar
el vino	vino blanco vino tinto vino de la casa	wine	white wine red wine house wine
la ensalada	la lechuga el tomate	salad	lettuce tomato
la sopa	una sopa de pescado una sopa de tomate	soup	fish soup tomato soup
la fruta	la manzana la naranja	fruit	apple orange
el postre	el helado fruta y queso	dessert	ice cream fruit and cheese

III. ¿Sí o no?

MODELO Student A El café es una sopa. →
Student B **¡Oh, no! El café es una bebida.**

1. La gente toma el vino con leche y azúcar.
2. La gente pone tomates en una ensalada.

3. La fruta es importante en la dieta.
4. El postre es más importante que la comida.
5. Después de comer en un restaurante, una persona deja una propina.
6. Con el pescado la gente toma vino blanco.
7. El agua y la cerveza son dos bebidas.
8. La naranja es un pescado.

IV. Para completar

1. Me gusta ______.
2. No me gustan ______.
3. ¿Qué te parecen ______?
4. El mesero va a traer ______.
5. Vamos a pedir ______.
6. Cuando tienes hambre ______.
7. Hay varios tipos de vino: ______.
8. Para el desayuno esta mañana tomé ______.

V. ¿Preparamos una comida?

Form small groups of two to four people each. One person may be very hungry (**tiene mucha hambre**), one may not be (**tiene poca hambre**). Another person wants to gain a little weight (**quiere engordar**), another is dieting (**está a dieta**). Each person plans a complete meal for him or herself. You should consult each other with questions like **¿Quieres. . . ?** or **¿Prefieres ______ o ______?** After you have practiced in class, why not join your group (or another group) in the student cafeteria or in a local restaurant and carry on a similar conversation. . . **¡en español!**

A Spanish toast

Salud, amor y pesetas y tiempo para gozarlos.
Health, love, and **pesetas** (Spanish money) and time to enjoy them.

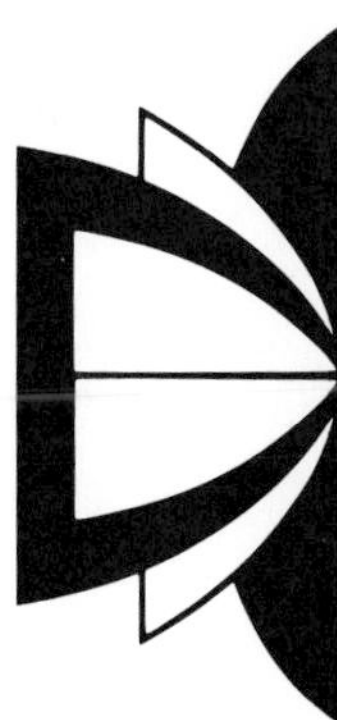

Capítulo 9

Despegue

Emilio estaciona el carro.

La mamá cuida al bebé.

El perro come un hueso.

Pronunciación

San José **en Costa Rica** **en Canadá** **en Cuba**	When **n** is followed by **j** or by **ca, co,** or **cu,** the **n** has the same sound as *ng* in English *sing.*
Rivero **Costa Rica** **carro** **perro**	Notice that the trilled (or rolled) **r** is pronounced when the tip of the tongue flaps several times against the hard upper ridge.
Avila **báscula** **propósito** **médico**	In words accented on the third-from-last syllable, care must be taken to pronounce all syllables very clearly.

Aplicación

I. Para pronunciar

Practice saying each of the following groups of words imitating the pronunciation of your instructor.

1. San José / en Costa Rica / en Canadá / en Cuba
2. La mamá cuida al bebé.
3. Rivero / Costa Rica / carro / perro
4. Emilio estaciona el carro.
5. Ávila / báscula / propósito / médico
6. El perro come un hueso.

II. Para contestar

1. 

¿Quién cuida al bebé?
¿Hay un bebé en su familia?
¿Le gusta a usted cuidar a los bebés?

2. 

¿Qué come el perro?
¿Tiene usted perro? ¿Cómo se llama?
¿Quién come huesos, usted o su perro?

3. 

¿Qué hace Emilio?
¿Tiene usted carro?
¿Es difícil estacionar un carro?
¿Están por las nubes los precios de los carros?

Tema del diálogo

A young couple visits the doctor in downtown San José, Costa Rica.

DIÁLOGO

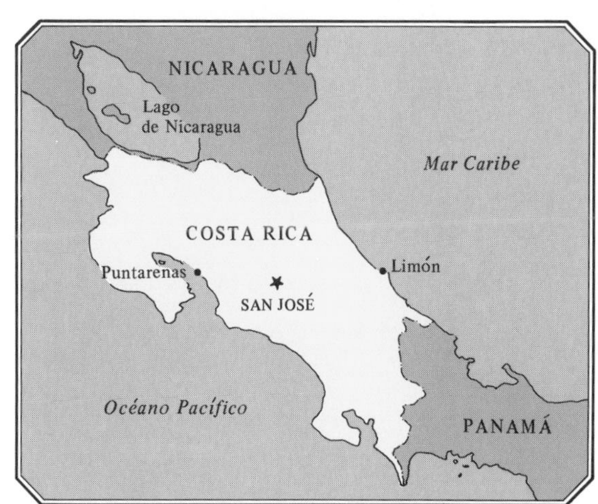

Una visita al médico

Marisela Rivero y su esposo Emilio están en el centro de la ciudad de San José, Costa Rica. Marisela tiene cita con la doctora Ávila[1].

DOCTORA Adelante, Marisela. ¿Cómo le va?
MARISELA Muy bien, supongo.
DOCTORA ¿Y Emilio? ¿Cómo está?
MARISELA También muy bien. Hoy me acompañó. Ahorita viene. Fue a estacionar el carro.
DOCTORA A ver. La presión arterial anda bien. . .
(Marisela sube a la báscula.)
DOCTORA Dos kilos más.[2] No está mal.
MARISELA Yo pensé que iba a ser más difícil.
DOCTORA No necesariamente. Tiene muy buen aspecto.
MARISELA Eso me dice Emilio. Piensa que el embarazo me prueba.

* * *

(Entra la enfermera. Anuncia que Emilio ya llegó. Entra Emilio.)
EMILIO Buenas, doctora.
DOCTORA Muy buenas.[3] A propósito, lo felicito. El bebé es para junio.
EMILIO Estupendo. ¿Y cómo encontró a Marisela?
DOCTORA Perfectamente bien. Pero hay que cuidarla y cuidar a su hijo.
EMILIO Naturalmente.
DOCTORA Nada de alcohol, nada de drogas.
EMILIO ¡Caramba! ¡La cosa va en serio!
MARISELA Menos mal que para la comida no hay prohibiciones.
DOCTORA Bueno, si no sube demasiado de peso. . .
MARISELA A otro perro con ese hueso.[4] ¡A mí me gusta comer bien!

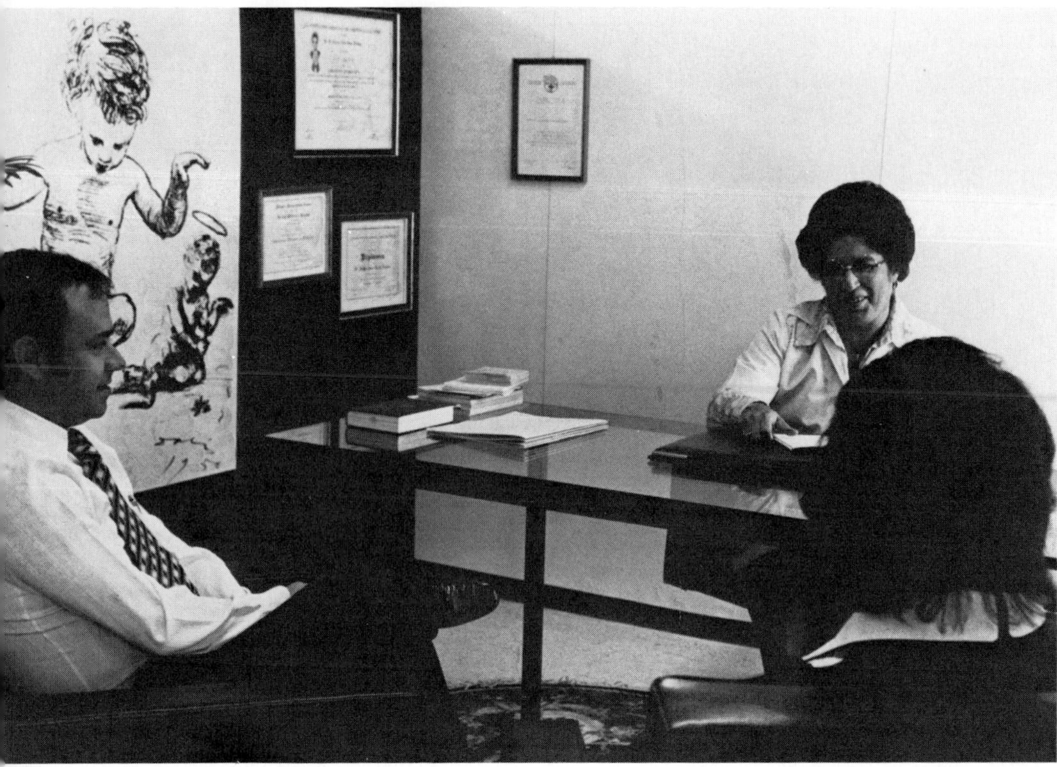

Congratulations, the baby is due in June.

A visit to the doctor

Marisela Rivero and her husband Emilio are in the downtown of the city of San José, Costa Rica. Marisela has an appointment with Doctor Ávila.

D: Come in, Marisela. How are you?
M: Very well, as far as I know (I suppose).
D: And Emilio? How is he?
M: Very well also. Today he came with me. He's coming right away. He went to park the car.
D: Let's see. Blood pressure O.K. . . .
(Marisela gets on the scale.)
D: Two kilos more. Not bad.
M: I thought it was going to be more difficult.
D: Not necessarily. You look very healthy.
M: That's what Emilio tells me. He thinks that pregnancy agrees with me.

* * *

(The nurse enters. She announces that Emilio has arrived. Emilio enters.)

E: Afternoon, Doctor.
D: Good afternoon. By the way, I congratulate you. The baby is due in June.
E: Great. And how do you find Marisela?
D: Perfectly fine. But it's necessary to take care of her and to take care of your child.
E: Naturally.
D: No alcohol, no drugs.
E: Christopher! This is getting serious.
M: Thank goodness there are no restrictions on food.
D: Well, so long as you don't gain too much weight. . .
M: Come off it! Me, I like to eat.

VARIACIONES

¿Está usted enfermo (enferma)?	Are you sick?
Sí, me duele la cabeza.	Yes, I have a headache.
el estómago.	I have a stomach ache.
la garganta.	I have a sore throat.
todo el cuerpo.	My whole body aches.
Sí, me duelen los ojos.	Yes, my eyes hurt.
las orejas.	ears ache
los brazos.	arms hurt
las piernas.	legs ache
los pies.	feet hurt
¿Está mejor ahora?	Are you better now?
Sí, pero tengo que bajar de peso.	Yes, but I have to lose weight.
¿Para qué mes es el bebé?	In what month is the baby due?
Para el mes de enero.	In the month of January.
febrero	February
marzo	March
abril	April
mayo	May
junio	June
julio	July
agosto	August
septiembre	September
octubre	October
noviembre	November
diciembre	December

Glosas

1. In Hispanic countries most physicians are general practitioners who, in a given day, will see a great variety of cases ranging from the broken leg of a **futbolista infantil** (pee-wee league soccer player) to pregnancies and the diseases of the elderly.
2. A kilo, or kilogram, is equal to 2.2 pounds. The U.S.A. is slowly changing over to the metric system, which the rest of the Western World has been using for almost 200 years. Some basic units in the metric system:

SPANISH	ENGLISH	
metro	*meter*	Measures length; approximately 40 inches.
litro	*liter*	Measures volume; approximately 60 cubic inches (i.e., larger than a quart)
gramo	*gram*	Measures weight; approximately 28 grams = one ounce.

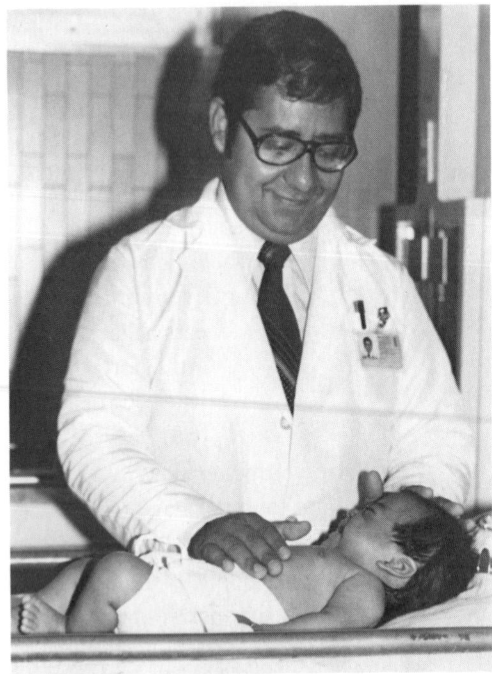

A warm and dedicated Hispanic doctor views his reward, a healthy baby.

3. In familiar Spanish it is common to shorten **buenos días** and **buenas tardes** (or **noches**) to **buenos** or to **buenas.** Speaker B will follow suit by using either identical greetings or a simple **muy buenos** (if it is morning) or **muy buenas** (during the P.M. hours).
4. Literally, "Throw that bone to another dog." Spanish conversation is seasoned with **refranes** (old sayings and proverbs). Regardless of formal education, Spanish-speakers constantly resort to these **refranes** when making a point.

SOBRE EL DIÁLOGO

I. Para contestar

1. ¿En qué país están Marisela y Emilio Rivero? 2. ¿Con quién tiene cita Marisela? 3. ¿Vino sola Marisela o la acompañó su esposo? ¿Dónde está él? 4. ¿Cuántos kilos subió Marisela? ¿Está bien o mal de peso? 5. ¿Qué anuncia la enfermera? 6. ¿Para cuándo es el bebé? 7. ¿Qué prohibiciones tiene Marisela? 8. ¿Cuáles son seis partes del cuerpo humano?

II. Complete each sentence with the logical word taken from the following list.

cabeza, ojos, bebé, estómago, garganta, piernas, pies, báscula, carro, enfermera, embarazo, peso, perro, centro, meses

MODELO La doctora dice que hay que cuidar al. . . → **La doctora dice que hay que cuidar al bebé.**

1. No puedo leer más. Me duelen los. . .
2. La oficina de la doctora Ávila está en el. . .
3. La señorita que trabaja con la doctora es una. . .

4. Comí demasiado. Me duele el. . .
5. ¿Quién va a conducir el. . . ?
6. Mi. . .se llama Atila.
7. Si como mucho, voy a subir de. . .
8. La profesora no puede hablar. Le duele la. . .
9. ¡Tres kilos! ¡No puede ser! Tengo que bajar de. . .
10. Estas botas me van a matar. Ay, Dios mío, mis. . . !
11. Marisela no tuvo problemas con el. . .
12. ¿Puedes caminar o te duelen las. . . ?
13. Cuando estudio por muchas horas siempre me duele la. . .
14. En cada año hay doce. . .

III. Respond to the following sentences using one of the expressions from the list. You may be able to respond in several ways.

¡Hombre! ¿Cómo te va?
A otro perro con ese hueso.
Sí, ahorita viene.
A ver. . . Todo está bien.
Buenas, Carmen.
A propósito, ¿cómo está Emilio?
¡Caramba !
Menos mal.
Cómo no. Adelante.

MODELO Usted va a tener que comer menos. → **¡A otro perro con ese hueso!**

1. Sólo subió un kilo.
2. Buenas tardes, Marta.
3. ¿Puedo entrar?
4. ¿Emilio fue a estacionar el carro?
5. El bebé es para la semana que viene.
6. ¿La acompañó Felipe?
7. ¿Cómo anda la presión arterial?
8. ¡Guillermo! ¡Mi viejo amigo!

IV. Complete the following sentences with the names of the appropriate months.

1. La Navidad es en _____.
2. Los meses de verano son _____.
3. Los meses de invierno son _____.
4. Las clases empiezan en _____.
5. Las clases terminan en _____.
6. Tenemos vacaciones en los meses de _____.
7. El mes que me gusta más es _____.
8. Los meses del año son _____.

HORARIOS
PARA NAVIDAD
La Candelaria informa
a su distinguida clientela que
para mayor comodidad en
sus compras de Navidad
abrirá sus puertas HOY
en jornada continua
de 8:30 a.m. a 5 p.m.
LA CANDELARIA
Los especialistas del supermercado

VOCABULARIO

nouns

el **alcohol**	alcohol
el **aspecto**	appearance
la **báscula**	scale
el **bebé**	baby
el **centro**	downtown
la **cita**	appointment
la **ciudad**	city
la **droga**	drug
el **embarazo**	pregnancy
el **enfermero**, la **enfermera**	nurse
el **esposo**	husband
la **esposa**	wife
los **esposos**	husband and wife
el **hueso**	bone
el **kilo(gramo)**	kilogram
el **mes**	month
el **perro**	dog
el **peso**	weight
la **presión**	pressure
la **presión arterial**	blood pressure
la **prohibición**	restriction
la **visita**	visit

parts of the body

el **brazo**	arm
el **cuerpo**	body
la **cabeza**	head
el **estómago**	stomach
la **garganta**	throat
el **ojo**	eye
la **oreja**	ear
el **pie**	foot
la **pierna**	leg

verbs

acompañar	to accompany
anunciar	to announce
bajar	to go down
bajar de peso	to lose weight
cuidar	to take care of
estacionar	to park
felicitar	to congratulate
probar (ue)	to suit, to agree with, to test, to prove
subir (a)	to get on, in
subir de peso	to gain weight
suponer (like **poner**)	to suppose

adjectives

arterial	of the blood
enfermo	sick, ill
mejor	better
serio	serious
solo	alone

other expressions

ahorita	right away
andar bien	to be doing fine (a person); to function well
¡a otro perro con ese hueso!	Go on! Forget it! Don't be silly!
a propósito	by the way
¡Buenas!	Hi! Good afternoon! Evening!
¡Caramba!	Christopher! Wow! Gee!

Los meses del año					
enero	marzo	mayo	julio	septiembre	noviembre
febrero	abril	junio	agosto	octubre	diciembre

¿Cómo le (te) va?	How are you? How's it going?
demasiado	too much
demasidos	too many
La cosa va en serio.	The thing is getting serious; this is for real.
menos mal	thank goodness
nada de + noun	no + noun, none of + modified noun
naturalmente	naturally; of course
necesariamente	necessarily
No está mal.	Not bad.
perfectamente	perfectly
tener buen aspecto	to look well, healthy
tener cita	to have an appointment

additional vocabulary

alguna vez	sometime
algún día	someday
algunos(-as)	some
examinar	to examine
humano	human
mayor	older, oldest
mejor	better, best
menor	younger, youngest
nadie	nobody
ni. . .ni	neither. . .nor
ninguno(-a, -os, -as); ningún	none
o. . .o	either. . .or
peor	worse, worst
la **selva**	jungle
tampoco	neither

ESTRUCTURA I

A. Indefinite and negative words

Yo **no** pido **nada.**

1. Indefinite words answer, in a general way, such questions as *what?*, *who?*, *which?*, and *when?*

2. The following chart contains important Spanish indefinite words and the negative words that correspond to them. Study the meaning and examples provided.

ENGLISH	INDEFINITE	NEGATIVE	
something / nothing	**algo**	**nada**	Hay algo para usted. / No hay nada para mí.
someone / nobody	**alguien**	**nadie**	Hay un puesto estupendo para alguien como yo. / Nadie me acompañó.

ENGLISH		INDEFINITE	NEGATIVE	
another (one) one (a person) some all	none	**otro** **uno** **algunos** **todos**	**ninguno**	El pan está rico. ¿Me das otro? Uno necesita bajar de peso. Algunos van a la ciudad. Todos están en el centro. / Ninguno de ellos trajo pan.
someday sometime at times always	never	**algún día** **alguna vez** **a veces** **siempre**	**nunca**	Algún día voy al Brasil. ¿Comiste alguna vez allá? A veces estamos preocupados. Siempre estaciono el carro aquí. / Nunca llegaste.
also / neither		**también**	**tampoco**	Manolo también lo conoce. / Yo tampoco lo conozco.
either. . .or neither. . .nor		**o. . .o**	 **ni. . .ni**	Quiero viajar o a México o al Canadá. Ni tu padre ni tu tío oyen bien.[1]

3. All of the negative words except **ni. . .ni** may be used either before or after the verb in a sentence. However, if the negative word appears after the verb, **no** is used before the verb.

negative word + verb	Nadie llamó.
no + verb + negative word	No llamó nadie.

When **no** is used, the sentence retains its negative meaning despite the double negative.

No compró nada.	He didn't buy anything.
¿No te gustan tampoco?	Don't you like them either?

4. When an indefinite or negative word referring to a person (**alguien, nadie, alguno, ninguno. . .**) functions as direct object, personal **a** is used before it.

No tengo que convencer a nadie.	I do not have to convince anyone.
No vimos a ninguno de ellos.	We didn't see any of them.
¿Llamamos a otro?	Should we call another (person)?

[1]If a verb follows **o. . .o** or **ni. . .ni,** it is usually plural.

5. **Alguno, otro, uno,** and **ninguno** may function as adjectives and show normal adjective agreement.

No puedo ganar ninguna plata.	I can't earn any money.
Algunos gobiernos son militares.	Some governments are military (ones).

Before a masculine singular noun, three of these words have special forms:

algún / **un** / **ningún** + masculine singular noun

No tomo ningún alcohol.	I don't drink any alcohol.
Algún día vas a ser doctor.	Someday you're going to be a doctor.

6. Note these final points about the use of indefinite and negative words: a) **Ninguno** is usually used in the singular; b) **Todo(s)** is not followed by **de;** and c) English *Me neither* is expressed in Spanish **Yo tampoco.**

No invitó a ningún amigo.	He didn't invite any friends.
Marisela estudia para todas sus clases.	Marisela studies for all of her classes.
Tú no quieres ir y yo tampoco.	You do not want to go and me neither (neither do I).

Aplicación

I. Para expresar en español

MODELO She studies some books. → **Ella estudia algunos libros.**

1. She's studying something.
2. She's studying with someone.
3. She's studying one of them.
4. She studies sometimes.
5. She studies also.
6. She either studies or sleeps.

II. Change the following sentences to the negative.

MODELO Alguien acompaña a Marisela. → **Nadie acompaña a Marisela.**

1. Algo molesta a Marisela.
2. Algún día Sandra va a tener un bebé.
3. Alguien llamó al doctor.
4. También vino la enfermera.
5. O la doctora o la enfermera entraron.
6. Alguna de ellas está en la oficina.

III. Change to a negative sentence starting with **no.**

MODELO Nada le interesa. → **No le interesa nada.**

1. Nunca voy al doctor.
2. Nada me duele.
3. Tampoco tengo un abogado.
4. A ninguno de los dos necesito.
5. Nadie me dice qué hacer.
6. Ni el doctor ni el abogado me lo dicen.

IV. Answer each question with a negative sentence.

MODELO ¿Va usted a llamar a alguien esta noche? → **No, no voy a llamar a nadie.**

1. ¿Va usted a salir con algunos amigos esta noche?
2. ¿Tiene usted algún problema?
3. ¿Ve usted algo? ¿Ve usted a alguien?
4. ¿Estudia usted o química o inglés?
5. ¿Va usted a ir a la Argentina algún día?
6. ¿Duerme usted en clase a veces?
7. ¿Va usted a salir o con Barbra Streisand o con Robert De Niro?
8. ¿No va a salir con Warren Beatty o con Jane Fonda tampoco?

V. Para expresar en español

MODELO No alcohol! → **Nada de alcohol.**

1. No drugs!
2. No food!
3. No wine!
4. No water!
5. No meat!

B. Uses of **por**

Repaso. The preposition **para** often translates the English word *for.* It is used to express destination (**para ti**), deadlines (**para las 9**), and disproportion (**para un niño de tres años. . .**).

Emilio fue **por** el carro.

Por also translates the English word *for.* But unlike **para, por** is used to express motive, movement, and means or manner. In addition, **por** expresses exchange.

1. Motive. **Por** expresses motive or cause for an action.

Sólo vengo a San José por la Dra. Ávila.	I come to San José only for (because of) Dr. Ávila.
Hice eso por ti.	I did that for (because of) you.

2. Movement. **Por** indicates movement through space or through time. It sometimes has the meaning *through.*

Anduve por las calles de San José.	I walked through the streets of San José.
Estuvimos en Washington por tres meses.	We were in Washington for three months.
¿Cuándo vas a ir, por la mañana, por la tarde o por la noche?	When are you going, in the morning, in the afternoon, or in the evening?

3. Exchange. **Por** can also mean *in exchange for, in place of, instead of.*

Dejé los estudios por un puesto en Caracas.	I quit my studies for a job in Caracas.
Muchas gracias por la copa.	Thanks very much for the drink.

4. **Por** is used in a number of set expressions.

ir por	to go for
pasar por	to stop by for
venir por	to come for

Aplicación

I. Express in Spanish using **por.**

MODELO For how long are you going to be in Costa Rica?
¿Por cuánto tiempo vas a estar en Costa Rica?

1. They walked down the street.
2. I did it for (because of) you.
3. They're coming for the boys.
4. Thanks for the books.
5. I'm there in the morning.
6. Marta spoke for (instead of) her dad.
7. She'll arrive in the afternoon.
8. No drugs, no alcohol for now.

II. Supply either **por** or **para,** as appropriate.

El otro día José pasó ___1___ nosotros muy temprano ___2___ la mañana. El tenía un viejo carro que le dio un hombre que se llama Juan el Honesto ___3___ $200. Parecía andar más o menos bien ___4___ un carro así de viejo.

Nosotros íbamos ___5___ el monte y ___6___ llegar íbamos a tener que pasar ___7___ toda una selva. En nuestras mochilas teníamos carne y pan ___8___ comer y agua ___9___ tomar. En el carro teníamos machetes ___10___ quitar maleza y matar víboras. Creo hablar ___11___ todos cuando digo que no teníamos nada de miedo.

Pero, ¡qué mala suerte! Una hora después de partir el carro ya andaba mal. Lo examinamos ___12___ ver si podíamos encontrar el problema. ¡Trabajamos ___13___ ocho horas! Cuando ___14___ fin vimos cuál era el problema ya era tarde y ¿___15___ qué seguir al monte? ¡Qué día!

III. Para completar

MODELO Ella fue al banco por. . . → **Ella fue al banco por su padre.**

1. Ellos andan por. . .
2. Salimos para. . .
3. Vamos a pasar por. . .
4. Emilio dejó una carta para. . .
5. Para una niña de tres años. . .
6. Este trabajo es para. . .
7. Sandra va a llegar por. . .
8. Él fue al banco por. . .

C. Verbs irregular in the imperfect

Repaso. All **-ar** verbs are regular in the imperfect (**pensaba, pensabas. . .**). All but three **-er** and **-ir** verbs are regular in the imperfect (**tenía, tenías. . .**)

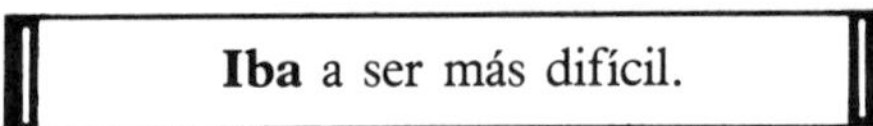

Iba a ser más difícil.

Only three verbs have irregular imperfect forms.

ir	ser	ver	
iba	era	veía	Yo iba a hablar con él.
ibas	eras	veías	Ibas a San José.
iba	era	veía	Emilio era su novio.
íbamos	éramos	veíamos	Éramos buenos amigos.
ibais	erais	veíais	Me veíais mucho, ¿no?
iban	eran	veían	¿Qué veían ustedes?

Note the written accent mark and pronunciation of the **nosotros** and **vosotros** forms.

Aplicación

I. Repeat each sentence changing the subject according to the cue.

MODELO Tú eras doctor. (yo, José) → **Yo era doctor. José era doctor.**

1. La veía los miércoles. (tú, las enfermeras, el doctor, yo, ustedes y yo)
2. Siempre íbamos al club. (yo, tú, Emilio, ustedes, María y yo)
3. Ella era doctora. (tú, yo, Marisela y Emilio, tú y yo)

II. Answer each question using **ser** first in the imperfect and then in the present tense.

MODELO ¿Es estudiante ella? → **Era estudiante, pero ya es profesora.**

1. ¿Soy estudiante yo?
2. ¿Es estudiante el señor López?
3. ¿Son estudiantes esos jóvenes?
4. ¿Es estudiante usted?
5. ¿Son estudiantes ustedes?
6. ¿Somos estudiantes nosotros?

III. Change the verbs in the following sentences to the imperfect.

MODELO Es la una de la mañana. → **Era la una de la mañana.**

1. Todos duermen. 2. Sólo yo trabajo. 3. Tengo sueño. 4. Pero sigo con mis libros. 5. —¡Qué chico!—siempre me dice mi padre. . . 6. . . .cuando me ve estudiar. 7. Pero nosotros somos gente fuerte. 8. Yo voy a la universidad. 9. Soy un estudiante serio. 10. Y me gusta trabajar.

IV. Answer each question any way you wish.

1. ¿Dónde estudiaba usted antes de entrar en la universidad? 2. ¿Era una buena escuela? ¿Le gustaba a usted? 3. ¿Eran buenos los profesores? 4. ¿Era usted un buen estudiante? 5. ¿Eran difíciles las clases? 6. ¿Qué hacían usted y sus amigos los sábados? ¿Adónde iban? 7. ¿Tenía usted muchos buenos amigos? ¿Quiénes eran? 8. ¿Los veía usted todos los días? ¿Todavía los ve?

Pausa oral

El cuerpo y los médicos

If you visit a doctor in a Spanish-speaking country you may need to use some of the vocabulary and phrases practiced in this section.

I. Para identificar

II. Para completar

MODELO A Pablo le duele la cabeza porque. . . → **A Pablo le duele la cabeza porque tomó demasiado vino anoche.**

1. Tengo que ir al médico porque. . .
2. Me duele(n). . .
3. Me duele la cabeza cuando. . .
4. (No) quiero tener hijos porque. . .
5. Es difícil bajar de peso cuando. . .
6. Mañana tengo cita con. . .
7. La cita es para. . .
8. Tengo muy buen aspecto cuando. . .
9. Tengo muy mal aspecto cuando. . .
10. Me gusta cuidar a. . .
11. Es fácil subir de peso si. . .
12. En la universidad no hay prohibiciones para. . .

III. Para conversar

Person A makes a statement and asks a question. Person B answers, using either of the two possibilities suggested.

PERSON A	PERSON B
1. Tienes cita con la doctora Ávila. ¿Estás enfermo (enferma)?	Me duele(n). . . / No me duele nada. Pero. . .
2. Marisela tiene muy buen aspecto. ¿Qué come esa mujer?	legumbres y fruta / Le gusta comer. . .
3. Emilio tiene muy mal aspecto. ¿Qué le pasa?	Está preocupado por. . . / Le duele(n). . .
4. El médico te encontró bien, ¿eh? Pero ¿qué prohibiciones te dio?	Hay prohibiciones para. . . / No hay prohibiciones pero. . .
5. Estás un poco enfermo. ¿Qué hiciste anoche?	Fui. . . / Estuve. . .
6. En el Paraguay buscan médicos jóvenes. ¿Quieres ir?	Sí, porque. . . / No, no me interesa. . .
7. ¿Por qué no puedes caminar más rápido?	Me matan. . .botas / Puedo, pero. . .
8. El viejo no oye bien. ¿Qué dice él?	le duelen. . .orejas / le molestan. . .cosas modernas
9. Siempre dices que no te gustan los médicos. ¿Por qué?	ganar dinero / muchas drogas
10. Estás muy bien ahora, ¿verdad?	muy mal / mejor

A. Comparisons (I): **más. . .que** and **menos. . .que**

¿Está **mejor** ahora?

1. To say that something is *more. . .than* something else, the construction **más** + noun or adjective + **que** is used.

Enero y marzo tienen más días que febrero.	January and March have more days (in them) than February.
Yo tengo más sueño que tú.	I am sleepier than you (are).
Marisela es más simpática que Olga.	Marisela is nicer than Olga.

2. To express that something is *less than* something else, use the construction **menos** + noun or adjective + **que.**

Mamá es menos terca que papá.	Mom is less stubborn than Dad.
La sesión de hoy fue menos provechosa que la sesión de ayer.	Today's session was less profitable than yesterday's session.

3. If **que** is followed by a personal pronoun, the subject pronoun (**yo, tú, él. . .**) is used.

La doctora Ávila sabe más que yo o que tú.	Dr. Ávila knows more than you or I (do).
Ellos tienen más dinero que nosotros.	They have more money than we (do).

4. There are four irregular comparative forms: **mejor, peor, mayor, menor.** They correspond to the following adverbs and adjectives.

bien well **bueno** good	**mejor**	better		Marisela está mucho mejor ahora. Vamos a brindar por un futuro mejor.
mal poorly **malo** bad	**peor**	worse		Tú juegas peor que yo. El primer mesero fue malo pero éste es peor.
viejo old	**mayor**	older		Paco es mayor que Elena.[1]
joven young	**menor**	younger		Ésta es mi hermana menor.

5. To express the maximum degree (the superlative) of any quality, an article (**el, la, los, las**) is used with an adjective in its comparative form. The article agrees in number and gender with the adjective and noun.

[1]**Más viejo** and **más joven** are used when the speaker is not just stating the relative ages of the two people, but is also stressing that both are old or that both are young.

Mi hija Liliana es mayor que mi hija Mariana. (Makes the point that Liliana is the older one.)
Esa mujer es más vieja que mi abuela. (Both are old but that woman is even older.)

Éste es el mejor año de mi vida.	This is the best year of my life.
Marisela es la mujer más simpática que conozco.	Marisela is the nicest woman I know.

Notice that **de** translates *in* after a superlative.

Es el chico mas inteligente de la clase.	He's the smartest boy *in* the class.

6. To express the idea *more than* or *less than* + any quantity, use **más de** or **menos de.**

Compré más de cuatro kilos.	I bought more than four kilos.
Tengo menos de doscientos dólares en el banco.	I have less than $200 in the bank.

Aplicación

I. Produce sentences containing a complete comparison with **más.**

MODELO un bebé / dar / trabajo / perro → **Un bebé da más trabajo que un perro.**

1. Emilio / estar / preocupado / Marisela
2. La doctora / ser / optimista / Marisela y Emilio
3. Un embarazo / ser / serio / todo eso
4. Los hombres / tener / problemas con los embarazos / mujeres
5. Los Rivero / querer / niños / sus amigos

II. Produce sentences containing a complete comparison with **menos.**

MODELO Marisela / tomar / vino / esposo →
Marisela toma menos vino que su esposo.

1. Marisela / estar / preocupada / Emilio
2. Esta doctora / ser / simpática / la otra
3. Marisela / estar / enferma / esposo
4. El alcohol / ser / malo / drogas
5. Los doctores / ganar / dinero / hombres de negocios

III. Respond to each statement in the pattern shown by the models.

MODELOS Esta clase es muy buena. → **La otra es mejor todavía.**
Esta comida está muy rica. → **La otra está más rica todavía.**

1. Esta situación es muy mala.
2. Esta muchacha es muy joven.
3. Ese señor es muy viejo.
4. Este muchacho es muy guapo.
5. Este vino es muy bueno.
6. Estos problemas son muy serios.
7. Estas clases son muy malas.
8. Estos estudiantes son muy buenos.

IV. Para expresar en español

MODELO There are more than a thousand people here.
There are more people here than before. →
Hay más de mil personas aquí.
Hay más personas aquí que antes.

1. I have more than twenty dollars.
   I have more money than you.
2. She has more than a hundred students.
   She has more students than Doctor Jara.
3. We bought more than three kilos.
   We bought more kilos than they.
4. He has less than fifteen books.
   He has fewer books than we.
5. You have fewer than five classes.
   You have fewer classes than I.

V. Answer each question by making a complete comparison.

MODELOS ¿Quién está más preocupado, Emilio o Marisela? → **Emilio está más preocupado que Marisela.**
¿Quién es la mejor estudiante de la clase? → **Sandra es la mejor estudiante de la clase.**

1. ¿Cuál es peor, un examen de química o un examen de español?
2. ¿Cuál es mejor, esta universidad o la Universidad de Madrid?
3. ¿Cuáles son más ricos, los anticuchos o los *hot dogs?*
4. ¿A usted le gusta más la comida americana o la comida mexicana?
5. ¿Cuál es peor, el alcohol o las drogas?
6. ¿Quién es mayor, usted o yo? ¿Quién es menor?
7. ¿Quién habla mejor el español, usted o yo?
8. ¿Quiénes son los peores estudiantes, los hombres o las mujeres?
9. ¿Quién es el mejor estudiante de la clase?
10. ¿Quién es el profesor más difícil de la universidad?
11. ¿Cuál es la mejor clase de todas?
12. ¿Quién es la mujer más inteligente del mundo?
13. ¿Tiene usted más de diez dólares o tiene menos?
14. ¿Subió usted más de dos kilos el mes pasado?

B. **Hace** + time

Hace seis meses que estamos aquí.

The third-person verb **hace** is used with expressions of time in sentences that correspond to several English structures: 1) *have been. . . ,* 2) *ago,* and 3) *How long. . . ?*

1. To express that an action has been going on or a condition has existed for a certain period of time, follow the pattern:

hace + time + **que** + present tense verb

Hace veinte años que vivimos en San Francisco.	We have been living in San Francisco for twenty years.
Hace mucho tiempo que no te veo.	I haven't seen you for a long time.
Hace una semana que Emilio está aquí.	Emilio has been here for a week.

2. To express the idea "period of time ago," follow either of these patterns:

preterit + **hace** + time *or* **hace** + time + **que** + preterit

Vi a Marisela hace un mes.	I saw Marisela a month ago.
Hace un mes que la vi.	I saw her a month ago.
Comimos hace poco tiempo.	We ate a little while ago.
Hace poco tiempo que comimos.	We ate a little while ago.

3. To ask the question *How long. . . ?*, use **¿Cuánto tiempo hace que. . . ?**

¿Cuánto tiempo hace que vives en Costa Rica?	How long have you been living in Costa Rica?
¿Cuánto tiempo hace que esperas a Marisela?	How long have you been waiting for Marisela?

Aplicación

I. Answer each question, using the information given in parentheses.

MODELO ¿Cuánto tiempo hace que María estudia? (dos horas) → **Hace dos horas que María estudia.**

1. ¿Cuánto tiempo hace que ustedes leen eso. (una hora)
2. ¿Cuánto tiempo hace que los Soto están en Centroamérica? (un mes)
3. ¿Cuánto tiempo hace que estamos aquí? (treinta minutos)
4. ¿Cuánto tiempo hace que ella espera un bebé? (cinco meses)
5. ¿Cuánto tiempo hace que ustedes vienen a este club. (tres años)
6. ¿Cuánto tiempo hace que espera a Marisela? (mucho tiempo)

II. Tell how long each person has been here.

MODELO María llegó a las dos. Ahora son las tres. → **Hace una hora que María está aquí.**

1. Juan llegó a las ocho. Ahora son las once.
2. José llegó a las diez. Ahora son las doce.
3. Los Soto llegaron el año pasado.
4. El señor Plá llegó en 1960.
5. Pedro llegó el mes pasado.
6. Usted llegó a clase hace media hora.
7. Ellos nos llamaron en julio.
8. La vi en agosto.

III. Answer each question using the information given in parentheses.

MODELO ¿Cuándo llamó? (diez minutos) → **Llamó hace diez minutos.**

1. ¿Cuándo llegó? (una hora)
2. ¿Cuándo estacionó el carro? (cinco minutos)
3. ¿Cuándo hablaron con el médico? (dos o tres días)
4. ¿Cuándo tuvo el bebé? (un mes)
5. ¿Cuándo vinieron sus padres? (cuatro años)
6. ¿Cuándo salieron los muchachos? (una hora)

IV. Restate each sentence starting with **hace.**

MODELO Lo vi hace un mes. → **Hace un mes que lo vi.**

1. Comimos hace dos horas.
2. Vinieron a este país hace treinta años.
3. Habló con la doctora hace unos minutos.
4. Tuvo el bebé hace tres días.
5. Encontraron donde estacionar hace un minuto.
6. Emilio llegó hace un rato.

V. Para expresar en español

MODELO He parked the car fifteen minutes ago. / He's been parking the car for fifteen minutes. → **Estacionó el carro hace quince minutos. Hace quince minutos que estaciona el carro.**

1. She studied an hour ago. / She has been studying for an hour.
2. He read that book a year ago. / He's been reading that book for a year.
3. I wrote this letter ten minutes ago. / I've been writing this letter for ten minutes.
4. We ate two hours ago. / We've been eating for two hours.

VI. Para contestar

1. ¿Cuántos meses hace que ustedes estudian español? 2. ¿Hace mucho tiempo que usted está en esta universidad? ¿Cuánto tiempo? 3. ¿Cuánto tiempo hace que usted fue al médico? 4. ¿Cuánto tiempo hace que el Presidente está en la Casa Blanca? 5. ¿Cuánto tiempo hace que yo llegué a clase?

VII. Ask your instructor five or six questions using a construction with **hace.**

MODELO **¿Hace mucho tiempo que usted trabaja en esta universidad?**

VIII. Ask another student questions using the **hace** constructions. Person B answers including **hace** in his or her response.

MODELO Person A **¿Cuánto tiempo hace que estás en el Club de Español?**
Person B **Hace tres meses que estoy en el Club.**

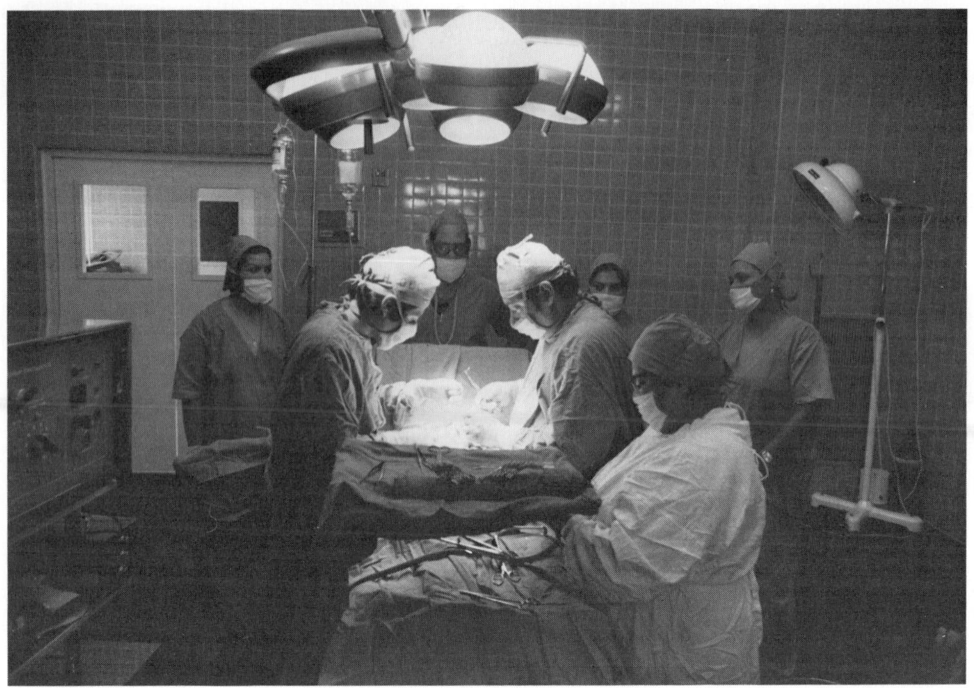

Surgeons at work at the Hospital Occidental, in Managua, Nicaragua.

 LECTURA

La medicina en Hispanoamérica

En Hispanoamérica la medicina está en una situación difícil. Por una parte[1], la mayoría de los pocos[1] médicos que hay dedican cuerpo y alma[1] a curar el mayor número de pacientes con la mejor técnica posible[1] y de una manera económica; por otra[1], la mayoría de ellos ejercen[1] la profesión médica en las grandes ciudades, en primer lugar, o en zonas urbanas no muy pequeñas, en segundo lugar. Son muy pocos los médicos que establecen sus consultorios[1] o clínicas en aldeas[1] remotas o en pueblos alejados[1] de la civilización. A consecuencia de esta distribución geográfica, millones de hispanoamericanos en el campo y en las montañas nunca reciben atención médica profesional, mientras que muchos de los habitantes de las metrópolis pueden ir a hospitales modernos y recibir buen tratamiento médico.

Por. . . On the one hand / **la. . .** Most of the few
dedican. . . devote body and soul
por otra on the other hand
practice

offices / villages / far away

Ahí donde termina la presencia de los médicos universitarios comienza la intervención de toda una brigada de interesantes personajes que practican la medicina de muy diversas maneras.

Las parteras[1] son las "ginecólogas empíricas[2]". Los boticarios—los propietarios de las farmacias de provincia[1]—recetan y dan inyecciones[1] con su semi-conocimiento de una ciencia[1] médica de segunda o tercera mano[1]. Los curanderos[1] usan toda clase de remedios; utilizan oraciones[1], encantaciones, hierbas[1] y muchas otras fórmulas y brebajes[1] mágicos. Estos paramédicos (los curanderos) son los más pintorescos; dan aliento[1] a los desesperados y psicológicamente hacen bien, pero la necesidad de obtener servicios médicos profesionales no desaparece.

No obstante[1], la medicina moderna es cara[1]. Los gobiernos de Hispanoamérica no tienen suficiente dinero para traerla a las zonas rurales. Cuando los productos agrícolas[1] produzcan[1] más dinero en el mercado internacional, y la economía de las zonas rurales mejore[1], los problemas médicos rurales se resolverán[1]. Mientras tanto[1] los campesinos[1] que necesitan servicios médicos no tienen otra alternativa más que unirse[1] a la masiva migración a las ciudades[3].

midwives
small-town pharmacies
recetan. . . prescribe and give shots / science /
de. . . second-or third-hand / healers
prayers / herbs
brews
dan aliento give hope

Yet / expensive

farm / produce

improves / **se. . .** will be resolved / In the meantime / peasants
join

In Taguales, Colombia, a government rural auxiliary nurse teaches the members of a women's organization to give shots.

Ecuador. A chief from the Colorado tribe explains the medical uses of various roots and shrubs.

Glosas

1. Some twentieth-century Hispanic physicians of note include the Nobel Prize winners Bernardo Alberto Houssay (Argentina) and Santiago Ramón y Cajal (Spain); Luis Agote (Argentina), inventor of a process to prevent coagulation of the blood used for transfusions; Juan Carlos Finlay (Cuba), the conqueror of yellow fever; and Marcelino Herrera Vegas (Venezuela), another pioneering researcher. Hispanic doctors often have interests in fields other than medicine—for example, the Spaniard Gregorio Marañón, a brilliant endocrinologist who was also a gifted historical and literary essayist; and Ernesto "Che" Guevara, Argentine revolutionary active in Cuba and the highlands of Bolivia.
2. "Empirical gynecologists," that is, women who have learned to help deliver children through experience rather than study in a school of medicine or nursing.
3. The massive migration of people from the rural areas of Latin America to the great urban centers has created monumental public-health problems for such Hispanic megacities as Mexico City (population 12,500,000), Buenos Aires (10,000,000) and Caracas, Bogotá, and Lima (4,000,000 each). The governments have responded by helping to set up hospitals and clinics, often known by perplexing **siglas** (acronyms) such as **ISSSTE (Instituto de Seguridad y Servicio Social para los Trabajadores del Estado** *Social Security and Service Institute for Civil Servants*). But none of the agencies, whether public, cooperative, or private, has the resources to provide adequate medical care for the ever-expanding belts of slum dwellings surrounding the megacities, which are the point of arrival for the migrants from the countryside.

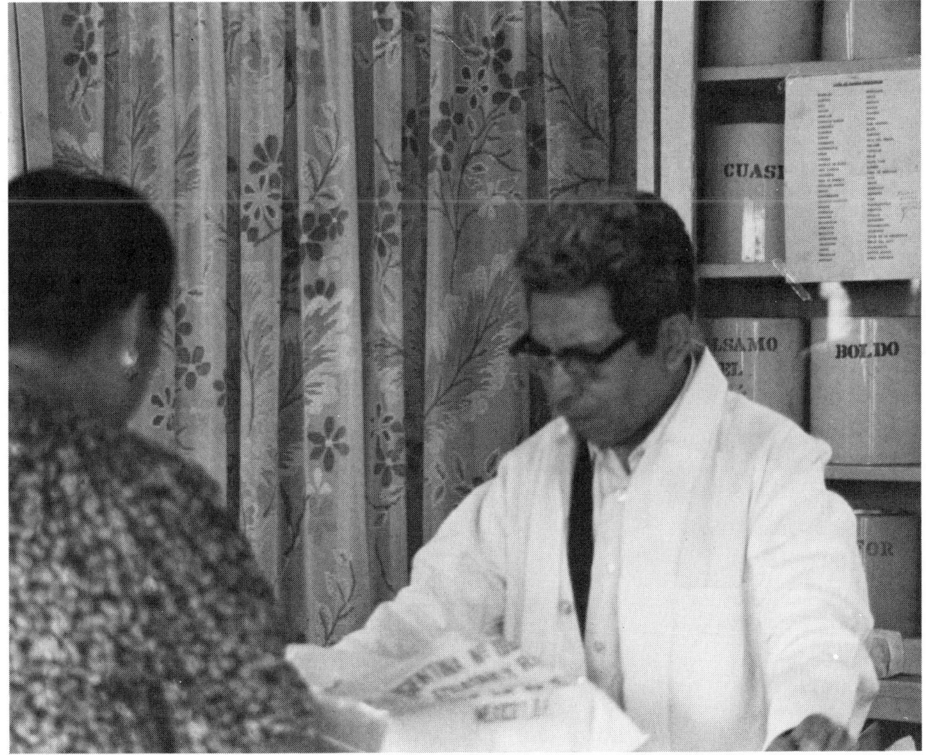

A **curandero** in his shop in Toluca, Mexico. **Boldo** is a powerful diuretic and **cuasia** is for the stomach.

SOBRE LA LECTURA

I. Para contestar

1. ¿Por qué está la medicina en una situación difícil en Latinoamérica?
2. ¿Por qué no reciben atención médica muchos hispanoamericanos que viven en el campo o en las montañas?
3. En los lugares en que no hay atención médica profesional, ¿quiénes ejercen la medicina?
4. ¿Por qué es difícil solucionar este problema?
5. ¿Qué hacen los campesinos que necesitan servicios médicos?

II. Debate

Is it more worthwhile to practice medicine in the country or in the city? Divide the class into two groups and debate the issue. Some topics you may want to mention are listed below.

ES MEJOR EJERCER EN LA CIUDAD.

1. el número de clínicas y hospitales
2. el equipo moderno
3. la concentración de personas
4. la posibilidad de ganar más dinero

ES MEJOR EJERCER EN EL CAMPO.

1. la necesidad de médicos profesionales
2. los boticarios y curanderos
3. la ignorancia de la gente
4. la satisfacción personal

Repaso oral

I. Una visita al médico

Imagine that you have an appointment with a doctor for a physical examination. Person A assumes the role of the doctor, and Person B is the patient. You may want to use some of the vocabulary and expressions listed below.

DOCTOR(A)	PACIENTE
Adelante	Muy bien (mucho mejor)
presión arterial	(no) me duele(n). . .
tener muy buen aspecto	. . .me prueba
dos kilos más (menos)	comida
báscula	subir (bajar) de peso
cuidar	el cuerpo
alcohol. . .drogas	prohibiciones

II. Para describir

Preguntas: ¿Quiénes son? ¿Dónde están? ¿Qué hacen? ¿Cuándo ocurre?

EMPRESA PETROLERA

Solicita para trabajar en hospital de clima cálido, médicos oftalmólogo, otorrinolaringólogo y urólogo.

Interesados enviar hoja de vida y sueldo deseado al Apartado Aéreo No. 6813 BOGOTA

Capítulo 10

Despegue

DIÁLOGO **Un negocio bien lindo**
Command forms (I) affirmative **tú** • (II) negative **tú** • (III) **usted** and **ustedes;** summary

PAUSA ORAL **Las cartas y el teléfono**
The preterit tense: irregular third-person forms • The subjunctive: regular present-tense forms; **ojalá**

Repaso oral

Despegue

la carta

Mandaron la carta por avión.

la escuela

Los niños van a la escuela.

¡Ay, bendito!

¡Ay, bendito! Vamos a volver a Puerto Rico.

Pronunciación

hay
hablaba
hacia

The letter **h** is not pronounced in any Spanish word.

dejar
trabajo
jueves
Germán

Spanish **j** and **g** (in **ge, gi**) are both pronounced like English *h*.

tía Amparo
¿Qué hay?
mucha experiencia

Remember to run together (but pronounce clearly) a word that ends in a vowel and one that begins with a vowel sound.

Aplicación

I. Para pronunciar

Pronounce very clearly the following words and word groups.

1. hay / hablaba / hacia
2. Mandaron la carta por avión.
3. dejar / trabajo / jueves / Germán
4. Los niños van a la escuela.
5. tía Amparo / ¿Qué hay? / mucha experiencia
6. ¡Ay, bendito! Vamos a volver a Puerto Rico.

II. Para contestar

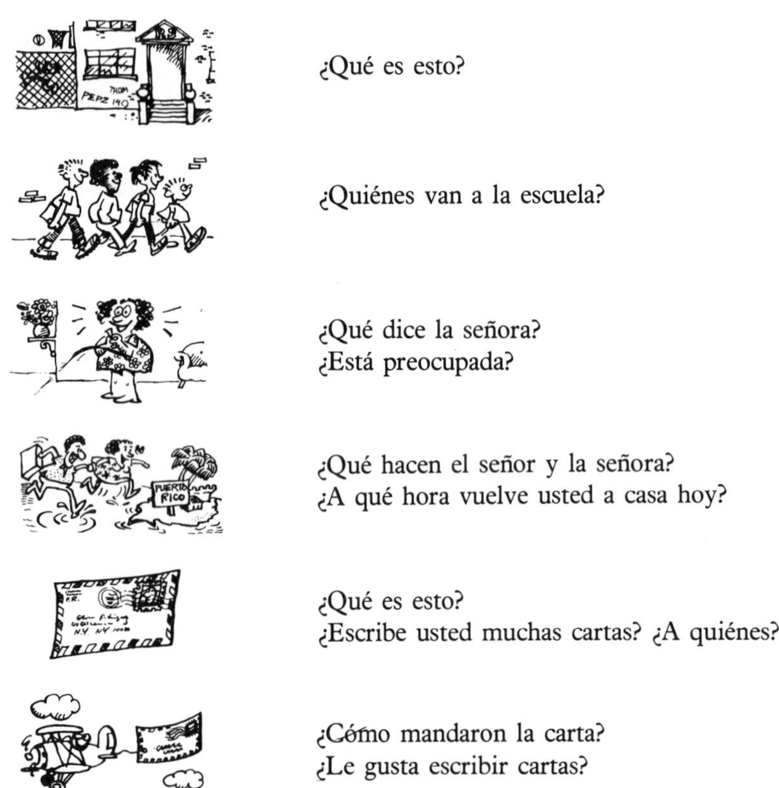

¿Qué es esto?

¿Quiénes van a la escuela?

¿Qué dice la señora?
¿Está preocupada?

¿Qué hacen el señor y la señora?
¿A qué hora vuelve usted a casa hoy?

¿Qué es esto?
¿Escribe usted muchas cartas? ¿A quiénes?

¿Cómo mandaron la carta?
¿Le gusta escribir cartas?

Tema del diálogo

Puerto Ricans can move freely between their island in the Caribbean and continental U.S.A. The choice often depends on personal commitments and economic opportunity.

DIÁLOGO

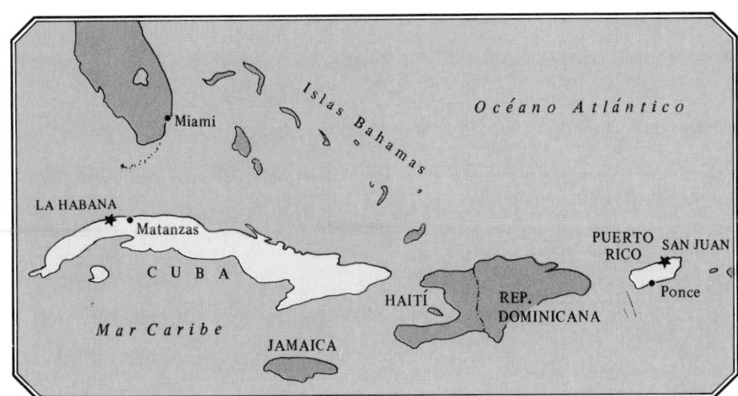

Un negocio bien lindo

Un domingo por la tarde Germán Rodríguez y su esposa, Adela, están en el Parque Central de la ciudad de Nueva York[1]*. Mientras sus dos niños juegan, Germán y Adela conversan.*

GERMÁN Oye, nena, ¿recuerdas la carta de tía Amparo que llegó el jueves?

ADELA Sí, mi vida. Pero no tuve tiempo de leerla.

GERMÁN Pues, escucha. Es una carta muy. . .

ADELA Espera un instante. Germancito le pegó al niño de la bicicleta. Trae a Germancito para acá.

* * *

GERMÁN Lo mismo de siempre. Problemas con los niños en el barrio, en el parque, en la escuela. . .

ADELA Ay, no digas eso. Ya viste que yo arreglé el problema de Rosita.

GERMÁN Es verdad. Pero luchaste seis meses para sacarla de "educación especial". ¡Y sólo porque no hablaba bien inglés![2]

* * *

(Adela, Germán, Rosita y Germancito empiezan a caminar hacia la estación del metro.)

ADELA Bueno, ¿y qué hay con la carta? Dime.

GERMÁN Fíjate que podemos volver a Puerto Rico[3].

ADELA ¿Vas a dejar tu buen trabajo del sindicato?

GERMÁN Calma, nena, calma. Yo bien sé que este trabajo paga muy bien.

ADELA ¡Ya lo creo!

GERMÁN Pero desde que murió tío Rafael la constructora en Ponce[4] anda mal.

ADELA Pues mira, sólo si te dan el puesto de gerente.

GERMÁN Así va a ser. Tía Amparo sabe que yo tengo mucha experiencia en cuestiones de construcción.

ADELA Ay, bendito. El nuestro sí que va a ser un negocio bien lindo.

GERMÁN Ojalá que todo salga bien.

A very nice business

One Sunday afternoon Germán Rodríguez and his wife Adela are in New York City's Central Park. While their two children play, Germán and Adela converse.

G: By the way, dear, do you remember the letter from Aunt Amparo that arrived Thursday?

A: Yes, sweetie. But I didn't have time to read it.

G: Well listen. It's a very. . .

A: Wait a second. Germancito hit the child with the bicycle. Bring Germancito over here.

* * *

G: The same as always. Problems with the kids in the neighborhood, in the park, at school. . .

A: Oh, don't say that. You saw that I settled Rosita's problem.

G: That's true. But you fought six months to get her out of "special education." And just because she didn't speak English well!

* * *

(Adela, Germán, Rosita, and Germancito begin to walk toward the subway station.)

A: Well then, and what's with the letter? Tell me.

G: Look, we can return to Puerto Rico.

A: You're going to give up your good union job?

G: Easy, honey, easy. Believe me, I know that this job pays very well.

A: It sure does!

G: But since Uncle Rafael died the construction company in Ponce is running badly.

A: Well look, only if they give you the job of manager.

G: That's the way it's going to be. Aunt Amparo knows that I have a lot of experience in construction matters.

A: Oh, thank God! Ours really is going to be a very nice business.

G: Let's hope everything turns out well.

VARIACIONES

¿Qué necesitas para escribir una carta?	What do you need to write a letter?
papel	paper
un lápiz	a pencil
una pluma	a pen
un bolígrafo	a ballpoint
una máquina de escribir	a typewriter
un sobre	an envelope
unos sellos	some stamps
¿Te escribió una carta Adela?	Did Adela write you a letter?
Sí, la recibí ayer.	Yes, I received it yesterday.
No, me mandó una bonita tarjeta postal.	No, she sent me a pretty postcard.
Me la mandó por avión.	She sent it to me airmail.
Me llamó por teléfono.	She called me on the phone.
No sé. ¿Dónde está el correo?	I don't know. Where's the mail?
¿Cuál es su dirección?	What's her address?
No recuerdo.	I don't remember.
¿Qué hizo Adela?	What did Adela do?
Repitió las mismas ideas.	She repeated the same ideas.
Prefirió ver televisión.	She preferred to watch (see) television.
Fue a la oficina de correos.	She went to the post office.

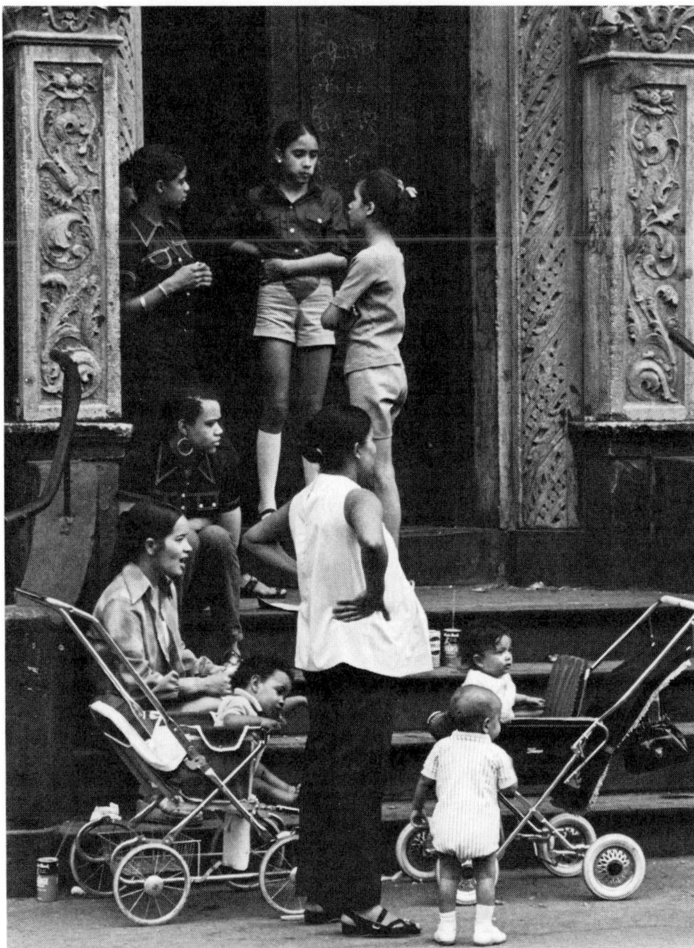

People from every Latin American country have made New York City their home, giving many sections of the city a definite Hispanic flavor.

Glosas

1. Of the approximately two million Hispanics living in New York City, about half are Puerto Ricans. The rest are Colombians, Cubans, Dominicans, Venezuelans, and smaller groups from other Spanish-speaking countries.
2. In the United States a disproportionate number of students of limited proficiency in English are assigned to special education classes on the basis of scores obtained from I.Q. and achievement tests administered in English. Many of these children would have different test results if the tests were administered in their primary language. In 1974 the U.S. Supreme Court ruled in *Lau vs. Nichols* that non-English-dominant students must be provided with an education that takes into account the linguistic and cultural characteristics of the student. Much remains to be done to realize that goal.
3. Since 1970 more Puerto Ricans have been returning to Puerto Rico than have been moving to the continental United States.
4. Historic Ponce, located on Puerto Rico's south coast, is the island's second largest city, with approximately 200,000 inhabitants. San Juan, Puerto Rico's booming capital, is located across the island on the north coast, and has a population of about one-half million.

SOBRE EL DIÁLOGO

I. Formulate questions that will elicit the following answers. More than one question may be possible for each answer.

MODELO (answer) En el Parque Central. →
(question) **¿Dónde están Germán y Adela?**

1. Ellos juegan.
2. Ellos conversan.
3. Llegó el jueves.
4. No, no la leyó.
5. El niño de la bicicleta.
6. Por seis meses.
7. Sí, lo va a dejar.
8. Sí, paga muy bien.
9. Murió.
10. Anda mal.
11. El puesto de gerente.
12. Va a ser un negocio bien lindo.

II. Respond to each sentence choosing one of the items in the list.

Sí, mi vida. / **No me digas.** / **Calma, hijo, calma.** / **Ya lo creo.** / **¡Ay, bendito!** / **Ojalá.** / **Así va a ser.**

MODELO Me dieron un puesto estupendo en Puerto Rico. → **¡Ay, bendito!** *or* **No me digas.**

1. ¿Me acompañas al parque, mi amor?
2. Seguro que todo va a salir bien.
3. Ana Vargas espera un bebé.
4. Nunca voy a trabajar para esa constructora. ¡Nunca! ¡Nunca!
5. El Dr. Salas es muy buen médico.
6. ¿Tú vas a ser el nuevo presidente del Club de Español?

III. Answer each question using the word in parentheses in your response.

MODELO ¿Cómo se llama la tía de Luis? (recordar) → **No recuerdo, pero creo que se llama Amparo.**

1. ¿Dónde están los niños? (parque)
2. ¿Van a seguir aquí en Nueva York? (volver a Puerto Rico)
3. ¿Qué puesto va a tener Germán en la compañía? (gerente)
4. ¿Va usted a llamar a Adela? (teléfono)
5. ¿Cuándo le llegó la carta a Germán? (recibir)
6. ¿Mandó su amiga una carta? (tarjeta postal)
7. ¿Va usted a mandar la carta hoy? (sobre)
8. ¿Quiere usted escribir algo? (pluma)
9. ¿Quiere usar mi pluma? (lápiz)
10. ¿Qué necesita usted para escribir una carta? (papel y una pluma)
11. ¿Dónde vive usted? (barrio)
12. ¿Cómo llega él a la universidad? (bicicleta)
13. ¿Necesita un bolígrafo para escribir la carta? (máquina de escribir)
14. ¿Dónde vive Andrea? (dirección)
15. ¿Necesita usted sellos? (oficina de correos)

VOCABULARIO

nouns

el **barrio**	neighborhood
la **bicicleta**	bicycle
el **bolígrafo**	ballpoint
la **carta**	letter
la **construcción**	construction
la **constructora**	construction company
el **correo**	mail
la **cuestión**	matter; question for discussion
la **dirección**	address
la **educación**	education
la **escuela**	school
la **estación**	station
la **experiencia**	experience
el, la **gerente**	manager
la **idea**	idea
el **instante**	instant; second
el **lápiz**	pencil
la **máquina de escribir**	typewriter
el **metro**	subway
la **nena,** el **nene**	(colloquial) sweetheart (*literally,* baby girl, baby boy)
el **niño,** la **niña**	child
la **oficina de correos**	post office
el **papel**	paper
el **parque**	park
la **pluma**	pen
el **sello**	stamp
el **sindicato**	labor union
el **sobre**	envelope
la **tarjeta postal**	postcard
el **teléfono**	telephone
la **televisión**	television

verbs

arreglar	to settle; to fix; to arrange
fijarse	to pay attention
fíjate	just imagine; look
luchar	to struggle; to fight
llamar (por teléfono)	to call (on the phone)
mandar	to send
mirar	to look (at), to watch
morir (ue, u)	to die
pagar (gu)	to pay, to pay for
pegar (gu)	to hit
recibir	to receive
recordar (ue)	to remember
repetir (i)	to repeat
sacar (qu)	to remove; to take out
volver (ue)	to return

adjectives

bonito	pretty
especial	special
lindo	attractive; nice; pretty

other expressions

ay, bendito	oh, (thank) God
bien	very
¿cuál(es)?	what?, which?
desde que	since
el nuestro	ours
hacia	toward(s)
mientras	while; during
mismo	same
lo mismo de siempre	the same as always
para acá	over here

por avión	airmail	**Yo bien sé**	Believe me, I know.
¿qué hay con. . . ?	what about. . . ?		
salir bien	to turn out alright		
tener tiempo de (+ infinitive)	to have the time to	***additional vocabulary***	
¡Ya lo creo!	I should say so!, It sure does!	la **clase**	type
		vender	to sell

ESTRUCTURA I

A. Command forms (I): affirmative tú

Espera un instante.

1. You may direct a command to a person you address as **tú,** to a person you address as **usted,** or to two or more persons at once—the sort of grouping you address as **ustedes.** A command may be affirmative *(Do this!)* or negative *(Don't do that!).*

2. The affirmative **tú** command is the same form as the third person present indicative.

él *(present indicative)*	**tú** *(affirmative command)*
él escucha	escucha (tú)
él trae	trae
él pide	pide

3. When expressing an affirmative **tú** command, the subject (**tú**) is used only for emphasis. Normally it is omitted.

Escucha, nena.	Listen, dear.
Cuida bien a tu hijo.	Take good care of your child.
Come mucho.	Eat a lot.
Prueba el vino.	Try the wine.
Habla más fuerte, por favor.	Speak up, please.
Sube a la báscula, Marisela.	Get up on the scale, Marisela.

New structures rise each day in Hato Rey and other communities in Puerto Rico.

Aplicación

I. Convert the following sentences into **tú** affirmative commands.

MODELO Germán escribe una carta. → **Germán, escribe una carta.**

1. Adela lee la tarjeta.
2. Jorge llama por teléfono.
3. Luisa compra sobres.
4. José juega con los niños.
5. Josefa espera a Pedro.
6. María piensa mucho.
7. Juan cuenta todo.
8. Roberto encuentra esas cartas.
9. Germán escribe una tarjeta.
10. Josefa trae el correo.

II. Tell another student to do the following.

MODELO Estudiar más. → **Estudia más, por favor.**

1. Leer el libro.
2. Escribir una carta.
3. Usar una pluma.
4. Buscar el correo.
5. Traer a un amigo a clase.
6. Hablar de un viaje.

III. Person A asks a second person a question. Person B answers with a **tú** command.

MODELO estudiar o dormir →
Person A **¿Estudio o duermo?**
Person B **Duerme.**

1. trabajar o estudiar
2. mandar una carta o llamar por teléfono
3. leer un libro o jugar tenis
4. hablar del amor o escuchar al profesor
5. caminar por el centro o visitar a Pedro

B. Command forms (II): negative **tú**

No **digas** eso.

1. In order to form the negative **tú** command of most verbs, start with the first-person (**yo**) form of the present indicative; delete the final **o**.

yo FORM	**yo** FORM
cenø	comø
piensø	pidø
cuentø	digø

2. Then, for verbs in **-ar,** add **-es.** For verbs in **-er** or **-ir,** add **-as.**

VERBS IN **-ar**	VERBS IN **-er** OR **-ir**
no cenes	no comas
no pienses	no pidas
no cuentes	no digas

No hables ahora.	Don't talk now.
No juegues en el parque.	Don't play in the park.
No me digas eso.	Don't tell me that.
No pidas más dinero.	Don't ask for more money.
No subas demasiado de peso, Marisela.	Don't gain too much weight, Marisela.

Aplicación

I. Change the following sentences to negative **tú** commands.

MODELO María, habla con ella. → **María, no hables con ella.**

1. Pedro, toma una Coca-Cola.
2. Juan, llama a Marisela.
3. Lupe, espera a los chicos.
4. Germán, busca la carta.
5. David, come ahora.
6. Jorge, pide más carne.
7. Sara, sigue con el trabajo.
8. José, piensa en eso.
9. Susana, juega con tus amigas.
10. Adela, duerme aquí.

II. The instructor will ask Student A a question. Student A will answer by directing another question to Student B. Student B will then answer with a negative command.

MODELO ¿Va usted a estudiar ahora? →
(A to B) **No sé, ¿estudio?**
(B) **No, no estudies.**

1. ¿Va usted a salir ahora?
2. ¿Va usted a hacer el trabajo ahora?
3. ¿Va usted a poner las cosas allí?
4. ¿Va usted a pedir más dinero?
5. ¿Va usted a decir la verdad?
6. ¿Va usted a seguir con el español?
7. ¿Va usted a cenar aquí?
8. ¿Va usted a comprar sellos?

III. Student A asks Student B a question. Student B answers first with an affirmative command, then with a negative one.

MODELO estudiar o dormir →
Person A **¿Estudio o duermo?**
Person B **Estudia. No duermas.**

1. trabajar o salir
2. leer o ver televisión
3. seguir con el español o dejar los estudios
4. mandar una carta o llamar por teléfono
5. pedir más plata o buscar otro trabajo

C. Command forms (III): **usted** and **ustedes;** summary

Escuche usted. **Escuchen** ustedes.

1. Commands directed to people you address as **usted** or **ustedes** have the same form whether affirmative or negative. To produce the form, start with the negative **tú** command and delete the final **-s.** For **usted,** add nothing; for **ustedes,** add **-n.**

tú NEGATIVE	**usted** / **ustedes**
no escuches	(no) **escuche** usted (no) **escuchen** ustedes
no digas	(no) **diga** (no) **digan**

While **tú** is rarely used after the informal command, **usted** or **ustedes** is often used following a formal command.

2. The following chart summarizes the **tú, usted,** and **ustedes** command forms, both affirmative and negative.

verb	person	command forms	
escuchar traer pedir	tú	**escucha** **trae** **pide**	**no escuches** **no traigas** **no pidas**
escuchar	usted ustedes	**escuche** **escuchen**	**no escuche** **no escuchen**
traer	usted ustedes	**traiga** **traigan**	**no traiga** **no traigan**
pedir	usted ustedes	**pida** **pidan**	**no pida** **no pidan**

Aplicación

I. Respond with an **usted** command in the pattern shown by the model.

MODELO ¿Pago la comida? → **Sí, pague usted la comida, por favor.**

1. ¿Llamo a Amparo?
2. ¿Mando la tarjeta?
3. ¿Ceno en el club?
4. ¿Visito a los viejos?
5. ¿Estaciono el carro?
6. ¿Escribo la carta?
7. ¿Leo el libro?
8. ¿Pido otra botella?
9. ¿Discuto el problema?
10. ¿Hago el trabajo?
11. ¿Digo la verdad?
12. ¿Conduzco yo?
13. ¿Pongo el correo aquí?
14. ¿Traduzco ahora?

II. Change first to an affirmative **usted** command, then to a negative command.

MODELO La señorita López toma más café. → **Srta. López, tome usted más café. Srta. López, no tome usted más café.**

1. El señor Alessandri paga todo.
2. El señor Soto manda la tarjeta.
3. La señora Pérez compra sellos.
4. El señor Pereda sale temprano.
5. La señorita Pereda discute la cuestión.
6. El señor Santos escribe la carta.
7. La señora Larra vuelve temprano.
8. La profesora García viene ahora.

III. Student A asks the question suggested by the cue. Student B responds with a **tú** command. The instructor asks a question. Student B responds with an **usted** command.

MODELO (comer ahora) →
A **¿Como ahora?**
B **Sí, come.**
Instructor **¿Y yo?**
B **Sí, señor, coma usted también.**

1. (mandar una tarjeta)
2. (mirar los papeles)
3. (sacar un mapa)
4. (volver a casa)
5. (escribir cartas)
6. (arreglar las cosas)

IV. Direct the following commands to the persons indicated. Use a **tú, usted,** or **ustedes** command form, as appropriate.

MODELO No tenga usted miedo.
a su hermano → **No tengas miedo.**
a dos amigos → **No tengan ustedes miedo.**
a un amigo de su papá → **No tenga usted miedo.**

1. Llega temprano.
   a su profesor de inglés / a su mamá / a dos señores / a mí
2. No diga usted nada.
   a dos niños / al doctor / a dos señoras / a un buen amigo
3. No vuelvas tarde.
   a su primo / a sus padres / a su abogado / a mí

4. Pide otra botella de vino.
   a los otros estudiantes / a su amiga / al contador / a mí
5. Pague usted esta vez.
   a su hermana / a tres amigos / al Dr. Gómez / a su prima

V. Convert the following statements into **tú** or **usted(es)** commands.

MODELOS ¿Por qué no piensas un poco más? → **Piensa un poco más.**
¿Por qué no dice la verdad? → **Diga usted la verdad.**

1. ¿Por qué no tomas otra copa?
2. ¿Por qué no estudian más?
3. ¿Por qué no visita a su familia?
4. ¿Por qué no sales ahora?
5. ¿Por qué no vuelve usted tarde?
6. ¿Por qué no compran sellos.
7. ¿Por qué no haces eso?
8. ¿Por qué no traduce la carta?
9. ¿Por qué no empiezan ahora?
10. ¿Por qué no traes los libros?

VI. Make up a series of five commands for the instructor to carry out.

MODELOS **Escriba usted algo.**
Diga usted cuál es su dirección.

Pausa oral

Las cartas y el teléfono

I. Para completar

Complete the following mini-dialogs with another person. Each refers to some type of communication (writing or calling on the phone).

PERSON A	PERSON B
1. Hoy tuve carta de. . .	Y yo tuve una de. . .
2. Esta tarjeta postal viene de. . .	Esta tarjeta postal viene de. . .
3. Me llamó por teléfono mi. . .	Me llamaron mis. . .
4. Necesito comprar. . .	Tengo que comprar. . .
5. Para escribir mis cartas uso. . .	Prefiero escribir mis cartas con. . .
6. No tuve tiempo de leer. . .	Yo no tuve tiempo de. . .
7. Me gusta llamar por teléfono a. . .	Yo prefiero llamar a. . .
8. Voy a escribirles a mis padres para decirles que. . .	Les voy a escribir a mis padres para decirles que. . .

II. Para contestar

1. ¿Es una lata escribir cartas?
2. ¿Qué clase de carta le gusta recibir? ¿Qué clase le gusta escribir?
3. ¿Cuesta más dinero mandar una tarjeta postal a Puerto Rico o a España? Y a México, ¿cuánto cuesta?
4. ¿Qué tipo de cartas escribe un hombre de negocios? ¿Y un diplomático?
5. ¿Qué clase de cartas escriben dos novios?
6. ¿Cuál prefiere usted, escribir una carta o visitar a un amigo (una amiga)? ¿Por qué?

III. Una carta

Choose either of the topics below and write a letter to someone. Using the past tense (preterit and imperfect), describe in your letter what you remember about either episode. Below each topic are some suggestions for inclusion in your letter.

FIN DE SEMANA EN EL MONTE

dos jóvenes y yo
caminar más rapido
tres horas de luz
la colina y las botas
el machete y la pala
una escalera y una pirámide
la mochila y el mapa
la cima
restos de un templo
¡Qué maravilla!

CARTA DE TÍA AMPARO

llegar el jueves
tener tiempo de leerla
poder volver a Puerto Rico
dejar el buen trabajo
pagar muy bien
la constructora anda mal
el puesto de gerente
tener mucha experiencia
un negocio bien lindo
¡Ojalá!

A. The preterit tense: irregular third-person forms

Repaso. The forms of the preterit tense may be regular (**pregunté, comí, escribí**) or irregular (**vine, tuve**). The verbs **ir (fui. . .)**, **ser (fui. . .)**, and **dar (di. . .)** are irregular in the preterit.

> ¿Qué **sugirió** tía Amparo?
> Tío Rafael **murió** el año pasado.

1. All **-ir** verbs with **e** → **i** or **e** → **ie** stem alternation in the present tense have an **i** in the third person preterit forms, singular and plural. All other persons are regular.

pedir	
pedí	Le pedí papel.
pediste	¿Qué me pediste?
pidió	Me pidió el dinero.
pedimos	Pedimos una botella de vino.
pedisteis	Pedisteis un mapa.
pidieron	¿Pidieron ustedes papel?

2. Some verbs which show the **e** → **i** change in the third persons are these:

	3RD PERSONS		
INFINITIVE	SINGULAR	PLURAL	
preferir	**prefirió**	**prefirieron**	¿Cuál prefirió ella?
repetir	**repitió**	**repitieron**	Pedro repitió sus ideas.
seguir	**siguió**	**siguieron**	Ellos siguieron muy optimistas.
sugerir	**sugirió**	**sugirieron**	Ustedes sugirieron otra cosa.

3. For two verbs (**dormir, morir**), **u** (instead of **o**) occurs in the third-person preterit forms.

dormir	morir	
dormí	morí	Anoche dormí ocho horas.
dormiste	moriste	Dormiste como un lirón.
durmió	**murió**	Marcos murió el año pasado.
dormimos	morimos	Dormimos en casa.
dormisteis	moristeis	¿Dormisteis bien anoche?
durmieron	**murieron**	Murieron hace seis meses.

Aplicación

I. Repeat each sentence, changing the subject according to the cue.

MODELO Yo pedí anticuchos. (él, tú) → **Él pidió anticuchos. Tú pediste anticuchos.**

1. Siguieron con el trabajo. (nosotros, ella)
2. ¿Qué pediste? (Sandra, nosotros)
3. ¿Sugirieron algo? (yo, el doctor)
4. Preferí volver. (los chicos, nosotros)
5. El perro casi murió. (yo, ellos)
6. Dormimos todo el día. (el estudiante, tú)

II. Answer each question in the pattern shown in the model.

MODELO ¿Pidió usted vino? → **Yo pedí vino pero él no pidió vino.**

1. ¿Prefirió usted salir?
2. ¿Sugirió usted eso?
3. ¿Siguió usted?
4. ¿Pidió usted plata?
5. ¿Durmió usted bien?

III. Change the verbs in the following sentences from the present to the preterit.

MODELO Prefiero estudiar. → **Preferí estudiar.**

1. Él no pide nada.
2. Sigo con el trabajo.
3. ¿Qué sugieres?
4. Los chicos prefieren jugar.
5. ¿Pides algo?
6. Los niños siguen en esta escuela.
7. El abogado sugiere esto.
8. Tú no duermes aquí.
9. Ese señor muere.
10. Prefiero dormir.

IV. Para contestar

1. ¿Prefirió usted salir o ver televisión anoche?
2. ¿Le pidió usted dinero a su padre la semana pasada? ¿Qué dijo él?
3. ¿Le contó usted sus problemas a un amigo? ¿Qué sugirió él?
4. ¿Comieron ustedes en un restaurante anoche? ¿Qué pidieron?
5. ¿Les pedí a ustedes mucho trabajo para hoy?
6. ¿Prefirieron Adela y Germán vivir en Nueva York o volver a Puerto Rico?
7. ¿Durmió usted bien o mal anoche?
8. ¿En qué año murió John F. Kennedy? ¿Y Martin Luther King?

V. Review all preterit and imperfect forms. Then rewrite the following story in the past.

Adela no está bien. Le duele la cabeza y no tiene ganas de comer. Su esposo Juan piensa que ella trabaja demasiado y que necesita pasar dos o tres semanas con su familia, que vive en un pueblo. Adela va al pueblo y pasa tres semanas en casa de su hermana, pero cuando vuelve a Santiago todavía tiene el mismo problema. ¿Qué le pasa? Nadie lo sabe.

Su esposo está preocupado. Él quiere hacer una cita para ella con el médico, pero Adela prefiere esperar. Dos o tres días después Juan sugiere una cita con el médico otra vez. Adela no quiere pero por fin dice que sí.

Juan acompaña a Adela a la oficina de la doctora Méndez. La doctora conversa con Adela y la examina. Después la felicita. ¿Por qué? Porque la doctora le dice que ella espera un bebé.

B. The subjunctive: regular present-tense forms; ojalá

Repaso. The indicative system, present tense, includes verbs that end in **-ar** (**cenar**), **-er** (**comer**), and **-ir** (**vivir**). Some are stem-changing (**pensar, contar, pedir**) or irregular (**tener, decir, ver**).

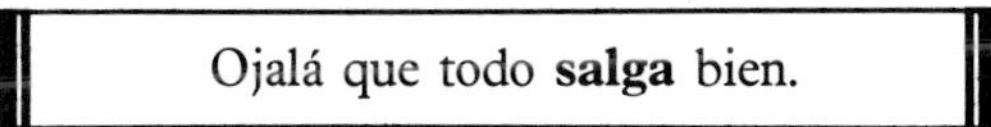

Ojalá que todo **salga** bien.

1. The subjunctive system is a special set of verb forms. This special set is used in statements which express a personal reaction of the speaker.

2. The present subjunctive forms are similar to the **usted** command form.

usted COMMAND	PRESENT SUBJUNCTIVE	
cene	yo **cen**	**e**
	tú **cen**	**es**
	ella **cen**	**e**
	nosotros **cen**	**emos**
	vosotros **cen**	**éis**
	ustedes **cen**	**en**
diga	yo **dig**	**a**
	tú **dig**	**as**
	él **dig**	**a**
	nosotros **dig**	**amos**
	vosotros **dig**	**áis**
	ellos **dig**	**an**

3. With stem-changing verbs, the stem-change appears in all subjunctive forms except the **nosotros** and **vosotros** forms.

yo	**piens**	**e**	yo	**cuent**	**e**
tú	**piens**	**es**	tú	**cuent**	**es**
usted	**piens**	**e**	ella	**cuent**	**e**
nosotros	pens	emos	nosotros	cont	emos
vosotros	pens	éis	vosotros	cont	éis
ellas	**piens**	**en**	ellos	**cuent**	**en**

4. One use of the subjunctive occurs after the expression **ojalá** *I hope, Let's hope.* The construction expresses a wish. (The word **que** sometimes follows **ojalá** but is not required.)

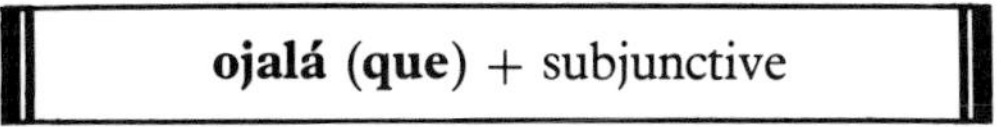

ojalá (**que**) + subjunctive

Ojalá cenes aquí con nosotros.	I hope you'll eat here with us.
Ojalá Marisela no suba de peso.	I hope Marisela doesn't gain any weight.
Ojalá que encontremos el metro.	Let's hope we find the subway.
Ojalá ellos no repitan las mismas ideas.	I hope they don't repeat the same ideas.

Aplicación

I. Repeat each sentence, changing the subject according to the cue.

MODELO Ojalá que vuelva. (nosotros, tú) → **Ojalá que volvamos. Ojalá que vuelvas.**

1. Ojalá que no hable. (el niño, yo, tú, tú y yo, los jóvenes)
2. Ojalá que llegue. (tú, nosotros, yo, el muchacho, las secretarias)
3. Ojalá que no pague él. (yo, nosotros, el profesor, los chicos, tú)
4. Ojalá que recuerde. (tú, ellos, yo, nosotros, el niño)
5. Ojalá que comas ahora. (mis hermanos, Germancito y yo, Alicia, tú y yo)
6. Ojalá que podamos seguir. (tú, él y yo, ustedes, yo, mi padre)
7. Ojalá que no conduzca él. (ustedes, yo, tú, ese hombre, nosotros)
8. Ojalá que lo haga. (ellos y yo, tú y ellas, tú, yo, el Sr. Rodríguez)

II. Respond in the negative using **ojalá.**

MODELO ¿Va a llamar Alberto? → **Ojalá que no llame.**

1. ¿Van a seguir ustedes?
2. ¿Va a empezar usted?
3. ¿Va a querer más postre ella?
4. ¿Voy a conducir yo?
5. ¿Vamos a salir ella y yo?
6. ¿Va a subir de peso Adela?
7. ¿La van a conocer ustedes?
8. ¿Va a morir ella?
9. ¿Van a volver los médicos?
10. ¿Van a tener miedo ellos?

III. Combine the elements to make sentences.

MODELO ojalá / María / recibir / plata → **Ojalá (que) María reciba la plata.**

1. ojalá / Marisela / bajar / peso
2. ojalá / comida / no costar / mucho
3. ojalá / contador / decir / verdad
4. ojalá / tío / no morir
5. ojalá / tú / dormir / bien / esta noche
6. ojalá / secretaria / traducir bien / carta
7. ojalá / yo / no tener / problemas / con la aduana
8. ojalá / médico / venir
9. ojalá / mamá / traer / al niño
10. ojalá / nadie / hacer / nada
11. ojalá / estudiante / seguir / con el español
12. ojalá / Juan / no sugerir / eso

IV. Respond to each statement with an original sentence using **ojalá.**

MODELO Germán tomó mucho vino. → **Ojalá que no le duela la cabeza.** *or* **Ojalá que conduzca otra persona.**

1. Mañana empiezo un nuevo trabajo.
2. Me van a mandar una carta.
3. Vamos a comer en casa de Alberto.
4. Vamos al monte este fin de semana.
5. Voy a pasar la noche en el Hotel María Isabel.
6. Van a dar una fiesta.

El Yunque rain forest overlooks one of the many perfect vacation spots in Puerto Rico.

Repaso oral

I. Para contestar

1. ¿Recibe usted muchas cartas? ¿De quién o de quiénes?
2. Cuando usted viaja, ¿qué les manda a sus amigos?
3. Cuando usted sale con un amigo, ¿quién paga, usted o él?
4. ¿Son muy fuertes los sindicatos en los Estados Unidos?
5. En su opinión, ¿son buenos o malos los sindicatos?
6. ¿Prefiere usted escribirles cartas a sus amigos o llamarlos por teléfono? ¿Por qué?

II. Para describir

Repaso 2

I. Verbs: Present tense and command forms

The present tense is the starting point for forming the commands in Spanish. First review the following present tense irregularities, and then review the formation of the command forms.

A. Present tense

1. Stem-consonant **c** becomes **zc** in the **yo** form; all other forms are regular.

   (conocer) **conozco;** (traducir) **traduzco;** (conducir) **conduzco**

2. Stem includes a **g.**

   (hacer) **hago,** (poner) **pongo,** (salir) **salgo**
   (tener) **tengo, tienes, tiene, tenemos, tenéis, tienen**
   (venir) **vengo, vienes, viene, venimos, venís, vienen**
   (decir) **digo, dices, dice, decimos, decís, dicen**
   (oír) **oigo, oyes, oye, oímos, oís, oyen**

B. Command forms

1. **Tú** affirmative command = **él** present indicative.

   escucha; vende, pide (tú)

2. **Tú** negative command = first-person (**yo**) form of present indicative; delete final **-o.** Then, for verbs in **-ar,** add **-es;** for verbs in **-er** or **-ir,** add **-as.**[1]

   no estaciones; no vengas; no comas

3. **Usted** / **ustedes** commands (affirmative and negative): Start with negative **tú** command and delete final **-s.** Then, for **usted,** add nothing; for **ustedes,** add **-n.**

   estacione(n); venga(n); coma(n); traiga(n)

[1]Some verbs require a spelling change when the ending is added.
a) Stem-consonant **z** becomes **c** before **e** or **i.**
   (empezar) empie**z**o → no empie**c**es
b) Stem-consonant **g** becomes **gu** before **e** or **i.**
   (llegar) lle**g**o → no lle**gu**es

Aplicación

A. Change each sentence to a command.

MODELOS Tú necesitas vender el carro. → **Vende el carro.**
Usted no necesita hacer eso. → **No haga usted eso.**

1. Tú necesitas llegar temprano.
2. Usted necesita empezar.
3. Ustedes no necesitan pedir nada.
4. Tú no necesitas esperar más.
6. Usted necesita oír esto.
6. Ustedes necesitan felicitar a mamá.
7. Usted necesita salir ahora.
8. Tú necesitas subir.
9. Ustedes necesitan comer algo.
10. Tú no necesitas leer la carta.

B. Choose two **tú** commands, two **usted,** and two **ustedes** commands. Make up a complete sentence for each one.

MODELO vender (tú) → **No vendas la casa.**

II. Object Pronouns: Direct and indirect

1. The following chart is a summary of the indirect and direct object pronouns and the pronouns used after a preposition.

INDIRECT	DIRECT	PREPOSITIONAL
me	**me**	(a) **mí**
te	**te**	(a) **ti**
le (**se**)	**lo, la**	(a) **él, ella, usted**
nos	**nos**	(a) **nosotros**
os	**os**	(a) **vosotros**
les (**se**)	**los, las**	(a) **ellos, ellas, ustedes**

2. When two third-person object pronouns appear together, the first one (**le** or **les**) changes to **se: se lo**(s) / **se la**(s).

Se la voy a mandar a tía Amparo. — I'm going to send it to Aunt Amparo.

3. There are two special forms used with **con: conmigo, contigo.**

Me gusta estar contigo. — I like to be with you.

4. In a sentence with an indirect object, quite often the object appears twice, once in its pronoun form (**me, te, le. . .**) and then as **a** + name of person or as **a** + **mí** (**ti, él, ella. . .**).

Le hablamos a Germán.
Voy a mandársela a ellas.

5. It is sometimes necessary to clarify to whom **lo, los, la,** or **las** refers. This is done by using both the object and the phrase **a + él, ella. . .**

   Míralo a él. Mírala a ella.

6. Pronoun repetition is always necessary in two cases:
   a) when **a** + object appears at the beginning of a sentence
      A ellos los vi en el parque.
   b) for the sake of emphasis
      Me vieron a mí ayer por la tarde.

Aplicación

Guided translation

Translate the following English sentences into Spanish. In each case, the model Spanish sentence given will help you with the basic structure of the sentence to be translated.

1. Nos quedan tres horas de luz solamente.
   They only have four maps left.
2. Mete la mano en su mochila y los saca.
   He put his hand in his backpack and took them out.
3. ¿A quién se lo das?
   Who(m) did you give them to?
4. ¿Qué le hizo a su aparato? ¿Por qué no lo usa?
   What did she do with the vegetables? Why isn't she using them?
5. A mí todo me gusta pero a ellos no les gusta nada.
   You (familiar) like everything but we don't like anything.
6. ¿Por qué no toma usted una copa y unas tapas conmigo?
   Why doesn't she have a cold beer with you (familiar)?
7. Me pareció excelente y a ella le pareció muy provechosa.
   It seemed excellent to us and they (feminine) found it very profitable.
8. Me duelen los ojos.
   Do your (familiar) feet hurt?
9. Adelante Marisela. ¿Cómo te va?
   Come on in, friends. How's it going?
10. Tengo que discutir esta carta contigo.
    Why don't you (formal) discuss your idea with me?
11. A Emilio lo vi esta tarde y se lo di.
    I saw Mrs. Avila this morning and I gave it to her.
12. ¿A usted qué le parecen los anticuchos?
    What do you (familiar) think of the pyramids?

III. Past Time: The preterit and the imperfect

A. When we use the preterit tense, we limit an action or an event to a specific point or segment of time in the past. A verb in the preterit can usually answer the question, *What specifically happened?*

B. When we use the imperfect tense, we convey an action or state as being continuous in the past. The imperfect usually answers the question, *What was happening?* or *What was generally true?*

Aplicación

A. Make the indicated substitutions. Be sure to retain the person and tense (preterit or imperfect) of the original sentence.

MODELOS Hablaste bien. (traducir) → **Tradujiste bien.**
Hablábamos mucho. (ir) → **Íbamos mucho.**

1. No caminó nada. (pensar)
2. Venían sus dos hijos. (ser)
3. ¿Encontraste algo? (ver)
4. Tú y yo nunca encontrábamos tiempo. (tener)
5. ¿Qué vio Guillermo? (saber)
6. Emilio y Marisela ya partían. (llegar)
7. Salimos ayer. (venir)
8. Esperábamos muchas cosas. (ver)
9. Mis tíos no vieron nada. (traer)
10. Marisela iba a la báscula. (subir)
11. Tomé un café. (pedir)
12. La veías mucho, ¿no? (cuidar)
13. ¿Quiénes te vieron anoche? (seguir)
14. Olga Velasco me dijo muchas cosas. (sugerir)
15. Estuvieron en casa de los Andrade. (dormir)
16. Yo no lo vi. (decir)
17. Federico Ovando llegó el año pasado. (morir)
18. No quisieron hacer eso. (poder)
19. ¿Adónde entraste anoche? (ir)
20. Le estacionamos el carro. (dar)

B. Read through the following narration, which is expressed in the present tense. Then go back and express the entire narration in the past, changing the verbs (but not the infinitives) to the preterit or the imperfect, as required by the meaning of the entire sentence.

Los dos novios

Es un viernes por la tarde. José Antonio espera a su novia Nancy; ella está en la clase de inglés. Por fin empieza a salir de la clase mucha gente, y allí está Nancy. Nancy y José Antonio quieren ir a una fiesta en casa de unos amigos. Van a cenar antes, pero como no tienen prisa, deciden salir a tomar una copa y unas tapas primero.

Entran en un café; Nancy pide una copa de vino y José Antonio pide una cerveza. Toman las copas, pero los dos todavía tienen sed. ¿Qué hacen? Pues piden dos copas más, por supuesto. Charlan de muchas cosas: de cómo la economía mejora cada día, de cómo un embarazo siempre prueba a a mujer, y de cómo el amor es universal. ¡Ahora sí que tienen hambre! Encuentran un restaurante que conocen bien y entran. José Antonio pide cebiche pero Nancy dice que prefiere comer anticuchos porque hace mucho tiempo que no los come. El mesero les trae una botella de vino blanco, y los dos brindan por el futuro. Después de cenar, todavía les queda una hora antes de ir a la fiesta. Van a un lugar donde Nancy y José Antonió toman dos copas de vino cada uno.

Nadie sabe qué pasa aquella noche porque Nancy y José Antonio nunca llegan a la fiesta. Pero un amigo me dice que los dos novios siguen juntos y que todo va bien. ¡Qué rico el amor!, ¿verdad?

Primera lectura sobre civilización hispánica

Los primeros hombres que llegaron al Nuevo Mundo cruzaron de Siberia a Alaska por el Estrecho de Bering. De Alaska los ancestros de nuestros indios se desplazaron por toda Norte, Centro y Sudamérica. Muchos antropólogos piensan que estos viajes entre Asia y América ocurrieron entre los años 18.000 y 14.000 a.C.; sin embargo, hoy día también sabemos que existe evidencia, descubierta en 1967 cerca de Puebla, México, que indica que ya había hombres en esa región desde hace 35.000 a 40.000 años.

Al principio, los primeros americanos se dedicaban a la caza, pero en México cerca de los años 7.000 a.C. aparecieron las primeras culturas basadas en la agricultura. Cultivaban el maíz principalmente. Al pasar el tiempo, estos primeros americanos crearon civilizaciones muy complejas. En la parte sur de Norte América y en Centroamérica, esta región que los antropólogos

crossed
Strait
moved
anthropologists / between
B.C.
however / nowadays
discovered / near
since
In the beginning / hunting
appeared
based / corn
mainly / As time went by
complex / southern

The Spanish Empire in America, showing the different viceroyalties in the 18th Century.

denominan "Mesoamérica", florecieron en diferentes épocas las grandes civilizaciones de los olmecas, toltecas, mayas y aztecas. En Sudamérica también hubo grandes civilizaciones; de estas civilizaciones es muy conocida la civilización incaica o de los incas. Los primeros europeos que llegaron al Nuevo Mundo, cerca del año 1.000 de la era cristiana, probablemente eran vikingos de origen noruego y viajaban desde Islandia y Groenlandia. Sabemos que llegaron a Nueva Escocia y a Nueva Inglaterra pero no dejaron huellas permanentes en el continente americano.

En 1492 Cristóbal Colón, el famoso explorador italiano, navegando bajo la bandera de Castilla llega a las Américas. En su primer viaje descubre San Salvador (Watling Island), Cuba y Española (Haití y la República Dominicana). En viajes subsiguientes en 1493, 1498, y 1502, Colón y sus tripulaciones españolas descubren las Antillas Menores, Guadalupe, Antigua, Puerto Rico, las Islas Vírgenes, Jamaica, Trinidad, la costa norte de Sudamérica, Honduras, Costa Rica y Panamá. Durante los siguientes noventa años (1492 a 1582) exploradores y conquistadores españoles se desplazan por las Américas. Por ejemplo: Vasco Núñez de Balboa descubre el Océano Pacífico y Juan Ponce de León llega a la Florida (ambos en 1513). Poco después, Juan de Solís explora el Río de la Plata en la parte sur de Sudamérica (1515) y Alonso Álvarez de Piñeda descubre la boca del río Misisipí (1519). También en 1519 Hernán Cortés inicia la conquista de México, concluida dos años más tarde con la derrota del imperio azteca, y unos diez años después Francisco Pizarro comienza la conquista del Perú que termina con la destrucción del imperio incaico en 1535.

flourished
Olmecs, Toltecs, Mayans, and Aztecs
there were
well known
1,000 A.D. / probably
Norwegian origin / from / Greenland
Nova Scotia / New England / traces (*literally,* footprints)
sailing under the flag
discovers
subsequent
Spanish crews / the Bahamas
northern coast
following ninety
both
River
mouth
conquest
concluded / defeat / empire
some

Hernán Cortés, Conqueror of Mexico, the most brilliant of the Spanish **conquistadores**, born in Extremadura in 1485.

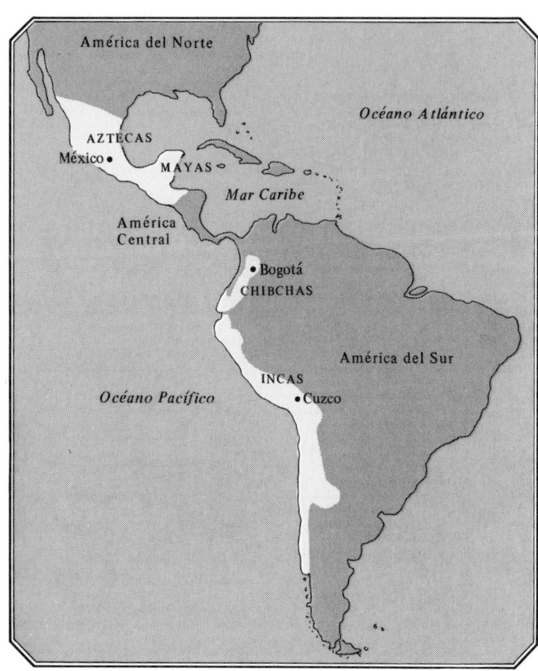

Areas where pre-Columbian civilizations flourished in the Americas.

Mientras tanto, otros españoles continúan explorando nuestro continente mientras España comienza a duplicar otras Españas aquí en el Hemisferio Occidental, comenzando con México (Nueva España) y siguiendo con el Perú. De los exploradores españoles más famosos deben ser mencionados Alvar Núñez Cabeza de Vaca, quien en 1536 llega a las costas de Texas y se interna, Francisco de Ulloa, quien en 1539 llega a las costas de California, y Hernando de Soto, quien también en 1539 descubre el río Misisipí en donde hoy está la ciudad de Memphis. También debemos mencionar a Francisco Vázquez de Coronado, quien en 1540 explora el sudoeste de los EE.UU., y a García de Cárdenas, descubridor del gran Cañón del Colorado (1540). Finalmente recordamos a Antonio de Espejo, quien unos cuarenta años más tarde explora Nuevo México.

exploring
while
Western / starting
following
must be mentioned
goes inland
Southwest
discoverer
remember

Y mientras la conquista y las exploraciones españolas se llevaban a cabo, otro fenómeno ocurría: la colonización. Sí, por medio de la colonización millones de indígenas se convirtieron al cristianismo y comenzaron a hablar español. Es decir, se "hispanizaron". Naturalmente esto representó un cambio muy drástico para los indios, y para la nobleza azteca y la nobleza inca—especialmente—significó la pérdida de todos sus privilegios y su poder.

se. . . were being carried out
por. . . through / natives / were converted / That is
they became Hispanic / Naturally / change
nobility
meant / loss

Miguel de Cervantes Saavedra, author of *Don Quijote de la Mancha, Part 1* (1605) and *Part 2* (1615).

España era una nación pequeña; América era muy grande. ¿Cómo fue posible hacer todo esto? Parte de la respuesta' es que los españoles tenían armas de fuego, armaduras, caballos y mastines'. . . cosas completamente desconocidas' entre' los indios. En parte, también, debemos comprender que, en el caso de México, los aztecas eran odiados enemigos' de otros indígenas mexicanos y, por eso, los españoles establecieron alianzas' fácilmente con los indios no aztecas. Además, Hernán Cortés llegó a México el año en que las profecías indígenas señalaban el retorno de Quetzalcóatl, un dios blanco y barbado'. Asimismo', en el Perú, Francisco Pizarro, aprovechando' una guerra civil' por la dinastía inca, capturó y mató a Atahualpa, el más legítimo sucesor al trono' de los incas, y en poco tiempo controlaba los destinos del imperio.

answer
firearms, armor, horses, and mastiffs / unknown / among
hated enemies
alliances
dios. . . white, bearded god / Likewise / taking advantage of / civil war
throne

Cada' conquista, pues, fue posible gracias a casualidades y coincidencias' históricas; sin embargo, aunque' las condiciones favorables al cambio siempre existieron, únicamente' cuando un individuo dinámico y arrojado' llega a explotar' estas condiciones es cuando ocurre el cambio. Es necesario recordar, además, que el español del siglo XVI tenía' una determinación sobrehumana' ante' dificultades y sufrimientos'. Hay que recordar, también, que con 800 años de entrenamiento' en las guerras contra' los "moros"', el español del siglo XVI era sencillamente' el mejor soldado' del mundo. Otra cosa es cierta también y es que el español tenía dos motivos que lo impulsaban': la propagación de la fe cristiana' y la adquisición de bienes materiales'.

Each
chance and coincidence / although
only
daring / exploit
had / superhuman / in the face of
suffering(s)
training / against / "Moors" (Moslem invaders)
simply / best soldier
drove / Christian faith
material goods

Acompañando' la tremenda expansión territorial de España, ocurre un fenómeno cultural notable conocido como el Siglo de Oro español'. Normalmente asociamos la frase "Siglo de Oro" con los años 1530 a 1680 en que la literatura, la arquitectura y la pintura'

Accompanying
Spanish Golden Age
art, painting

Lope de Vega, the most prolific playwright of Spain's Golden Age. To say that something was first-class, Spaniards in the 17th century would often say it was **de Lope.**

españolas florecieron en forma extraordinaria. Durante este siglo y medio aparece la novela picaresca', madre de la sátira moderna. Miguel de Cervantes (1547–1616) inventa en los personajes' de Don Quijote y Sancho una obra maestra' y la primera novela moderna. En el teatro', Lope de Vega (1562–1635) escribe unas 1800 comedias', y forma una nueva escuela dramática española con una docena' de dramaturgos' de excepcional calidad'.

En cuestiones de arquitectura, España produce dos estilos' distintivamente españoles. Uno al principio del Siglo de Oro—el plateresco—en el que' aparecen combinados' elementos clásicos y

picaresque novel
characters
masterpiece
theater
plays
dozen / playwrights / quality
styles
which / combined

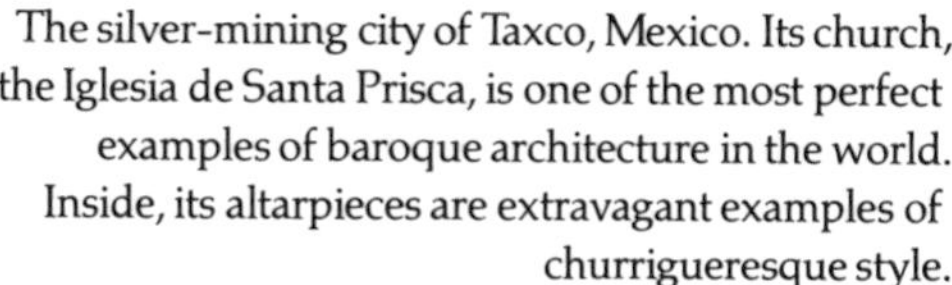

The silver-mining city of Taxco, Mexico. Its church, the Iglesia de Santa Prisca, is one of the most perfect examples of baroque architecture in the world. Inside, its altarpieces are extravagant examples of churrigueresque style.

Diego Velázquez, *The Surrender of Breda*, an incident in the wars of Philip IV in Holland.

góticos[1] con una ornamentación inspirada en el arte de los plateros[1]. Otro, al final del Siglo de Oro, es el estilo churrigueresco, una variedad del estilo barroco[1], en el que la libertad en los aspectos decorativos es tan[1] exagerada que, consecuentemente, produce formas de ornamentación extremas muy interesantes y bellas[1].

Finalmente la pintura española, después de recibir[1] influencias de los retratistas flamencos[1] y de los pintores[1] religiosos italianos, asimila genialmente[1] esos estímulos y produce artistas inmortales como El Greco (1584–1614), Diego Velázquez (1599–1660), José Ribera (1588–1652), Bartolomé Murillo (1618–1862), Francisco Ribalta (1564–1628), Francisco Herrera (1576–1656) y Francisco de Zurbarán (1598–1664).

Las obras[1] de estos artistas las encontramos en todos los grandes museos del mundo, pero especialmente en el Museo del Prado en Madrid. Una visita al Prado convence a cualquiera[1] de que la grandeza del Siglo de Oro español no es mito[1], sino[1] una realidad palpable[1]. Además, es el Siglo de Oro una de las grandes floraciones[1] del espíritu humano de todos los tiempos.

gothic / silversmiths
baroque
so
beautiful
después. . . after receiving
Flemish portraitists / painters
masterfully
works
anyone
myth / but rather
tangible / flowerings

El Greco, *View of Toledo*. Toledo, capital of Spain from 1085 to 1560, is so rich in cultural monuments that tourists with just one day to spend in Spain are frequently advised to spend it in Toledo.

SOBRE LA LECTURA

I. Para contestar

1. ¿Quiénes son los primeros hombres que descubrieron el Nuevo Mundo? ¿Cuándo llegaron?
2. ¿A qué se dedicaban los primeros americanos al principio? ¿Y después?
3. ¿Cuáles son las civilizaciones más importantes de México y Centroamérica? ¿De Suramérica?
4. ¿Quiénes son los primeros europeos que llegaron al Nuevo Mundo? ¿Cuándo llegaron? ¿De dónde vinieron?
5. ¿Qué regiones del Nuevo Mundo descubrió Cristóbal Colón?
6. ¿Quiénes son los primeros exploradores y conquistadores que vinieron al Nuevo Mundo? ¿Qué partes de las Américas exploraron y conquistaron?
7. ¿Dónde estableció España centros de cultura española?
8. ¿Qué pasó durante el período de la colonización?
9. ¿Cómo pudo España, que era una nación pequeña, conquistar un territorio tan grande?
10. ¿Qué es el Siglo de Oro español?
11. ¿Cuáles son algunas de las grandes obras maestras literarias que los españoles produjeron durante este período?
12. ¿Cuáles son algunas de las características del Siglo de Oro con respecto a la pintura y la arquitectura?

II. Discusión

¿Es la temprana historia de nuestro país similar o diferente a la temprana historia de Hispanoamérica?

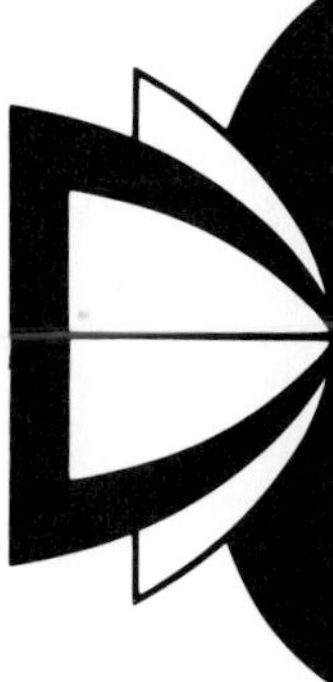

Capítulo 11

Despegue
DIÁLOGO **Una reseña**
Reflexive constructions (I): physical condition • The present subjunctive: irregular verbs • The subjunctive after verbs of persuasion and emotion
PAUSA ORAL **Comentarios personales**
Commands: irregular forms • Object pronouns + command or infinitive
LECTURA **La población hispánica de los EE.UU.**
Repaso oral

Despegue

Descripción del dibujo[1]

1. Mariana Portilla es una pianista cubana que dio un concierto en Chicago.
2. En el periódico salió una reseña (artículo sobre el concierto) que no era muy buena.
3. El agente de Mariana está furioso.
4. Dice que va a ir a la oficina del hombre que escribió la reseña.
5. Le va a decir que es un animal y que necesita clases de música.

Pronunciación

1. Mariana Portilla / Chicago
2. el periódico / un artículo
3. va a ir / la oficina / el hombre que escribió
4. es un animal / necesita clases de música

[1] *Description of the drawing.*

Aplicación

I. Relación[1]

Make as many statements as you can about the picture on page 251. Try to make at least eight sentences.

II. Para contestar

1. ¿A usted le gusta la música?
2. ¿Va a muchos conciertos?
3. ¿Es usted un buen pianista (una buena pianista)?
4. ¿Necesita usted un agente o todavía no?
5. ¿Siempre lee usted las reseñas que salen en el periódico?
6. ¿Piensa usted a veces que las personas que escriben reseñas son animales?
7. ¿Qué hace usted cuando lee una mala reseña de un buen concierto?
8. ¿Toma usted clases de música?

Tema del diálogo

A Cuban pianist and her agent visit the office of a newspaper critic in Chicago.

[1] *Report.*

Columbia Artists
presents
the internationally acclaimed piano virtuoso
Horacio Gutiérrez
"His virtuosity is of the kind of which legends are made."
—The London Times

Horacio Gutiérrez, winner of the silver medal in the 1970 Tchaikowsky piano competition in Moscow. He was born in Havana and performed with the Havana Symphony Orchestra at age eleven. In 1967 he became an American citizen.

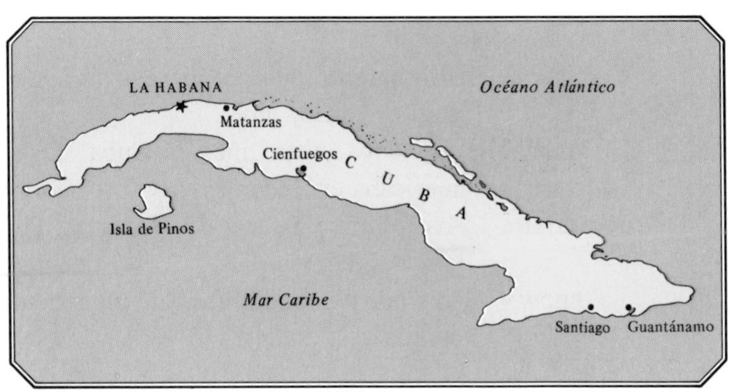

DIÁLOGO

Una reseña

Mariana Portilla, pianista cubana[1]*, y su agente, Edmundo Javier Pereda, reaccionan ante la reseña en el periódico sobre el concierto en Chicago la noche anterior.*

MARIANA Edmundo, quiero que te sientes y te calmes, chico.

EDMUNDO ¡Ese infame! ¿Cómo esperas que yo esté tranquilo? La reseña de ese animal me pone tan furioso. . . (Se pasea de un lado a otro de la sala.)

MARIANA Ven acá, mi vida. Dame el periódico.

EDMUNDO Ten. Ojalá vaya Brown a su oficina esta mañana. Le dejé un recado con la secretaria.

MARIANA Hazme el favor de sentarte y ponerte cómodo.

EDMUNDO Lo siento, pero no puedo. Tengo que ir a buscarlo. ¡Vamos! Ese tío necesita unas clases de música.

* * *

(Mariana y Edmundo salen a la calle, detienen el primer taxi que pasa y suben.)

MARIANA Ay, Edmundo Javier. Ya leí la reseña dos veces y no está mal.

EDMUNDO Es un animal. ¿Cómo es capaz de criticar tu interpretación de Manuel de Falla?[2]

MARIANA Bueno, pero el resto del programa le pareció excelente.

* * *

(El taxi llega a las oficinas del periódico. Los dos entran al edificio y encuentran el despacho de George Brown.)

EDMUNDO ¿Mr. Brown? This is Mariana Portilla. She. . .

BROWN ¡Qué coincidencia! Ahora mismo iba yo a llamarla por teléfono.

MARIANA (muy sorprendida porque Brown les habló en español): Pero es que usted es latino, ¿no?

BROWN Casi. Viví quince años en Cuba. Trabajaba con una compañía americana en Matanzas. . .[3]

MARIANA ¡Ave María![4] Yo soy de Matanzas. Pero dígame, ¿por qué me iba a llamar usted?

BROWN Pues porque quiero escribir un artículo sobre su carrera artística con fotografías y todo. . .

A Review

Mariana Portilla, a Cuban pianist, and her agent, Edmundo Javier Pereda, react to the review in the newspaper about the concert in Chicago the previous night.

M: Edmundo, I want you to sit down and make yourself comfortable, honey.

E: That scoundrel. How do you expect me to be calm? That brute's review makes me so mad. . . (He walks from one side of the room to the other.)

M: Come here, sweetheart. Give me the paper.

E: Here. I hope Brown goes to his office this morning. I left a message for him with his secretary.

M: Please sit down and calm yourself.

E: I'm sorry, but I can't. I have to go look for him. Let's go! That guy needs some music classes.

* * *

(Mariana and Edmundo go out to the street, stop the first taxi that passes, and get in.)

M: Oh, Edmundo Javier. I've read the review twice now and it's not bad.

E: He's a blockhead (an animal). How can he criticize your interpretation of Manuel de Falla?

M: OK, but the rest of the program seemed excellent to him.

* * *

(The taxi arrives at the offices of the newspaper. The two enter the building and find the office of George Brown.)

E: Mr. Brown? This is Mariana Portilla. She. . .

B: What a coincidence! I was just going to call her on the phone.

M: (very surprised because Brown spoke to them in Spanish) But you are a Latino, aren't you?

B: Almost. I lived fifteen years in Cuba. I worked for an American company in Matanzas. . .

M: Good Lord! I'm from Matanzas. But tell me, why were you going to call me?

B: Why because I want to write an article about your artistic career, with photographs and everything. . .

VARIACIONES

Hazme el favor de:	Do me the favor of:
ducharte o bañarte	showering or bathing
lavarte y vestirte	getting washed and getting dressed
acostarte y dormirte	going to bed and going to sleep
¿Puedes quedarte un rato más?	Can you stay for a little while longer?
No, debo irme.	No, I must leave.
Tengo que darme prisa.	I have to hurry.
No, voy a ponerme el abrigo.	No, I'm going to put my coat on.

¿Vas a comprar boletos para el concierto?
No, son muy caros.
Sí, son baratos.
Es una lástima que sean caros.

Are you going to buy tickets for the concert?
No, they're very expensive.
Yes, they're cheap.
It's too bad (a pity) that they are expensive.

Glosas

1. Many of the children who left Cuba with their parents during the first years of Fidel Castro's regime have become talented musicians, painters, and sculptors.
2. Manuel de Falla (1876–1946), Spanish composer of classical music. His passionate, often mysterious, impressionistic music, perfectly framed within precise classical forms, harks back to the **cante jondo,** or fatalistic deep song, tradition of the Andalusian region of southern Spain. *Nights in the Gardens of Spain, Four Spanish Pieces,* and a *Concerto* are among his works that form part of the standard international repertory for piano and orchestra.
3. Matanzas is a city in Cuba some 50 miles east of the capital, **La Habana.**
4. Familiar expressions in Spanish frequently involve a mention of God, the Virgin Mary, or one of a large number of popular saints—for example, **Ave María** *Hail, Mary,* **Dios mío** *My God,* **Válgame Dios** *God help me,* **Válgame la Virgen (del Carmen)** *May the Virgin* (of the miracle of Carmen) *assist me.* These expressions are reflections of the personal nature of the religious feelings and beliefs of the Hispanic peoples.

SOBRE EL DIÁLOGO

I. Choose the word that logically completes each sentence.

carrera, sienta, reseña, tranquilo, periódico, cómodo, prisa, abrigo, caro, edificios, despacho, boletos, lástima

1. Siempre hay artículos excelentes en ese ______.
2. ¡Qué frío! Voy a ponerme el ______.
3. Hay muchos ______ altos en Chicago.
4. Don Alejandro tiene un ______ en la calle Medellín.
5. ¿Leíste la ______ sobre el concierto?
6. Si no me doy ______, voy a llegar tarde.
7. Vas a tener una gran ______ como ingeniero.
8. Edmundo Javier está furioso. No está ______.
9. ¿Por qué no se ______ usted aquí, Mariana?
10. No hay concierto esta noche. Es una ______.
11. Voy a comprar ______ para el concierto.
12. El abrigo no es barato, es ______.

II. Respond to each of the sentences using one of the expressions in the list.

¡Qué coincidencia! / Casi. Viví veinte años en Guadalajara. / Lo siento mucho. / Me pone tan furioso ese animal. / ¡Ese infame!

1. ¡Yo también soy de Matanzas!
2. Brown criticó su interpretación de Manuel de Falla.
3. ¿Cómo? ¿Es usted mexicano?
4. ¿No puede usted acompañarnos al concierto? ¡Qué lástima!
5. ¡Ese muchacho siempre dice cosas tan feas!

III. Para contestar

1. ¿Quién es Mariana Portilla? ¿Y Edmundo Javier Pereda?
2. ¿Por qué no está tranquilo Edmundo Javier?
3. ¿Cómo van a la oficina de Brown, en el carro de Edmundo o en taxi?
4. ¿A Mariana también le parece mala la reseña?
5. ¿Qué interpretación criticó Brown?
6. A Brown, ¿qué le pareció el resto del programa?
7. ¿Por qué habla el Sr. Brown muy bien el español?
8. ¿Por qué iba Brown a llamar a Mariana?

VOCABULARIO

nouns

el **abrigo** coat
el (la) **agente** agent
el **animal** animal, brute
el **artículo** article
el **boleto** ticket
la **carrera** career
la **coincidencia** coincidence
el **concierto** concert
el **despacho** office
el **edificio** building
la **fotografía** photograph
el (la) **infame** scoundrel, cad
la **interpretación** interpretation
el **lado** side
la **música** music
el **periódico** newspaper
el (la) **pianista** pianist
el **programa** program
el **recado** message
la **reseña** review
el **resto** rest
el **taxi** taxi
el **tío** guy (*colloquial*)

verbs

acostarse (ue) to go to bed
bañarse to bathe, to take a bath
calmarse to calm down, to calm oneself

criticar (qu)	to criticize	**caro**	expensive
darse prisa	to hurry	**cómodo**	comfortable
deber	to have to, must, should, ought	**cubano**	Cuban
		furioso	furious
detener (like **tener**)	to stop	**infame**	infamous
dormirse (ue)	to go to sleep	**latino**	Latin, Hispanic, Latin American
ducharse	to take a shower		
irse (me voy)	to leave, to go away	**sorprendido**	surprised
lavarse	to get washed	**tranquilo**	calm
pasearse	to walk, pace; to take a walk, ride		
		other expressions	
ponerse (me pongo)	to get, to become	**acá**	over here
poner + adjective	to make + adjective; to become	**ahora mismo**	right now, this very moment
ponerse + noun	to put on	**Ave María**	my God (*literally,* Hail, Mary)
quedarse	to remain, to stay		
reaccionar	to react	**es una lástima**	it's a pity, shame; it's too bad
sentarse (ie)	to sit down		
sentirse (ie, i)	to feel	**hacer el favor de** + infinitive	please + verb; to do the favor of
subir	to get in (a car, train, etc.)		
		lo siento	I'm sorry
tener (ie) (tengo)	to take, to hold	**sobre**	on, about
vestirse (i)	to get dressed	**ten**	here, here it is
adjectives		***additional vocabulary***	
anterior	previous	**cortarse**	to cut oneself
artístico	artistic	**dejar**	to let, to allow
barato	cheap	**despertarse (ie)**	to wake up
capaz	capable	el **tráfico**	traffic

ESTRUCTURA I

A. Reflexive constructions (I): physical condition

Siéntate por favor y **cálmate,** chico.

1. A reflexive pronoun in Spanish is an object pronoun that refers to the same person as the subject: **Me corto** *I cut myself.*

2. Reflexive constructions often describe some type of change in the physical or mental condition of the subject. The use of a reflexive pronoun with the verb relates the indicated change directly to the subject.

REFLEXIVE PRONOUNS		
me	*myself*	Me siento
te	*yourself*	Te sientas.
se	*herself (him-, your-, itself)*	Se sienta.
nos	*ourselves*	Nos sentamos.
os	*yourselves*	Os sentáis.
se	*themselves (yourselves)*	Se sientan.

3. The verbs that follow are all used with a reflexive pronoun to convey some type of physical change in the subject.

acostarse (ue)	*to go to bed*	Siempre me acuesto temprano.
bañarse	*to take a bath*	¿Te bañaste ya?
calmarse	*to calm down*	¡Cálmate, chico!
cortarse	*to cut oneself*	¿Se cortó usted la mano?
darse prisa	*to hurry up*	Vamos a darnos prisa.
despertarse (ie)	*to wake up*	Ellos se despertaron a las 8.
dormirse (ue)	*to fall asleep*	¿A qué hora se durmió la niña?
ducharse	*to take a shower*	Me duché esta mañana.
irse	*to go away*	¿Ya se va usted?
lavarse	*to wash oneself*	¿Te lavaste?
levantarse	*to get up*	Ojalá nos levantemos temprano.
llamarse	*to be named*	Me llamo Edmundo.
morirse (ue, u) (de)	*to die (of)*	Ellos se murieron de frío.
pasearse	*to walk (around)*	Nos paseamos mucho en el parque.
ponerse	*to put (clothing)*	Mariana se pone el abrigo.
	on; to get (+ adjective)	Mariana se puso furiosa.
quedarse	*to remain, to stay*	¿Te quedas aquí conmigo?
quitarse	*to take off (clothing)*	Se quitó el abrigo.
sentarse (ie)	*to sit down*	El pianista se sentó.
sentirse (ie, i)	*to feel*	¿Te sientes mal?
vestirse (i)	*to get dressed*	Nos vestimos muy rápido.

4. A few verbs that are used reflexively in Spanish may also be used reflexively in English: **cortarse** *to cut oneself.* However, many verbs used reflexively in Spanish are not used this way in English: **despertarse** *to wake up.*

5. The following chart is a summary of reflexive, indirect object, and direct object pronouns.

REFLEXIVE	INDIRECT	DIRECT
me	me	me
te	te	te
se	le (se)	lo, la
nos	nos	nos
os	os	os
se	les (se)	los, las

REFLEXIVE

Me siento aquí.	I'll sit down here.
Te fuiste temprano.	You left early.
Mamá se puso furiosa.	Mom got furious.

INDIRECT

Me hablaron por teléfono.	They spoke to me on the phone.
Te dimos el dinero, ¿no?	We gave you the money, right?
Le vamos a escribir ahora.	We're going to write to you (her, him) now.

DIRECT

Me dejó aquí.	He (you, she) left me here.
Te buscamos esta mañana.	We looked for you this morning.
A mis hermanas casi nunca las veo.	I almost never see my sisters.

Aplicación

I. Change the subject and verb form as indicated.

MODELO Me siento aquí. (él, nosotros) → **Se sienta aquí. Nos sentamos aquí.**

1. ¿Me baño ahora? (los niños, tú, nosotros, él, yo)
2. ¿Cuándo se viste? (tú, tú y yo, Mariana, ustedes, él)
3. Si no me doy prisa, llego tarde. (tú, ellas, usted, nosotros)
4. ¿Te quedas o te vas? (ustedes, yo, los chicos, nosotros, tú)
5. Siempre nos acostamos temprano. (yo, tú, mis padres, la familia)

II. Answer each question using **ya** + preterit tense.

MODELO Pero ¿cuándo vas a bañarte? → **Cálmate, chico. Ya me bañé.**

1. Pero ¿cuándo va a acostarse el niño?
2. Pero ¿cuándo vas a ducharte?
3. Pero ¿cuándo va a sentarse ella?
4. Pero ¿cuándo va a vestirse Mariana?
5. Pero ¿cuándo van a lavarse las manos ustedes?
6. Pero, ¿cuándo vas a quitarte el abrigo?

III. Tell what you do in the morning. Use as many of the following expressions as you can, and add any additional words you need.

MODELO despertarse a las 6 → **Me despierto a las 6 pero me levanto a las 6 y media.**

1. despertarse a las 7
2. levantarse temprano
3. ducharse
4. lavarse
5. vestirse
6. ponerse el abrigo
7. darse prisa
8. pasearse con los amigos

IV. Pronoun Review

Restate each sentence directing it to a person you address as **usted.**

MODELOS Te vas temprano. → **Se va temprano.**
Te escriben cartas. → **Le escriben cartas.**
Te buscan ahora, Edmundo. → **Lo buscan ahora, Edmundo.**

1. Te sientas aquí.
2. Te llaman por teléfono.
3. Te dieron el dinero.
4. Te pones furioso.
5. Te sirven el vino.
6. Te levantas y te vas.
7. ¿Dónde te dejó, Mariana?
8. Te hablan en español.

V. Para contestar

1. ¿Se siente usted preocupado (preocupada) antes de un examen? ¿Se calma después?
2. ¿Se quedan ustedes aquí durante las vacaciones o se van?
3. ¿Se acuestan tarde o temprano los estudiantes?
4. ¿Dónde se sienta usted en esta clase? ¿Dónde me siento yo?
5. ¿Cuándo se pasean ustedes? ¿Dónde se pasean?
6. ¿Se pone usted furioso a veces? ¿Cuándo?

B. The present subjunctive: irregular verbs

Ojalá **vaya** Brown a su oficina.

1. Six verbs in Spanish have irregular present subjunctive forms.

dar	**estar**
dé	esté
des	estés
dé	esté
demos	estemos
deis	estéis
den	estén

ir	**haber**
vaya	haya
vayas	hayas
vaya	haya
vayamos	hayamos
vayáis	hayáis
vayan	hayan

ser	**saber**
sea	sepa
seas	sepas
sea	sepa
seamos	sepamos
seáis	sepáis
sean	sepan

Ojalá alguien me dé plata.	I hope someone gives me money.
Ojalá que estés cómodo.	I hope that you're comfortable.
Ojalá que vayamos al concierto.	I hope we go to the concert.
Ojalá no haya más problemas.	I hope there aren't any more problems.
Ojalá sea un negocio bien lindo.	I hope it will be a very fine business.
Ojalá mis padres no sepan la verdad.	I hope my parents don't know the truth.

2. In addition, all **-ir** verbs with **o** or **e** in their stems have the change **o** → **u** or **e** → **i** in the **nosotros** (and **vosotros**) form of the present subjunctive.

Ojalá durmamos tranquilos.	I hope we sleep peacefully.
Ojalá nos sintamos mejor mañana.	I hope we'll be feeling better tomorrow.
Ojalá no nos muramos de calor.	I hope we don't roast.

Aplicación

I. Supply the correct subjunctive form of the verbs listed in the key.

ANA: Ojalá que __1__ boletos para el concierto.
EVA: Y ojalá que no __2__ muy caros.
ANA: Espero que papá me __3__ plata.
EVA: Ojalá que todos __4__ aquí a las siete, porque si llegamos tarde, va a ser imposible comprar boletos.
ANA: Sí, y que nosotros __5__ un taxi, y que el hombre __6__ adónde llevarnos.
EVA: Y que no __7__ por el centro, porque en el centro siempre hay mucho tráfico.
ANA: Espero que todo __8__ bien y que no nos __9__ de frío.
EVA: ¡Y que no nos __10__ en el concierto!

1. haber
2. ser
3. dar
4. estar
5. encontrar
6. saber
7. ir
8. salir
9. morir
10. dormir

II. Answer each question using **No sé** and **ojalá** + subjunctive.

MODELO ¿Estudian los chicos ahora? → **No sé; ojalá que estudien.**

1. ¿Va Mariana al concierto?
2. ¿Están en casa ahora?
3. ¿Hay boletos para todos?
4. ¿Saben llegar al despacho?
5. ¿Dan precios especiales para los estudiantes?
6. ¿Se duermen ustedes en los conciertos?

III. Answer each question using **ojalá** + **no** + subjunctive.

MODELO ¿Y si se duermen ustedes en clase? → **Ojalá que no nos durmamos en clase.**

1. ¿Y si saben ellos la verdad?
2. ¿Y si hay mucha gente allí?
3. ¿Y si se sienten ustedes mal?
4. ¿Y si se mueren ustedes de sueño?
5. ¿Y si es usted demasiado optimista?
6. ¿Y si estoy aquí a esa hora?
7. ¿Y si van ellos al centro?
8. ¿Y si tú das una fiesta?

C. The subjunctive after verbs of persuasion and emotion

> Quiero que **te sientes** y **te calmes,** chico.
> Es una lástima que **sean** caros.

1. Most sentences that contain a verb in the subjunctive have these characteristics: a) they contain two separate parts or clauses joined by **que;** b) each of the two clauses has a different subject and verb; and c) the subjunctive appears in the second clause only.

   > subject one + indicative + **que** + subject two + subjunctive

2. Not all sentences that include two clauses contain a verb in the subjunctive. The subjunctive form is used in the *subordinate* (dependent) clause when the verb in the *main* clause expresses a personal reaction of some kind to the subordinate statement. Typical examples are when the main clause expresses the desire of its subject to persuade or influence another person; when it expresses emotion on the part of the subject; or when it expresses the subject's reservation or doubt.

3. The following verbs express suasion.

dejar	to let, to allow	**sugerir**	to suggest
pedir	to ask	**querer**	to want

No dejo que Germancito vaya al parque.	I don't allow Germancito to go to the park.
Le pido que se dé prisa.	I ask you to hurry up.
¿Me sugieres que vaya a su despacho?	Are you suggesting that I go to his office?
Queremos que usted lea el periódico.	We want you to read the newspaper.

4. The following verbs express various kinds of emotion. When they are used to express a personal reaction to an event or an action performed by someone else, they are followed by a clause in which the subjunctive is used.

esperar	to hope, to expect	**sentir**	to be sorry
gustar	to be pleasing to, to like	**tener miedo**	to be afraid
necesitar	to need		

Necesito que alguien se quede conmigo.	I need for someone to stay with me.
Ellos esperan que yo llegue el jueves.	They expect me to arrive on Thursday.
¿Te gusta que los niños jueguen en la calle?	Do you like the kids to play in the street?
Él siente que haya tantos problemas.	He is sorry there are so many problems.
¿Tienen miedo ustedes que no sepamos nada?	Are you people afraid that we don't know anything?

5. Verbs that do not fall into the categories mentioned above, that is, verbs that do *not* express a personal reaction or doubt, are followed by the *indicative* in the subordinate clause.

Me cuentan que las reseñas son estupendas.	They tell me the reviews are terrific.
Creo que están aquí.	I think they're here.

6. An impersonal expression is one that has no definite subject. Many impersonal expressions are formed by using **ser** or **parecer** + adjective or, occasionally, a noun. A few common impersonal expressions are the following.

Es posible
Es probable
Es necesario
Es mejor
Es una lástima

When impersonal expressions are followed by a subordinate clause, the verb of this clause is nearly always in the subjunctive.[1]

Es mejor que nos vayamos.	It's better that we leave.
Es posible que haya más cartas.	It is possible there are more letters.
No es probable que se queden aquí.	It's not probable they will stay here.
Es necesario que leas el periódico.	It is necessary for you to read the paper.
Es una lástima que yo tenga que salir.	It is too bad I have to go out.

7. When a sentence has just one subject, do not use a second verb in the subjunctive. Use an infinitive instead, and omit **que.**

No quiero estudiar esta noche.	I don't want to study tonight.
¿A ti te gusta ir a conciertos?	Do you like to go to concerts?
Espero poder ir.	I hope I can go.

Aplicación

I. Combine the two clauses and make any necessary changes.

MODELO Mariana sube al taxi. Edmundo quiere que _____. → **Edmundo quiere que Mariana suba al taxi.**

1. Yo salgo. Ellos prefieren que _____.
2. Discutes el concierto. Brown quiere que _____.
3. Vamos al despacho. Esperan que _____.
4. Ella se sienta. Le piden que _____.
5. Llamo por teléfono. Sugiere que _____.
6. Leen la reseña. Tengo miedo que _____.
7. Hago eso. No les gusta que _____.
8. Dejas un recado. Prefieren que _____.

[1]Some impersonal expressions indicate certainty and are followed by a verb in the indicative: **Es seguro que lo saben** *It's certain that they know it.* This principle will be taken up in the next chapter; for now, just remember that most impersonal expressions are followed by the subjunctive not because they are impersonal expressions, but because they express a reaction or reservation of some kind about the clause that follows them.

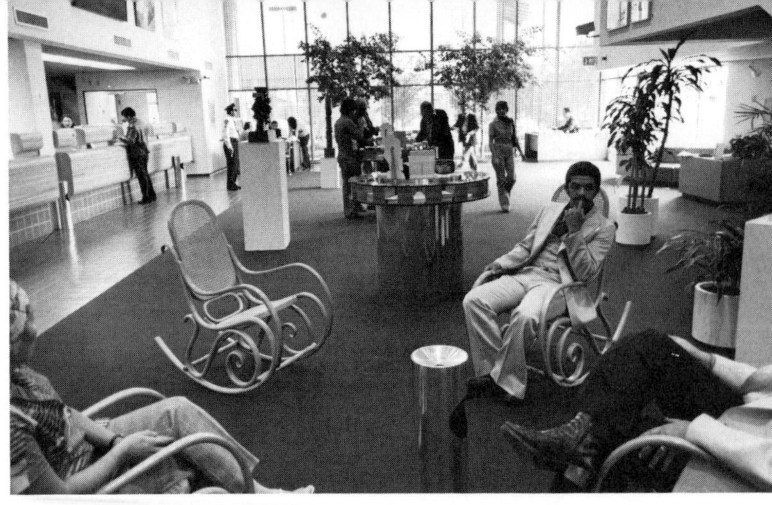

A Cuban bank in Miami, Florida. The Cuban presence in Dade County has been felt in all walks of life.

II. Combine the following elements to make sentences.

MODELO Josefa / querer / Eduardo / irse → **Josefa quiere que Eduardo se vaya.**

1. María / tener miedo / los amigos / llegar tarde
2. Ella / querer / todos / estar allí temprano
3. Yo / sentir / tú / no poder ir a la fiesta
4. Ellos / sugerir / nosotros / traer vino
5. Nuestros padres / no dejar / nosotros / volver tarde
6. Yo / esperar / ustedes / saber dónde vivimos
7. Nosotros / querer / todo el mundo / venir
8. María / esperar / haber muchas personas

III. Restate each sentence, adding the subject in parentheses.

MODELO Quiero salir. (que tú).→ **Quiero que salgas.**

1. Necesito buscar un taxi. (que ellos)
2. Prefiero llamar por teléfono. (que Ud.)
3. Es mejor leer la reseña. (que ella)
4. Espero poder hacer eso. (que tú)
5. Sentimos no tener tiempo. (que ustedes)
6. Quiere escribir un artículo. (que yo)
7. Me gusta recibir tarjetas postales. (que las niñas)
8. Es imposible encontrar un taxi. (que Edmundo)

IV. Para contestar

1. ¿Es probable que usted estudie esta noche? ¿Es muy probable o poco probable?
2. ¿Es posible que leamos ese libro hoy?
3. ¿Qué quieren sus padres que usted estudie? ¿Qué quiere estudiar usted?
4. ¿Qué sugiere usted que yo haga después de esta clase?
5. ¿Tienen ustedes miedo que yo les dé más trabajo para mañana?
6. ¿Es necesario que ustedes estudien mucho? ¿Es necesario que yo estudie también?
7. ¿Quieren ustedes que yo los invite a un concierto?
8. ¿Prefieren ustedes que yo los invite a comer a mi casa? ¿Prefieren ir a un restaurante?

Pausa oral

Comentarios personales

Language is used to make personal comments as well as to report facts.

I. Exclamaciones

Choose from the following list the exclamation that could most logically be used as a personal reaction to each of the statements below.

¡Vamos!
¡La cosa va en serio!
¡Qué maravilla!
¡Ya doy!
¡Ay, bendito!
¡Ave María!
¡No hombre! ¡Qué va!
Ya era tiempo.
Uff. ¡Qué difícil!
Salud.
Ya lo creo.

MODELO ¿Quieres ir al concierto conmigo? → **¡Vamos!**

1. La reseña de Brown me pone furioso.
2. Tengo que ir a buscarlo ahora mismo.
3. Fíjate que podemos volver a Puerto Rico.
4. Pero tú, mi vida, ¿vas a cambiar de opinión ahora?
5. No esperaba yo un pacto así de bueno.

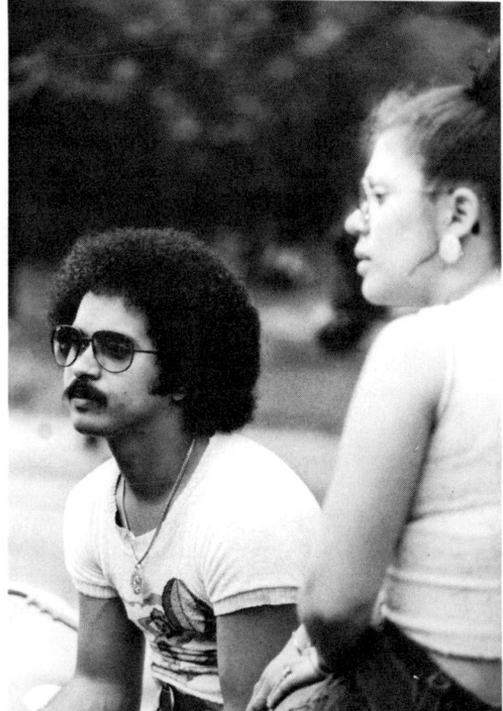

Americans of Puerto Rican origin in New York City are sometimes called *Neo-Ricans* or *Nuyoricans*.

6. Más vale escuchar al Dr. Varela.
7. Ahora vamos a brindar por el progreso de la patria.
8. Hay un puesto estupendo en la compañía para alguien como yo.
9. Por fin quité la maleza.
10. ¡Hombre! ¡Hay una víbora aquí!

II. Modificaciones

Adjectives and adverbs may be used to modify or to reinforce another word within a sentence. Choose the word in the list which fits in best with the meaning of the sentences below. Use each adjective in its correct form.

adjectives	*adverbs*
sorprendido	rápido
emocionado	solamente
preocupado	temprano
joven	ahorita
terco	claro está
cómodo	naturalmente
estupendo	afortunadamente
furioso	perfectamente bien

MODELO Adela estuvo muy _____ porque Brown le habló en español. → **Adela estuvo muy sorprendida porque Brown le habló en español.**

1. Los precios de la carne me ponen tan _____.
2. En el Paraguay buscan médicos _____.
3. Si una mujer espera un bebé, pues _____ no debe tomar alcohol.
4. Estoy muy _____ porque el nuevo apartamento no tiene dos baños.
5. Siéntese usted aquí y póngase _____.
6. Mis padres van a estar _____ porque dejo los estudios.
7. No me duele la garganta. Me encuentro _____.
8. No podemos caminar más _____.
9. Nos quedan tres horas de luz _____.
10. No esperaba yo una reseña tan buena. Estoy muy _____.
11. Es aún muy _____ para ir a clase.
12. Papá nunca come en restaurantes. Ya lo conoces, es muy _____.
13. Emilio está muy bien. Hoy me acompañó; _____ viene.
14. _____, en este aeropuerto no hay problemas con las maletas.

III. State what you think the people in the following drawings might be thinking.

ESTRUCTURA II

A. Commands: irregular forms

Repaso. Regularly formed **tú** affirmative commands are the same as the third-person **(él)** present indicative: **Entra a la oficina.**

> **Ven** acá, mi vida.

1. The following verbs have irregular **tú**-form commands.

infinitive	*irregular* **tú**	
poner	**pon**	Pon las cosas aquí, por favor.
tener	**ten**	Ten paciencia.
venir	**ven**	Ven acá, chico.
decir	**di**	Di la verdad.
hacer	**haz**	Haz esto, ¿quieres?
salir	**sal**	Sal a la calle.
ir	**ve**	Ve al despacho.
ser	**sé**	Sé bueno.

2. For most verbs, the first-person **(yo)** form, present indicative, provides the basis for the **tú** negative command.

salir → yo salgo → **no salgas**
venir → yo vengo → **no vengas**
buscar → yo busco → **no busques**

No salgas a la calle.	Don't go out into the street.
No vengas ahora, por favor.	Don't come now, please.
No busques al Sr. Brown.	Don't look for Mr. Brown.

3. The exceptions are:

ir → **no vayas**
dar → **no des**
estar → **no estés**
saber → **no sepas**
ser → **no seas**

4. All verbs whose present subjunctive forms are irregular have irregular **usted, ustedes** command forms.

No vaya usted al centro hoy.	Don't go downtown today.
Sean amables con ella.	Be nice to her.

Aplicación

I. Change each sentence to an affirmative **tú** command.

MODELO María hace el trabajo. → **María, haz el trabajo.**

1. Edmundo sale temprano.
2. Pedro es bueno.
3. Mariana pone la comida aquí.
4. Josefa va al despacho.
5. Jorge dice la verdad.
6. José tiene paciencia.
7. Antonio viene ahora.
8. Susana hace algo.

II. Complete each sentence by adding a **tú** command.

MODELO Sra. García, venga con nosotros. Y tú también, Edmundo, ______. → **Y tú también, Edmundo, ven con nosotros.**

1. Sr. Soto, tenga paciencia. Y tú también, José, ______.
2. Sra. Sánchez, salga ahora. Y tú también, Alicia, ______.
3. Profesor Pereda, vaya con la enfermera. Y tú también, Olga, ______.
4. Srta. Portilla, diga la verdad. Y tú también, Javier, ______.
5. Sra. García, haga el trabajo. Y tú también, Miguel, ______.
6. Sr. Gaviria, sea amable. Y tú también, Pepe, ______.
7. Dr. Gómez, venga ahora. Y tú también, Pedro, ______.
8. Srta. Franco, ponga eso aquí. Y tú también, Mónica, ______.

III. Change to the negative.

MODELO Di esa palabra. → **No digas esa palabra.**

1. Sé así.
2. Sal por aquí.
3. Ven pronto.
4. Haz una reseña.
5. Ve al concierto.
6. Pon el periódico allí.
7. Di eso.
8. Ten miedo.

IV. Direct the following statements to a classmate.

MODELO Profesor: Dígale a su amigo que venga a la fiesta. →
Estudiante: **Ven a la fiesta.**

1. Dígale a su amigo que haga el trabajo.
2. Pídale a su amigo que salga con usted esta noche.
3. Dígale a su amigo que no diga cosas malas.
4. Dígale a su amigo que no venga a clase tarde.
5. Pídale a su amigo que vaya con usted al centro.
6. Dígale a su amigo que ponga los libros aquí.

V. Change the following statements to informal **tú** commands or formal **usted, ustedes** commands.

MODELOS Tú debes leer la reseña. → **Lee la reseña, por favor.**
Usted no debe llegar tarde. → **No llegue tarde, por favor.**

1. Tú debes tener paciencia.
2. Usted debe saber eso para mañana.
3. Ustedes deben detener un taxi.
4. No debes hablar inglés.
5. Ustedes deben estar aquí a las ocho.
6. No debes decir eso.

7. Usted no debe comenzar ahora.
8. No debes seguir así.
9. Ustedes no deben llamar a Brown.
10. No debes pensar mucho.
11. Ustedes no deben escuchar el programa.
12. No debes criticar su interpretación.
13. No debes ir con ellos.
14. No debes dar una fiesta.

B. Object pronouns with commands or infinitives

Repaso. When used with a conjugated verb that isn't an affirmative command, indirect, direct object, and reflexive pronouns appear directly before the verb: **¿Te sirvo un café? ¿Lo sirvo ahora? Me siento aquí.**

> Siéntate y cálmate, chico.
> No te sientes, chico.

1. When used with an affirmative command, all object pronouns, including the reflexives, follow the command form and are attached to it.

Haznos ese favor, ¿quieres?	Do us that favor, will you?
Dame el periódico.	Give me the paper.
Siéntate.	Sit down.

A written accent mark is placed over the stressed vowel of the command form in a combination with three or more syllables.

Siéntense ustedes.	Sit down.
Tráigame un café con leche, por favor.	Bring me coffee with cream, please.

2. When used with a negative command, all object pronouns, including the reflexives, are placed directly before the command.

No se acuesten ustedes todavía.	Don't go to bed yet.
No nos vayamos todavía.	Let's not leave yet.
No me lo des.	Don't give it to me.

3. When used in sentences with a verb + infinitive, the object pronouns may occur: a) before the conjugated verb, or b) attached to the end of the infinitive.

PRONOUN + VERB + INFINITIVE

La iba yo a llamar por teléfono, Sra. Pérez.	I was going to call you on the phone, Mrs. Pérez.
¿Me vas a escribir?	Are you going to write to me?

VERB + INFINITIVE + PRONOUN

Iba yo a llamarla por teléfono.	I was going to call you on the phone.
¿Vas a escribirme?	Are you going to write to me?

4. If both an indirect and direct object pronoun are used with a command or an infinitive, they are never separated by other words. (The indirect object pronoun always occurs first.)

No se lo des a ella.	Don't give it to her.
¿Me lo quieres dar?	Do you want to give it to me?
¿Quieres dármelo?	Do you want to give it to me?

Aplicación

I. A. Replace the noun with a pronoun.

MODELO Lea usted la reseña. → **Léala.**

1. Mire el artículo.
2. Escuche el concierto.
3. Haga el trabajo.
4. Llame al abogado.
5. Discutan los programas.
6. Lea el periódico.
7. Busquen a la secretaria.

B. Replace the noun with a second pronoun.

MODELO Déjame las cosas allí. → **Déjamelas allí.**

1. Tráenos el periódico.
2. Dile la verdad.
3. Detenme el taxi.
4. Enséñale la tarjeta.
5. Explícales el trabajo.
6. Ponte el abrigo.

II. A. Answer each question with an **usted, ustedes** command.

MODELO ¿Lo hago ahora? → **Sí, hágalo ahora.**

1. ¿Les digo eso?
2. ¿Lo pongo aquí?
3. ¿Los llamo por teléfono?
4. ¿Le escribo una carta?
5. ¿La busco?
6. ¿Le doy el dinero?
7. ¿Las escucho?
8. ¿Le hablamos a ella?
9. ¿Las invitamos a ellas?
10. ¿Lo visitamos a él?

B. Answer with an **usted, ustedes** command, replacing the noun with a pronoun.

MODELO ¿Le leo la carta a usted? → **Sí, léamela.**

1. ¿Le doy la reseña a ella?
2. ¿Les escribo la carta a ellos?
3. ¿Le doy el periódico a usted?
4. ¿Les pido el dinero a ustedes?
5. ¿Le leemos el artículo a él?
6. ¿Le enseñamos el libro a usted?

C. Answer with an **usted, ustedes** command plus a reflexive pronoun.

MODELOS ¿Me siento? → **Sí, siéntese.**
¿Nos lavamos las manos? → **Sí, lávenselas.**

1. ¿Me acuesto?
2. ¿Me visto?
3. ¿Me pongo el abrigo?
4. ¿Me ducho?
5. ¿Me quito las botas?
6. ¿Nos levantamos?
7. ¿Nos damos prisa?
8. ¿Nos sentamos aquí?
9. ¿Nos vamos ahora?
10. ¿Me doy prisa?

III. Make each command negative.

MODELO Tráigamelo. → **No me lo traiga.**

1. Hágalas ahora.
2. Díganlo, por favor.
3. Enséñeselo.
4. Póngase cómodo.
5. Míralo.
6. Vete, por favor.

IV. Answer each question using a negative **usted** or **ustedes** command.

MODELO Voy a sentarme aquí, ¿está bien? → **¡No, no! No se siente allí.**

1. Voy a llamarla ahora, ¿está bien?
2. Voy a escribirle más tarde, ¿está bien?
3. Voy a ducharme, ¿está bien?
4. Voy a enseñarles la carta, ¿está bien?
5. Voy a dejar un recado, ¿está bien?
6. Vamos a decírselo, ¿está bien?
7. Vamos a dárselo, ¿está bien?
8. Vamos a lavarnos las manos, ¿está bien?
9. Vamos a vestirnos ahora, ¿está bien?
10. Vamos a quitárselo, ¿está bien?

V. Place each pronoun after the infinitive.

MODELO Lo quiero ver. → **Quiero verlo.**

1. Se quieren sentar.
2. Le tengo que hablar.
3. Te lo voy a mandar.
4. Los necesitamos ver.
5. ¿Cuándo le vas a escribir?
6. ¿Lo quieren conocer?
7. No lo podemos comprar.
8. Te tienes que calmar.

VI. Answer the following questions, replacing the noun with a pronoun.

MODELO ¿Quieren ustedes escuchar el concierto? → **Sí, queremos escucharlo.**

1. ¿Prefieren ustedes leer el artículo ahora?
2. ¿Quiere usted ver el programa?
3. ¿Tienen ustedes que estudiar el diálogo?
4. ¿Puedo ver la reseña del concierto?
5. ¿Vamos a estudiar el libro?
6. ¿Puede usted detener ese taxi?
7. ¿Necesitamos encontrar la oficina de Brown?
8. ¿Quiere usted escuchar esta música?

EXCLUSIVO
"Confirmamos sus Vacaciones"
MEXICO - MIAMI
Visitando LIMA (2 dias)
MEXICO (3 días)
TAXCO y CUERNAVACA (1 día)
ACAPULCO (3 días)
MIAMI y ORLANDO (11 días)
Hoteles de 1ª categoría,
precio por persona en habitación doble.
U$S 2.330 incluido pasaje aéreo.
Salidas: 6 y 19 de Enero
8 y 23 de Febrero - 1 y 8 de Marzo,
consulte otras fechas.
aconcagua turismo s.a.
Corrientes 1291 8º piso - Tel. 35-3168/4681/7160.

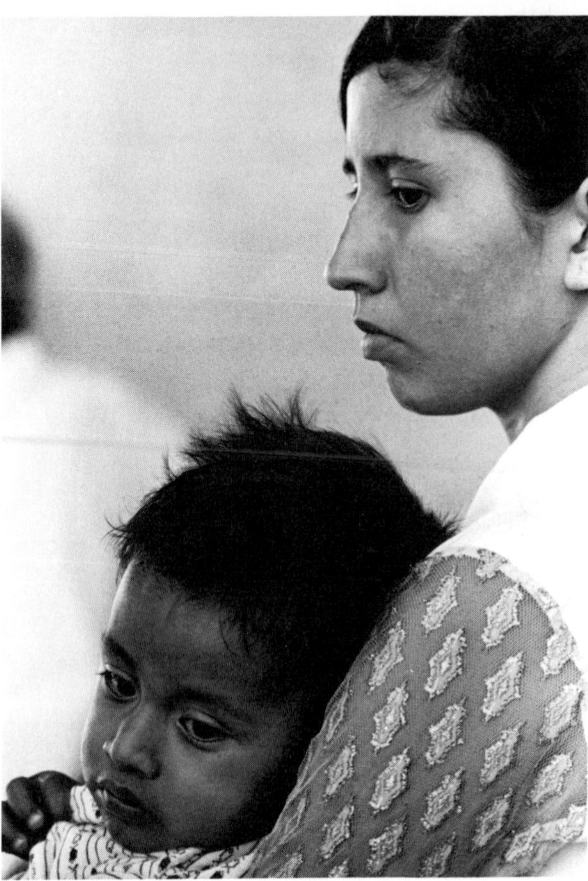

Mother and child in South Texas. For many Chicanos, love of family is one of the most important things in life.

LECTURA

La población hispánica de los EE.UU.

En la década de los 80, los EE.UU., con una población hispánica de más de 20 millones, es ya la quinta nación hispánica del mundo. Sólo las respectivas poblaciones de México, España, Argentina y Colombia son más grandes que la población hispánica de los EE.UU. Muchos piensan que para el siglo XXI, habrá cuarenta millones de hispanos en tierras del Tío Sam y por consiguiente, los hispanos van a ser la minoría étnica más grande de los EE.UU.

La historia de los EE.UU. es una historia de inmigraciones. En diferentes épocas grupos de diversas nacionalidades vinieron a empezar una nueva vida en territorio americano.

En el caso de algunos americanos de origen hispánico se puede decir que exactamente lo contrario ocurrió. Los Estados Unidos vinieron adonde estaban ellos. En 1848, al final de la guerra entre los EE.UU. y México, la República Mexicana perdió más

the USA
the fifth (largest)
populations
century
there will be / lands
por. . . therefore
begin
lo. . . the opposite
war
lost

de la mitad[1] de su territorio (California, Arizona, Nevada, Utah, Nuevo México, Colorado y Texas); México también perdió aproximadamente cincuenta mil personas que residían en estas tierras, quienes se convirtieron en[1] los primeros méxico-americanos o "chicanos". Cincuenta años más tarde, como resultado de otra guerra (la guerra entre los EE.UU. y España de 1898), Puerto Rico pasó a ser parte[1] de los EE.UU[2].

Sin embargo[1], sólo los "primeros hispanos" no son técnicamente inmigrantes; otros hispanos han inmigrado[1] a diferentes regiones de los EE.UU. Recientemente, el porcentaje (%) de hispanos muestra[1] un incremento[1] gradual y un 50% de los inmigrantes que vinieron a los EE.UU. entre los años 1950 y 1980 son de origen hispánico.

México ha contribuido[1] con el mayor número de hispanos, es decir, con un poco más de dos millones. De Cuba vino un millón de habitantes. Puerto Rico contribuye a la población hispánica de los EE.UU. con unos tres millones que viven en Puerto Rico y otros dos millones en "tierra firme[1]". Sin embargo, los puertorriqueños no son inmigrantes puesto que[1] son ciudadanos americanos. Otros hispanos han venido[1] a este país de la Argentina, Colombia, España, la República Dominicana y otros países hispánicos.

Los mexicanos y los puertorriqueños generalmente han seguido[1] el molde[1] clásico para inmigrantes, trabajando en la agricultura o como obreros no cualificados[1] en la industria. Los inmigrantes de otros países hispánicos—por ejemplo, la Argentina o Colombia—muy a menudo[1] obtienen mejores trabajos porque, generalmente, sólo emigran aquellas personas que tienen más dinero y más años de instrucción.

El caso de los cubanos es algo muy especial porque, debido a[1] la dictadura comunista de Fidel Castro (1959), casi toda la clase media[1] y toda la clase alta[1] cubanas salieron del país. Muchos cubanos fueron a España, otros a Puerto Rico, algunos otros a países de Hispanoamérica; pero la mayoría vino a los EE.UU., residiendo[1] primero en Miami y después estableciéndose[1] por todas las grandes ciudades del país.

Al pasar los años[1], los hispanos van integrándose[1] en la sociedad americana, y la sociedad americana va hispanizándose[1] un poco.

half
became
pasó. . . became part of
However
have immigrated
shows / increase
has contributed
en. . . on the mainland
puesto que since
come
followed / pattern
obreros. . . unskilled laborers
muy. . . very often
because of
middle class / upper class
residing / settling
As the years pass / **van. . .** are becoming integrated / **va. . .** is becoming hispanicized

Chicano cowboy, Hidalgo County, Texas. Most of the early cowboys, or **vaqueros,** were Mexican.

Glosas

1. Of these 20 million Hispanic Americans, over 50% are of Mexican origin. The second largest group is comprised of Americans of Puerto Rican origin (about 25%); Cubans and Cuban-Americans represent about 5%. Besides the 20 million Hispanics legally in the country, hundreds of thousands of others, looking for jobs, have slipped across the borders, overstayed their visitor's visas, or jumped ship in American ports and settled here. Many believe that up to 90% of these undocumented workers come from Mexico. Typically they take the lowest-paying, most menial jobs, and often pay their federal, state, and local taxes (to stay out of trouble with the taxing authorities). Because of their status—not legally admitted into the United States—they make little use of the social services available to citizens and residents of this country.

2. In 1917, U.S. citizenship was granted to Puerto Ricans by an act of Congress. Puerto Rico's elected resident commissioner pleaded that a referendum be held to determine the wishes of the Puerto Rican people on the issue; his plea, however, went unheeded. In recent years, referendums have been held; most Puerto Ricans vote either for maintaining the island's current status as a commonwealth associated with the U.S. or for seeking full statehood. A smaller group votes for independence.

SOBRE LA LECTURA

I. Para contestar

1. ¿Por qué son los Estados Unidos la quinta nación hispánica del mundo?
2. ¿Por qué podemos decir que en el siglo pasado "los Estados Unidos vinieron adonde estaban" los mexicanos?
3. ¿Inmigraron muchos hispanos a los Estados Unidos entre los años 1950 y 1980?
4. ¿Qué país ha contribuido con el mayor número de inmigrantes?
5. ¿De qué otros países son los inmigrantes hispánicos?
6. ¿Qué tipo de trabajos tienen los inmigrantes mexicanos y puertorriqueños generalmente?
7. ¿Por qué obtienen mejores trabajos los otros inmigrantes hispánicos?
8. ¿Por qué es especial el caso de los cubanos?

II. Discusión

1. ¿Qué problemas tienen los inmigrantes en general?
2. ¿Qué problemas tienen los inmigrantes hispánicos en particular?
3. ¿Debe Puerto Rico ser un país independiente? ¿Por qué (no)?

III. Entrevista[1]

¿Conoce usted a algún inmigrante hispánico? Converse usted con él. Dígale que a usted le interesa saber si le gusta vivir en los Estados Unidos. En general, cuáles son las cosas que le gustan y cuáles son las cosas que no le gustan de la vida norteamericana, por qué vive aquí, qué trabajo tiene, si le gustaría volver a su país, etc. Después, dígales a los otros estudiantes que están en su clase de español cuáles son las impresiones de su amigo hispánico.

[1] *Interview.*

Repaso oral

I. Make up an original sentence incorporating the words in each pair.

MODELO edificios / universidad → **Hay muchos edificios viejos en esta universidad.**

1. pianista / concierto
2. artículo / periódico
3. recado / secretaria
4. tener frío / abrigo
5. escribir / reseña

II. Para contestar

1. ¿A usted le gusta la música? ¿Qué clase de música le gusta?
2. ¿Qué tipo de artículos lee usted en el periódico? ¿Lee las reseñas?
3. ¿A qué hora se acuesta usted? ¿A qué hora se levanta?
4. ¿Qué tiene usted que hacer este fin de semana?
5. ¿Qué quiere que hagamos en la clase de español?

III. Para describir

What thoughts might be going through the mind of the woman pictured sitting in her office?

Capítulo 12

Despegue

DIÁLOGO **Una entrevista**

The future and conditional tenses: regular and irregular forms • Ways to express probability • Reflexive constructions (II): mental condition

PAUSA ORAL **El tiempo libre**

Reservation: indicative or subjunctive • Verbs + **a** + infinitive

Repaso oral

Despegue

Descripción del dibujo

1. Nancy López es una famosa golfista.
2. Oscar Morales es un reportero para la Cadena Hispana de Televisión.
3. Oscar entrevista a Nancy. Es una buena entrevista.
4. Nancy sonríe.
5. Nancy muestra la llave de la ciudad de Indianápolis.

Pronunciación

1. la señorita López / La señorita López sonríe.
2. la llave / Ella muestra la llave.
3. golfista / entrevista / una famosa golfista / una buena entrevista

Aplicación

I. Relación

Make as many statements as you can about the picture on page 277. Try to make at least ten sentences.

II. Para contestar

1. ¿Quién es Nancy López?
2. ¿Quién es Oscar Morales?
3. ¿Qué hace Oscar?
4. ¿Sonríe Nancy o no?
5. ¿Qué tiene Nancy en la mano?
6. ¿A usted le gustan las entrevistas?

Tema del diálogo

What would it be like to interview a famous athlete? Do athletes have secret formulas that explain their success?

Nancy López, Chicana from Rosswell, New Mexico, winner of the European Women's Golf Championship, 1978. In the same year, she won five consecutive LPGA tournaments, an unprecedented feat.

gracias mil	thanks a million
hace	ago
hace unos diez años	about ten years ago
no hay tal cosa	There's no such thing
se	each other
se dan la mano	they shake hands

additional vocabulary

el **autógrafo**	autograph
comenzar (ie, c)	to begin
el **éxito**	success
fanático	enthusiastic; fan
preguntarse (si)	to wonder (if)
terminar	to finish

ESTRUCTURA I

A. The future and conditional tenses: regular and irregular forms

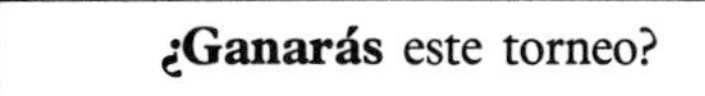

¿**Ganarás** este torneo?

1. The future tense expresses what will happen at a moment yet to come. The conditional tense expresses what would happen at a time which is left undetermined.

2. To form the future and conditional tenses, take the entire infinitive and add the endings which appear below. There is just one set of future endings and one set of conditional endings for all verbs in **-ar, -er,** and **-ir.**

endings		**andar**	
FUTURE	CONDITIONAL	FUTURE	CONDITIONAL
-é	**-ía**	**andaré**	**andaría**
-ás	**-ías**	**andarás**	**andarías**
-á	**-ía**	**andará**	**andaría**
-emos	**-íamos**	**andaremos**	**andaríamos**
-éis	**-íais**	**andaréis**	**andaríais**
-án	**-ían**	**andarán**	**andarían**

FUTURE

Me divertiré con los amigos esta noche.	I'll have a good time with friends tonight.
¿Ganarás otro torneo?	Will you win another tournament?
Oscar esperará a Nancy.	Oscar will wait for Nancy.
Dejaremos un recado con la secretaria.	We'll leave a message with the secretary.

CONDITIONAL

La llamarían.	They would call her.
Yo hablaría español con ella.	I would speak Spanish with her.
Al público le gustaría saberlo.	The audience would like to know it.
Veríamos los partidos de fútbol.	We would see the football games.

3. The endings for the conditional are the same as those used to form the imperfect tense of **-er** and **-ir** verbs. (The stem for the conditional, however, is different from the stem for the imperfect.)

creer

IMPERFECT	CONDITIONAL
creía	creería
creías	creerías
creía	creería
creíamos	creeríamos
creíais	creeríais
creían	creerían

4. The following verbs do not use the entire infinitive to form the future and conditional. They use the same endings in the future and conditional as all other verbs.

Irregular verbs—**yo**-forms

	FUTURE	CONDITIONAL		FUTURE	CONDITIONAL
decir	**diré**	**diría**	hacer	**haré**	**haría**
haber	**habré**	**habría**	poner	**pondré**	**pondría**
poder	**podré**	**podría**	salir	**saldré**	**saldría**
querer	**querré**	**querría**	tener	**tendré**	**tendría**
saber	**sabré**	**sabría**	venir	**vendré**	**vendría**

Te diré la verdad	I'll tell you the truth.
¿Quién hará la entrevista?	Who will do the interview?
¿Podrías decírmelo?	Could you tell it to me?
No tendríamos tiempo.	We wouldn't have time.

5. Do not confuse the verbs **poder (podré, podría)** and **poner (pondré, pondría)** in the future and conditional.

Aplicación

I. Answer each question using **no sé cuándo** + future tense.

MODELO ¿Ya llega la gente? → **No sé cuándo llegará.**

1. ¿Ya se va el reportero?
2. ¿Ya terminan ustedes?
3. ¿Ya empieza la entrevista?
4. ¿Ya hablo yo bien?
5. ¿Ya comprenden los estudiantes?
6. ¿Ya juegan ustedes?
7. ¿Ya están mejor ustedes?
8. ¿Ya entra la golfista?

II. Supply the future tense of each verb listed in the key.

1. ser
2. jugar, yo
3. entrevistar
4. ver
5. ganar, yo
6. estar
7. ser
8. pasar, nosotros
9. conversar, nosotros
10. hablar, nosotros
11. visitar
12. comprar, yo
13. pasear
14. cenar
15. esperar
16. pedir
17. dar, yo
18. contar
19. saber
20. sonreír
21. saludar
22. ser

Algún día yo ____1____ un gran golfista. ____2____ en torneos en todas las ciudades de los Estados Unidos. Los reporteros me ____3____ y Josefa, el gran amor de mi vida, me ____4____ en la televisión. Claro que no ____5____ siempre, pero si pierdo, Josefa ____6____ allí para decirme que no importa, que ella me quiere.

Nancy López, Lee Treviño, Jack Nicklaus y yo ____7____ amigos y ____8____ mucho tiempo juntos. ____9____ del golf y también ____10____ de muchas otras cosas. Tú me ____11____ en la casa estupenda que me ____12____ en Hollywood. Tú y yo nos ____13____ en mi carro y más tarde ____14____ en el club campestre. Todo el mundo ____15____ mi llegada y me ____16____ el autógrafo. Se lo ____17____ con gusto, pero no les ____18____ la fórmula de mi éxito. No, eso el público nunca lo ____19____. Si salgo a la calle, todo el mundo me ____20____ y me ____21____. Ay, qué bonita ____22____ mi vida. Claro que hay un problemita. ¡No sé jugar golf!

III. Answer each question in the negative using the conditional tense.

MODELO Él no se lo pediría. ¿Y tú? ¿Y ellos? →
Yo no se lo pediría tampoco.
Ellos no se lo pedirían tampoco.

1. Yo no la esperaría. ¿Y ustedes? ¿Y Pedro? ¿Y tú?
2. Él no se lo contaría a nadie. ¿Y usted? ¿Y ellas? ¿Y yo?
3. No nos quedaríamos aquí. ¿Y ella? ¿Y los chicos? ¿Y usted?
4. Ella no le pegaría. ¿Y nosotros? ¿Y él? ¿Y Mariana?
5. Ellos no se irían. ¿Y ustedes? ¿Y yo? ¿Y Osvaldo?
6. No me moriría de frío. ¿Y tú? ¿Y Oscar? ¿Y tú y Oscar?

IV. Change each sentence to the future tense.

MODELO Mariana da un concierto. → **Mariana dará un concierto.**

1. Hay mucha gente allí.
2. Hace su interpretación de Manuel de Falla.
3. Escucho el concierto.
4. Pedro tiene que llegar tarde.
5. ¿Vienes tú?
6. ¿Qué dicen los reporteros?
7. Yo no sé nada.
8. Nunca leo los periódicos.
9. ¿Quieren ustedes acompañarme?
10. Podemos ir en taxi.
11. ¿A qué hora salimos?
12. ¿Qué me pongo para salir?

V. Complete each sentence with a conditional form.

MODELO Pedro dice esas cosas pero yo no las . . . → **Pedro dice esas cosas pero yo no las diría.**

1. Oscar hace eso, pero tú no lo . . .
2. Todos mis amigos salen, pero yo no . . .
3. Tú lo puedes hacer, pero nosotros no lo . . .
4. Él tiene tiempo, pero ellas no lo . . .
5. Yo digo la verdad, pero él no la . . .
6. Nosotros queremos ir, pero mamá no . . .

VI. Answer each question in the negative using the conditional tense.

MODELO ¿Vas a salir con él? → **No señor, yo no saldría con él.**

1. ¿Vas a decírselo a papá?
2. ¿Va a haber tiempo?
3. ¿Van ustedes a hacerlo ahora?
4. ¿Van ellos a ponerlo allí?
5. ¿Va usted a venir con su novia (novio)?
6. ¿Voy yo a saber hacerlo?

VII. Para contestar

1. ¿Cuándo terminará sus estudios?
2. ¿Recibirán todos los estudiantes una A en esta clase?
3. ¿Estudiarán ustedes español el año que viene?
4. ¿Estudiará química también?
5. ¿Qué deporte le gustaría jugar?
6. ¿Sería necesario comprar muchas cosas para jugar ese deporte?
7. ¿A usted le gustaría conocer a Nancy López? ¿Qué le diría?
8. ¿Qué hará este verano? ¿Trabajará? ¿Estudiará?

B. Ways to express probability

Nancy **tendrá** un secreto. *Nancy probably has a secret.*

Simple statements of fact indicate what happens, did happen, or will happen. Such statements can be modified to express probability—they indicate what is or was likely to happen. Probability can be expressed in several ways in Spanish.

1. The future tense may be used in Spanish to express probability. (English uses words like *probably, must, could, might.*)

Los boletos serán muy caros.	The tickets must be very expensive.
¿Cuántos años tendrá Oscar?	How old could Oscar be?
¿Dónde andarán los novios?	Where might the **novios** be?

2. The conditional tense may be used to express probability in the past.

¿Quién sería?	I wonder who it was?
La entrevista se prolongaría un poco.	The interview probably ran a little long.

3. The adverb **probablemente** or the expression **es probable** (+ subjunctive) may also be used to express probability.

Probablemente está aquí ella.	She is probably here.
Es probable que ella esté aquí.	It's probable that she's here.
Probablemente salieron a la calle.	They probably went out into the street.
Es probable que Nancy gane el otro torneo.	It's probable that Nancy will win the other tournament.

4. To pose the question *I* (*you, we . . .*) *wonder if . . .*, either use the verb **preguntarse** *to wonder* or formulate a question with the future of probability.

Me pregunto qué hace Edmundo.	I wonder what Edmundo is doing.
¿Estará aquí Mariana?	I wonder if Mariana is here.

Aplicación

I. Restate the following sentences using the future of probability.

A. MODELO ¿Dónde está Nancy? → **¿Dónde estará Nancy?**

1. ¿Quién es ese señor?
2. ¿Qué hay allí?
3. ¿Dónde andan esos chicos?
4. ¿Qué cree él?
5. ¿Por qué quiere salir?

B. MODELO Probablemente está en el aeropuerto. → **Estará en el aeropuerto.**

1. Ese señor probablemente es un reportero.
2. Probablemente hay cámaras allí.
3. Probablemente andan con la golfista.
4. Probablemente te gustan los deportes.
5. Probablemente quieren ir al club.

Nancy López won $203,400 in prize money during 1978.

II. Para expresar en español

MODELOS I wonder what time it is. → **¿Qué hora será?**
It must be late. → **Será tarde.**

1. I wonder how old she is.
2. She must be twenty or twenty-one.
3. I wonder who is there.
4. It's probably Mariana.
5. She probably doesn't remember.
6. Where might she be now?

III. Restate each sentence using the conditional of probability.

MODELO Probablemente se retrasó el avión. → **Se retrasaría el avión.**

1. Probablemente se divertía.
2. Al público probablemente le gustó saberlo.
3. El reportero probablemente era Oscar Morales.
4. La golfista probablemente tenía una fórmula especial.
5. Probablemente pensaba mal de nosotros.

C. Reflexive constructions (II): mental condition

Repaso. Reflexive constructions often indicate a change in the physical condition of the subject: **me acuesto, te bañas, se despierta.**

Date cuenta que no hay tal cosa.

1. The following verbs, when used reflexively, all indicate a change in the mental condition of the subject.

aburrirse (de)	to get bored (with)	Los estudiantes se aburren de estudiar.
acordarse (ue) (de)	to remember	Siempre me acordaré de ti.
alegrarse (de)	to become (be) happy	Nos alegramos de estar aquí.
casarse (con)	to get married (to)	Nancy no se casará con Oscar.
darse cuenta (de)	to realize	Me di cuenta de que había más problemas.
divertirse (ie, i)	to have a good time	Ojalá ustedes se diviertan mucho.
enamorarse (de)	to fall in love (with)	Él se enamoró de Celia.
enojarse (con)	to get mad (at)	No me enojé contigo anoche.
equivocarse (qu) (de)	to be wrong (about)	Tú te equivocaste de casa.
olvidarse (de)	to forget	No se olvide usted de llamar.
ponerse (+ adjective)	to get, to become	Edmundo se puso furioso.
quejarse (de)	to complain (about)	¡Claro que nos quejamos de los precios!

2. Notice that most of these verbs require **de** or **con** before a noun or a verb phrase. However, **de** and **con** are not always translated in the English sentence.

Me acuerdo muy bien de Nancy.	I remember Nancy very well.
¿Te olvidaste de traer las llaves?	Did you forget to bring the keys?
Nos dimos cuenta de que no había tal cosa.	We realized that no such thing existed.
Mis padres se alegran de estar aquí.	My parents are happy to be here.

Aplicación

I. Replace the verb with the new one suggested.

MODELO Ella comprende el problema. (darse cuenta de) → **Ella se da cuenta del problema.**

1. Ellos están en la fiesta. (divertirse)
2. No recuerdo nada. (acordarse de)
3. Tú duermes en clase. (aburrirse)
4. Todos los chicos quieren a Susana. (enamorarse de)
5. Edmundo Javier sonríe. (enojarse)
6. Nosotros hablamos de la situación. (quejarse de)
7. Sé todo eso. (darse cuenta de)
8. Ustedes esperan. (alegrarse)

II. Make sentences using the items listed.

MODELO Edmundo / quejarse / reseña → **Edmundo se queja de la reseña.**

1. Ella / no darse cuenta / situación
2. Roberto / enamorarse / todas las chicas
3. Yo / no acordarse / entrevista
4. Tú / olvidarse / amigos
5. Nosotros / alegrarse / verte
6. El golfista / quejarse / reporteros
7. María / equivocarse / calle
8. Ustedes / aburrirse / estas conversaciones

III. For each blank supply a verb from the following lists. In each case, also supply the appropriate reflexive pronoun, **me, se,** or **nos.**

yo	**él**	**nosotros**
aburro	acuerda	alegramos
doy cuenta	divierte	
enamoré	alegra	
equivoco	enoja	
quejo	pone	

(Habla una señora que se llama Lola.)
A mí no me gustan los deportes, pero ____ 1 ____ de un hombre que es un golfista fanático. Yo no ____ 2 ____ porque sé que él ____ 3 ____ mucho con el golf. Pero, para decirle la verdad, los niños y yo ____ 4 ____ cuando hace mal tiempo y papá no puede jugar golf. Cuando mi esposo no gana, ____ 5 ____ mucho y ____ 6 ____ imposible. No quiere hablar. ____ 7 ____ del partido y dice que va a buscar un nuevo profesor. Pero cuando gana, ____ 8 ____ mucho. A veces yo ____ 9 ____ de escuchar estas largas descripciones, pero no digo nada porque ____ 10 ____ de que él necesita divertirse. Si no ____ 11 ____, hay muchos hombres que son golfistas fanáticos. Y además, yo también tengo mis cosas. Yo soy fanática de la ópera.

IV. Para contestar

1. ¿Se divierte usted en la universidad? ¿Se divierte en esta clase? ¿Me divierto yo?
2. ¿Quiénes se quejan más, los hombres o las mujeres? ¿los profesores o los estudiantes?
3. ¿Me enojo yo con ustedes? ¿Por qué?

4. ¿Se acuerdan ustedes del primer diálogo del libro?
5. ¿Se enamora usted fácilmente? ¿De qué tipo de persona se enamora usted?
6. ¿Se equivoca usted a veces o siempre tiene razón?
7. ¿Me alegro yo cuando ustedes hacen bien el trabajo?
8. ¿En qué clases se aburren ustedes? No se aburren en la clase de español, ¿verdad?
9. ¿Se olvida usted de las cosas a veces? Cuando usted habla español, ¿se olvida del vocabulario?
10. ¿Se dan cuenta ustedes de la suerte que tienen de poder hablar español? ¿Me doy cuenta yo de la suerte que tengo de tener estudiantes tan excelentes?

Pausa oral

El tiempo libre

I. ¿Qué hace usted con su tiempo libre?

Carry on several exchanges with another person by completing the following statements.

MODELO (PERSON A) En mi tiempo libre me gusta divertirme con mis amigos.
(PERSON B) A mí me gusta ver televisión y jugar tenis.

1. Me gustan mucho los partidos de . . .	A mí me gustan los partidos de . . .
2. Me alegro mucho cuando . . .	Yo me alegro cuando . . .
3. Mis amigos y yo siempre nos divertimos en (cuando) . . .	Pues nosotros nos divertimos mucho . . .
4. En mi tiempo libre no me gusta . . .	A mí no me gusta . . .
5. Me aburro un poco en (cuando) . . .	Y yo me aburro en (cuando) . . .
6. Para ir al monte es necesario . . .	También es necesario . . .
7. Este año pasaré la Navidad con (en) . . .	Esta Navidad la pasaré con (en) . . .
8. Hay una fiesta . . .	También hay una fiesta . . .
9. Mi hermano disfruta mucho cuando . . .	Mi hermana disfruta mucho cuando . . .
10. Este fin de semana voy a . . .	Yo voy a . . .
11. Durante las vacaciones quiero . . .	Y yo quiero . . .
12. Cuando estoy en el centro siempre . . .	Yo siempre . . .

II. ¿Sabe usted qué palabra usar?[1]

Complete each sentence with any logical word from the dialog or **Variaciones.**

MODELO Nancy es una ____ famosa. → **Nancy es una golfista famosa.**

1. Llego en avión en el ____ número 479.
2. Los chicos juegan mucho ____.
3. Tengo mucho trabajo. No tengo mucho tiempo ____.
4. El avión va a llegar tarde. Va a haber una ____ de veinte minutos.
5. El deporte que más me gusta es el ____.
6. Ese señor es un ____ con el *Washington Post.*
7. No puedo entrar a la casa porque no tengo mis ____.
8. En la televisión vimos una ____ con un famoso golfista.
9. Te darán una cordial ____ a su ciudad.
10. Para jugar bien, tienes que pegarle fuerte a la ____.

III. ¿Puede usted contestar?

1. ¿Le gusta a usted ver televisión? ¿Qué programas de televisión le gustan?
2. ¿Qué deportes le interesan más? ¿Prefiere usted jugar deportes o ver televisión?
3. ¿Sabe usted jugar tenis? ¿Juega usted bien o necesita clases?
4. ¿Le gusta más el fútbol americano o el *soccer*?
5. ¿Tiene usted bicicleta? ¿Le gusta andar en bicicleta?
6. ¿Qué otras cosas hace usted en su tiempo libre?

ESTRUCTURA II

A. Reservation: indicative or subjunctive

Repaso. The subjunctive is used following verbs of persuasion (**querer, pedir . . .**), after verbs of emotion (**esperar, alegrarse . . .**), and after certain impersonal expressions (**es necesario, es probable . . .**).

> Tal vez lo **gane;** tal vez no.
> Tal vez lo **ganaré;** creo que sí.

Three expressions of reservation in Spanish are followed sometimes by the indicative, sometimes by the subjunctive.

1. **Quizás** (or **quizá**) and **tal vez** are expressions of reservation; both mean *perhaps* or *maybe.* If the speaker uses them to imply doubt, the verb that follows is in the subjunctive. However, if the speaker regards what he is stating as likely to occur, the verb that follows is in the indicative.

quizá **tal vez**	+ subjunctive / indicative

[1] *Do you know what word to use?*

Quizá él no tuvo tiempo de leer la carta.	Maybe he did not have time to read the letter.
Tal vez volvieron a Puerto Rico.	Maybe they went back to Puerto Rico.
Quizá ella ya no quiera hacer la entrevista.	Maybe she no longer wants to do the interview.
Tal vez haya una fórmula especial.	Maybe there's a special formula.

2. When a question begins with **¿Cree(s) que . . . ?,** the subjunctive follows if the questioner believes the information contained in the dependent clause is doubtful or false. The indicative is used if the questioner believes the information in the dependent clause is true.

¿Cree(s) que . . . ? + subjunctive / indicative

¿Crees que van a llegar tarde?	Do you think they're going to arrive late? (questioner expects an affirmative answer)
¿Cree usted que los deportes son importantes?	Do you think that sports are important? (questioner expects an affirmative answer)
¿Cree usted que él tenga razón?	Do you think he's right? (questioner expects a negative answer)
¿Crees que ella esté en perfectas condiciones?	Do you think she's in perfect shape? (questioner expects negative answer)

3. The following verbs, when used to make a positive statement, are not followed by the subjunctive: **leer que, decir que, saber que, parecer que.**

Leo que Nancy está en Indianápolis.	I read that Nancy is in Indianapolis.
Dicen que Nancy jugará este fin de semana.	They say that Nancy will play this weekend.
Sé que el postre te gustará.	I know that you'll like the dessert.
Me parece que ella es americana.	It seems to me that she is American.

4. The following impersonal expressions, which indicate certainty, are followed by the indicative.

Es seguro	It's certain
Es cierto	It's true
Es evidente	It's evident
Es obvio	It's obvious
Es verdad	It's true

Es seguro que lo saben.	It's certain that they know it.
Es cierto que ella viene.	It's true that she's coming.
Es evidente que la quiere.	It's evident that he loves her.
Es obvio que no estudiaste.	It's obvious you didn't study.
Es verdad que lo dijeron.	It's true that they said it.

Aplicación

I. Restate each sentence twice using **tal vez** or **quizás.**
First speak as a pessimist, then as an optimist.

MODELO Nancy nos espera.

(Pessimist, subjunctive:) **Tal vez Nancy nos espere.**
(Optimist, indicative:) **Tal vez Nancy nos espera.**

1. Oscar tiene la llave.
2. Al público le gusta.
3. Hay una fórmula especial.
4. Ella se siente en perfectas condiciones.
5. La ceremonia termina ahora.

II. Each item consists of a question and a statement of your own belief about the answer. Formulate a question to find out what a classmate thinks about the same question, using the indicative or subjunctive, as appropriate.

MODELOS ¿Vendrán ellos? Creo que sí. → **¿Crees que vienen?**
¿Vendrán ellos? Creo que no. → **¿Crees que vengan?**

1. ¿Ganará Nancy? Creo que sí.
2. ¿Llegará tarde el vuelo? Creo que no.
3. ¿Hablará ella con los reporteros? Creo que sí.
4. ¿Se casará pronto? Creo que no.
5. ¿Se enojarán con nosotros? Creo que no.
6. ¿Nos acordaremos del concierto? Creo que sí.
7. ¿Dirán la verdad? Creo que no.
8. ¿Tenemos razón? Creo que no.

III. Repeat each sentence, replacing the underlined portion with the cues in parentheses.

MODELO <u>Es posible</u> que lo haga. (es verdad, es necesario) →
Es verdad que lo hace.
Es necesario que lo haga.

1. <u>Es mejor</u> que lo sepan. (es cierto, es dudoso, es seguro, es posible)
2. <u>Quiero</u> que salga. (es verdad, prefiero, estoy seguro, no me gusta)
3. <u>Es evidente</u> que te conocen. (es imposible, es verdad, es seguro, es probable)
4. <u>Me cuentan</u> que es verdad. (leí, es posible, me alegro, tengo miedo)
5. <u>Tengo miedo</u> que le digas algo. (es posible, es necesario, es mejor, es obvio)
6. <u>Sentimos</u> que no te guste. (estamos seguros, es evidente, tenemos miedo, no nos importa)

IV. Para contestar

1. ¿Cree usted que es importante jugar deportes?
2. ¿Cree que es necesario saber hablar español?
3. ¿Cree que los hombres jueguen mejor los deportes que las mujeres?
4. ¿Cree que el tenis sea más fácil que el golf?

C. Verbs + a + infinitive

¿Vas a esperar el vuelo?

Several verbs in Spanish require **a** when they are used before an infinitive. The **a** is not translated into English.

1. Certain of these verbs indicate physical movement.

entrar a	to go in to	Entramos a tomar un café.
salir a	to go out to	¿Salieron ustedes a cenar anoche?
venir a	to come to	Vengo a verte.

2. The following verbs also require **a** before the infinitive.

ir a	to be going	Vas a llegar tarde.
comenzar a	to begin	Comencé a estudiar a las 8.
empezar a	to begin	¿Empiezas a tener sueño?
enseñar a	to teach how	Ella me enseñó a hablar español.
invitar a	to invite	Te invito a ver el partido.

3. With most other verbs in Spanish, **a** is not used before an infinitive.

No sé jugar fútbol.	I don't know how to play soccer.
No queremos ver televisión esta noche.	We don't want to watch T.V. tonight.
¿Qué prefiere hacer usted?	What do you prefer doing?

Aplicación

I. Replace the conjugated verb with the one in parentheses.

MODELO Quiero estudiar. (voy) → **Voy a estudiar.**

1. Necesitamos pagar. (venimos)
2. Prefirió hablar con ella. (entró)
3. Quisieron comer. (empezaron)
4. Desea jugar tenis. (salió)
5. Me hizo salir. (invitó)
6. ¿Te dejan hablar español? (enseñan)
7. Podemos cenar. (salimos)
8. Sé traducir la carta. (comienzo)

II. Supply the preposition **a** whenever necessary.

A las ocho de la mañana Rosa entró __1__ decirme que ya era tarde. Yo no quería __2__ ir a clase. Tenía ganas de dormir todo el día, pero cinco minutos más tarde Rosa vino otra vez __3__ decirme que ya era muy tarde. Empecé __4__ pensar: primero voy __5__ ir a la clase de química. Prefiero __6__ no ir, pero hoy empezamos __7__ estudiar no sé qué cosa que es muy importante. A ver . . . ¿puedo __8__ no ir a la clase de español? No, porque hoy la profesora nos enseña __9__ escribir cartas y eso también es importante; yo necesito __10__ saber __11__ escribir cartas en español. Y necesito __12__ ir a la clase de inglés porque hoy vamos __13__ empezar un libro nuevo. Bueno, ¿qué puedo __14__ hacer? Voy __15__ tener que ir a clase. ¡Qué lata!

Repaso oral

A. Para conversar

1. You ask your friend if he/she thinks he/she will win the match. Person B says, "Maybe I'll win it, maybe not."
2. You say that maybe there is something special in his/her game. Person B says you should realize that there is no such thing.
3. You ask your friend if he/she will get married soon. Person B says that he/she probably will not be getting married this year.

B. Para describir

What might Oscar and Nancy be saying to each other in the following drawing? State five to ten possibilities.

Comunicación 3

Las diversiones

Familiarize yourself with the following vocabulary and expressions, some of which you already know. They all relate to various diversions.

hacer camping	to go camping
ir al campo	to go to the country
estar en el monte	to be in the mountains
nadar	to swim
ir a la playa	to go to the beach
nadar en el mar	to swim in the sea
nadar en una piscina	to swim in a pool
llevar un traje de baño	to wear a bathing suit
tomar sol	to sunbathe
jugar deportes	to play sports
ganar	to win
perder	to lose
esquiar	to ski
el, la atleta	the athlete
leer	to read
leer una revista	to read a magazine
terminar una novela	to finish a novel
el escritor	writer (man)
la escritora	writer (woman)

escuchar música	to listen to music
poner el radio	to put the radio on
tocar un disco	to play a record
el, la cantante	the singer
la música lenta	slow music
tocar un instrumento	to play an instrument
tocar la guitarra	to play the guitar
tocar el piano	to play the piano
ver televisión	to watch T.V.
poner (prender) la televisión	to put the T.V. on
ver un programa	to see a program
ir de compras	to go shopping
comprar	to buy
gastar	to spend
devolver (devuelvo. . .)	to return (I return. . .)
ir al cine	to go to the movies
ver una película	to see a film
sacar las entradas	to get the tickets
el actor	actor
la actriz	actress
divertirse	to have a good time
ir a un baile	to go to a dance
bailar	to dance

I. ¿Qué le gusta hacer?

How do you spend your free time? Starting with what you most like to do, tell the class how you spend your time. Use **Me gusta. . . , Prefiero. . . ,** etc.

leer (¿revistas o una novela?)
escuchar música (¿popular o clásica?)
jugar deportes (¿fútbol o tenis?)
tocar un instrumento (¿el piano o la guitarra?)
nadar (¿en el mar o en una piscina?)
ver televisión (¿dramas o deportes?)
hacer camping (¿en el monte o en la playa?)
ir de compras (¿aquí o en otra ciudad?)
ir al cine (¿películas musicales o películas de detectives?)
bailar (¿música lenta o música rápida?)

Now make a more specific statement about yourself and about each of your activities.

MODELO **Cuando quiero nadar, voy a la playa a nadar en el mar.**

II. ¿Puede usted comentar?

A person from the class (or the instructor) will make the following statements; some are true and some are false. If a statement is true, person B responds by agreeing (**Sí, seguro; Claro. . .**). If a statement is false, person B should correct it to make a true statement.

MODELO Sales a bailar todos los días. → **No, hombre. Salgo a bailar los sábados.**

1. Para hacer camping, vas a la playa.
2. Cuando estás en el monte, vas mucho al cine.
3. Cuando quieres nadar, vas a una piscina.
4. Jugar fútbol es más difícil que jugar tenis.
5. Lees novelas cuando estás en el cine.
6. Tocas discos en la clase de química.
7. Tocas el piano cuando estás en la playa.
8. Si compras mucho, gastas poco.
9. Si compras poco, puedes economizar.
10. La mejor diversión es dormir.

III. ¿Físico o mental?

Certain of the activities listed below are physical while others are mental. Make up two lists, one for **actividades físicas** and one for **actividades mentales.** If there is disagreement about a certain activity, one member of the class states why he or she thinks it is mainly physical. Another person tells why it may be a mental activity.

MODELO (tocar el piano) →

A: Tocar el piano es una actividad física. Muchas personas tocan pero no saben leer música.

B: Tocar el piano es una actividad mental. Para tocar bien, necesitas estudiar música.

hacer camping
nadar en el mar
jugar tenis
leer una novela
escuchar radio
tocar la guitarra
ver televisión
ir de compras
ver una película
bailar

IV. ¿Dónde le gustaría estar?

The class should now divide into small groups of two or three people each. One member of the group states that he or she prefers activities which can be enjoyed at home (**en casa**). Another person prefers outdoor activities (**al aire libre**). A third person likes to be downtown (**en el centro**). Each person states what can be enjoyed in his or her preferred place and tells something about each of these activities: what he or she reads, which music he or she listens to, which beach or pool he or she goes to, which movies, etc.

Capítulo 13

Despegue

Descripción del dibujo

1. Ramón acaba de llegar a casa de Pilar; Ramón llegó a la casa de Pilar hace poco tiempo.
2. Tiene un periódico bajo el brazo.
3. Pilar es la prometida de Ramón; Pilar y Ramón van a casarse.
4. La mamá de Pilar está muy agitada; está muy preocupada porque sabe que al papá de Pilar no le gusta Ramón.
5. El papá de Pilar está furioso. —Márchese—le dice a Ramón. Quiere que Ramón se vaya.

Pronunciación

1. Ramón llega. / Ramón acaba de llegar.
2. un periódico / el brazo
3. Está muy agitada. / Está muy preocupada.
4. Márchese. / Quiere que se vaya.

Aplicación

I. Relación

Make as many statements as you can about the picture on page 301. Try to make at least ten sentences.

II. Para contestar

1. ¿Quién acaba de llegar a la casa de Pilar?
2. ¿Acaba usted de llegar a la universidad?
3. ¿Tiene usted un periódico bajo el brazo ahora?
4. ¿Cómo se llama la prometida de Ramón?
5. ¿Tiene usted un prometido (una prometida)?
6. ¿Se siente usted muy agitado (agitada) a veces? ¿Por qué?
7. ¿Quiere el papá de Pilar que Ramón se marche o que se quede?
8. ¿Se marcha usted ahora?

Tema del diálogo

Psychological scars from the Spanish Civil War of 1936–1939 still complicate the lives of some Spaniards.

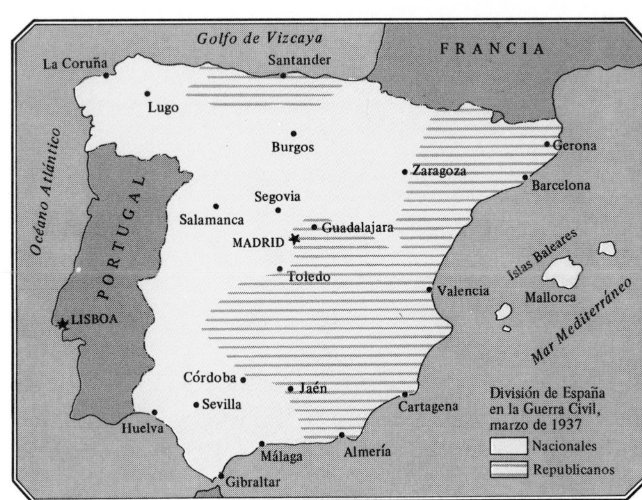

DIÁLOGO

La guerra continúa. . .

Ramón Suárez acaba de llegar a casa de su prometida[1]*, Pilar Iglesias, con un periódico bajo el brazo y la cara larga.*

PILAR ¿Qué haces por aquí a estas horas? ¿Se te olvidó algo anoche?

RAMÓN No, encanto. Nada de eso.

PILAR Ya doy. . .tu abuela está muy grave de nuevo y la boda. . .

RAMÓN No, no. Mira esto. (Ramón le muestra un artículo de *El Sol* a Pilar.)

PILAR (Lee el periódico en voz alta.) "El General Juan Francisco Suárez Heredia implicado en las matanzas de civiles en Huelva durante la Guerra."[2] Dios mío, ¡tu abuelo!

* * *

(Entra en la sala e interrumpe muy agitada la madre de Pilar.)

MADRE Ramón, ya veo que tiene usted el periódico. Por favor, váyase inmediatamente. Si no, mi marido. . .

(Entra el padre de Pilar con cara de pocos amigos.)

PADRE Mire, Ramón. ¡Márchese ahora mismo!

RAMÓN Pero, don Martín[3], yo no soy responsable de. . .

PADRE ¡Fuera de aquí!

* * *

(La tarde de ese día Ramón habla por teléfono con Pilar.)

RAMÓN ¡Cómo no voy a saber que tu abuelo y tu tío Armando perdieron la vida en esa masacre! Te quiero locamente. . .y ¿tú a mí?

PILAR Sí, mi vida, pero no podemos tratar de resolver tú y yo todos los problemas del pasado.

RAMÓN Pues no hay otra alternativa. ¿Quedamos en vernos mañana a las tres en la estación? Saca todos nuestros ahorros del banco[4]. Y no se te olvide el pasaporte.

A Republican soldier felled by Nationalist bullets, one of the first of more than a million deaths in the Spanish Civil War.

The war continues . . .

Ramón Suárez has just arrived at the house of his fiancée, Pilar Iglesias, with a newspaper under his arm and a long face.

P: What are you doing around here at this hour? Did you forget something last night?

R: No, my love. Nothing like that.

P: I know . . . Your grandmother is critically ill again and the wedding . . .

R: No, no. Look at this. (Ramón shows an article in *El Sol* (*The Sun*) to Pilar.)

P: (reads the newspaper aloud) "General Juan Francisco Suárez Heredia implicated in the killings of civilians in Huelva during the War." My God, your grandfather!

* * *

(Pilar's mother, very upset, enters in the room and interrupts.)

M: Ramón, I see you have the paper. Please leave immediately. If not, my husband . . . (Pilar's father enters looking angry.)

F: Look Ramón. Get out of here immediately.

R: But Don Martín, I am not responsible for . . .

F: Out of here!

* * *

(That afternoon Ramón is speaking with Pilar by telephone.)

R: Of course I know (how am I not going to know) that your grandfather and your uncle Armando lost their lives in that massacre! I love you madly . . . and you me?

P: Yes, darling, but you and I can't try to resolve all the problems of the past.

R: Then we have no choice (there's no other alternative). We agree to see each other at three tomorrow at the station? Take all our savings out of the bank. And don't forget your passport.

VARIACIONES

¿Cómo está tu abuela?	How is your grandmother?
Está { sana. / bien de salud.	She's healthy.
Está en el hospital.	She's in the hospital.
Está débil.	She's weak.
Está resfriada.	She has a cold.
Está más loca que nunca.	She's crazier than ever.
¿Cómo es don Martín?	What is don Martin like?
Es rico y famoso.	He's rich and famous.
Es muy pobre.	He's very poor.
Es antipático.	He's unpleasant.

Glosas

1. The Spanish word **prometido (prometida)** is the equivalent of English *fiancé* (*fiancée*). The progression in a Hispanic couple's relationship is **novia → prometida → esposa (novio → prometido → esposo)**.
2. The Spanish Civil War has not been forgotten; on the contrary, with their recently acquired freedom, Spain's newspapers and magazines have been printing articles on heretofore never discussed incidents from the 1936–1939 war, a conflict which claimed one million lives. Hundreds of American volunteers died fighting with the Abraham Lincoln Battalion in defense of the Spanish Republic, which eventually lost the war to the Nationalists led by Francisco Franco.
3. In most Hispanic countries **don (doña** for women) is used to show respect for age, superior social status, or political prestige. Hispanics characteristically have a high regard for older members of society.
4. In Hispanic countries, it is quite common for the **prometida** to be in charge of the finances for the future home. Most purchases (furniture, linen, etc.) will be stored in the home of the **prometida** until shortly before the wedding.

SOBRE EL DIÁLOGO

I. Match the items at left with a logical definition from the list at the right.

MODELO abuelo → **el padre de la madre o del padre**

1. guerra	a. perder la vida
2. abuela	b. la madre de la madre o del padre
3. boda	c. novia
4. marido	d. muy enfermo
5. rico	e. tiempo agitado cuando muere mucha gente
6. prometida	f. ceremonia en que dos personas se casan
7. grave	g. esposo
8. estación	h. de donde sale el tren, el autobús
9. morir	i. que tiene mucho dinero
	j. el padre de la madre o del padre

II. Respond to each sentence using one of the expressions in the list. You may be able to respond in more than one way.

Nada de eso. / **¡Váyase!** / **Fuera de aquí.** / **No hay otra alternativa.** / **Dios mío.**

1. ¿No podemos hacer otra cosa?
2. Tu abuela está enferma de nuevo.
3. Don Martín, necesito hablar con usted. Por favor déjeme entrar.
4. Pero, pero don Martín. . .
5. ¿Puedo quedarme un rato más?

III. **Antónimos.** Replace the underlined word with a word that means the opposite.

MODELO Ella es muy <u>alta</u>. → **Ella es muy baja.**

1. Es un hombre muy <u>rico</u>.
2. Ella es muy <u>simpática</u>.
3. Son gente <u>fuerte</u>.
4. Mis hermanos están <u>tranquilos</u>.
5. La abuela está muy <u>enferma</u>.

IV. **Para contestar**

1. ¿Quién es Pilar Iglesias?
2. ¿Qué tiene Ramón bajo el brazo?
3. ¿Qué le muestra Ramón a Pilar?
4. ¿Qué dice el artículo?
5. ¿Qué le dice la mamá de Pilar a Ramón?
6. ¿Qué quiere don Martín que haga Ramón?
7. ¿Qué hace Ramón, se queda o se va?
8. ¿Va Ramón a la casa de Pilar esa tarde? ¿Cómo hablan?
9. ¿Quiénes perdieron la vida en la masacre?
10. ¿Cree Pilar que Ramón y ella pueden resolver el problema?
11. ¿En qué quedan Ramón y Pilar? ¿Qué van a hacer?
12. ¿Qué quiere Ramón que Pilar haga?

VOCABULARIO

nouns

la **abuela**	grandmother
el **abuelo**	grandfather
la **alternativa**	alternative
la **boda**	wedding
la **cara**	face
el, la **civil**	civilian
el **general**	general
la **guerra**	war
el **hospital**	hospital, clinic
el **marido**	husband
la **masacre**	massacre
la **matanza**	killing
el **pasado**	past
el **prometido**	fiancé
la **prometida**	fiancée
el **sol**	sun
la **voz**	voice

verbs

continuar (ú)	to continue
interrumpir	to interrupt
marcharse	to leave
olvidar	to forget
¿se te olvidó. . . ?	did you forget . . . ?
quedar en	to agree to
resolver (ue)	to resolve

adjectives

agitado	excited, agitated, upset
antipático	unpleasant
débil	weak
grave	critically ill, grave, serious
implicado	implicated
loco	crazy
pobre	poor
responsable	responsible
rico	rich
sano	healthy

other expressions

a estas horas	at this hour
acabar de + infinitive	to have just + verb
bajo	under, underneath
cómo no voy a saber. . .	of course I know . . .
con cara de pocos amigos	looking mad
de nuevo	again
en voz alta	out loud, aloud
encanto	my love
estar bien de salud	to be healthy
estar resfriado	to have a cold
estar sano	to be healthy
fuera	out
fuera de aquí	get out of here
inmediatamente	immediately
locamente	madly
más ___ que nunca	as ___ as ever
nada de eso	nothing like that
tratar de + infinitive	to try to (do something)

additional vocabulary

acabar	to finish
bastante	enough
dejar de	to stop
demasiado	too much, too many
dudar	to doubt
insistir en	to insist upon
la **manera**	manner
ocurrir	to occur
realmente	really
varios	several

ESTRUCTURA I

A. The subjunctive after expressions of reservation

Repaso. The expressions **quizá(s), tal vez,** and the question **¿Cree(s). . .que?** are used with the subjunctive if doubt or a reservation is implied. If no doubt is implied, the indicative is used.

Dudo que haya problemas.

After verbs and expressions of reservation, the second verb is sometimes subjunctive, sometimes indicative.

1. After the verb **dudar,** the subjunctive is used.[1]

Dudo que él venga.	I doubt that he's coming.
Dudamos que Pilar y Ramón vayan a casarse.	We doubt that Pilar and Ramón are going to get married.

2. When the following verbs and expressions are used in the negative, they express reservation or doubt. In this form only, they are followed by the subjunctive.

reservation + **que** + subjunctive	
no creer	not to think
no estar seguro	not to be sure
no es cierto	it's not true
no es evidente	it's not evident
no es seguro	it's not certain
no es verdad	it's not true

Sus padres no creen que Pilar quiera a Ramón.	Her parents don't think that Pilar loves Ramón.
No es cierto que yo vaya a España este verano.	It's not true that I'm going to Spain this summer.
No es verdad que Ramón sea responsable.	It's not true that Ramon is responsible.

[1]When **dudar** is used in the negative to say that the speaker has no reservation or doubt, the second verb is in the indicative.

No dudo que ganarás. I don't doubt that you'll win.

3. When these verbs and expressions are used in the affirmative, they do not convey reservation or doubt. Therefore, the second verb is in the indicative.

affirmation + **que** + indicative	
creer	to believe
estar seguro	to be sure
es cierto	it is true
es evidente	it is evident
es seguro	it is certain
es verdad	it is true

Tú creías que la clase iba a ser más difícil.	You thought the class was going to be more difficult.
Estamos seguros que Marisela va a tener un bebé.	We are sure that Marisela is going to have a baby.
Es evidente que a Emilio le gusta comer bien.	It's evident that Emilio likes to eat well.
Era verdad que no sabíamos nada.	It was true we did not know anything.

Aplicación

I. Answer each question using **No sé** and **Dudo** + subjunctive.

MODELO Ella ganará, ¿verdad? → **No sé. Dudo que gane.**

1. Ella irá con nosotros, ¿verdad?
2. Meterá las cosas en la mochila, ¿verdad?
3. Ellos jugarán tenis, ¿verdad?
4. Ustedes llegarán temprano, ¿verdad?
5. Juan hará algo, ¿verdad?
6. Podremos salir, ¿verdad?
7. Me aburriré, ¿verdad?
8. Los chicos se divertirán, ¿verdad?

II. Change the following sentences to the negative. The subjunctive will be required.

MODELO Creo que juega bien. → **No creo que juegue bien.**

1. Estoy seguro que están resfriados.
2. Es verdad que gana siempre.
3. Es evidente que lo saben.
4. Es cierto que él es un buen golfista.
5. Creemos que se divierte.
6. Es seguro que hay una fórmula especial.

III. Restate each sentence making the indicated substitutions. Use the indicative or subjunctive, as appropriate.

MODELO Creo que esperan a Mariana. (Dudo, estoy seguro) →
(subjunctive) **Dudo que esperen a Mariana.**
(indicative) **Estoy seguro que esperan a Mariana.**

1. No creo que sea así. (creo, dudo, estoy seguro)
2. Es imposible que se calme. (es seguro, no es verdad, no es cierto, estoy seguro)

3. Quieren que me vaya. (dudan, prefieren, creen, están seguros)
4. No me gusta que ella lo diga. (creo, me contaron, dudo)
5. Creemos que hay otra alternativa. (es imposible, esperamos, no es seguro)
6. Es mejor que no lo sepan. (es cierto, es lástima, es seguro, es posible)
7. Quiero que salga. (es verdad, prefiero, estoy seguro, no me gusta)
8. Es evidente que te conocen. (es imposible, es verdad, es seguro, es probable)
9. Tengo miedo que estés resfriado. (es posible, es una lástima, creo, espero)
10. Sentimos que no te guste el artículo. (estamos seguros, es evidente, tenemos miedo, no nos importa)

B. Adverbs: forms and uses

Te quiero **locamente.**

An adverb is a word used to modify a verb, an adjective, or another adverb. Many English adverbs end in *-ly: immediately, quickly, only.*

1. You are already familiar with several adverbs in Spanish. Adverbs may be one word or a combination of two or more words.

muy	**pronto**
demasiado	**un poco**
quizás	**por fin**
siempre	**de nuevo**
bien	**por la tarde**

Mi abuelo está grave de nuevo.	My grandfather is critical again.
Sé que el trabajo es muy difícil.	I know that the work is very difficult.
Quizás haya una fórmula especial.	Maybe there is a special formula.

2. A simple way to form many additional adverbs is to add the ending **-mente** to the feminine singular form (or invariable form) of an adjective.

(sola + mente) → **solamente**

(fácil + mente) → **fácilmente**

Por favor, márchese inmediatamente.	Please leave immediately.
Los tres muchachos subieron rápidamente.	The three boys climbed up quickly.

3. Adverbs never change their ending for gender agreement. Normally they appear just before or just after the word (a verb, an adjective, or another adverb) they modify. Adverbs modify by answering, in a general way, one of the following questions:

   a. Where? (**aquí, allá. . .**)

Aquí se habla español.	Spanish is spoken here.

b. When? **(ayer, hoy, a veces, pronto, por la tarde. . .)**

Ayer fue martes, hoy es miércoles, y mañana es jueves.	Yesterday was Tuesday, today is Wednesday, and tomorrow is Thursday.

c. How? **(bien, mal, fácilmente. . .)**

Hablo bien el español.	I speak Spanish well.
Ganamos fácilmente.	We won easily.

d. Really? **(posiblemente, quizás. . .)**

Quizás te veo esta noche.	Maybe I'll see you tonight.
Tal vez lo gane; tal vez, no.	Maybe I'll win it; maybe not.

e. To what degree? **(locamente, muy, demasiado. . .)**

José Antonio come demasiado.	José Antonio eats too much.
Está muy preocupado.	He's very worried.
Te quiero locamente.	I love you madly.

Aplicación

I. Answer each question, including the word in parentheses in your response.

MODELO ¿Está grave? (muy) → **Sí, está muy grave.**

1. ¿Habla por teléfono Ramón con Pilar? (demasiado)
2. ¿Ganará Nancy? (quizás)
3. ¿Habla usted español? (un poco)
4. ¿Se marchará Ramón? (muy pronto)
5. ¿Cuándo lee usted el periódico? (por la mañana)
6. ¿Tienen plata ellos? (nunca)
7. ¿Cuándo hablamos del problema? (hoy)
8. ¿Llama usted a su prometida (prometido)? (siempre)
9. ¿Llegaron a la estación? (por fin)
10. ¿Comprende Juan el inglés? (bien)

II. Give the adverb that corresponds to each adjective.

MODELO inmediato → **inmediatamente**

1. fácil 2. nuevo 3. solo 4. cordial 5. agitado 6. anterior 7. especial 8. loco 9. inteligente 10. débil

III. Change the adjective in parentheses to an adverb and insert it in the sentence.

MODELO (loco) Te quiero. → **Te quiero locamente.**

1. (fácil) Ganaron.
2. (rápido) Se marchó.
3. (largo) Sonreíste.
4. (solo) Es una niña.
5. (nuevo) Está enferma.
6. (loco) Se enamoraron.
7. (débil) Habló.
8. (claro) Lo dijo.

C. Ordinal numbers

> **Primero,** pégale a la pelota.

The ordinal numbers in English are *first, second, third* . . .

1. The first ten Spanish ordinals are as follows.

1° **primero**	6° **sexto**
2° **segundo**	7° **séptimo (sétimo)**
3° **tercero**	8° **octavo**
4° **cuarto**	9° **noveno**
5° **quinto**	10° **décimo**

2. When an ordinal number is used as an adjective, it appears before the noun and agrees with it in number and gender.

Elena llegará en el segundo vuelo de Miami.	Elena will arrive on the second flight from Miami.
Ésta es la quinta vez que lo digo.	This is the fifth time that I am saying it.
¡Dios mío! Ésta es la tercera reseña mala.	My gosh! This is the third bad review.

These changes are reflected in the abbreviation: **7° vuelo, 7ª reseña.**

3. **Primero** and **tercero** have special forms used before a masculine singular noun.

primer
tercer + masculine singular noun

Detuvieron el primer taxi.	They stopped the first taxi.
¿Cuándo será el tercer torneo?	When will the third tournament be (held)?

The forms are abbreviated **1ʳ** and **3ʳ.**

4. The ordinal numbers are used from **primero** to **décimo.** After **décimo,** use a noun followed by the cardinal number.

Ésta es la décima vez que estoy aquí en Madrid.	This is the tenth time that I've been here in Madrid.
Estamos en el siglo veinte.	We're in the twentieth century.

5. In order to express the English pronouns *the first* (*one*), *the second* (*one*) . . . , use a definite article + ordinal number. Both the article and the ordinal correspond in number and gender to the noun they are replacing.

Mis amigos siempre son los primeros en llegar.	My friends are always the first to arrive.
Su oficina es la tercera.	His office is the third one.
Suban ustedes al décimo.	Go up to the tenth (floor).

6. When an ordinal number is modified by an infinitive, **en** precedes the infinitive.

Eres el segundo en llamar.	You're the second one to call.
Fuimos las primeras en salir.	We were the first to leave.

Aplicación

I. Repeat each sentence making the indicated substitutions.

MODELO Es el primer torneo. (entrevista) → **Es la primera entrevista.**

1. ¿Fuiste a la segunda fiesta? (concierto, clase, partido)
2. ¿Es la tercera muchacha que vino? (estudiante, reportero, persona)
3. ¿Es la décima vez? (mes, semana, día)
4. Detuvieron a la primera persona que vieron. (americano, médico, muchachas, extranjeros)
5. Es la quinta recepción del año. (fiesta, mes, sesión, partido)

II. Supply the ordinal numbers.

MODELO Ésta es la 3ª vez que te lo digo. → **Ésta es la tercera vez que te lo digo.**

1. Ésta es la 10ª persona que veo.
2. Ésta es la 4ª vez que llama.
3. Enero es el 1^r mes del año.
4. La familia Iglesias vive en la 3ª casa.
5. Éste es el 5° recado que dejo.
6. Hablan de la 2ª Guerra.
7. Éste es el 7° estudiante que viene.
8. Hoy es el 6° día de la semana.
9. Ésta es la 9ª reseña que escribe.
10. Hay que leer el 8° capítulo para mañana.

III. Express in Spanish using an ordinal pronoun + **en** + infinitive.

MODELO You're the third one to arrive. → **Usted es el tercero en llegar.**

1. You're the first one to know.
2. She's the fifth one to call.
3. I'm the tenth one to come.
4. He's the third one to leave.
5. They're the first ones to read the article.

Pausa oral

La familia Iglesias

I. Listed below are the groups of a typical family listed from oldest to youngest. Identify one member of each group in relation to one or two of the other family members.

MODELO el padre → **El padre es el hijo del abuelo y la abuela. También es el hermano de uno de los tíos.**

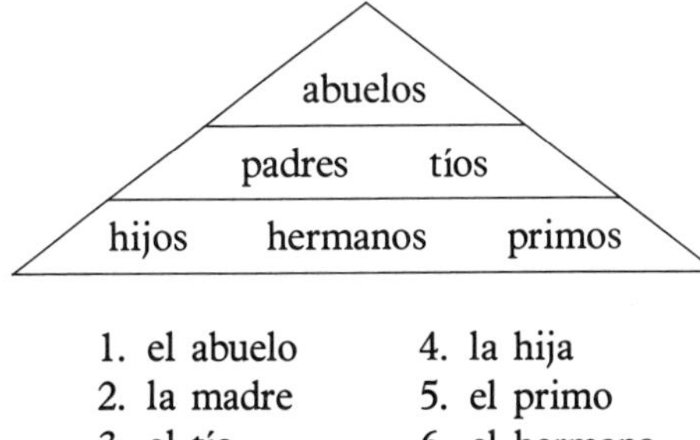

1. el abuelo
2. la madre
3. el tío
4. la hija
5. el primo
6. el hermano

II. Review the dialog at the beginning of the chapter. Then, together with two classmates, recreate the general scene and conversation or a similar conversation. The first few words of each exchange are listed below to help you along.

(Pilar, Ramón, la madre de Pilar, el padre de Pilar)

PILAR ¿Qué haces. . . ?
RAMÓN No, encanto. Nada. . .
PILAR Ya doy; tu abuela. . .
(Pilar lee el periódico en voz alta.)
PILAR Dios mío, tu. . .

* * *

MADRE Ramón, por favor. . .
PADRE Mire, Ramón.
RAMÓN Pero, don Martín, yo. . .
PADRE ¡Fuera. . . !

* * *

RAMÓN Cómo no voy a saber que. . .
PILAR No podemos tú y yo. . .
RAMÓN Quedamos en. . .

III. How does the Iglesias family feel about the relationship between Pilar and Ramón? Use some of the expressions listed below to explain how four or five members of the family might react.

ser optimista	equivocarse
estar emocionado	apresurar las cosas
estar preocupado	analizar todo
estar tranquilo	cambiar de opinión
estar sorprendido	tener razón
estar (muy) agitado	resolver el problema
ser muy terco	ser responsable (de)
calmarse	quedar (en)
ponerse furioso	convencer (a)
enojarse (con)	darse cuenta (de)

MODELO (la abuela) **La abuela de Pilar está muy agitada porque recuerda a su hijo Armando. Armando perdió la vida en la masacre de Huelva. Pero la abuela comprende que Ramón no es responsable por esa masacre. Ella se da cuenta que Pilar quiere mucho a Ramón.**

The International Brigades were made up of foreign volunteers fighting on the side of the Spanish Republic. Over 2800 American volunteers, of whom more than 500 were killed, were organized in the Lincoln Battalion.

ESTRUCTURA II

A. Reflexive constructions (III): unplanned occurrences

¿Se te olvidó algo anoche?

1. The reflexive **se** is used in sentences which express an unplanned occurrence. An indirect object pronoun (**me, te, le . . .**) follows **se** and indicates who the person affected by the occurrence is. The verb is third-person singular or plural, depending on the subject. This subject often appears at the end of the sentence.

se + indirect object + third-person verb + subject

¿Se te olvidó la llave?	Did you forget the key?
¿Se te olvidaron las llaves?	Did you forget the keys?

2. The noun to which **le** or **les** refers may or may not be stated.

Se le ocurrirá algo.	Something will occur to her.
Se le ocurrirá algo a María.	Something will occur to María.

3. The verb used to indicate the unplanned occurrence is often, but not always, in the preterit tense. Here are some typical verbs used in this way.

se me acabó	(acabaron)
se te cayó	(cayeron)
se le ocurrió	(ocurrieron)
se nos olvidó	(olvidaron)
se les perdió	(perdieron)
se me rompió	(rompieron)

Se nos acabó la leche.	We ran out of milk.
Se me cayeron los papeles.	I dropped the papers.
Se les ocurrió una idea estupenda.	They had a wonderful idea.
Se te van a perder las llaves.	You're going to lose the keys.
Se le rompieron las botellas.	He broke the bottles.

Aplicación

I. Make the indicated substitutions and change the verb as required.

MODELO Nunca se me pierden las llaves. (el pasaporte) → **Nunca se me pierde el pasaporte.**

1. Se me olvidaron los libros. (el periódico, las llaves, el abrigo)
2. ¿Se te ocurre una idea? (una solución, alguien, una pregunta, algo)

3. Se me acabó el café. (el postre, la paciencia, las papas)
4. ¿Se le rompieron las cosas? (la mochila, el machete, las botas)
5. Se les perdió la botella. (los ahorros, el dinero, los libros)

II. Repeat each sentence changing the indirect object pronoun according to the cue.

MODELO ¿Se te olvidó algo? (a Juan, a nosotros) → **¿Se le olvidó algo? ¿Se nos olvidó algo?**

1. Se me rompió el lápiz. (a mamá, a ustedes, a ti, a nosotros, a Pilar)
2. Se te perdieron las llaves. (a los chicos, a mi hermana, a mí, a nosotros, a usted)
3. Siempre se le olvida todo. (a mis amigos, a Ramón, a nosotros, a mí, a ti)
4. Se les acabaron los problemas. (a nosotros, a mí, a ti, a ustedes, a mi tía)
5. ¿Dónde se te quedaron las cosas? (a mí, a usted, a nosotros, a los estudiantes, a ti)

III. Para contestar

1. ¿A usted se le olvidan las cosas fácilmente? ¿Qué se le olvida?
2. ¿A ustedes se les ocurren buenas ideas? ¿Y a los profesores?
3. ¿Se me cayó el libro? ¿A veces se me caen las cosas en clase?
4. ¿A usted se le perdieron las llaves alguna vez? ¿Cómo entró usted a la casa?
5. ¿Se nos acabaron las preguntas para hoy o se les ocurren más a ustedes?

B. Adjectives of indefinite quantity

No podemos resolver **todos** los problemas.

1. Adjectives of indefinite quantity are those that indicate amount in a very general way. They give a general answer to the question *How many?* With one exception (the word **cada**), they all show agreement for number and gender with the noun that follows them.

poco	(a) little	poco dinero
mucho	a lot, much, many	muchos años
demasiado	too much, too many	demasiados problemas
otro	another	otra copa
bastante	enough	bastante tiempo
varios	several	varios amigos
algunos	some	algunas clases
unos	some, a few	unas mujeres
todos	every, all	todos los días
cada	each	cada muchacho

Note that nouns of indefinite quantity appear before the noun they modify.

2. The special form **algún** is used before a masculine singular noun.

Algún día iré a España.	Someday I'll go to Spain.
Vamos a hacer un viaje a algún país extranjero.	We're going to take a trip to some foreign country.

3. The word **un** (**una. . .**) is never used before **otro** (**otra. . .**).

¿Quieres otro café, mamá?	Do you want another (cup of) coffee, mom?
¿Voy a trabajar para otra compañía.	I'm going to work for another company.

4. The word **cada** is invariable in form. It is always followed by a singular noun or by **uno** or **una.**

Tú y yo no podemos resolver cada problema.	You and I can't solve every problem.
En cada guerra hay matanzas de civiles.	In every war there are killings of civilians.
Hay tres señores aquí y cada uno tiene una pregunta.	There are three gentlemen here and each has a question.

Aplicación

I. Form a new sentence using both adjectives.

MODELO Tengo dinero. (poco / mexicano) → **Tengo poco dinero mexicano.**

1. Conozco a gente. (mucha / extranjera)
2. Vimos edificios. (varios / famosos)
3. Pilar tiene tiempo. (demasiado / libre)
4. Compré tazas. (algunas / muy caras)
5. Resuelven los problemas. (todos / difíciles)
6. Hay detalles que discutir. (otros / importantes)
7. Oigo voces. (unas / amables)
8. Tenemos amigos. (pocos / argentinos)
9. Hay clases. (pocas / fáciles)
10. ¿Estuviste en el hospital? (otro / nuevo)
11. Vimos botas. (algunas / baratas)
12. Leo periódicos. (muchos / españoles)

II. Para expresar en español

MODELO Each has another book. → **Cada uno tiene otro libro.**

1. Each has another question.
2. Each asks for (**pide**) another dessert.
3. Each has another job.
4. Each writes another article.
5. Each looks for another apartment.

C. Verbs + **de** / Verbs + **en**

Repaso. Several verbs require the preposition **a** when used before an infinitive: **ir a, empezar a, volver a. . .**

> Ramón **acaba de** llegar.
> **Quedamos en** vernos mañana.

1. A number of verbs require the preposition **de** when used before an infinitive.

acabar de	to have just	Acabamos de llegar.
dejar de	to stop	Ella no deja de interrumpir.
tratar de	to try	Traté de estudiar.

Acabo de lavarme las manos.	I just washed my hands.
Trata de calmarte, chico.	Hey, try to calm down.
Osvaldo ya dejó de jugar golf.	Osvaldo has already quit playing golf.

2. When used in the present tense, **acabar de** means *have (has) just* (+ verb). When used in the imperfect, **acabar de** means *had just* (+ verb).

El profesor acaba de ir a su despacho.	The professor has just gone to his office.
Acaba de morirse la abuela de Pilar.	Pilar's grandmother just died.
Acabábamos de ponernos cómodos.	We had just gotten comfortable.
Acababan de morirse mis abuelos cuando salimos de Cuba.	My grandparents had just died when we left Cuba.

3. Still other verbs require **en** before an infinitive.

insistir en	to insist upon	Insisto en hablarte.
quedar en	to agree to	¿En qué quedamos?

Ramón insiste en venir a casa de Pilar.	Ramon insists upon coming to Pilar's house.
Oscar y Nancy quedaron en verse a las 5 en la estación.	Oscar and Nancy agreed to meet at 5 o'clock in the station.

Aplicación

I. Form sentences by combining the items in each list.

MODELO nosotros / alegrarse / poder resolver / el problema → **Nos alegramos de poder resolver el problema.**

1. yo / acabar / hacer el trabajo
2. ellos / aburrirse / escuchar al profesor
3. Susana / alegrarse / vernos / de nuevo
4. ellos / nunca / dejar / divertirse

5. nosotros / tratar / encontrar otra alternativa
6. ustedes / acabar / leer el periódico
7. Pilar y yo / olvidarse / traer el libro
8. Ramón / quejarse / tener que hacerlo
9. Ella y yo / quedar / vernos en el café
10. yo / insistir / discutirlo contigo

II. Para expresar en español

MODELO My family just left. / They had just left. → **Mi familia acaba de salir.** / **Acababan de salir.**

1. My grandparents just arrived. / They had just arrived.
2. My parents just called. / They had just called.
3. My uncle just came in. / He had just come in.
4. My sister just won. / She had just won.
5. My cousin just lost. / He had just lost.

III. Supply the correct preposition: **a, en, de.**

Cada vez que Ramón va a casa de don Martín, los dos hombres empiezan ______ discutir *(to argue).* Me acuerdo ______ una noche en que comenzaron ______ discutir más o menos a las siete y no dejaron ______ hablar hasta la una de la mañana. Mamá insiste ______ que Ramón y Martín se hablen de una manera cordial en casa, pero es imposible. Cada vez que don Martín ve ______ Ramón, recuerda ______ su padre y ______ su hermano: los dos murieron en esa masacre horrible de Huelva. Una vez, por mamá, quedaron ______ no discutir más, por lo menos no en casa. Yo creo que realmente trataron ______ dejar ______ discutir, pero fue imposible. Ninguno de los dos puede olvidar la Guerra.

Ser español, mayor de 21 años y estar en el Censo. Es todo lo que necesitas para participar en tu futuro político. Medita tu voto.

Spain, June 15, 1975. First free elections since 1936.

Madrid, 1978. First feminist demonstration in Spain, with 15,000 women marching.

 LECTURA

La España joven

1 No hace mucho tiempo[1], hace unos cinco o diez años, la gente
tenía una impresión muy negativa de la juventud[1] española.
3 Muchos pensaban que los españoles de 17 a 25 años eran o
exageradamente conservadores o[1] francamente "reaccionarios".
5 Pensaban que su manera de pensar estaba completamente
dominada por las Instituciones—con mayúscula[1]—es decir, por
9 un gobierno inflexible y rígido, una iglesia[1] conservadora y
anticuada y una familia dominante y tradicionalista. Lógicamente,
11 pensaba la gente, los colegios[1], los institutos y las universidades
funcionaban como agentes de las "tres grandes instituciones" y
13 nada más.

Not too long ago
youth
o. . .o either . . . or
capital letter
church
schools (K–12)

Pero ocurre que un veinte de noviembre de 1975 España pierde a su Jefe Máximo—el Generalísimo Francisco Franco. El "Caudillo de España por la gracia de Dios" muere a los ochenta y dos años después de gobernar a España desde 1939. El Generalísimo Franco—quien con la ayuda de Hitler y Mussolini derrota a la República Española cuyo gobierno tenía el apoyo de Stalín—inicia la Guerra Civil (1936–1939) y después, por casi cuarenta años, domina por completo los destinos de España. Con la muerte de Franco, España entra en una nueva etapa.

Naturalmente que son los jóvenes españoles los primeros en lanzarse a esta "modernidad" que la desaparición del Caudillo proporciona. Los jóvenes españoles, hombres y mujeres, buscan la emancipación, la liberación y la integración de España dentro del concierto de naciones europeas modernas. Ansiosamente la juventud española trata de recuperar el terreno perdido durante la dictadura de Francisco Franco, la cual trajo prosperidad y paz a expensas de la libertad de expresión, de los derechos humanos y de la diversidad cultural y política de millones de españoles.

España, después de Franco, es cambio, es exploración. Las transformaciones empiezan a ocurrir muy pronto, especialmente en los sectores que más deseaban el cambio: los jóvenes españoles de clase media. Sus actitudes tocante a pólitica, religión y sexo contrastan en forma tan marcada con las actitudes de las generaciones viejas que es conveniente describirlas. En los 80, los jóvenes Juan Pérez y María Sánchez no son de extrema derecha ni de extrema izquierda: son de centro izquierda. Su nacionalismo es muy moderado y no les gustan las intervenciones militares fuera de España. Favorecen las autonomías de las diferentes regiones españolas como Cataluña y los Países Vascos[1], pero están opuestos al terrorismo utilizado por unos de los separatistas.

A la religión, Juan y María—como más del cincuenta porciento (50%) de la juventud—le prestan poca o nada de atención. Favorecen el divorcio y piensan que no es necesario establecer la religión católica (o cualquier otra religión) como religión oficial de España[2].

Tocante a la sexualidad, Juan y María tienen una actitud liberada. Son realistas, racionales y tolerantes; aceptan cosas en

- Supreme Chief
- **"Caudillo . . ."** Chief of State of Spain by the Grace of God
- defeats / whose / support
- **por completo** completely
- death / era
- **en . . .** to lunge for
- makes available
- **dentro del** within the
- ground / lost
- **la cual trajo** which brought
- **derechos humanos** human rights
- change
- soon
- **que . . .** who desired change the most
- middle class / **tocante a** regarding
- worthwhile
- **Juan . . .** John and Jean Q. Public
- right (wing) / nor / left (wing)
- opposed
- pay
- sexual matters

Two Valencians reading of the visit of King Juan Carlos and Queen Sofía to their city.

otras personas que ellos no harían. Tres cuartas partes ($^3/_4$) de los jóvenes españoles, por ejemplo, no consideran las relaciones sexuales premaritales como problema. Y la emancipación femenina gana más y más terreno en España cada día porque los hombres y las mujeres jóvenes españoles se inclinan a pensar que la mujer, como el hombre, tiene derecho a trabajar fuera de casa y a ganar tanto dinero como el hombre. Hoy día' la inmensa mayoría' también favorece la idea de compartir' las labores del hogar'.

Nowadays
majority / share
labores . . . household chores

Sí, España está muy cambiada. Y son, en gran parte, los jóvenes españoles los responsables de estas transformaciones. Gracias a su juventud, España es una vez más parte de Europa. Los jóvenes españoles, armados con su sentido práctico de la vida y sin tener que observar programas ideológicos, combaten cada día grandes batallas y obtienen triunfos significativos. Tal parece que hasta los viejos españoles, normalmente poco inclinados a escuchar a la gente joven, están copiando poco a poco el estilo de vida de la juventud española.

Después de todo, ¿por qué no imitar un estilo de vida que sólo requiere vivir y dejar vivir?

changed

una vez más once more

armed / sense

battles

It would appear that even

style

Glosas

1. Throughout recorded history Spain has lived with strong regional tensions. Portugal, once part of Spain, broke away permanently. **Cataluña** (the region centering on Barcelona, once an independent kingdom, where many people speak Catalan as well as Spanish) and **los Países Vascos** (the Basque provinces, centering on Bilbao, where many people speak Basque as well as Spanish) have agitated for more than a century, when not for outright independence, at least for governmental autonomy within a federal framework. In the early 1930's, when the Spanish Republic granted significant autonomous powers to Catalonia and the Basque country, many Spaniards, envisioning the breakup of Spain, joined the conservative, nationalistic opposition which soon rose up against the Republic and began the Civil War. It is a sign of how swiftly the process of liberalization is proceeding in Spain that young people today can casually advocate regional autonomy. A certain measure of autonomy has already been granted by the new central government.
2. Other factors leading Spanish conservatives to revolt in 1936 were the Republic's attempts to stop funding the Catholic Church, to permit divorce, and to curtail the Church's dominance of the country's educational system. Acts of violence against priests and churches by some anticlerical supporters of the Republic were increasingly common; when war broke out, they occurred on a massive scale in many parts of Spain.

SOBRE LA LECTURA

I. Comment on each of the following topics:

1. la opinión que los extranjeros tenían de los jóvenes españoles.
2. Francisco Franco.
3. la muerte del Generalísimo.
4. los primeros españoles en lanzarse a la "modernidad".
5. las ideas del típico joven español en cuanto a la política.
6. la importancia de la Iglesia.
7. la actitud de los jóvenes con respecto al divorcio.
8. sus opiniones con respecto a cuestiones sexuales.
9. la emancipación de la mujer.
10. la importancia de los jóvenes en la transformación de España.

II. Para discutir

1. Antes de leer este artículo, ¿qué opinión tenía usted de los jóvenes españoles?
2. En los Estados Unidos, ¿tienen los jóvenes mucha influencia en la política? ¿en las actitudes sociales y morales?
3. Compare las opiniones de los jóvenes españoles en cuanto a la política con las opiniones de los jóvenes americanos.
4. ¿Tiene la religión mucha importancia en la vida de un típico joven americano? Explique.
5. En cuanto a cuestiones sexuales, ¿tienen los americanos una actitud liberada?
6. ¿Qué piensa usted de la emancipación femenina?
7. ¿Deben el hombre y la mujer compartir las labores del hogar? ¿Por qué?
8. En los Estados Unidos, ¿copian los viejos el estilo de vida de la juventud? ¿Es bueno o malo esto?

Repaso oral

I. Combine the elements in each list to form a complete sentence.

1. Abuela / estar / sano / ahora / estar / resfriado
2. yo / no creer / el abuelo / ser responsable / las matanzas
3. la abuela de Pilar / darse cuenta / Pilar / querer / Ramón
4. siempre / se me / perder / llaves
5. algún día / yo / tratar / resolver / ese problema
6. nosotros / acabar / salir de casa / cuando / llamar / Pilar

II. Para comentar

There might be many reasons why the young woman and young man in the drawing are unhappy. State as many reasons as you can think of. Some possible reasons are suggested by the smaller drawings.

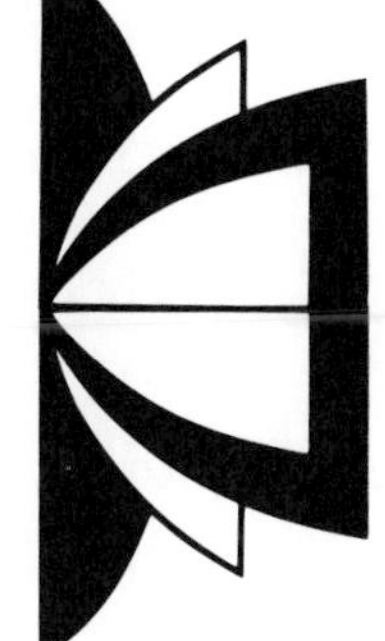

Capítulo 14

Despegue

DIÁLOGO **En un aserradero en Oaxaca, México**
The present perfect and past perfect tenses • Comparisons (II): equality • Three ways to express obligation

PAUSA ORAL **La vida rural**
The passive: **se** + verb / **ser** + participle • Commands (IV): **nosotros**

Repaso oral

Despegue

Descripción del dibujo

1. En el aserradero cortan muchos árboles.
2. Un día hay un accidente en el aserradero.
3. Cae un puente.
4. El administrador está muy preocupado.
5. Dice que reconstruir el puente sería muy caro.

Pronunciación

1. Cae el puente.
2. Hugo Bernal / Oaxaca / México
3. No se reconstruye el puente.
4. una vez / mil veces
5. Hay un accidente.

Aplicación

I. Relación

Make as many statements as you can about the picture on page 327. Try to make at least ten sentences.

II. Para contestar

1. ¿Qué hacen los hombres que trabajan en el aserradero?
2. ¿Sabría usted cortar un árbol?
3. ¿Qué es un aserradero?
4. ¿Qué accidente ocurrió?
5. ¿Hay un puente en esta ciudad?
6. ¿Cayó el puente alguna vez?
7. ¿Qué dice el administrador?
8. ¿A usted le gustaría ser administrador (administradora) de un aserradero?

Tema del diálogo

The owner of a sawmill in Oaxaca, Mexico, and his foreman survey the damage suffered by a bridge in a mountainous lumber camp.

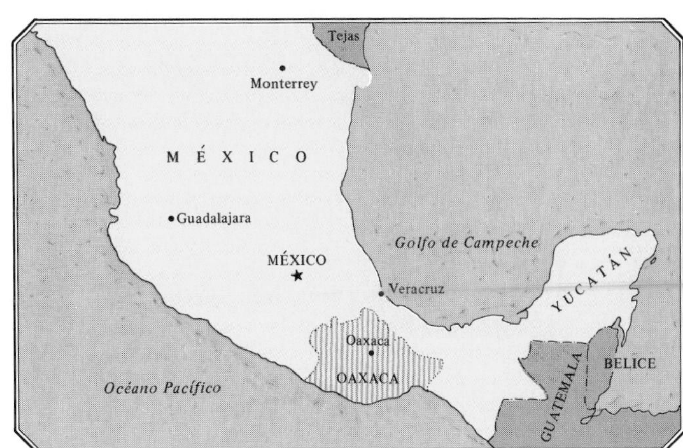

DIÁLOGO

En un aserradero en Oaxaca[1], México

El ingeniero Hugo Bernal, dueño de un aserradero, habla con su administrador.

BERNAL Una y mil veces te[2] he dicho que hay que proteger al trabajador ante todo.

ADMINISTRADOR Sí, ingeniero[3], pero el accidente de ayer era inevitable.

BERNAL ¿Inevitable? ¡Ja! ¿Habías revisado los cables del puente?

ADMINISTRADOR Sí, don Hugo. Es que ha llovido tanto y la tierra está muy blanda.

BERNAL Bueno, por suerte no murió nadie. (El ingeniero Bernal se dirige a la ventana, mira hacia el cielo y cierra la ventana.)

BERNAL Vamos a ver si el daño es tan extenso como dices.

ADMINISTRADOR Ya le he ensillado un caballo que le va a gustar.

BERNAL (Para sí.) ¡Ojalá no sea tan malo como el caballo de la semana pasada!

* * *

(Montan a caballo los dos. Después de un buen rato, llegan al lugar del accidente.)

BERNAL ¡Mi madre![4] Aquí parece que ha caído una bomba. ¡Del puente no ha quedado casi nada!

ADMINISTRADOR Sí, ingeniero. Los árboles que habíamos cortado ayer pesaban demasiado para el puente. . .y, pues, allá en el valle se ven los troncos.

BERNAL ¡Qué remedio! Ahora yo pienso que reconstruir el puente saldría más caro que hacer otro camino por allí.

ADMINISTRADOR ¿Por el lado sur?

BERNAL Allí mismo.

ADMINISTRADOR Bueno pues, ¿cuándo empezamos?

BERNAL Empecemos esta misma tarde. No debemos perder un instante.

ADMINISTRADOR De acuerdo, don Hugo. El aserradero tiene que seguir produciendo.

Timber from the Mexican states of Oaxaca and Chiapas is used throughout the nation.

In a sawmill in Oaxaca, Mexico

Hugo Bernal, engineer and owner of a sawmill, is talking with his foreman.

B: Time and again I've told you that it's necessary to protect the worker above all else.

A: Yes, Engineer, but yesterday's accident was unavoidable.

B: Unavoidable? Ha! Had you inspected the cables of the bridge?

A: Yes, Don Hugo. It's just that it has rained so much and the ground is very soft.

B: Well, luckily no one died. (Bernal goes toward the window, looks at the sky, and closes the window.)

B: Let's see if the damage is as extensive as you say.

A: I've already saddled you a horse that you're going to like.

B: (to himself) Hopefully it won't be as bad as the horse (I had) last week!

* * *

(The two mount up. After quite a while, they arrive at the scene of the accident.)

B: My God! It looks like a bomb has fallen here. Almost nothing of the bridge is left (has remained).

A: Yes, Engineer. The trees that we had cut yesterday weighed too much for the bridge . . . and, well, down here in the valley you can see (are seen) the trunks.

B: What can you do? Now I'm thinking that to rebuild the bridge would turn out more expensive than making another road over there.

A: On the South Side?

B: Exactly there.

A: Well then, when do we start?

B: Let's start this very afternoon. We shouldn't lose a moment.

A: Agreed, Don Hugo. The sawmill has got to go on producing.

VARIACIONES

¿Trabajas en un aserradero?	Do you work in a lumbercamp?
No, trabajo en una finca[5].	No, I work on a farm.
¿Está en el sur la finca?	Is the farm in the south?
No, está en el norte.	No, it's in the north.
Está en el este.	It's in the east.
Está en el oeste.	It's in the west.
¿Qué hay en la finca?	What is there on the farm?
cerdos	pigs
gallinas	chickens
gatos	cats
ovejas	sheep
pájaros	birds
vacas	cows
¿Qué tiempo hace?	How's the weather?
Hace buen tiempo.	It's nice weather.
mal tiempo.	bad weather.
calor.	hot.
frío.	cold.
sol.	sunny.
viento.	windy.

Glosas

1. **Oaxaca** (pronounced Wa-HA-ca) is a large state in Southern Mexico; its remarkably beautiful capital city has the same name. Oaxaca's forests are rich in pines and other valuable trees. Historically speaking, Oaxaca is a very special state. Benito Juárez (1806–1872), one of the greatest figures in the history of Mexico, and Porfirio Díaz (1830–1915), once a patriotic general and later a notorious dictator, were **oaxaqueños.** Hernán Cortés, the conqueror of Mexico, was given the title **Marqués del Valle de Oaxaca** by **Carlos V** (King Charles V of Spain) as a reward for his exploits in conquering Mexico for the Spanish crown.
2. When two Spanish-speakers are noticeably different in social standing, backgrounds, professional status, or age, conversations in which one person addresses the other as **usted,** and the other responds with **tú,** often occur. In the dialog, don Hugo Bernal is the owner of the sawmill and he is also college educated. The foreman's social credentials are less impressive. Notice how the two men address each other.
3. In Hispanic countries not only doctors are addressed by their titles, but also **ingenieros, licenciados** (lawyers), **químicos, arquitectos,** and so on. In writing these titles are often abbreviated: **Ing., Lic., Quim., Arq.** Thus, Mr. Bernal, who is an engineer, would be called **el ingeniero Bernal.** When addressing him one would say, **Buenos días, ingeniero Bernal.**

4. In Spanish America motherhood is considered to be sacred. The word **madre** should be handled with care as most people are hypersensitive about casual references to their mother. In Venezuela and Mexico, the situation is such that one can hardly inquire about someone's mother without resorting to **¿cómo está su <u>señora</u> madre?** In conversations conducted on a **tú** basis, one may refer to **tu mamá** without risk of offending.
5. **Finca** is just one of a large number of Spanish terms for *farm.* Others are **rancho, hacienda, granja, fundo, estancia.** Some of these words are used in certain regions or countries (e.g., **fundo** in Chile, **rancho** in Mexico and in the U.S. Southwest). Other words convey differences in size; increase the size of a **rancho** and it may be called a **hacienda. Finca** may be relied upon until the particular terms used in an area become clear. In many parts of Spanish America **rancho** means *hut.*

SOBRE EL DIÁLOGO

I. ¿Sí o no?

MODELO Hugo Bernal es de los Estados Unidos. → **No, Hugo Bernal es mexicano, de Oaxaca.**

1. Bernal es dueño de un aserradero.
2. Habla con uno de sus amigos.
3. Bernal dice que los trabajadores no son importantes.
4. El administrador había revisado los cables del puente.
5. Don Hugo espera que el caballo sea bueno.
6. Bernal y su administrador van en taxi al lugar del accidente.
7. El puente no está en malas condiciones.
8. Allá en el valle se ven casas.
9. Bernal quiere reconstruir el puente.
10. Van a empezar a hacer el camino la semana que viene.
11. Bernal dice que no hay que darse prisa.
12. El aserradero tiene que dejar de producir.

II. Tell which sentence in the righthand column is a logical response to each statement at the left.

MODELO ¿Es médico tu tío? → **No, es ingeniero.**

1. Mi tío tiene una finca.	a. Hombre, esta misma tarde.
2. Tiene muchos animales.	b. Les va a gustar el oeste.
3. Vamos a vivir en California.	c. No, es ingeniero.
4. Tenemos que llegar al otro lado.	d. ¿Caballos, vacas y cerdos?
5. ¿Es de tu abuelo la finca?	e. Tendrán que pasar por el puente.
6. Va a llover, ¿verdad?	f. ¿Tiene mucha tierra?
7. Llueve mucho, ¿verdad?	g. Él es el dueño, sí.
8. El daño es muy extenso.	h. Claro, mira esas nubes.
9. Vamos a empezar inmediatamente.	i. No queda casi nada.

VOCABULARIO

nouns

el **accidente**	accident
el **administrador**, la **administradora**	foreman, administrator
el **árbol**	tree
el **aserradero**	lumber camp, sawmill
la **bomba**	bomb
el **caballo**	horse
el **cable**	cable
el **camino**	road
el **cerdo**	pig
el **cielo**	sky
el **daño**	damage
el **dueño**	owner
el **este**	east
la **finca**	farm
la **gallina**	chicken, hen
el **gato**	cat
el **norte**	north
el **oeste**	west
la **oveja**	sheep
el **pájaro**	bird
el **puente**	the bridge
la **suerte**	luck
por suerte	luckily
el **sur**	south
el **tiempo**	weather
la **tierra**	ground, land, earth
el **trabajador**, la **trabajadora**	worker
el **tronco**	tree trunk
la **vaca**	cow
el **valle**	valley
la **ventana**	window

verbs

cerrar (ie)	to close
dirigirse (j) (a)	to go (towards)
ensillar	to saddle
llover (ue)	to rain
pesar	to weigh
producir (zc)	to produce
proteger (j)	to protect
reconstruir (y)	to reconstruct
revisar	to check, to revise

adjectives

blando	soft
extenso	extensive
inevitable	unavoidable, inevitable
mismo	same, very
rural	rural

other expressions

allí mismo	right there
ante todo	above all
anteayer	the day before yesterday
ja	ha
los dos	both (of them)
mi madre	oh, my God
montar a caballo	to mount a horse, to go horseback riding
para sí	to himself (herself, yourself, themselves. . .)
salir más caro	to turn out to be more expensive
tan. . .como	as . . . as
tanto	so much
una y mil veces	time and time again, a thousand and one times

additional vocabulary

el **coche**	car
fresco	fresh
romper	to break

ESTRUCTURA I

A. The present perfect and past perfect tenses

> **Ha llovido** mucho.
> **¿Habías revisado** los cables?

1. The Spanish present perfect generally corresponds to English *have (has)* + past participle: *I have eaten.* The past perfect corresponds to *had* + past participle: *We had arrived.*

2. The present perfect and past perfect tenses are compound tenses: the verb **haber** is used together with a past participle. In Spanish, the regular past participles are formed by dropping the infinitive ending and, for **-ar** verbs, adding **-ado;** for **-er** and **-ir** verbs, add **-ido.**

INFINITIVE		PARTICIPLE
revisar	→	**revisado**
llover	→	**llovido**
discutir	→	**discutido**

3. To form the present perfect tense, use the present tense of **haber** + participle, as follows:

empezar		**salir**	
he	+ **empezado**	**he**	+ **salido**
has		**has**	
ha		**ha**	
hemos		**hemos**	
habéis		**habéis**	
han		**han**	

No ha llovido mucho este año.	It has not rained much this year.
Han llegado al lugar del accidente.	They have arrived at the place of the accident.
Ya lo hemos discutido mil veces.	We've already discussed it a thousand times.
¿Nunca has estado en una finca?	You've never been on a farm?
¿Se ha cortado usted?	Did you cut yourself?

4. Several common verbs have irregular participles; these must be memorized.

VERB	PARTICIPLE	
abrir *to open*	**abierto**	He abierto la botella.
escribir	**escrito**	¿Has escrito la carta?
decir	**dicho**	Ha dicho la verdad.
ver	**visto**	Han visto un accidente.
morir	**muerto**	Han muerto muchas personas.
poner	**puesto**	¿Dónde has puesto el dinero?
volver	**vuelto**	Pilar no ha vuelto todavía.
hacer	**hecho**	Hemos hecho la comida.
romper *to break*	**roto**	Ya has roto la ventana.

When **-ido** is added to a verb stem that ends in **a, e,** or **o,** an accent is written on the **i.**

caer → caído
leer → leído
oir → oído

5. The past perfect (or pluperfect) tense expresses what had happened in the past. This tense is formed by using the imperfect of **haber** + participle.

llegar		**volver**	
había	**llegado**	**había**	**vuelto**
habías		**habías**	
había		**había**	
habíamos		**habíamos**	
habíais		**habíais**	
habían		**habían**	

¿Qué habías visto?	What had you seen?
Tus amigos habían llegado antes que tú.	Your friends had arrived before you.
Yo te había dicho eso mil veces.	I had told you that a thousand times.

6. When it functions as part of a compound tense, the participle does not change its ending to show agreement. **Haber** and the participle form a unit; except when **haber** is used as an infinitive, no other word can separate the form of **haber** and the participle.

¿Ha llegado Mariana?	Has Mariana arrived?
No habíamos comido todavía.	We had not yet eaten.
¿Han vivido ustedes aquí mucho tiempo?	Have you people lived here for a long time?

7. The past participle (without the verb **haber**) can also be used as an adjective. In this case, it does show agreement with the noun it modifies.

Las tazas ya están rotas.	The cups are already broken.
Mamá va a estar preocupada.	Mom is going to be worried.
No te vi la semana pasada.	I didn't see you last week.
Los caballos ya están ensillados.	The horses are already saddled.

Aplicación

I. Repeat each sentence, changing the subject according to the cue.

A. MODELO He revisado el trabajo. (el dueño, nosotros) →
Ha revisado el trabajo. Hemos revisado el trabajo.

1. ¿Han empezado? (tú, ellos, usted, nosotros)
2. Hemos viajado un buen rato. (yo, tú y yo, ustedes, tú)
3. Ya ha llegado. (los trabajadores, ustedes y yo, yo, Hugo Bernal, tú)
4. Siempre he protegido al trabajador. (ellos, el dueño, tú, nosotros, yo)
5. Se han ido. (el niño, nosotros, tú, yo, los chicos)

B. MODELO Había llamado tres veces. (tú, nosotros) →
Habías llamado tres veces. Habíamos llamado tres veces.

1. Yo había pensado mucho. (ellos, tú, nosotros, usted)
2. Había hecho el trabajo. (yo, ustedes, Hugo, tú, nosotros)
3. ¿Habías visto el accidente? (ustedes, tú, yo, nosotros)

II. Change the verb to the present perfect.

MODELO Llueve mucho. → **Ha llovido mucho.**

1. El puente cae.
2. El dueño habla con el administrador.
3. Salen a ver el puente.
4. Van a caballo.
5. El daño es extenso.
6. No quiero ir con ellos.
7. Los chicos y yo nos quedamos en casa.
8. ¿Acompañas a don Hugo?

III. Change the verb form from the present perfect to the past perfect.

1. Ya te lo he dicho.
2. No los hemos protegido.
3. No has revisado los cables.
4. Nadie ha visto el puente.
5. Yo no he hecho nada tampoco.
6. Hemos tenido muchos problemas.
7. Por eso la gente se ha quejado.
8. Y el administrador se ha ido.

IV. Answer each question using **ya** + present perfect.

MODELO ¿Vas a hacer el trabajo? → **Ya he hecho el trabajo.**

1. ¿Van a volver los chicos?
2. ¿Vas a escribir la reseña?
3. ¿Va a morir el hombre?
4. ¿Van ustedes a decir la verdad?
5. ¿Van los señores a romper el contrato?
6. ¿Voy a abrir la carta?
7. ¿Van ustedes a ver el puente?
8. ¿Vamos a poner las cosas allí?

V. Complete the following sentences with any past perfect form.

MODELO Cuando yo llegué, mis amigos. . .→
Cuando yo llegué, mis amigos ya se habían ido. *or*
Cuando yo llegué, ya habían terminado el trabajo.

1. Cuando el profesor entró. . .
2. Cuando el dueño habló conmigo. . .
3. Yo te dije que. . .
4. Ella me preguntó si. . .
5. Cuando empezó a llover. . .
6. El dejó de trabajar en la finca porque. . .

VI. Answer each question using past participles functioning as adjectives.

MODELO ¿Vas a cortar los árboles? → **No, hombre. Los árboles ya están cortados.**

1. ¿Vas a comprar las cosas?
2. ¿Vas a terminar el trabajo?
3. ¿Vas a hacer la ensalada?
4. ¿Vas a ensillar los caballos?
5. ¿Vas a escribir la carta?

VII. Para contestar

1. ¿Ha estado usted en una finca alguna vez?
2. ¿Ha visitado usted algún país extranjero? ¿Cuál? ¿Ha estado en México?
3. ¿Ha salido mucho esta semana? ¿Ha conocido a gente interesante?
4. ¿Ha tenido usted mucha vida social o ha estudiado este año?
5. ¿Han revisado ustedes su trabajo?
6. ¿Dónde ha puesto usted sus libros?
7. ¿He llegado tarde a clase alguna vez? ¿Y usted?
8. ¿Es verdad que algunos estudiantes no han abierto un libro en todo el año?

Monte Alban, capital of the ancient Zapotec civilization, in the Western Sierra Madre of Oaxaca.

9. ¿Han escrito ustedes muchos trabajos en esta clase?
10. ¿Ha montado usted a caballo alguna vez? ¿Sabe montar bien?
11. ¿Está usted preocupado (preocupada)? ¿enojado (enojada)? ¿por qué?
12. ¿Están abiertos sus libros?

B. Comparisons (II): equality

Repaso. In order to express that something is "more. . .than" or "less. . .than" something else, the expressions **más. . .que** and **menos. . .que** are used. There are four irregular comparative forms: **mejor, peor, mayor,** and **menor.**

El daño no es **tan** extenso **como** dices.

1. To express the idea *as. . .as,* use **tanto** (or **tan**) **como.**

tanto como		
tan +	{adjective, adverb}	+ **como**
{**tanto(s)**, **tanta(s)**}	+ noun + **como**	

2. **Tanto como** means *as much as:* it modifies a verb.

Yo no me quejo tanto como tú.	I do not complain as much as you (do).
Este año ha llovido tanto como el año pasado.	This year it has rained as much as last year.
Ya no montamos a caballo tanto como antes.	We no longer go horseback riding as much as before.

3. **Tanto** used alone to modify a verb means *so much.*

Ha llovido tanto.	It has rained so much.

4. **Tanto (-a, -os, -as). . .como** means *as much as* or *as many as* + noun.

Tú y yo no tenemos tantos problemas como ellos.	You and I do not have as many problems as they (do).
En la finca hay tantos cerdos como vacas.	On the farm there are as many pigs as cows.

5. **Tan. . .como** means *as* + adjective or adverb + *as.*

Mamá no está tan preocupada como papá.	Mother is not as worried as Dad.
Esto no es tan difícil como yo esperaba.	This isn't as difficult as I expected.

Aplicación

I. Repeat each sentence replacing the noun with the ones in parentheses.

MODELO Tienen tantos animales. (vacas, caballos) → **Tienen tantas vacas. Tienen tantos caballos.**

1. Necesitan tantas cosas. (dinero, tierra, trabajadores)
2. Compramos tanta comida. (leche, carne, gallinas)
3. Hacen tanto trabajo. (artículos, cosas, comida)

II. Make a new sentence which expresses the same idea.

A. MODELO Papá se queja mucho, y mamá, también. → **Mamá se queja tanto como papá.**

1. El año pasado llovió mucho, y este año, también.
2. El dueño se enoja mucho, y el otro señor, también.
3. Este caballo me gusta mucho, y el otro, también.
4. Los abogados trabajan mucho, y los médicos, también.
5. La finca produce mucho, y la compañía, también.

B. MODELO Josefa es menos simpática que María. → **Josefa no es tan simpática como María.**

1. Mi abuelo está menos enfermo que mi abuela.
2. Un coche es menos caro que un caballo.
3. Yo juego menos bien que Nancy.
4. El tenis es menos difícil que el golf.

C. MODELO Yo tengo tres hermanos y tú tienes tres hermanos. → **Yo tengo tantos hermanos como tú.**

1. Esta finca tiene tres mil vacas y la otra finca tiene tres mil vacas.
2. Ellos cortaron cien árboles y nosotros cortamos cien árboles.
3. Él escribió nueve artículos y yo escribí nueve artículos.
4. Tú invitaste a veinte personas y yo invité a veinte personas.

III. Answer each question using a comparison of equality.

MODELOS María monta a caballo bien, ¿y Susana? → **Susana monta a caballo tan bien como María.**
La otra finca tiene muchas vacas, ¿y ésta? → **Ésta tiene tantas vacas como la otra finca.**

1. Las mujeres se quejan mucho, ¿y los hombres?
2. Las ovejas producen dinero, ¿y los cerdos?
3. El dueño es inteligente, ¿y el administrador?
4. Ustedes trabajan mucho, ¿y yo?
5. El camino es malo, ¿y el puente?
6. El profesor tiene problemas, ¿y los estudiantes?
7. Juan juega mucho fútbol, ¿y José?
8. Usted sabe muchas cosas, ¿y los otros estudiantes?
9. Yo tengo buenas ideas, ¿y ustedes?
10. Don Martín es rico, ¿y Mariana Portilla?

IV. Para contestar en español

1. ¿Sabe usted tanto como sus amigos?
2. ¿Hablan ustedes tan rápido como yo en español?
3. ¿Sabe usted jugar golf? ¿Juega tan bien como Nancy López?
4. ¿Le gusta el tenis tanto como el fútbol?
5. ¿Hay tantos hombres como mujeres en esta universidad?

C. Three ways to express obligation

Hay que proteger al trabajador.

1. **Hay que** + infinitive is an impersonal expression of obligation.

Hay que discutirlo ahora mismo.	It must be discussed right now.
Hay que proteger al trabajador.	It is necessary to protect the worker.

2. In order to state what a specific person or persons must do, **tener que** + infinitive is used.

Tengo que ir a buscar a Brown.	I have to go look for Brown.
Tiene usted que marcharse inmediatamente.	You have to leave immediately.

3. In order to express what a specific person or persons should or must do, **deber** + infinitive is used.

No debemos perder un instante.	We should not lose a moment.
Debes estar en el despacho a las nueve.	You must be in the office at 9 o'clock.

Aplicación

I. Respond to each remark using **Vamos, hombre** and **hay que** + infinitive.

MODELO ¿Estudiar? ¡Qué lata! → **Vamos, hombre. Hay que estudiar.**

1. ¿Trabajar? ¡Qué lata!
2. ¿Ir al concierto? ¡Qué lata!
3. ¿Revisar el artículo? ¡Qué lata!
4. ¿Levantarse? ¡Qué lata!

II. Respond to each remark using **tener que** + infinitive.

MODELO No quiero salir ahora. → **Pero tienes que salir.**

1. No quiero estudiar.
2. Ellos no quieren quedarse aquí.
3. No queremos empezar ahora.
4. Ella no quiere seguir con la clase.
5. No quiero leer el libro.

Above: Acapulco, Mexico, circa 1930. Below: Acapulco, 1980.

III. Restate each sentence using **deber** + infinitive.

MODELO Es necesario que él hable con el dueño. → **Él debe hablar con el dueño.**

1. Es necesario que tú hagas el trabajo.
2. Es necesario que yo me vaya.
3. Es necesario que ellos empiecen.
4. Es necesario que ustedes hablen conmigo.
5. Es necesario que Juan se acueste.
6. Es necesario que los jóvenes estudien.

IV. Para contestar

1. ¿Por qué hay que estudiar el español?
2. ¿Qué hay que hacer para hablar bien el español?
3. ¿Trabaja usted en una oficina? ¿Qué tiene que hacer?
4. ¿Qué hay que hacer si hay un accidente?
5. ¿Por qué hay que jugar deportes? ¿Son importantes?
6. Cuando uno llega tarde a una fiesta, ¿qué debe decir?
7. ¿Debe el profesor (la profesora) hablar con los estudiantes de los problemas de ellos?

Bandstand in the central plaza, Cuernavaca, Mexico.

Pausa oral

La vida rural

I. Descripción de una finca

You are on a ranch in rural Mexico and want to describe the ranch to a Spanish-speaking friend. Include in your description comments on the following points.

1. situación geográfica: ¿Dónde está la finca? ¿en el norte de México?
2. animales que hay en la finca: ¿Hay vacas? ¿perros? ¿otros animales?
3. actividades en la finca: ¿Monta usted mucho a caballo? ¿Corta muchos árboles? ¿Cuida las vacas?
4. ¿Ha llovido mucho este año? ¿Hay muchos accidentes?
5. ¿Le gusta o no le gusta la vida en la finca? ¿Por qué?

II. Los animales

Can you give two or three examples of animals you have seen or know which display the traits listed on the right?

MODELO **Una vez yo tenía un gato que era muy terco. Nunca quería comer la comida que yo le daba.**

caballo	ser terco
perro	ser fuerte
gato	ser tranquilo
cerdo	ser bonito
pájaro	ser feo
oveja	ser inteligente
burro	estar loco

III. ¿Vida rural o vida en la gran ciudad?

Certain activities are likely to occur in the country and others in a large city. Choose between ten and fifteen of the following activities and tell why you associate each with rural life or with city life.

MODELO estudiar para abogado → **Es más fácil estudiar para abogado en la ciudad porque hay universidades en muchas ciudades.**

ir a un concierto	tomar una copa y unas tapas	cortar unos árboles
quedarse en un gran hotel	trabajar en una oficina	aburrirse un poco
gastar mucho dinero	detener el primer taxi que pasa	divertirse mucho
vivir en un apartamento	montar a caballo	
tener un patio	estar tranquilo	
trabajar como burro	comer frutas y legumbres muy frescas	
visitar la Embajada Boliviana	tener una casa muy grande	

ESTRUCTURA II

A. The passive: **se** + verb / **ser** + participle

Repaso. An active verb tells what the subject does or is: *The workers built the bridge.*

Se construye el puente.

1. A verb in the passive form tells what happens or happened to the subject: *We were invited to the party.*

2. The most common passive construction in Spanish is formed with **se** followed by a third-person verb. The passive subject often appears at the end of the sentence.

se + third-person verb + passive subject

If the passive subject is one person or thing, a singular verb is used. If the subject is plural, a plural verb appears.

SINGULAR SUBJECT

Aquí se habla español.	Spanish is spoken here.
La ceremonia se prolongó un poco.	The ceremony was prolonged a little.

PLURAL SUBJECT

En una finca se ven muchos animales.	On a farm many animals are seen.
No siempre se resuelven los problemas del pasado.	The problems of the past are not always solved.

3. Another kind of passive construction is formed with the verb **ser** followed by a past participle. The participle agrees in number and gender with the subject.

subject + **ser** + participle

Los árboles fueron cortados ayer.	The trees were cut down yesterday.
La finca fue abandonada por los dueños.	The farm was abandoned by the owners.

Ser + participle is more emphatic, but less commonly used, than the construction with **se.**

Aplicación

I. Change the noun in each sentence to the one given in parentheses; modify the verb as necessary.

MODELOS a) Se necesitan libros. (dinero) → **Se necesita dinero.**
b) Ahora se mejora la situación. (las cosas) → **Ahora se mejoran las cosas.**

1. No se abandona una casa. (el trabajo)
2. Los problemas no se discuten de sobremesa. (el dinero)
3. No se apresura un matrimonio. (estas cosas)
4. Se van a analizar los detalles. (el caso)
5. El contrato se va a revisar. (los detalles)

II. Respond using **aquí no** + a construction with **se.**

MODELOS En la Argentina necesitan médicos. → **Aquí no se necesitan médicos.**
En Chile hablan español. → **Aquí no se habla español.**

1. Allá estudian medicina.
2. Allá abandonan el trabajo.
3. En Perú toman Inka-Cola.
4. En México pasan las Navidades con la familia.
5. En los Estados Unidos apresuran mucho las cosas.

III. Change to a passive construction with **ser.**

MODELO El pasaporte se perdió. → **El pasaporte fue perdido.**

1. Las llaves se encontraron.
2. La casa se construyó.
3. Los caballos se ensillaron.
4. Los artículos se revisaron.
5. El problema se discutió.
6. Las cosas se compraron.

IV. Express in Spanish using **se.**

MODELO Spanish is spoken in Cuba. → **Se habla español en Cuba.**

1. The house was sold.
2. The bridge was built.
3. The problems were solved.
4. Spanish is taught here.
5. These things are studied in class.
6. The cables were broken.
7. Coffee is produced in Colombia.
8. Trees are cut at the sawmill.
9. The papers were lost.
10. The letter was found.

B. Command forms (IV): **nosotros**

Vamos a ver el puente.
Empecemos esta misma tarde.

1. The most common way to express a **nosotros** command (*Let's* + verb) is with **vamos a** + infinitive.

Vamos a comer.	Let's eat.
Vamos a salir por aquí.	Let's go out this way.

2. A second way to express *Let's* + verb is with the **nosotros** command form, which is the same as the subjunctive **nosotros** form.

Esperemos.	Let's wait.	Pensemos.	Let's think.
Comamos.	Let's eat.	Traduzcamos.	Let's translate.

Aplicación

I. Change the **nosotros** command to **vamos a** + infinitive.

MODELO Comamos aquí. → **Vamos a comer aquí.**

1. Comencemos ahora.
2. Escuchemos al profesor.
3. Partamos mañana.
4. Oigamos el concierto.
5. Analicemos la situación.
6. Estemos allí temprano.
7. Hagamos eso.
8. Veamos el caballo.

II. Answer each question with a **nosotros** command.

MODELO ¿Entramos o salimos? → **Entremos.** *or* **Salgamos.**

1. ¿Trabajamos o jugamos?
2. ¿Traducimos o leemos?
3. ¿Hablamos o estudiamos?
4. ¿Seguimos o volvemos?
5. ¿Empezamos o esperamos?
6. ¿Subimos o bajamos?
7. ¿Vemos televisión o conversamos?
8. ¿Comemos o tomamos una copa?

III. Express in Spanish two ways.

MODELO Let's eat. → **Vamos a comer. Comamos.**

1. Let's walk.
2. Let's tell the truth.
3. Let's return.
4. Let's visit Juan.
5. Let's pay.
6. Let's begin.
7. Let's write a postcard.
8. Let's spend Christmas here.

Repaso oral

I. Para conversar

Act out the following situation with another member of the class.

MODELO Usted es dueño (dueña) de un aserradero. Le dice al administrador que los trabajadores tienen que producir más. Él cree que es imposible porque ha llovido tanto. →

A: **La finca produce muy poco.**

B: **Es que ha llovido mucho, don Roberto. Los trabajadores no pueden trabajar cuando llueve.**

A: **Bueno, pero hemos perdido mucho dinero. Tendrán que producir más.**

1. Usted necesita entrar a casa. Pero a su amigo o amiga se le perdió la llave.
2. Usted y su amigo (amiga) están en una finca. Usted quiere montar a caballo. La otra persona tiene miedo porque ha llovido tanto y la tierra está muy blanda.
3. Usted y su amigo o amiga están en un coche. Usted quiere pasar por un puente, pero son las ocho y media de la mañana y hay mucho tráfico. Su amigo o amiga está muy preocupado (preocupada) porque tiene una clase en la universidad a las nueve y tiene miedo de llegar tarde.
4. Usted quiere estudiar para ingeniero porque le gusta la idea de construir caminos y puentes. Su padre cree que no es buena profesión para usted.

II. Para describir

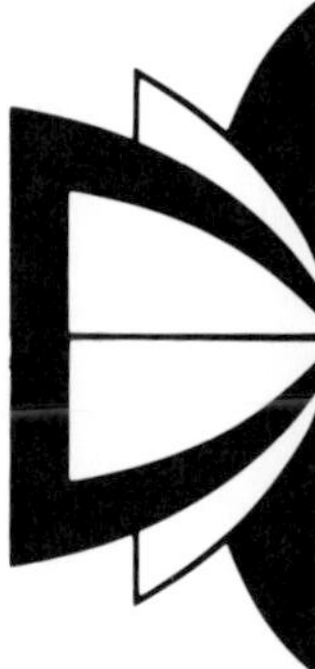

Capítulo 15

Despegue

Descripción del dibujo

1. Asunción y Aurora son gemelas bolivianas.
2. Van a pasar las vacaciones en Miami con su tía.
3. En el avión hay una azafata—una señorita que sirve la comida y habla con la gente que viaja.
4. Asunción piensa en toda la ropa que pueden comprar en Miami.
5. Aurora quiere comprar un estéreo, discos y tal vez una televisión a colores.

Pronunciación

1. Asunción / Asunción y Aurora
2. el avión / una azafata
3. la ropa / Piensa en toda la ropa.
4. un estéreo / discos / una televisión a colores

Aplicación

I. Relación

Make as many statements as you can about the picture on page 349. Try to make at least ten sentences.

II. Para contestar

1. ¿Son gemelas Asunción y Aurora?
2. ¿Qué son "gemelas"?
3. ¿Tiene usted un hermano gemelo?
4. ¿Dónde pasa usted las vacaciones?
5. ¿Qué es una "azafata"?
6. ¿A usted le gustaría ser azafata? ¿Por qué (no)?
7. ¿A usted le gusta comprar ropa?
8. ¿Tiene usted muchos discos? ¿un estéreo?
9. ¿Cuáles son los discos que le gustan más?
10. ¿Tiene usted una televisión a colores? ¿Le gusta o no le gusta ver televisión? ¿Por qué?

Tema del diálogo

An unexpected incident changes the character of an airplane trip.

El Alto Airport in La Paz, Bolivia. To the landlocked nations of Bolivia and Paraguay, airlines sometimes seem the only way out—the only contact with the rest of the world.

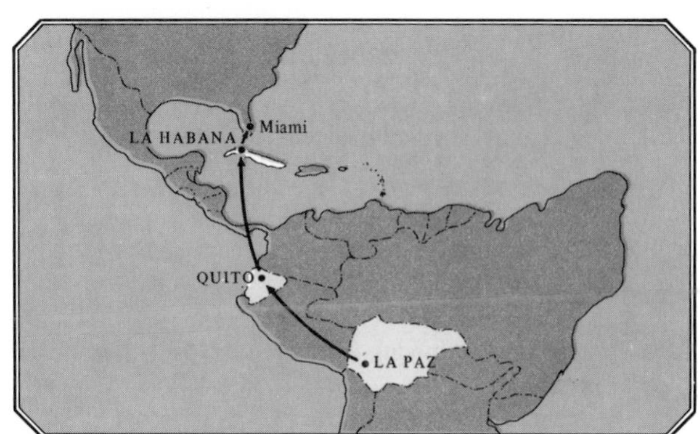

DIÁLOGO

Viajando por América

Asunción y Aurora Arizmendi, gemelas bolivianas de 18 años, van de viaje en avión a los EE.UU. donde pasarán un mes de vacaciones con una tía en Miami[1].

AURORA ¡Qué lindo! Todo un mes de vacaciones con tía Emilia.

ASUNCIÓN Ay, sí. Y toda la plata que nos dio papá.

AURORA Me pongo nerviosa pensando en toda la ropa que vamos a comprar.

ASUNCIÓN Yo pienso comprar un estéreo, discos y una televisión a colores.

AURORA A propósito, ¿le habrá llegado el telegrama a tía Emi?

ASUNCIÓN Lo sabremos al llegar al aeropuerto.

* * *

(Tres horas más tarde el 727 empieza el descenso en Quito, Ecuador, la única escala del vuelo. Las gemelas se despiertan en ese momento.)

ASUNCIÓN ¡Qué vista tan estupenda!

AURORA Sí, pero mira. Ya estamos sobre la pista.

(El avión toma tierra suavemente y avanza hacia la terminal, pero de repente se detiene.)

AURORA Asunción, fíjate qué raro. El avión no va a la terminal.

ASUNCIÓN Cierto. Sería conveniente preguntarle a la azafata. . .

(Por el parlante se oye una voz desconocida de mujer.)

VOZ Atención, todo el mundo. Aquí desde la cabina de mando les habla Sonya, comandante del Frente de Liberación Panamericano.

AURORA ¡Jesús, María y José! Probablemente nos van a matar!

ASUNCIÓN No, chica. No te espantes ya que no va a pasar nada. O casi nada.

VOZ Favor de no abandonar sus asientos. Después de cargar combustible, este vuelo liberado irá a la Habana.

AURORA ¡Caramba! ¿Quién habría pensado en una desviación a Cuba?

ASUNCIÓN No está tan mal la cosa. ¿No crees que habrá algo que podremos comprar en la Habana?[2]

Traveling through the Americas

Asunción and Aurora Arizmendi, 18-year old Bolivian twins, are going on a plane trip to the United States where they will spend a month of vacation with an aunt in Miami.

AS Really super! A whole month of vacation with Aunt Emilia.

AU Um hm. And all the money Dad gave us.

AS I get nervous thinking of all the clothes we can buy.

AU I'm thinking of buying a stereo, records, and a color T.V.

AS By the way, I wonder if the telegram reached Aunt Emi?

AU We'll find out when we arrive (upon arriving) at the airport.

* * *

(Three hours later the 727 begins its descent into Quito, Ecuador, the only stop on the flight. The twins wake up at this moment.)

AS What a great view!

AU Yes, but look. We're already on the landing strip.

(The plane lands softly and advances toward the terminal, but suddenly it stops.)

AU Asunción, something strange is happening (notice how strange). The plane is not going to the terminal.

AS Right. It would be a good idea to ask the stewardess.

(Over the loudspeaker the unfamiliar voice of a woman is heard.)

V Attention, everybody. This is Sonya, Commander of the Pan American Liberation Front, speaking to you from the controls.

AS Good grief! They're probably going to kill us!

AU No, sis. Don't be scared, since nothing's going to happen. Or almost nothing.

V Please do not leave your seats. After taking on fuel, this liberated flight will go to Havana.

AU Wow! Who would have thought of a detour to Cuba?

AS Things aren't so bad. Don't you think there will be something that we will be able to buy in Havana?

VARIACIONES

¿Vas a comprar ropa, Emilia?	Are you going to buy clothes, Emilia?
Sí, un vestido.	Yes, a dress.
una blusa	a blouse
una falda	a skirt
medias	stockings
zapatos	shoes
¿Tú también, Pedro?	You too, Pedro?
Claro, una camisa.	Of course, a shirt.
calcetines	socks
pantalones	pants
pantalones vaqueros / unos blue jeans	blue jeans
ropa interior	underwear

La Habana, capital of the Republic of Cuba. Approximately one-fifth of the island's ten million inhabitants live in the capital city.

Glosas

1. Every year several million Latin Americans come to the United States as tourists. They visit Disneyland, Disneyworld, and other attractions; they also spend millions in department stores in Miami (most South Americans favor Florida), San Antonio, Dallas, Houston, and Los Angeles (which Mexican tourists prefer).
2. Many goods are rationed in Cuba, but special shops have been set up for tourists where rationed goods can be purchased.

SOBRE EL DIÁLOGO

I. Choose the word which corresponds to each definition.

MODELO dos hermanos de exactamente la misma edad → **gemelos**

1. donde uno se sienta en un avión
2. mujer que trabaja en un avión
3. tener mucho miedo
4. un hombre se pone éstos antes de ponerse los zapatos
5. ropa de mujer
6. una mujer se pone éstas antes de ponerse los zapatos

a. vestido
b. azafata
c. gemelos
d. asiento
e. calcetines
f. espantarse
g. medias

II. Para contestar

1. ¿Tienen la misma edad Asunción y Aurora? ¿Cuántos años tienen?
2. ¿Adónde van? ¿Por qué?
3. ¿En qué van las chicas a gastar el dinero que les dio su papá?
4. ¿En qué cosa rara se fija Aurora?
5. ¿Quién les habla por el parlante, la azafata?
6. ¿Quién es Sonya?
7. ¿Qué piensa Aurora que va a pasar? ¿Y Asunción?
8. ¿Adónde dice Sonya que va el avión?

VOCABULARIO

nouns

el **asiento**	seat
la **atención**	attention
la **azafata**	stewardess
la **blusa**	blouse
la **cabina de mando**	controls, cockpit
el **calcetín**	sock
la **camisa**	shirt
el (la) **comandante**	commander
el **combustible**	fuel
la **desviación**	detour
el **descenso**	descent
el **disco**	record
la **escala**	stopover, intermediate stop
el **estéreo**	stereo
la **falda**	skirt
el **frente**	front
el **gemelo,** la **gemela**	twin
la **liberación**	liberation
la **media**	stocking
los **pantalones**	pants
los **pantalones (de) vaqueros**	blue jeans (*literally,* cowboy pants)
el **parlante**	loud speaker
la **pista**	landing strip, runway
la **ropa**	clothes
la **ropa interior**	underwear
el **telegrama**	telegram
la **televisión a colores**	color television
la **terminal**	terminal
el **vestido**	dress
la **vista**	view
el **zapato**	shoe

verbs

avanzar (c)	to go forward, to advance
cargar (gu)	to load, to take aboard
detenerse	to stop
espantarse	to be afraid
preguntar	to question, to ask (a question)

adjectives

conveniente	suitable, advisable
desconocido	unknown, unfamiliar
liberado	liberated
nervioso	nervous
panamericano	Pan American
raro	strange
único	only

other expressions

de repente	all of a sudden, suddenly
de vacaciones	on vacation
de viaje	traveling
desde	from
efectivamente	That's right, Really
favor de	please, kindly
ser conveniente	to be a good idea
suavemente	softly
todo el mundo	everyone
todo un mes	a whole month
tomar tierra	to land
ya que	since

additional vocabulary

ahora que	now that
la **edad**	age
pronto	soon
puesto que	since
tener ganas de + infinitive	to feel like (doing something), to be anxious to (do something)
volverse (ue)	to become

ESTRUCTURA I

A. The future perfect and conditional perfect tenses

> **Habremos llegado** a Miami.
> ¿Quién **habría pensado** en eso?

1. The future perfect tense corresponds to English *will have* + past participle *(I will have eaten).* To form this tense in Spanish, use the future of **haber** + past participle.

viajar	
habré	viajado
habrás	
habrá	
habremos	
habréis	
habrán	

Para mañana yo me habré ido.	By tomorrow I will have gone.
Habremos terminado a las cinco.	We will have finished at 5 o'clock.
Ellos habrán trabajado en el oeste.	They will have worked in the West.

2. The conditional perfect tense corresponds to *would have* + participle *(We would have helped).* To form this tense, use the conditional of **haber** + past participle.

volver	
habría	vuelto
habrías	
habría	
habríamos	
habríais	
habrían	

Yo habría comprado mucha ropa.	I would have bought lots of clothes.
Asunción y Aurora habrían ido de viaje este mes.	Asunción y Aurora would have gone on a trip this month.
A mí me habría gustado ser más alto.	I would have liked to be taller

3. The future perfect tense may be used to express probability in the past (sometimes expressed as *wonder* in English).

Habrá sido Aurora.	It probably was Aurora.
Ellas habrán ido de viaje.	They probably went on a trip.
¿Habrá llegado el telegrama?	I wonder if the telegram arrived.

Aplicación

I. Repeat each sentence changing the subject according to the cue.

MODELO Habrán terminado para las seis. (tú, yo) →
Habrás terminado para las seis.
Habré terminado para las seis.

1. A esa hora ya habrá llegado. (yo, ellos, tú, nosotros, ustedes)
2. Habremos empezado antes de la una. (los estudiantes, tú, mi amigo y yo, yo, la azafata)
3. ¿Tú habrías hecho eso? (ustedes, el dueño, las gemelas, yo, nosotros)
4. Ella no habría dicho nada. (yo, tú, nosotros, la secretaria, los gemelos)

II. Answer each question using the future perfect in part A. Use the conditional perfect in part B.

A. MODELO ¿Llegarán a las cinco? → **¡Qué va! A las cinco ya habrán llegado.**

1. ¿Se despertarán ellas a las siete?
2. ¿Empezará usted a las nueve?
3. ¿Llegaré a las tres?
4. ¿Terminarán ustedes a las cuatro?
5. ¿Saldrá el avión a las diez?
6. ¿Se irán ellos a las doce?
7. ¿Se abrirán las oficinas a las ocho?
8. ¿Los verás a las once?

B. MODELO ¿María dijo eso? → **¡No hombre! María no habría dicho eso.**

1. ¿Ellos jugaron golf?
2. ¿Elena tomó el avión?
3. ¿Usted se vistió?
4. ¿Yo me olvidé?
5. ¿Se oyó su voz?
6. ¿Abandonaron sus asientos?

III. Express probability in the past by using the future perfect.

MODELO ¿Quién sería? → **¿Quién habrá sido?**

1. ¿Qué creería Asunción?
2. ¿Dónde estarían los chicos?
3. ¿Cuántos años tendría José?
4. ¿Quién podría hacerlo?
5. ¿Por qué dirían eso las chicas?

IV. Para expresar en español

MODELO He probably bought a stereo. → **Habrá comprado un estéreo.**

1. They probably left.
2. She probably forgot.
3. I probably fell asleep.
4. You probably bought records.
5. He probably sent a telegram.

V. Complete the sentences by using a future perfect construction.

MODELO A los cinco de la tarde yo ______. →
(Possible answers) **A las cinco de la tarde yo habré terminado mi trabajo.** *or* **A las cinco de la tarde yo habré vuelto a casa.**

1. A esa hora todo el mundo ______.
2. Para el mes de junio nosotros ya ______.
3. A las ocho de la mañana tú no ______.
4. A la hora de la fiesta, todos mis amigos ______.
5. Para la semana que viene, nosotros ______.

VI. Para contestar

1. ¿A usted le habría gustado estudiar en otra universidad? ¿Por qué?
2. ¿Le habría gustado tener un hermano gemelo?
3. ¿Le habría gustado jugar tenis hoy?
4. ¿Dónde le habría gustado pasar las vacaciones?
5. A las doce de la noche, ¿ya se habrá acostado usted?

B. Long-form possessive adjectives; possessive pronouns

Repaso. The short-form possessive adjectives are used before the noun that names the object possessed and agrees with it in number (and, in the case of **nuestro** and **vuestro,** in gender): **mis cartas, su idea, nuestra hermana.**

Aurora y Asunción son amigas **mías.**

1. Corresponding to each short-form possessive adjective is a long form. The long-form possessive adjectives may be used either for emphasis or to express the idea *of mine, of yours,* etc. They always follow the noun they modify and agree with it in number and in gender.

SINGULAR		PLURAL	
masculine	feminine	masculine	feminine
mío	mía	míos	mías
tuyo	tuya	tuyos	tuyas
suyo	suya	suyos	suyas
nuestro	nuestra	nuestros	nuestras
vuestro	vuestra	vuestros	vuestras
suyo	suya	suyos	suyas

Ésta es la casa mía, no es la casa tuya. — This is *my* house, it's not *your* house.
Me llamó un amigo mío. — A friend of mine called me.
¿Bernardo es primo tuyo? — Is Bernard a cousin of yours?
Esta patria nuestra tiene que progresar. — This country of ours has got to progress.
Hay algún dinero suyo aquí. — There is some money of his here.

2. The long-form possessives are used with the definite article or a demonstrative to form the possessive pronouns (English *mine, yours, hers . . .*). Both the article and the possessive correspond in number and gender with the object referred to.

article + long-form possessive

El suyo es un puesto estupendo.	His is a great job.
La casa tuya es bonita, pero la nuestra es más cómoda.	Your house is pretty, but ours is more comfortable.
El vestido de María es caro; el mío es barato.	Mary's dress is expensive; mine is cheap.

3. Following the verb **ser,** the definite article may be omitted.

Este dinero no es mío.	This money is not mine.
¿Son tuyas estas medias?	Are these stockings yours?
¿Es suya esta ropa?	Is this clothing yours?
Estas camisas no son nuestras.	These shirts are not ours.

The Bodeguita del Medio in Havana, a favorite hangout of the late American writer Ernest Hemingway.

Aplicación

I. Modify each item following the model.

A. MODELO mi idea → **la idea mía**

1. tus opiniones 2. nuestros zapatos 3. mi teléfono 4. su esposa 5. nuestro problema 6. su compañía 7. sus negocios 8. tu ropa interior 9. mis pantalones 10. su falda

B. MODELO la carta de Juan → **la carta suya**

1. la escuela de ellos 2. los vestidos de la secretaria 3. la falda de mi tía 4. el médico de Germán y de Adela 5. las ideas del muchacho 6. los hijos de la señora

II. Answer each question according to the model.

MODELO ¿Es mío este libro? → **¿Tuyo? No.**
¿Es de Juan esta carta? → **¿Suya? No.**

1. ¿Es de ustedes este carro?
2. ¿Son de María estas blusas?
3. ¿Es del dueño este teléfono?
4. ¿Es de usted este perro?
5. ¿Son mías estas tarjetas?
6. ¿Es del profesor esta oficina?
7. ¿Es de Pedro y de Juan esta ropa?
8. ¿Es de los empleados este sindicato?

III. Para expresar en español

MODELO a friend of mine → **un amigo mío**

1. a son of his 2. an aunt of ours 3. a problem of theirs 4. an idea of yours (plural) 5. a daughter of theirs 6. a sister of yours (familiar singular) 7. a shirt of mine 8. a dog of ours

C. Conjunctions

No te espantes **ya que** no va a pasar nada.

1. Some sentences contain only one clause.

Tú te fuiste.	You went away.
No he comido bien.	I have not eaten well.

Others contain two different clauses, one of which cannot function as a separate sentence.

Desde que te fuiste, no he comido bien.	Since you went away, I have not eaten well.

The expression **desde que** is a conjunction. A conjunction connects two separate clauses to form one sentence.

2. Two common conjunctions which express a relationship of time are **desde que** *since* and **ahora que** *now that.*

Los conocemos desde que viven aquí.	We've known them since they've lived here.
Ahora que te conozco mejor, empiezo a comprenderte más.	Now that I know you better, I'm beginning to understand you better.

3. If the verb following **desde que** expresses an idea which begins in the past and continues in the present, the present tense is used.

Desde que Asunción y Aurora están en Miami, hace muy buen tiempo.	Since Asunción and Aurora have been in Miami, the weather has been good.
Desde que trabajo en ese restaurante, he subido mucho de peso.	Since I've been working in that restaurant I've gained lots of weight.

4. Three common conjunctions which express relationships of cause and effect are **porque** *because* and **puesto que** and **ya que,** both meaning *since* (considering the fact that).

Estoy muy contento porque quedamos en vernos mañana a las tres.	I'm very happy because we agreed to meet tomorrow at three o'clock.
Puesto que ha llovido tanto la tierra está muy blanda.	Since it has rained so much the earth is very soft.
Pronto lo sabremos ya que Sonya va a explicar todo.	We'll know soon since Sonya is going to explain everything.

5. The conjunction **porque** always begins the second clause of a sentence. It seldom appears at the beginning.

Asunción y Aurora tienen la misma edad porque son gemelas.	Asunción and Aurora are the same age because they are twins.
No he comprado discos porque todavía no tengo estéreo.	I have not bought any records because I still don't have a stereo.

To translate *because* at the beginning of a sentence, use **como.**

Como llovía, no salimos.	Because it was raining, we didn't go out.

Aplicación

I. Form one sentence by using the conjuncton in parentheses.

MODELO (Ahora que) Estoy aquí. Te puedo hablar. → **Ahora que estoy aquí, te puedo hablar.**

1. (puesto que) Él es presidente de la compañía. Puede llegar tarde.
2. (ya que) La azafata está ocupada. No voy a molestarla.
3. (ahora que) Llegamos al aeropuerto. Lo sabremos pronto.
4. (porque) Vamos a pasar las vacaciones en Colombia. Tenemos una tía que vive allí.
5. (desde que) Ellos viven en esa casa. Yo los conozco.

II. Make sentences by combining the items listed.

MODELO Juan / ser / así / desde que / (yo) conocerlo → **Juan es así desde que lo conozco.**

1. ahora que / (nosotros) estar / aquí / (nosotros) poder / preguntárselo.
2. (yo) comprarme / disco / porque / música / gustarme

3. (nosotros) ir a / viajar / ya que / estar de vacaciones
4. azafata / necesita / sentarse / porque / avión / empezar a / tomar tierra
5. puesto que / ella / ser / pianista / necesitar / tocar / todos los días
6. Juan / hablar / situación / desde que / (nosotros) estar / aquí

III. Complete the sentences any way you wish.

MODELO Me gusta viajar en avión porque. . . →
Me gusta viajar en avión porque es rápido. *or* **Me gusta viajar en avión porque las azafatas son simpáticas.**

1. Yo vivo aquí desde que. . .
2. Voy a comprar una televisión a colores ya que. . .
3. Sería conveniente mandar un telegrama porque. . .
4. Podemos oír discos ahora que. . .
5. Es mejor no abandonar los asientos puesto que. . .

Pausa oral

La ropa y la gente

I. Everyone follows a certain order while getting dressed. Describe the order you follow each day starting with what you do first. You may need some of the following verbs:

bañarse, darse prisa, despertarse, ducharse, lavarse, ponerse (+ ropa), **vestirse**

MODELO **Me despierto a las 7 de la mañana. Cuando me levanto, voy al cuarto de baño y me ducho. Después. . .**

II. By this time in the school year you have come to know other individuals in the class. Make up a short description of several class members. Include facts like the following:

¿dónde viven?
su familia: ¿tienen hermanos?
su trabajo y sus estudios
la comida que les gusta
cómo pasan su tiempo libre
la ropa que llevan

During the description, you may ask the person you are describing for any information you may need: **¿Dónde vives? ¿Te gusta la comida mexicana?**

ESTRUCTURA II

A. Ways to express change

Me pongo nervioso en clase.

Several different verbs are used to express change in Spanish.

1. **Ponerse** is used to indicate change in a physical or emotional state.

Ponte cómodo, Edmundo.	Make yourself comfortable, Edmundo.
Nos pusimos furiosos.	We got furious.
Mi tía se ha puesto grave.	My aunt has become critically ill.
La situación se puso fea.	The situation got nasty.

2. **Volverse.** If the change is of a sharper or more intense nature, the verb **volverse** is used.

Un amigo mío se ha vuelto loco.	A friend of mine has gone crazy (insane).

3. **Hacerse.** When the change involves conscious effort with a fixed goal in mind, **hacerse** is used.

Hugo Bernal se hizo dueño de la finca.	Hugo Bernal became owner of the farm.
Quiero hacerme famoso un día.	I want to become famous one day.

4. **Llegar a** (+ infinitive) is used to indicate prolonged effort.

Nancy llegó a ser una golfista profesional.	Nancy became a professional golfer.
Después de muchos años llegué a ser el mejor médico de la ciudad.	After many years I became the best doctor in the city.

5. Sometimes a reflexive verb is used to express change.

Me enfermé.	I got sick.
Se enojó.	He got mad.
Se enamoraron.	They fell in love.

Empresa de Turismo Nacional e Internacional de Cuba
Calle 23 No. 156, Vedado, Habana.
Telex: Cubatour 051-243
Teléfono: 32-4521

Aplicación

I. Choose the correct verb.

MODELO María Luisa (llegó a ser / se puso) dueña de la compañía. → **María Luisa llegó a ser dueña de la compañía.**

1. El hombre (llegó a ser / se volvió) loco.
2. Juan Carlos (se hizo / se puso) furioso.
3. Todo el mundo (se puso / se volvió) cómodo.
4. Susana quiere (hacerse / volverse) doctora.
5. Antonio (llegará a ser / se pondrá) un buen abogado.
6. El día (ha llegado a ser / se ha puesto) lindo.
7. Cuando oí eso (me hice / me puse) nerviosa.
8. Aurora (se volverá / llegará a ser) una pianista famosa.

II. Para expresar en español

A. MODELO He got nervous. → **Se puso nervioso.**

1. He got furious.
2. She got nervous.
3. We got optimistic.
4. I got sick.
5. The clouds got black.

B. MODELO He got to be president of the company. → **Llegó a ser presidente de la compañía.**

1. She got to be a professional golfer.
2. We got to be good friends.
3. He got to be owner of everything.
4. They got to be the best students in the school.
5. He got to be a famous pianist.

B. Ways to express *each other*

¿Cuándo **nos** vemos?

1. The plural pronouns **nos** and **se** are often used with a verb to convey the idea *each other.* Both the subject and verb are always plural (**nosotros, ellos, ellas,** or **ustedes**).

Las gemelas se quieren mucho.	The twins love each other a lot.
Mis padres se conocieron cuando eran estudiantes.	My parents met each other when they were students.
Ella y yo nos escribimos.	She and I write to each other.

2. In order to emphasize the meaning *each other,* the words **uno a otro** (**una a otra, unos a otros,** etc.) may be added to the end of the sentence.

Siempre nos llamamos uno a otro.	We always call each other.
Aurora y Asunción se cuentan todo una a otra.	Aurora and Asunción tell each other everything.
Los trabajadores se dan la mano unos a otros.	The workers shake hands with each other.

Aplicación

I. Produce a new sentence that expresses the same idea. Use **se** in part A and **nos** in part B.

A. MODELO Juan conoce a Mariana. Mariana conoce a Juan. → **Juan y Mariana se conocen.**

1. José ve a Javier en clase. Javier ve a José en clase.
2. Luisa le escribe a Antonia. Antonia le escribe a Luisa.
3. María le cuenta todo a Lupe. Lupe le cuenta todo a María.
4. Marco quiere a Josefa. Josefa quiere a Marco.

B. MODELO Usted me conoce a mí. Yo lo conozco a usted. → **Usted y yo nos conocemos.**

1. Yo le hablo a usted. Ustedes me hablan a mí.
2. Yo los saludo a ustedes. Ustedes me saludan a mí.
3. Yo te quiero a ti. Tú me quieres a mí.
4. Usted me llama a mí. Yo lo llamo a usted.

II. Para contestar

1. ¿Usted y su mejor amigo se cuentan todo?
2. ¿Se ven ustedes en clase todos los días?
3. ¿Se llaman por teléfono?
4. ¿Usted y yo nos conocemos bien?
5. ¿Nos hablamos después de la clase?
6. ¿Ustedes y yo nos saludamos si nos vemos en la calle?
7. ¿Usted y sus padres se escriben mucho?
8. ¿Dónde se conocieron usted y su mejor amigo?

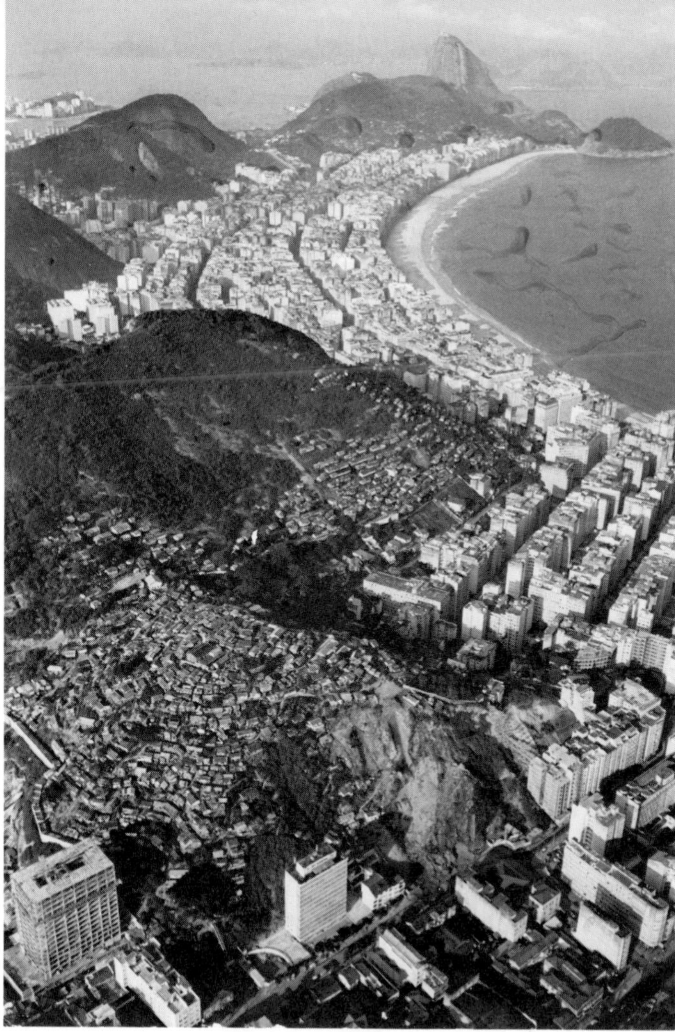

Rio de Janeiro, Brazil's former capital, a city of five million people, situated on one of the most beautiful bays in the world.

 LECTURA

Distorsiones geográficas

A pesar de que la geografía—por ser muy importante—se estudia en todo el mundo, muchas personas tienen conceptos muy curiosos y nociones muy raras tocante a ciertas regiones del planeta. En otros casos, las lagunas mentales producen ciertas confusiones o ciertas situaciones muy cómicas. Echemos un vistazo al mapa mental de un ciudadano americano típico y mencionemos algunas de estas distorsiones:

1. Los nombres *Estados Unidos* y *América* son sinónimos.
2. Los términos Latinoamérica y Sudamérica (Suramérica) son intercambiables.

In spite of the fact / **por ser** because it is

funny, strange / **tocante a** with respect to

blindspots

Let's take a look / citizen

interchangeable

3. México está ubicado[1] en Centro o en Sudamérica.

located

4. Las Antillas[1] sólo se mencionan en casos de revoluciones o tormentas tropicales.

West Indies

5. En el Brasil la lengua nacional es el español.

Cuando ocurre un problema de este tipo y se quiere resolverlo, la gente se dirige a la biblioteca. Ahí se consulta el *Atlas* y se estudian algunas enciclopedias. Y puesto que nuestros amables lectores[1] no siempre tienen tiempo de ir a la biblioteca a buscar las respuestas[1] correctas a los "cinco errores más comunes", pues damos las correcciones aquí mismo:

amables lectores kind readers

answers

1. Los Estados Unidos (de América) es el nombre oficial que ha recibido U.S.A.; la palabra *América* identifica a todo el continente americano, es decir, *Norte, Centro* y *Sur* y todas las islas[1].

islands

2. *Latinoamérica* significa todas las naciones americanas de cultura predominantemente latina[1]; *Sudamérica* significa sólo la porción sur de América. México, las Antillas y los países de Centroamérica no estarían incluidos en el concepto *Sudamérica.*

3. La República Mexicana[2], al igual[1] que el Canadá, siempre ha sido parte de Norteamérica.

al igual just as

The Cathedral of Santo Domingo, Dominican Republic, is the oldest in the New World. Columbus is buried there. Santo Domingo, founded in 1496, is the oldest settlement by Europeans in the Western Hemisphere.

4. Las Antillas, islas situadas en forma de arco entre la América del Norte y la América del Sur, incluyen entre otras, a Cuba, Puerto Rico, la República Dominicana, Haití, Jamaica y las Bahamas. Tienen más de 22,000,000 de habitantes y producen café, cacao, tabaco y ron.

5. El Brasil es un país latino pero no de habla hispana' ya que los primeros colonizadores europeos vinieron de Portugal y no de España. La lengua nacional del Brasil, claro está, es el portugués.

de habla hispana Spanish-speaking

Sólo así, estudiando' la geografía, se eliminan contratiempos' como aquel' de un banquero' de Alaska que llegó a Chile en julio con sólo ropa tropical[3].

studying / mishaps

the one / banker

Glosas

1. From Latin, the official language of the Roman Empire, many other languages evolved, including Spanish, Portuguese, and French. The term Latin America includes the 18 Spanish-speaking nations of the New World plus Puerto Rico; Brazil, where Portuguese is spoken; and Haiti and various smaller islands in the Caribbean where the official language is French. Defined in terms of territory, Latin America means Mexico and all of Central and South America except Jamaica and several other small English and Dutch-speaking islands and countries.
2. Mexico is a federal republic with a political system patterned after the political system of the U.S.A. The official name of the country, **los Estados Unidos Mexicanos** (the United Mexican States), is used mainly in government documents. Most people prefer the shorter name, **México** or **la República Mexicana.** Note also that the official spelling of **México** is with an **x,** and not a **j,** despite the tendency of non-Mexicans to modify the spelling to conform to its modern pronunciation (**Méjico**).
3. The seasons in the northern hemisphere are the reverse of those in the southern hemisphere. When it is snowing in Chicago, the summer sun warms Santiago de Chile.

SOBRE LA LECTURA

I. Para escoger[1]

Choose the correct answer.

1. Estados Unidos es
   a) sinónimo de América   b) el nombre de todo el continente americano   c) el nombre de nuestro país

[1] *To choose.*

2. América es
   a) otro nombre de EE.UU. b) el nombre de todo el continente—Norte, Centro, Sur y las islas del Caribe c) el nombre oficial de Sudamérica
3. Latinoamérica y Sudamérica
   a) son sinónimos b) significan dos cosas diferentes c) son nombres que ya no se usan
4. Latinoamérica incluye
   a) sólo los países donde se habla español b) Brasil, México, Cuba y otros países c) sólo los países donde la lengua oficial no es el español
5. México está
   a) en Sudamérica b) en las Antillas c) en Norteamérica
6. Las Antillas
   a) están en Sudamérica b) son un grupo de islas c) no incluyen Cuba y Puerto Rico
7. La lengua oficial del Brasil es
   a) portugués b) español c) francés
8. La ropa del banquero de Alaska no es apropriada porque
   a) Chile es un país tropical b) en julio los chilenos están en verano c) Chile está en invierno en julio

II. Para conversar

1. ¿Cuáles son algunas de las idea incorrectas que tiene mucha gente tocante a la geografía del Hemisferio Occidental?
2. ¿Cuáles son algunas ideas incorrectas que tienen algunos extranjeros sobre los Estados Unidos?
3. ¿Quiere usted viajar a Latinoamérica? ¿A qué país? ¿Por qué?
4. ¿Qué lenguas se necesitan saber para visitar todos los países de Latinoamérica?
5. ¿Cúales son los países favoritos de los turistas norteamericanos?

III. Para enseñar la geografía

Identify on an outline map of America each of the areas discussed in the **lectura,** using their Spanish names. Then, using vocabulary and expressions from the **lectura** as necessary, make five additional statements concerning other areas of North, Central, or South America or the Caribbean.

Repaso oral

I. Para conversar

Act out the following situations with a classmate.

MODELO Usted está en un avión que va a Los Ángeles. Tiene muchas ganas de llegar porque lo (la) espera una tía suya. Le pregunta a la azafata cuándo van a llegar.

USTED **Señorita, ¿me puede usted decir cuándo vamos a llegar?**
AZAFATA **En una hora más, señor.**
USTED **¡Una hora más!**
AZAFATA **¿Tiene usted mucha prisa, señor?**
USTED **No, pero me espera una tía y tengo muchas ganas de verla.**

1. Usted está en un avión que ya toma tierra. Por el parlante se oye una voz desconocida que dice que el avión no va a la terminal. Va a seguir para la Habana.
2. Usted es azafata. Todo el mundo quiere pedirle algo, o preguntarle algo. Usted no tiene tiempo para toda la gente.
3. Usted sale con una amiga a comprar ropa. Ustedes miran vestidos, faldas, blusas, pantalones, zapatos. . .de todo.
4. Usted y sus amigos discuten sus ideas para las vacaciones.

II. Para describir

Describe as completely as you can what Asunción and Aurora's visit to Miami might be like. The drawings may suggest some ideas.

Repaso 3

I. PRESENT SUBJUNCTIVE Its forms

1. The present subjunctive forms are similar to the **usted**-form command. They are shown in the following chart.

USTED COMMAND	PRESENT SUBJUNCTIVE
tenga (usted)	yo **tenga** tú **tengas** él **tenga** nosotros **tengamos** vosotros **tengáis** ellos **tengan**

2. With stem-changing verbs, the stem-changes **e** → **ie** and **o** → **ue** appear in all subjunctive forms except for **nosotros** (and **vosotros**). Model, **pensar:** yo **piense,** tú **pienses,** ella **piense,** nosotros **pensemos,** ellas **piensen.**

3. The stem-change **e** → **i,** however, appears in all forms. Model, **pedir:** yo **pida,** tú **pidas,** usted **pida,** nosotros **pidamos,** ustedes **pidan.**

4. There are six verbs with irregular forms in the present subjunctive:

   dar (yo dé, tu des, él dé. . .)
   estar (yo esté, tú estés, ella esté. . .)
   ir (yo vaya, tú vayas, usted vaya. . .)
   haber (yo haya, tú hayas, él haya. . .)
   ser (yo sea, tú seas, ella sea. . .)
   saber (yo sepa, tú sepas, usted sepa. . .)

Aplicación

A. Answer each question using **No sé** and **ojalá** + subjunctive.

MODELO ¿Estudian tus amigos? → **No sé; ojalá estudien.**

1. ¿Se siente mejor ella?
2. ¿Vienen aquí los novios?
3. ¿Va a su despacho la profesora?
4. ¿Anda por aquí Nancy?
5. ¿Quiere ella salir conmigo esta noche?
6. ¿Le dan una cordial bienvenida?
7. ¿Están en perfectas condiciones físicas los padres?
8. ¿No es responsable el abuelo por las matanzas?
9. ¿Se despiertan las gemelas?
10. ¿Llueve mucho allí?

B. Combine both phrases to form a complete sentence. Use the indicative or subjunctive, as required.

MODELO Ella viene a vernos. Creo que. . . → **Creo que viene a vernos.**

1. Las azafatas trabajan como burros. Me dicen que. . .
2. Escuchas muy bien. Quiero que. . .
3. Compramos mucha ropa. No creo que. . .
4. Nos esperan en el aeropuerto. Les pedimos que. . .
5. Papá nos da mucha plata. Ojalá. . .
6. Nancy sonríe para las cámaras. Espero que. . .
7. Pasamos un mes de vacaciones con tía Emilia. Tal vez. . .
8. Se retrasa el vuelo. Dudamos que. . .
9. Ha llovido mucho. Es evidente. . .
10. Vemos el partido en la televisión. Es muy posible que. . .
11. El accidente era inevitable. Creemos que. . .
12. Te marchas inmediatamente. Es necesario que. . .
13. La clase es muy mala. No es cierto. . .
14. Mamá se pone furiosa. Dudo que. . .
15. Pueden hacerlo. Adela no cree que. . .

II. REFLEXIVE VERBS

1. Most of the following verbs are used with a reflexive pronoun (**me, te, se, nos**) in order to convey a physical change in the subject:

   acostarse, bañarse, calmarse, darse prisa, despertarse, ducharse, dormirse, irse, sentarse, vestirse. . .

   Date prisa, ya es tarde.

2. The verbs which follow all indicate a change in the mental condition of the subject:

   acordarse (de), casarse (con), darse cuenta (de), divertirse (con), enamorarse (de), olvidarse (de)

   Nunca me olvidaré de ti.

3. The reflexive **se** is used in sentences which express an unplanned occurrence for which the subject (usually a person) is caught unprepared.

se + indirect object + third-person verb + subject

   Some typical verbs used in this way follow:

   se me acabó, se te cayó, se le ocurrió, se nos olvidó, se les perdió, se me rompió

   Se me perdió tu dirección.

4. The most common passive construction is formed with **se** followed by a verb in either the third-person singular or plural:

   Se perdieron muchas vidas en la Guerra Civil.

5. A second passive construction is formed with **ser** (usually in the preterit) followed by the past participle.

   La finca fue abandonada por los dueños.

6. The plural pronouns **nos** and **se** are used to convey the idea *each other.*

   Hugo Bernal y su administrador se ven y se hablan todos los días.

Aplicación

Combine each group of words to form a complete sentence. Add any additional words you need to complete the meaning.

MODELO Edmundo / quejarse / reseña → **Edmundo se quejó de la reseña.**

1. si no / darme prisa / llegar / tarde
2. mis hermanos / comprarse / camisas y ropa interior
3. siempre / ponerme nervioso (nerviosa) / antes / clase
4. en la universidad / hablarse / inglés y español
5. quedarnos aquí / durante / vacaciones
6. en una finca / encontrarse / cerdos, caballos y vacas
7. ellos / divertirse / fiesta / anoche
8. él y yo / saludarnos / si / vernos / calle
9. todos los chicos / enamorarse de / Susana
10. María y Lupe / contarse / todo / una a otra
11. ustedes / no darse cuenta / nada
12. perdérsenos / dinero / centro
13. acabársele / café / por fin
14. rompérsele / taza / cocina
15. ¿acordarte de / dos gemelas que / llamarse / Aurora y Asunción?

III. ADDITIONAL VERB TENSES

1. The future and conditional tenses are formed by adding to the infinitive standard sets of endings.

   dar (FUTURE): **daré, darás, dará, daremos, daréis, darán**
   dar (CONDITIONAL): **daría, darías, daría, daríamos, daríais, darían**

Iré al despacho del profesor esta tarde.	I'll go to the professor's office this afternoon.
Iría a buscarlo en su oficina.	I would go to find him in his office.

Córdoba, Spain. Arches of the Mezquita, an immense mosque begun by the Moors in 785 A.D.

Segovia. The Alcázar, one of Spain's most famous castles, begun early in the Middle Ages.

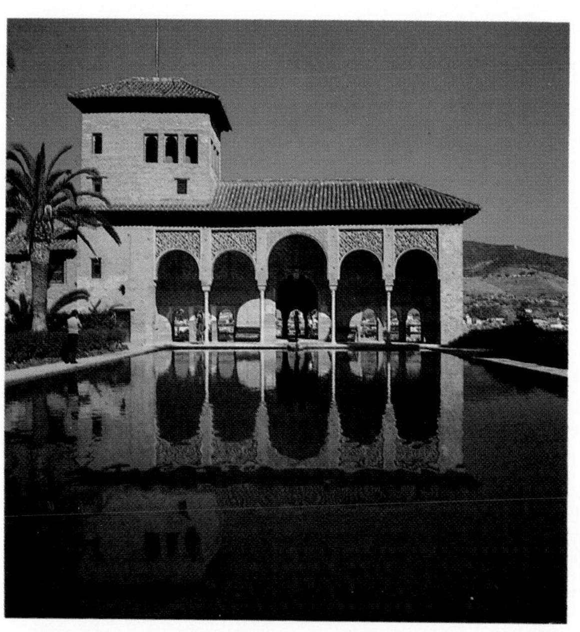

Granada. The Alhambra, Moorish palace overlooking the Darro River, completed in the 14th century.

El Greco, *Fray Hortensio Félix de Paravicino.* Portrait of a Spanish poet and court preacher at age 29. The Spanish masters strove to record the essential reality of living individuals.

Diego Velázquez, *Juan de Pareja.* Portrait of the painter's black assistant, who later became a noted painter himself.

Armies of occupation. Francisco Goya, *The Executions of the Third of May, 1808*. Reprisals by the French occupational forces against the citizens of Madrid after an uprising.

Diego Rivera, *The Betrayal.* Detail of a mural in the Palacio de Cortés, Cuernavaca, Mexico, depicting an aspect of the conquest of Mexico.

Pablo Picasso, *The Muse.* A work from 1935 characteristic of much of the painter's later production.

Salvador Dalí, *The Discovery of America.* Columbus's first landing interpreted by the leading surrealist painter.

2. A number of verbs do not use the entire infinitive to form the future or conditional; these irregular forms, in the future tense, are as follows: (yo) **diré, habré, podré, querré, sabré, haré, pondré, saldré, tendré, vendré.**

Él no dirá nada.	He won't say anything.
¿Podrías acompañarme?	Could you accompany me?

3. The present perfect tense generally corresponds to English *have (has)* + past participle *(I have eaten; She has arrived).* In order to form this tense, use the present of **haber** + past participle.

Por fin hemos llegado al club.	We've finally arrived at the club.
Mis amigos nunca han querido venir aquí.	My friends have never wanted to come here.

4. Several commonly used past participles are irregular in form: **dicho, ido, visto, muerto, puesto, vuelto, hecho, roto, sido.**

¿Qué has hecho?	What have you done?
Ya he visto el periódico.	I've already seen the newspaper.

5. The past perfect (or pluperfect) tense corresponds to English *had* + past participle *(I had seen her).* The past perfect is formed by using the imperfect of **haber** + participle.

Yo no había dicho eso.	I hadn't said that.
Habíamos discutido todas las alternativas.	We had discussed all the alternatives.

6. The future perfect tense conveys what will have happened or what might have happened. To form this tense, use the future of **haber** + past participle: **A esa hora ya habrán terminado.** This tense is also used to express probability in the past: **¿Habrá llegado el telegrama?**

7. The conditional perfect tense conveys what would have happened. To form this tense, use the conditional of **haber** + past participle.

¿Quién habría pensado en una cosa así?	Who would have thought of such a thing?

Aplicación

Express the following sentences in Spanish. In each case a model is provided which will help you with the basic structure.

1. Me lavaré y me vestiré.
   I'll go to bed and I'll fall asleep.
2. Tendríamos que irnos.
   They would have to hurry up.
3. No querrías sentarte allí.
   You (**tú**) wouldn't be able to take a shower there.

4. ¿Has oído muchos conciertos de piano?
   Have you seen many soccer games?
5. No he hecho más que aburrirme.
   We haven't done anything but have a good time.
6. La abuela de Pilar había estado bien de salud.
   Pilar's grandfather had been in poor health.
7. Habrán tenido que ir a buscar al Sr. Brown.
   You (**usted**) will have had to go to see Mrs. Álvarez.
8. Puesto que no habrá pasado nada, no estoy preocupado.
   Since probably no one came, we're not worried.
9. En tu lugar, no habría hecho nada.
   In her place, we wouldn't have said anything.
10. ¿Le habría dicho la verdad, Mariana?
    Would you have told us the truth, Mrs. Pérez?
11. Hugo Bernal llegó a ser dueño de la compañía.
    Hugo Bernal had become first secretary of the Bolivian Embassy.
12. Tú y yo no tendremos tantos problemas como antes.
    You and Pilar will not want as much money as before.
13. Ella no iría contigo a la fiesta.
    She would come with you to the reception.
14. ¿Dónde andarán los novios?
    Where might my parents be?

Capítulo 16

Despegue

DIÁLOGO **Tres aventureros**

Past subjunctive • Uses of the present subjunctive and past subjunctive • Number variants

PAUSA ORAL **Más comentarios personales**

The reflexive (IV): involved condition • Two word endings: **-ito** and **-ísimo**

Repaso oral

Despegue

Descripción del dibujo

1. Estos tres aventureros están en un bote.
2. Tienen pepitas de oro que van a contrabandear.
3. También tienen jaulas con loros y monos.
4. Ponen las pepitas de oro en el fondo doble de la jaula de los monos.

Pronunciación

1. tres aventureros / un bote
2. pepitas de oro / contrabandear
3. jaulas / loros y monos
4. el fondo doble / la jaula de los monos

Aplicación

I. Relación

Say at least ten sentences about the drawing on page 375.

II. Para contestar

1. ¿Son estudiantes los tres chicos?
2. ¿Ha sido usted aventurero alguna vez?
3. ¿Qué contrabandean los tres chicos?
4. ¿Para qué usan las jaulas?
5. ¿A usted le gustan los monos? ¿Le gustaría tener uno en casa?
6. ¿Qué es un loro?
7. ¿Qué hacen los loros que no hacen los otros animales?
8. ¿Le gustaría a usted tener un bote? ¿Por qué?

Tema del diálogo

Midnight. Northeastern Peru. Three smugglers load a boat with gold nuggets and push off into a tributary of the Amazon River.

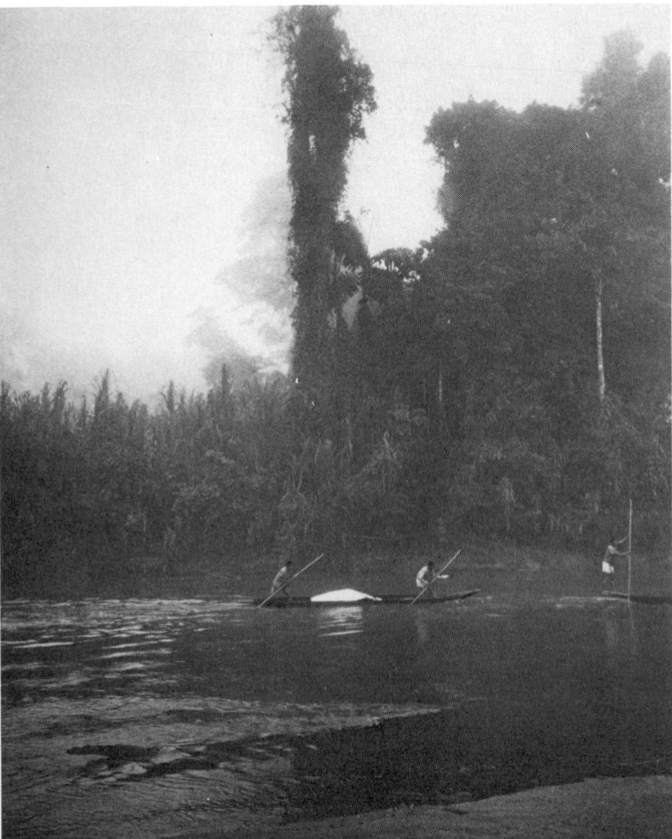

The rainy, tropical lowlands of Eastern Ecuador contrast sharply with the temperate highlands of the Andes.

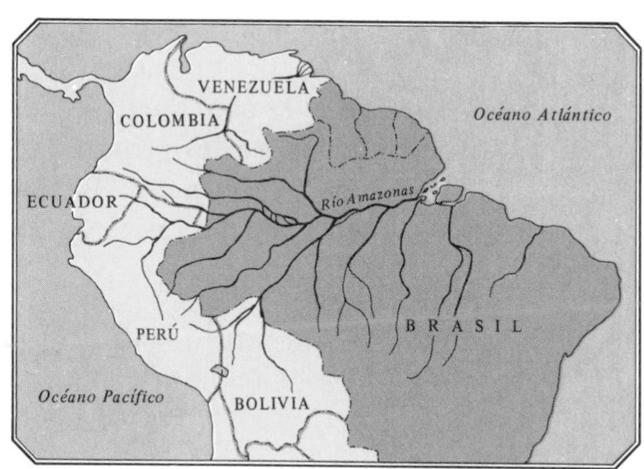

DIÁLOGO

Tres aventureros

Medianoche. Una venezolana, un dominicano y un uruguayo, disfrazados de biólogos, se peparan para navegar por el río Madre de Dios en la selva amazónica[1]. Llevan gran cantidad de pepitas de oro que van a contrabandear. Cristina Rico, Manolo Fajardo y Santiago Jiménez son sus respectivos nombres.

CRISTINA ¡Manos a la obra! El oro va a ir escondido en el fondo doble de las jaulas de los monos.

MANOLO Sí, y a las jaulas de los loros sólo les pondremos piedritas.

SANTIAGO De acuerdo. Así tendrán todas las jaulas un peso semejante.

CRISTINA Una recomendación final. Si tenemos complicaciones, deshágganse de todo. Pero traten de salvar por lo menos una jaulita dorada.

* * *

(Ahora es de madrugada. Los tres jóvenes han navegado por varias horas. Durante los últimos diez minutos han viajado con el motor apagado y sin luces para no ser vistos por los guardias.)

MANOLO ¡Uff! Espero que no nos vieran los guardias.

SANTIAGO Más les vale que no. . .porque de lo contrario cada guardia tendría que comerse medio kilo de plomo de esta metralleta.

CRISTINA Ay, Santiago, no. Ni lo pienses.

* * *

MANOLO Oye, Cristi. Tocante a este oro, ¿estás segura que vale la pena sacarlo de contrabando[2]?

CRISTINA Claro que sí, hombre. Fíjate que aun si perdiéramos la mitad de las jaulas, todavía podríamos irnos ricos de este bello infierno verde[2].

SANTIAGO Es muy cierto, Manolo.

CRISTINA ¡Chitón! se acerca un bote.

MANOLO (Mirando por los prismáticos.) Tranquilos. Parecen ser dos misioneros con un cargamento de Biblias.

CRISTINA U otros aventureros con mejor disfraz que el nuestro, ¿eh?

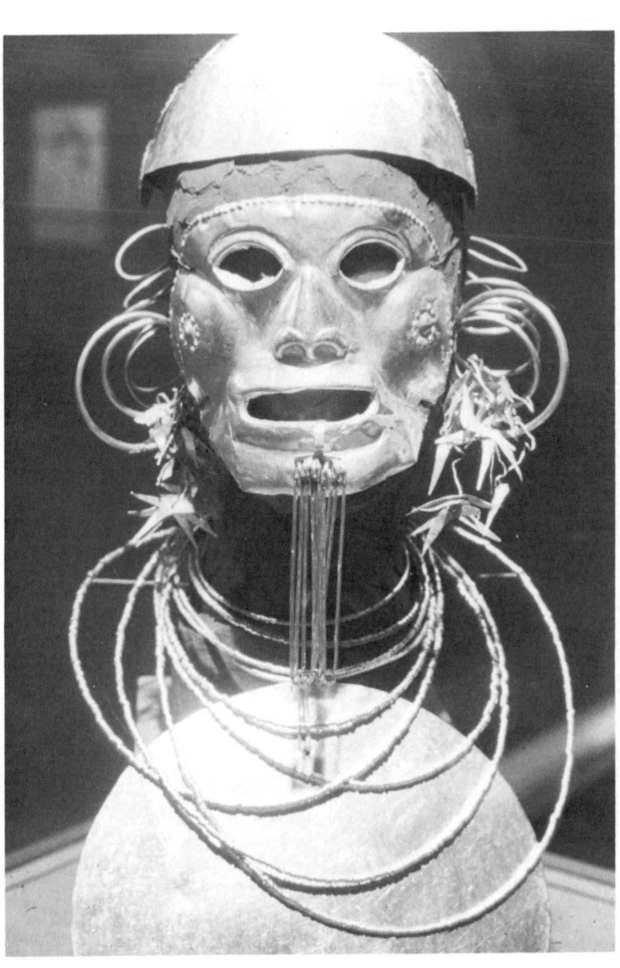

Gold mask produced by the master metalsmiths of Colombia's ancient Chibcha civilization.

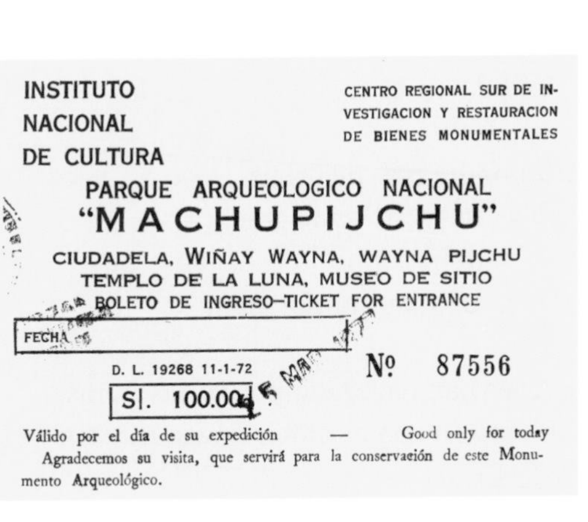

INSTITUTO NACIONAL DE CULTURA

CENTRO REGIONAL SUR DE INVESTIGACION Y RESTAURACION DE BIENES MONUMENTALES

PARQUE ARQUEOLOGICO NACIONAL

"MACHUPIJCHU"

CIUDADELA, WIÑAY WAYNA, WAYNA PIJCHU

TEMPLO DE LA LUNA, MUSEO DE SITIO

BOLETO DE INGRESO–TICKET FOR ENTRANCE

FECHA

D. L. 19268 11-1-72

Nº 87556

S/. 100.00

Válido por el día de su expedición — Good only for today

Agradecemos su visita, que servirá para la conservación de este Monumento Arqueológico.

AERO-CONDOR S.A.
Edif. "Centro Lider" — Bajada Balta Nº 131
2do. Piso — Of. 9 Miraflores. Telf. 463042.

Three adventurers

Midnight. A Venezuelan, a Dominican, and an Uruguayan, disguised as biologists, are getting ready to go by boat along the Madre de Dios River in the Amazon jungle. They are carrying a large quantity of gold nuggets which they are going to smuggle (traffic as contraband). Cristina Rico, Manolo Fajardo, and Santiago Jiménez are their respective names.

C: Let's get to work! The gold is going to go hidden in the false bottom of the monkey cages.

M: Yes, and in the parrot cages we'll just put pebbles.

S: O.K. That way all the cages will have a similar weight.

C: One last piece of advice. If we run into (have) complications, get rid of everything. But try to save at least one golden cage.

* * *

(Now it's dawn. The three youths have traveled for several hours. During the last ten minutes they have traveled with the motor turned off and without lights in order not to be seen by the border patrols.)

M: Oof! Let's hope that the border patrols didn't see us.

S: They'd better not . . . because otherwise each patrol is going to have to swallow half a kilo of lead from this submachine gun.

C: Ah, no, Santiago. Don't even think of it.

* * *

M: Listen, Cristi. About this gold, are you really sure it's worth the trouble to smuggle it out?

C: Of course it is. Listen, even if we were to lose half the cages, we would still leave this beautiful green inferno rich.

S: That's for sure, Manolo.

C: Shh! A boat is coming this way (approaching).

M: (looking through the binoculars) Cool it ([everybody stay] calm). They seem to be two missionaries with a load of Bibles.

C: Or some other adventurers with a better disguise than our own, eh?

VARIACIONES

¿Dónde están las jaulas?	Where are the cages?
delante de Cristina	in front of Cristina
detrás de Manolo	behind Manolo
debajo del asiento	under the seat
encima de un banco	on top of a bench
cerca de Santiago	near Santiago
lejos de Santiago	far from Santiago
¿Dónde llevan el oro?	Where are they carrying the gold?
en una cartera	in a purse
en una bolsa	in a bag, pouch
en un maletín	in a briefcase
¿Navegan por un río?	Are they traveling (sailing) along a river?
No, por el mar.	No, across the sea.
No, por un lago.	No, across a lake.
¿Qué es de oro?	What is (made) of gold?
Mi reloj.	My watch.
Mi collar.	My necklace.
Mi pulsera.	My bracelet.

Glosas

1. The Madre de Dios River runs through the Peruvian **departamento** (= state-like political subdivision) of Madre de Dios and then into the Bolivian **departamento** of Pando, where it joins the Beni River, a tributary of the Amazon River. Large quantities of gold nuggets abound in eastern Madre de Dios.
2. Gold is tightly controlled by many governments. In some countries, people with gold to sell are required by law to take it to a government bank that offers an arbitrary, low price. This situation gives rise to smuggling.

SOBRE EL DIÁLOGO

I. ¿Sí o no?

If the statement is true, say **sí** and repeat it. If the statement is false, say **no** and make a statement which is true.

MODELO Tres hombres se preparan para navegar por un río. → **No, dos hombres y una mujer se preparan para navegar por un río.**

1. Los tres tienen mucho oro que han comprado en el Uruguay.
2. Cristina Rico lleva el oro en su cartera.
3. A las jaulas de los pájaros les pondrán piedritas.
4. Si hay complicaciones, van a deshacerse de todo.
5. Navegan con el motor apagado.
6. Si los guardias ven a los muchachos, Santiago quiere matarlos.
7. Cristina piensa que ésta es una buena idea.
8. Cristina dice que no van a ganar mucho dinero con el oro.
9. Se acerca otro bote.
10. En el otro bote hay tres aventureros que también llevan jaulas.

II. For each word in the list, say another word which is in some way related.

MODELO perro → **mono (Los dos son animales.)**

1. gato
2. pájaro
3. plata
4. avión
5. detrás
6. lago
7. jaula
8. selva
9. maletín
10. Biblia
11. madrugada
12. encima

III. Respond to each remark with one of the items in the list.

¡Manos a la obra! / De acuerdo. / Ni lo pienses. / Sí, pero vale la pena. / ¡Chitón! Más les vale que no.

MODELO Hay problemas con el motor del coche. Tendremos que tomar un taxi. → **De acuerdo.**

1. Ese muchacho quiere pegarte.
2. Hay mucho trabajo que hacer.
3. Es difícil estudiar y trabajar de noche.
4. Quiero quedarme aquí toda la noche.
5. Mira, se acercan dos guardias.

IV. Make sentences by combining the following groups of words.

MODELO llave / plata / cartera → **Llevo mis llaves y mi plata en la cartera.**

1. bote / navegar / lago
2. ir / mar / verano
3. tigre / mono / jaula
4. misionero / Biblia / selva
5. papel / periódico / maletín
6. gato / comer / pájaro

V. Para contestar

1. ¿Tiene usted algunas cosas de oro? ¿Qué, por ejemplo?
2. ¿Tiene usted un animal en casa? ¿Qué tipo de animal? ¿un perro? ¿un gato? ¿un pájaro?
3. ¿Tiene usted una jaula? ¿Para qué se usa una jaula?
4. ¿Qué hay en su cartera? ¿llaves? ¿papeles? ¿dinero?
5. ¿Le gustan a usted los botes? ¿Vive cerca de un río o de un lago?
6. ¿Trae usted un maletín a clase? ¿Qué hay en su maletín?
7. ¿Lleva usted muchos libros? ¿Los lleva en una bolsa?
8. ¿A usted le gustaría ser rico (rica)? ¿Qué cosas compraría?
9. ¿A usted le gustaría ser aventurero? ¿Por qué?
10. ¿Preferiría usted trabajar en una oficina o contrabandear?

VOCABULARIO

nouns

el **aventurero** adventurer
el **banco** bench
la **Biblia** Bible
el **biólogo,** la **bióloga** biologist
la **bolsa** bag, pouch
el **bote** boat
la **cantidad** quantity
el **cargamento** shipment
la **cartera** purse
el **collar** necklace
la **complicación** complication
el **contrabando** contraband
el **disfraz** disguise
el **dominicano,** la **dominicana** Dominican
el **fondo** bottom
  el **fondo doble** false bottom
el (la) **guardia** guard, (border, highway) patrol, policeman (woman)
el **infierno** hell, inferno
la **jaula** cage
la **jaulita** little cage
el **lago** lake
el **loro** parrot
la **madrugada** dawn
el **maletín** briefcase
el **mar** sea
la **metralleta** submachine gun
el **misionero** missionary
la **mitad** half
el **mono** monkey
el **motor** motor
el **nombre** name

la **obra**	work
el **oro**	gold
la **pepita**	nugget
la **piedra**	stone
la **piedrita**	pebble
el **plomo**	lead
los **prismáticos**	binoculars
la **pulsera**	bracelet
la **recomendación**	recommendation
el **reloj**	watch, clock
el **río**	river
el **uruguayo,** la **uruguaya**	Uruguayan
el **venezolano,** la **venezolana**	Venezuelan

verbs

acercarse (qu)	to come near, to approach
apagar (gu)	to turn off
contrabandear	to smuggle, to traffic as contraband
deshacerse de	to get rid of
escaparse	to escape
llevar	to carry, to take
navegar	to navigate, to sail
preparar	to prepare
salvar	to save

adjectives

amazónico	Amazon
bello	beautiful
contrario	opposite
disfrazado	disguised
dorado	golden
escondido	hidden
final	final
medio	half
respectivo	respective
semejante	similar
último	last

prepositions

cerca de	near
debajo de	underneath
delante de	in front of
detrás de	behind
encima de	on top of
lejos de	far from
por	along, across
sin	without
tocante a	about, with respect to, relative to

other expressions

aun	even
claro que sí	of course (it is)
chitón	jeez, shh
de lo contrario	otherwise
manos a la obra	let's get to work
más les vale que no	they'd better not
ni lo pienses	don't even think of it
oye	hey; listen
por lo menos	at least
sacar de contrabando	smuggle out
u	or
vale la pena	it's worthwhile

additional vocabulary

beber	to drink
beberse	to drink up
comerse	to eat up
llevarse	to carry off (away)
el millón	million
morirse (ue, u)	to pass away
perderse (ie)	to miss out on (a party, etc.)

ESTRUCTURA I

A. Past subjunctive

Repaso. Certain grammatical contexts require the present subjunctive: **Quiero que lo hagas. Duda que lo sepamos.**

> Espero que no nos **vieran.**

1. To form the past subjunctive of a verb, begin with the third-person plural (**ellos**) form of the preterit.

(preparar)	(ver)	(ir)
prepararon	**vieron**	**fueron**

Delete the **-ron** ending:

prepara~~ron~~	**vie~~ron~~**	**fue~~ron~~**

Then add the following endings: **-ra, -ras, -ra, ´ramos, -rais, -ran.**

preparara	**viera**	**fuera**
prepararas	**vieras**	**fueras**
preparara	**viera**	**fuera**
preparáramos	**viéramos**	**fuéramos**
prepararais	**vierais**	**fuerais**
prepararan	**vieran**	**fueran**

2. Note that a written accent mark is placed on the stem of the **nosotros** form only.

Ojalá que yo fuera más rico.	I wish I were richer.
Ojalá estuvieras seguro de eso.	I wish you were sure of that.
Ojalá tuviéramos más tiempo.	I wish we had more time.
Ojalá pudiéramos escaparnos.	I wish we could escape.

3. One use of the past subjunctive is after **ojalá** to refer to a situation that is hypothetical or nonexistent (sometimes expressed in English as *would, were,* etc.).

Ojalá vinieran.	I wish they would come.
Ojalá que estudiaras más.	I wish you studied more (but you don't).
Ojalá que Juan estuviera aquí.	I wish John were here (but he's not).
Ojalá que yo fuera famosa.	I wish I were famous.

Aplicación

I. Repeat each sentence, changing the subject as indicated.

MODELO Ojalá supiera hacerlo. (ellos, tú) → **Ojalá supieran hacerlo.**
Ojalá supieras hacerlo.

1. Ojalá hablara como Elena, (los chicos, tú, nosotros, yo, usted)
2. Ojalá trabajara allí. (ustedes, yo, tú, mi novio y yo, el Dr. López)
3. Ojalá comiera menos. (yo, ese señor, mis padres, tú, nosotros)
4. Ojalá tuviéramos tiempo. (yo, los profesores, mis amigos y yo, tú, el médico)
5. Ojalá estuvieran en la selva. (tú, mis padres, yo, todo el mundo, mi familia y yo)

II. Respond to each remark using **¡Qué lástima!** and **Ojalá** + past subjunctive.

MODELO Yo no hablo español. → **¡Qué lástima! Ojalá que hablaras español.**

1. Yo no puedo quedarme.
2. Yo no sé cómo se llama.
3. Ella no tiene tiempo.
4. Ellos no tratan de comprender.
5. Usted no se siente bien.
6. Él no comprende la situación.
7. El reloj no es de oro.
8. Ella no encuentra la pulsera.

B. Uses of the present subjunctive and the past subjunctive

Cristina esperaba que no **se acercara** el otro bote.

1. In chapter 11, we studied two-clause sentences. The verb in the second clause was subjunctive because the (indicative) verb in the first clause expressed a personal reaction to it. The tenses of the two verbs commonly follow a certain sequence.

verb one (indicative)	verb two (subjunctive)
present future imperative	present subjunctive
imperfect preterit conditional	imperfect subjunctive

2. In the following examples, note that English often uses an infinitive phrase in the situations in which Spanish uses the present or the past subjunctive.

PRESENT SUBJUNCTIVE

Quiero que te acuestes temprano. — I want you to go to bed early.
Les pediremos que se vayan. — We'll ask them to leave.
Dile que no juegue en la calle. — Tell him not to play in the street.

PAST SUBJUNCTIVE

Era imposible que nos divirtiéramos mucho.	It was impossible for us to have a good time.
Le dije a Ramón que se marchara.	I told Ramón to leave.
Sería una lástima que no estuvieras bien.	It would be too bad for you not to be well.

3. If, however, the independent clause expresses a reaction in the present to an action or event that took place in the past, the present indicative + past subjunctive may be used.

Espero que no nos vieran.	I hope they didn't see us.
Tenemos miedo que muriera mucha gente.	We're afraid that lots of people died.
Es posible que Aurora se fuera.	It's possible that Aurora left.

Aplicación

I. Respond in the negative using **mamá no quería que** + past subjunctive.

MODELO ¿Fuiste al lago? → **No, mamá no quería que fuera al lago.**

1. ¿Estudiaste anoche?
2. ¿Volvieron los chicos?
3. ¿Se acostó papá?
4. ¿Se fueron los niños?
5. ¿Te pusiste un disfraz?
6. ¿Invitó Juan a Olga?
7. ¿Leíste la carta?
8. ¿Salieron los gemelos?

II. Make a new sentence by adding **que** + a second clause with the past subjunctive.

MODELO Ellos esperaban casarse. (que yo) → **Ellos esperaban que yo me casara.**

1. Yo quería salvar una jaula. (que Cristi)
2. Preferíamos ir en coche. (que usted)
3. Ellos querían comprar oro. (que nosotros)
4. Era imposible vernos. (que los guardias)
5. Fue necesario deshacerse de la pulsera. (que ella)
6. Tuve miedo de hacerlo. (que ustedes)

III. Change the following sentences to the past.

MODELO Yo no quiero que los chicos entren a esa casa. → **Yo no quería que los chicos entraran a esa casa.**

1. No me gusta que los chicos vayan allí.
2. Les digo que no se acerquen.
3. Pero ellos me dicen que no me preocupe.
4. Tengo miedo que algo les pase.
5. No creo que sea buena idea.
6. Es posible que viva allí el misionero sin cabeza.
7. No es verdad que esas cosas no pasen.
8. Nadie duda que el misionero sea malo.
9. Y nadie duda que viva en el infierno.
10. Yo prefiero que los chicos no salgan.

IV. Repeat each sentence using the imperfect indicative or past subjunctive, as required.

MODELO Yo creía que ustedes venían. (quería, sabía) → **Yo quería que ustedes vinieran. Yo sabía que ustedes venían.**

1. Tú decías que ellos se preparaban. (dudabas, estabas seguro)
2. Ellos sabían que teníamos un bote. (esperaban, se alegraron de)
3. Se me olvidó que tú eras abogado. (no creía, dudaba)
4. María dijo que ellos se casaban. (estaba contenta, leyó)
5. El dueño creía que se caía el puente. (tenía miedo, no quería)
6. Me parecía que la pulsera costaba demasiado. (no me parecía, se me había olvidado)

V. Supply the correct form of the verbs in parentheses.

MODELOS Voy a decirle que _____. (jugar) → **Voy a decirle que juegue.**
Era imposible que ella _____. (venir) → **Era imposible que ella viniera.**

1. Quiero que tú _____. (volver, empezar, irse, decirlo)
2. Sería estupendo que nosotros _____. (ganar, terminar, salir, hacerlo)
3. No fue fácil que él _____. (venir, probarlo, avanzar, verlo)
4. Dígale a Juan que _____. (estudiar más, sentarse, escribirnos)
5. Les pediremos a ellos que _____. (acercarse, hacer una cita, apagar el motor)

VI. Restate each sentence, replacing the underlined portion with the words in parentheses and making any necessary changes.

MODELO Le digo que vaya al partido. (Dígale, Ayer le dije) → **Dígale que vaya al partido. Ayer le dije que fuera al partido.**

1. Es mejor que estudie. (Era importante, Será necesario, Sería mejor, Pídale)
2. Espero que ganemos. (Yo quería, Sería bueno, Es importante, Nos dijeron)
3. Dudo que lo haga. (Sería imposible Voy a pedirle, Sugiérale, Fue imposible)
4. Querían que volviéramos. (Nos pedirán, No es fácil, Sería estupendo, No creen)

VII. Complete each sentence with the words in the list.

MODELO Espero que (argentinos / ganar). → **Espero que los argentinos ganen.**
Sería mejor que (ustedes / ir / partido) → **Sería mejor que ustedes fueran al partido.**

1. Quiero que (niño / ponerse / abrigo)
2. Sería mejor que nosotros (usar / prismáticos / también)
3. Voy a decirle que (no olvidarse de / radio)
4. Espero que (el / llevar / boletos)
5. Pídele que (volver / pronto)
6. Hace mucho frío y no me gusta que (Roberto / salir)
7. Yo preferiría que (él / quedarse / en casa)
8. No quiero que (ese nino / ponerse / enfermo)

Clearing the jungle in Yacapani, in Bolivia's Amazonian interior. Bolivia's chief industry is mining, especially tin, but the country also exports potatoes, sugar, coffee, and other crops.

C. Number variants

Doscientos **millones** de dólares.

Spanish has a few special number forms. Here is how they are used.

1. **Un** / **una** / **unos** / **unas** (+ noun)

un + masculine singular	un viaje
una + feminine singular	una botella
unos + masculine plural	unos problemas
unas + feminine plural	unas casas

Remember that **unos** or **unas** (+ noun) means *some.* **Unos (unas)** + number means *about* (+ number).

Veo unos árboles.	I see some trees.
Tiene unos cincuenta años.	He's about 50 years old.

2. **Ciento** / **cien**

ciento +	smaller number	ciento noventa estudiantes
cien +	plural noun	cien camiones / cien familias
	larger number	cien mil personas
	when counting	noventa y ocho, noventa y nueve, cien

3. **Cientos / cientas**

cientos + masculine plural noun	doscientos bancos
cientas + feminine plural noun	cuatrocientas personas

4. **Un millón / millones**
Un millón (dos millones. . .) are followed directly by smaller numbers.

un millón doscientos argentinos
cuatro millones novecientos puestos

5. **Un millón (millones) de**

If the next item in the phrase is a noun, **de** is inserted: **un millón (millones) de** + noun.

cien millones de dólares

Aplicación

I. Make the substitutions and any necessary changes.

MODELO Tengo un primo. (prima) → **Tengo una prima.**

1. Hay doscientos chicos aquí. (chicas)
2. Necesito un libro. (libros)
3. Vinieron cien personas. (hombres)
4. Vio un carro. (casas)
5. Recibieron quinientas cartas. (dólares)
6. Hay veintiún libros. (cosas)

II. Say the following.

MODELO 1 muchacha → **una muchacha**

1. 100 personas 2. 115 estudiantes 3. 200 abogados 4. 715 cartas 5. $1.000.000 6. 1 economista chileno 7. 900 chicas 8. 31 muchachas 9. 21 hombres 10. $2.894.243

Pausa oral

Más comentarios personales

You are now prepared to make statements of personal reaction in the present and in the past.

I. Para completar

Complete the following statements in any logical way.

MODELO Yo quería salir pero mis padres querían que. . . → (Possible answers). . .**me quedara en casa.** *or*. . .terminara mi trabajo.

1. Nosotros íbamos a comprar un bote pero mi amiga dijo que era mejor que. . .
2. Ella iba a estudiar pero su novio prefería que. . .
3. Yo quería ponerme un disfraz para la fiesta pero los otros me pidieron que. . .
4. Ella decía que sabía navegar muy bien pero sus compañeros dudaban que. . .

II. Para conversar

Respond to the following situations with a sentence beginning with **ojalá** + past subjunctive. Add an additional sentence to complete your response.

MODELO María no está bien. Le duele la cabeza y no tiene ganas de hacer nada. → (Possible answers) **Ojalá se sintiera mejor. Tal vez se levante mañana.** *or* **Ojalá no estuviera enferma. Espero que mañana se sienta mejor.**

1. No puedo ir con ustedes porque tengo mucho que hacer. Tengo que comprar comida, preparar la cena y después, tengo que lavar la ropa.
2. No vale la pena llamar a Isabel porque no está en casa. No sé dónde está. He llamado cuatro o cinco veces pero no hay nadie.
3. Ya van a empezar las vacaciones de Navidad y todavía no he comprado nada para nadie. A Mariana le quiero comprar un reloj y a mamá una cartera nueva.
4. ¡Qué calor! Este lugar parece un infierno. Tengo ganas de ir a bañarme, pero no hay ni un río ni un lago cerca de aquí.
5. Javier quiere estacionar el carro, pero ¿dónde? Ha pasado hora y media y no ha podido encontrar sitio. Tal vez tenga que volver a casa sin comprar las cosas que necesita.
6. ¡Qué bueno el concierto! ¡Qué estupendo el pianista! ¡Qué lástima que se nos olvidaran los prismáticos!

III. Para describir

What are the people in the following drawings thinking or doing? Tell why you think they are reacting the way they are. Use expressions and verbs like **ojalá, querer, es (era) mejor, preferir, pedir, dudar, es (era) imposible, sentir. . .**

MODELO **Nancy sonríe para las cámaras de televisión. Ella dice que siente mucho que la ceremonia en el aeropuerto se prolongara tanto.**

A. The reflexive (IV): involved condition

Repaso. Verbs which are used with a reflexive pronoun fall into several categories: physical condition (**Me ducho**), mental condition (**Te olvidaste**), unprepared condition (**Se le cayó**), and passive condition (**Se escondió el oro**).

Podríamos **irnos** ricos.

1. A final category of verbs is used with a reflexive pronoun only at certain times. If the subject of the sentence—usually a person—is affected either favorably or unfavorably by the idea expressed by the verb, a reflexive pronoun is used with certain verbs to indicate this special involvement of the subject. Note the following shades of meaning conveyed when a reflexive pronoun is used:

beber to drink	**beberse** to drink up (completely)
caer to fall	**caerse** to fall down
comer to eat	**comerse** to eat up (completely)
ir to go	**irse** to go away; to get going
llevar to carry	**llevarse** to carry off (away)
morir to die	**morirse** to pass away, to die
perder to lose	**perderse** to miss (out on) (a party, etc.)
reír to laugh	**reírse** to laugh [more conversational in tone]

Notice the difference in tone when the reflexive is used; **morirse,** for example, is a less blunt way of saying **morir.**

2. The use of a reflexive pronoun with these verbs is especially common in informal conversation.

Vámonos.	Let's get going.
Me comí todos los anticuchos.	I ate (up) all the anticuchos.
Se ha muerto la tía Amparo.	Aunt Amparo has passed away.
Si tú te vas, yo me muero.	If you go away, I'll die.
Te perdiste una fiesta estupenda.	You missed out on a great party.

Aplicación

I. Translate each of the following pairs.

MODELO María is going with Juan. / María is going away with Juan. → **María va con Juan.** / **María se va con Juan.**

1. He died. / He passed away.
2. They eat dessert. / They eat up all the dessert.

3. She lost the bracelet. / She missed the party.
4. I'm going to class. / I'm going away.
5. The child drank milk. / The child drank up all the milk.
6. He carried a briefcase. / He carried off the briefcase.

II. Para contestar

1. ¿Se queda usted aquí durante las vacaciones o se va? ¿Adónde va usted?
2. ¿Come usted en clase? Cuando usted era niño (niña), ¿ se enojaba su mamá cuando no se comía toda la comida?
3. ¿Se tomó usted una cerveza antes de venir a clase? ¿Toman los estudiantes mucha cerveza?
4. ¿Se perdió un buen programa de televisión anoche? ¿Por qué?
5. ¿Se ha muerto algún amigo suyo?
6. ¿Se muere usted de hambre ahora? ¿Se muere de sueño?
7. ¿Se rieron los estudiantes cuando yo pregunté si tomaban mucha cerveza?
8. ¿Se llevó alguien su cartera alguna vez? ¿Cuándo? ¿Dónde?

B. Two word endings: -ito and -ísimo

la jaula → la jaulita
rico → riquísimo

1. The diminutive **-ito** is a word ending used to express smallness, cuteness, familiarity, intimacy, or fondness (compare English *John, Johnny*). It is attached to the base of a noun or an adjective (and occasionally to an adverb); the base of a noun or adjective is the word minus final **-o** or **-a.** If the word does not end in **-o** or **-a,** the ending is added to the entire word.

un gatito	a cute cat
un perrito	a nice little dog
una pulserita	a pretty little bracelet
ahorita	right now; in a little while

2. The diminutive ending **-cito** is used: a) with nouns and adjectives of more than one syllable that end in **-n** or **-r;** and b) with all nouns and adjectives that end in **-e.**

Carmencita	(dear) Carmen
jovencito	(quite) young
mujercita	a (small) woman
botecito	a (little) boat
verdecito	soft (light) green

3. The diminutive ending reflects both the number and gender of the base form.

una bolsita	a (small) bag
los gatitos	the kittens
las jaulitas	the (little) cages

4. To express the idea *extremely* (+ adjective), the ending **-ísimo** (**-ísima**) is added to the base of an adjective or adverb. When **-ísimo** is attached to an adjective, it is modified to express both number and gender agreement. Note that sometimes a spelling change will be required.

Este caballo corre rapidísimo.	This horse runs extremely fast.
La recepción se prolongó muchísimo.	The reception got drawn out a whole lot.
Muchísimas gracias.	Many, many thanks.
Me gusta mucho este postre; está riquísimo.	I like this dessert very much; it's very delicious.

Aplicación

I. Give the diminutive of each of the following words.

MODELO bolsa → **bolsita**

1. jaula 2. bote 3. cartera 4. puente 5. gato 6. café 7. pájaro 8. loro 9. amor 10. motor 11. verde 12. azul

II. Answer each question, including a diminutive form in your response.

MODELO ¿Le gusta el gato? → **Claro que me gusta el gatito. Es muy lindo.**

1. ¿Le gusta el perro?
2. ¿Le gustan los zapatos?
3. ¿Le gusta el vestido?
4. ¿Le gustan los loros?
5. ¿Le gusta la camisa?

III. Change the adverb to the **-ísimo** form.

MODELO Ha llovido mucho. → **Ha llovido muchísimo.**

1. Es temprano.
2. Este aserradero produce poco.
3. Ya es tarde.
4. Hay que trabajar rápido.
5. La finca está cerca.

IV. Answer each question using an **-ísimo** form in your response.

MODELO ¿Es viejo este caballo? → **Claro, es viejísimo.**

1. ¿Es grande la finca?
2. ¿Es importante la clase?
3. ¿Son pocos los trabajadores?
4. ¿Es cara la carne?
5. ¿Es guapo este muchacho?
6. ¿Es linda su casa?
7. ¿Es difícil el español?
8. ¿Son inteligentes ustedes?

Repaso oral

I. Para describir

Describe the action of the dialog **Tres aventureros** including in your description comments on the following:

> pepitas de oro, el fondo doble, piedritas, complicaciones, los guardias, el contrabando, el bello infierno verde, un botecito, dos misioneros

II. Para completar

MODELO No le gustaba a Cristina que. . .→ **No le gustaba a Cristina que los guardias estuvieran cerca del bote.**

1. Cristina quería que. . .
2. Manolo le pidió a Santiago que. . .
3. Santiago le dijo a Cristina que. . .
4. Era imposible que los tres. . .
5. Sería una lástima que Cristi y Santiago. . .
6. Los tres esperaban que. . .
7. Tenían miedo que. . .
8. No creían que. . .

La conquista del Peru.

Comunicación 4

El teléfono y el banco

When visiting a Spanish-speaking country you will need to use Spanish on the telephone and when banking.

El teléfono

Study the following vocabulary items. Practice saying out loud the short sentences that appear at the right.

llamar por teléfono	to call on the phone	Hay que llamar por teléfono.
contestar (**el teléfono**)	to answer (the telephone)	Llamé pero nadie contestó.
la llamada	the telephone call	Esperé tu llamada toda la tarde.
el número de teléfono	the telephone number	¿Me das tu número de teléfono?
la guía telefónica	the telephone book	Voy a buscar el número en la guía telefónica.
el número ocupado	the busy line	Está ocupado el número.
Diga.	Hello (used in Spain).	Diga. ¿Quién habla, por favor?
Bueno.	Hello (used in Mexico).	Bueno. ¿Quién habla, por favor?
Aló.	Hello (used in most other Spanish-speaking countries).	Aló, ¿está Pepito?
el (**la**) **telefonista**	telephone operator	Mi hermana es telefonista.

I. Entre nosotros

Student A (or the instructor) asks the following questions. Student B answers using either of the possibilities suggested at the right.

MODELO ¿Vas a llamar a tu familia? ¿De qué van a hablar? — los detalles del matrimonio / un puesto estupendo

STUDENT A (asks the questions)

STUDENT B **Vamos a discutir los detalles del matrimonio.**

STUDENT A	STUDENT B
1. ¿Vas a llamar a tu familia? ¿De qué van a hablar?	los estudios / el novio (la novia)
2. Esperé tu llamada toda la tarde. ¿Qué pasó?	mi primo Bernardo / Salí a. . .
3. Voy a buscar el número en la guía. ¿Sabes dónde está?	la mesa / el dormitorio
4. ¿Me das tu número de teléfono?	Sí, es. . . / No puedo porque. . .
5. ¿Está ocupado el número?	Claro. Adela habla con. . . / Por supuesto. Germán habla con. . .
6. Mi hermana es telefonista. ¿Sabes dónde trabaja?	Sí, trabaja en. . . / No, no sé. . .
7. Llamé pero nadie contestó. ¿Sabes por qué?	Ah, es porque. . . / Ah, no sé. . .
8. ¿Vas a contestar el teléfono?	Sí, debe ser. . . / No, no puedo porque. . .

El banco

la cuenta	account	Tengo una cuenta en ese banco.
el cheque	check	¿Cuántos cheques te quedan?
el cheque de viajero	traveler's check	Tengo que comprar más cheques de viajero.
economizar	to be thrifty	Tratamos de economizar.
ser rico	to be rich	Mi tía es una señora muy rica.
ser pobre	to be poor	Son muy pobres. No tienen nada.
firmar	to sign	Usted no firmó el cheque, señor.

despositar	to deposit	¿Ya depositaste el dinero?
sacar dinero	to withdraw money	Saqué cien dólares de la cuenta.
cambiar un cheque	to cash a check	¿Dónde puedo cambiar estos cheques?
empleado bancario	bank clerk	El padre de Juan Carlos es empleado bancario.

I. Person A asks the following questions to another person. Person B answers using either of the possibilities which appear at the right.

PERSON A	PERSON B
1. Allí está el Banco de España. ¿Necesitas entrar?	Sí, tengo que entrar para. . . / No, no quiero porque. . .
2. ¿Sabes cuánto dinero tengo en la cuenta?	Sí, tienes. . . / No, no me importa. . .
3. Necesito comprar más cheques de viajero. ¿Cuántos voy a necesitar?	Pues, creo que. . . / Pues, no sé. . .
4. Usted no firmó el cheque. ¿Cuándo lo puede firmar?	Lo puedo firmar. . . / No lo puedo firmar. . .
5. ¿Cuándo me pagas el dinero?	Te lo pago. . . / No te lo voy a pagar porque. . .
6. ¿Dónde puedo cambiar estos cheques de viajero?	Puedes cambiar los cheques en. . . / No sé. Pero por qué no. . .?
7. ¿Tienes mucha plata o no?	Ahora estoy rico (rica) porque. . . / Ahora estoy pobre porque. . .
8. ¿Depositas o sacas dinero del banco?	Deposito. . . / Saco. . .

II. Situación

Form groups of two or three people. One person wants to call a friend in another part of the country, or in a foreign country. A second person needs to go to the bank. The third is heading for the post office. You discuss what you're going to do. Each person asks another to do him or her a favor while making the call or while at the bank or post office.

Capítulo 17

Despegue

Descripción del dibujo

1. Raúl y Leandro están en el estadio.
2. Es un partido de fútbol estupendo.
3. Holanda y Argentina juegan por la Copa del Mundo.
4. Los espectadores se vuelven locos.
5. Raúl prende su radio para ver qué dice el cronista.

Pronunciación

1. Raúl y Leandro / el estadio
2. un partido / un partido de fútbol estupendo
3. Holanda y Argentina / la Copa del Mundo
4. el radio / Vamos a prender el radio.

Aplicación

I. Relación

Say at least ten sentences about the drawing on page 397.

II. Para contestar

1. ¿A usted le gusta el fútbol?
2. ¿Hay un estadio de fútbol cerca de aquí?
3. ¿Qué país tiene la Copa del Mundo de fútbol ahora?
4. ¿Se vuelven locos los espectadores aquí?
5. Cuando usted va a un partido, ¿prende la radio para ver qué dice el cronista?
6. ¿Vio usted uno de los partidos en que jugaron Holanda y Argentina?

Tema del diálogo

Buenos Aires. The decisive moment in the World Soccer Cup Championship final between Argentina and Holland.

Mario Kempes after scoring the decisive goal in the World Cup final between Argentina and Holland, 1978.

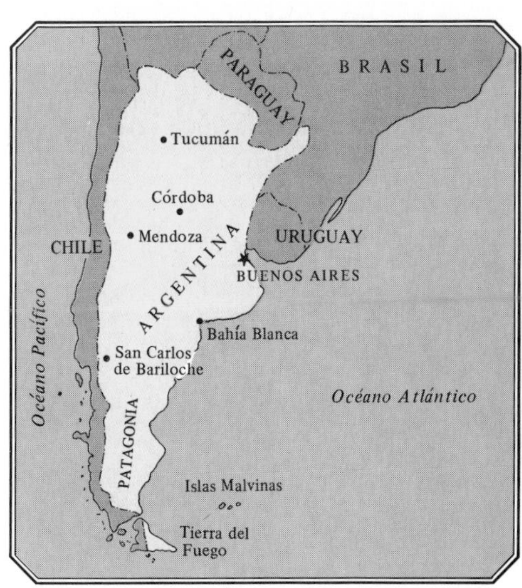

DIÁLOGO

Un partido de fútbol memorable

En el estadio River Plate[1] de Buenos Aires, Argentina, se juega el último juego de la Copa del Mundo[2]. Raúl Garmendia y un amigo, Leandro Porras, ya han visto 90 minutos de furioso juego y el marcador dice Argentina 1, Holanda 1. Puesto que es el último juego, se jugarán 30 minutos adicionales para decidir quién será el campeón. El estadio es un manicomio.

RAUL ¡Che Leandro! Si papá pudiera ver esto.

LEANDRO ¡Sí, claro! ¡Este juego ha estado macanudo!

RAÚL Ahora sólo se necesita que Argentina anote un gol, un solo gol. . .

LEANDRO Ya empieza el juego de nuevo.

RAÚL ¡A sentarse todo el mundo! ¡Que no se puede ver bien el campo!

* * *

LEANDRO (Raúl vuelve a prender su radio para ver qué dice el cronista. Se escucha el animado comentario de Ñato Pelicano.)
"Mario Kempes avanza con la pelota por la mitad del campo holandés. Burla a la defensa holandesa. Kempes se acerca a la meta y suelta un tremendo disparo. . .¡como si tuviera un cañón! ¡Pero la pelota pega en el marco!"

RAÚL ¡Pronto, Mario! ¡Dispara! ¡Que vienen dos defensas! (Kempes vuelve a disparar.)

LOS ESPECTADORES ¡GOL! ¡GOL! ¡GOL!

* * *

Celebration in Buenos Aires following Argentina's qualification for the World Cup final, 1978.

(Una hora más tarde el juego ha terminado y Raúl y Leandro van en el colectivo[3] hacia casa. Raúl vuelve a prender su radio y se escucha el comentario final de Ñato.)

"Marcador final, Argentina 3, Holanda 1. . .lo que se suele decir en estos casos, se ha demostrado ampliamente la superioridad del fútbol nacional. También se ha probado que el estilo del fútbol sudamericano es infinitamente superior al estilo europeo. Y ahora, amigos, un importante mensaje comercial. . ."

(Se escucha el anuncio.)

"Hablando de campeones, si hubiera una Copa del Mundo de hojas de afeitar, las Faconazo también serían el número uno de este siglo. . ."

A memorable soccer game

In the River Plate Stadium in Buenos Aires, Argentina, the final game of the World Cup is being played. Raúl Garmendia and a friend, Leandro Porras, have already seen 90 minutes of furious play and the scoreboard says Argentina 1, Holland 1. Since it is the final game, they will play an additional 30 minutes to decide who will be the champion. The stadium is a madhouse.

R: Wow, Leandro. If Dad could only see this.

L: Right you are! This game has been fabulous.

R: Now the only thing we need is that Argentina score a goal, a single goal . . .

L: The game is starting again.

R: Everybody sit down! (The reason is that) one can't see the field well!

* * *

L: Raúl, turn your radio on again to see what our announcer is saying.
(The excited commentary of Ñato Pelicano is heard.)
"Mario Kempes advances with the ball through the middle of Dutch territory (the Dutch field). He fools the Dutch defense. Kempes approaches the goal and lets go a tremendous shot . . . as if he had a cannon! But the ball hits the post (frame)!"

R: Quick, Mario! Shoot! Two defensemen are coming. (Kempes shoots again.)

SPECTATORS Goal! Goal! Goal!

* * *

(An hour later the game has ended and Raúl and Leandro are going home in the bus. Raúl turns his radio on again and the final commentary of Ñato is heard.)
"Final score, Argentina 3, Holland 1 . . . as one usually says in these cases, the superiority of our national soccer has been amply shown. It has also been proved that the South American style of soccer is infinitely superior to the European style. And now, friends, an important commercial message . . ."
(The advertisement is heard.)
"Speaking of champions, if there were a World Cup of razor blades, Faconazo blades (those [with the brand name] Faconazo) would also be Number One in this century . . ."

VARIACIONES

¿Quiénes son esos muchachos?	Who are those boys?
Son atletas.	They're athletes.
Un equipo de fútbol.	A soccer team.
Jugadores de fútbol.	Soccer players.
Son aficionados.	They're fans.
¿De dónde son los muchachos?	Where are the boys from?
De Europa. . .son europeos.	Europe . . . they are Europeans.
De Inglaterra. . .son ingleses.	England . . . they are English.
De Alemania. . .son alemanes.	Germany . . . they are Germans.
De Francia. . .son franceses.	France . . . they are French.
De Italia. . .son italianos.	Italy . . . they are Italians.
De Portugal. . .son portugueses.	Portugal . . . they are Portuguese.
De Rusia. . .son rusos.	Russia . . . they are Russians.
¿Vamos al partido?	Shall we go to the game?
Primero me pongo la chaqueta.	I'll put my jacket on first.
Me pongo los guantes.	I'll put my gloves on.
Me pongo la bufanda.	I'll put my scarf on.
Me pongo el sombrero.	I'll put my hat on.
¿Dónde te encontraste el domingo?	Where were you on Sunday?
¿Sueles ir a los partidos?	Do you usually go to the games?
No, los aficionados gritan demasiado.	No, the fans shout too much.
Tengo la costumbre de verlos en televisión.	I usually see them on television.

Glosas

1. *River Plate* is the name in British English for the **Río de la Plata,** the enormous South American river that empties into the sea at Buenos Aires. The fact that the largest sports arena in the Argentine capital has a British name is symbolic of Argentina's orientation toward Europe, and in particular, Italy and England. British influence in Argentina, reflecting Britain's role at the turn of the century as Argentina's principal customer for agricultural products, British ownership of all the railroads, and many other factors, remained very great until the World Depression of the 1930's caused Britain to exclude Argentine products in favor of imports from Canada and Australia. In Argentina the term **gringo** once meant *Englishman;* today it usually means *Italian.* (A **gringo** is really *someone speaking "that" strange language;* in South American countries other than Argentina, the term often means *Englishman.* Only in Mexico, Central America, and the Caribbean does it inevitably mean *American.*) Rich Argentines still share a conspicuous fondness for polo and British tailoring.
2. A World Cup championship is truly an outstanding event for most of the sports aficionados of the world. All continents participate in the preliminary rounds of elimination, and the final playoffs are accordingly the one athletic event that can honestly be described as producing a "world" champion. For Argentine fans, winning the World Cup in 1978—their first championship—was the dream of a lifetime.
3. Most urban Hispanics depend on mass transit systems (**sistemas de transporte colectivo**) for their transportation. The largest cities have trains, buses, and occasionally subways (**el metro,** short for **el metropolitano;** in Buenos Aires, **el subte,** short for **el subterráneo**). Buses are the most prevalent form of public transportation. Different terms for *bus* are used in different countries; **el autobús** is understood everywhere, though **el colectivo** is favored in Argentina, **la guagua** in Cuba and Puerto Rico, **el camión** in Mexico, etc.

SOBRE EL DIÁLOGO

I. Complete the sentence with the appropriate word or words from the following list.

chaqueta	**equipo**	**mensajes comerciales**
guantes	**jugador**	**estadio**
sombrero	**siglo**	**manicomio**
espectadores	**probar**	**se volvieron**
juego		

MODELO Mi hermano es ____ de fútbol. → **Mi hermano es jugador de fútbol.**

1. ¡Qué frío! Voy a ponerme la ____.
2. Jugaron tenis, pero yo no vi el ____.
3. Tenemos que ____ que nuestro estilo es superior.
4. En la cabeza llevo un ____.
5. Tienes las manos muy frías. Debes ponerte los ____.
6. Cien años son un ____.
7. Tienen a los locos en el ____.

8. En la televisión hay muchos _____.
9. Muchos _____ fueron a ver el juego.
10. El juego va a ser en el _____ nuevo.
11. ¿Cuántos jugadores hay en un _____ de fútbol?
12. Los espectadores _____ locos.

II. Replace the underlined words with a synonym from the list.

de nuevo, los espectadores, estupendo, se encuentran, más tarde, manicomio

MODELO Llegaron una hora después. → **Llegaron una hora más tarde.**

1. Mario avanza con la pelota otra vez.
2. El estadio parece una casa de locos.
3. Raúl y Leandro están en el estadio.
4. Sonríe para el público.
5. Este partido ha sido macanudo.

III. Supply the appropriate adjective.

MODELO Compré este reloj en Alemania. Es un reloj _____. → **Es un reloj alemán.**

1. Esa muchacha es de Inglaterra. Es una muchacha _____.
2. El vino es de Francia. Es un vino _____.
3. Compramos estas tazas en Portugal. Son tazas _____.
4. Estos guantes son de Italia. Son guantes _____.
5. Mis padres son de Europa. Son _____.
6. Estudiamos el gobierno de Rusia. Estudiamos el gobierno _____.
7. Hacen buenos coches en Alemania. Voy a comprar un coche _____.
8. Tengo una amiga de Holanda. Es una chica _____.

IV. Para contestar

1. ¿Dónde se encuentran Raúl y Leandro? ¿Qué van a ver?
2. ¿Quién querría Raúl que pudiera ver el partido?
3. ¿Quién es Mario Kempes? ¿Qué hace?
4. ¿Por qué se vuelve loco el público? ¿Qué grita todo el mundo?
5. ¿Por qué es este partido especialmente importante para la Argentina?
6. ¿Qué se ha demostrado?
7. ¿Qué se oye en el radio después del comentario de Ñato Pelicano?
8. ¿Cuáles son seis países europeos? ¿Cuál le gustaría visitar más?

VOCABULARIO

nouns

el **aficionado**	fan
Alemania	Germany
el **anuncio**	advertisement, announcement
el (la) **atleta**	athlete
la **bufanda**	scarf
el **campeón,** la **campeona**	champion
el **campo**	field
el **cañón**	cannon
el **colectivo**	bus
el **comentario**	commentary
la **copa**	cup
la **costumbre**	custom
el (la) **cronista**	announcer, sportscaster
la **chaqueta**	jacket
la **defensa**	defense
el (la) **defensa**	defenseman
el **disparo**	shot
el **equipo**	team
el **espectador,** la **espectadora**	spectator
el **estadio**	stadium
el **estilo**	style
Europa	Europe
Francia	France
el **gol**	goal
el **guante**	glove
la **hoja de afeitar**	razor blade
Holanda	Holland
Inglaterra	England
Italia	Italy
el **jugador,** la **jugadora**	player
el **manicomio**	madhouse, insane asylum
el **marcador**	scoreboard
el **marco**	frame
el **mensaje comercial**	advertisement, message from the sponsor
la **meta**	goal
Portugal	Portugal
el (la) **radio**	radio
Rusia	Russia
el **siglo**	century
el **sombrero**	hat
la **superioridad**	superiority

verbs

anotar	to chalk up, to add on, to get, to score
burlar	to mock, to fool
decidir	to decide
demostrar (ue)	to demonstrate
disparar	to shoot
encontrarse (ue)	to be
gritar	to shout, to yell
prender	to turn on
soler (ue) + infinitive	to usually + verb
soltar (ue)	to let loose, to let go
volver (ue) a + infinitive	to (do something) again

adjectives

adicional	additional
alemán, alemana	German
animado	excited
europeo	European
francés, francesa	French
holandés, holandesa	Dutch
italiano	Italian
macanudo	(regional) great, fantastic
memorable	memorable
portugués, portuguesa	Portuguese
ruso	Russian

superior	superior	**pronto**	quick
tremendo	tremendous		
		other expressions	
adverbs		**a sentarse**	sit down
ampliamente	amply	**lo que**	what
infinitamente	infinitely		

ESTRUCTURA I

A. Relator words

1. A relator word introduces a clause that refers back to a word mentioned earlier in the sentence. The relator clause provides additional information concerning this word.

¿Quién es el chico que está con Raúl ?	Who is the boy who is with Raúl?
Me gusta el sombrero que lleva Leandro .	I like the hat that Leandro is wearing.
Ñato vio el colectivo que se acercaba .	Nato saw the bus that was approaching.

2. The most frequently used relator is **que**. It appears directly after the word—referring to either a person or a thing—to which it relates. **Que** means *who, which,* or *that*. It is never omitted from a Spanish sentence the way its equivalents are sometimes omitted in English.

person(s) / thing(s) } + **que**

Raúl es el chico que vi ayer en el estadio.	Raúl is the boy that I saw yesterday in the stadium.
¿Dónde están las maletas que vamos a llevar?	Where are the suitcases we're going to take?

3. The relator **quien (quienes)** refers to people and is used following a preposition to express the idea *who* or *whom*. **Quien** refers back to one person; **quienes** refers to more than one.

person(s) + preposition + **quien(es)**

Allí están los jugadores de quienes te hablé.	There are the players about whom I spoke to you.
Ése es el muchacho a quien le vendimos el coche.	That is the boy to whom we sold the car.
Raúl y Leandro son los amigos con quienes iré al partido.	Raúl and Leandro are the friends with whom I'll go to the game.

4. **Que** is used after a preposition to refer to a thing or things. Note that in sentences with a preposition followed by a relator word, the preposition and relator appear directly after the noun to which they refer.

Ésta es la chaqueta de que te hablaba.	This is the jacket I was telling you about.

5. Another relator word is **lo que.** It refers to nothing specific but rather has the general meaning *what* or *that which.*

No entiendo lo que dicen en el radio.	I don't understand what they're saying on the radio.
¡Quién sabe lo que quiere María!	Who knows what Mary wants!

Aplicación

I. Combine the following sentences by using the relator **que.**

A. MODELO Juan es la persona. Me enseñó a jugar tenis. → **Juan es la persona que me enseñó a jugar tenis.**

1. Éste es el equipo. Ganó el partido.
2. ¿Dónde están los jugadores? Burlaron a la defensa.
3. Éstos son los espectadores. Gritaban.
4. ¿Conoces al chico? Vino ayer.
5. Escuchábamos al cronista. Hablaba del partido.
6. Éste es el partido. Ha demostrado la superioridad del fútbol argentino.

B. MODELO Ésta es la chaqueta. Tú me la compraste. → **Ésta es la chaqueta que tú me compraste.**

1. Compré el abrigo. Tú me lo mostraste.
2. Me puse los guantes. Mamá me los dio.
3. Necesito el sombrero. Ella lo usa.
4. Dame la bufanda. Yo te la compré.
5. No me acuerdo de esa muchacha. Ustedes la invitaron.
6. Se fueron los espectadores. Ellos los conocían.

II. Restate each sentence to include a preposition followed by **quien** or **quienes.**

A. MODELO Yo te hablaba de esos jugadores. → **Ésos son los jugadores de quienes te hablaba.**

1. Compré los guantes para esta muchacha.
2. Yo jugaba tenis con ese señor.
3. Nosotros le hablamos de ese jugador.
4. María salía con ese joven.
5. Él compró una pulsera de oro para esa mujer.

B. MODELO Yo le vendí el coche a ese muchacho. → **Ése es el muchacho a quien le vendí el coche.**

1. Les doy dinero a estos jóvenes.
2. Le cuento mis problemas a este doctor.
3. Le pagamos el dinero a ese hombre.
4. Le mostré la carta a ese abogado.
5. Les digo la verdad a estos estudiantes.

C. MODELO Yo te hablaba de este libro. → **Éste es el libro de que yo te hablaba.**

1. Nosotros jugábamos con esta pelota.
2. Ellos caminaban en este parque.
3. Siempre me habla de ese equipo.
4. Tengo mi dinero en este banco.
5. Me gusta escribir con esta pluma.

III. Para expresar en español

MODELO That's the girl I was sitting with. → **Ésa es la chica con quien yo estaba sentado.**

1. That's the young woman I was speaking of.
2. That's the child I bought it for.
3. Those are the boys we were playing with.
4. That's the ball we were playing with.
5. That's the student I showed it to.
6. That's the game we were speaking of.
7. Those are the players we were listening to.
8. That's the fan we were talking with.

IV. Answer each question following the pattern shown in the model.

MODELO ¿Qué quiere María? → **¡Dios mío! ¡Quién sabe lo que quiere!**

1. ¿Qué hizo Mario?
2. ¿Qué dijeron tus hermanos?
3. ¿Qué gritaron los aficionados?
4. ¿Qué contó el cronista?
5. ¿Qué vieron Raúl y Federico?

V. Para expresar en español

MODELO I don't understand what she says. → **No entiendo lo que dice.**

1. We don't know what they want.
2. Do they have what you asked for?
3. I read what they give me.
4. Who knows what she did?
5. Do you know what happened?
6. Did you hear what the announcer said?

B. Sentences with **si** and **como si**

Si Argentina gana el partido, daremos una fiesta.

1. In a clause with **si,** the verb may be either indicative or subjunctive. If the condition expressed in the **si**-clause may actually become fulfilled, the indicative, not the subjunctive, is used in the **si**-clause.

Si vamos al partido, tendremos que salir temprano.	If we go to the game, we'll have to leave early.
Si hay complicaciones, no me llamen.	If there are problems, don't call me.

2. When, however, the condition differs from what is known to be true, the past subjunctive is used following **si** and the conditional is used in the result clause.

si + past subjunctive + conditional

Si Nancy López fuera amiga mía, yo jugaría tenis con ella.	If Nancy López were a friend of mine, I'd play tennis with her.
Si tú trabajaras más, ganarías más dinero.	If you worked more, you would earn more money.
Si no lloviera tanto, nos divertiríamos mucho más.	If it weren't raining so much, we would have a much better time.

3. **Si** may either begin a sentence or introduce a clause in the middle of a sentence.

Compraría el reloj si no fuera tan caro.	I would buy the watch if it weren't so expensive.
Si el reloj no fuera tan caro, lo compraría.	If the watch weren't so expensive, I'd buy it.

4. Another expression, **como si** *as if*, is always followed by a past subjunctive.

Cristina me miró como si no me conociera.	Cristina looked at me as if she didn't know me.
¡Qué loco estás! Les hablas a los animales como si fueran personas.	Boy, are you ever crazy! You speak to animals as if they were people.

Argentina's team leaving the field after defeating Holland in the World Cup final, June 22, 1978.

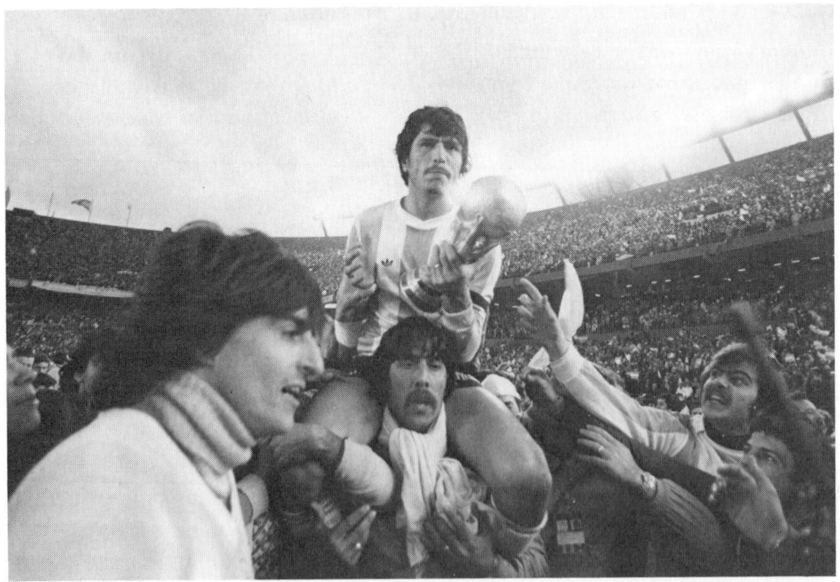

Aplicación

I. Modify the following sentences to express an unfulfilled condition; use the past subjunctive and the conditional.

MODELO Si yo tengo dinero, haré un viaje. → **Si yo tuviera dinero, haría un viaje.**

1. Si tú te sientas, podremos ver.
2. Si Kempes juega, ganarán.
3. Si vamos al partido, me pondré una chaqueta.
4. Si es de Italia, habla italiano.
5. Si son de Rusia, saben ruso.
6. Si me pongo el abrigo, tendré calor.
7. Si tenemos ganas de viajar, iremos a Francia.
8. Si te molesta ese hombre, le pegarás en la cara, ¿no?

II. Combine the items listed to form sentences.

MODELO si / (yo) tener / tiempo / (yo) hacerlo. → **Si tuviera tiempo, lo haría.**

1. si / (tú) ser / novia / yo / darte / pulsera / oro
2. si / no / gustarte / pulsera / (yo) comprarte / reloj
3. si / tú / no querer / reloj / yo / darte / unas botas / bonito
4. si / no gustarte / botas / yo / pedirles / dinero / hermanos / para comprarte / casa
5. si / ellos / no darme / dinero / (yo) hacerme / aventurero
6. si / yo / hacerme / aventurero / (yo) contrabandear / oro
7. si / yo / ser / rico / tú / casarte / conmigo
8. si / tú / no casarte / conmigo / yo / buscarme / otro / novia

III. Respond to each remark using **hablar** and **como si** + past subjunctive.

MODELO Él no es un gran aventurero. → **Pero habla como si fuera un gran aventurero.**

1. Ella no lo sabe todo.
2. Ellos no son ricos.
3. Yo no estoy preocupado.
4. Ellos no quieren plata.
5. Él no tiene problemas.
6. Ella no necesita una cartera nueva.

IV. Complete the following sentences any way you wish.

MODELO Ella me mira como si _____. → **Ella me mira como si me conociera.** *or* **Ella me mira como si quisiera pegarme.**

1. El niño sonríe como si _____.
2. Doña Teresa se preocupa como si _____.
3. El presidente habló como si _____.
4. Yo iría a Inglaterra si _____.
5. Los novios se casarán si _____.
6. Ella me llamaría si _____.
7. Yo te esperaré si _____.
8. Si tú me quisieras, _____.
9. Si ellos me invitan, _____.
10. Si yo fuera dueño de una gran compañía, _____.

V. Para contestar

1. ¿Qué haría usted si fuera presidente de esta universidad?
2. ¿Qué haría usted si se encontrara en la selva y no supiera cómo salir?
3. ¿Qué cree usted que yo haría si no tuviera que enseñar hoy?
4. ¿Dónde estudiaría usted si no estudiara en esta universidad?
5. ¿Qué haría usted si fuera la persona más rica del mundo?
6. ¿Hablan los hombres a veces como si fueran más inteligentes que las mujeres? Y las mujeres, ¿cómo hablan ellas?
7. ¿Jugará usted fútbol esta tarde si tiene tiempo?
8. ¿Qué digo yo si usted llega tarde?

Pausa oral

Actividades

Imagine that you are going to go to a concert, a soccer game, or some other event at your university or in a city.

I. To begin, review the vocabulary in the following list, which is organized according to the stages of getting ready, going, and returning from the event. Add as many additional words as you can, and ask your instructor if you need others.

prepararse	bañarse ducharse	sentarse	gustar interesar
llevar	zapatos pantalones	salir	a cenar para ir a un bar estudiantil *(coffee shop)*
encontrarse	en un café en el centro	irse a casa	temprano a medianoche a las 2 de la mañana
ir	en el colectivo en el metro en taxi	parecerle	bueno malo estupendo excelente
llegar	a tiempo tarde		

II. Now, together with a friend from the class, plan a date to go to the event you have selected. Use some of the vocabulary in the list.

MODELO (STUDENT A) **¿A qué hora nos encontramos para ir al concierto esta noche?**
(STUDENT B) **Pues a las siete. ¿Te parece bien?**
(STUDENT A) . . .
(STUDENT B) . . .

III. Para describir

What activities do the following drawings depict? Describe what you see by answering these questions: **¿Quiénes están? ¿Dónde se encuentran? ¿Qué hacen? ¿Por qué?**

ESTRUCTURA II

A. Al / soler / volver a + infinitive

Raul **vuelve a** prender su radio.

1. **Al** + infinitive is used to express a time relationship between two actions that occur simultaneously or one right after the other. English uses *when, as,* or *upon* + gerund in similar contexts.

Al prender el radio, oí el comentario de Ñato.	When I put the radio on, I heard Ñato's commentary.
Leandro se quitó la chaqueta al entrar.	Leandro took off his jacket when (as) he came in.
Al tomar tierra, el avión se detuvo de repente.	When the airplane landed, it stopped suddenly.

2. **Soler** + infinitive is used to express customary action. In similar contexts, English uses *usually* + verb.

Mario Kempes suele jugar muy bien.	Mario Kempes usually plays very well.
Cuando yo era niño, solía pasar las vacaciones en Europa.	When I was a kid I usually spent my vacation in Europe.

3. **Volver a** + infinitive is used to express repetition of an action, with the idea *to do something again.*

Volvimos a visitar Inglaterra.	We visited England again.
Vuelvo a leerlo.	I'll read it again.
El verano pasado volvieron a visitar la selva amazónica.	Last summer they visited the Amazon jungle again.

Aplicación

I. Restate the following sentences using **al** + infinitive.

MODELO Lo vi cuando entré. → **Lo vi al entrar.**

1. Te llamé cuando lo oí.
2. Se volvieron locos cuando vieron el partido.
3. Cambiamos de opinión cuando oímos eso.
4. Le pegó a la pelota cuando vio a los defensas.
5. Apagó el radio cuando empezaron los anuncios.
6. Todos gritaron cuando se terminó el partido.

II. Para expresar en español

MODELO I did it upon arriving (when I arrived). → **Lo hice al llegar.**

1. We left upon hearing it.
2. She calmed down upon realizing the truth.
3. I spoke to her upon entering.
4. He stood up upon seeing her.
5. They came back upon receiving the letter.

III. Restate the following sentences using **soler** + infinitive.

MODELO Tiene la costumbre de llegar tarde. → **Suele llegar tarde.**

1. Tengo la costumbre de usar sombrero.
2. Tiene la costumbre de cenar tarde.
3. Tenemos la costumbre de encontrarnos en un café.
4. Tienen la costumbre de escuchar música los sábados.
5. ¿Tiene usted la costumbre de comer en casa?

IV. Answer each question using **soler** + infinitive.

MODELO ¿Llegará temprano esta noche? → **Probablemente. Suele llegar temprano.**

1. ¿Jugarán fútbol esta noche?
2. ¿Escuchará el radio esta noche?
3. ¿Irá al concierto esta noche?
4. ¿Tomarán el colectivo esta noche?
5. ¿Ganarán ellos esta noche?

V. Restate the following sentences using **volver a** + infinitive.

MODELO Se puso el abrigo otra vez. → **Volvió a ponerse el abrigo.**

1. Se calmó otra vez.
2. Nos encontramos allí otra vez.
3. El público se volvió loco otra vez.
4. Me quité el sombrero otra vez.
5. Kempes se acercó a la meta otra vez.

VI. Answer each question using **volver a** in the future tense.

MODELO ¿Hablarás con él de nuevo? → **¿Cómo no? Volveré a hablar con él.**

1. ¿Empezará él de nuevo?
2. ¿Vendrás de nuevo?
3. ¿Jugaré de nuevo?
4. ¿Trabajaremos juntos de nuevo?
5. ¿Prenderán el radio de nuevo?

B. Acabar de + infinitive

El partido **acaba de** empezar.

To express an action which takes place immediately before the present moment or a moment in the past, **acabar de** is used as follows.

1. The present tense of **acabar de** + infinitive corresponds to English *has (have) just* + past participle.

Acaba de llamar mi primo Bernardo.	My cousin Bernardo just called.
Josefa y Marco Aurelio acaban de dejar los estudios.	Josefa and Marco Aurelio have just quit their studies.

2. The imperfect of **acabar de** + infinitive corresponds to English *had just* + past participle.

Emilio acababa de ir por el coche.	Emilio had just gone for the car.
Marisela y Emilio acababan de entrar en la oficina de la Dra. Ávila.	Marisela y Emilio had just gone into Dr. Ávila's office.

3. **Acabar** may also be used alone (without **de**) with the meaning *to finish.*

Josefa y Marcos acaban sus estudios este año.	Josefa and Marcos finish their studies this year.
¿Acabaste todo el vino?	Did you finish all the wine?

Aplicación

I. Answer each question using **acabar de** in the present tense.

MODELO ¿Ya salió Emilio? → **Sí, acaba de salir.**

1. ¿Ya estacionó el coche José Antonio?
2. ¿Ya llegó el médico?
3. ¿Ya hablaron la doctora y Marisela?
4. ¿Ya entró el esposo?
5. ¿Ya cenó usted?
6. ¿Ya estudiaron ustedes?

II. Make complete sentences using **acabar de** in the imperfect followed by a second clause beginning with **cuando.**

MODELO Ella / salir / usted / llamar → **Ella acababa de salir cuando usted llamó.**

1. Yo / comer / mamá / llegar
2. Los muchachos / entrar / el profesor / venir

3. Emilio / estacionar el carro / Marisela / salir
4. Nosotros / salir / eso / ocurrir
5. José / subir al dormitorio / sus amigos / llamar
6. Tú / ver el partido / yo / prender / radio

III. Complete each sentence any way you wish, but use some form of **acabar** in each.

MODELOS Ella no quiere salir porque _____. → **Ella no quiere salir porque acaban de llegar sus amigos.**
¿Cuándo vas a _____ el trabajo? → **¿Cuándo vas a acabar el trabajo?**

1. Pedro no puede hablar con usted porque _____.
2. Ellos no pueden cenar con nosotros porque _____.
3. Marisela no quiere comer mucho porque _____.
4. Yo _____ cuando usted _____.
5. Los muchachos _____ cuando la profesora _____.
6. El espectador _____ cuando los jugadores _____.
7. Yo _____ el trabajo anoche a las once.
8. Parece que ella ya va a _____ el libro.

IV. Review of special expressions. Repeat each sentence inserting the cues in parentheses.

MODELO Acabo de decirlo. (tengo que, vuelvo a, hay que) → **Tengo que decirlo. Vuelvo a decirlo. Hay que decirlo.**

1. Suelen cenar en el club. (acaban de, vuelven a, tienen que)
2. Hay que ir. (tenemos que, acabamos de, solemos)
3. Tienen que esperarlos. (hay que, acaban de, vuelven a)

V. Para expresar en español

MODELO I just studied. / I have to study. / I studied again. → **Acabo de estudiar.** / **Tengo que estudiar.** / **Volví a estudiar.**

1. He just went out. / He has to go out. / He went out again.
2. They usually arrive late. / They arrived late again. / They have to arrive late.
3. Kempes usually plays. / Kempes has to play. / Kempes plays again.
4. One has to prove it. / We proved it again. / We just proved it.

VI. Para contestar

1. ¿Volvió usted a estudiar el diálogo antes de venir a clase?
2. ¿Cuál es la primera cosa que usted hizo al llegar a la universidad?
3. ¿Acaban ustedes de ver un partido de fútbol?
4. ¿Por qué hay que jugar deportes?
5. ¿Suelen los estudiantes ir a los partidos de fútbol?
6. ¿Qué hay que hacer al llegar a la casa de alguien? ¿A quién hay que saludar? ¿Qué hay que hacer antes de irse?
7. ¿Volverá a tomar una clase de español el año que viene? ¿Qué clase tomará?
8. ¿Suelen los profesores encontrarse con los estudiantes después de las clases?

Jai alai, Spain's oldest sport and one of the newest in the USA.

LECTURA

Deportes hispánicos

Muchas personas piensan que el deporte hispánico más típico es el toreo, o corrida de toros[1]. Por eso se llevan la sorpresa de su vida[1] al darse cuenta de que al toreo, primero, no se le considera *deporte* sino un espectáculo simbólico. Segundo, las corridas de toros sólo se encuentran en España, México, Perú, Panamá, Ecuador, Colombia y Venezuela.

Para la inmensa mayoría hispánica, el fútbol (*soccer*) es el verdadero emperador de los deportes. El fútbol es sin duda alguna[1] el deporte que más se juega en tierras hispánicas; es también el deporte que, jugado en forma profesional, cuenta con el mayor[1] número de aficionados. Se calcula que más de 600 millones de personas de todo el mundo vieron por televisión, vía satélite, el juego por la Copa del Mundo entre Holanda y Argentina. En verdad la popularidad del fútbol en todo el mundo es suprema. Inclusive[1], en los EE.UU. en los últimos años se ha visto un gran desarrollo[1] en su popularidad.

corrida de toros bullfight

sorpresa . . . surprise of their life

sin duda alguna without a doubt

cuenta . . . has the greatest

Even

great increase

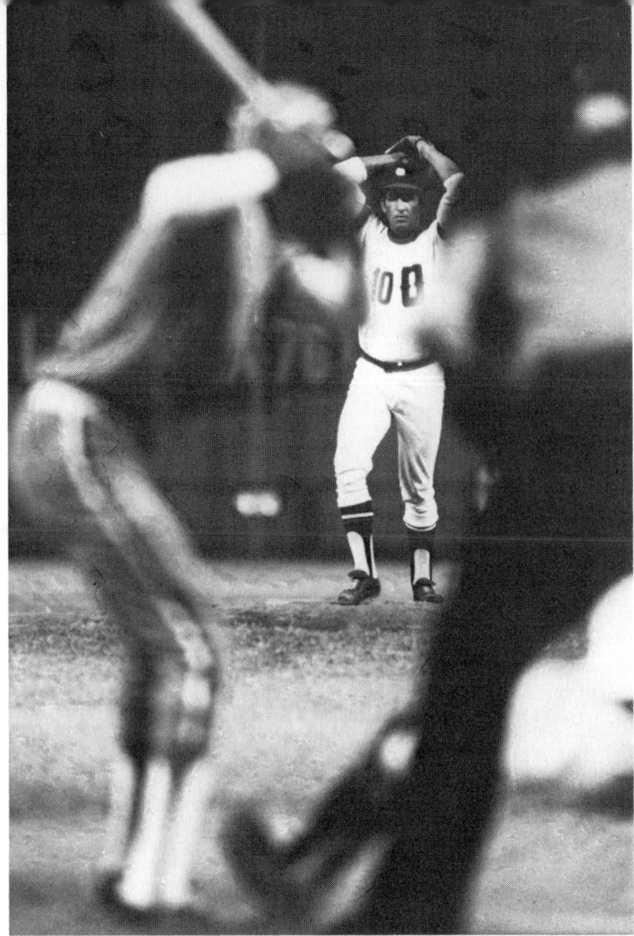

Cuba, Las Villas batting against Oriente in the National Series final. Baseball is still Cuba's national sport.

Además del fútbol, el básquetbol es bastante popular en países hispánicos a ambos lados del Atlántico. El básquetbol generalmente se practica en forma *amateur* y casi todos los países hispanos tienen equipos nacionales—conocidos como "selecciones nacionales"[1]—que participan en torneos y competencias internacionales de toda clase. En Hispanoamérica el "básquet" es uno de los pocos deportes principales en que las mujeres hispánicas participan activamente.

"all-star teams"

El béisbol es prácticamente desconocido[1] en España y en la mayoría de los países hispanoamericanos. Pero en Puerto Rico, la República Dominicana, Cuba, Venezuela, Panamá y México, el béisbol compite o supera[1] al fútbol en popularidad. En Cuba el béisbol es el deporte nacional y el fútbol es casi desconocido. En la capital mexicana coexisten ambos deportes, pues los domingos es fútbol por la mañana y béisbol por la tarde. El béisbol, por cierto[1], es uno de los deportes profesionales practicados en los EE.UU. en los cuales se ha dejado sentir[1] en forma sobresaliente[1] la presencia hispánica[1].

unknown

surpasses

por cierto by the way

en los cuales . . . in which has been felt/ outstanding

Quedan por mencionar muchos otros deportes que en ciertas partes de Hispanoamérica gustan mucho. Entre otros, hablemos del ciclismo que se practica entusiásticamente en Colombia, Centroamérica y México. En Chile y en Argentina se esquía en parajes andinos realmente hermosísimos. A la gente también le gusta esquiar sobre las dunas de arena; este deporte se practica en Chile y en el Perú. Además hay otros tres deportes muy populares en España y en toda Hispanoamérica. Nos referimos a la caza, la pesca, y la natación. Para estos deportes hay oportunidades ilimitadas porque todos los países hispánicos tienen una gran variedad de animales en los campos y montes para la caza. Para la pesca, siempre hay abundancia de peces de agua dulce en todos los países y de agua salada en casi todos los países. En estos mismos ríos, lagos, y mares (con excepción de Bolivia y Paraguay que no tienen salida al mar) se practica la natación y otros deportes acuáticos.

There remain
bicycling
parajes andinos Andean spots / most beautiful
dunas de arena sand dunes
hunting / fishing / swimming
campos y montes open fields and woods
peces . . . fresh-water fish / **de . . .** saltwater (fish)
lakes / seas
no . . . landlocked

Por último, hay que mencionar un juego cuyo origen se pierde en las tradiciones de los Países Vascos en España y en la zona vasca de Francia. Es el *jai alai*, el cual es un juego aparentemente muy sencillo—se juega como el *handball* o *squash*—y pueden jugar dos, cuatro o seis jugadores. Cada jugador tiene una "cesta" y la pelota es muy dura, como pelota de béisbol. Se calcula que la pelota en juego llega a alcanzar velocidades de más de 250 kilómetros por hora. Fuera de las tierras vascas, el jai alai se juega en México, las Filipinas, Macao, Indonesia y en Italia. En los EE.UU. existen "frontones" en la Florida, Nevada, Connecticut y Rhode Island. El jai alai es un juego rápido y emocionante.

whose
Basque Country
paddle / hard
It is estimated / **llega a alcanzar** reaches
jai alai courts

Glosa

1. Major League players of Hispanic origin include Rod Carew (Panama), Bobby Ávila (Mexico), Dave Concepción (Venezuela), Tony Oliva (Cuba), and José Cruz (Dominican Republic). One name that would surely appear on any Hispanic all-star team is Roberto Clemente. Clemente, who died in an airplane crash as he was taking a planeload of medicine, clothes, and food from Puerto Rico to an earthquake-torn Nicaragua, is not only the best Hispanic baseball player ever to play in the Major Leagues, but he is also considered a national hero in Puerto Rico. Baseball is just one of the sports in which Hispanic players have achieved stardom. The Hispanic presence is also felt in boxing, golf, tennis, and horse racing. Hispanics dominate the lower-weight classifications in boxing.

SOBRE LA LECTURA

I. Sí o no

If the information is true, say **sí** and repeat the sentence. If it is false, say **no** and make a sentence that is true.

1. Hay corridas de toros en todos los países de Latinoamérica.
2. El fútbol es el deporte más popular de todos en los países hispánicos.
3. El básquetbol no se conoce en Hispanoamérica.
4. En los países latinos, las mujeres no practican ningún deporte.
5. El béisbol es muy popular en todos los países hispánicos.
6. Hay varios jugadores de béisbol hispánicos en los Estados Unidos.
7. El jai alai es un juego similar al béisbol.
8. El jai alai no se juega en los Estados Unidos.

II. Para discutir

1. ¿A usted le gustaría ver una corrida de toros? ¿Por qué (no)?
2. ¿Ha visto usted un partido de soccer? ¿Cuál prefiere usted, el soccer o el fútbol americano? ¿Por qué?
3. ¿Cuántas personas vieron el juego por la Copa del Mundo? ¿Recuerda usted alguna vez cuando los espectadores que estaban en el estadio se volvieron locos? ¿Cuándo?
4. ¿Cuál es el deporte más popular de los Estados Unidos?
5. En los Estados Unidos, ¿participan las mujeres en los deportes? ¿En cuáles? ¿Es bueno o malo esto?
6. ¿Cuál es el deporte que le gusta más a usted? ¿Le gusta el béisbol? ¿Cuál es su equipo favorito? ¿Tiene algunos jugadores hispánicos? ¿Quiénes?
7. ¿Qué es el jai alai? ¿Cuál es su origen?
8. En su opinión, ¿es la caza un deporte cruel? ¿Por qué?

Young Hondurans shoot a few baskets in Tegucigalpa.

Repaso oral

I. Para conversar

Act out each of the following situations with a classmate.

MODELO Usted quiere ir al partido de fútbol pero su amiga quiere ir al club campestre.

A. Bueno, ¿vamos al partido?
B. Ay, tú y tus partidos de fútbol. ¿Por qué no nos quedamos aquí?
A. Pero Marta, éste va a ser un partido estupendo. Si ganamos este partido. . .
B. No me importa. A veces parece que quieres más a Mario Kempes que a mí. . .
A. Pero, mi amor. . .
B. Por favor, Javier, vamos al club campestre esta tarde.
A. Bueno. . .muy bien. . .si tú quieres. . .

1. Usted y su amigo (amiga) están en el estadio donde ven un partido de fútbol. Parece que su equipo favorito va a ganar, pero un jugador del otro equipo mete un gol.
2. Usted y su amigo (amiga) se encuentran en el estadio. Su equipo favorito va a perder. Su amigo cree que no existe ninguna posibilidad de que gane, pero usted no está de acuerdo.
3. Usted y su amigo (amiga) se encuentran en un colectivo después de un partido de fútbol estupendo. Discuten lo que van a hacer esta noche.
4. Usted quiere ser jugador de fútbol, pero sus padres quieren que estudie para abogado.
5. Usted escucha el radio y hace comentarios. El cronista habla del partido de béisbol.

II. Para describir

Make a statement about each of the drawings below using the word or construction that appears below it.

MODELO

quienes

Raúl y Leandro son los amigos argentinos con quienes fui al partido de fútbol.

1. 

como si

4. 

al + infinitive

2. 

volver a + infinitive

5. 

acabar de + infinitive

3. 

si + past subjunctive

Capítulo 18

Despegue

Descripción del dibujo

1. Rebeca Flores es dueña de un taller mecánico—un lugar donde arreglan coches, camiones, etc.
2. En el taller hay muchos camiones y camionetas.
3. Muchos mecánicos trabajan en el taller.
4. Rebeca le dice a uno de los mecánicos que ella se marcha (se va).
5. Tiene mucha prisa porque tiene una cita con el gobernador.

Pronunciación

1. Rebeca / Rebeca Flores
2. el taller / camiones y camionetas
3. mecánicos / Muchos mecánicos trabajan.
4. le dice / Le dice que se marcha.
5. prisa / Tiene mucha prisa.

Aplicación

I. Relación

Say at least ten sentences about the picture on page 421.

II. Para contestar

1. ¿Qué es un taller mecánico?
2. ¿Trabajó usted en un taller mecánico alguna vez?
3. ¿Es difícil estacionar un camión? ¿una camioneta?
4. ¿A qué hora se marcha usted?
5. ¿Quién es el gobernador de este estado?
6. ¿Ha tenido una cita con él alguna vez?
7. ¿Tiene usted una cita con el médico hoy?
8. ¿A usted le gustaría ser mecánico? ¿Por qué (no)?

Tema del diálogo

A modern Hispanic businesswoman adroitly concludes a major business deal with an old-fashioned politico.

avisos limitados
EL TIEMPO
¿VENDE SU VEHICULO?
Anuncie en las siguientes secciones y venda INMEDIATAMENTE:
11 PARTICULARES
12 TAXIS
13 JEEPS
14 CAMIONETAS
15 CAMIONES
16 BUSES
17 OTROS

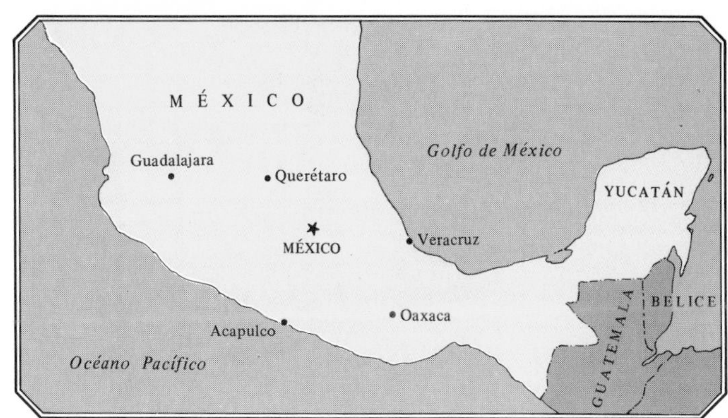

DIÁLOGO

Una mujer de negocios

Rebeca Flores, dueña de un taller mecánico en Querétaro, México[1], está charlando con Esteban, un empleado suyo, en el momento en que sale a la calle.

REBECA En caso de que vuelva Ortiz antes de que yo regrese, dígale que el pedido es urgentísimo.

ESTEBAN Así se hará, Srta. Flores. ¡Se nos está acabando el tiempo!

REBECA ¡Y a mí se me está agotando la paciencia! Bueno, Esteban, gracias. Ahora me marcho. Tengo cita en la oficina del gobernador a las cinco. Hasta luego.

* * *

(Después de esperar como una hora en la antesala del gobernador, Rebeca se entera de que el general y licenciado don Rosalío Pérez Herrera[2] la atenderá en unos minutos.)

SECRETARIO (Abre la puerta.) Adelante, Srta. Flores. Pase usted.

GOBERNADOR (Levantándose y dando la mano.) ¡Dichosos los ojos! Es un gran placer volver a verla aquí. ¡Siéntese, por favor!

REBECA Señor gobernador, yo comprendo lo ocupado que está usted y. . .

GOBERNADOR Nada, nada. Para usted siempre hay tiempo.

REBECA Pues para que yo no me sienta culpable de monopolizar su tiempo, iré directamente al grano.

GOBERNADOR Permítame hacer un comentario. Ésta es la ventaja que tienen las mujeres de negocios. . .(buscando un tabaco en su elegante escritorio). Se combinan en ellas la belleza y la eficiencia.

REBECA Ay, general. Usted tan galante como siempre. Este. . .pero yo le empezaba a decir que. . .

GOBERNADOR Oh, sí. Por supuesto, dígame.

REBECA ¿Qué le parece si hacemos un contrato de servicio por dos años para toda la flotilla de camiones y camionetas del estado?

The manager of a Mexican agricultural implements firm. Latin American women have begun taking their rightful places in the worlds of business, politics, the arts, and the professions.

GOBERNADOR Ummm, pues. . .

REBECA Ya usted sabe que Flores S.A. tiene los mejores precios y los mejores mecánicos.

GOBERNADOR Eso es indiscutible, sin embargo. . .(prendiendo el tabaco y caminando hacia la ventana).

REBECA Además, mi general, ya estamos terminando la ampliación de los talleres y. . .usted recordará que Arturo es el único mécanico especialista en Mercedes Benz[3]. . .

GOBERNADOR ¡Huelgan los comentarios! (Llamando al secretario[4].) Marcelino, arregla un contrato con Flores S.A. por dos años. ¡Faltaba más!

A businesswoman

Rebeca Flores, owner of an auto repair shop in Querétaro, Mexico, is talking with Esteban, an employee of hers, as she is about to go out the door (in the moment in which she is going out to the street).

R: In case Ortiz comes back before I return, tell him the order is extremely urgent.

E: Will do, Srta. Flores. Time is running out on us!

R: And my patience is running out! Well, Esteban, thanks. I'm leaving now. I have an appointment in the governor's office at five. See you later.

* * *

(After waiting about an hour in the governor's anteroom (waiting room), Rebeca learns that General and Lawyer don Rosalío Pérez Herrera will see (attend) her in a few minutes.)

S: (Opens the door.) Come right in, Srta. Flores. Come in.

G: (Getting up and extending his hand.) How wonderful to see you! It's a great pleasure to see you here again. Sit down, please.

R: Mr. Governor, I know (understand) how busy you are, and . . .

G: Not at all. For you there's always time.

R: Well, so that I don't feel guilty of monopolizing your time, I'll get directly to the point.

G: Permit me to make an observation. This is the advantage that businesswomen have . . . (looking for a cigar in his elegant desk). Beauty and efficiency are combined in them.

R: Ah, General. As gallant as always. Umm . . . but I was starting to tell you that . . .

G: Oh yes. Of course, tell me.

R: What (do you think) if we make a service contract for two years for the whole fleet of the state's trucks and vans?

G: Umm, well . . .

R: You know that Flores S.A. has the best prices and the best mechanics.

G: That is beyond question; however . . . (lighting up the cigar and walking toward the window).

R: Furthermore, my General, we are completing the expansion of the shops and . . . you may remember that Arturo is the only qualified Mercedes Benz mechanic . . .

G: Enough said (give rest to explanations)! (Calling the secretary.) Marcelino, draw up a contract with Flores Inc. for two years. Harumph!

VARIACIONES

¿ Adónde va Rebeca, al taller?	Where is Rebeca going, to the shop?
No, al cine.	No, to the movies.
a la iglesia	to church
al mercado	to the market
al museo	to the museum
a la tienda	to the store
al zoológico	to the zoo
Ella va de compras.	She's going shopping.
Ella va a ver una película.	She's going to see a film.
¿Cenó usted con el Sr. Pérez?	Did you have dinner with Sr. Pérez?
No, desayuné con él.	No, I had breakfast with him.
Almorcé con él.	I had lunch with him.

Glosas

1. Querétaro, historic capital city of a state with the same name, is located about 250 kilometers north of Mexico City. In 1867 Maximilian, who had been installed with French support as Emperor of Mexico in 1864, was captured and subsequently executed in Querétaro by the republican armies of Benito Juárez, the constitutionally elected president of Mexico. Querétaro is also famous because the Mexican Constitution that governs the country was drafted there in 1916 and 1917.
2. It is not uncommon in Spanish America, and especially in Mexico, for politicians to have both a military and an academic background. In such cases, both their rank and their academic title (**general** and **licenciado**) are religiously used. Governor Pérez Herrera's full official name on documents and proclamations would be **el ciudadano gobernador del estado libre y soberano de Querétaro, general y licenciado Rosalío Pérez Herrera.**
3. Mercedes Benz cars are highly prized and obvious status symbols for prominent politicos in Mexico and other Hispanic countries.
4. **Secretario** to a governor or a president usually means *executive assistant.*

SOBRE EL DIÁLOGO

I. Complete each of the following sentences with information from the dialog.

MODELO Rebeca es dueña de _____. → **Rebeca es dueña de un taller mecánico.**

1. Esteban es _____.
2. La Srta. Flores se marcha porque _____.
3. Rebeca espera al gobernador en _____.
4. Después de esperar como una hora _____.
5. El gobernador le pide que entre y que _____.
6. Dice que para ella siempre _____.
7. Rebeca va directamente al grano porque _____.
8. Rebeca sugiere que hagan _____.
9. Rebeca dice que Flores S.A. tiene _____.
10. El gobernador decide hacer el contrato porque Arturo _____.

II. Respond to each sentence using one of the expressions in the list. More than one response may be possible.

Adelante. Pase usted.
¡Dichosos los ojos!
Sería un gran placer.
Para usted siempre hay tiempo.
Iré directamente al grano.
Por supuesto.
Sin embargo, son muy caras.
Así se hará, señor.

MODELO Buenos días, Guillermo. Hace mucho tiempo que no nos vemos. → **¡Dichosos los ojos!**

1. ¿Puedo entrar, don Roberto?
2. ¿Cuál es el problema, Sr. Sánchez?
3. No quiero perder tiempo.
4. Son las mejores camionetas.
5. Quiero que se arregle el contrato inmediatamente.
6. ¿Podría usted ayudarnos con este problema?
7. Me siento culpable de monopolizar su tiempo, señorita.
8. ¿Quieres acompañarme a la iglesia, abuelita?

III. Para contestar

Respond to each sentence using the word in parentheses.

MODELO ¿Sabe Arturo arreglar carros? (mecánico) → **Claro, Arturo es mecánico y sabe arreglar carros y camiones.**

1. Si su carro no anda bien, ¿adónde lo lleva usted? (taller mecánico)
2. Ya son las doce. ¿Tiene usted hambre? (almorzar)
3. ¿Necesita usted comprar carne? (mercado)
4. ¿Cómo se llevan los productos de la finca a la ciudad? (camión)
5. ¿Comió usted algo esta mañana? (desayunar)
6. ¿Qué hago yo con todas estas cartas? (la oficina de correos)
7. Nunca he visto un tigre. ¿Dónde puedo ver uno? (zoológico)
8. ¿A qué hora va usted a encontrarse con el abogado? (cita)
9. ¿Quién mató al Sr. Contreras? (culpable)

10. Ese reloj no anda bien. ¿Qué hago? (arreglar)
11. ¿Qué hace usted los domingos? (iglesia)
12. A mí me encantan Picasso y Dalí. ¿Y a usted? (museo)
13. El médico no nos puede ver todavía. ¿Dónde esperamos? (antesala)
14. Tengo ganas de ver una buena película. ¿y ustedes? (cine)
15. Ya es tarde, ¿verdad? (marcharse)

VOCABULARIO

nouns

la **ampliación**	enlargement, expansion
la **antesala**	anteroom, waiting room
la **belleza**	beauty
la **camioneta**	van, pickup truck, station wagon
el **cine**	movies, movie theater
el **comentario**	observation, explanation, comment
el **contrato de servicio**	service contract
la **eficiencia**	efficiency
el **escritorio**	desk
el **estado**	state
la **flotilla**	fleet
el **gobernador,** la **gobernadora**	governor
la **iglesia**	church
el **licenciado**	lawyer
el **mecánico**	mechanic
el **mercado**	market
el **museo**	museum
la **mujer de negocios**	businesswoman
la **paciencia**	patience
el **pedido**	order
la **película**	film, movie
el **placer**	pleasure
el **servicio**	service
el **tabaco**	tobacco, cigar
el **taller**	workshop
el **taller mecánico**	auto workshop
la **tienda**	store
la **ventaja**	advantage
el **zoológico**	zoo

verbs

acabarse	to run out, to be used up
agotarse	to run out, to be used up
almorzar (ue) (c)	to have lunch
atender (ie)	to attend to, to see; to take care of
combinar	to combine
desayunar	to have breakfast
enterarse	to learn, to find out
monopolizar (c)	to monopolize
permitir	to permit
prender	to light up
regresar	to return

adjectives

culpable	guilty
elegante	elegant
especialista	skilled, expert, qualified (in)
galante	gallant
indiscutible	unquestionable, beyond question

mecánico	mechanical
ocupado	busy
urgente	urgent

conjunctions and prepositions

antes de que	before
en caso de que	in case
en el momento en que	at the moment that
hasta	until
para que	so that, in order that

other expressions

así se hará	will do; it'll be done
como una hora	about an hour
dichosos los ojos	how wonderful to see you
directamente	directly
este. . .	uh . . .
(no) faltaba más	of course, absolutely; harumph
hasta luego	see you later
huelgan los comentarios	enough said
ir al grano	to get to the point
ir de compras	to go shopping
mi general	my (honored) general
nada, nada	think nothing of it; not at all
pase usted	come in
S.A. (**sociedad anónima**)	Inc. (incorporated)
sin embargo	nevertheless
tan	so; just as

additional vocabulary

a menos que	unless
con tal (de) que	provided that
sin que	without

ESTRUCTURA I

A. The progressive tenses

Rebeca **está charlando** con Esteban.

1. In English the progressive tenses consist of the verb *to be* + the *-ing* form of a main verb: *I am thinking; they were traveling.* The *-ing* form is often called the *gerund.*
2. When we want to emphasize the on-going nature of an action—and show that the action is in progress—a construction with **estar** + gerund is used.

Rebeca está almorzando con Esteban.	Rebeca is having lunch with Stephen.
El mecánico está trabajando.	The mechanic is working.

3. To form the gerund, first drop the infinitive ending. Then, for **-ar** verbs, add **-ando;** for **-er** and **-ir** verbs, add **-iendo.**

charlar → **charlando**
volver → **volviendo**
salir → **saliendo**

4. Several changes which appear in the preterit tense also appear in the gerund; these include: a) the stem-changes **e** → **i** and **o** → **u** in **-ir** verbs; b) the spelling change **i** → **y** in **-er** and **-ir** verbs.

estoy pidiendo	I am asking (for)
estás diciendo	you are saying
está durmiendo	she is sleeping
estamos leyendo	we are reading
están oyendo	they are hearing

5. The progressive construction is used in all tenses. The form of **estar** indicates the tense reference.

Ahora mismo estamos acabando el trabajo.	We're finishing the work right now.
¿Estarás esperando en la estación?	Will you be waiting at the station?
Yo estaba almorzando cuando vino Rebeca.	I was having lunch when Rebecca came.

6. While English often uses the present progressive with a future meaning, Spanish never does. The simple present tense, **ir a** + infinitive, or the future is used instead.

Ellos salen esta tarde.	They are leaving this afternoon.
¿Van a venir mañana?	Are you coming tomorrow?

7. When reflexive or direct or indirect object pronouns are used, they either precede the verb **estar** or they follow and are attached to the gerund.

¿Me estás contando la verdad?	Are you telling me the truth?
La estamos esperando en la estación.	We're waiting for her in the station.
Estaba haciéndolo.	I was doing it.
Rebeca está divirtiéndose muchísimo.	Rebeca is having a wonderful time.

Aplicación

I. Supply the gerund of the following verbs.

A. MODELO comer → **comiendo**

1. charlar
2. salir
3. empezar
4. desayunar
5. almorzar
6. volver
7. llegar
8. entrar
9. hacer
10. beber

B. MODELO pedir → **pidiendo**

1. sentir
2. servir
3. morir
4. venir
5. divertir
6. dormir
7. repetir
8. poder
9. despedir
10. sugerir

II. Repeat each sentence, changing the subject according to the cue.

MODELO Estamos desayunando ahora. (él, tú) → **Está desayunando ahora. Estás desayunando ahora.**

1. Están charlando. (yo, la dueña y yo, tú y él, la secretaria)
2. Estamos discutiendo el contrato. (el jefe, los empleados, yo, tú, mi agente y yo)
3. Estaban almorzando. (yo, los trabajadores, tú, el gobernador, el dueño y yo)
4. Estábamos esperando. (Olga, los abogados, mis amigos y yo, tú)

III. Change the verb to the present progressive.

MODELO Rebeca almuerza con el gobernador. → **Rebeca está almorzando con el gobernador.**

1. Comen en un pequeño restaurante.
2. Piden cebiche.
3. El mesero lo trae.
4. Charlan mucho.
5. ¿Escuchas?
6. Hablan del contrato.
7. Rebeca sonríe.
8. Veo a Rebeca ahora.
9. Mira los papeles.
10. Nosotros arreglamos coches también.
11. Tratamos de hacer un contrato con el estado.
12. Pero perdemos la oportunidad.

IV. Answer the following questions using the present progressive.

MODELO ¿Cuándo vas a estudiar? → **Estoy estudiando ahora.**

1. ¿Cuándo va Rebeca a salir?
2. ¿Cuándo van ustedes a empezar?
3. ¿Cuándo van los chicos a comer?
4. ¿Cuándo voy a hablar español?
5. ¿Cuándo van ustedes a volver?

V. Change the verb to the imperfect progressive.

MODELO Caminábamos por el zoológico. → **Estábamos caminando por el zoológico.**

1. Mirábamos los animales.
2. Los tigres dormían.
3. Un mono gritaba.
4. El loro hablaba.
5. Yo buscaba las otras jaulas.
6. ¿Qué hacías tú?

VI. Repeat each sentence, attaching the pronoun to the end of the gerund.

MODELO Lo estoy llamando. → **Estoy llamándolo.**

1. Los estamos esperando.
2. Rebeca se está fijando.
3. El gobernador se está despidiendo.
4. Me estoy durmiendo.
5. Los estamos empezando.
6. Le estoy escribiendo.
7. Se están sentando.
8. Nos estamos levantando.

VII. Restate each sentence two ways, changing the verb to the present progressive.

MODELO Lo leo ahora. → **Lo estoy leyendo ahora. Estoy leyéndolo ahora.**

1. Me doy cuenta.
2. Se vuelve loco.
3. Nos saludan.
4. Les doy las gracias.
5. La llamo por teléfono.

VIII. Answer each question using the present progressive + pronoun.

MODELO ¿Vas a llamar a Juan? → **Estoy llamándolo ahora.**

1. ¿Vas a hacer el trabajo?
2. ¿Vas a escribir la carta?
3. ¿Vas a sentarte?
4. ¿Vas a levantarte?
5. ¿Vas a leer el libro?
6. ¿Vas a llamar a los guardias?
7. ¿Vas a tomar la cerveza?
8. ¿Vas a arreglar la camioneta?

IX. Para contestar

1. ¿Está usted hablando español o inglés ahora?
2. ¿Estamos haciendo el diálogo o estamos conversando ahora?
3. ¿Qué estaba haciendo usted cuando empezó la clase?
4. ¿Estaba usted leyendo algo cuando yo entré?
5. ¿Estaba usted escribiendo cuando yo entré?
6. ¿Qué estamos haciendo ahora?
7. ¿Qué va a hacer usted esta noche?
8. ¿Vienen ustedes a clase mañana?

B. Uses of the infinitive

Repaso. The infinitive of a verb generally provides the stem or base-form from which the various tenses are formed: **marcharse** → **me marcho** / **me marchaba** / **me marché** / **me marcharé.**

> Después de **esperar** una hora, me marché.

1. The infinitive may function in a sentence as a noun. It appears with or without the article **el** and conveys the general idea *the act of* + verb.

Ver es creer.	Seeing is believing.
Nos gusta ver buenas películas.	We like to see good films.
Para muchas personas (el) ir a la iglesia es muy importante.	For many people going to church is very important.

2. When a pronoun is used, it is attached to the end of the infinitive.

(El) casarse es una cosa muy especial.	Getting married is a very special thing.
(El) conocerte ha sido un placer.	Meeting you has been a pleasure.

3. In Spanish, prepositions are followed by an infinitive, not by a gerund or a second clause as in English.

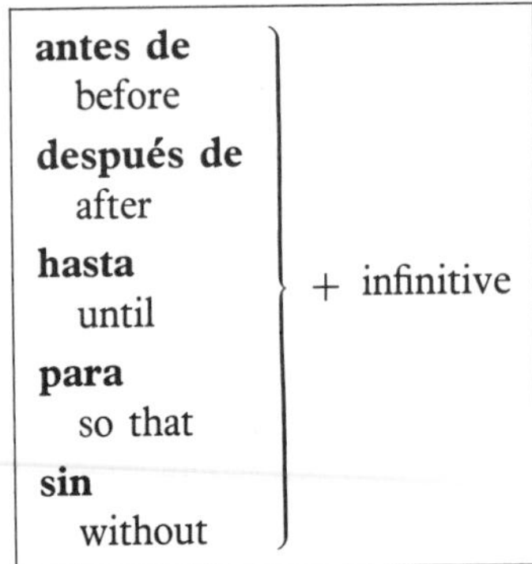

antes de before **después de** after **hasta** until **para** so that **sin** without	+ infinitive

Quiero ducharme antes de desayunar.	I want to take a shower before having breakfast.
Después de salir el avión, volvimos a casa.	After the airplane left, we went home.
Los alemanes ganaron el partido sin haber practicado mucho.	The Germans won the game without having practiced very much.

Aplicación

I. Repeat each sentence, replacing the noun with the infinitive phrase in parentheses and making any required changes.

A. MODELO Los negocios son importantes. (trabajar) → **Trabajar es importante.**

1. Los deportes son estupendos. (jugar tenis)
2. Los hombres de negocios son difíciles. (hablar con hombres de negocios)
3. Los hoteles son caros. (viajar)
4. Este trabajo tomará tiempo. (terminar este trabajo)
5. El puesto es difícil. (arreglar coches)

B. MODELO Nos marchamos después de la comida. (comer) → **Nos marchamos después de comer.**

1. Comimos sin los chicos. (decir nada)
2. Lo compré para mi abuela. (usarlo)
3. Voy a quedarme hasta las seis. (terminar)
4. Se fueron después del partido. (ver quién había ganado)
5. Voy a terminar antes de la fiesta. (marcharme)

II. Para expresar en español

MODELO He left without eating. → **Se fue sin comer.**

1. Finish the work before leaving. / Finish the work before playing. / Finish the work before calling. / Finish the work before asking.
2. Don't come without knowing them. / Don't come without having them. / Don't come without seeing them first. / Don't come without talking to her first.
3. It's a good day for sleeping. / It's a good day for studying. / It's a good day for playing football. / It's a good day for staying at home.
4. Learning is important. / Working is important. / Sleeping is important. / Smiling is important.
5. Knowing you has been a pleasure. / Speaking with you has been a pleasure. / Having lunch with you has been a pleasure. / Going out with you has been a pleasure.
6. I like playing football. / I like going to the movies. / I like reading. / I like walking.

III. Complete each sentence with any logical infinitive phase.

MODELO ______ sería estupendo. → **Hacer un viaje sería estupendo.**

1. ______ sería muy difícil.
2. ______ ha sido un gran placer.
3. ______ es una buena idea.
4. ______ es necesario.
5. Quiero terminar la lección antes de ______.
6. Me gustaría almorzar después de ______.
7. Es un buen día para ______.
8. Vamos a esperar hasta ______.

Venezuelan Maritza Sayalero, Miss Universe, 1979. While some Hispanic women pursue careers in white collar occupations, others are still drawn to traditional roles involving beauty and charm.

Pausa oral

Problemas de todos los días

I. Para conversar

Act out each of the following situations with another person in the class.

MODELO Usted y su amigo tienen cita con el profesor de inglés a las cuatro. Ya son las cuatro menos diez pero su amigo todavía no sale.

A: **Ya son las cuatro menos diez y la cita es a las cuatro.**
B: **Cálmate, chico. Todavía tenemos tiempo.**
A: **No lo tenemos, hombre. Y no quiero llegar tarde. Tú sabes cómo es el profesor de inglés.**
B: **Pero la oficina está cerca. No te preocupes. No vamos a llegar tarde.**

1. Su coche no anda bien y usted lo lleva a un taller mecánico. Allí le dicen que van a necesitar una semana para arreglarlo.
2. Usted es una mujer de negocios. Usted llega a la oficina del gobernador para discutir un contrato importantísimo, pero él sólo quiere hablar del amor.
3. Usted y su amigo van al mercado a comprar comida. Necesitan comprar carne, fruta, legumbres, pan y algo para beber.
4. Usted es dueña de una tienda de ropa. Hay muchas mujeres en la tienda comprando. Llama por teléfono una de las empleadas y dice que no puede ir a trabajar hoy.
5. Usted y su mamá se están preparando para ir a la iglesia con toda la familia. Hay muchos problemas: el coche no anda bien, su hermanito le ha pegado a otro niño y papá quiere ver televisión.
6. Hoy es domingo y usted no trabaja. Usted y sus amigos están tratando de decidir qué van a hacer. Algunos quieren ir al museo, otros quieren ir al cine, otros tienen otras ideas.

II. Para describir

ESTRUCTURA II

A. Conjunctions + subjunctive

Repaso. In chapter 15 we saw that certain conjunctions of time **(desde que. . .)** or of cause **(porque. . .)** may be used to introduce a dependent idea or clause. The verb of this clause is indicative: **Desde que estoy aquí en Querétaro, estoy muy ocupado** *Since I've been here in Querétaro I've been very busy.*

> En caso de que **llame** Ortiz, dígale que esto es urgente.

1. Spanish has a great many other conjunctions. The ones in the following list, however, are always followed by a dependent clause with a verb in the subjunctive.

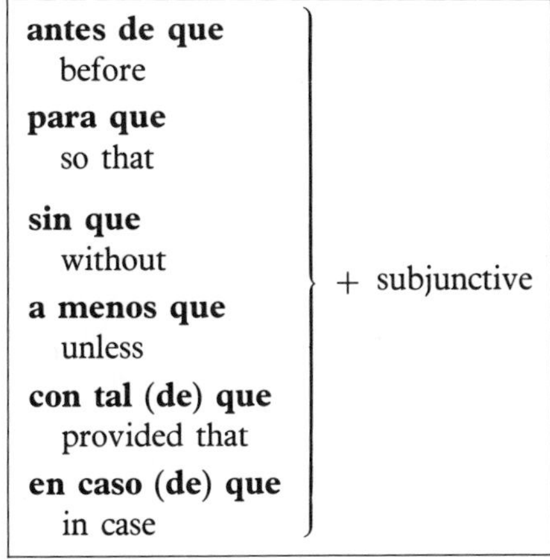

antes de que before **para que** so that **sin que** without **a menos que** unless **con tal (de) que** provided that **en caso (de) que** in case	+ subjunctive

Ya comprendemos sin que digas nada más.	We understand without your saying anything else.
En caso de que llame Ortiz, dígale que no estoy.	In case Ortiz calls tell him that I'm not in.
Te llamo para que sepas que no me he olvidado de ti.	I'm calling you so that you'll know that I haven't forgotten you.

2. If the indicative verb in the main clause is expressed in the present or future tense, the subjunctive verb in the dependent clause is also in the present tense.

Antes de que empiece el partido, quiero comprarme una cerveza.	Before the game starts I want to buy a beer.
A menos que haya problemas, Rebeca irá a Francia y a Alemania este verano.	Unless there are problems, Rebeca will go to France and to Germany this summer.

Para que ellas lo sepan antes.
abrótano
macho
Productos Masculinos
en Toda La Linea.

3. If the main clause is past or conditional, the subjunctive clause is normally past also.

Yo quería llegar temprano para que pudiéramos almorzar juntos.	I wanted to arrive early so that we could have lunch together.
Con tal de que papá viniera con nosotros, mamá estaría contenta.	Provided that Dad came with us, Mom would be happy.

4. If there is no change in subject, a preposition followed by an infinitive is used.

Llegué temprano para poder conversar con usted.	I arrived early so I could talk with you.

Aplicación

I. Complete each sentence with the present subjunctive of the verb in parentheses.

A. MODELO (llegar) No quiero empezar antes de que ellos. . . → **No quiero empezar antes de que ellos lleguen.**

1. (regresar) Te llamo en caso de que Juan. . .
2. (marcharse) No me voy antes de que tú. . .
3. (esperar) Yo lo hago con tal de que ustedes me. . .
4. (traer) No puedo terminar el trabajo a menos que tú me lo. . .
5. (saber) Nunca salimos sin que papá lo. . .
6. (poder) Yo me quedo en casa para que ella. . .salir.

B. Now use the past subjunctive of the verb.

MODELO (volver) Almorcé antes de que ella. . . → **Almorcé antes de que ella volviera.**

1. (ver) Fuimos al centro para que los niños. . .las tiendas.
2. (llegar) No quería ir de compras antes de que tú. . .

3. (desayunar) Me levanté temprano para que los chicos. . .
4. (saber) Ella no se marcharía sin que yo lo. . .
5. (acompañar) Yo no iría al museo a menos que ustedes me. . .
6. (dar) Ella compraría un vestido nuevo con tal de que yo le. . .el dinero.

II. Make the indicated substitutions and any modifications they require.

A. MODELO Arreglo la casa porque ellos vienen. (antes de que) → **Arreglo la casa antes de que ellos vengan.**

1. Yo lo haré ya que él lo hace. (con tal de que)
2. Nosotros nos quedamos puesto que ella se marcha. (a menos que)
3. No podemos empezar ahora que él está aquí. (sin que)
4. Papá dice que puede ir ya que Pedro viene. (a menos que)
5. Ella estudia desde que su hermano estudia. (para que)
6. Rebeca regresa porque los otros llegan. (antes de que)
7. Estoy aquí porque tú me necesitas. (en caso de que)
8. Ustedes van directamente al grano, ya que todos nos damos cuenta de la situación. (para que)

B. MODELO Yo lo hice porque ellos lo hacían. (para que) → **Yo lo hice para que ellos lo hicieran.**

1. Tú te marcharías ya que ellos regresaban. (con tal de que)
2. Yo no saldría porque Olga salía. (sin que)
3. Él volvió ya que yo regresaba. (antes de que)
4. Dijo que lo haría porque nosotros lo hacíamos. (a menos que)
5. Dije que yo me quedaría porque él venía. (en caso de que)

III. Introduce a new second clause that contains the subject given in parentheses.

MODELO Vamos al centro para ver las tiendas. (los niños) → **Vamos al centro para que los niños vean las tiendas.**

1. Nunca mando una carta sin leerla. (mi abogado)
2. Siempre almorzamos antes de volver al despacho. (papá)
3. Vamos a la oficina de correos para mandar una carta. (mamá)
4. Te llamo en caso de retrasarme. (nosotros)
5. Salieron a la calle para jugar. (los chicos)
6. Fui al mercado antes de regresar a casa. (los otros)
7. Lo iban a hacer con tal de tener tiempo. (Hugo)
8. No hablaría sin entender el problema. (todo el mundo)

IV. Para expresar en español

MODELO Don't come without calling. / Don't come without his calling. →
No venga usted sin llamar. / No venga sin que él llame.

1. Don't leave before finishing. / Don't leave before he finishes.
2. Go to bed after having lunch. / Go to bed after the children have lunch.
3. Don't fix the car without asking him. / Don't fix the car without my asking him.
4. Go to the market to buy vegetables. / Go to the market so mom can buy vegetables.

V. Complete the following composition by filling the blanks with any appropriate words.

La Srta. Flores, que es dueña de la compañía, quería que yo ___1___. Le dije que lo haría con tal de que ___2___. Pero ella no estaba de acuerdo.

—Mire usted—me dijo—. Es muy importante que usted ___3___ porque ___4___.

—Muy bien, señorita—le contesté—. Le prometo hacerlo a menos que ___5___.

—En caso de que yo ___6___ antes de que usted ___7___—me dijo—, va a haber problemas.

—Para que yo ___8___ antes de que usted ___9___, voy a tener que empezar ahora mismo.

—Muy bien—dijo ella—. Empiece.

Entonces comencé a trabajar como loco. No terminé antes de que la Srta. Flores ___10___, pero ella no me hizo nada porque ___11___. Y ya que ella no me ___12___, yo pensaba que sería mejor ___13___.

B. Pero / sino / sino que

Ya desayuné **pero** todavía tengo hambre.

Two Spanish words, **pero** and **sino,** both correspond to the English word *but.*

1. When two parts of a sentence are joined with **pero,** the clause that follows **pero** serves to modify what is said in the first clause.

pero + modification

Yo no quería ir al mercado hoy, pero va a ser necesario.	I did not want to go to the market today, but it's going to be necessary.
Trabajo en Querétaro pero vivo en un pueblo pequeño.	I work in Querétaro but I live in a small town.

2. When the second part of a sentence presents a contrast with what was said in the first part, **sino** is used. The meaning of **sino** is *but rather.*

sino + contrast

No voy al mercado sino a la oficina de correos.	I'm not going to the market but rather to the post office.
No estamos cerca sino lejos del museo.	We're not near but rather far from the museum.

3. **Sino** is also used to express *but* in sentences that express the idea *not only . . . but also.*

No estudio sólo el español sino también el ruso.	I don't study only Spanish but also Russian.

4. In a sentence that expresses contrast, the variant **sino que** is used if a conjugated verb follows directly.

No desayunamos sino que almorzamos con él.	We didn't have breakfast but rather had lunch with him.
No te pido que te marches sino que te quedes aquí conmigo.	I'm not asking you to leave but rather to stay here with me.

Aplicación

I. Answer each question in the negative using **sino** and the word in parentheses.

MODELO ¿Estudia usted francés? (español) → **No señor. No estudio francés sino español.**

1. ¿Arreglan coches? (camionetas)
2. ¿Es dueño de un taller? (tienda)
3. ¿Va usted a la iglesia? (mercado)
4. ¿Lleva a los niños al cine? (museo)
5. ¿Juegan en el patio? (calle)
6. ¿Quiere usted el abrigo? (chaqueta)

II. Complete each sentence with **pero** or **sino.**

MODELO Lo siento _____ no puedo ir a la fiesta. → **Lo siento pero no puedo ir a la fiesta.**

1. Sé que sus precios son baratos, _____ no tiene un buen mecánico.
2. No vienen en colectivo _____ en taxi.
3. No la conozco _____ me gustaría conocerla.
4. No voy a comprar un vestido _____ un abrigo.
5. Quería ir al museo _____ no tengo tiempo.
6. No es absolutamente necesario _____ sería una buena idea.

III. Complete each sentence with **sino** or **sino que.**

MODELO No estudian _____ juegan fútbol. → **No estudian sino que juegan fútbol.**

1. No almuerzan _____ cenan.
2. No toman cerveza _____ vino.
3. No es secretaria _____ dueña de una compañía.
4. No hablan por teléfono _____ se visitan.
5. No está en la iglesia _____ en casa de su amiga.
6. No esperó _____ se fue.

IV. Complete each sentence in any appropriate way.

MODELO Me gustaría comprar una camioneta pero _____. → **Me gustaría comprar una camioneta pero no tengo dinero.**

1. No hablan de política sino que _____.
2. No es un taller mecánico sino _____.
3. No le dio las gracias a la dueña sino que _____.
4. Ella no es economista, pero _____.

5. Yo nunca almuerzo en casa sino ____.
6. Rebeca no trabaja con nadie sino que ____.
7. No pasamos la tarde en el museo sino que ____.
8. No tenemos un coche nuevo, pero ____.
9. No leía el periódico sino ____.
10. No pude ir al banco esta mañana, pero ____.

Repaso oral

For each of the headings listed below, make up two sentences. In each sentence include one of the words or phrases that appear below the items.

MODELO **correos**
sin → **Cuando yo estaba en Querétaro salí a buscar la oficina de correos sin conocer muy bien la ciudad.**
pero → **Nunca encontré la oficina de correos pero vi muchas cosas interesantes.**

una mujer de negocios
está charlando
estaba cenando

el mercado
el ir
después de comprar

el zoológico
antes de que
para

el cine
. . .pero la película. . .
. . .no al cine sino. . .

Capítulo 19

Despegue

Descripción del dibujo

1. Dolores y Maricarmen estudian para los exámenes finales.
2. Dolores tiene un examen en la clase de química orgánica.
3. Está muy cansada. Se le cierran los ojos.
4. Su amiga Maricarmen va a la biblioteca para conseguirle un manual de química.
5. También va a buscar tiza y una pequeña pizarra.
6. Pobre Dolores. No tiene ganas de estudiar más.

Pronunciación

1. Dolores y Maricarmen / Dolores y Maricarmen estudian.
2. química / la clase de química orgánica
3. la biblioteca / Maricarmen va a la biblioteca.
4. una pequeña pizarra / tiza y una pequeña pizarra
5. ganas / No tiene ganas de estudiar.

Aplicación

I. Relación

Say at least 12 sentences about the picture on page 441.

II. Para contestar

1. ¿Cuándo son sus exámenes finales?
2. ¿Cómo se prepara usted para los exámenes?
3. ¿Cómo es la biblioteca de esta universidad? ¿Es buena? ¿Por qué?
4. ¿Estudia usted química orgánica?
5. ¿Usa usted tiza y una pizarra cuando estudia?
6. ¿Dónde consigue usted los manuales que necesita?
7. ¿Va a la biblioteca todos los días? ¿Es un buen lugar para estudiar?
8. ¿Se le cierran los ojos ahora? ¿Por qué? ¿Estudió hasta tarde anoche?

Tema del diálogo

Final examinations at the University of Barcelona can seem as threatening as elsewhere. Is there a miraculous solution?

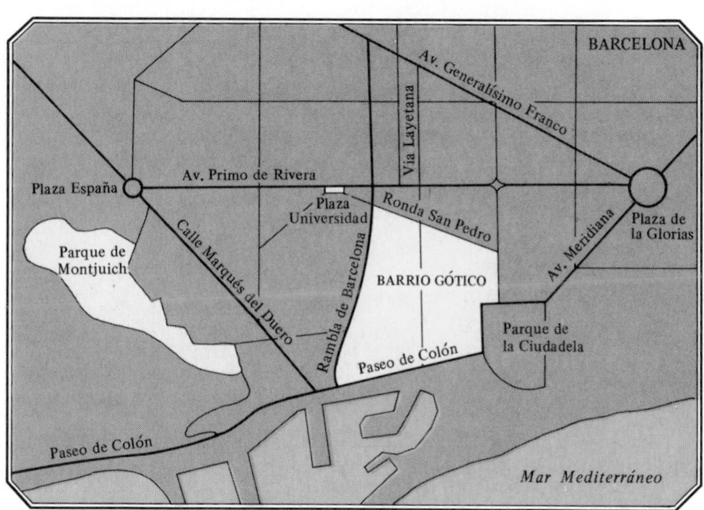

DIÁLOGO

Dos estudiantes en época de exámenes

Una tarde en Barcelona, dos estudiantes charlan mientras estudian. Una es Dolores Alsina; la otra es Maricarmen Carbonell.

DOLORES ¡Dios mío! Se me están cerrando los ojos y todavía me falta un capítulo más de química orgánica que aprender.

MARICARMEN Pues espero que te hayas convencido de que lo más fácil es matricularse y. . .

DOLORES Sí, y que lo más difícil es aprobar un examen final cuando empiezas a estudiar dos días antes de la "ejecución".

MARICARMEN Yo ya te lo había dicho. Si hubieras escuchado mis consejos, no andarías con este problema.

* * *

DOLORES Mira, Maricarmen. Antes de que yo pierda la calma, ¿por qué mejor no me ayudas?

MARICARMEN Lola[1], tú bien sabes que era broma. Tan pronto como me digas qué necesitas, yo lo haré encantada.

DOLORES Pues mientras yo termino el último capítulo, consígueme una pizarra, tiza por kilos[2], un manual de la biblioteca y un santo muy milagroso.[3]

MARICARMEN Ay, mujer, con las tres primeras cosas no hay problema. Pero un santo especializado en química orgánica. . .¡es difícil!

DOLORES Sí, claro, sobre todo en época de exámenes finales.

* * *

MARICARMEN Bien, ya está todo listo. Ahora concéntrate en esta materia y no pienses más en las otras asignaturas.

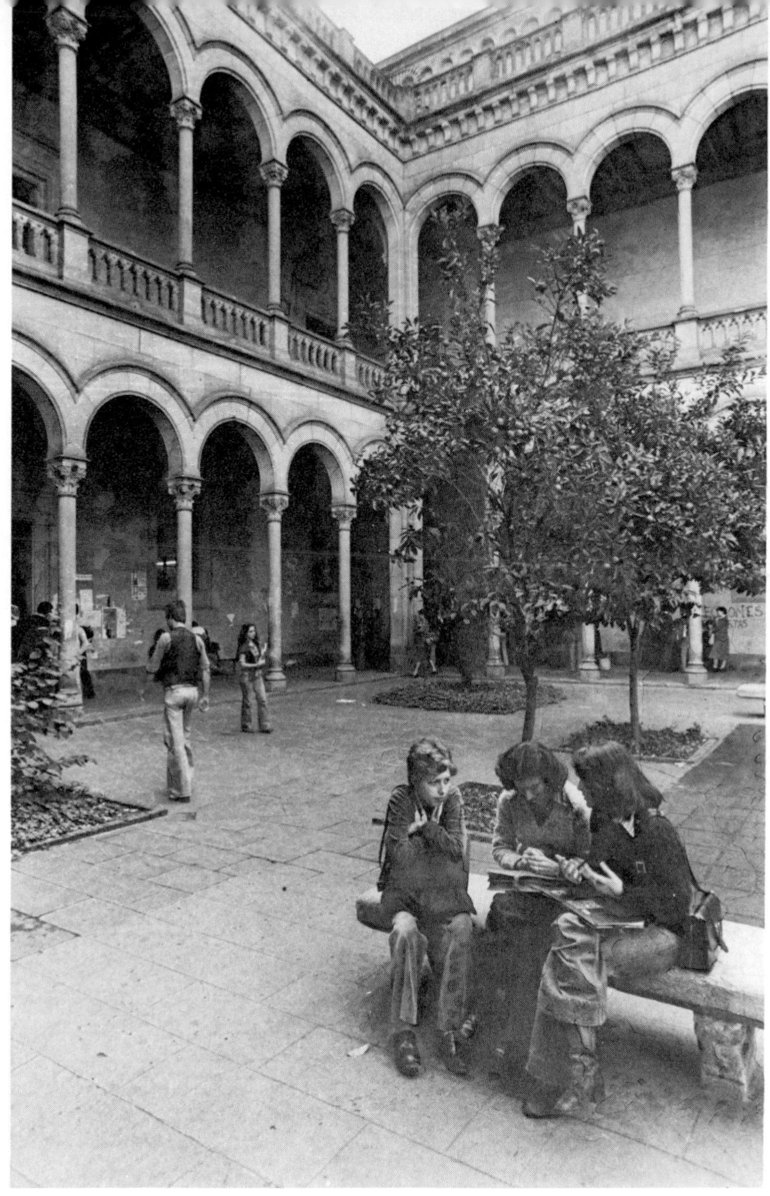

The University of Barcelona.

DOLORES Buen consejo. Así lo haré. Cuando termine con este primer examen, me preocuparé de las otras asignaturas.

MARICARMEN Tal vez no tengas que pensar en los otros exámenes por algún tiempo.

DOLORES ¿Cómo? ¿Qué dices?

MARICARMEN Pues, Mariano me ha dicho que en un par de días es posible que estalle una huelga de empleados universitarios.

DOLORES ¿Por qué motivo?

MARICARMEN Eso es lo de menos, chica, con tal que haya huelga y se suspendan los exámenes, ¿no?

Two students at exam time

One afternoon in Barcelona two students are talking while they study. One is Dolores Alsina; the other is Maricarmen Carbonell.

D: Good grief! My eyes are closing on me and I still have a chapter of organic chemistry left to learn.

M: Then I hope you've become convinced that the easiest thing is to register and . . .

D: Yes, and the hardest thing is to pass a final exam when you start to study two days before the "execution."

M: I told you so. If you had listened to my advice, you wouldn't be having this problem.

* * *

D: Look, Maricarmen. Before I get upset, why don't you help me?

M: Lola, you know perfectly well that it was a joke. As soon as you tell me what you need, I'll do it happily.

D: Then while I finish the last chapter, get me a blackboard, chalk by the kilo, a textbook from the library, and a very miraculous saint.

M: Oh, brother (ay, woman), with the first three things there's no problem. But a saint specialized in organic chemistry . . . that's tough!

D: Yes, sure, especially at final-exam time.

* * *

M: So, everything is ready. Now concentrate on this subject and don't think about the other courses.

D: Good advice. That's what I'll do. When I finish this first exam, I'll worry about the other subjects.

M: Perhaps you won't have to think about the other exams for a while.

D: What? What are you saying?

M: Well, Mariano told me that in a couple of days it's possible a strike of university employees will break out.

D: For what reason?

M: Who cares (that's the least important part), honey, provided that there's a strike and the exams are suspended, right?

VARIACIONES

¿En qué te especializas?	What are you majoring in?
en biología	in biology
en historia	in history
en matemáticas	in mathematics
en lenguas extranjeras	in foreign languages
¿Qué llevas en el maletín?	What do you have in the briefcase?
unos cuadernos	some notebooks
un diccionario	a dictionary
mis tareas	my homework
mis apuntes	my notes
un libro de gramática	a grammar book
¿Qué pasa si no sales bien en el examen?	What happens if you don't pass the exam?
Seré reprobado.	I'll fail.
No podré graduarme.	I won't be able to graduate.
El profesor se enojará.	The professor will get mad.
Tendré que matricularme en otro curso.	I'll have to register for another course.

Glosas

1. **Lola** and **Lolita** are nicknames for **Dolores,** just as **Maricarmen** and **Maribel** are nicknames for **María del Carmen** and **María Isabel,** respectively.
2. In Hispanic universities, undergraduate students take quite a few oral examinations. Each student is usually examined individually by one to three professors; therefore, chalk and blackboards are standard equipment during exam time so that the students can practice their presentation. Organic chemistry with its many formulas lends itself especially well to blackboard explanations.
3. Devout Hispanic Catholics, depending on the region they live in, pray to a variety of saints and virgins on different occasions. For example, many pray to **San Antonio** (St. Anthony) for locating lost persons or objects; **San Nicolás de Bari** (St. Nicholas of Bari) for difficult financial situations; and until recently, **San Cristóbal** (St. Christopher) for the safety of travellers.

SOBRE EL DIÁLOGO

I. ¿Sí o no?

If the statement is true, say **sí** and repeat it. If the statement is false, say **no** and make a statement that is true.

MODELO Las dos estudiantes que hablan son colombianas. → **No, son españolas, de Barcelona.**

1. Dolores tiene muchas ganas de seguir estudiando.
2. Maricarmen piensa que es más fácil matricularse en un curso que aprobar el examen.
3. Dolores quiere que su amiga la ayude.
4. Dolores le pide a Maricarmen que vaya a la biblioteca y que saque cuatro o cinco libros de química.
5. Maricarmen no puede ayudar a su amiga porque está muy ocupada.
6. Maricarmen le dice a Dolores que vaya a la iglesia y que pregunte si hay un santo especializado en química orgánica.
7. Maricarmen le sugiere a su amiga que estudie para el examen de química y que no se preocupe de los otros exámenes.
8. Es posible que se suspendan todos los exámenes por una huelga de empleados universitarios.

II. Complete each sentence with the most logical word.

MODELO El profesor escribe en (el maletín, la pizarra, la huelga). → **El profesor escribe en la pizarra.**

1. Se escribe en la pizarra con (tiza, materias, bromas).
2. En este curso hay que trabajar mucho. Hay mucha (tiza, broma, tarea).
3. Si apruebo estos cursos podré (ser reprobado, graduarme, estallar).
4. Los trabajadores declararon (un examen, una huelga, una tarea).
5. En este libro hay veinte (diccionarios, capítulos, asignaturas).
6. En la clase de español estudiamos (matemáticas, gramática, biología).
7. Estudio para médico. Tengo que tomar muchos cursos de (lenguas extranjeras, historia, biología).

8. Ella no está hablando seriamente. Es (un cuaderno, una broma, una huelga).
9. Todos mis apuntes están en mi (cuaderno, asignatura, idea).
10. Le dijo que estudiara; fue un buen (curso, diccionario, consejo).
11. Cuando el profesor habla, nosotros tomamos (apuntes, cuadernos, tareas).
12. Si no sé una palabra, la busco en el (libro de historia, diccionario, escritorio).
13. ¿En qué cursos vas a (graduarte, matricularte, levantarte)?
14. En la iglesia hay muchos (apuntes, santos, cuadernos).
15. No tengo ese libro. Tendré que sacarlo de la (tarea, historia, biblioteca).

III. Para contestar en español

1. ¿Qué hay en esta sala?
2. ¿Qué materias estudia usted? ¿Cuál es la asignatura que le gusta más?
3. ¿En qué se especializa usted?
4. ¿Cuándo va a graduarse? ¿Qué va a hacer después de graduarse?
5. ¿Qué se estudia en la clase de historia?
6. ¿Tienen ustedes mucha tarea en esta clase? ¿En qué curso tiene usted más tarea?
7. ¿Toman ustedes apuntes en todas las clases? ¿Por qué?
8. ¿Qué es lo que más le gusta de esta clase, la conversación, la gramática. . .?
9. ¿Por qué trae usted un cuaderno a clase?
10. ¿Aprobará usted el examen final en este curso? ¿Son fáciles o difíciles los exámenes de español?
11. ¿Qué hace usted cuando no sabe una palabra?
12. ¿En qué cursos va usted a matricularse el año que viene?

Barcelona. Students demonstrating in front of the Cathedral for better vocational education facilities. Barcelona is Spain's chief port and a major European industrial center.

VOCABULARIO

nouns

los **apuntes**	notes
la **asignatura**	assignment, subject
la **biblioteca**	library
la **biología**	biology
la **broma**	joke
el **campo**	academic area of specialization, field
el **consejo**	piece of advice
los **consejos**	advice
el **cuaderno**	notebook
el **curso**	course
el **diccionario**	dictionary
la **ejecución**	execution
la **época**	time, period, epoch
el **examen**	exam
la **gramática**	grammar
la **historia**	history
la **huelga**	strike
el **manual**	textbook, manual
las **matemáticas**	mathematics
la **materia**	subject
el **motivo**	motive, reason
el **par**	couple
la **pizarra**	chalkboard
el **santo**	saint
la **tarea**	homework, task
la **tiza**	chalk

verbs

aprender	to learn
aprobar (ue)	to pass (an exam, a course)
ayudar	to help
concentrarse en	to concentrate on
conseguir (i)	to get
convencerse (z) (de)	to become convinced (of)
enojar	to anger
enojarse	to get mad
especializarse (c)	to major, to specialize
estallar	to break out, erupt
faltar	to be left
graduarse (ú)	to graduate
matricularse	to register
preocuparse de	to worry about
suspender	to suspend, call off

adjectives

cansado	tired
encantado	delighted
especializado	specialized
listo	ready
milagroso	miraculous
orgánico	organic
reprobado	failed
universitario	university

other expressions

bien saber	to know perfectly well
eso es lo de menos	who cares?
perder la calma	to get upset
¿por qué mejor no. . .?	Why not . . ., why wouldn't it be better to . . .?
salir bien	to pass (an exam, a course)
ser reprobado	to fail (an exam, a course)
sobre todo	especially
tan pronto como	as soon as

additional vocabulary

aunque	although, even though

después de que	after	**opinar (de)**	to think (of)
en cuanto	as soon as	**siempre que**	whenever
estudiantil	student	**tener la intención de**	to plan to, to intend to
hasta que	until		

ESTRUCTURA I

A. Present perfect and past perfect subjunctive tenses

Espero que **te hayas convencido.**

1. To form the present perfect subjunctive tense, use the present subjunctive of **haber** + past participle.

comer	
haya	comido
hayas	
haya	
hayamos	
hayáis	
hayan	

2. The present perfect subjunctive tense is used in two-clause sentences of personal reaction or reservation to express what has happened or may have happened.

Dudo que hayas estudiado.	I doubt you have studied.
Espero que ustedes se hayan divertido mucho.	I hope you've had a wonderful time.

3. The Spanish present perfect subjunctive is often translated as a simple past tense in English.

No es probable que hayamos salido bien en el examen.	It's not probable that we passed the exam.
¡Qué lástima que no te hayas especializado en lenguas extranjeras!	What a shame you didn't major in foreign languages!

4. To form the past perfect subjunctive, use the past subjunctive of **haber** + past participle.

decir	
hubiera hubieras hubiera hubiéramos hubierais hubieran	dicho

5. The past perfect subjunctive is used in two-clause sentences of personal reaction to express what had happened or had not happened in the past.

Yo esperaba que hubieras estudiado más.	I expected (hoped) that you had studied more.
Nadie creería que te hubieras especializado en biología.	No one would believe that you had majored in biology.

6. The past perfect subjunctive is also used in clauses with **si** that state a non-existent condition. In sentences of this type, the past subjunctive is *present* in meaning, while the past perfect subjunctive is *past* in meaning.

PAST SUBJUNCTIVE

Si tuviera tiempo, lo haría.	If I had time *(right now)*, I'd do it.

PAST PERFECT SUBJUNCTIVE

Si hubiera tenido tiempo, lo habría hecho.	If I had had time *(last week)*, I'd have done it.

7. When the past perfect subjunctive is used in clauses with **si,** the result clause will be in one of the following tenses: conditional, conditional perfect, or past perfect subjunctive.

Si hubieras traído un maletín, podrías llevar los cuadernos en él.	If you had brought a briefcase, you could carry the notebooks in it.
Si Carmen hubiera escuchado mis consejos, no habría tenido ese problema.	If Carmen had listened to my advice, she would not have had that problem.
Si hubieras salido bien en el examen, hubieras podido graduarte.	If you had passed the test, you would have been able to graduate.

Aplicación

I. Begin each sentence with the material in parentheses and make any other necessary changes.

MODELO Los argentinos han ganado. (Dudo que. . .) → **Dudo que los argentinos hayan ganado.**

1. Kempes ha metido un gol. (Todos se alegran de que. . .)
2. El público se ha vuelto loco. (Es probable que. . .)
3. Los holandeses han perdido. (Los argentinos están encantados que. . .)
4. Yo he visto todo el partido. (No creen que. . .)
5. Hemos probado nuestra superioridad. (Tú dudas que. . .)

II. Answer each question using **ojalá** + present perfect subjunctive.

MODELO ¿Han llegado los jugadores? → **¡Quién sabe! Ojalá que hayan llegado.**

1. ¿Ha venido el equipo de fútbol?
2. ¿Han pagado los espectadores?
3. ¿Hemos hablado con todos los jugadores?
4. ¿Has traído el radio?
5. ¿Ha terminado el programa?
6. ¿Hemos ganado el partido?

III. Provide two English translations for each of the following sentences.

MODELO Me alegro que hayan venido. → *I'm happy they came.* / *I'm happy they have come.*

1. Dudo que se hayan matriculado.
2. Es mejor que hayas estudiado biología.
3. No me gusta que hayan escrito en el diccionario.
4. Es imposible que ustedes se hayan graduado.
5. No es verdad que ellas hayan estudiado para el examen.
6. ¿Por qué te enoja que yo haya venido?

IV. Combine the following sentences as shown in the model.

MODELO ¿Se fue? No es verdad. → **No es verdad que se haya ido.**

1. ¿Terminaron? Me alegro.
2. ¿Aprobaste el examen? Estoy encantado.
3. ¿Llegaron tarde? Me enoja.
4. ¿Estalló una huelga? No me gusta.
5. ¿Dijeron eso? Es imposible.
6. ¿Sacó un diccionario? Es mejor.
7. ¿No viste el manual de química? Es una lástima.
8. ¿Yo fui reprobado? Es imposible.
9. ¿Estuvieron aquí? Es probable.
10. ¿Se acostó sin estudiar? Es una lástima.

V. Make each of the following sentences negative and modify the second verb as required.

MODELO Es verdad que ellos nos esperaron. → **No es verdad que ellos nos hayan esperado.**

1. Es seguro que ellos vinieron.
2. Es obvio que estuvieron aquí.
3. Es verdad que Dolores aprobó el examen.
4. Es evidente que ella lo vio.
5. Es cierto que salió bien.

VI. Respond to each remark with a sentence beginning with **ojalá.**

A. MODELO Los argentinos no ganaron. → **Ojalá que hubieran ganado.**

1. Yo no fui al partido.
2. Kempes no metió un gol.
3. Tú no trajiste el radio.
4. Ustedes no escucharon los comentarios.
5. Nosotros no nos divertimos.

B. MODELO Yo fui al restaurante. → **Ojalá que no hubiera ido.**

1. Comí mucho.
2. Juan me acompañó.
3. Pedimos carne y ensalada.
4. Tomamos una botella de vino.
5. Juan se puso enfermo.
6. Tuvo que ir al médico.

VII. Change the following sentences to the past.

MODELO No creo que hayan empezado. → **No creía que hubieran empezado.**

1. Dudo que hayan estudiado.
2. Me alegro que se haya ido.
3. Estamos encantados que lo hayas dicho.
4. Es estupendo que hayamos ganado.
5. Es imposible que haya llamado.
6. No creemos que se hayan divertido.
7. Es posible que no se haya dado cuenta.
8. Siento que hayas tenido tantos problemas.

VIII. Supply either the past subjunctive or the past perfect subjunctive, as required.

MODELOS (tener) Si ellos _____ el tiempo, me ayudarían. → **Si ellos tuvieran el tiempo, me ayudarían.**
(preguntar) Si ellos me lo _____, se lo habría dicho. → **Si ellos me lo hubieran preguntado, se lo habría dicho.**

1. (trabajar) Si tú no _____ tanto, no te cansarías.
2. (cenar) Si nosotros _____ en el restaurante, habríamos pedido anticuchos.
3. (venir) Si ella _____, habría traído una ensalada.
4. (estar) Si yo _____ en Lima, comería cebiche.
5. (comer) Si tú no _____ tanto, no te habrías puesto enfermo.
6. (tomar) Si yo no _____ tanto vino, no me sentiría tan mal.
7. (servir) Si nosotros _____ legumbres, la comida habría sido mejor.
8. (ponerse) Si papá no _____ enfermo, habríamos ido al cine.

IX. Change each sentence so both verbs are past in meaning.

MODELO Si tuviera tiempo, lo llamaría. → **Si hubiera tenido tiempo, lo habría llamado.**

1. Si no estuviera cansado, iría contigo.
2. Si tuviera frío, se pondría un abrigo.
3. Si necesitara los guantes, te los pediría.
4. Si le doliera la garganta, usaría una bufanda.
5. Si te pusieras el sombrero, no tendrías frío.
6. Si yo no encontrara la chaqueta, me compraría otra.
7. Si saliéramos, me cambiaría de ropa.
8. Si fuéramos a la embajada, me pondría vestido azul.

X. Para contestar

1. Si usted no hubiera estudiado español, ¿qué lengua habría estudiado?
2. Si usted no hubiera entrado en esta universidad, ¿dónde habría estudiado?
3. Si usted no fuera estudiante, ¿qué le gustaría ser?
4. Si ustedes hubieran estudiado más este año, ¿habrían aprendido más?
5. Si usted no se hubiera quedado en casa anoche, ¿adónde habría ido?
6. Si yo no fuera profesor(a), ¿saben ustedes lo que me gustaría ser?

B. Uses of **lo**

Repaso. In the combination **lo que** + verb, **lo que** is a relator pronoun which conveys the meaning *what* or *that which:* **¿Entiendes lo que te estoy diciendo?**

Lo más fácil es matricularse.

1. The combination **lo** + adjective (in its masculine singular form) conveys the meaning *the* + adjective + *part* (or *thing*).

Lo malo es que no podré graduarme.	The bad thing is that I won't be able to graduate.
Lo bueno de esta clase es la conversación.	The good part of this class is the conversation.

2. In a sentence with **todo** as direct object, **lo** is often used before the verb. The meaning conveyed is *everything* or *all.*

En cosas de gramática Maricarmen lo comprende todo.	In matters of grammar Maricarmen understands everything.
Yo ya te lo había explicado todo mil veces.	I had already explained everything to you a thousand times.

Aplicación

I. Combine the following pairs of sentences by forming a new sentence with **lo que.**

MODELO Ellos se matricularon. Eso no me gusta. → **Lo que no me gusta es que ellos se hayan matriculado.**

1. Estudiaron muy poco. Eso me enoja.
2. No fueron a la biblioteca. Eso no nos divierte.
3. Ganaron los argentinos. Eso me gusta.
4. Se suspendieron los exámenes. Eso es estupendo.
5. Los chicos tomaron cerveza antes del examen. Eso nos divierte.

II. Restate each sentence, changing the underlined section to **lo** + adjective.

MODELO La parte interesante de la clase son las conversaciones. → **Lo interesante de la clase son las conversaciones.**

1. La cosa difícil son los exámenes.
2. La parte estupenda es que aprendemos mucho.
3. La cosa interesante es la gramática.
4. La parte mala es que tenemos que tomar apuntes.
5. La cosa importante es hablar en español.

III. Para expresar en español

MODELO That's the hard part. → **Eso es lo difícil.**

1. That's the good stuff.
2. That's the bad thing.
3. That's the easy part.
4. That's the great thing.
5. That's the last part.

IV. Para contestar

1. ¿Qué es lo bueno de esta clase? ¿Qué es lo difícil? ¿Qué es lo fácil?
2. ¿Siempre comprende usted lo que yo digo? ¿Qué es lo que me pide cuando usted no comprende?
3. ¿Siempre hace usted lo que quieren sus padres? ¿Por qué (no)?
4. Cuando usted va a un partido de fútbol, ¿comprende usted todo lo que pasa? ¿Qué es lo que no comprende?
5. ¿Sabe usted lo que va a hacer después de terminar los estudios?

Pausa oral

La vida estudiantil

I. Para conversar

Act out the following situations with another student.

MODELO Mañana hay un examen de química y usted no sabe nada. Su amigo tampoco comprende la materia. →

A: **¿Qué vamos a hacer? Yo no comprendo nada.**

B: **Yo tampoco. ¿Por qué no vamos a la biblioteca a ver si hay algún manual. . . ?**

A: **Mejor sería ir a la iglesia a preguntar si hay un santo especializado en química orgánica.**

B: **Nada de bromas, amigo. Tenemos que aprobar este examen.**

1. Usted necesita estudiar para un examen de historia pero no encuentra sus apuntes. Le pide los apuntes a un amigo (amiga), pero él (ella) no se los quiere dar porque también tiene que estudiar.
2. Usted y su amigo (amiga) están tratando de decidir en qué cursos quieren matricularse.
3. Usted está en la clase de español y no ha preparado la tarea. El profesor está muy enojado.
4. Los estudiantes están en huelga porque la comida en el restaurante estudiantil es malísima. A usted no le parece muy buena la idea.

II. Para describir

Why would students organize **una huelga estudiantil**? Look at the following drawing and list as many motives for a strike as you can think of.

ESTRUCTURA II

A. Conjunctions + indicative or subjunctive

Repaso. Certain conjunctions of time (**ahora que. . .**) and of cause (**puesto que. . .**) are always followed by a verb in the indicative. Other conjunctions (**antes de que, para que, sin que. . .**) are always followed by the subjunctive.

> **Tan pronto como** me digas qué necesitas, yo lo haré encantada.

1. A final set of conjunctions, most of which refer to time, sometimes introduce the subjunctive, sometimes the indicative.

cuando when **hasta que** until **después (de) que** after **siempre que** whenever **en el momento en que** at the time that **en cuanto** as soon as **tan pronto como** as soon as	+ indicative or subjunctive

2. When one of these conjunctions introduces a clause that refers to the future or to an indefinite time, the verb is in the subjunctive. When the conjunction introduces a clause that refers to an action that actually takes place or took place, the indicative is used.

SUBJUNCTIVE

Te daré el dinero cuando te vea.	I'll give you the money when I see you.
Tan pronto como usted me lo diga, yo lo haré.	As soon as you tell me to, I'll do it.
Dijo que en cuanto tuviera el dinero, me lo mandaría.	She said as soon as she has *(or* had—*the time is indefinite)* the money, she would give it to me.

INDICATIVE

Cuando terminé el examen, salí del cuarto.	When I finished the exam, I left the room.
Tan pronto como usted me lo dijo, yo lo hice.	As soon as you told me to, I did it.
Lo saludo cuando lo veo.	I say hello to him when(ever) I see him.
En cuanto terminamos de almorzar, nos fuimos.	As soon as we finished having lunch, we left.

3. The conjunctions **aunque** *although, even though* and **mientras (que)** *while, as long as* function differently. When they introduce a clause that refers to a situation that is a reality (i.e., that is happening), the indicative is used. When the clause refers to a situation that is only a possibility (i.e., that may happen), the subjunctive is used.

INDICATIVE

Aunque está lloviendo, iremos al centro.	Even though it is raining, we'll go downtown.
Mientras Mercedes desayunaba yo fui de compras.	While Mercedes was having breakfast, I went shopping.

SUBJUNCTIVE

Aunque esté lloviendo, saldremos.	Although it may be raining, we'll go out.
Mientras yo sea el presidente de esta compañía, se hará así.	As long as I'm president of this company, it will be done that way.

Aplicación

I. Choose the correct verb form.

MODELO El profesor se enojará cuando (vea / ve) esta tarea. → **El profesor se enojará cuando vea esta tarea.**

1. Comprenderás cuando (lees / leas) los apuntes.
2. Siempre hago la tarea tan pronto como (llego / llegue) a casa.
3. En cuanto se (graduó / graduara), encontró trabajo.
4. Dijo que en cuanto (pudiera / pudo), lo haría.
5. Se me perdió el libro de gramática cuando (fuera / fui) al café.
6. En el momento en que lo (supe / supiera), te llamé.
7. Vamos a estudiar hasta que lo (sepas / sabes).
8. Trabajaste hasta que se te (acabó / acabe) la paciencia.
9. Después de que (compro / compre) el diccionario, te lo mostraré.
10. Tan pronto como (aprobemos / aprobamos) el examen, podremos divertirnos.

II. Change the verb in the past to one in the future.

MODELO Esperé hasta que vino. (Esperaré. . .) → **Esperaré hasta que venga.**

1. Estudió cuando llegó. (Estudiará. . .)
2. Buscaron empleo tan pronto como se graduaron. (Buscarán. . .)
3. Estuviste en la biblioteca hasta que lo aprendiste. (Estarás. . .)
4. Usamos la pizarra hasta que se rompió. (Usaremos. . .)
5. Lo llamaba siempre que podía. (Lo llamaré. . .)
6. Fuimos a Barcelona tan pronto como terminaron las clases. (Iremos. . .)
7. Lo reconocí en el momento en que lo vi. (Lo reconoceré. . .)
8. Los profesores suspendieron los exámenes después de que se anunció la huelga. (Suspenderán. . .)

III. Read each sentence. When the instructor says **¿Cómo?,** restate the sentence, starting each with **Dije que** and changing the verbs so that they express indefinite time.

MODELO Te llamaré cuando llegue la carta. (¿Cómo?) → **Dije que te llamaría cuando llegara la carta.**

1. Daré una fiesta cuando me gradúe. (¿Cómo?)
2. Te lo diré tan pronto como lo sepa. (¿Cómo?)
3. Te ayudaré siempre que quieras. (¿Cómo?)
4. Estaré en la biblioteca hasta que se cierre. (¿Cómo?)
5. Me especializaré tan pronto como me dejen. (¿Cómo?)
6. Te mostraré el cuaderno cuando lo encuentre. (¿Cómo?)

IV. Para expresar en español

A. MODELO I always buy a bracelet when I go to Mexico. / I'll buy a bracelet when I go to Mexico. → **Siempre compro una pulsera cuando voy a México. / Compraré una pulsera cuando vaya a México.**

1. I waited until he came. / I'll wait until he comes.
2. We always went to the museum when we lived there. / We'll go to the museum when we live there.
3. He changed after we graduated. / He'll change after we graduate.
4. We always have lunch as soon as they arrive. / We'll have lunch as soon as they arrive.

B. MODELO I told him it when you called. / I said I'd tell him it when you called. → **Se lo dije cuando llamaste. / Dije que se lo diría cuando llamaras.**

1. I waited until they knew. / I said I'd wait until they knew.
2. We bought it when we were there. / We said we'd buy it when we were there.
3. He asked her as soon as they arrived. / He said he'd ask her as soon as they arrived.
4. She studied until they suspended classes. / She said she'd study until they suspended classes.

C. MODELO Even though it may be raining, I'll go. / Even though it's raining, I'll go. → **Aunque esté lloviendo, iré. / Aunque está lloviendo, iré.**

1. Even though they may be intelligent, they have to study. / Even though they're intelligent, they have to study.
2. Even though they may suspend classes, I'll stay here. / Even though they are suspending classes, I'll stay here.

3. We listen as long as they talk. / We listen while they talk.
4. She won't study as long as they talk about a strike. / She studies while they talk about the strike.

V. Review exercise

Complete each sentence with the correct form of the verb in parentheses.

MODELO (perder) Dímelo antes de que yo _____ la calma. → **Dímelo antes de que yo pierda la calma.**

1. (terminar) Cuando yo _____ con este examen, estudiaré para los otros.
2. (llegar) No podemos hacer nada hasta que él _____.
3. (haber) No me importa nada, con tal de que _____ una huelga.
4. (estallar) Eso no pasará sin que _____ una huelga.
5. (preparar) Yo siempre estudio mientras ella _____ la cena.
6. (conseguir) Vamos a la biblioteca para que Maricarmen _____ un manual.
7. (graduarse) Cuando él _____, le ofrecieron un puesto estupendo.
8. (comprar) Fuimos a la tienda para que los chicos _____ cuadernos.
9. (dar) Yo no podría hacer esta lección a menos que alguien me _____ un diccionario.
10. (acompañar) Dijo que no iría a la biblioteca a menos que nosotros la _____.
11. (concentrarse) A menos que tú _____ en una sola materia, no vas a aprobar el examen.
12. (dejar) No pude estudiar hasta que ella me _____ ver sus apuntes.
13. (suspender) No sé si van a suspender las clases o no, pero aunque las _____, nosotros vamos a estudiar.
14. (ayudar) Lo podré entender siempre que tú me _____.
15. (hacer) Después de que Juan _____ su tarea, todos fueron al cine.

B. The verb **pensar**

No **pienses** más **en** las otras asignaturas.

Pensar has several uses in Spanish.

1. **Pensar que** (+ a clause) is used to express a thought; it has the same meaning as **creer que.**

¿Piensas que le habrá llegado el telegrama?	Do you think the telegram arrived?
Pienso que le dejó un recado con la secretaria.	I believe that he left a message for him with the secretary.

2. The expression **¿Qué piensa(s) de. . . ?** is used when asking someone's opinion. It is similar in meaning to **¿Qué le (te) parece?** or **¿Qué opina(s)?**

¿Qué piensas de esta clase?	What do you think of this class?
¿Qué piensan tus padres de Ramón?	What do your parents think of Ramón?

3. **Pensar en** (+ noun or pronoun) conveys the meaning *to think about.*

¿En qué piensas?	What are you thinking about?
Pienso en toda la ropa que voy a comprar.	I'm thinking about all the clothes I'm going to buy.

4. **Pensar** + infinitive is used to state an intended plan of action. It has the same meaning as **tener la intención de** *to plan* or *intend.*

¿Qué piensas hacer esta noche?	What do you plan on doing tonight?
Pensamos llamarla por teléfono.	We intend to call her on the phone.

Aplicación

I. Restate each of the following sentences using a form of **pensar.**

MODELO Tengo la intención de hacerlo. → **Pienso hacerlo.**

1. ¿Qué opinan ustedes de esta situación?
2. Creo que está malísima.
3. Tenemos la intención de llamar al dueño.
4. ¿Y qué opinan del dueño?
5. Creemos que es una buena persona.
6. Yo tengo la intención de hablar con él.

II. Para expresar en español

MODELO I'm thinking about the trip. → **Pienso en el viaje.**

1. When do you intend to travel?
2. I plan to leave tomorrow.
3. I'm thinking of my farm.
4. We plan to be there all summer.
5. What do you think of my idea?
6. I think it's very good.

The University of Barcelona. Exams or no exams, there is always time for romance.

University of Salamanca facade honoring Fernando de Aragón and Isabel de Castilla. When Ferdinand and Isabel married in 1469, the Spanish nation was created. They were granted the title **Reyes Católicos,** the Catholic Monarchs, by Spanish Pope Alexander VI.

LECTURA

El mundo universitario hispánico

La Universidad de Salamanca, que comparte[1] con Oxford, París y Bologna la distinción de ser uno de los primeros centros de estudio[1] medievales[1] de Europa, se estableció al principio del siglo XIII de nuestra era[1] en la Península Ibérica[1]. Sin embargo, ya existían actividades de creación literaria y se cultivaba "el comercio con las cosas de la mente" desde unos quince siglos antes[1].

En efecto[1], la vida intelectual y artística de España había sido grandemente enriquecida[1] con la mezcla[1] de diversas razas y culturas—romanas[2], visigóticas[3], hebreas[4] y musulmanas[5]—que habían invadido la península; por eso, sin tener que exagerar, es posible hablar de una larga tradición académica hispánica.

En 1492, cuando Cristóbal Colón descubre América—iniciando así[1] la hispanización de una gran parte del hemisferio occidental[1]—España extiende al Nuevo Mundo sus viejas tradiciones académicas y artísticas. De esta manera vemos como en 1536 los españoles fundan en la Ciudad de México el Colegio de Santa Cruz de Tlatelolco para enseñar a muchos indios filosofía, música, medicina, religión, latín y retórica. Dos años después se funda en Santo Domingo—hoy la República Domini-

shares
learning
era (A.D.) / Iberian Peninsula (Spain and Portugal)
desde . . . for some fifteen centuries earlier
As a matter of fact
enriched / mixture
iniciando así thus beginning
Western

cana—la Universidad de Santo Tomás de Aquino. Esta universidad se funda unos cien años antes que Harvard[6]. Para 1551 la Ciudad de México y Lima cuentan con sendas universidades[1], las cuales aún[1] funcionan hoy en día. Con el tiempo, todos los países hispánicos del hemisferio acabarán con una o más universidades. Muchas de estas universidades evolucionarán con el paso del tiempo, convirtiéndose algunas en[1] mega-universidades como la Universidad Autónoma de México o la Universidad de Buenos Aires, contando con un estudiantado[1] de más de cien mil personas.

con . . . with one university each
las . . . which still
convirtiéndose . . . some turning into
contando . . . having a student body

El sistema educativo actual[1] de los países hispánicos se divide normalmente en tres niveles[1] de enseñanza: la instrucción primaria o elemental, la instrucción secundaria o media y la instrucción universitaria o superior. La duración de cada uno de los niveles varía un poco de un país a otro; sin embargo, la siguiente gráfica dará una idea general de la situación actual.

current
levels

ESTRUCTURA EDUCATIVA

EDAD: 3–5 y 6–11	12–14	15–16 o 17	17 o 18–22
Pre-primaria 3 años **Primaria** 6 años	**Secundaria, primer ciclo** 3 años	**Secundaria, segundo ciclo** Puede ser: Académico o general, 2 años Técnico, 3 años Normal[1], 3 años	**Universitaria**[2] Puede ser: Universidad, 5 años Instituto pedagógico[3], 4 años Instituto politécnico[4], 5 años Colegio universitario[5], 3 años Academia militar, 4 años

GLOSAS 1. **Normal:** teacher training. 2. Hispanic college degrees take from 4 to 6 years to obtain. Most degrees are professional. 3. **Instituto pedagógico:** graduate school of education. 4. **Instituto politécnico:** college-level technical institute offering courses in engineering and basic sciences like chemistry. 5. **Colegio universitario:** similar to junior college.

La educación universitaria hispánica ha tenido siempre un carácter más bien[1] público. Además, la mayoría de las universidades hispánicas han concentrado sus esfuerzos[1] en la preparación de sus estudiantes para las carreras o profesiones como leyes, medicina e ingeniería civil. Así que el estudiante universitario hispánico típico ocupa la mayor parte de su tiempo (un 99%) en

más bien rather, relatively
efforts

estudiar los cursos ya programados de su carrera o especialización. Esto es posible de llevar a cabo porque el segundo ciclo de la enseñanza media es en realidad una combinación de estudios secundarios y estudios pre-universitarios. El plan de estudios (*curriculum*) del segundo ciclo incluye cursos semejantes a los que se estudian en los últimos dos años del *high school* y los dos primeros de la universidad americanos. Por su carácter "profesional", el plan de estudios de las universidades admite muy pocos cursos "electivos".

Otra característica compartida por casi todas las universidades hispánicas públicas es la de ser no sólo una institución académica sino también un lugar de marcada actividad política. Y puesto que tantos aspectos de la vida de una persona se deciden en el campo de la política nacional, es natural que los estudiantes hispánicos pronto comprendan que participar en la política es muchas veces más significativo que la misma carrera que estudian. Lógicamente, muchos conflictos han ocurrido entre los

llevar . . . carry out
similar
shared
la de ser that of being
very

The medical school of the Universidad Nacional Autónoma de México, Mexico City.

estudiantes, tratando de introducir cambios en el sistema político nacional, y el gobierno, luchando por mantener el statu quo.[7] Uno de los resultados de estas luchas ha sido el conceder a muchas universidades la autonomía, cosa que significa no sólo la libertad de enseñanza intelectual sino también el derecho de gobernarse internamente en forma independiente.

struggles / to grant
cosa que which
derecho de right to / govern themselves

Los gobiernos democráticos o semidemocráticos mantienen relaciones cordiales con las universidades y respetan su autonomía. Los gobiernos dictatoriales, ya sean de izquierda o derecha, ven con muy malos ojos el activismo político de los estudiantes. Por consiguiente, tratan de minar la autonomía universitaria, llegando a veces a ocupar militarmente los edificios universitarios o, como en el caso de la Universidad de San Marcos en Lima, mudando la universidad fuera del centro de la ciudad hacia un suburbio remoto y desolado.

ya sean be they
izquierda . . . left or right (wing) / **ven . . .** disapprove
Consequently / undermine
going so far
moving

Al acercarnos al final del siglo XX, se puede decir que la condición actual del mundo universitario hispánico se resume en dos palabras: persistencia y variedad. Persistencia que se hace patente en los largos años de existencia; variedad que se manifiesta en las diversas características—externas e internas—de tantas universidades hispánicas a ambos lados del Atlántico.

se resume can be summed up
que . . . which becomes evident
both

Con respecto al futuro, es de rigor formular esta pregunta: ¿Serán capaces las universidades de responder eficaz y eficientemente a las nuevas condiciones que la ciencia y la tecnología rápidamente van creando? La respuesta no es fácil. Sin embargo, la evidencia indica que ya muchas universidades están haciendo frente a los problemas del mundo moderno y que lenta pero seguramente van ganando la batalla por conseguir un desarrollo social y económico más justo para todos los miembros de la sociedad.

es . . . it is absolutely necessary
eficaz . . . effectively and efficiently
van creando are creating
haciendo frente are facing
lenta . . . slowly but surely / **van ganando** are winning
por. . . to obtain
development

Glosas

1. The medieval period of European history is the period of the Middle Ages, between Ancient and Modern times. Conventionally, the period is said to begin with the fall of Rome (476 A.D.) and to end in the late 1400's.
2. Spain was part of the Roman Empire from the third century B.C. to the beginning of the fourth century A.D. Seneca, a famous Stoic philosopher and playwright born in Córdoba, was one of many talented Romans of Hispanic origin.

3. The Visigoths were one of the Germanic tribes that invaded Italy and destroyed the Roman Empire. They established a monarchy in Spain that lasted from the fifth to the eighth century.
4. Jewish people made their way to the Iberian Peninsula and settled as early as the third century A.D. The Hispanic Jews, or Sephardim, coexisted with other ethnic groups and cultures until 1492 A.D., when most were expelled from Spain on the orders of **los Reyes Católicos** *the Catholic Kings,* Queen Isabel and King Ferdinand. The Sephardic genius Maimónides, one of the most brilliant men Spain ever produced, was a physician and a philosopher. He, too, was born in Córdoba.
5. The invasion of Spain by **los musulmanes** *Moslems* is known in Spanish history as **la invasión árabe,** but in fact the invaders were racially a mixed lot. The vast majority of the first invaders were Berbers from the Atlas Mountains in Northern Africa. They were later joined by men from all the former Roman colonies of Northern Africa and, eventually, by Arabs from Arabia. Finally, toward the end of the Moslem domination, came the Almoravids and the Almohads, wild mountain people from Northern Africa, recent converts to Mohammedanism who thought the Arabic leadership in Spain was ignoring the true teachings of the Prophet. Córdoba won its independence from Damascus in 756 and remained an independent state, or Caliphate, until 1236. The City of Córdoba, which became the capital of the Caliphate, had, at one time during the tenth century, a population of over 500,000 people, and was famous for its splendid gardens, palaces, libraries, and factories. During the reign of the Caliph Abdur'r-Rahman III, Córdoba became the intellectual and artistic center not only of the Iberian Peninsula but also of most of Europe.
6. The oldest university in the United States, Harvard, was founded in 1636.
7. **Statu quo** (in English *status quo*) is the Spanish spelling of the Latin phrase meaning *the way things are.*

SOBRE LA LECTURA

I. Para completar

Complete the following sentences with information from the reading selection.

1. La Universidad de Salamanca es uno de los primeros ______.
2. Quince siglos antes de la creación de la primera universidad española ya ______.
3. La vida intelectual y artística de España había sido enriquecida con ______.
4. En 1536 los españoles fundaron en México ______.
5. Allí los indios aprendían ______.
6. Ahora todas las repúblicas latinoamericanas ______.
7. El sistema educativo de los países hispanos se divide ______.

8. En los países hispanos, la educación universitaria tiene un carácter ____.
9. Las universidades preparan a sus estudiantes para ____.
10. Hay pocos cursos "electivos" porque ____.
11. La universidad hispana no es sólo una institución académica sino también ____.
12. Uno de los resultados de las luchas políticas ha sido ____.
13. Con respecto al futuro, el problema principal es ____.
14. La evidencia indica que ____.

II. Para discutir

1. ¿Es la política importante en las universidades norteamericanas? ¿Es bueno o malo esto?
2. ¿Le gusta más a usted el sistema educativo hispano o el norteamericano? ¿Por qué?
3. ¿Deberían las universidades norteamericanas dar más importancia a la preparación profesional?
4. ¿Son importantes los electivos o no? ¿Por qué?
5. ¿A usted le gustaría estudiar en una universidad extranjera por un año? ¿En cuál? ¿Por qué?

Repaso oral

I. Add to each of the following phrases to form complete sentences.

MODELO Pensamos. . . → **Pensamos concentrarnos en esta materia y no en las otras asignaturas.**

1. Ojalá Dolores haya comprendido. . .
2. Si hubiera escuchado. . .
3. ¿Qué piensa Dolores de. . . ?
4. Dolores y Maricarmen ya no quieren pensar en. . .
5. Cuando llegue la época de exámenes, nosotros. . .
6. Aunque no salgamos bien en el examen. . .

II. Make several statements about the following picture. In each sentence use one of these words or constructions:

1) **hubiera** + past participle; 2) **lo;** 3) **mientras;** 4) **pensar** + infinitive.

Capítulo 20

Despegue

Descripción del dibujo

1. Anita Archuleta y David Walker viajan de El Salvador a Honduras.
2. En la frontera la gente les muestra sus pasaportes a los soldados.
3. Después todos hacen cola para mostrar sus documentos.
4. De repente una señora se pone a gritar.
5. Su nene tiene convulsiones. Alguien tiene que atender al niño inmediatamente.
6. Anita mata un alacrán que se había metido en la ropa del niño.

Pronunciación

1. El Salvador / de El Salvador a Honduras
2. pasaportes / La gente les muestra sus pasaportes.
3. de repente / inmediatamente
4. alacrán / Anita mata un alacrán.

Aplicación

I. Relación

Say at least 12 sentences about the picture on page 467.

II. Para contestar

1. ¿Con qué países tienen fronteras los Estados Unidos?
2. ¿Hay que mostrar los documentos en la frontera? ¿A quiénes?
3. ¿A usted le gustaría ser soldado?
4. ¿Hay que hacer cola para muchas cosas en la universidad? ¿Cuándo se tiene que hacer cola?
5. ¿Le gritan a usted sus padres algunas veces? ¿Por qué?
6. ¿Sabría usted atender a un nene con convulsiones?
7. ¿Ha visto usted alguna vez un alacrán?
8. ¿Qué haría usted si se encontrara en la misma situación que Anita?

Tema del diálogo

Knowing Spanish, being friendly, and having some technical skills are three passports that are welcomed in the Hispanic world.

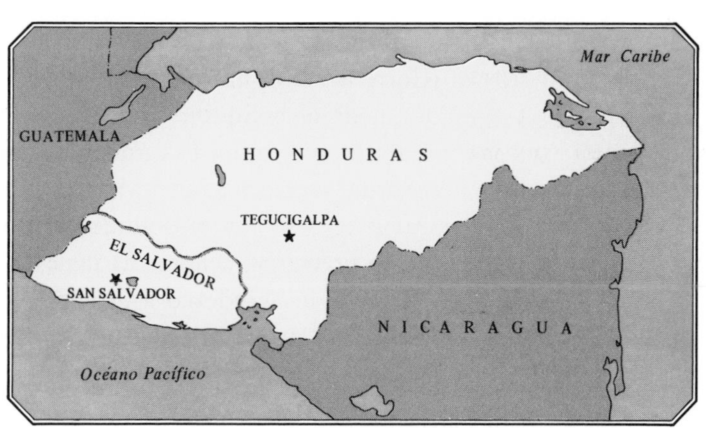

DIÁLOGO

Yanqui, ven a casa

David Walker y Anita Archuleta[1] *son dos geólogos americanos haciendo investigaciones para predecir temblores de tierra*[2] *en Centroamérica, utilizando magnetómetros y sismómetros. Viajan ahora de El Salvador a Honduras.*

DAVID (Manejando el jeep mientras Anita estudia varios mapas.) Creo que allí adelante está la frontera con Honduras.

ANITA Ahora sólo necesitamos encontrar un aduanero que nos facilite la entrada.

DAVID Sí, uno que no nos haga bajar todo el equipo de la canastilla del jeep. (Un soldado hondureño aparece en mitad de la carretera. El soldado se acerca y los saluda.)

SOLDADO Muy buenas tardes. Bienvenidos. (Los observa detenidamente.) ¿Hablan español?

DAVID Y ANITA Sí. Lo hablamos.

SOLDADO ¿Su nacionalidad?

DAVID Somos americanos.

ANITA (Anita saca los documentos de un portafolio.) Aquí tiene los pasaportes, señor.

SOLDADO Estacionen el jeep detrás de ese autobús y vengan conmigo, por favor.

* * *

(David y Anita entran en una pequeña oficina y hacen cola. Los pasajeros del autobús van mostrando uno a uno sus documentos. De repente, una señora grita desesperadamente.)

SEÑORA ¡Pronto, pronto! ¡Alguien que me ayude! Mi nene se muere. ¡Tiene convulsiones!

ANITA (Corre a ver al niño.) Vamos a ver. . .David, ve al jeep y baja el baúl que tiene el botiquín.

SEÑORA (La señora le quita la camisita al niño. Un animal cae al suelo.) Ay, señorita, es un alacrán. ¡Mátelo! ¡Mátelo! (Anita mata el alacrán y David regresa con el botiquín. Entre los dos atienden al niño.)

ANITA No se preocupe, señora. El nene se compondrá muy pronto.

SEÑORA ¡Cómo se lo agradezco a ustedes! Son una maravilla. . .

DAVID Estamos a sus órdenes, señora.

* * *

SEÑORA Bueno, si algún día pasan por Sabanagrande, pregunten por la familia Orellana Ortiz. Y mi esposo y mis hermanos y yo. . .

DAVID No me diga. ¡Qué casualidad! Mañana y pasado estaremos cerca de Marcala[3], pero la semana próxima tenemos que ir a Sabanagrande[3].

ANITA Y claro está, pasaremos a verlos.

SEÑORA Nada de eso. Ustedes se quedarán en casa con nosotros, y Ludovico, mi hermano menor, les servirá de guía. (Saca un papel del bolso y escribe algo.) Aquí tienen: nombre, dirección y teléfono.

DAVID Muchas gracias, señora. Ah, y no se le olvide llevar al nene al médico cuando llegue a casa.

SEÑORA De ninguna manera, pero a ustedes tampoco se les olvide que los esperamos en nuestra casa ¿eh?

ANITA Claro que no. Allá nos veremos el jueves.

Yankee come home

David Walker and Anita Archuleta are two American geologists who are doing research in order to predict earthquakes in Central America, using magnetometers and seismometers. They are now traveling from El Salvador to Honduras.

D: (Driving the jeep while Anita studies several maps.) I think up ahead is the border with Honduras.

A: Now we only need to find a customs official who will make it easy for us to get through (facilitate our entry).

D: Yes, one who will not make us take down all the equipment from the luggage rack of the jeep.
(A Honduran soldier appears in the middle of the highway. The soldier approaches and greets them.)

S: Good afternoon. Welcome. (He looks them over carefully.) Do you speak Spanish?

D, A: Yes, we do.

S: Your nationality?

D: We are Americans.

A: (Anita takes their papers out of a folder.) Here are the documents, sir.

S: Park the jeep behind that bus and come with me, please.

* * *

(David and Anita enter a small office and wait in line. The bus passengers are showing their papers one by one. Suddenly a lady cries out desperately.)

L: Quickly, quickly! Somebody help me! My little boy is dying. He's having convulsions!

A: (Runs to see the child.) Let's see . . . David, go to the jeep and get down the trunk that has the first-aid kit.

L: (The lady takes off the child's little shirt. A bug falls to the ground.) Oh, Miss, it's a scorpion. Kill it! Kill it! (Anita kills the scorpion and David returns with the first-aid kit. Between the two (of them) they tend to the child.)

A: Don't worry, ma'am. The little boy will get better very soon.

L: I am very grateful to you. You're a wonder.

D: We're pleased to help, ma'am.

* * *

L: Well, if some day you are passing through Sabanagrande, ask for the Orellana Ortiz family. My husband, my brothers, and I . . .

D: No kidding. What a coincidence. Tomorrow and the day after we will be near Marcala, but next week we have to go to Sabanagrande.

A: And, of course, we'll stop by to see you.

L: Absolutely not. You will stay at our house, and Ludovico, my younger brother, will serve you as guide. (She takes out a paper from her bag and writes something.) Here you are: name, address, and telephone.

D: Thanks very much, ma'am. Ah, and don't forget to take the little boy to the doctor when you get home.

L: I certainly won't, but neither will you forget that we are expecting you in our home, right?

A: Of course not. We will see you there Thursday.

VARIACIONES

Si voy al campo, tendré que llevar:	If I go to the country, I'll have to take:
un peine	a comb
un cepillo	a brush
un cepillo de dientes	a toothbrush
pasta de dientes	toothpaste
jabón	soap
un espejo	a mirror
unas toallas	some towels
También voy a llevar:	I'll also take:
un paraguas	an umbrella
un impermeable	a raincoat

Border crossing in Nicaragua. "All we need now is a customs official who will make it easy for us to get through."

Glosas

1. Archuleta, Baca, Montoya, and Griego are some of the old Hispanic last names that have been around New Mexico and southern Colorado since the beginning of the seventeenth century.
2. Specially trained geologists (with fluency in Spanish and survival skills) have been trying to predict scientifically the occurrence of earthquakes. Geologists deploy their instruments to monitor phenomena related to an active surface fault or to a buried fault formation. Some of these geologists work for the Office of Earthquake Studies of the U.S. Department of the Interior.
3. Marcala and Sabanagrande are small towns located in the southern part of Honduras.

SOBRE EL DIÁLOGO

I. Complete each sentence with the appropriate word from the list below.

cepillo	**impermeable**	**baúl**
espejo	**paraguas**	**aduanero**
jabón	**carretera**	**soldado**
toalla	**guía**	**cola**
peine	**dirección**	**nene**
cepillo de dientes	**manejas**	**compone**
pasta de dientes	**adelante**	**agradeceré**

MODELO Si tú _____ muy rápido, puedes tener un accidente. → **Si tú manejas muy rápido, puedes tener un accidente.**

1. Para lavarse la cara se necesitan _____ y _____.
2. Si llueve, tendrás que ponerte _____ y llevar un _____.
3. Hay muchos carros, camiones, camionetas y autobuses en la_____.
4. Si me ayuda con el nene, se lo _____.
5. Para arreglarse el pelo se necesita un _____ o un _____.
6. Un hombre que trabaja en la aduana es _____.
7. ¿Dónde vive usted? ¿Cuál es su _____?
8. Cuando uno se baña, usa _____ y agua, y después, una _____.
9. El _____ está jugando en la calle.
10. Está en el ejército. Es _____.
11. A veces se pone enfermo, pero siempre se _____ rápido.
12. Mírate al _____ y verás que tienes algo en la cara.
13. Hay mucha gente esperando. Vamos a tener que hacer _____.
14. Tiene muchas cosas: cinco maletas y un _____.
15. ¿Quién nos servirá de _____ en esta ciudad?
16. La frontera está allí _____.

The mountainous Republic of Honduras is slightly larger than Tennessee and has a population of about three million inhabitants.

II. Para contestar

1. ¿Por qué están en Centroamérica David Walker y Anita Archuleta?
2. ¿A qué país van ahora?
3. ¿Quiere David bajar todo el equipo de la canastilla del jeep?
4. ¿Qué les pregunta el soldado hondureño? ¿Qué les pide que hagan?
5. ¿Por qué se pone a gritar una de las señoras que están en la oficina?
6. ¿Qué animal ha causado las convulsiones?
7. ¿Por qué le dice Anita a la señora que no se preocupe?
8. ¿Adónde invita la señora a Anita y a David?
9. ¿Piensan ellos estar en Sabanagrande algún día?
10. ¿Qué escribe la señora en un papel?

III. Respond to each remark with one of the sentences in the list. There is more than one possible response to some of the remarks.

Aquí. . .tiene. / **¡Cómo se lo agradezco!** / **Estamos a sus órdenes.** / **No me diga.** / **¡Qué casualidad!** / **Nada de eso.** / **Bienvenidos.**

MODELO Acabamos de llegar a Colombia. → **Bienvenidos.**

1. Yo también soy de San Fernando.
2. ¡Cómo les agradezco el ayudar a mi nene!
3. Cuando lleguemos allí, tomaremos un cuarto en un hotel.
4. ¿Puedo ver sus documentos, señorita?
5. Yo puedo ayudarla con ese trabajo, señora.
6. María y Juan se casan la semana que viene.

IV. Supply a new leading statement that will elicit each of the expressions in the list in exercise III.

MODELO **¿Me permite usar su bolígrafo, por favor?** ← Aquí lo tiene.

VOCABULARIO

nouns

el **aduanero**	customs official
el **alacrán**	scorpion
el **baúl**	trunk
el **bolso**	bag, purse
el **botiquín**	first-aid kit
el **campo**	country
la **canastilla**	luggage rack
la **carretera**	highway
la **casualidad**	accident, coincidence
el **cepillo**	brush
el **cepillo de dientes**	toothbrush
la **cola**	line (*literally,* tail)
la **convulsión**	convulsion
el **diente**	tooth
el **documento**	document
la **entrada**	entrance, entry
el **equipo**	equipment
el **espejo**	mirror
la **frontera**	border
el **geólogo,** la **geóloga**	geologist
el (la) **guía**	guide
el **impermeable**	raincoat
la **investigación**	investigation
las **investigaciones**	research
el **jabón**	soap
el **jeep**	jeep
el **magnetómetro**	magnetometer
la **nacionalidad**	nationality
el **paraguas**	umbrella
el **pasajero**	passenger
la **pasta de dientes**	tooth paste
el **peine**	comb
el **portafolio**	portfolio, folder
el **sismómetro**	seismometer
el **soldado**	soldier
el **suelo**	floor, ground
el **temblor**	tremor
el **temblor de tierra**	earthquake
la **toalla**	towel
yanqui	Yankee

verbs

agradecer (**zc**)	to thank
aparecer (**zc**)	to appear
bajar	to get down
componerse (like **poner**)	to get better
correr	to run
facilitar	to facilitate
gritar	to yell, to scream
manejar	to drive
observar	to observe
pasar	to stop by
predecir (like **decir**)	to predict
servir (**de**)	to serve (as), to function (as)
utilizar (**c**)	to use, to utilize

adjectives

bienvenido	welcome
hondureño	Honduran
próximo	next

other expressions

a sus órdenes	at your service
allí adelante	up ahead
aquí tiene	here is, here are
desesperadamente	desperately
detenidamente	carefully
entonces	then
entre	between, among
hacer cola	to wait in line
nada de eso	oh, no; absolutely not
no me diga	you don't say; no kidding
pasado mañana	the day after tomorrow
uno a uno	one by one
venir (**ir**) **a casa**	to come (to go) home

A. Indefinite or negative reference + subjunctive

> Necesitamos encontrar un aduanero que nos **facilite** la entrada.

1. An adjective clause is one that modifies a noun. It occupies the same position in a sentence as an adjective.

Tengo un coche | blanco.	I have a white car.
Tengo un coche | que va muy rápido.	I have a car that goes very fast.

2. The verb in an adjective clause may be either indicative or subjunctive. If the noun being modified refers to something that does not exist in reality, or if the speaker is unsure whether it exists or not, the subjunctive is used.

Buscamos un guía que hable inglés.[1]	We're looking for a guide who speaks English.
Quiero comprar una casa que tenga jardín.	I want to buy a house that has a garden.

3. Sentences that begin with negative expressions nearly always take the subjunctive in an adjective clause, since they deny the existence of the noun modified.

No conozco a nadie que viva cerca de aquí.	I don't know anyone who lives near here.
Busco una tienda donde vendan jabón y pasta de dientes.	I'm looking for a store where they sell soap and toothpaste.
Quiero casarme con una persona que sea buena, inteligente y rica.	I want to marry a person who is good, intelligent, and rich.

Aplicación

I. Explain the difference between the following pairs of sentences.

MODELO Conocemos a un aduanero que nos facilitará la entrada. / Hay que buscar un aduanero que nos facilite la entrada.
In the first sentence, the speaker refers to a specific customs official whom he knows. / In the second, the speaker does not know if such a customs official exists.

1. Tengo un paraguas que no es caro. / Busco un paraguas que no sea caro.
2. Compraron una casa que tiene un patio grande. / Quieren comprar una casa que tenga un patio grande.

[1]Notice that because the person referred to is indefinite, personal **a** is not used. Personal **a** is used, however, with **alguien, nadie,** and other indefinite or negative expressions:
Buscamos a alguien que hable inglés. We're looking for somebody who speaks English.

3. Necesito encontrar un carro que no cueste tanto. / Encontré un carro que no cuesta tanto.
4. No había ningún médico que pudiera atender al niño. / Por suerte había un médico que podía atender al niño.
5. Conocimos a un señor que sabía inglés. / No encontramos a nadie que supiera inglés.

II. Replace the underlined portion of the sentence with the words in parentheses and make any other necessary changes.

MODELOS Tengo una secretaria que sabe español. (Necesito. . .) → **Necesito una secretaria que sepa español.**
Buscaba una tienda donde vendieran jabón. (Allí había. . .) → **Allí había una tienda donde vendían jabón.**

1. Hablamos con un señor que entendía el problema. (Necesitábamos encontrar a alguien. . .)
2. Buscan un periódico que tenga buenos artículos. (Leen. . .)
3. Hay alguien aquí que la conoce. (No hay nadie. . .)
4. Conocíamos a un soldado que hablaba inglés. (No conocíamos a ningún soldado. . .)
5. Quería vivir en un lugar donde no lloviera mucho. (Compré una casa en un lugar. . .)
6. Buscábamos alguien que nos lo mostrara. (Encontramos a alguien. . .)

III. Change the following sentences to the negative.

MODELO Tengo un amigo que es geólogo. → **No tengo ningún amigo que sea geólogo.**

1. Veo a un niño que necesita ayuda.
2. Conozco a una persona que puede atenderlo.
3. Lleva una mochila que contiene medicinas.
4. Hay un pueblo que está cerca de aquí.
5. Allí tienen un restaurante que es bueno.

IV. Complete each sentence with the correct form of the verb.

A. MODELO Éste es el jeep que nosotros ____. (necesitar) → **Éste es el jeep que nosotros necesitamos.**

1. Vamos a ver si encontramos algún soldado que no nos ____ bajar todo el equipo. (hacer)
2. Allí hay uno que ____ simpático. (parecer)
3. Pero tiene que ser alguien que ____ español. (saber)
4. Veo a uno que ____ hablando español. (estar)
5. Esperemos a ése que ____ a esa señora. (atender)

B. MODELO Necesitábamos encontrar a alguien que nos ____ ayudar. (poder) → **Necesitábamos encontrar a alguien que nos pudiera ayudar.**

1. Había varios aduaneros que ____ allí. (trabajar)
2. Pero no había ninguno que ____ el problema. (comprender)
3. Por fin vino un soldado que nos ____ entrar. (hacer)
4. Una mujer gritó, pero no había nadie que la ____. (atender)
5. Bajamos el baúl que ____ el botiquín. (tener)
6. Por suerte, mi amiga era una chica que ____ medicina. (estudiar)

V. Complete the following paragraph any way you wish.

Cuando yo me gradúe, quiero encontrar un trabajo que. . .Quiero trabajar con personas que. . .y que. . .Me gustaría tener una oficina que. . .Prefiero estar en un edificio que. . .

Tal vez yo vaya a otro lugar a vivir. Quiero vivir en un lugar donde. . .y donde. . .Quiero tener una casa que. . . , que. . .y que. . .

Después de trabajar por dos o tres años, me casaré. Quiero casarme con un hombre (una mujer) que. . . , que. . .y que. . .

B. Nominalization

el pasaporte de David y **el de Anita**

In order to avoid repeating the same noun within a sentence or paragraph, the noun may be deleted by a process known as *nominalization.*

1. Nominalization can be achieved simply by deleting the noun after the article or adjective that modifies it. When a noun is deleted after a demonstrative adjective, the adjective is written with an accent mark.

¿Qué toalla quieres, ésta o la que está en el baño?	Which towel do you want, this one or the one that's in the bathroom?

2. Note that when a noun is deleted, the article and adjective that remain continue to show number and gender agreement. Masculine singular **un,** however, becomes **uno.**

Aquí están mi pasaporte y el de Anita.	Here are my passport and Anita's.
De todos los radios me gustan más los alemanes.	Of all radios I like the German ones the most.
Sugiero que compres dos camisas: una negra y otra roja.	I suggest you buy two shirts: a black one and a red one.
Con este libro y uno más, podremos aprobar el examen.	With this book and one other, we'll be able to pass the test.

Aplicación

I. Repeat each sentence, eliminating the noun. Then translate the new sentence into English.

MODELO Me gusta el caballo blanco. → **Me gusta el blanco.** *(I like the white one.)*

1. Es el mejor caballo de la finca.
2. No es tan malo como el caballo de la semana pasada.
3. Me gusta la casa blanca más que la casa amarilla.
4. Este puente se ha caído pero el otro puente no.
5. Las vacas de aquí son muy buenas.
6. El coche nuevo es peor que el coche viejo.
7. Los exámenes de español son tan difíciles como los exámenes de historia.
8. Si ese espejo está roto, usa este espejo.

II. Para expresar en español

A. MODELO this farm and my uncle's → **esta finca y la de mi tío**

1. that comb and María's
2. those towels and my mom's
3. this raincoat and my father's
4. these boots and Oscar's

B. MODELO that book and the one you bought → **ese libro y el que compraste**

1. these exams and the ones he wrote
2. this umbrella and the one you have
3. that soap and the one that's in the bathroom
4. these brushes and the ones you have

C. MODELO I like this umbrella and the red one. → **Me gustan este paraguas y el rojo.**

1. I like this raincoat and the white one.
2. I like these brushes and the other ones.
3. I like those boots and the black ones.
4. I like these towels and the new ones.

III. Para contestar

1. ¿A usted le gusta esta clase tanto como la de matemáticas?
2. ¿Son tan difíciles los exámenes de español como los de inglés?
3. ¿Son mejores los estudiantes de español o los de francés?
4. ¿Quiénes son más guapos, los chicos americanos o los extranjeros?
5. ¿Prefiere usted la vida de ciudad o la del campo?

The Presidential Palace in Tegucigalpa, capital of Honduras.

Pausa oral

Más problemas de todos los días

I. Para comunicar

Act out the following situations with another person.

MODELO Usted está en la frontera. Un soldado le pide sus documentos, pero usted no encuentra el pasaporte.

A: **Sus documentos, por favor, señor.**
B: **Aquí tiene.**
A: **¿Y su pasaporte?**
B: **¿Cómo? ¿No está allí?**
A: **No, señor.**
B: **Pero estoy seguro que lo puse en mi maletín. A ver. . .¿dónde puede estar?**
A: **Bueno, venga conmigo, señor.**
B: **Un momentito, un momentito. Estoy seguro que lo tengo. . .**

1. Usted está haciendo cola en una oficina. De repente una señora empieza a gritar y pide ayuda. Parece que su hijo tiene convulsiones. Usted es estudiante de medicina.
2. Usted pasa la noche en casa de un amigo (una amiga). Él (ella) le muestra todas las cosas que usted podría necesitar: toallas, jabón, donde ducharse. . .Usted le pregunta a qué hora se levantan en la casa, cuándo desayunan y otras cosas.
3. Usted entra a una tienda. Sólo quiere comprar un cepillo de dientes, pero tiene mucha prisa. Hay mucha gente allí que está haciendo cola. Usted le pide a una señora que deje que usted pague primero.
4. Usted escucha el radio. De repente se oye un anuncio para una nueva pasta de dientes estupenda que lo (la) hará a usted más guapo (guapa). Usted piensa que el anuncio es muy malo.
5. Usted está en la aduana y el aduanero examina todo lo que hay en sus maletas. ¡Y tiene muchas!
6. Usted y su amigo están sentados conversando. De repente usted ve un alacrán que se acerca a la mano de su amigo.

II. Para describir

ESTRUCTURA II

A. The words e and u

1. Before a word whose first sound is /**i**/, the word **e** is used instead of **y** to mean *and.*

Anita e Isabel son amigas mías.	Anita and Isabel are friends of mine.
Me interesan mucho las clases de matemáticas e historia.	The mathematics and history classes interest me a lot.

2. Before a word whose first sound is /**o**/, **u** is used instead of **o** to mean *or.*

Pedro y Maricarmen tendrán siete u ocho hijos.	Pedro and Maricarmen probably have seven or eight kids.
Quiero visitar Inglaterra u Holanda.	I want to visit England or Holland.

Aplicación

I. Reverse the order of items in each pair.

A. MODELO hijos y padres → **padres e hijos**

1. ingleses y españoles
2. ideas y problemas
3. historia y biología
4. inglés y francés
5. inteligente y guapo
6. interesante y fácil

B. MODELO horas o minutos → **minutos u horas**

1. Olga o Liliana
2. otros o éste
3. oficinas o apartamentos
4. hombres o mujeres
5. hoteles o iglesias
6. oír música o estudiar

II. Complete each sentence with either **y** or **e.**

MODELO Estudio química _____ biología. → **Estudio química y biología.**

1. Habla español _____ italiano.
2. Tiene muchas opiniones _____ ideas.
3. Ha habido discusiones _____ huelgas.
4. Necesitamos libros _____ cuadernos.
5. Es interesante _____ importante.

III. Complete each sentence with either **o** or **u.**

MODELO No sé si es abogado _____ contador. → **No sé si es abogado o contador.**

1. ¿Necesitas este cuaderno _____ otro?
2. ¿Son casas _____ oficinas?
3. Llevan plata _____ oro.
4. ¿Es en septiembre _____ octubre?
5. ¿Tienes un abrigo _____ un impermeable?

B. Review of the indicative

David y Anita **son** geólogos que **están haciendo** investigaciones.

The indicative system of verbs contains regular and irregular verbs which fall into the general categories of present tense, past tense, future and conditional tenses, and compound tenses. The following is a review of stem-changing and of irregular verb forms in the indicative.

1. A stem-changing verb has two stems. The changes (except for **nosotros** and **vosotros**) in the present are from **e** to **ie, o** to **ue,** and **e** to **i.**

   (pensar) pienso, piensas, piensa, pensamos, pensáis, piensan
   (volver) vuelvo, vuelves, vuelve, volvemos, volvéis, vuelven
   (seguir) sigo, sigues, sigue, seguimos, seguís, siguen

2. The following **yo**-forms are irregular: **sé, veo, doy, estoy, caigo, oigo, traigo, hago, pongo, salgo, conozco;** also all verbs ending in **-ucir: conduzco, traduzco**

3. The following verbs are also irregular.

   (ser) soy, eres, es, somos, sois, son
   (decir) digo, dices, dice, decimos, decís, dicen
   (ir) voy, vas, va, vamos, vais, van
   (tener) tengo, tienes, tiene, tenemos, tenéis, tienen
   (venir) vengo, vienes, viene, venimos, venís, vienen

   The form **hay** *there is, there are* is also irregular and is always singular.

   Hay un alacrán.
   Hay varios alacranes.

4. Only three verbs are irregular in the imperfect.

   (ir) iba, ibas, iba, íbamos, ibais, iban
   (ser) era, eras, era, éramos, erais, eran
   (ver) veía, veías, veía, veíamos, veíais, veían

5. Three irregularities commonly occur in the preterit stem of certain verbs: some verbs contain a **-u** stem (**anduve, estuve, pude, puse, supe, tuve**); others have an **-i** stem (**hice, quise, vine**); and others have a **-j** stem (**conduje, dije, traduje, traje**).

6. Several **-ir** verbs are irregular in the preterit only in the third-person singular or plural. In certain ones **e** changes to **i** (**pidió, prefirió, repitió, siguieron, sugirieron**); in two verbs—**dormir** and **morir—o** changes to **u** (**durmió, murieron**).

7. Three verbs in the preterit are irregular in all forms.

   (ir and ser) fui, fuiste, fue, fuimos, fuisteis, fueron
   (dar) di, diste, dio, dimos, disteis, dieron

   Note that **ir** and **ser** have the same preterit forms.

8. Some common irregular future stems (with the ending for **yo**) are: **diré, habré, pondré, querré, sabré, haré, podré, saldré, tendré, vendré.** The conditional tense uses these same stems: **yo diría, tú pondrías, usted sabría, nosotros haríamos,** etc.

9. Some common irregular past participles are: **abierto, escrito, dicho, ido, visto, muerto, puesto, vuelto, hecho, roto.** These participles are used to form the present perfect and other perfect tenses: **hemos abierto, yo habría ido, habrás visto, ella había dicho,** etc.

10. In the progressive tenses, two basic changes affect the gerund: a) **-ir** verbs with **e** or **o** in their stem change **e** to **i** or **o** to **u** (**siguiendo, durmiendo**); b) **-er** and **-ir** verbs show the spelling change **i** to **y** (**cayendo, leyendo**).

Aplicación

I. Give the present perfect, the present progressive, the preterit, the imperfect, the future, and the conditional.

MODELO Me gradúo. → **Me he graduado.** / **Me estoy graduando.** / **Me gradué.** / **Me graduaba.** / **Me graduaré.** / **Me graduaría.**

1. No salen.
2. ¿Dónde pone las cosas?
3. Termino la tarea.
4. Rompen las tazas.
5. Se acuesta temprano.
6. Lo hacemos.
7. ¿Qué dicen?
8. ¿Ves algo?
9. Oyen el programa.
10. Se siente mal.
11. Traigo algunas cosas.
12. ¿Se caen?

II. Fill in each blank with the correct present tense form of the verb in the list.

1. deber
2. saber
3. tener
4. comprender
5. decir
6. poder
7. sacar
8. gustar
9. haber
10. tener
11. venir
12. estudiar
13. querer
14. conocer
15. poder
16. terminar, nosotras
17. cenar, nosotras
18. ir, nosotras
19. poder
20. mostrar
21. parecer

¿Qué __1__ hacer? Yo no __2__. Esta tarde __3__ un examen en la clase de historia y no __4__ nada. La profesora __5__ que estos exámenes son muy importantes y que nadie __6__ pasar a la próxima clase si no __7__ una buena nota (*good mark*). Pero la verdad es que a mí no me __8__ la historia. __9__ tantos nombres que aprender. ¿Tú __10__ el mismo problema? ¿De veras? Pues, mira, chica, ¿por qué no __11__ a mi casa esta tarde y entonces tú y yo __12__ juntas. O si tú no __13__ venir a mi casa, yo __14__ un lugar muy tranquilo donde nosotras __15__ repasar los apuntes. Y si __16__ temprano, __17__ juntas y __18__ al cine. Mira, tú __19__ traer tus apuntes y libros y yo te __20__ los míos. ¿Qué te __21__ la idea?

III. Write the following story using verbs in the past.

Liliana está estudiando como loca porque tiene un examen de francés y todavía no ha aprendido todos los verbos. O por lo menos Liliana piensa que no sabe los verbos. La verdad es que Liliana es una de esas personas que siempre creen que no saben nada, pero que en realidad lo saben todo.

Liliana le pide ayuda a su hermana Mariana, pero Mariana está viendo un programa de televisión y no quiere levantarse. Le dice que tal vez más tarde. Mariana está segurísima que Liliana ya lo sabe todo y no necesita estudiar más. Liliana estudia hasta muy tarde pero finalmente ya no puede concentrarse más y se acuesta.

A la mañana siguiente Liliana se levanta temprano. Se baña y se viste. No come nada porque está demasiado nerviosa. —Buena suerte—le dicen sus padres cuando sale.

Finalmente llega el autobús y la muchacha sube. Hay mucha gente. Liliana saca sus libros y empieza a repasar los verbos una vez más. Cuando llega a la universidad, va directamente a la clase de francés. Pero no hay nadie. ¿Dónde están los otros estudiantes? Liliana no comprende. Espera un rato y entonces se marcha a la oficina central. Las secretarias se ríen cuando ella les pregunta.

—¿No sabe usted, señorita?—dice una de ellas. Entonces le cuenta que los profesores están en huelga y la universidad ha tenido que suspender todas las clases. Claro que estas cosas siempre se anuncian en la televisión, pero Liliana nunca ve televisión.

Dos semanas después, cuando finalmente termina la huelga, Liliana tiene que repetir toda la experiencia de nuevo. Excepto que esta vez hace el examen y claro que el suyo es el mejor examen de la clase.

IV. Rewrite the following story, changing the subject from **Pedro** to **yo.**

Pedro está haciendo planes. En septiembre se graduará. Entonces buscará un buen trabajo. ¿Qué hará entonces? Pues ganará muchísimo dinero que meterá en el banco. Se comprará una casita y un cochecito y finalmente podrá casarse con Maricarmen. Pedro y Maricarmen tendrán siete u ocho hijos. A Pedro le gustaría tener una familia grande. Jugaría con los niños y ayudaría a su esposa a bañarlos y a vestirlos. Claro que no sería un marido muy típico, pero eso no le importa. Maricarmen y Pedro serían un matrimonio ideal. Todas las noches Pedro vendría a la casa temprano y repasaría la tarea con sus hijos. Entonces Pedro y su familia se sentarían a cenar. ¡Qué hermosa sería la vida!, ¿verdad?

Repaso oral

I. Para contestar

1. ¿A usted le gustaría visitar Centroamérica? ¿Por qué? ¿Qué lugares le gustaría visitar?
2. Si usted fuera geólogo (geóloga), ¿dónde trabajaría? ¿Qué estudiaría?
3. ¿Qué lleva usted cuando va a pasar unos días en casa de un amigo (una amiga)?
4. ¿A usted le gusta la lluvia? ¿Qué hace usted cuando llueve? ¿Qué cosas necesita cuando sale en la lluvia?
5. ¿Qué haría usted si estuviera en una oficina y de repente alguien se pusiera enfermo? ¿Trataría de ayudar? ¿Llamaría a un doctor? ¿Qué haría?
6. ¿A usted le gusta que le digan "yanqui" o no? ¿Por qué?
7. Cuando uno viaja, ¿por qué debe llevar siempre sus documentos?
8. ¿Le gustaría ser guía? ¿Qué le mostraría a la gente?
9. ¿Preferiría usted manejar un jeep o un Cadillac? ¿Por qué?
10. De todas las clases en que se matriculó usted este año, ¿cuál ha sido la más difícil, la más fácil, la más provechosa, la más divertida?

II. Para describir

Describe an imaginary trip you might take with a friend to Central America. The following drawings should provide some suggestions.

Repaso 4

I. Tenses of the Subjunctive

For a review of the formation of the present subjunctive, see Repaso 3, p. 370.

1. To form the past subjunctive tense, begin with the third-person (**ellos**) form of the preterit (**fueron**); delete the **-ron** ending (**fue-**). Then add the following endings: **-ra, -ras, -ra, -́ramos, -rais, -ran.**

   (ser) **fuera, fueras, fuera, fuéramos, fuerais, fueran**

2. To form the present perfect subjunctive tense, use the present subjunctive of **haber** + past participle:

   (volver) **haya (hayas, haya, hayamos, hayáis, hayan) vuelto.**

3. To form the past perfect subjunctive tense, use the imperfect subjunctive of **haber** + past participle:

   (irse) **me hubiera (te hubieras, se hubiera, nos hubiéramos, se hubieran) ido.**

4. In sentences with two clauses in which the verb in one expresses a personal reaction to the verb in the other, there is a normal relationship of tenses between the indicative verb of the first clause and the subjunctive verb of the second clause.

verb one (indicative)	verb two (subjunctive)
present future imperative	present subjunctive
imperfect preterit conditional	past or past perfect subjunctive

5. In sentences with **si** which express an unreal condition, the past subjunctive or past perfect subjunctive is used in the **si**-clause depending on whether the condition applies to the present (past subjunctive) or to the past (past perfect subjunctive).

si-clause	result
(condition in present)	
past subjunctive	conditional
(condition in past)	
past perfect subjunctive	conditional perfect

Si viviéramos en Europa, sería fácil visitar París y Roma. — If we lived in Europe, it would be easy to visit Paris and Rome.
Si yo no hubiera desayunado tan tarde, habría podido almorzar ahora. — If I had not had breakfast so late, I would have been able to have lunch now.

6. If, however, a sentence with **si** expresses a condition which may actually come about, the indicative is used; the tenses correspond to those used in English.

Si voy al campo, tendré que llevar jabón y pasta de dientes. — If I go to the country I'll have to take soap and toothpaste.
Si almorzamos juntos, ¿por qué no buscamos un restaurante barato? — If we have lunch together, why don't we look for a cheap restaurant?

Aplicación

A. Repeat each sentence replacing the underlined portion with the material in parentheses; modify the verb as required.

MODELO Dudo que nos facilite la entrada. (Creo, espero) →
(indicative) **Creo que nos facilita la entrada.**
(subjunctive) **Espero que nos facilite la entrada.**

1. No me gusta que diga eso. (Estoy seguro, me alegro de, estoy enojado de)
2. Busco un coche que no sea caro. (Tengo, necesito encontrar, aquí hay)
3. Te doy la dirección para que vengas. (con tal de que, ya que, puesto que)
4. Quiero que tú me ayudes. (insisto en, necesito, me parece)
5. Es necesario que lo hagan. (es verdad, es imposible, es estupendo)
6. Yo me quedé porque ellos salían. (ya que, para que, puesto que)
7. Terminé después de que tú viniste. (antes de que, sin que, cuando)
8. Sabíamos que ellos estaban allí. (preferíamos, dudábamos, creíamos)

B. Supply the correct form: indicative, subjunctive, or infinitive.

MODELO (seguir) El soldado quiere que ellos lo ____. → **El soldado quiere que ellos lo sigan.**

(sacar) Anita abre su portafolio para ____ los documentos. → **Anita abre su portafolio para sacar los documentos.**

1. (venir) Si tú ____ a mi casa, vamos a montar a caballo.
2. (nadar) Yo preferiría ____ en el lago.
3. (llevar) No te olvides de ____ una toalla.
4. (tener) Si nosotros ____ el coche, podríamos partir ahora.
5. (haber) Buscamos algún lugar donde no ____ tanta gente.
6. (volver) David nos da el jeep con tal de que nosotros ____ temprano.
7. (empezar) Queremos volver antes de que ____ a llover.
8. (ver) Vamos al campo para que nuestros amigos ____ la finca.
9. (llegar) Cuando nosotros ____ allí, te diré lo que pasó en la aduana.
10. (facilitar) Anita y David esperaban que el aduanero les ____ la entrada.
11. (hacer) Querían encontrar uno que no les ____ bajar el equipo.
12. (estacionar) El soldado les pidió que ____ el jeep.
13. (hacer) A mí no me gusta ____ cola.
14. (buscar) Había una señora que ____ un médico.
15. (estar) Ella tenía miedo de que su hijito ____ muy enfermo.
16. (entender) Pero no había ningún médico que ____ el problema.
17. (poder) Yo creía que Anita ____ ayudar.
18. (dar) Cuando yo me ____ cuenta de lo que había pasado, me puse furioso.
19. (llevar) La señora quería que nosotros la ____ a Sabanagrande.
20. (haber tenido) Si nosotros ____ tiempo, habríamos ido.
21. (querer) Pasaremos la noche en la finca a menos que ustedes no ____.
22. (traer) No puedo ir porque yo no ____ mi cepillo y las otras cosas que necesito.
23. (llover) Y ¿qué hacemos si ____?
24. (estar) Si el día no ____ bonito, no podremos ir.
25. (empezar) Tendremos que esperar hasta que ____ el verano.

II. Review

Translate the English sentences which follow into Spanish. For each sentence a Spanish model is provided with the basic structure of the sentence to be translated.

1. Llevan una gran cantidad de oro que van a contrabandear.
   They are carrying $1,000,000 which they're going to hide.
2. Ellos esperaban que yo me casara.
   They wanted the kids to get up.
3. Cada persona va a tener que hacer eso.
   No one will have to miss the party.
4. Aun si perdiéramos la mitad de las jaulas, todavía podríamos irnos ricos de aquí.
   Even if we found the highway, we would still arrive there late.
5. Raúl y Leandro acababan de llegar al estadio cuando empezó el partido.
   Cristina and Manolo had just left Paris when the French lost the World Cup.

6. Quiero ducharme antes de desayunar.
   I want to go to bed after seeing the film.
7. En caso que te acuestes temprano, dime lo que quieres.
   Before you get married, look at what you're doing.
8. Si Anita hubiera escuchado mis consejos, habría terminado el trabajo.
   If we had gone shopping, we would have bought a stereo.
9. Tan pronto como me digan qué necesitan, yo lo haré encantado.
   After they told me what they wanted, I did it happily.
10. No pensamos ni verla, ni escribirle.
    I don't plan on majoring either in biology or in mathematics.
11. No encontré nada que yo pudiera usar.
    I didn't meet anyone who could help me.
12. Lo inevitable es que todos nos vamos a morir.
    The sure thing is that we'll all have a good time.
13. Al saber lo que querían, él dejó de preguntar.
    Upon realizing what was happening, he stopped talking.
14. Querer es poder.
    Seeing is believing.

Segunda lectura sobre civilización hispánica

A principios del siglo XX España empezaba a recuperarse del tremendo golpe[1] que los Estados Unidos le habían dado en la guerra del '98[1]. El precio de la guerra para España había sido perder Cuba, Puerto Rico y las Filipinas, las últimas posesiones ultramarinas[1]. El trauma y la humillación de la derrota a manos del nuevo coloso[1] obligaron a los intelectuales en España a considerar muy seriamente la decadencia del país y a estudiar muy a fondo[1] el espíritu del pueblo español y el futuro de la nación.

blow
overseas
colossus
in depth

Estas investigaciones, aunque no dieron una visión nítida[1] del futuro de España, provocaron un mini-renacimiento[1] de las letras españolas[1]. Por primera vez desde el tiempo de Cervantes, había escritores españoles con impacto considerable en la vida intelectual del mundo occidental.

clear
mini-renaissance
Spanish literature

El versátil Miguel de Unamuno (1864–1936), quien era catedrático universitario[1] y ensayista filosófico, poeta, novelista y dramaturgo, dejó una obra[1] muy extensa—solamente contando sus ensayos y artículos pasamos de[1] 3.000. En 1912 Unamuno escribe *Del sentimiento trágico de la vida* en donde examina en forma brillante el conflicto entre la razón y la fe[1]. Unamuno, humanista ciento por ciento[1], sostenía que el individuo, y no la civilización ni la sociedad ni la cultura, era el tema y objeto supremo de todo pensamiento[1].

college professor
body of work
we count more than
reason and faith / one hundred percent
thought (thinking)

Miguel de Unamuno, oil painting by Ignacio Zuloaga y Zamora.

"Adelita," woman soldier in the Mexican Revolution, in a classic photograph by Agustín Víctor Casasola, 1913.

José Ortega y Gasset (1883–1955) empieza a darse a conocer[1] en 1914 cuando publica sus *Meditaciones del Quijote,* explorando temas que los filósofos existencialistas[2] popularizarían unos diez años después en Europa. De Ortega se conocen bien en el mundo occidental *La deshumanización del arte* (1925), en la cual Ortega insiste en un arte "puro", alejado[1] de la realidad y sin función social, y *La rebelión de las masas* (1930), en donde Ortega explica cómo la "hiperdemocracia" de las masas vulgares[1], desgraciadamente[1], ha creado una dictadura basada en falsos valores[1], derrotando[1] a la "minoría selecta" *(élite),* a la antigua clase directiva.

begins to be known
removed from
popular / unfortunately
values / displacing

Por esa misma época[1] y al otro lado del Atlántico, México experimentaba[1] una tremenda revolución que trasciende[1] límites políticos y que transforma toda una sociedad. Durante una década la Revolución Mexicana de 1910 efectúa[1] grandes cambios tan drásticos que empujan[1] violentamente a un país medieval hacia el siglo XX con todos los

About the same time
was undergoing / goes beyond
accomplishes / push

problemas y esperanzas de una nación en desarrollo[1]. Por todo el mundo los nombres de los revolucionarios Emiliano Zapata, Pancho Villa y Francisco I. Madero van de boca en boca[1].

Sin embargo, otras figuras mexicanas fueron destinadas a obtener aun[1] más fama: los pintores, novelistas e intelectuales mexicanos que captaron[1] a través de[1] diferentes medios[1] el espectáculo terrible y fascinante de una verdadera revolución. Diego Rivera (1887-1957) pintó sus maravillosos murales en edificios públicos en México y también en el extranjero[1][3]. Rivera combinó las formas del arte moderno europeo con las tradiciones artísticas locales (las indígenas y las españolas) para presentar en forma vívida a México. Mariano Azuela (1873-1952), novelista que participó en persona en la lucha armada[1], da al mundo en 1915 su obra *Los de abajo*[4], la cual ilustra perfectamente uno de los aspectos negativos de la revolución—la inutilidad de mucho de los esfuerzos[1] humanos por llevar a cabo cambios.

developing country
van... are widely talked about
even
captured / through / mediums
en . . . abroad
armed struggle
efforts

Mural by Diego Rivera in a public market, Mexico City.

Rubén Darío, Nicaraguan poet, in a portrait by Vázquez Díaz.

Fuera ya de México, pero en el centro de la vida artística de Hispanoamérica, dos poetas contribuyen notablemente a la literatura del mundo. Ruben Darío (1867–1916), poeta y diplomático nicaragüense, creó un nuevo estilo poético e inició una nueva escuela estética en la literatura en español de España y de Hispanoamérica conocida con el nombre de *modernismo*[5]. Gabriela Mistral (1889–1957), poetisa, diplomática y educadora chilena—premio Nobel en literatura en 1946—se distingue[1] por su profunda compasión por los humildes[1] y los necesitados[1]. Su obra la ha colocado entre las primeras figuras de la poesía de habla española de este siglo[6].

stands out / humble
needy

Por estos años, siguiendo[1] la renovación iniciada por la debacle militar de 1898, había otros artistas vigorosamente activos. En la música, Pablo Casals (1876–1973) revolucionó ciertamente la forma de tocar el violoncello mientras que Andrés Segovia (1894) se ha destacado[1] como gran guitarrista clásico. El virtuosismo de Segovia, indudablemente[1], ha ayudado a elevar la importancia de la guitarra como instrumento para solos. Claudio Arráu (1903), pianista chileno, goza de[1] fama internacional como intérprete de Beethoven.

following
stands out
undoubtedly
enjoys

Y si en la música ha habido[1] artistas de primera categoría, ni que decir de[1] la pintura, la cual ha tenido famosísimos artistas como Pablo Picasso, Salvador Dalí, Joan Miró y Juan Gris.

there have been
needless to say

Hablemos del más famoso, del super-estrella[1], Pablo Ruiz Picasso (1881–1973), cuya cuantiosa[1] y valiosa[1] aportación[1] al desarrollo del arte moderno europeo ha sido rivalizada por muy pocos. Picasso, colaborando con Georges Braque, echó a andar[1] el cubismo, y, si no creó el surrealismo[7], Picasso no está enteramente desligado[1] de tal movimiento. Picasso, sin embargo, es realmente inclasificable porque siempre fue muy individualista.

super-star
copious / valuable / contribution
initiated
not entirely unrelated

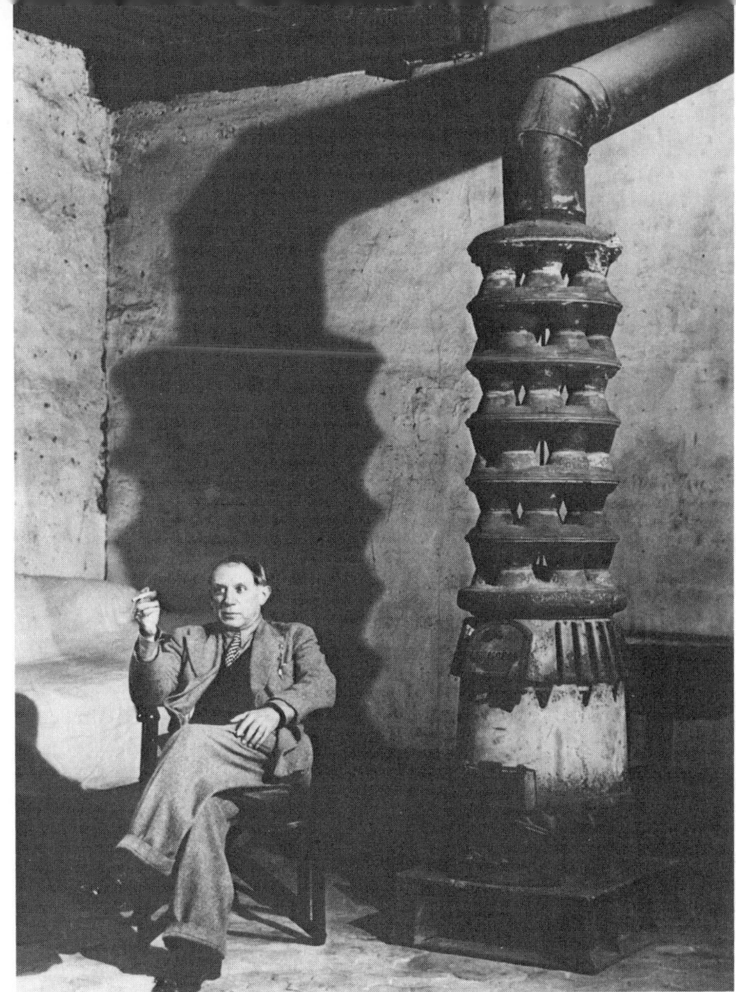

Pablo Picasso in his studio in Paris, 1939, in a photograph by Brassaï.

El arte de Picasso desafía el punto de vista tradicional del observador y desafía también la forma tradicional de clasificar a un artista. Muchos han dicho que Picasso es como el siglo XX: muy complejo. No obstante, se puede hablar de varios períodos o fases. Su primer estilo personal fue el *período azul,* con temas melancólicos y predominio del color azul. Después vino otra época con colores más vivos y, con frecuencia, aparecieron escenas de circos. Más tarde Picasso pintó grandes figuras macizas. En 1907 Picasso pintó *Les Demoiselles d'Avignon* y esta obra marcó un hito en el arte moderno. De este cuadro de cinco mujeres monstruosas con máscaras se origina el cubismo. Después de la Primera Guerra Mundial, Picasso pinta imágenes de los sueños, pero también pinta en forma "clásica" figuras grandes y dignas. Después de 1945 Picasso empieza a pintar en forma menos tormentosa y de una manera más suave y tranquila.

challenges
viewer
circus scenes
massive
marcó . . . became a landmark
painting / monstrous / masks
World War I
dignified, stately
troubled / gentle

En las letras hay por lo menos unos veinte nombres de "estrellas refulgentes". Mencionemos sólo a cuatro:

shining

Pablo Neruda (1904–1973), chileno, poeta y premio Nobel de literatura en 1971. Su obra es muy extensa y variada. Neruda tiene poesía° amorosa (el amor sereno), poesía surrealista (los sueños dominan en gran parte), poesía política (sus creencias° marxistas se manifiestan) y poesía de temas sociales y americanistas, es decir, latinoamericanistas. Muchos críticos lo consideran el mejor poeta de Hispanoamérica.

poetry
beliefs

Jorge Luis Borges (1899), argentino, ensayista, poeta y gran maestro del cuento°. Utilizando tanto temas hispanoamericanos como universales, Borges ha logrado capturar un numeroso público por todo el mundo.

maestro . . . master of the short story

Octavio Paz (1914), mexicano, el poeta vivo° más importante de su país. Paz, además° de la poesía, cultiva el ensayo en forma magistral°. Ha estudiado a fondo el ser del mexicano° y el lugar de Latinoamérica en el mundo.

alive, living
besides / masterly, superb
the Mexican soul (being)

Gabriel García Márquez (1928), colombiano, novelista de fama internacional, la cual obtuvo con su novela *Cien años de soledad* (1967). García Márquez con esta interesante obra no sólo nos ha dado una gran historia—la de la familia Buendía—sino también una representación mítica° de una cultura del "tercer mundo"°.

mythical / "third world"

Las últimas dos décadas del siglo XX prometen ser años de intensa, variada y abundante actividad cultural, tanto en España como en Hispanoamérica. En España, desde la muerte de Francisco Franco (1892–1975), se ha observado un gran incremento° en la producción de la obra literaria, de la pintura, de la escultura y de la música. El pueblo español acude° a conciertos, museos y exposiciones° en mayores° números cada día. Los teatros se encuentran llenos de bote en bote° cuando se estrenan° nuevas obras de dramaturgos españoles.

increase
attends / exhibitions / larger
filled to capacity
are premiered

En Hispanoamérica se observa algo parecido°. La cultura continúa floreciendo, sobre todo° en aquellos países que han gozado de estabilidad política y económica durante los últimos treinta años. México, la nación más grande de habla española con 80 millones de habitantes, ha llogrado° mantener un sistema de gobierno constitucional con sus respectivos cambios pacíficos de presidentes. Su economía, por muchos años en aprietos°, con toda seguridad° mejorará pues en estos últimos años se han descubierto grandes yacimientos petrolíferos superiores a los 200 mil millones° de barriles de petróleo. La opinión general es de que si la situación ya era propicia a las actividades culturales en el México "pre-petrolero", un México más próspero cultivará las artes a una escala mucho mayor°.

similar
especially
managed
en. . . troubled / **con. . .** surely
yacimientos. . . oil deposits surpassing 200 billion
on a larger scale

Finalmente, en los últimos cinco o seis años España ha comenzado a desarrollar muy fuertes relaciones comerciales y artísticas con México y con la mayoría de los países hispanoamericanos de Sudamérica. Estas actividades, indudablemente, contribuirán a crear una situación ideal para el progreso económico de los países participantes. También se espera, claro está, una revitalización general del ambiente[1] artístico y literario.

[1] climate

Glosas

1. Spain was defeated by the United States in the short Spanish-American War of 1898. The United States justified its participation in the war on the grounds that it was fighting to free the oppressed Cubans. However, the immediate excuse for its taking up arms was provided by a mysterious explosion aboard the battleship *Maine* as it lay at anchor in the Havana harbor in February, 1898. The Treaty of Paris (October, 1898) re-established peace between the two countries, rang down the curtain on Spain's overseas empire, left Puerto Rico and the Philippines under American sovereignty, and placed Cuba under temporary American custody.
2. Existentialist philosophers hold that existence is prior to essence, that man makes himself what he is, and that individuals are responsible only to themselves for what they become.
3. Rivera's murals decorate the Presidential Palace, the Palace of Fine Arts, and the Ministry of Education in Mexico City as well as the National Agricultural School of Chapingo, outside Mexico City, and the Palace of Cortés in Cuernavaca. In the United States, murals are found in the City College of San Francisco and the Detroit Institute of Fine Arts.
4. Mariano Azuela, an M.D., was a lieutenant colonel in charge of medical services for the troops of Julián Medina, a revolutionary general who had allied himself with the army of Pancho Villa. When Villa's forces were defeated in 1915, Azuela took refuge in El Paso, Texas, where he finished and first published *Los de abajo (The Underdogs).* The novel was published in serial form by the El Paso newspaper, *El Paso del Norte,* between October and December, 1915.
5. *Modernismo* was an aesthetic movement destined to revitalize Hispanic literature, especially poetry, with new sounds, images, and themes. Modernist works emphasize sensuality, refinement, sophistication, and exquisiteness; they also frequently involve deep analysis, serious meditation, and profound concern for philosophical, religious, historical, and political matters.
6. Gabriela Mistral also taught for a while in the United States, at Barnard College. Her books of poetry include *Desolación,* 1922; *Ternura,* 1924; *Tala,* 1938; and *Lagar,* 1954. Mistral's language is strong, simple, and direct. Her themes include frustrated love, children, maternal love, and the future of the Hispanic peoples.
7. *Cubism* is a style of painting, drawing, and sculpture in which objects are represented by cubes or other geometrical forms rather than by realistic details. *Surrealism,* another style of painting and sculpture that made itself felt in literature as well, tries to show what takes place in the subconscious mind. Surrealistic images often combine the conventional and unconventional. (In Spanish, the words **surrealismo, superrealismo,** and **suprarrealismo** all refer to surrealism.)

Gabriela Mistral, in an oil painting by José María López Mezquita.

SOBRE LA LECTURA

I. Para contestar

1. ¿Qué golpe sufrió España a principios del siglo XX?
2. ¿Qué provocó un mini-renacimiento de las letras españolas?
3. ¿Quién fue Miguel de Unamuno?
4. ¿Cuáles son algunas de las ideas más importantes de Ortega y Gasset?
5. ¿Qué pasaba en México durante este período?
6. ¿En qué año empezó la Revolución Mexicana? ¿Qué efecto tuvo?
7. ¿Cuáles son algunos artistas mexicanos que obtuvieron fama durante la primera parte del siglo XX?
8. ¿Quiénes fueron Rubén Darío y Gabriela Mistral?
9. Mencione usted a tres grandes músicos hispánicos.
10. ¿Cuál es el pintor español más famoso del siglo XX? ¿Con qué movimientos artísticos está asociado?
11. Describa usted algunos de los estilos de Picasso.
12. ¿Qué sabe usted de Pablo Neruda?
13. ¿Quién es Jorge Luis Borges? ¿Octavio Paz? ¿Gabriel García Márquez?
14. ¿Participan los españoles en muchas actividades culturales?
15. ¿Pasa lo mismo en Hispanoamérica? Explique.

II. Discusión

1. ¿Conoce usted algunos cuadros de Pablo Picasso? ¿Qué opina usted de su forma de pintar? ¿Le gusta o no? ¿Por qué?
2. ¿Ha leído usted alguna historia o novela de un escritor hispánico? ¿Cuál? ¿Sobre qué era?
3. ¿Piensa usted que ocurre en los EE.UU. una revitalización artística? ¿Por qué?

Appendix

THE SPANISH ALPHABET

LETTER	NAME	LETTER	NAME	LETTER	NAME
a	a	**j**	jota	**r**	ere
b	be	**k**	ka	**rr**	erre
c	ce	**l**	ele	**s**	ese
ch	che	**ll**	elle	**t**	te
d	de	**m**	eme	**u**	u
e	e	**n**	ene	**v**	ve (uve)
f	ele	**ñ**	eñe	**w**	doble ve (uve)
g	ge	**o**	o	**x**	equis
h	hache	**p**	pe	**y**	i griega
i	i	**q**	cu	**z**	zeta

Spanish is written with the same 26 letters used to write English, plus **ch, ll, ñ,** and **rr.** These four letters or letter combinations each represent a specific sound. The letters **k** and **w** occur only in a few words of foreign origin—for example, **Kremlín, whiski.**

SPANISH SPELLING CONVENTIONS

1. The three consonantal sounds /k/, /g/, and /x/ are represented by different letters, depending on the vowel that follows them.

/k/ Written **c** before **a, o, u** and **qu** before **e, i.**

ca	café	**que**	pequeño
co	banco	**qui**	quince
cu	Cuba		

/g/ Written **g** before **a, o, u** and **gu** before **e, i.**

ga	llegar	**gue**	despegue
go	diálogo	**gui**	guía
gu	gusto		

/x/ Often written **j** before all vowels; before **e** and **i,** written **g** in some words.

ja	viajar	**ge**	inteligente
jo	joven	**gi**	corregir
ju	junio		
je	extranjero		
ji	hijito		

2. The vowel **i,** when it appears between two vowels and is not accented, is written **y.**

creyó	leyó
creyeron	leyeron
creyendo	leyendo

But, when the **i** is accented, it is written **i.**

creía
leían

STEM CHANGE MARKERS

In the chapter vocabulary lists and the vocabularies at the back of the book, verb entries have been marked with a series of letter symbols to show that in certain tenses and forms, changes in the stem occur. The symbols are as follows.

1. *Stem-vowel changes.*
   (ie)
   (ue)
   (i)
   (ie, i)
   (ue, u)
   (í)
   (ú)
   } See the Verb Tables following the Appendix.

2. *Irregularity.*
   (zc) Signals an irregularity in the first-person singular of the present indicative and the related subjunctive and command forms: **parecer → yo parezco; parezca usted,** etc. Verbs marked this way behave like **conocer,** entered in the list of irregular verbs in the Verb Tables.

3. *Spelling changes.* See Spanish Spelling Conventions in this Appendix. To recapitulate:
   (c) **z** changes to **c** before **e,** as in **economizar → economicé.**
   (qu) **c** changes to **qu** before **e,** as in **buscar → busqué.**
   (gu) **g** changes to **gu** before **e,** as in **pagar → pagué.**
   (j) **g** changes to **j** before **o** or **a,** as in **proteger → protejo.**
   (y) **i,** when it appears between two vowels and is not accented, is written **y,** as in **creer → creyó.**

Verb Tables

REGULAR VERBS

	-ar	**-er**	**-ir**
INFINITIVE	llamar	comprender	vivir
GERUND	llamando	comprendiendo	viviendo
PAST PARTICIPLE	llamado	comprendido	vivido

Indicative

PRESENT	llamo	comprendo	vivo
(**llamo** *I call, do*	llamas	comprendes	vives
call, am calling)	llama	comprende	vive
	llamamos	comprendemos	vivimos
	llamáis	comprendéis	vivís
	llaman	comprenden	viven
IMPERFECT	llamaba	comprendía	vivía
(**llamaba** *I was*	llamabas	comprendías	vivías
calling, called)	llamaba	comprendía	vivía
	llamábamos	comprendíamos	vivíamos
	llamabais	comprendíais	vivíais
	llamaban	comprendían	vivían
PRETERIT	llamé	comprendí	viví
(**llame** *I called,*	llamaste	comprendiste	viviste
did call)	llamó	comprendió	vivió
	llamamos	comprendimos	vivimos
	llamasteis	comprendisteis	vivisteis
	llamaron	comprendieron	vivieron

FUTURE (**llamaré** *I will call, shall call*)	llamaré llamarás llamará llamaremos llamaréis llamarán	comprenderé comprenderás comprenderá comprenderemos comprenderéis comprenderán	viviré vivirás vivirá viviremos viviréis vivirán
CONDITIONAL (**llamaría** *I would call*)	llamaría llamarías llamaría llamaríamos llamaríais llamarían	comprendería comprenderías comprendería comprenderíamos comprenderíais comprenderían	viviría vivirías viviría viviríamos viviríais vivirían

PRESENT PERFECT (**he llamado** *I have called*)	he has ha hemos habéis han	llamado, compren-dido, vivido	PAST PERFECT (**había llamado** *I had called*)	había habías había habíamos habíais habían	llamado, compren-dido, vivido
FUTURE PERFECT (**habré llamado** *I will have called*)	habré habrás habrá habremos habréis habrán	llamado, compren-dido, vivido	CONDITIONAL PERFECT (**habría llamado** *I would have called*)	habría habrías habría habríamos habríais habrían	llamado, compren-dido, vivido

Subjunctive

PRESENT (**llame** *that I call*)	llame llames llame llamemos llaméis llamen	comprenda comprendas comprenda comprendamos comprendáis comprendan	viva vivas viva vivamos viváis vivan
PAST (**llamara** *that I called*)	llamara llamaras llamara llamáramos llamarais llamaran	comprendiera comprendieras comprendiera comprendiéramos comprendierais comprendieran	viviera vivieras viviera viviéramos vivierais vivieran

PRESENT PERFECT (**haya llamado** *that I have called*)	haya hayas haya hayamos hayáis hayan	llamado, compren-dido, vivido	PAST PERFECT (**hubiera llamado** *that I had called*)	hubiera hubieras hubiera hubiéramos hubierais hubieran	llamado, compren-dido, vivido

Commands

FAMILIAR (**tú**) COMMANDS (**llama** *call,* **no llames** *don't call*)	llama (tú), no llames (tú)	comprende, no comprendas	vive, no vivas
FAMILIAR (**vosotros**) COMMANDS (**llamad** *call,* **no llaméis** *don't call*)	llamad (vosotros), no llaméis (vosotros)	comprended, no comprendáis	vivid, no viváis
FORMAL (**usted**) COMMANDS (**llame** *call,* **no llame** *don't call*)	llame (usted), no llame (usted)	comprenda, no comprenda	viva, no viva
FORMAL (**ustedes**) COMMANDS (**llamen** *call,* **no llamen** *don't call*)	llamen (ustedes), no llamen (ustedes)	comprendan, no comprendan	vivan, no vivan
Let's (**nosotros**) COMMANDS (**llamemos** *let's call,* **no llamemos** *let's not call*)	llamemos (nosotros), no llamemos (nosotros)	comprendamos, no comprendamos	vivamos, no vivamos

STEM-CHANGING VERBS

	(e → ie)	**(o → ue)**	**(u → ue)**	**(e → i)**
INFINITIVE	pensar	contar	jugar (gu)	pedir
GERUND	pensando	contando	jugando	pidiendo
PAST PARTICIPLE	pensado	contado	jugado	pedido
PRESENT INDICATIVE	pienso piensas piensa pensamos pensáis piensan	cuento cuentas cuenta contamos contáis cuentan	juego juegas juega jugamos jugáis juegan	pido pides pide pedimos pedís piden
PRESENT SUBJUNCTIVE	piense pienses piense pensemos penséis piensen	cuente cuentes cuente contemos contéis cuenten	juegue[1] juegues juegue juguemos juguéis jueguen	pida pidas pida pidamos pidáis pidan

[1]The change from **g** to **gu** before **e** is a regular spelling change.

COMMANDS	piensa,	cuenta,	juega,	pide,
tú	no pienses	no cuentes	no juegues	no pidas
usted	(no) piense	(no) cuente	(no) juegue	(no) pida
nosotros	(no) pensemos	(no) contemos	(no) juguemos	(no) pidamos
vosotros	pensad,	contad,	jugad,	pedid,
ustedes	no penséis	no contéis	no juguéis	no pidéis
	(no) piensen	(no) cuenten	(no) jueguen	(no) pidan
PRETERIT	*(no stem change)*	*(no stem change)*	*(no stem change; spelling change in* ***jugué****)*	pedí
				pediste
				pidió
				pedimos
				pedisteis
				pidieron
PAST SUBJUNCTIVE	*(no stem change)*	*(no stem change)*	*(no stem change)*	pidiera
				pidieras
				pidiera
				pidiéramos
				pidierais
				pidieran

	(e → ie, i)	**(o → ue, u)**
INFINITIVE	preferir	dormir
GERUND	prefiriendo	durmiendo
PAST PARTICIPLE	preferido	dormido
PRESENT INDICATIVE	prefiero	duermo
	prefieres	duermes
	prefiere	duerme
	preferimos	dormimos
	preferís	dormís
	prefieren	duermen
PRESENT SUBJUNCTIVE	prefiera	duerma
	prefieras	duermas
	prefiera	duerma
	prefiramos	durmamos
	prefiráis	durmáis
	prefieran	duerman
COMMANDS	prefiere,	duerme,
tú	no prefieras	no duermas
usted	(no) prefiera	(no) duerma
nosotros	(no) prefiramos	(no) durmamos
vosotros	preferid,	dormid,
ustedes	no prefiráis	no durmáis
	(no) prefieran	(no) duerman

PRETERIT	preferí preferiste prefirió preferimos preferisteis prefirieron	dormí dormiste durmió dormimos dormisteis durmieron
PAST SUBJUNCTIVE	prefiriera prefirieras prefiriera prefiriéramos prefirierais prefirieran	durmiera durmieras durmiera durmiéramos durmierais durmieran
	(i → í)	**(u → ú)**
INFINITIVE	variar	continuar
GERUND	variando	continuando
PAST PARTICIPLE	variado	continuado
PRESENT INDICATIVE	varío varías varía variamos variáis varían	continúo continúas continúa continuamos continuáis continúan
PRESENT SUBJUNCTIVE	varíe varíes varíe variemos variéis varíen	continúe continúes continúe continuemos continuéis continúen
AFFIRMATIVE **tú** COMMAND	varía	continúa

IRREGULAR VERBS

Each verb entry begins with the infinitive, gerund, and past participle. Only tenses with irregularities are listed. For the other tenses, keep in mind the following:

1. In all tenses, *spelling changes* occur if appropriate. (See the summary of spelling-change rules at the beginning of the Appendix.)
2. The *present subjunctive,* when regularly formed, will have in every form any irregularity found in the stem of the first-person singular of the present indicative.
3. *Commands.* Affirmative and negative **usted, ustedes,** and **nosotros** commands; negative **tú;** and negative **vosotros** commands will have the same stem irregularities found in the corresponding subjunctive forms.

4. The *past subjunctive* will have in every form any irregularity found in the stem of the third-person plural of the preterit.

abrir (abriendo, **abierto**) *to open*

andar (andando, andado) *to walk*

PRETERIT	**anduve, anduviste, anduvo, anduvimos, anduvisteis, anduvieron**

caer (cayendo, caído) *to fall*

PRESENT INDICATIVE	**caigo,** caes, cae, caemos, caéis, caen

conducir (zc) (conduciendo, conducido) *to drive*

PRESENT INDICATIVE	**conduzco,** conduces, conduce, conducimos, conducís, conducen
PRETERIT	**conduje, condujiste, condujo, condujimos, condujisteis, condujeron**

conocer (zc) (conociendo, conocido) *to know*

PRESENT INDICATIVE	**conozco,** conoces, conoce, conocemos, conocéis, conocen

dar (dando, dado) *to give*

PRESENT INDICATIVE	**doy,** das, da, damos, dais, dan
PRETERIT	**di, diste, dio, dimos, disteis, dieron**
PRESENT SUBJUNCTIVE	**dé,** des, **dé,** demos, deis, den

decir (diciendo, dicho) *to say, to tell*

PRESENT INDICATIVE	**digo, dices, dice,** decimos, decís, **dicen**
PRETERIT	**dije, dijiste, dijo, dijimos, dijisteis, dijeron**
FUTURE	**diré, dirás, dirá, diremos, diréis, dirán**
CONDITIONAL	**diría, dirías, diría, diríamos, diríais, dirían**
AFFIRMATIVE **tú** COMMAND	**di**

escribir (escribiendo, **escrito**) *to write*

estar (estando, estado) *to be*

PRESENT INDICATIVE	**estoy, estás, está,** estamos, estáis, **están**
PRETERIT	**estuve, estuviste, estuvo, estuvimos, estuvisteis, estuvieron**
PRESENT SUBJUNCTIVE	**esté, estés, esté, estemos, estéis, estén**

haber (habiendo, habido) *to have* (auxiliary)

PRESENT INDICATIVE	**he, has, ha, hemos,** habéis, **han**
PRETERIT	**hube, hubiste, hubo, hubimos, hubisteis, hubieron**
FUTURE	**habré, habrás, habrá, habremos, habréis, habrán**
CONDITIONAL	**habría, habrías, habría, habríamos, habríais, habrían**
PRESENT SUBJUNCTIVE	**haya, hayas, haya, hayamos, hayáis, hayan**

hacer (haciendo, **hecho**) *to do, to make*

PRESENT INDICATIVE	**hago,** haces, hace, hacemos, hacéis, hacen
PRETERIT	**hice, hiciste, hizo, hicimos, hicisteis, hicieron**
FUTURE	**haré, harás, hará, haremos, haréis, harán**
CONDITIONAL	**haría, harías, haría, haríamos, haríais, harían**
AFFIRMATIVE **tú** COMMAND	**haz**

ir (**yendo,** ido) *to go*

PRESENT INDICATIVE	**voy, vas, va, vamos, vais, van**
IMPERFECT	**iba, ibas, iba, íbamos, ibais, iban**
PRETERIT	**fui, fuiste, fue, fuimos, fuisteis, fueron**
PRESENT SUBJUNCTIVE	**vaya, vayas, vaya, vayamos, vayáis, vayan**
AFFIRMATIVE **tú** COMMAND	**ve**

morir (**ue, u**) (muriendo, **muerto**) *to die*

oír (oyendo, oído) *to hear*

PRESENT INDICATIVE	**oigo,** oyes, oye, oímos, oís, oyen

poder (**ue**) (**pudiendo,** podido) *to be able*

PRETERIT	**pude, pudiste, pudo, pudimos, pudisteis, pudieron**
FUTURE	**podré, podrás, podrá, podremos, podréis, podrán**
CONDITIONAL	**podría, podrías, podría, podríamos, podríais, podrían**

poner (poniendo, **puesto**) *to put, to place*

PRESENT INDICATIVE	**pongo,** pones, pone, ponemos, ponéis, ponen
PRETERIT	**puse, pusiste, puso, pusimos, pusisteis, pusieron**
FUTURE	**pondré, pondrás, pondrá, pondremos, pondréis, pondrán**
CONDITIONAL	**pondría, pondrías, pondría, pondríamos, pondríais, pondrían**
AFFIRMATIVE **tú** COMMAND	**pon**

querer (**ie**) (queriendo, querido) *to want, to love*

PRETERIT	**quise, quisiste, quiso, quisimos, quisisteis, quisieron**
FUTURE	**querré, querrás, querrá, querremos, querréis, querrán**
CONDITIONAL	**querría, querrías, querría, querríamos, querríais, querrían**

romper (rompiendo, **roto**) *to break*

saber (sabiendo, sabido) *to know*

PRESENT INDICATIVE	**sé,** sabes, sabe, sabemos, sabéis, saben
PRETERIT	**supe, supiste, supo, supimos, supisteis, supieron**
FUTURE	**sabré, sabrás, sabrá, sabremos, sabréis, sabrán**
CONDITIONAL	**sabría, sabrías, sabría, sabríamos, sabríais, sabrían**
PRESENT SUBJUNCTIVE	**sepa, sepas, sepa, sepamos, sepáis, sepan**

salir (saliendo, salido) *to go out*

PRESENT INDICATIVE	**salgo,** sales, sale, salimos, salís, salen
FUTURE	**saldré, saldrás, saldrá, saldremos, saldréis, saldrán**
CONDITIONAL	**saldría, saldrías, saldría, saldríamos, saldríais, saldrían**
AFFIRMATIVE **tú** COMMAND	**sal**

ser (siendo, sido) *to be*

PRESENT INDICATIVE	**soy, eres, es, somos, sois, son**
IMPERFECT	**era, eras, era, éramos, erais, eran**
PRETERIT	**fui, fuiste, fue, fuimos, fuisteis, fueron**
PRESENT SUBJUNCTIVE	**sea, seas, sea, seamos, seáis, sean**
AFFIRMATIVE **tú** COMMAND	**sé**

tener (ie) (teniendo, tenido) *to have*

PRESENT INDICATIVE	**tengo,** tienes, tiene, tenemos, tenéis, tienen
PRETERIT	**tuve, tuviste, tuvo, tuvimos, tuvisteis, tuvieron**
FUTURE	**tendré, tendrás, tendrá, tendremos, tendréis, tendrán**
CONDITIONAL	**tendría, tendrías, tendría, tendríamos, tendríais, tendrían**
AFFIRMATIVE **tú** COMMAND	**ten**

traer (trayendo, traído) *to bring*

PRESENT INDICATIVE	**traigo,** traes, trae, traemos, traéis, traen
PRETERIT	**traje, trajiste, trajo, trajimos, trajisteis, trajeron**

traducir (zc) (traduciendo, traducido) *to translate*

PRESENT INDICATIVE	**traduzco,** traduces, traduce, traducimos, traducís, traducen
PRETERIT	**traduje, tradujiste, tradujo, tradujimos, tradujisteis, tradujeron**

venir (ie) (viniendo, venido) *to come*

PRESENT INDICATIVE	**vengo,** vienes, viene, venimos, venís, vienen
PRETERIT	**vine, viniste, vino, vinimos, vinisteis, vinieron**
FUTURE	**vendré, vendrás, vendrá, vendremos, vendréis, vendrán**
CONDITIONAL	**vendría, vendrías, vendría, vendríamos, vendríais, vendrían**
AFFIRMATIVE **tú** COMMAND	**ven**

ver (viendo, **visto**) *to see*

PRESENT INDICATIVE	**veo,** ves, ve, vemos, veis, ven
IMPERFECT	**veía, veías, veía, veíamos, veíais, veían**
PRETERIT	**vi,** viste, **vio,** vimos, visteis, vieron

volver (volviendo, **vuelto**) *to return*

Spanish-English Vocabulary

This vocabulary includes all the Spanish words used in the textbook except the numbers, names of the letters, conjugated forms of verbs, and words mentioned only in the **glosas.** Following each English equivalent is a number that tells in which chapter the word first appeared. *L* following the number means **lectura,** and indicates that the word is for passive recognition only unless later introduced as active. *Civ 1* and *Civ 2* refer to the **Primera** and **Segunda lectura sobre civilización hispánica;** *com 1, 2, 3,* and *4* refer to the four interchapter *Comunicación* sections. Words so marked are also passive unless a second number indicates that they are later introduced as active.

Four abbreviations are used:

adj adjective *f* feminine
adv adverb *inf* infinitive

A

a to, at, 2; from, 6; **a cambio de** in exchange for, 8; **a consecuencia de** because of, as a consequence of, 9L; **a dieta** on a diet, *Com 2;* **a eso de** at about, 7; **a estas horas** at this hour, 13; **a menos que** unless, 18; **a otro perro con ese hueso** get out of here!, forget it!, don't be silly!, 9; **a precios fijos** at fixed prices, 8; **a propósito** by the way, 9; **¡a sentarse!** sit down!, 17; **a sus órdenes** at your service, 20; **a veces** sometimes, 7; at times, 9; **a ver** let's see, 6;
abajo: los de abajo the underdogs, *Civ 2*
abandonar to abandon, 4; to leave, 15
abastecido stocked, 7L
abierto open, opened, 14
el **abogado** lawyer, 4
el **abrigo** coat, 11
abril April, 9
abrir to open, 8
el **abuelo** grandfather, 13; la **abuela** grandmother, 13; los **abuelos** grandparents, 13
abundante abundant, copious, *Civ 2*
aburrirse (de) to get bored (with), 12
acá over here, 10
acabar to end, to finish, 13; **acabar con** to end up with, to wind up with, 19L; **acabar de** + *inf* to have just + verb, 13; **acabarse** to run out, to be used up, 18
académico academic, 19L
aceptar to accept, 13L
el **accidente** accident, 14
la **acción** action, act, 3L
acercarse (qu) to come near, to approach, 16
acompañar to accompany, 9
acordarse (ue) (de) to remember, 12
acostarse (ue) to go to bed, 11
activamente actively 17L
la **actividad** activity, 19L
el **activismo** activism, 19L
activo active, *Civ 2*
el **actor,** la **actriz** actor, *Com 3*
actual current, 19L
acuático *adj* water, 17L
acuerdo: de acuerdo agreed, 3
acudir a to attend, to turn out for, *Civ 2*
adelante ahead, 1; **¡adelante!** come in, 1; **allí adelante** up ahead, 20
además besides, 4
adicional additional, 17
adiós good-bye, 1
el **administrador,** la **administradora** administrator, foreman, 9L, 14
admitir to allow (for), 19L
adonde where, 2
la **adquisición** acquisition, *Civ 1*
la **aduana** customs, 2
el **aduanero** customs official, 20
adverso adverse, 5L
el **aeropuerto** airport, 2
el **aficionado** fan, 17
afirmar affirm, 7L
afortunadamente fortunately, luckily, 2
el **Africa** *f* Africa, 3

el, la **agente** agent, 11
agitado excited, agitated, upset, 13
agosto August, 9
agotarse to run out, 18; **agotarse la paciencia** run out of patience, 18
agradable pleasant, 3L
agradecer (zc) to thank, 20
agrícolo *adj* farm, agricultural 9L
la **agricultura** agriculture, *Civ 1*
el **agua** *f* water, 7; **agua dulce** fresh water, 17L; **agua salada** salt water, 17L
ahí there, right there, 9L
ahora now, 2; **ahora bien** now then, 7L; **ahora mismo** right now, this very moment, 11; **ahora que** now that, 15; **ahorita** right away, 9
los **ahorros** savings, 13
¡ajá! Hey!, 6
al (contraction of **a** + **el**) to the, 2; **¿vamos al centro?** shall we go downtown?, 9
el **alacrán** scorpion, 20
alcanzar (c) to reach, 17L; **llegar a alcanzar** to reach, 17L
el **alcohol** alcohol, liquor, 9
la **aldea** village, 9L
alegrarse (de) to be happy, 12
alejado far away, distant, 9L; removed, *Civ 2*
alemán, alemana German, 17
Alemania, Germany, 17
algo something, 7
alguien someone, 5
algún, alguno some, 9; **algún día** someday, 9; **alguna vez** sometime, ever, 9
la **alianza** alliance, *Civ 1*
aliento: dar aliento to give hope, 9L
el **alma** *f* soul, 9L
almorzar (ue) to have lunch, 18
aló hello (on the phone), *Com 4*
altamente highly, 7L
la **alternativa** alternative, choice, 9L, 13
alto tall, 4; **clase alta** upper class, 11L; **en voz alta** out loud, aloud, 13
allá there, 4
allí there, 14; **allí adelante** up there, up ahead, 20; **allí mismo** right there, 14
el **ama** *f* **de casa** housewife, 4
amable kind, 8
amarillo yellow, 4
el **Amazonas** Amazon, 7L
amazónico Amazon, 16
el **ambiente** climate, environment, *Civ 2*
ambos both, *Civ 1*
la **América** America, 15; la **América del Norte** North America, 15L; la **América del Sur** South America, 15L
americanista *adj* having to do with Latin America, *Civ 2*
americano American, 1
el **amigo,** la **amiga** friend, 4
el **amor** love, 3
amoroso *adj* love, *Civ 2*
la **ampliación** enlargement, expansion, 18
ampliamente amply, 17
analizar (c) to analize, to think over, 3
la **anarquía** anarchy, 5L
el **ancestro** ancestor, *Civ 1*
andar to go, to walk, 2; **andar bien** to be doing fine (a person); to function well, 9; **¿dónde anda?** where is he?, 12
los **Andes** Andes Mountains, 7L
andino Andean, in the Andes Mountains, 17L
animado excited, 17
el **animal** animal, brute, 11
el **año** year, 2; **de 70 años** 70 years old, 7; el **Año Nuevo,** New Year, 3; **tener 18 años** to be 18 years old, 7
anoche last night, 6
anotar to chalk up, to score, 17
ansiosamente eagerly, anxiously, 13L
ante in the face of, *Civ 1;* **ante todo** above all, 14
anteayer the day before yesterday, 14
antecedente antecedent, early development, 7L
anterior previous, 11
antes before, beforehand, 8; **antes de** before, 5; **antes de que** *conjunction* before, 18
la **antesala** anteroom, waiting room, 18
anticuado antiquated, outdated, 13L
los **anticuchos** Peruvian shish kebob, 7
antiguo former, old, *Civ 2*
las **Antillas** West Indies, 14L; las **Antillas Menores** the Bahamas, *Civ 1*
antipático unpleasant, 13
el **antropólogo,** la **antropóloga** anthropologist, *Civ 1*
anunciar to announce, 9
el **anuncio** advertisement, announcement, 17
apagar (gu) to turn off, 16
el **aparato** device, gadget, 7
aparecer (zc) to appear, *Civ 1,* 20
aparentemente seemingly, 17L
el **apartamento** apartment, *Com 1,* 5
la **aplicación** application, 1
la **aportación** contribution, *Civ 2*
el **apoyo** support, 13L
aprender to learn, 19
apresurar to hurry, to rush, 3
aprieto: en aprietos troubled, *Civ 2*
aprobar (ue) to pass (an exam), 19
aprovechar to take advantage, *Civ 1,* 17
aproximadamente approximately, 11L
el **apunte** note, 19
aquel, aquella *adj* that, 7; **aquellos, aquellas** those, 7;

aquél *pronoun* the one, 15L
aquello *pronoun* that, 7
aquí here, 4; **aquí mismo** right here, 15L; **aquí tiene** here is, here are, 20
árabe Arab, 7L
el **árbol** tree, *Com 1,* 14
el **arco** arc, 15L
la **arena** sand, 17L
argentino Argentine, 4
el **arma** *f* **de fuego** firearm, *Civ 1*
armado armed, 5L
la **armadura** armor, *Civ 1*
el **arquitecto** architect, 8
la **arquitectura** architecture, *Civ 1*
arreglar to settle, to fix, [illegible]o arrange, 10
arrojado daring, *Civ 1*
el **arte** art, *Civ 1*
arterial of the blood, 9
el **artículo** article, 11
el, la **artista** artist, *Civ 1*
artístico artistic, 11
el **aserradero** sawmill, lu[illegible]ber camp, 14
así so, this (that) way, [illegible]us, 3; **así de bueno** so goo[illegible]uch a good, that good, 8; **a**[illegible] **pensé** just as I thou[illegible]6; **así que** so, 19L; **así se**[illegible] that's the way, 12; **a**[illegible] **hará** will do, it'll be done [illegible]
el **asiento** seat, 15
la **asignatura** subj[illegible]gnment, 19
asimilar to assimilate, *Civ 1*
asimismo likewise, *Civ 1*
asociar to associate, *Civ 1*
el **aspecto** aspect, appearance, *Civ 1*; **tener buen aspecto** to look well, healthy, 9
el **asunto** matter, 5
la **atención** attention, 15; **prestar atención** to pay attention, 13L
atender (ie) to attend to, to see; to take care of, 18
el **Atlántico** Atlantic Ocean, 17L
el, la **atleta** athlete, *Com 3,* 17
aun even, 16
aún still, 8; **aún más** + *noun* even greater, *Civ 1*
aunque although, even though, *Civ 1*, 19
el **autobús** bus, 8
el **autógrafo** autograph, 12
la **autonomía** autonomy, 13L
avanzar (c) to go forward, to advance, 15
Ave María my God (literally, Hail Mary), 11
el **aventurero** adventurer, 16
el **avión** airplane, 3
¡Ay, bendito! Oh, thank God!, Oh, bless you!, 10
ayer yesterday, 5
la **ayuda** help, aid, 13L
ayudar to help, 19
la **azafata** stewardess, 15
el, la **azteca** Aztec Indian, *Civ 1*
el **azúcar** sugar, *Civ 2*
azul blue, 4

B

bailar to dance, 3L
el **baile** dance, *Com 3*
bajar to go down, 9; to get down, 20; **bajar de peso** to lose weight, 9
bajo short, 4; *preposition* under, *Civ 1*, 13; underneath, 13
bancario *adj* bank, banking, 4
el **banco** bank, 3; bench, 16
la **bandera** flag, *Civ 1*
bañarse to bathe, 11
el **baño** bath, *Com 1;* el **cuarto de baño** bathroom, *Com 1;* **tomar un baño** to have a bath, *Com 1*
el **banquero** banker, 15L
barato cheap, 11
barbado bearded, *Civ 1*
el **barril** barrel, *Civ 2*
el **barrio** neighborhood, 10
barroco baroque, *Civ 1*
basado (en) based (on), *Civ 1*
la **báscula** scale, 9
el **básquetbol** basketball, 12
bastante *adj* enough, 13; *adv* quite, 17L
la **batalla** battle, 13L
el **baúl** trunk, 20
el **bebé** baby, 9
beber to drink, *Com 2;* **beberse** to drink up, 16
la **bebida** drink, *Com 2*
el **béisbol** baseball, 12
la **belleza** beauty, 18
bello beautiful, *Civ 1*, 16
la **Biblia** Bible, 16
la **biblioteca** library, 15L, 19
la **bicicleta** bicycle, 10
bien well, 1; fine, O.K., 2; *adv* very, 4; **ahora bien** now then, 7L; **bien saber** to know perfectly well, 10; **bien valer** to be well worth, 6; **más bien** rather, 19L; los **bienes materiales** material goods, *Civ 1*
la **bienvenida** welcome, 12
bienvenido welcome, 20
el **biólogo,** la **bióloga** biologist, 16
la **biología** biology, 19
blanco white, 4
blando soft, 14
la **blusa** blouse, 15
la **boca** mouth, *Civ 1*; **ir de boca en boca** to be widely talked about, *Civ 2*
la **boda** wedding, 13
el **boleto** ticket, 11
el **bolígrafo** ballpoint, 10
el **bolívar** monetary unit of Venezuela, 5
boliviano Bolivian, 8
la **bolsa** bag, pouch, 16
el **bolso** bag, purse, 20
la **bomba** bomb, 14
bonito pretty, 5
la **bota** boot, 6
el **bote** boat, 16; (literally, jar) **lleno de bote en bote** filled to capacity, packed, *Civ 2*
la **botella** bottle, 7
el **boticario** druggist, owner of a small-town pharmacy, 9L
el **botiquín** first-aid kit, 20
el **brazo** arm, 9

el **brebaje** brew, potion, 9L; **brebaje mágico** magic brew, 9L

breve brief, short, 7L; **de manera breve** briefly, 7L

la **brigada** brigade, group, 9L

brillante brilliant, *Civ 2*

brindar to toast, 7

el **brindis** toast, 7

la **broma** joke, 19

buen, bueno good, well, 1; **¡buenas!** hi!, 9; (on the phone) **¡bueno!** hello!, *Com 4;* **buenos días** hello, good morning, 1; **un buen rato** quite a while, 14

la **bufanda** scarf, 17

burlar to fool, to mock, 17

el **burro** donkey, 4; **trabajar como burro** to work like a horse, 4

buscar (qu) to look (for), 4

C

el **caballo** horse, *Civ 1*, 14

la **cabeza** head, 9

la **cabina de mando** controls, cockpit, 15

el **cable** cable, 14

el **cacao** cacao, chocolate, 15L

cada each, 4; every, 13

la **cadena** chain, network, 12

caer (caigo) to fall, 5; **caerse** to fall down, 16; **caer bien** to please, to be just right, to hit the spot, 8

el **café** café, 2; coffee, 4; **café con leche** coffee with milk, *Com 2;* **café solo** black coffee, *Com 2*

el **calcetín** sock, 15

calcular to calculate, 11L; to estimate, 17L; **se calcula que** it is estimated that, 17L

la **calidad** quality, *Civ 1*

caliente hot, 7L

calificado qualified, 11L; **obrero no calificado** unskilled worker, 11L

el **calor** warmth, heat, 8; **hace calor** it's hot, 14; **tener calor** to be warm, hot, 8

la **calle** street, 8

la **calma** calm, 19; **¡calma!** take it easy!, 6; **perder (ie) la calma** to get upset, to lose one's composure, 19

calmarse to calm down, 11

la **cama** bed, *Com 1;* **tender (ie) la cama** to make the bed, *Com 1*

la **cámara** camera, 12

cambiar to change, 3; **cambiar de opinión** to change (one's) mind, 3; **cambiar un cheque** to cash a check, *Com 4;* **cambiarse de ropa** to change clothes, 19

el **cambio** change, exchange, 8; **a cambio de** in exchange for, 8

caminar to walk, 6

el **camino** road, 14

el **camión** truck, 8

la **camioneta** van, pick-up truck, station wagon, 18

la **camisa** shirt, 15

la **camisita** little shirt, 20

el **campeón,** la **campeona** champion, 17

el **campesino,** la **campesina** peasant, 9L

el **camping** camping, *Com 3;* **hacer camping** to go camping, *Com 3*

el **campo** country, 9L; field, 17; major, academic area of specialization, 19; el **campo de la política** political arena, 19L; **ir al campo** to go to the country, *Com 3*

la **canastilla** luggage rack, 20

cansado tired, 19

cansar to tire (you out), 2

el,la **cantante** singer, *Com 3*

la **cantidad** quantity, 16

el **cañón** canyon, *Civ 1*; cannon, 17

capaz capable, 5L, 11

el **capítulo** chapter, 1

la **capital** capital (city), 17L

captar to capture, *Civ 2*

capturar to capture, *Civ 1*

la **cara** face, 13; **con cara de pocos amigos** looking angry, 13

el **carácter** character, nature, 19L

la **característica** characteristic, trait, 19L

¡caramba! Christopher!, Wow!, Gee!, 9

cargar (gu) to load, to take aboard, 15

el **cargamento** shipment, 16

la. **carne** meat, 7

caro expensive, 9L, 11

la **carrera** studies leading to a professional degree, 11; career, profession, 19L

la **carretera** highway, 20

el **carro** car, 4

la **cart[illegible]** letter, 10; menu, *Com 2*

la **cart[illegible]ra** purse, 16

la **cas[illegible]** house, home, 2; la **casa c[illegible]ercial** business firm, c[illegible]pany, 4; **en casa** at home, 2[illegible]**star en casa** to be at h[illegible]e, *Com 1;* **ir (venir) a c[illegible]** to go (come) home, 20; [illegible]**iar la casa** to clean [illegible]e, *Com 1*

cas[illegible] to get married, 12; [illegible]**se con José** to marry J[illegible] 12

casi almost, 7

el **caso** matter, case, 3; **en caso de que** in case, 18

la **casualidad** chance, coincidence, accident, *Civ 1*, 20; **¡Qué casualidad!** What a coincidence!, 20

cartaginés Carthaginian, 7L

catalogado catalogued, 6

el **catedrático** professor, *Civ 2*

el **cebiche** marinated raw fish, 7

la **categoría** category, 3L; **de primera categoría** first-class, *Civ 2*

católico Catholic, 13L

el **caudillo** chief of state, 13L

la **caza** hunting, *Civ 1*
la **cena** dinner, supper, *Com 2*
cenar to have dinner (supper), 2
el **centro** downtown, 9; center, 19L; **¿vamos al centro?** shall we go downtown?, 9; el **centro de estudio** center of learning, 19L
la **Centroamérica** Central America, 7L
el **cepillo** brush, 20; el **cepillo de dientes** toothbrush, 20
cerca de near, close, *Civ 1*, 16; (with expressions of time or quantity) about, nearly, *Civ 1*
el **cerdo** pig, 14
la **ceremonia** ceremony, 12
cerrar (ie) to close, 14
el **cesta** (literally, basket) wicker paddle used to play jai alai, 17L
la **cerveza** beer, 4
el **ciclismo** bicycling, 17L
el **ciclo** period of secondary school, 19L; **primer ciclo** seventh, eighth, and ninth grade, 19L; **segundo ciclo** tenth, eleventh, and twelfth grade
el **cielo** sky, 14
la **ciencia** science, 9L
ciento por ciento one hundred percent, *Civ 2*
cierto certainly, that's right, true, 2; **no es cierto** it's not true, 13; **cierto caso** a certain matter, 3; **por cierto** by the way, 17L
la **cima** top (of a hill), 6
el **cine** movies, movie theater, 3L, 18; **ir al cine** to go to the movies, 3L
el **circo** circus, *Civ 2*
la **cita** appointment, 9
la **ciudad** city, 7L, 9
el **ciudadano,** la **ciudadana** citizen, 5L
civil civil, 5L; el, la **civil** civilian, 13
la **civilización** civilization, 9L
claro of course, sure, 3; light, 13; **claro está** of course, 5; **claro que sí** of course (it is), 16; *adv* plainly, 4
la **clase** class, 1; type, kind, 9L, 10; social class, 11L; **clase alta** upper class, 11L; **clase media** middle class, 11L; la **clase de inglés** English class, 1; **toda clase de** all kinds of, 9L
clásico classical, *Civ 1*
clasificar (qu) to classify, *Civ 2*
el **clima** climate, 7L
la **clínica** private hospital, clinic, 9L
el **club campestre** country club, 2
el **cobre** copper, 8
la **cocina** kitchen, *Com 1*, 5; stove, *Com 1*
cocinar to cook, *Com 1*
el **coche** car, 14
coexistir to coexist, 17L
la **coincidencia** coincidence, *Civ 1*, 11
la **cola** line (literally, tail), 20; **hacer cola** to wait in line, 20
la **colección** collection, 7L
el **colectivo** bus, 17
el **colegio** school (K-12), 13L
la **colina** hill, 6
colocar (qu) to place, *Civ 2*
colombiano Colombian, 5
la **colonización** colonization, *Civ 1*
el **colonizador** colonist, settler, 15L
el **color** color, 4
el **coloso** colossus, *Civ 2*
el **collar** necklace, 16
el, la **comandante** commander, 15
combatir to fight, to combat, 13L
la **combinación** combination, 19L
combinar to combine, 18
el **combustible** fuel, 15
la **comedia** play, *Civ 1*
el **comedor** dining room, *Com 1*, 5
el **comentario** commentary, observation, explanation, 18
comenzar (ie, c) (a) to begin (to), to start, 5
comer to eat, 3; **comerse** to eat up, 16
comercial commercial, business, 4
el **comercio** commerce, business, 19L; el **comercio con las cosas de la mente** intellectual pursuits, 19L
la **comida** meal, food, lunch, dinner, *Com 1*, 7; **servir la comida** to serve the food, *Com 1*
como as, like, since, 1, 4; **como a** at about, 7; **como una hora** about an hour, 18
cómo what, how, 1; **¿cómo es. . .?** what is. . .like?, 4; **¿cómo le (te) va?** How are you?, How's it going?, 9; **cómo no** of course, 8; **cómo no voy a saber** of course I know, 13; **¿cómo se llama usted?** what is your name?, 1
cómodo comfortable, 11
la **compañía** company, 5
compartir to share, 13L
la **compasión** compassion, *Civ 2*
la **competencia** competition, 17L
competir (i) to rival, compete with, 17L
complejo complex, *Civ 1*
completamente completely, *Civ 1*
completo complete, 13L; **por completo** completely, 13L
la **complicación** complication, 16
componerse (like **poner**) to get better, 20
la **compra** purchase, *Com 3*, 18; **ir de compras** to go shopping, *Com 3*
comprar to buy, 4
comprender to understand, 3
común common, 5L, 15L
comunista Communist, 11L
con with, 2; **con cara de pocos amigos** looking angry, 13; **con tal de que** provided that, 18

conceder to concede, 11L; to grant, 19L
concentrar to concentrate, 19L
concentrarse en to concentrate on, 19
el **concepto** concept, idea, 15L
el **concierto** concert, 11; el **concierto de naciones** the world community, 13L
concluído concluded, *Civ 1*
concreto particular, concrete, special, 3
la **condición** condition, *Civ 1*; **en buenas condiciones** in good shape, 12
conducir (zc) to drive, 6
confirmar to confirm, 5L
el **conflicto** conflict, 19L
la **confusión** confusion, 15L
el **congreso** congress, 11L
conmigo with me, 7
conocer (zc) to know, to be acquainted with, 6; (preterit) to meet, 8; **darse a conocer** to become known, *Civ 2*
conocido known, 7L; **muy conocido** well known, *Civ 1*
el **conocimiento** knowledge, 9; **semi-conocimiento** partial knowledge, 9L
la **conquista** conquest, *Civ 1*
el **conquistador** conquistador, conqueror, *Civ 1*
la **consecuencia** consequence, 9L; **a consecuencia de** as a result of, because of, 9L
consecuentemente consequently, *Civ 1*
conseguir (i) to get, to obtain, 19
el **consejo** piece of advice, 19; los **consejos** advice, 19
conservador conservative, 13L
considerable considerable, *Civ 2*
considerar to consider, 3
consiguiente: por consiguiente therefore, consequently, 11L
constitucional constitutional, *Civ 2*
la **construcción** construction, 10
la **constructora** construction company, 10
construir (y) to construct, 9L
consultar to consult, 15L
el **consultorio** doctor's office, 9L
el **contador** accountant, 8
contar (ue) to tell, relate, 5: to count, 5L; to include, *Civ 2*; **contar con** to count on, 5L; to have, 17L
contestar to answer, 8
contigo with you, 7
el **continente** continent, *Civ 1*
continuar (ú) to continue, *Civ 1*, 11L, 13
contra against, *Civ 1*
contrabandear to smuggle, to traffic as contraband, 16
el **contrabando** contraband, 16; **sacar (qu) de contrabando** to smuggle out, 16
contrario opposite, 16; **de lo contrario** otherwise, 16; **lo contrario** the opposite, 11L
contrastar to contrast, 13L
el **contratiempo** mishap, 15L
el **contrato** contract, 2; **contrato de servicio** service contract
contribuir (y) to contribute, 11L, *Civ 2*
controlar to control, *Civ 1*
convencer (z) to convince, 5; **convencerse (de)** to become convinced, to be convinced, 19
conveniente advisable, useful, 13L; **ser conveniente** to be advisable, 13L; to be a good idea, 15
la **conversación** conversation, 7
conversar to converse, 3L, 8
convertirse (ie, i) to be converted, *Civ 1*; **convertirse en** to become, 11L; to turn into, 19L
la **convulsión** convulsion, 20
la **copa** drink, stem glass, wine glass, 8; cup, 17; la **Copa del Mundo** World Cup, 17L
copiar to copy, 13L
cordial cordial, 12
la **corrección** correction, 15L
correcto correct, 15L
el **correo** mail, 10; la **oficina de correos** post office, 10
correr to run, 20
la **corrida de toros** bullfight, 17L
cortar to cut, *Com 1*, 14; **cortarse** to cut oneself, 11
la **cosa** thing, 3; **la cosa va en serio** you really mean business, this is for real, 9
la **costa** coast, 7L; la **costa norte** northern coast, *Civ 1*
costar (ue) to cost, 4
la **costumbre** custom, 17
la **creación** creation, 19L
crear to create, *Civ 1*
la **creencia** belief, *Civ 2*
creer (y) to think, to believe, 4
el **cristianismo** Christianity, *Civ 1*
cristiano Christian, *Civ 1*; **de la era cristiana** A.D., *Civ 1*
criticar (qu) to criticize, 11
el, la **cronista** announcer, sportscaster, 17
cruzar (c) to cross, *Civ 1*
el **cuaderno** notebook, 19
el **cuadro** picture, 7L; painting, *Civ 2*
cual: el cual, la cual, los cuales, las cuales which, who, 13L
¿cuál?, ¿cuáles? which, what?, 1
cualquier any, 11L, 18
¿cuándo? when? 1; **cuando** when, 6
cuantioso copious, *Civ 2*
cuánto how much, 3; **cuántos** how many, 3; **en cuanto** as soon as, 19
cuarto fourth, 13; el **cuarto** quarter, 7; room, *Com 1*, 5; el **cuarto de baño (el baño)** bathroom, *Com 1*, 5
cubano Cuban, 11
el **cubismo** cubism, *Civ 2*
cubrir to cover, 6

la **cuenta** bill, *Com 2;* account, *Com 4*
el **cuento** short story, *Civ 2*
el **cuerpo** body, 9; **cuerpo y alma** body and soul, 9L
la **cuestión** matter, question for discussion, 7L, 10
el **cuidado** care, 11L; **¡cuidado!** careful!, 17
cuidar to take care of, 9
culpable guilty, 18
cultivar to cultivate, to grow, *Civ 1*
la **cultura** culture, *Civ 1*
cultural cultural, *Civ 1*
el **curandero,** la **curandera** healer, 9L
curar to cure, 9L
curioso funny, strange, 15L
el **curso** course, 19
cuyo whose, 5L

CH

la **chaqueta** jacket, 17
charlar to converse, to chat, 5
el **cheque** check, *Com 3;* el **cheque de viajero** traveler's check, *Com 4;* **cambiar un cheque** to cash a check, *Com 4*
¡che! listen!, hey!, 4
¡chévere! (regional) Great!, fantastic, 5
chicano Chicano, Mexican-American, 11L, 12
el **chico** boy, 1; la **chica** girl, 1
chileno Chilean, 8
chino Chinese, 7L
chitón shh, jeez, 16
churrigueresco one of the baroque styles of architecture, *Civ 1*

D

el **daño** damage, 14
dar (doy) to give, 2; **dar la mano** to shake hands, 2; **darse a conocer** to become known, *Civ 2*; **darse cuenta (de)** to realize (that), 12; **darse prisa** to hurry up, 11
de of, 1; from, 4; **de acuerdo** O.K., I agree, 3; **de ahora en adelante** from now on, 7; **¿de dónde?** (from) where?, 4; **de. . .en adelante** from. . .on, 11L; **de habla española** Spanish-speaking, 7L; **de lo contrario** otherwise, 16; **de manera breve** briefly, 7L; **de nada** you're welcome, 1; **de nuevo** again, 13; **de otra manera** otherwise, 4; **de primera** first class, 16; **de repente** all of a sudden, suddenly, 15; **de sobremesa** after dinner, 4; **de vacaciones** on vacation, 15; **de veras** that's right, really, 1; **de viaje** traveling, 15
la **debacle** catastrophe, disaster, *Civ 2*
debajo de underneath, 16
deber should, ought, 11; **unas cosas deben ser mencionadas** some things must be mentioned, *Civ 1*
debido a because of, 11L
débil weak, 13
la **década** decade, 11L
la **decadencia** decadence, decline, *Civ 2*
decidir to decide, 3L, 17
décimo tenth, 13
decir (i) (digo) to say, to tell, 3L, 6; **decir que sí (no)** to say yes (no), 6; **es decir** that is, 3L; **no me diga** you don't say, no kidding, 20
decorativo decorative, *Civ 1*
dedicar (qu) to dedicate, 9L; **dedicarse a** to devote oneself to, *Civ 1*
el, la **defensa** defenseman, 17
dejar to leave, to quit, 5; to let, to allow, 11; **dejar de** to stop (doing something), 13; **dejar una propina** to leave a tip, *Com 2*
del (contraction of **de** + **el**) of the, from the, 2
delante de in front of, 16
delgado thin, *Com 2;* **estar delgado** to be thin, *Com 2*
demasiado *adv* too, too much, 9; *adj* too much, too many, 13
democrático democratic, 5L
la **demora** delay, 12
demostrar (ue) to demonstrate, 17
denominar to name, call, *Civ 1*
dentro de in, within, 2; **dentro de un rato** in a little while, 2
depender (de) to depend (on), 5L
el **deporte** sport, 12
depositar to deposit, *Com 4*
la **derecha** right (wing), 13L
el **derecho** right, 13L; los **derechos humanos** human rights, 13L; **tener derecho a** to have a right to, 13L
la **derrota** defeat, *Civ 1*
derrotar to defeat, 13L
desafiar (í) to challenge, *Civ 2*
desaparecer (zc) to disappear, 15L
la **desaparición** disappearance, 13L
el **desarrollo** increase, 17L; development, 19L; el **país en desarrollo** developing country, *Civ 2*
desayunar to have breakfast, *Com 2,* 18
el **desayuno** breakfast, *Com 2*
desconocido unknown, unfamiliar, *Civ 1*, 15
describir to describe, 13L
la **descripción** description, 11
descubierto discovered, *Civ 1*
el **descubridor** discoverer, *Civ 1*
descubrir to discover, *Civ 1*
desde from, *Civ 1*, 15; **desde**

hace since, *Civ 1*; **desde que** since, 10
desear to desire, to wish, 3L, 7
el **disequilibrio** imbalance, 5L
desesperadamente desperately, 20
desesperado desperate, despairing, 9L
desgraciadamente unfortunately, *Civ 2*
deshacerse de (like **hacer**) to get rid of, 16
la **deshumanización** dehumanization, *Civ 2*
el **desierto** desert, 7L
desligado unrelated, *Civ 2*
desolado desolate, 19L
el **desorden** disorder, 5L
el **despacho** office, 11
despertarse (ie) to wake up, 11
el **despegue** takeoff (airplane), 1
desplazarse (c) to move, *Civ 1*
después after, afterwards, 8; **después de** after, 3L; **después de que** after, 19; **después de todo** after all, 13L
destinar; ser destinado a to be destined to, *Civ 2*
el **destino** destiny, fate, *Civ 1*
la **desviación** detour, 15
la **destrucción** destruction, *Civ 1*
el **detalle** detail, 3
detener (like **tener**) to stop, 11; **detenerse** to stop, 15
detenidamente carefully, 20
la **determinación** determination, *Civ 1*
detrás de behind, 16
devolver (ue) to return (something), *Com 3*
el **día** day; **buenos días** hello, good morning, 1; **hoy día** nowadays, *Civ 1*; **todos los días** every day, 4
el **diálogo** dialog, 1
el **dibujo** drawing, 11
el **diccionario** dictionary, 19
diciembre December, 9
la **dictadura** dictatorship, 11L
dictatorial dictatorial, 19L
dicho said, told, 14
dichoso lucky, 18; **dichosos los ojos** how wonderful to see you, 18
el **diente** tooth, 20; el **cepillo de dientes** toothbrush, 20; la **pasta de dientes** toothpaste, 20
la **dieta** diet, *Com 2;* **estar a dieta** to be on a diet, *Com 2*
la **diferencia** difference, 3L
diferente different, 5L; **en diferentes épocas** in various periods, 11L
difícil difficult, 6
diga hello (on the phone), *Com 4;* **no me diga** you don't say, no kidding, 20
digno dignified, stately, *Civ 2*
el **dios** god, *Civ 1*; **¡Dios mío!** oh my gosh!, My God, 6
dinámico dynamic, *Civ 1*
la **dinastía** dynasty, *Civ 1*
el **dinero** money, 4; **sacar (qu) dinero** to withdraw money, *Com 4*
el, la **diplomático** diplomat, 8
la **dirección** address, 10
directamente directly, 18
directivo ruling, *Civ 2*
dirigirse (j) (a) to go (towards), 14; to head for, 15L
el **disco** record, *Com 3,* 15; **tocar (qu) un disco** to play a record, *Com 3*
la **discoteca** discotheque, 3L
discutir to discuss, 3
el **disfraz** disguise, 16
disfrazado disguised, 16
disfrutar de + *noun* to enjoy (something), 4
disminuir (y) to diminish, to cut down, 4
disparar to shoot, 17
el **disparo** shot, 17
la **distinción** distinction, 19L
distinguirse to stand out, to distinguish oneself, *Civ 2*
distintamente distinctively, *Civ 1*
la **distorción** distortion, 15L
la **distribución** distribution, 9L
la **diversidad** diversity, 13L
diverso diverse, different, 7L; **diversos** several, various, 9L
divertir (ie,i) to amuse, 12; **divertirse** to enjoy oneself, to have a good time, 12
dividir to divide, 19L
el **divorcio** divorce, 13L
el **documento** document, 20
el **doctor,** la **doctora** doctor, 4
el **dólar** dollar, 6
doler (ue) to hurt, 7; **me duele la mano** my hand hurts, 7
la **dominación** domination, 7L
dominante domineering, 13L; **una familia dominante** a strong family
dominar to dominate, 13L; to predominate, *Civ 2*
el **domingo** Sunday, 1
el **dominicano,** la **dominicana** Dominican, 16
don, doña title of respect, 8
donde where, 1; **¿dónde?** where?, 4
dorado golden, 16
dormir (ue, u) to sleep, 3; **dormir como un lirón** to sleep like a log, 3; **dormirse** to go to sleep, to fall asleep, 11
el **dormitorio** bedroom, *Com 1,* 5
dramático dramatic, *Civ 1*
el **dramaturgo** playwright, *Civ 1*
drástico drastic, *Civ 1*
la **droga** drug, 9
la **ducha** shower, *Civ 1*; **tomar una ducha** to take a shower, *Civ 1*
ducharse to take a shower, 11
la **duda** doubt, 17L; **sin duda alguna** without a doubt, 17L
dudar to doubt, 13
el **dueño,** la **dueña** owner, 14
dulce: el **agua dulce** fresh water, 17L
la **duna** dune, 17L; **dunas de arena** sand dunes, 17L

duplicar (qu) to duplicate, *Civ 1*
la **duración** duration, 19L
durante during, 6
duro hard, 17L

E

la **economía** economy, economics, 4
económico economic, economical, 4
el, la **economista** economist, 3
echar: echar un vistazo to take a look, to glance, 15L
economizar (c) to save, to be thrifty, 4
la **edad** age, 15
el **edificio** building, 11
la **educación** education, 10
el **educador,** la **educadora** educator, *Civ 2*
educativo educational, 19L
efectivamente exactly, that's right, really, 5
efecto: en efecto as a matter of fact, 19L
efectuar (ú) to accomplish, to bring about, *Civ 2*
eficazmente effectively, 19L
EE.UU. (*abbreviation for* Estados Unidos) U.S.A., 11L
la **eficiencia** efficiency, 18
eficientemente efficiently, 19L
¿eh? hm?, 8
la **ejecución** execution, 19
el **ejemplo** example, 11L; **por ejemplo** for example, 11L
ejercer (z) to practice, 9L
el **ejército** army, 7
el the, 1
él he, 2; *after preposition* him, 7
elemental elementary, primary, 19L
el **elemento** element, *Civ 1*
elevar to elevate, *Civ 2*
eliminar eliminate, 5L
ella she, 2; *after preposition* her, 7
ellos, ellas they, 2' *after preposition* them, 7
la **emancipación** emancipation, 13L; la **emancipación femenina** women's lib, 13L
la **embajada** embassy, 8
el **embarazo** pregnancy, 9
embargo: sin embargo however, *Civ 1*; nevertheless, 11L, 18
emigrar to emigrate, 11L
emocionado excited, 5
emocionante exciting, 17L
el **emperador** emperor, 17L
empezar (ie, c) (a) to start (to), 8
el **empleado,** la **empleada** employee, 4; el **empleado bancario** bank clerk, *Com 4*
empírico empirical, 9L
empujar to push, *Civ 2*
en in, at, 1; **en caso de que** in case, 18; **en cuanto** as soon as, 19; **en efecto** as a matter of fact, 19L; **en el momento en que** at the moment that, at the time that, 19; **en punto** exactly, on the dot, 7; **en voz alta** out loud, 13
enamorarse de to fall in love with, 12
la **encantación** charm, spell, enchantment, 9L
encantado delighted, 19
encanto my love, 13
la **enciclopedia** enclyclopedia, 15L
encima de on top of, 16
encontrar (ue) to find, 5L, 6; **encontrarse** to be found, 9L; to be, 17
el **enemigo,** la **enemiga** enemy, *Civ 1*
enero January, 9
el **enfermero,** la **enfermera** nurse, 9
enfermo sick, ill, 9
engordar to gain weight, to get fat, *Com 2*
enojar to anger, 19; **enojarse con** to get mad at, 12
enriquecer (zc) to enrich, 19L
la **ensalada** salad, 7
el, la **ensayista** essayist, *Civ 2*
el **ensayo** essay, *Civ 2*
la **enseñanza** education, teaching, 19L
enseñar to show, to teach, 1
ensillar to saddle, 14
enteramente entirely, *Civ 2*
enterarse (de) to learn, to find out, 18
entero whole, *Civ 2*
entonces then, 3L, 20
la **entrada** ticket, *Com 3;* entry, entrance, 20; **sacar (qu) las entradas** to get the tickets, *Com 3*
entrar (en, a) to enter, 3L, 8
entre between, among, 3L, 20
el **entrenamiento** training, *Civ 1*
la **entrevista** interview, 12
entrevistar to interview, 12
entusiasticamente enthusiastically, 17L
la **época** epoch, period, time, *Civ 1*, 19
el **equipo** team, 17; equipment, 20
equivocarse (qu) (de) to be mistaken (about), 12
el **error** error, mistake, 15L
esa that, 7; **esas** those, 7
la **escala** scale, *Civ 2*
la **escalera** staircase, stairway, 6
escaparse to escape, 16
la **escena** scene, *Civ 2*
escoger (j) to choose, 15
esconder to hide, 7
escribir to write, 8
escrito written, 14
el **escritor,** la **escritora** writer, *Com 3*
el **escritorio** desk, 18
escuchar to listen (to), *Com 1*, 4
la **escuela** school, 10
la **escultura** sculpture, *Civ 2*
ese, esa *adj* that, 1, 7; **esos, esas** those, 7
ése that one, 1
el **esfuerzo** effort, 19L

eso that, 10; **a eso de** at about, 10; **nada de eso** oh, no; absolutely not, 20
espantarse to be afraid, 15
España Spain, 7L
español Spanish, 1; el **español** Spanish (language), 1; el **español,** la **española** Spaniard, 7L; **de habla española** Spanish-speaking, 7L
especial special, 10
especialista skilled, expert, qualified (in), 18
la **especialización** major, field of specialization, 19L
especializado specialized, 19
especializarse (c) to major, 19
especialmente especially, 7L
el **espectáculo** spectacle, show, 17L
el **espectador,** la **espectadora** spectator, 17
el **espejo** mirror, 20
la **esperanza** hope, *Civ 2*
esperar to wait, to hope, 5; to expect, 8
el **espíritu** spirit, *Civ 1*
el **esposo** husband, 9; la **esposa** wife, 9; los **esposos** husband and wife, 9
esquiar (í) to ski, *Com 3*
esta this, 6; **estas** these, 6
ésta this one, 1
la **estabilidad** stability, *Civ 2*
estable stable, 5L
establecer (zc) to establish, set up, 9L; **establecerse** to settle down 11L
la **estación** station, 10
estacionar to park, 9
el **estadio** stadium, 17
el **estado** state, 18
los **Estados Unidos** United States, 2
estallar to break out, to erupt, 19
el **estaño** tin, 8
estar (estoy) to be, 1; **estar bien de salud** to be in good health, 12; **estar resfriado** to have a cold, 13; **estoy para servirle** it's my pleasure, 8
este, esta this, 6; **este. . .** uh. . ., 18; **estos, estas** these, 6, 7
el **este** east, 14
el **estéreo** stereo, 15
estético aesthetic, *Civ 2*
el **estilo** type, style, 7L, 17; el **estilo de vida** life style, 13L
el **estímulo** stimulus, *Civ 1*
esto uh. . ., 3; this, 10
el **estómago** stomach, 9
estos, estas these, 6
el **estrecho** strait, *Civ 1*; el **Estrecho de Bering** Bering Strait, *Civ 1*
la **estrella** star, *Civ 2*
estrenar to premiere, to open (a new play, movie), *Civ 2*
el **estudiantado** student body, 19L
el, la **estudiante** student, 1
estudiantil *adj* student, 19
estudiar to study, 3; **estudiar para** to study to be, 8
el **estudio** study, 5; el **centro de estudio** center of learning, 19L; los **estudios** studies, 5; el **plan de estudios** curriculum, 19L
estupendo fantastic, superb, delicious, great, 5
la **etapa** era, phase, 13L
eterno eternal, 7L
étnico ethnic, 7L
Europa Europe, 17
europeo European, *Civ 1*, 17; el **europeo,** la **europea** European (person), 17
la **evidencia** evidence, proof, *Civ 1*
evolucionar to evolve, to change, 19L
exactamente exactly, 11L
exageradamente overly, excessively, 13L
exagerado exaggerated, *Civ 1*
exagerar to exaggerate, 19L
el **examen** exam, 19
examinar to examine, 9
excelente excellent, 1
la **excepción** exception, 17L; **con excepción de** except, 17L
excepcional exceptional, *Civ 1*
el **excusado** toilet, *Com 1*
la **existencia** existence, 19L
existencialista existentialist, *Civ 2*
existir to exist, 3L
el **éxito** success, 12
la **expansión** expansion, *Civ 1*
especialmente especially, *Civ 1*
la **expensa** expense, 13L; **a expensas de** at the cost of, 13L
la **experiencia** experience, 10
experimentar to undergo, to experience, *Civ 2*
explicar (qu) to explain, 5L
la **exploración** exploration, *Civ 1*
el **explorador,** la **exploradora** explorer, *Civ 1*
explorar to explore, *Civ 1*
explotar to exploit, *Civ 1*
la **exportación** exportation, 5L
la **exposición** exhibition, *Civ 2*
extender (ie) to spread, extend, 19L
extenso extensive, 14; **obra extensa** extensive writings, *Civ 2*
el **extranjero,** la **extranjera** foreigner, 2; **en el extranjero** abroad, *Civ 2*
extraordinaria extraordinary, *Civ 1*
extremo extreme, *Civ 1*

F

la **facción** faction, extremist group, 5L
fácil easy, 6
fácilmente easily, *Civ 1*
facilitar to facilitate, 20
la **falda** skirt, 15
falso false, *Civ 2*
la **falta** lack, absence, 5L
faltar to be lacking; **me falta un capítulo** I have a chapter left

(to do), 19; **(no) faltaba más** absolutely, harumph, 18
la **fama** renown, fame, *Civ 2*
la **familia** family, 3
famoso famous, *Civ 1*, 12
la **farmacia** pharmacy, 9L; **farmacia de provincia** small-town pharmacy, 9L
fanático fanatic, 12; el **fanático,** la **fanática** fan, 13L
fascinante fascinating, *Civ 2*
la **fase** phase, *Civ 2*
el **favor** favor, 8; **favor de** + *inf* please, kindly, 15
favorable favorable, *Civ 2*
favorecer (zc) to favor, 13L
favorito favorite, 15L
la **fe** faith, *Civ 1*; la **fe cristiana** Christian faith, *Civ 1*
febrero February, 9
federal federal, 9L
felicitar to congratulate, 7
femenina feminine, 13L; la **emancipación femenina** women's lib, 13L
el **fenómeno** phenomenon, *Civ 1*
feo ugly, 5
la **fiesta** party, 8
la **figura** figure, personage, *Civ 2*
fijarse to pay attention, notice, 10; **fíjate** just imagine, look, 15
fijo fixed, 8; **a precios fijos** at fixed prices, 8
la **filosofía** philosophy, 19L
filosófico philosophical, *Civ 2*
el **filósofo** philosopher, *Civ 2*
el **fin** end, 6; el **fin de semana** weekend, 6
final final, 15; **al final de** at the end of, *Civ 1*
finalmente finally, *Civ 1*
financiero *adj* finance, 2
la **finca** farm, 14
firmar to sign, *Com 4*
firme: en tierra firme on the mainland, 11L
físico physical, 7L, 12
la **fisonomía** face, 7L
flamenco Flemish, *Civ 1*
la **flor** flower, *Com 1*
la **floración** flowering, *Civ 1*
florecer (zc) to flourish, *Civ 1*
la **flotilla** fleet, 18
el **fondo** bottom, 16; **a fondo** in depth, *Civ 2*; el **fondo doble** false bottom, 16
la **forma** way, form, 9L; **en forma tan marcada** in such a pronounced way, 13L
formar to form, 3L
formalizar (c) to formalize, 3L
la **fórmula** formula, 9L, 12
formular to formulate, 19L; **formular una pregunta** to ask a question, 19L
la **fotografía** photograph, 11
francamente frankly, 13L
francés French, 17; el **francés** French (language), 17; el **francés,** la **francesa** French person, 17
Francia France, 17
la **frase** phrase, *Civ 1*
frecuencia: con frecuencia frequently, often, *Civ 2*
el **frente** front, 15; **hacer frente,** to face, 19L
fresco fresh, 14
frío cold, 5; el **frío** cold, 8; **hace frío** it's cold, 14; **tener frío** to be cold, 8
la **frontera** border, 20
el **frontón** jai alai court, 17L
la **fruta** fruit, 7
fuera out, 13; **fuera de aquí** get out of here, 13; **fuera de** outside, 7L
fuerte loud, strong, 7
la **fuerza** force, 5L
la **función** use, function, *Civ 2*
funcionar to funcion, 9L; to be in operation, 19L
fundar to found, to establish, 19L
furioso furious, 11
el **fútbol** soccer, 12; el **fútbol americano** football, 12
el **futuro** future, 5

G

galante gallant, 18
la **gallina** chicken, hen, 14
ganar to earn, 4; to gain, to win, 13L
ganas: tener ganas de + *inf* to be anxious to, to feel like (doing something), 8
el **garage** garage, 5
la **garganta** throat, 9
gastar to spend (money), 5
el **gato** cat, 14
el **gemelo,** la **gemela** twin, 15
la **generación** generation, 13L
el **general** general, 13; el **Generalísimo** title used by Francisco Franco, 13L
generalmente generally, usually, 11L
genialmente masterfully, with genius, *Civ 1*
la **gente** people, 4
la **geografía** geography, 7L
geográfico geographic, 7L
el **geólogo,** la **geóloga** geologist, 20
el, la **gerente** manager, 10
el **ginecólogo,** la **ginecóloga** gynecologist, 9L
el **gitano** gypsy, 7L
el **gobernador** governor, 18
gobernar (ie) to rule, to govern, 13L; **gobernarse** to govern oneself, 19L
el **gobierno** government, 4
el **gol** goal (soccer), 17
el **golf** golf, 12
el, la **golfista** golfer, 12
el **golpe** blow, *Civ 2*
gordo fat, *Civ 2*; **estar gordo** to be heavy, *Com 2*
gótico gothic, *Civ 1*
gozar (c) de to enjoy, to have, *Civ 2*
la **gracia** grace, 13L; **por la gracia de Dios** by the grace of God, 13L

gracias thank you, 1; **gracias a** thanks to, *Civ 1*; **gracias mil** thanks a million, 12
gradual gradual, 11L
graduarse (ú) to graduate, 19
la **gráfica** chart, 19L
la **gramática** grammar, 19
gran, grande big, great, 5; **gran futuro** great future, 5
grandemente greatly, 19L
la **grandeza** greatness, *Civ 1*
grano: ir al grano to get to the point, 18
grave grave, serious, critically ill, 5L, 13
gritar to shout, to yell, 17; to scream, 20
el **grupo** group, 3L
el **guante** glove, 17
guapo handsome, good-looking, 1
el, la **guardia** guard, (border, highway) patrol, policeman (woman), 16
la **guerra** war, 11L, 13; la **guerra civil** civil war, *Civ 1*
el, la **guía** guide, 20; la **guía telefónica** telephone book, *Com 4*
la **guitarra** guitar, *Com 3*
el, la **guitarrista** guitarist, *Civ 2*
gustar to be pleasing, to please, to be appealing, 7; **me gusta el vino** I like wine, 7
el **gusto** pleasure, 2; taste, 7L; **mucho gusto** glad to meet you, 2; **con gusto** gladly, 12

H

el, la **habitante** inhabitant, 9L
hablar to speak, 1; **de habla hispana** Spanish-speaking, 7L; **hablar de** to talk about, 2
hacer (hago) to make, 4; to do, 1; **hace** for, since, ago, 10; **hace 10 minutos que está aquí** he has been here for 10 minutes, 9; **hace unos 10 años** about 10 years ago, 12; **no hace mucho tiempo** not too long ago, 13L; **hacer cola** to wait in line, 20; **hacer el favor de** + *inf* please + verb, 11
hacia toward, 10
el **hambre** *f* hunger 8; **tener hambre** to be hungry, 8; **tener un hambre de huérfano** to be dying of hunger, 8
hasta even, 13L; until, 18; **hasta luego** see you later, 18; **hasta que** until, 19
hay there is, there are, 1; **hay que salir** it is necessary to go out, 3
hebreo Hebrew, 19L
hecho done, made, 14
el **helado** ice cream, *Com 2*
el **hemisferio** hemisphere, *Civ 1*; el **Hemisferio Occidental** Western Hemisphere, *Civ 1*
el **hermano** brother, 3; la **hermana** sister, 3; los **hermanos** brothers, brother(s) and sister(s), 3
hermoso beautiful, 17L
la **hierba** grass (lawn), *Com 1;* herb, 9L; **cortar la hierba** to cut the grass, *Com 1*
el **hijo** son, 3; la **hija** daughter, 3; los **hijos** children, sons, sons and daughters, 3
la **hiperdemocracia** hyper-democracy, *Civ 2*
hispánico Hispanic, 3L, 12
la **hispanización** hispanization, hispanification, 19L
hispanizarse (c) to become hispanicized, to become Spanish-like, 11L
hispano Hispanic, 7L; el **hispano, la hispana** Hispanic person, person of Hispanic extraction, 7L, 12
la **Hispanoamérica** Hispanic America, Spanish America, 7L
hispanoamericano Spanish American, 9L
la **historia** story, 5L; history, 19
histórico historical, *Civ 1*
el **hito** landmark, milestone, *Civ 2*
el **hogar** home, 13L; las **labores del hogar** household chores, 13L
la **hoja de afeitar** razor blade, 17
hola hello, hi, 1
Holanda Holland, 17
holandés Dutch, 17; el **holandés** Dutch (language), 17; el **holandés,** la **holandesa** Dutch person, 17
el **hombre** man, 2; el **hombre de negocios** businessman, 2
hondureño Honduran, 20
la **hora** hour, 6; **¿a qué hora?** (at) what time?, 76; **a estas horas** at this hour, 13; **como una hora** about an hour, 18; **¿qué hora es?** what time is it?, 7
el **hospital** hospital, clinic, 9L, 13
el **hotel** hotel, 2
hoy today, 3; **hoy día** nowaday, *Civ 1*
el **hoyo** hole, 12
hubo (preterit of **haber**) there was, there were, *Civ 1*
la **huelga** strike, 19
el **huérfano,** la **huérfana** orphan, 8
la **huella** trace (literally, foot-print), *Civ 1*
el **hueso** bone, 9; **¡a otro perro con ese hueso!** go on!, forget it!, don't be silly!, 9
el,la **humanista** humanist, *Civ 2*
humano human, *Civ 1*, 9
el **humilde** humble, poor person, *Civ 2*
la **humillación** humiliation, *Civ 2*

I

ibérico Iberian, 7L
ibero Iberian, 7L
la **idea** idea, 10
ideal ideal, 3L

identificar (**qu**) to identify, 15L
ideológico ideological, 13L
la **iglesia** church, 13L, 18
igual the same, equal, 11L; **al igual** just as, 15L
ilimitado unlimited, 17L
ilustrar to illustrate, *Civ 2*
la **imagen** image, picture, *Civ 2*
imitar to imitate, 13L
el **impacto** impact, *Civ 2*
el **imperio** empire, *Civ 1*
el **impermeable** raincoat, 20
implicado implicated, 13
importante important, 15L
importar to be important, 7; **no me importa** I don't mind, I don't care, 7
imposible impossible, 1
la **impresión** impression, 13L
impulsar to drive, *Civ 1*
el, la **inca** Inca, *Civ 1*
incaica Incan, *Civ 1*
inclasificable unclassifiable, *Civ 2*
inclinarse a to be inclined to, to tend to, 13L
inclusive even, 17L
el **incremento** increase, 11L
independiente independent, 19L
indicar (**qu**) to indicate, *Civ 1*
indígeno native, indigenous, 7L; el, la **indígena** native, *Civ 1*
el **indio,** la **india** Indian, 7L
indiscutible unquestionable, beyond question, 18
individualista individualistic, *Civ 2*
el **individuo** individual, person, *Civ 1*
indudablemente undoubtedly, *Civ 2*
la **industria** industry, 11L
inevitable inevitable, unavoidable, 14
infame infamous, 11;
el, la **infame** scoundrel, cad, 11
el **infierno** hell, inferno, 7L, 16
la **infinidad** infinity, 7L
infinitamente infinitely, 17
inflexible inflexible, 13L
la **influencia** influence, *Civ 1*
la **ingeniería** civil engineering, 19L
el **ingeniero** engineer, 8
Inglaterra England, 17
el **inglés** English (language), l; el **inglés,** la **inglesa** English person, 17
iniciar to initiate, to begin, *Civ 1*
inmediatamente immediately, 7L, 13
inmenso immense, great, 13L
la **inmigración** immigration, 11L
el, la **inmigrante** immigrant, 7L
inmigrar to immigrate, 11L
inmortal immortal, *Civ 1*
insistir en to insist upon, 13
inspirado inspired, *Civ 1*
el **instante** instant, second, 10
la **institución** institution, 13L
el **instituto** institute, high school, vocational school, 13L
la **instrucción** instruction, education, 19L
el **instrumento** instrument, *Com 3*
la **integración** integration, 13L
integrarse to become part of, 11L
intelectual intellectual, 19L
inteligente intelligent, 1
la **intención** intention, 3L; **tener la intención de** to plan to, to intend to, 19
la **intensidad** intensity, 3L
intenso intense, 7L
intercambiable interchangeable, 15L
interesante interesting, 3L
interesar to interest, 7
internacional international, 2
internamente internally, 19L
internarse to go inland, *Civ 1*
interno internal, 19L
la **interpretación** interpretation, 11
el, la **intérprete** interpreter, performer, *Civ 2*
interrumpir to interrupt, 13
la **intervención** intervention, 9L
introducir (**zc**) to introduce, 19L
la **inutilidad** futility, uselessness, *Civ 2*
invadir to invade, 19L
inventar to invent, *Civ 1*
la **investigación** investigation, 20; las **investigaciones** research, 20
el **invierno** winter, 6
invitar (**a**) to invite (to), to treat (to), 5
la **inyección** shot, injection, 9L
ir to go, 3; **ir a** + *inf* to be going to (do something), 3; **ir a casa** to go home, 20; **ir al cine** to go to the movies, *Com 3;* **ir al grano** to get to the point, 18; **ir de compras** to go shopping, *Com 3,* 18; **irse** to leave, to go away, 11; **¡vamos!** come on, let's go, 6; **vamos a** + *inf* let's + verb, 5; **voy** I'm going, 3; I'm coming, 6
la **isla** island, 15L; las **Islas Vírgenes** Virgin Islands, *Civ 1*
Italia Italy, 17
italiano Italian, 7L, 17; el **italiano,** la **italiana** Italian person, 17
la **izquierda** left (wing), 13L; **de centro izquierda** center left, 13L

J

ja ha, 14
el **jabón** soap, 20
el **jai alai** jai alai (sport), 17L
jamás never, 9
la **jaula** cage, 16
la **jaulita** little cage, 16
el **jeep** jeep, 20
el **jefe,** la **jefa** boss, 13L; el **Jefe Máximo** Supreme Chief, 13L

joven young, 1; el **joven** young man, 3; la **joven** young woman, 3
el **judío,** la **judía** Jew, 7L
el **juego** game, 12
el **jueves** Thursday, 1
el **jugador,** la **jugadora** player, 17
jugar, (ue) to play, 4
julio July, 9
junio June, 9
juntos, juntas together, 3
justo fair, just, 19L
la **juventud** youth, 13L

K

el **kilo,** el **kilogramo** kilogram, 9
el **kilómetro** kilometer, 17L

L

la the, 1; *direct object pronoun* her, you, it, 6
la **labor** chore, work, 13L; las **labores del hogar** household chores, 13L
el **laboratorio de lenguas** language laboratory, 7
el **lado** side, 11
el **lago** lake, 7L, 16
la **laguna** gap, 15L; la **laguna mental** mental blindspot, 15L
la **lana** wool, 5L
lanzar (c) to throw, to hurl, 13L; **lanzarse a** to lunge for, to rush into, 13L
el **lápiz** pencil, 10
largo long, 8
las the, 1; *direct object pronoun* you, them, 6
la **lástima** shame, pity, 11; **es una lástima** it's a pity, shame; it's too bad, 11
la **lata** pain, nuisance, 2
latino Latin (relating to people that speak Spanish or other languages derived from Latin), Hispanic, Latin American, 11
la **Latinoamérica** Latin America, 15L
lavarse to get washed, to wash up, 11
le *indirect object pronoun* (to, from, for) him, her, you, it, 6
el **lector,** la **lectora** reader, 15L
la **lectura** reading, 3L
la **leche** milk, 7
la **lechuga** lettuce, *Com 2*
leer (y) to read, 8
legítimo legitimate, 7L
la **legumbre** vegetable, 7
lejos de far from, 16
la **lengua** language, 7
lentamente slowly, 19L
lento slow, *Com 3*
les *indirect object pronoun* (to, from, for) you, them, 6
las **letras** letters, literature, *Civ 2*; las **letras españolas** Spanish literature, *Civ 2*
la **ley** law, 5; las **leyes** law, 5; **estudia leyes** he is studying law, 5
libanés Lebanese, 7L
la **liberación** liberation, 13L, 15
liberado liberated, 13L, 15
la **libertad** freedom, liberty, 5; la **libertad de expresión** freedom of expression, 5
libre free, 12
el **libro** book, 8
el **licenciado** lawyer, 18
el **límite** limit, *Civ 2*
la **limosina** limousine, 12
lindo attractive, nice, pretty, 10
el **lirón** dormouse, 3; **dormir como un lirón** to sleep like a log, 3
listo ready, 19
literario literary, 19L
la **literatura** literature, *Civ 1*
lo *direct object pronoun* him, you, it, 6; **lo de menos** the least of it, 19; **lo que** what, that which, 17
local local, *Civ 2*
locamente madly, 13
loco crazy, 13
lógicamente logically, 3L
lograr to manage, *Civ 2*
el **loro** parrot, 16
los the, 1; *direct object pronoun* you, them, 6; **los (Alessandri)** the (Alessandri) family, 4; **los dos** both (of them), 14
la **lucha** struggle, 19L
luchar to fight, to struggle, 10
luego then, 18; **hasta luego** see you later, 18
el **lugar** place, 7L, 8; **en primer lugar** in the first place, 9L
el **lunes** Monday, 1
la **luz** light, sunlight, 6

LL

la **llamada** call, telephone call, *Com 4*
llamar to call, 5; **llamarse** to be called, 1; **llamar por teléfono** to call on the phone, 10; **¿cómo se llama usted?** what's your name?, 1
la **llanura** plain, 7L
la **llave** key, 12
la **llegada** arrival, 12
llegar (gu) to arrive, 2; **llegar a alcanzar** to reach, 17L
lleno full, *Civ 2*; **lleno de bote en bote** filled to capacity, *Civ 2*
llevar to carry, to take, 16; **llevarse** to carry off, 16; to wear, *Com 3;* **llevarse a cabo** to carry out, *Civ 1*; **llevarse una sorpresa** to get quite a surprise, 17L
llover (ue) to rain, 14

M

macanudo (Argentina) great, fantastic, 17
macizo massive, solid, *Civ 2*
el **machete** machete, 6
la **madre** mother, 3; **mi**

madre oh, my God, 14
la **madrugada** dawn, 16
el **maestro** master, *Civ 2*
mágico magic, 9L
magistral masterly, superb, *Civ 2*
el **magnetómetro** magnetometer, 20
el **maíz** corn, *Civ 1*
mal bad, ill, 1; badly, 1; **menos mal** thank goodness, 9; **no está mal** not bad, 9
la **maleta** suitcase, 2
el **maletín** briefcase, 16
la **maleza** vegetation, growth, weed, 6
malo bad, 4
la **mamá** mom, 3
mandar to send, 10
manejar to drive, 20
la **manera** manner, way, 9L; **de manera breve** briefly, 7L
el **manicomio** madhouse, insane asylum, 17
manifestarse (ie) to become evident, to be shown, 19L
la **mano** *f* hand, 2; **a manos de** at the hands of, *Civ 2*; **de segunda (tercera) mano** second- (third-) hand, 9L; **manos a la obra** let's get to work, 16; **se dan la mano** they shake hands, 12
el **manual** textbook, manual, 19
la **manzana** apple, *Com 2*
mañana tomorrow, 2; **9 de la mañana** 9 in the morning, 9 A.M., 7; **pasado mañana** the day after tomorrow, 20
el **mapa** map, 6
la **máquina de escribir** typewriter, 10
el **mar** sea, *Com 3*, 16
la **maravilla** wonder, marvel, 6
maravilloso marvelous, wonderful, *Civ 2*
marcado marked, strongly pronounced, 13L; **en forma tan marcada** in such a pronounced way, 13L
el **marcador** scoreboard, 17
marcar (qu): marcar un hito to become a landmark, *Civ 2*
el **marco** post, frame, 17
marcharse to leave, 13
el **marido** husband, 13
el **martes** Tuesday, 1
marxista Marxist, *Civ 2*
marzo March, 9
más plus, more, most, 3; **la chica más bonita** the prettiest girl, 5; **más. . .que** more than, 9; **más. . .que nunca** as. . .as ever, 13; **más vale** it's better, one had better, it would be better, 4; **más les vale que no** they had better not, 16; **un poco más (de)** a little more, 4
la **masa: las masas** the masses, *Civ 2*
la **masacre** massacre, 13
la **máscara** mask, *Civ 2*
masivo massive, 9L
el **mastín** mastiff, *Civ 1*
la **matanza** killing, 13
matar to kill, 6
las **matemáticas** mathematics, 19
la **materia** subject, 19
matricularse to register, 19
el **matrimonio** wedding, marriage, 3
maya Mayan, of the Mayan Indians, 6; el, la **maya** Mayan Indian, *Civ 1*
mayo May, 9
mayor older, oldest, largest, most, 9; greatest, 11L; el **mayor número de** the greatest number of, 9L
la **mayoría** majority, 9L; la **mayoría de** the majority, most of, 9L
la **mayúscula** capital letter, 13L
me me, to me, 6; myself, 11
mecánico mechanical, 18; el **mecánico** mechanic, 18; el **taller mecánico** auto workshop, 18
la **media** stocking, 15
la **medianoche** midnight, 4
la **medicina** medicine, 4
médico medical, 9L; el **médico, la médica** doctor, 4
medieval medieval, 19L
medio middle, 11L; half, 16; **media** half-past, 7; la **clase media** middle class, 13L; la **instrucción media** secondary education, 19L; el **medio** artistic medium, *Civ 2*; **por medio de** through, *Civ 1*
el **mediodía** noon, 7
mejor better, best, 9; rather, instead, 19; **¿por qué mejor no. . .?** why not. . ., why wouldn't it be better to . . . ?, 19
mejorar to improve, 4
melancólico melancholy, *Civ 2*
memorable memorable, 17
mencionar to mention, 7L
menor younger, youngest, 9
menos less, minus, 4; before (the hour), 7; **a menos que** unless, 18; **es lo de menos** who cares?, 19; **lo de menos** the least of it, the least important part, 19; **menos mal** thank goodness, 9; **menos. . .que** less than, 9; **por lo menos** at least, 16; **son las dos menos cinco** it's five minutes to two, 7
el **mensaje** message, 17; el **mensaje comercial** advertisement, message from the sponsor, 17
mental mental, 76, 12
la **mente** mind, 19L
el **menú** menu, *Com 2*
menudo: a menudo often, 11L
el **mercado** market, 5L, 18
el **mes** month, 9
la **mesa** table, *Com 1;* **a la mesa** at the table, *Com 2*
el **mesero** waiter, 8; la **mesera** waitress, 8

Mesoamérica Pre-Hispanic area of Mexico and Central America sharing one general civilization, *Civ 1*
la **meta** goal, 17
meter to put into, to stick, to insert, 6; to put, 12
la **metralleta** sub-machine gun, 16
el **metro** subway, 10
la **metrópoli** metropolis, 9L
mexicano Mexican, 11L; el **mexicano, la mexicana** Mexican, 2
México Mexico, 2
la **mezcla** mixture, 7L
mezclar to mix, 7L
mi, mis my, 2, 5
mí *after preposition* me, 7
el **miedo** fear, 8; **tener miedo** to be afraid, 8
el **miembro** member, 19L
mientras while, during, 9L; **mientras que** whereas, 9L; **mientras tanto** in the meantime
el **miércoles** Wednesday, 1
la **migración** migration, 9L
mil thousand, 12; **gracias mil** thanks a million, 12
milagroso miraculous, 19
militar military, 4; el **militar** solider, military man, 5L
militarmente militarily, 19L
el **millón** million, 8; **dos millones de dólares** two million dollars, 8; **millones de** millions of, 8
minar to undermine, 19L
la **minoría** minority, 11L; la **minoría selecta** elite, *Civ 2*
el **minuto** minute, 3
mío my, (of) mine, 15
mirar to look at, to watch, 10
el **misionero,** la **misionera** missionary, 16
mismo same, 8; very, 14; **allí mismo** right there, 14; **aquí mismo** right here, 15L; la **misma persona** the very person, 19L; **lo mismo de siempre** the same as always, 10
la **mitad** half, 11L, 16
mítico mythical, *Civ 2*
el **mito** myth, *Civ 1*
la **mochila** backpack, 6
moderado moderate, 13L
la **modernidad** modernity, 13L
el **modernismo** modernism, *Civ 2*
moderno modern, 7
el **molde** pattern, 11L
molestar to bother, to annoy 7
el **momento,** 6; **en el momento en que** at the time that, at the moment that, 18
el **mono** monkey, 16
monopolizar (c) to monopolize, 18
monstruoso monstrous, *Civ 2*
la **montaña** mountain, 7L
montar a caballo to mount a horse, to go horseback riding, 14
el **monte** wilderness, jungle, forest, 6; the mountains, *Com 3*; **estar en el monte** to be in the mountains, *Com 3*
morir (ue, u) to die, 10; **morirse** to pass away, 16; **morirse (de)** to die (of), 11
el **moro** "Moor", Moslem invader, *Civ 1*
mostrar (ue) to show, to display, 12
el **motivo** motive, *Civ 1*, 19
el **motor** motor, 16
el **movimiento** movement, *Civ 2*
el **muchacho** boy, 6; la **muchacha** girl, 16
mucho much, a lot, 2; **muchos** many, 2
mudar to move, 19L
mueble: los **muebles** furniture, *Com 1*
la **muerte** death, 13L
muerto dead, died, 14
la **mujer** woman, 2; la **mujer de negocios** businesswoman, 18
mundial world, *Civ 2*
el **mundo** world, 2; **"tercer mundo"** Third World, *Civ 2*; **todo el mundo** everybody, 3L, 15; the whole world, 17L
el **mural** mural, *Civ 2*
el **museo** museum, *Civ 1*, 18
la **música** music, 11
musulmán Moslem, 19L
muy very, 1

N

la **nación** nation, *Civ 1*
nacional national, 2
la **nacionalidad** nationality, 20
el **nacionalismo** nationalism, 13L
nada nothing, anything, 4; **nada, nada** think nothing of it, not at all, 18; **nada de** + *noun* no + *noun*, none of + *modified noun*, 9; **nada de eso** oh, no, absolutely not, nothing like that, 13
nadar to swim, *Com 3*
nadie no one, nobody, 9
la **naranja** orange, *Com 2*
la **natación** swimming, 17L
naturalmente naturally, 3L, 9
el **náufrago,** la **náufraga** shipwrecked person, 8
navegar (gu) to sail, to navigate, *Civ 1*, 16
la **Navidad** Christmas, 3; las **Navidades** Christmas season, 3
necesariamente necesarily, 7L, 9
necesario necessary, 3L
la **necesidad** need, 9L
los **necesitados** needy people, *Civ 2*
necesitar to need, 2; **necesitar** + *inf* to need to do something, 3
negativo negative
el **negocio** business matter, 2; los **negocios** business, 2; el **hombre de negocios** busi-

nessman, 2; la **mujer de negocios** businesswoman, 18
negro black, 4; el **negro,** la **negra** black person, 7L
el **nene,** la **nena** child, little boy, or girl, 20; (colloquial) sweetheart, dear, 10
nervioso nervous, 15
ni nor, 13L; **ni. . .ni** neither. . .nor, 9; **ni hablar de** don't even mention, 4
nicaragüense Nicaraguan, *Civ 2*
ningún, ninguno no, not any, 9; **ninguno** pronoun none, no one, 9
el **niño,** la **niña** child, 10
nítido clear, *Civ 2*
el **nivel** level, 19L
no no, 1; **¡no, hombre!** not at all, 5; **no obstante** yet, nevertheless, however, 9L
la **nobleza** nobility, *Civ 1*
la **noción** notion, idea, 15L
la **noche** night, 2; **buenas noches** good night, 2; **esta noche** tonight, 2; **por la noche** at night, 4
el **nombre** name, *Civ 1*, 16
normalmente normally, usually, 3L
norte northern, *Civ 1*; el **norte** north, 14
la **Norteamérica** North America, *Civ 1*
norteamericano American, 11
noruego Norwegian, *Civ 1*
nos us, to us, 6; ourselves, 11; each other, 15
nosotros, nosotras we, 2; *after preposition* us, 7
la **nota** grade, mark, 20; **sacar (qu) una buena nota** to get a good mark, 20
notable noteworthy, *Civ 1*; outstanding, *Civ 2*
notablemente notably, *Civ 2*
la **novela** novel, *Civ 1*; la **novela picaresca** picaresque novel, *Civ 1*
el, la **novelista** novelist, *Civ 2*
noveno ninth, 13
el **novio** suitor, fiancé, steady boyfriend, 3L, 13; la **novia** fiancée, steady girlfriend, 3L, 13; los **novios** (steady, engaged) couple, 3L, 13
noviembre November, 9
la **nube** cloud, 4; **por las nubes** sky-high (literally, in the clouds), 4
nuestro our, 5; our, (of) ours, 15
Nueva Escocia Nova Scotia, *Civ 1*
Nueva Inglaterra New England, *Civ 1*
nuevo new, 1; **de nuevo** again, 13
el **número** number, 4; el **mayor número** the greatest number of, 9L; el **número de teléfono** telephone number, *Com 4;* el **número ocupado** busy line, *Com 4*
numeroso numerous, 7L
nunca never, 5; **no. . .nunca** not ever, 5; **nunca pensé, jamás soñé** never in my wildest dreams, 6

O

o or, 2; **o. . .o** either. . .or, 9
el **objeto** goal, object, *Civ 2*; el **objeto supremo** the chief goal, *Civ 2*
obligar (gu) to force, to oblige, *Civ 2*
la **obra** work, 16; body of work, *Civ 2* ; **manos a la obra** let's get to work, 16; **obra maestra** masterpiece, *Civ 1*
el **obrero,** la **obrera** worker, 11L; el **obrero no calificado** unskilled worker, 11L
la **observación** observation, 5
el **observador,** la **observadora** viewer, *Civ 2*
observar to observe, 5L, 20
obstante: no obstante yet, nevertheless, however, 9L
obtener (like **tener**) to obtain, to get, 7L
ocasionar to create, 5L
occidental Western, 7L
el **océano** ocean, *Civ 1*
octavo eighth, 13
octubre October, 9
ocupado busy, *Com 4*, 18
ocupar to spend, to occupy, 19L; to take over 19L
ocurrir to occur, *Civ 1*; to take place, to happen, 13
odiado hated, *Civ 1*
el **oeste** west, 14
oficial official, 13L
la **oficina** office, 2; la **oficina de correos** post office, 10
oír (oigo, y) to hear, 7; **¡oye!** hey, listen!, 16
ojalá! I hope so!, 4; let's hope, 10
el **ojo** eye, 9; **dichosos los ojos** how wonderful to see you, 18; **ver con malos ojos** to disapprove, 19L
el, la **olmeca** Olmec Indian, *Civ 1*
olvidar to forget, 13; **olvidarse (de)** to forget (to), 12
opinar (de) to think (of), 19
la **opinión** opinion, 3
la **oportunidad** opportunity, 17L
optimista optimistic, 4
opuesto opposite, 11L; **estar opuesto a** to be opposed to, 13L
la **oración** sentence, 6
el **orden** order, 5; **a sus órdenes** at your service, 20
la **oreja** ear, 9
orgánico organic, 19
organizar (c) to organize, 3L
el **origen** origin, *Civ 1*
originarse to originate, *Civ 2*
la **ornamentación** ornamentation, *Civ 1*
el **oro** gold, 16

os you, to you, 6; yourselves, 11
el **otoño** fall, 6
otro other, another, 3; **otra vez** again, another time, 3
la **oveja** sheep, 14

P

la **paciencia** patience, 18
el, la **paciente** patient, 9L
pacífico Pacific, *Civ 1*; peaceful, *Civ 2*
el **pacto** pact, 8
el **padre** (el **papá**) father, 3; los **padres** mother and father, parents, 3
pagar (gu) to pay, to pay for, *Com 2*, 10
el **país** country, nation, 3L, 4
el **pájaro** bird, 14
la **pala** shovel, 6
la **palabra** word, 15L, 19
palpable concrete, tangible, *Civ 1*
el **pan** bread, 7
panamericano Pan American, 15
los **pantalones** pants, 15; los **pantalones vaqueros** blue jeans, 15
la **papa** potato, 7
el **papá** dad, 3
el **papel** paper, 10
el **par** couple, 19
para for, to, in order to, 2; headed for, to become, due for, 8; **estudio para profesor** I'm studying to become a professor, 8; **para acá** over here, 10; **para el martes** by Tuesday, 8; **para que** so that, in order that, 18; **para sí** to himself, herself, yourself, itself, themselves, yourselves, oneself, 14
el **paraíso** paradise, 7L
el **paraguas** umbrella, 20
el **paraje** spot, place
el **paramédico**, la **paramédica** paramedic, 9L
parecer (zc) to seem, 6; **¿qué te parece?** what do you think?, how do you like?, 7
parecido similar, *Civ 2*
la **pareja** couple, 3L
el **parlante** loudspeaker, 15
el **parque** park, 3L, 10
la **parte** part, 5L, 6; **en gran parte** to a large extent, 13L; **en todas partes** everywhere, 15L; **por una parte. . .por otra** on the one hand . . .on the other hand, 9L
la **partera** midwife, 9L
participante participating, *Civ 2*; el, la **participante** participant, 8
participar to participate, 17L
el **partido** match, game, 12
partir to leave, to depart, 3
pasado last, past, 6; el **pasado** past, 13; el **año pasado** last year, 6; **pasado mañana** the day after tomorrow, 20
el **pasajero**, la **pasajera** passenger, 20
el **pasaporte** passport, 2
pasar to spend, to pass (time), *Civ 1*; to happen, 5; to come in, enter, 18; to stop by, 20; **al pasar el tiempo** as time goes by, *Civ 1*; **pasar a ser** to become, 11L; **pasar de** to count more than, to exceed, *Civ 2*; **pase usted** please come (go) in, 18
pasearse to walk, to pace, to take a walk or ride, 11
el **paseo** outing, 3L
la **pasta de dientes** toothpaste, 20
patente evident, obvious, 19L
el **patio** patio, yard, *Civ 1*, 5
la **patria** fatherland, homeland, 7
la **paz** peace, 5L; la **paz y el orden** law and order, 5L
el **pedido** order, 18
pedir (i) to order, to ask for, 4
pegar (gu) to hit, 10
el **peine** comb, 20
la **película** film, 3L, 18
la **pelota** ball, 12
la **península** peninsula, 7L; la **Península Ibérica** Iberian Peninsula, 19L
el **pensamiento** thought, *Civ 2*
pensar (ie) to think, 4; **pensar de** to think of (have an opinion about), 19; **pensar en** to think about, 15; **pensar + *inf*** to plan on, to intend to do something, 19; **ni lo pienses** don't even think of it, 16; **pensándolo bien** thinking it over, 8; **¿qué piensan de él?** what do they think of him?, 19
peor worse, 9; el **peor** worst, 9
la **pepita** nugget, 16
pequeño small, little, 5
perder (ie) to lose, 12; to miss (a train), 16; **perder la calma** to get upset, 19; **perderse** to miss out on (a party, etc.), 16
la **pérdida** loss, *Civ 1*
perdonar to forgive, 12
perfectamente perfectly, 9
perfecto perfect, 12
el **periódico** newspaper, 11
el **período** period, *Civ 2*
permanente permanent, *Civ 1*
permitir to permit, 18
pero but, 1
el **perro** dog, 9; **¡a otro perro con ese hueso!** get out of here!, forget it!, don't be silly!, 9
la **persistencia** persistence, 19l
la **persona** person, 3
el, la **personaje** person, character, 9L
personal personal, 5
peruano Peruvian, 7
pesar to weigh, 14; **a pesar de que** in spite of the fact that, 15L
la **pesca** fishing, 17L
el **pescado** fish, 7

el **peso** weight, 9
el **petróleo** oil, petroleum, *Civ 2*
petrolero *adj* oil, petroleum, *Civ 2*
el **pez** fish, 17L; **peces de agua dulce** fresh-water fish, 17L
el, la **pianista** pianist, 11
el **piano** piano, *Com 3*, **tocar (qu) el piano,** to play the piano, *Com 3*
picaresco picaresque, *Civ 1*
el **pie** foot, 9
la **piedra** stone, 16
la **piedrita** pebble, 16
la **pierna** leg, 9
pintar to paint, *Civ 2*
el **pintor,** la **pintora** painter, *Civ 1*
pintoresco picturesque, 9L
la **pintura** art, painting, *Civ 1*
la **pirámide** pyramid, 6
la **piscina** swimming pool, *Com 3*
la **pista** landing strip, runway, 15
la **pizarra** chalkboard, 19
el **placer** pleasure, 18
el **plan:** el **plan de estudios** curriculum, 19L
el **planeta** planet, 15L
la **plata** money (literally, silver), 4
plateresco plateresque (a style of architecture), *Civ 1*
el **platero** silversmith, *Civ 1*
el **plato** dish, *Com 2*
la **playa** beach, 7L
pleno: en plena in the middle of, 18
el **plomo** lead, 16
la **pluma** pen, 10
la **población** population, 11L
pobre poor, 13
poco little, few, 3L; **poco a poco** little by little, gradually, 13L; **un poco** a little, somewhat, 2; **un poco más (de)** a little more, 4
poder (ue, u) to be able, can, 4; el **poder** power, *Civ 1*; **se puede** one can, 5L
el, la **poeta** poet, *Civ 2*
poético poetic, *Civ 2*
la **poetisa** woman poet, *Civ 2*
la **política** politics, 5L
político political, 5L
poner (pongo) to put, 5; to turn on, to put on (radio, television), *Com 3;* **poner furioso** to make furious, 11; **ponerse** to get, to become, 11; **ponerse el abrigo** to put on one's coat, 11
popular popular, 17L
la **popularidad** popularity, 17L
popularizar (c) to popularize, *Civ 2*
por for, through, 3; around, by, 8; because of, for the benefit of, instead of, in place of, in exchange for, 9; along, across, 16; **por aquí** around here, 8; **por avión** airmail, 10; **por ciento** per cent, 13L; **por cierto** by the way, 17L; **por completo** completely, 13L; **por consiguiente** consequently, 11L; **por ejemplo** for example, 11L; **por favor** please, 1; **por fin** finally, at last, 6; **por hora** per hour, 17L; **por la noche** at night, 4; **por la tarde** in the afternoon, 2; **por las nubes** sky-high (literally, in the clouds), 4; **por lo menos** at least, 16; **por medio de** through, *Civ 1*; **por una parte. . .por otra parte** on the one hand. . .on the other hand, 9L; **¿por qué?** why?, 3; **por ser** because it is, 15L; **por supuesto** of course, 7; **por último** finally, 17L
el **porcentaje** percent, 11L
la **porción** portion, part, 15L
porque because, 4
el **portafolio** portfolio, folder, 20
Portugal Portugal, 17
portugués Portuguese, 17; el **portugués** Portuguese (language), 17; el **portugués,** la **portuguesa** Portuguese person, 17
la **posesión** possession, *Civ 2*
posible possible, 5
el **postre** dessert, 4
prácticamente practically, 7L
practicar (qu) to practice, 9L
práctico practical, 13L
el **precio** price, 4; **a precios fijos** at fixed prices, 8
predecir (like **decir**) to predict, 20
predominantemente predominately, 15L
el **predominio** predominance, *Civ 2*
preferible preferable, 8
preferir (ie, i) to prefer, 4
la **pregunta** question, 12
preguntar to question, to ask (a question), 15; **preguntarse (si)** to wonder (if), 12
la **prehistoria** pre-history, 7L
premarital premarital, 13L
el **premio** prize, *Civ 2*
prender turn on, 17; to light up, 18
preocupado worried, 5
preocuparse de to worry about, 19
la **preparación** preparation, 19L
preparar to prepare, *Com 1*, 16; **prepararse** to get ready, 17
la **presencia** presence, 9L
presentar to present, 7L
la **presidencia** presidency, 7
el, la **presidente** president, 5
la **presión** pressure, 9; la **presión arterial** blood pressure, 9
prestar atención to pay attention, 13L
primario primary, elementary, 19L
la **primavera** spring, 6
primer, primero first, 2, 13; **de primera** first class, 16
el **primo,** la **prima** cousin, 5
principal principal, main, 17L

principalmente mainly, 7L
el **principio** beginning, 11L; **al principio** at or in the beginning, at first, *Civ 1*; **a principios de** at the beginning of, *Civ 2*
la **prisa** hurry, 8; **darse prisa** to hurry up, 11; **tener prisa** to be in a hurry, 8
los **prismáticos** binoculars, 16
el **privilegio** privilege, *Civ 1*
probable probable, 11
probablemente probably, *Civ 1*, 12
probar (ue) to try, to taste, 7; to suit, to agree with, to test, to prove, 9
el **problema** problem, 2
la **producción** production, *Civ 2*
producir (zc) to produce, 9L, 14
el **producto** product, 5L, 17
la **profecía** prophecy, *Civ 1*
la **profesión** profession, 8
profesional professional, 9L
el **profesor,** la **profesora** teacher, professor, 1
la **profundidad** depth, profundity, 3L
profundo deep, Civ 2
el **programa** program, 3L, 11
programado planned, 19L
el **progreso** progress, 7
la **prohibición** restriction, 9
prolongar (gu) to prolong, 12
prometer to promise, *Civ 2*
el **prometido** fiancé, 13; la **prometida** fiancée, 13
pronto soon, 13; quick, quickly, 17; **tan pronto como** as soon as, 19
la **propagación** propagation, spreading, *Civ 1*
propício propitious, favorable, *Civ 2*
el **propietario** owner, 9L
la **propina** tip, *Com 2*
proporcionar to make available, 13L
propósito: a propósito by the way, 9
la **prosperidad** prosperity, 13L
próspero prosperous, *Civ 2*
proteger (j) to protect, 14
provechoso beneficial, 8
la **provincia** province, 9L; la **farmacia de provincia** small-town pharmacy, 9L
provocar (qu) to bring about, *Civ 2*
próximo next, 20
psicológico psychological, 9L
psicológicamente psychologically, 9L
publicar (qu) to publish, *Civ 2*
público public, 19L; el **público** audience, public, 12
el **pueblo** town, village, 7; people, nation, *Civ 2*
la **puente** bridge, 14
la **puerta** door, *Com 2*, 8
puertorriqueño Puerto Rican, 11L
pues well, 3L; since, 4; then, 14; **pues bien** all right, well, 5
puesto put, placed, 14
el **puesto** position, job, 5
puesto que since, 11L, 15
la **pulsera** bracelet, 16L
el **punto** point, 7; el **punto de vista** viewpoint, *Civ 2*; **en punto** exactly, on the dot, 7
puro pure, *Civ 2*

Q

que who, that, 3; *relator word* who, which that, 17; **lo que** what, that which, 17
qué what, what a, 1; **¿qué?** what?, 3; **¡qué!** what!, how!, 7; **¡qué (bueno)!** how (good it is)!, 2; **¡qué (comida) más (sabrosa)!** what a (delicious meal)!; **qué cosa** hey, what's that, 4; **qué hay con. . .** what about. . ., 10; **¿qué le pareció?** what did you think of?, 8; **¡qué maravilla!** how fantastic!, 6; **¿qué remedio?** what is to be done?, there's nothing you can do about it, 7; **¿qué te parece. . .?** what do you think of. . .?, how do you like. . .?, 7; **¡qué va!** go on!, of course not!, 5; **¿Y qué (con eso)?** so what?, what's the connection?, 5
quedar to be left, 7; to remain, 17L; **quedar en** to agree to, 13; **quedarse** to remain, to stay, 11
quejarse (de) to complain (about), 12
querer (ie, i) to want, to love, 4; (in the preterit) to try, 7; (preterit negative) to refuse, 7; **querer decir** to mean, 6; **no quiso venir** he refused to come, 7
el **queso** cheese, *Com 2*
quien, quienes who, whom, 1; **¿de quién(es)?** whose?, 5
la **química** chemistry, 5
quinto fifth, 11L, 13
quitar to remove, 6; **quitarse** to take off (clothing), 11
quizá(s) perhaps, 12

R

racial racial, 7L
racional rational, reasonable, 13L
el **radio,** la **radio** radio, *Com 1*, 17; **poner el radio** to turn on the radio, *Com 3*
rápidamente quickly, 6
rápido fast, rapidly, 6; **más rápido** faster, 6
raro rare, 5L; strange, 15; **rara vez** rarely, 5L
el **rato** a little while, 2
la **raza** race, 7L
la **razón** reason, *Civ 2*; **tener razón** to be right, 8

reaccionar (ante) to react (to), 11
reaccionario reactionary, 13L
realmente really, 7L
la **realidad** reality, *Civ 1*; **en realidad** really, in fact, 19L
realista realistic, 13L
la **rebelión** revolt, rebellion, *Civ 2*
el **recado** message, 11
la **recepción** reception, 2
recetar to prescribe, 9L
recibir to receive, 5L, 10
recientemente recently, 11L
la **recomendación** recommendation, 16L
reconstruir (y) to reconstruct, 14
recordar (ue) to remember, 10
recuperar to recover, recuperate, 13L
referir (ie, i) to refer, 17L
el **refresco** soft drink, *Com 2*
el **refrigerador** refrigerator, *Com 1*
refulgente shining, *Civ 2*
la **región** region, 7L
regresar to return, 18
reír, reírse to laugh, 16
la **relación** relation, 3L; **relaciones comerciales** commercial ties, *Civ 2*; **relaciones sexuales** sexual relations, 13L
la **religión** religion, 13L
religioso religious, *Civ 1*
el **reloj** watch, clock, 16
el **remedio** remedy, cure, 9L; **¿qué remedio?** what's to be done?, there's nothing you can do about it, 7
remoto remote, 9L
el **renacimiento** renaissance, rebirth, *Civ 2*
la **renovación** renovation, *Civ 2*
la **renta** rent, *Com 1*
repetir (i) to repeat, 10
repente: de repente all of a sudden, suddenly, 15
el **reportero** reporter, 12
la **representación** representation, *Civ 2*
representar to represent, *Civ 1*
reprobado: ser reprobado to fail (an exam, a course), 19
la **república** republic, 5L
requerir (ie, i) to require, to need, 13L
la **reseña** review, 11
resfriado: estar resfriado to have a cold, 13
residir to reside, 11L
resolver (ue) to resolve, 9L, 13; **resolverse** to resolve itself, 9L
respectivamente respectively, 7
respectivo respective, 11L, 16
respetar to respect, 19L
respecto: con respecto a with regard to, 19L
responder to reply, 19L
la **responsabilidad** responsibility, 3L
responsable responsible, 13
la **respuesta** answer, 15L
restablecer (zc) reestablish, 5L
el **restaurante** restaurant, 2
el **resto** rest, 11
los **restos** ruins, remains, 6
el **resultado** result, 11L; **como resultado de** as a result of, 11L
resumir to summarize, 7L; to sum up, 19L
retirarse to leave, to retire, 12
la **retórica** rhetoric, 19L
el **retorno** return, *Civ 1*
retrasarse to be late, 12
el, la **retratista** portrait painter, *Civ 1*
la **reunión** reunion, meeting, 3L, 8
revisar to review, 7L; to check, to revise, 14
la **revista** magazine, *Com 3*
la **revitalización** revitalization, *Com 2*
la **revolución** revolution, 15L
revolucionar to revolutionize, *Civ 2*
el **revolucionario,** la **revolucionaria** revolutionary, *Civ 2*
rico tasty, delicious, 7: rich, wealthy, 13
el **rifle** rifle, 8
rígido rigid, strict, 13L
rigor: es de rigor it is absolutely necessary, 19L
el **río** river, *Civ 2*, 16
rivalizar (c) to rival, *Civ 2*
rojo red, 4
romano Roman, 7L
romper to break, 13,
el **ron** rum, 15L
la **ropa** clothes, 15; la **ropa interior** underwear, 15
roto broken, 14
rural rural, 9L, 14
Rusia Russia, 17
ruso Russian, 17

S

S.A. (Sociedad Anónima) Inc. (Incorporated), 18
el **sábado** Saturday, 1
saber (sé) to know (information), 5; (in the preterit) to find out, 7; **saber** + *inf* to know how to (do something), 8; **bien saber** to know perfectly well, 19; **cómo no voy a saber** of course I know, 13; **yo bien sé** believe me, I know, 10
sabroso tasty, delicious, 7
sacar (qu) to pull out, to remove, to take out, 6; to withdraw, 13; **sacar de contrabando** to smuggle out, 16; **sacar dinero** to withdraw money, *Com 4;* **sacar las entradas** to get the tickets, *Com 3*
la **sala** living room, *Com 1*, 5
salado salty, 17L
la **salida** exit, *Com 2;* **salida al mar** access to the sea, 17L

salir (salgo) to go out, to leave, 3; to come out, 5; **salir bien** turn out all right, 10; to pass (an exam, a course), 19; **salir más caro** to turn out (to be) more expensive, 14
saltar a la vista to become obvious, 7L
la **salud** health, 7; **¡Salud!** to your health!, 7; **estar bien de salud** to be healthy, 13
saludar to greet, 12
salvar to save,
sano healthy, 13; **estar sano** to be healthy, 13
el **santo,** la **santa** saint, 19
el **satélite** satellite, 17L
la **sátira** satire, *Civ 1*
sazonado witty, expressive, distinct, 7L
se *indirect object pronoun for* **le, les,** 6; himself, herself, yourself, itself, themselves, yourselves, oneself, 11; each other, 15; **se dan la mano** they shake hands, 12; **se llama María** her name is María, 5; **se quieren** they love each other, 15
el **secretario,** la **secretaria** secretary, 8
el **secreto** secret, 8
el **sector** sector, 13L
secundario secundary, 19L
la **sed** thirst, 8; **tener sed** to be thirsty, *Com 1,* 8; **tener una sed de náufrago** to be dying of thirst, 8
seguir (i) to follow, to continue, 4
segundo second, 9L, 13
seguramente surely, 19L
la **seguridad** security, *Civ 2*; **con toda seguridad** surely, *Civ 2*
seguro of course, (for) sure, 3
seleccionar to select, 3L
la **selección nacional** "all-Star team," 17L
la **selva** jungle, 7L, 9
el **sello** stamp, 10
la **semana** week, 6; la **semana pasada** last week, 6; la **semana que viene** next week, 6
semejante similar, 16
semi: semi-conocimiento partial knowledge, 9L; **semidemocrático** half-democratic, 19L
sencillamente simply, 3L
sencillo easy, simple, 17L
sendos: con sendas universidades with one university each, 19L
sensacional sensational, 17
sentarse (ie) to sit down, 11
el **sentido** sense, 13L
el **sentimiento** feeling, sense, *Civ 2*; ***Del sentimiento trágico de la vida*** *The Tragic Sense of Life, Civ 2*
sentir (ie, i) to be sorry, 11; **sentirse** to feel, 12; **lo siento** I'm sorry, 11
señalar to announce, *Civ 1*
señor, Sr. gentleman, sir, Mr., 1; los **señores X** Mr. and Mrs. X, 5
señora, Sra. woman, lady, ma'am, Mrs., 1
señorita, Srta. young lady, young woman, miss, Miss, 1
el, la **separatista** separatist, 13L
septiembre September, 9
séptimo (sétimo) seventh, 13
ser to be, 1; **ser conveniente** to be a good idea, 15; **ser reprobado** to fail (an exam, a course), 19
sereno serene, *Civ 2*
seriamente seriously, 3
serio serious, 3L, 9; **la cosa va en serio** the thing is getting serious, this is for real, 9
el **servicio** service, 9L, 18; **contrato de servicio** service contract, 18; **servicios médicos** medical services, 9L
servir (i) (de) to serve (as), to function (as), *Com 1,* 8; **estoy para servirle** it's my pleasure, 8
la **sesión** session, 8
el **sexo** sex, 3L
sexto sixth, 13
la **sexualidad** sexual matter, sexuality, 13L
si if, 4; **como si** as if, 17
sí yes, 1; *reflexive pronoun* **para sí** to himself (herself, yourself, themselves), 14; **sí, hombre** oh, yes, 2
siempre always, 1; **siempre que** whenever, 19
el **siglo** century, *Civ 1,* 17; el **Siglo de Oro español** Spanish Golden Age (16th-17th centuries), *Civ 1*
significar (qu) to mean, to signify, 3L
significativo significant, 13L
siguiente following, next, *Civ 1*
la **silla** chair, *Com 1*
simbólico symbolic, 17L
simpático nice, 4
sin without, 13L, 16; **sin embargo** however, *Civ 1*; nevertheless, 18; **sin que** without, 18
el **sindicato** labor union, 10
sino but rather, *Civ 1,* 18; **sino que** but rather, 18
sinónimo synonymous, 15L
el **sismómetro** seismometer, 20
el **sistema** system, 5L
el **sitio** place, 8
la **situación** situation, 2; la **situación económica** economic situation, 4
situado located, 15L
sobre about, on, *Civ 1,* 11; **sobre todo** especially, 19
sobrehumano superhuman, *Civ 1*
la **sobremesa** after-dinner conversation, 4; **de sobremesa** after dinner, 4
sobresaliente outstanding, 17L

social social, *Civ 2*
la **sociedad** society, 11L
el **sofá** sofa, *Com 1*
el **sol** sun, 7L, 13; **hace sol** it's sunny, 14; **tomar (el) sol** to sunbathe, *Com 1*
solamente only, 6
el **soldado** soldier, *Civ 1*, 20
la **soledad** solitude, *Civ 2*
soler (ue) + *inf* to usually + *verb*, 17
solo alone, 3L, 9; **café solo** black coffee, *Com 2;* el **solo** solo (performance), *Civ 2*
sólo only, 3
soltar (ue) to let loose, to let go, 17
el **sombrero** hat, 17
soñar (ue) to dream, 6
sonreír (í) to smile, 12
la **sopa** soup, *Com 2*
sorprender to surprise, 7L
la **sorpresa** surprise, 17L
sostener (like **tener**) to maintain, to hold (an opinion), *Civ 2*
el **statu quo** the status quo, 19L
su, sus his, her, your, its, one's, their, 5
suave gentle, *Civ 2*
suavemente softly, 15
subir (a) to climb, to go up, 6; to get on, in, 9; **subir de peso** to gain weight, 9
subsiguiente subsequent, *Civ 1*
el **suburbio** suburb, poor area on the outskirts of the city, 19L
subvertir (ie, i) to subvert, 5L
el **sucesor** successor, *Civ 1*
la **Sudamérica** South America, *Civ 1*
el **sudamericano,** la **sudamericana** South American, 8
el **sudoeste** southwest, *Civ 1*
el **suelo** floor, ground, 20
el **sueño** dream, *Civ 2*; **tener sueño** to be sleepy, 8
la **suerte** luck, 8; **por suerte** luckily, 14; **tener suerte** to be lucky, 8
suficiente enough, sufficient, 9L
el **sufrimiento** suffering, *Civ 1*
sufrir to suffer, 5L
sugerir (ie, i) to suggest, 4
la **super-estrella** super-star, *Civ 2*
superar to surpass, 17L
superior superior, 17L; **instrucción superior** higher education, 19L; **superior a** surpassing, exceeding, *Civ 2*
la **superioridad** superiority, 17
el **supermercado** supermarket, 7L
suponer (like **poner**) to suppose, 9
supremo supreme, 17L; el **objeto supremo** the chief goal, *Civ 2*
supuesto: por supuesto of course, 7
sur southern, *Civ 1*; el **sur** south, 14
surrealista surrealist, surrealistic, *Civ 2*
suspender to suspend, to call off, 19
suyo his, her, its, your, their, (of) his, (of) hers, (of) yours, (of) its, (of) theirs, 15

T

el **tabaco** tabacco, 15L; cigar, 18
tal this, such as, so, 12; **con tal (de) que** provided that, 18; **no hay tal cosa** there's no such thing, 12; **tal parece** it would appear, so it seems, 13L; **tal vez** maybe, 2
el **taller** workshop, 18; el **taller mecánico** auto workshop, 18
el **tamaño** size, 7L
también also, 1
tampoco neither, not. . .either, 9; **yo tampoco** me neither, 9
tan so, just as, 7L, 18; **tan. . .como** as. . .as, 14
tanto so much, 14; **tanto como** as much as, 14; **tanto(s)** + *noun* + **como** as many. . .as, as much. . .as, 14
las **tapas** (Spain) snacks, hors d'oeuvres, 8
tarde late, 3; la **tarde** afternoon, 2; **buenas tardes** good afternoon, 2; **más tarde** later, 11L; **por la tarde** in the afternoon, 2
la **tarea** homework, task, 19
la **tarjeta postal** postcard, 10
el **taxi** taxi, 11
la **taza** cup, 4
te you, (to) you, 6; yourself, 11
el **teatro** theater, *Civ 1*
la **técnica** technique, method, 9L
técnicamente technically, 11L
la **tecnología** technology, 19L
telefónico: la guía telefónica telephone book, *Com 4*
el, la **telefonista** telephone operator, *Com 4*
el **teléfono** telephone, 10; **contestar el teléfono** to answer the telephone, *Com 4*; el **número de teléfono** telephone number, *Com 4;* **llamar por teléfono** to telephone, 10
el **telegrama** telegram, 15
la **televisión** television, *Com 1*, 10; la **televisión a colores** color television, 15; **ver televisión** to watch television, *Com 1*
el **televisor** television set, *Com 1*
el **tema** theme, topic, *Civ 2*
el **temblor** tremor, 20; el **temblor de tierra** earthquake, 20
templada moderate, temperate, 7L
el **templo** temple, 6
temprano early, 3
tender (ie) la cama to make the bed, *Com 1*
tener (ie, tengo) to have, 5; to take, to hold, 11; **aquí tiene** here is, here are, 20;

ten here, here it is, 11; **tener. . .años** to be. . . years old, 7; **tener buen aspecto** to look well, healthy, 9; **tener calor** to be warm, hot, 8; **tener cita** to have an appointment, 9; **tener frío** to be cold, 8; **tener ganas de** + *inf* to feel like (doing something), to be anxious to (do something), 8; **tener hambre** to be hungry, 8; **tener la intención de** to plan to, to intend to, 19; **tener miedo** to be afraid, 8; **tener prisa** to be in a hurry, 8; **tener que** + *inf* to have to (do something), 5; **tener razón** to be right, 8; **tener sed** to be thirsty, 8; **tener sueño** to be sleepy, 8; **tener suerte** to be lucky, 8; **tener tiempo de** + *inf* to have the time to, 10; **tener un hambre de huérfano** to be dying of hunger, 8; **tener una sed de náufrago** to be dying of thirst, 8

el **teniente** lieutenant, 7

el **tenis** tennis, 4

tercer, tercero third, 13

terco stubborn, 7

la **terminal** terminal, 15

el **tío** uncle, 7; (slang) guy, 11

terminar to end, 7L, 12; to complete, 18

el **término** term, word, 15L

terrenal earthly, on earth, 7L

el **terreno** land, terrain, 7L; ground, 13L

terrible terrible, awful, *Civ 2*

territorial territorial, *Civ 1*

el **territorio** territory, 11L

el **terrorismo** terrorism, 13L

el, la **terrorista** terrorist, 5L

ti (after preposition) you, 7

el **tiempo** time, 8; weather, 14; **al pasar el tiempo** as time went by, *Civ 1*; **antes de tiempo** ahead of time, 8; **con el paso del tiempo** with time, 19L; **¿cuánto tiempo hace que . . . ?** how long . . . ?, 9; **hace buen (mal) tiempo** it's nice (bad) weather, 14; **no hace mucho tiempo** not too long ago, 13L; **¿qué tiempo hace?** how's the weather, 13

la **tienda** store, 18

la **tierra** land, earth, ground, 7L, 14; el **temblor de tierra** earthquake, 20; la **tierra firme** mainland, 11L; las **tierras vascas** Basque region, 17L; **tomar tierra** to land, 15

el **tigre** tiger (in Latin America **tigre** also is used to refer to jaguars, cougars, and bobcats), 6

tinto red (wine), *Com 2*

el **tío** uncle, 7; (slang) guy, 11; la **tía** aunt, 7; los **tíos** aunt and uncle, 7; **Tío Sam** Uncle Sam, 11L

típico typical, 15L

el **tipo** type, kind, 7L

la **tiza** chalk, 19

la **toalla** towel, 20

tocante a about, with respect to, relative to, 13L, 16

tocar (qu) to play (a record or instrument), *Com 3*

todavía still, yet, 3

todo everything, 3; all (of), 5; *plural* all, every, 4; **ante todo** above all, 14; **en todas partes** everywhere, 15L; **sobre todo** especially, *Civ 2;* **toda la tarde** the whole afternoon, 5; **todo un mes** a whole month, 15; **todo el mundo** everyone, 3L, 15; the whole world, 17L; **todos los días** every day, 4

tolerante tolerant, 13L

tolerar tolerate, 5L

el, la **tolteca** Toltec Indian, *Civ 1*

tomar to drink, to take, 4; **tomar (el) sol** to sunbathe, *Com 1, Com 3;* **tomar tierra** to land, 15

el **tomate** tomato, *Com 2*

la **tormenta** storm, 15L

tormentoso troubled, stormy, *Civ 2*

el **toreo** bullfighting, 17L

el **torneo** tournament, 12

trabajador hardworking, 4; el **trabajador,** la **trabajadora** worker, 14

trabajar to work, 3; **trabajar como burro** to work like a horse, 4; **trabajar con** to work for (with), 5; **trabajar de** to work as, 8

el **trabajo** work, job, 4

la **tradición** tradition, 17L

tradicionalista traditionalistic, 13L

traducir (zc) to translate, 6

traer (traigo) to bring, 5

el **tráfico** traffic, 11

trágico tragic, *Civ 2*

el **traje** suit, *Com 3*; el **traje de baño** bathing suit, *Com 3*

tranquilo calm, quiet, 11

la **transformación** transformation, change, 5L

transformar to transform, change, *Civ 2*

trascender (ie) to transcend, to go beyond, *Civ 2*

el **tratamiento** treatment, 9L

tratar de + *inf* to try to (do something), 4; **tratarse de** to be a matter of, 7L

el **trauma** trauma, *Civ 2*

través: a través de through, *Civ 2*

tremendo tremendous, 17

la **tripulación** crew, *Civ 1*

el **triunfo** triumph, 13L

el **tronco** trunk (of a tree), 14

el **trono** throne, *Civ 1*

tropical tropical, 7L

tu, tus your, 1
tú you, 1
el, la **turista** tourist, 15L
tuyo your, (of) yours, 15

U

u or, 16
ubicar (qu) to locate, 15L; **estar ubicado** to be located, 15L
Ud., Uds. (abbreviations for **usted, ustedes**) you, 2
uff wow (used to express great difficulty), 6
último last, 5L, 16; **por último** finally, 17L
ultramarino overseas, *Civ 2*
un, una a, an, one, 1; **una y mil veces** time and time again, a thousand and one times, 14
únicamente only, *Civ 1*
único only, 15
unirse to join, 9L
universal universal, *Civ 2*
la **universidad** university, 1
universitario university, 9L; university-trained, 19
uno one, 1; a person, 9; **uno a otro** each other, 15; **uno a uno** one by one, 20; **uno necesita viajar** a person (one) needs to travel, 9; **uno y otro** both, 3L
unos, unas a few, some, 3; **hace unos 10 años** about 10 years ago, some 10 years ago, *Civ 1*
urbano urban, 9L
urgente urgent, 18
el **uruguayo,** la **uruguaya** Uruguayan, 16
usar to use, 7
usted, ustedes you, 1, 2
utilizar (c) to use, to utilize, 9L, 20

V

la **vaca** cow, 14
las **vacaciones** vacation, 6; **de vacaciones** on vacation, 15
valer (valgo) to be worth, 6; **más les vale que no** they'd better not, 16; **valer la pena** to be worthwhile, 16
valioso valuable, *Civ 2*
el **valor** value, *Civ 2*; **falsos valores** false values, *Civ 2*
el **valle** valley, 14
vaquero cowboy, 15; **pantalones vaqueros** blue jeans, 15
la **variación** variation, 1
variado varied, 7L
variar (í) to vary, 19L
la **variedad** variety, 7L
varios several, 13
vasco Basque, 7L
el **vaso** glass, *Com 2*
la **velocidad** speed, 17L
vender to sell, 10
venezolano Venezuelan, 5; el **venezolano,** la **venezolana** Venezuelan person, 16
venir (ie, vengo) to come, 6; **venir a casa** to come home, 20
la **ventaja** advantage, 18
la **ventana** window, *Com 1,* 14
ver (veo) to see, 3; **a ver** let's see, 9; **ver con malos ojos** to disapprove, 19L; **ver televisión** to watch television, *Com 1,* 12
el **verano** summer, 6
la **verdad** truth, 4; **en verdad** really, truly, 17L; **es verdad** it's true, 4; **¿verdad?** true?, right?, isn't it?, 3
verdadero real, true, 17
verde green, 4
versátil versatile, *Civ 2*
el **vestido** dress, 15
vestirse (i) to get dressed, 11
la **vez** time (in a series), 3; **a veces** at times, 9; sometimes, 7; **una vez más** once more, 13L
vía *preposition* via, by way of, 17L
viajar to travel, 2
el **viaje** trip, 2; **de viaje** traveling, 15
viajero: el **cheque de viajero** traveler's check, *Com 4*
la **víbora** snake, 6
la **vida** life, 13; **mi vida** sweetheart, 3
viejo old, 4; el **viejo** "old man" (dad, father, husband), 7; **los viejos** parents (literally, old people), 4
el **viento** wind, 14; **hace viento** it's windy, 14
el **viernes** Friday, 1
vigorosamente vigorously, *Civ 2*
el **vikingo** Viking, *Civ 1*
el **vino** wine, 7; **vino tinto (blanco, de la casa)** red (white, house) wine, *Com 2*
violentamente violently, *Civ 2*
violento violent, 5L
el **violoncello** cello, *Civ 2*
el **virtuosismo** virtuosity, *Civ 2*
visigótico Visigothic, 19L
la **visión** vision, *Civ 2*
la **visita** visit, 9
visitar to visit, 3
vista view, sight, 7L; el **punto de vista** viewpoint, *Civ 2*; **saltar a la vista** to become obvious, 7L
el **vistazo** look, glance, 15L; **echar un vistazo** to take a look, 15L
visto seen, 14
vívido vivid, *Civ 2*
vivir to live, 5
vivo alive, living, bright, vivid, *Civ 2*
el **vocabulario** vocabulary, 1
volar (ue) to fly, 12
volver (ue) to return, 10; **volver a** + *inf* to (do something) again, 17; **volverse** to become, 15
vosotros, vosotras you, 2

la **voz** voice, 13; **en voz alta** out loud, aloud 13
el **vuelo** flight, 12
vuelto returned, 14
vuestro your, 5; your, (of) yours, 15
vulgar popular, common, *Civ 2*

Y

y and, 1; **¿y qué (con eso)?** so what?, what's the connection?, 5
ya already, 3; anymore, 12; **ya doy** I see, I get it, 5; **ya era tiempo** it was about time, 8; **ya es tarde** it's already late, 3; **¡ya lo creo!** I should say so!, it sure does!, 10; **ya no** no longer, 3L; not any more, 8; **ya que** since, 15
el **yacimiento petrolífero** oil deposit, *Civ 2*
el, la **yanqui** Yankee, 20
yo I, 1

Z

el **zapato** shoe, 15
la **zona** zone, area, 9L, 20; **zona urbana** urban area, 9L
el **zoológico** zoo, 18

English-Spanish Vocabulary

This vocabulary includes only the Spanish words needed to complete the translation exercises in the textbook.

A

a un, una
after después
again otra vez, de nuevo
ago hace + *expression of time*
alcohol el alcohol
all todo
already ya
also también
American americano
an un, una
and y
another otro
any: there isn't any more no hay más
anyone ninguno; (after negatives) nadie
anything cualquier cosa; (after negatives) nada
apartment el apartamento
arrive llegar (gu)
article el artículo
as como
ask (for something) pedir (i); (question) preguntar
asleep dormido
at en
aunt la tía

B

bad malo
ball la pelota
bank el banco
bathroom el (cuarto de) baño
be ser *or* estar; **to be able** poder(ue)
been sido *or* estado
beer la cerveza
become hacerse (me hago)
before antes
begin empezar (ie, c), comenzar (ie, c)
best mejor
biology la biología
black negro
Bolivian boliviano
book el libro
boot la bota
bother molestar
bought comprado
bottle la botella
boy el chico, el muchacho
bracelet la pulsera
bridge el puente
briefcase el maletín
bright brillante
bring traer (traigo)
broken roto
brush el cepillo
built construido; **houses are built** se construyen casas
business los negocios; **business (deal)** el negocio
but pero, sino
buy comprar

C

cable el cable
café el café
call llamar
calm down calmarse
can poder (ue)
car el carro, el coche
carry llevar; **to carry off** llevarse
class la clase
child niño
children los niños, los hijos
cloud la nube
coffee el café
cold frío
comb el peine
come venir (ie) (vengo); **to come back** volver (ue), regresar; **come in!** ¡adelante!
congratulalte felicitar
cost costar (ue)
country el país
cousin el primo, la prima
cup la taza
customs la aduana
cut cortar; *past participle* cortado; **trees are cut** se cortan árboles; **to cut down** (to diminish) disminuir (y)

D

dad el papá
daughter la hija
day el día
delicious rico, sabroso
dessert el postre
die morir (ue)
dinner (supper) la cena
discuss discutir
do hacer (hago)
doctor el doctor, la doctora
drink tomar, beber; **to drink up** beberse, tomarse

drug la droga

E

each *adj* cada; *pronoun* cada uno, cada una
early temprano
easy fácil
eat comer; **to eat up** comerse
economize economizar (c)
eight ocho
eighth octavo
either. . .or o. . .o
embassy la embajada
English inglés; (language) el inglés
enter entrar
even aun
everything todo
exam el examen
excellent excelente
experience la experiencia

F

fall asleep dormirse (ue, u)
family la familia
famous famoso
fan el aficionado, la aficionada; el fanático, la fanática
farm la finca
favor el favor
feel sentir (ie, i); **to feel good** estar bien, estar bueno
feet los pies
fewer menos
fifteen quince
fifth quinto
find encontrar (ue)
finish acabar, terminar
first primer, primero
five cinco
fix arreglar
food la comida
foot el pie
for para, por
foreigner el extranjero, la extranjera
forget olvidar
forgotten olvidado
found encontrado; **students are found there** allí se encuentran estudiantes
four cuatro
fourth cuarto
French francés; (language) el francés
friend el amigo, la amiga
Friday (el) viernes
from de; **from now on** de ahora en adelante
future el futuro
film la película

G

game el juego, el partido
gentleman el señor
get: to get (turn) black ponerse (pongo) negro; **to get furious** ponerse furioso; **to get going** irse; **to get married** casarse; **to get nervous** ponerse nervioso; **to get optimistic** ponerse optimista; **to get sick** ponerse enfermo; **to get to be** llegar (ue) a ser; **to get up** levantarse
girl la chica
give dar
go ir; **to go away** irse; **to go back** volver (ue), regresar; **to go on** seguir (i); **to go shopping** ir de compras; **to go to a movie** ir al cine; **to go to bed** acostarse (ue)
golfer el, la golfista
good bueno
grandparents los abuelos
great fantástico

H

hand la mano
handsome guapo
happen pasar
happy feliz
happily felizmente
hard duro, difícil
have tener (ie) (tengo); **to have a good time** divertirse (ie, i); **to have dinner** cenar; **to have left** quedar; **to have lunch** almorzar (ue, c), comer; **to have to** tener que + *inf*
he él
head for dirigirse (j) a
health la salud; **to be in good (poor) health** estar bien (mal) de salud
hear oír (y)
hello hola
her *direct object pronoun* la; *indirect object pronoun* le; *possessive pronoun* su
hide esconder
highway la carretera
him *direct object pronoun* lo; *indirect object pronoun* le
his su
home la casa
hotel el hotel

I

I yo
idea la idea
if si
imagine imaginar(se)
important importante
impossible imposible
in en; **in her place** en su lugar; **in order to** para
intelligent inteligente
invite invitar
it *direct object pronoun* lo; **it is necessary** es necesario

J

job el trabajo
just sólo

K

kid el chico, la chica; el niño, la niña
know (information) saber; (acquaintance) conocer (zc)

L

last: last night anoche; **last Tuesday** el martes pasado

late tarde
learn aprender
leave salir (salgo)
left *past participle* salido
less menos
letter la carta
like gustar, querer (ie, i)
listen escuchar
look mirar; **to look at** mirar; **to look for** buscar (qu); **to look great** estar fantástico, estar bien
lose perder (ie); **to lose weight** bajar de peso
lost perdido; **you are lost** ustedes se pierden
lot: a lot of mucho; **lots of** mucho
loud fuerte; **louder** más fuerte
luckily afortunadamente

M

major *verb* especializarse
make hacer (hago); **to make a call** hacer una llamada
map el mapa
market el mercado
match el partido, el juego
mathematics las matemáticas
maybe quizá, quizás, tal vez
meat la carne
meet conocer (zc), encontrar (ue)
mention mencionar
milk la leche
million el millón
minute el minuto
miss la señorita
miss out perderse (ie)
modern moderno
mom la mamá
Monday (el) lunes
money el dinero, la plata
more más
morning la mañana
movie la película
must deber; **must be, must have, must** *use future or conditional of probability* (deberá, debería)
Mrs. señora

N

name el nombre; **what is your name?** ¿cómo se llama usted?
need necesitar
neighborhood el barrio
new nuevo
next siguiente, próximo
ninth noveno
no no; **no one** ninguno
now ahora
number el número

O

of de
old viejo
on en
one uno, un, una; **one has to** hay que; **one of them** uno de ellos, una de ellos, una de ellas; **one ought** hay que
only *adj* solo; *adv* solamente, sólo
on time a tiempo
optimistic optimista
owner el dueño, la dueña

P

painter el pintor, la pintora
paper el papel
parents los padres
park el parque; *verb* estacionar
part la parte
party la fiesta
pass away morirse (ue)
passport el pasaporte
pay pagar (gu)
play jugar (ue, gu)
player el jugador, la jugadora
please por favor
pleasure el placer
point out señalar
portable radio el radio portátil, la radio portátil
post office la oficina de correos
president el presidente, la presidenta
pretty bonito
price el precio
probable probable
probably probablemente
problem el problema
produced producido; **potatoes are produced** se producen papas
professional profesional
professor el profesor, la profesora
profitable provechoso

Q

question la pregunta

R

radio el radio, la radio
raincoat el impermeable
read leer (y)
realize darse cuenta (de)
receive recibir
reception la recepción
record el disco
red rojo
remember recordar (ue)
restaurant el restaurante
return volver (ue), regresar
right? ¿no?, ¿verdad?, ¿no es verdad?
room el cuarto
running corriendo

S

Saturday (el) sábado
say decir
school la escuela
second segundo
secretary el secretario, la secretaria
see ver
seem parecer (zc); **to seem (appear) new, good** estar nuevo, bueno
send enviar (í), mandar
sent enviado, mandado
seventh séptimo
she ella
show enseñar
sir: yes, sir sí, señor
sister la hermana
sit sentarse (ie)
sixth sexto
sky-high por las nubes
sleep dormir (ue, u)
smile sonreír (í)
soap el jabón

soccer el fútbol
soccer ball la pelota de fútbol
sold vendido; **newspapers are sold** se venden periódicos
solved resuelto; **problems are solved** se resuelven problemas
so: so many tantos; **so much** tanto
someone alguien
something algo
sometimes a veces
son el hijo
soon pronto
Spanish español; (language) el español
speak hablar
special especial
spend (money) gastar; (time) pasar
stadium el estadio
stand up levantarse
stay quedarse
stereo el estéreo
stop detenerse (*like* tener); **(stop doing something)** dejar de + *inf*
strong fuerte
stubborn terco
student el, la estudiante
studied estudiado; **books are studied** se estudian libros
study estudiar
such tal
suggest sugerir (ie, i)
suitcase la maleta
summer el verano
Sunday el domingo
sure sí, chico; sí, chica

T

take tomar, llevar; **to take a shower** ducharse; **to take out** sacar (qu)
talk hablar
taste probar (ue); **to taste good** estar bueno, estar bien
taught enseñado; **Spanish and French are taught** se enseñan español y francés
teach enseñar
telegram el telegrama
tell contar (ue), decir
ten diez
tenth décimo
than que, de
thanks gracias; **thank you** gracias
that *demonstrative adj* ese, aquel; *demonstrative pronoun* eso, aquello; **that one** ése, aquél
the el, la, los, las
them *direct object pronoun* los, las
there ahí, allí; **there is, there are** hay; **there was, there were** había
they ellos, ellas
thing la cosa
think: what do you think? ¿qué te parece?
third tercer, tercero
this *demonstrative adj* este; *demonstrative pronoun* esto; **this one** éste
Thursday (el) jueves
to a
tomorrow mañana
tonight esta noche
towel la toalla
travel viajar
tree el árbol
trip el viaje
try tratar, probar (ue)
Tuesday (el) martes
two dos

U

ugly feo
umbrella el paraguas
uncle el tío
United States los Estados Unidos
university la universidad
upon + -ing al + *inf*
us *direct, indirect, and reflexive object pronoun* nos
usually normalmente
use usar
used to + verb *use a conjugated verb in the imperfect, e.g.,* **we used to ski** esquiábamos

V

vegetables las legumbres
very muy
visit visitar

W

wait esperar
walk andar, caminar; **to walk down the street** andar por la calle, caminar por la calle
want querer (ie, i)
water el agua *f*
we nosotros, nosotras
Wednesday el miércoles
week la semana
well bien
what qué; **what is your name?** ¿cómo se llama usted?; **what about . . . ?** ¿Y . . . ?
when cuándo
where dónde
which cuál
while mientras (que)
white blanco
who quién
whom a quíen
win ganar
wine el vino
wish desear, querer (ie, i)
with con; **with you** contigo, con usted
without sin
woman la mujer
wonder preguntarse *or use future or conditional of probability, e.g.,* **I wonder if he's there** ¿estará allí?
wonderful lindo, maravilloso
work el trabajo; **to work out (solve)** resolver (ue)
worried preocupado
worry preocuparse
write escribir

Y

year el año
yes sí
yesterday ayer
you tú, usted, ustedes
young joven; **young man** el joven; **young woman** la señorita, la joven
your tu, su

Index

Numbers refer to pages, often the first page of a discussion that continues for an additional page.

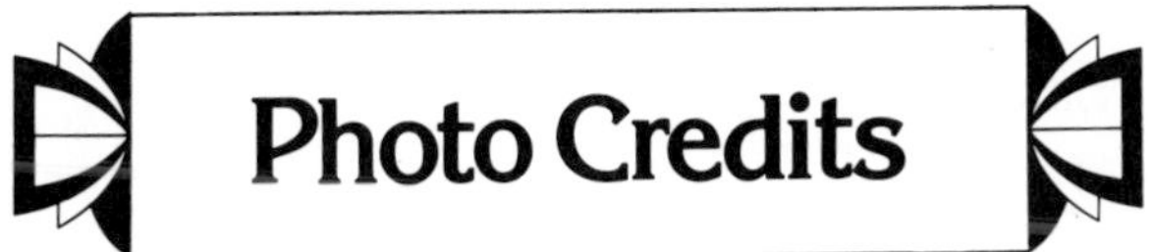

Photo Credits

Black and White Photographs

Page

2 Ana M. Redford
4 Peter Menzel
9 Peter Menzel
18 Ana M. Redford
23 Peter Menzel
25 David Mangurian
36 Ana M. Redford
44 Photo by Lupe/Peter Menzel
52 Beryl Goldberg
56 Peter Menzel
58 Peter Menzel
65 Diego Goldberg/Sygma
70 Courtesy of the Organization of American States
74 Peter Menzel
79 Carl Frank/Photo Researchers
88 George Gerster/Photo Researchers
90 Ana M. Redford
100 (left) Peter Menzel/Stock, Boston; (right) Carl Frank/Photo Researchers
107 David Mangurian
109 Cornell Capa/Magnum Photos, Inc.
120 WHO photo by Paul Almasy
122 George W. Gardner
129 WHO photo by Paul Almasy
146 Ernst Schrader
150 Ernst Schrader
155 Inge Morath/Magnum Photos, Inc.
163 Josip Ciganovic/Spanish National Tourist Office
164 Carl Frank/Photo Researchers
166 George Holton/Photo Researchers
172 Leo Pelissier/Rapho/Photo Researchers
173 Ernst Schrader
176 Ernst Schrader
187 Spanish National Tourist Office
196 Ana M. Redford
198 Ana M. Redford
208 WHO photo by Paul Almasy
214 David Mangurian
215 David Mangurian
216 WHO photo by D. Henrioud
217 Ana M. Redford
223 Michael Weisbrot from Black Star
227 Tom Hollyman/Photo Researchers
237 Fritz Henle/Photo Researchers
244 Courtesy of the Hispanic Society of America
246 Courtesy of the Hispanic Society of America
247 (top) Courtesy of the Hispanic Society of America; (bottom) Ernst Schrader
248 Spanish National Tourist Office
249 The Metropolitan Museum of Art, Bequest of Mrs. H. O. Havemeyer, 1929. The H. O. Havemeyer Collection.
252 Courtesy Columbia Artists Management, Inc.
264 Alex Webb/Magnum Photos, Inc.
265 I. A. González from Black Star
272 Baldwin-Watris/Woodfin Camp & Associates
274 Watris-Baldwin/Woodfin Camp & Associates
276 David Mangurian
278 United Press International Photo
288 Courtesy Ladies Professional Golf Association
304 Robert Capa/Magnum Photos, Inc.
315 Robert Capa/Magnum Photos, Inc.
320 William Dyckes
321 Photos: Archives/Sygma
323 William Braga/Photo Researchers
330 Ana M. Redford

337 George W. Gardner
341 (top) Courtesy Richard Woehr; (bottom) Ernst Schrader
342 Ernst Schrader
347 Colombia Information Service
350 David Mangurian
353 Fred Ward from Black Star
358 Photos Laffont/Sygma
365 Georg Gerster/Photo Researchers
366 Ernst Schrader
376 Cornell Capa/Magnum Photos, Inc.
378 Courtesy Inter-American Development Bank
387 Cornell Capa/Magnum Photos, Inc.
398 A.P. Wirephoto
400 Diego Goldberg/Sygma
408 Diego Goldberg/Sygma
415 Jim Anderson
416 Fred Ward/Black Star
418 Peter Menzel/Stock, Boston
424 Ana M. Redford
433 United Press International Photo
434 Peter Menzel
436 Ernst Schrader
444 Peter Menzel
447 Peter Menzel
460 Sybil Shelton/Peter Arnold, Inc.
461 Ernst Schrader
463 Peter Menzel
466 Alex Webb/Magnum Photos, Inc.
471 David Mangurian
473 Peter Menzel
478 Peter Menzel
479 Emilio Mercado/Jeroboam
489 Miguel de Unamuno y Jugo, oil painting by Ignacio Zuloaga y Zamora, courtesy of the Hispanic Society of America
490 Agustín Víctor Casasola/Courtesy, Prakapas Gallery, New York City
491 Kurt Severin from Black Star
492 Courtesy Editorial Afrodisio Aguado, Madrid
493 Picasso in his studio on the rue des Grands Augustins next to his stove which he had just acquired from a collector. Copyright 1939 by Brassaï.
496 Gabriela Mistral, oil painting by José María López Mezquita, courtesy of the Hispanic Society of America

Color Photographs

FIRST SECTION

Plate 1

(top left) Peter Frey-Arepi/The Image Bank; (top right) Ana M. Redford; (bottom left) Inter-American Development Bank; (bottom right) Vera Alicia Lentz

Plate 2

(top left) Ernst Schrader; (top right) Mauro E. Mujica; (center) Peter Menzel; (bottom) Ernst Schrader

Plate 3

(top) Ernst Schrader; (bottom left) Vera Alicia Lentz; (bottom right) W. H. Hodge/Peter Arnold, Inc.

Plate 4

(top left) Peter Menzel; (top right) G. Ziesler/Peter Arnold, Inc. (bottom) Peter Menzel

SECOND SECTION

Plate 5

(top) Harry Crosby/Photophile; (center) Mary Kathryn Boland; (bottom) Harry Crosby/Photophile

Plate 6

(top) *Fray Hortensio Felix de Paravicino*. El Greco. Isaac Sweetser Fund 04.234. Courtesy, Museum of Fine Arts, Boston. (bottom) Velázquez, *Portrait of Juan de Pareja*. Dated 1650. Oil on canvas. The Metropolitan Museum of Art, Isaac D. Fletcher Fund, Jacob S. Rogers Fund and Bequest of Adelaide Milton de Groot (1876-1967). Bequest of Joseph H. Durkee, by exchange, supplemented by Gifts from Friends of the Museum, 1971.

Plate 7

(top) Goya, *The Executions of the Third of May, 1808*. Scala/Editorial Photocolor Archives. (bottom) Diego Rivera, *The Betrayal*. The Palacio de Cortés, Cuernavaca, Mexico. Courtesy, Consulate General of Mexico.

Plate 8

(top) Picasso, *The Muse*. Editorial Photocolor Archives. (bottom) Salvador Dalí, *The Discovery of America by Christopher Columbus,* oil on canvas, 1959. Collection Mr. & Mrs. Reynolds Morse. Salvador Dali Museum. Cleveland (Beachwood), Ohio.

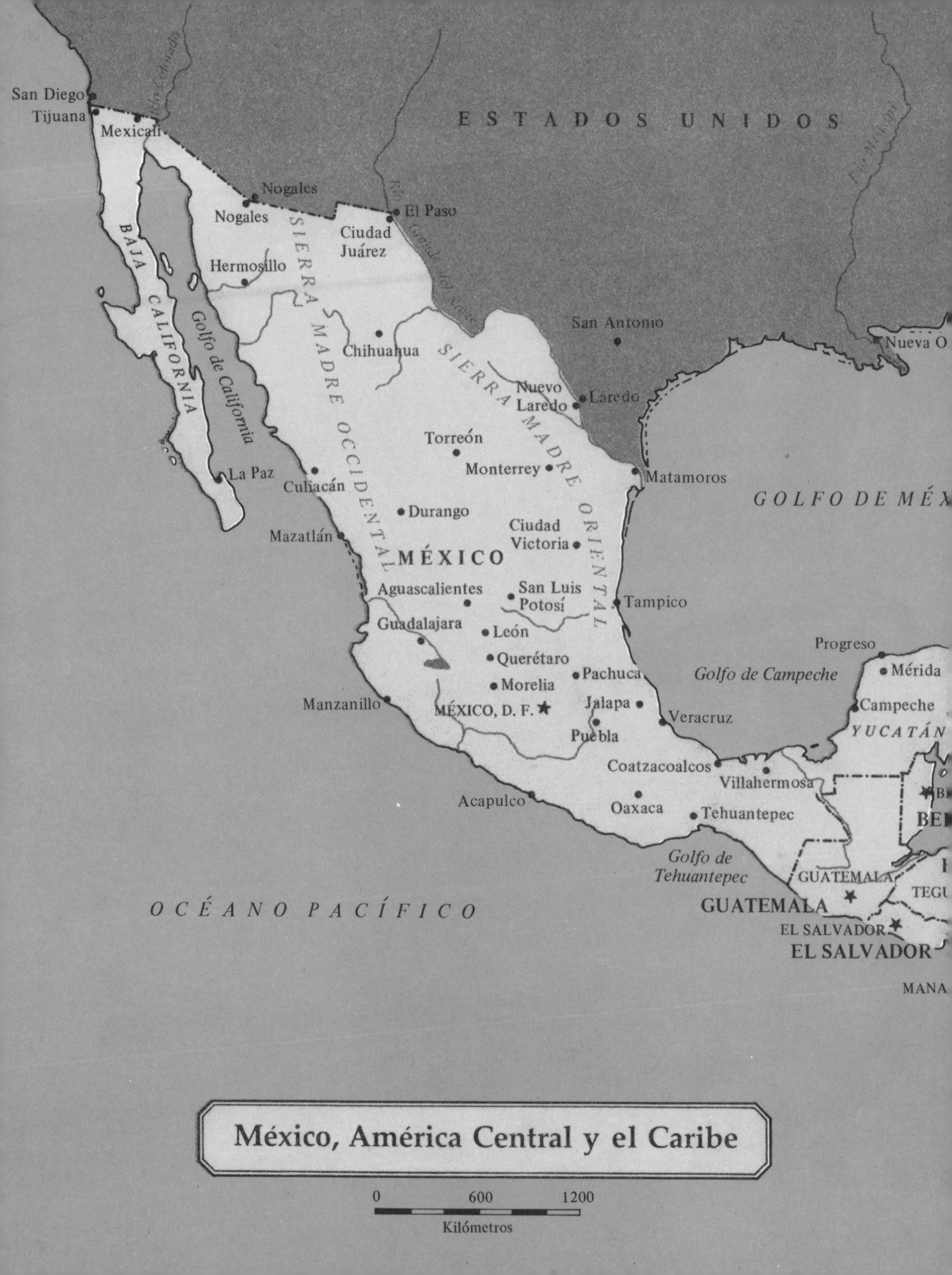

ESTADOS UNIDOS
San Diego
Tijuana
Mexicali
Río Colorado
Nogales
Nogales
El Paso
Ciudad Juárez
Río Grande del Norte
Río Misisipí
BAJA CALIFORNIA
Golfo de California
Hermosillo
SIERRA MADRE OCCIDENTAL
SIERRA MADRE ORIENTAL
Chihuahua
San Antonio
Nueva O
Nuevo Laredo
Laredo
Torreón
Monterrey
La Paz
Culiacán
Matamoros
GOLFO DE MÉX
Durango
Mazatlán
Ciudad Victoria
MÉXICO
Aguascalientes
San Luis Potosí
Tampico
Guadalajara
León
Querétaro
Progreso
Pachuca
Golfo de Campeche
Mérida
Morelia
Manzanillo
MÉXICO, D. F.
Jalapa
Campeche
Veracruz
Puebla
YUCATÁN
Coatzacoalcos
Villahermosa
Acapulco
Oaxaca
Tehuantepec
Golfo de Tehuantepec
GUATEMALA
GUATEMALA
TEGU
EL SALVADOR
EL SALVADOR
OCÉANO PACÍFICO
MANA

México, América Central y el Caribe

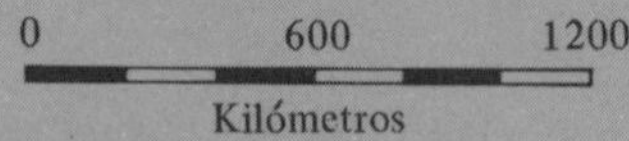